A Question of
Loyalty

A Question of
Loyalty

GEN. BILLY MITCHELL AND
THE COURT-MARTIAL
THAT GRIPPED THE NATION

Douglas Waller

HarperCollins*Publishers*

HarperCollins books may be purchased for educational, business, or sales promotional use. For information, please write: Special Markets Department, HarperCollins Publishers Inc., 10 East 53rd Street, New York, NY 10022.

FIRST EDITION

Designed by Nancy Singer Olaguera

Printed on acid-free paper

Library of Congress Cataloging-in-Publication Data

Waller, Douglas
    A question of loyalty : Gen. Billy Mitchell and the court-martial that gripped the nation / Douglas Waller.—1st ed.
        p. cm.
        Includes bibliographical references.
        ISBN 0-06-050547-8 (alk. paper)
        1. Mitchell, William, 1879–1936—Trials, litigation, etc. 2. Trials (Military offenses)—United States. 3. Courts-martial and courts of inquiry—United States. I. Title.

KF7642.M58W35 2004
343.73'0143—dc22   2004042899

04 05 06 07 08 ❖/RRD 10 9 8 7 6 5 4 3 2 1

To Matt, Susan, and Matthew

Contents

1 Exile   1

2 Flight of the *Shenandoah*   11

3 "Criminal...Treasonable"   17

4 The Mitchell Problem   24

5 Tribunal   36

6 The Challenge   46

7 Promise   63

8 "Not Guilty"   83

9 Love   93

10 Insubordination and the Truth   107

11 War   119

12 Preparing for Battle   132

13 Triumph   136

14 Tables Turned   168

15 Pearl Harbor   183

16 Bombshell   195

17 Reinforcements   203

18 Prelude   213

19 Cross-Examination   239

20 "Crushing"   253

21 "Damned Rot"   260

22 Siege   276

23 "Lawless"   291

24 The Verdict   316

25 Resignation   327

26 Periphery   333

27 The End   346

   Epilogue   353

   Source Notes   365

   Selected Bibliography   419

   Acknowledgments   425

   Index   429

1 Exile

It was evening when Billy Mitchell finally sat down in the parlor of his quarters at Fort Sam Houston to write to Betty (as his wife, Elizabeth, was known) about the plane accident. Shade from leafy trees, some ripe with figs and pecans in the front yard, surrounded the home and cooled the dry air in the evening. But summer at the army post, just outside San Antonio, Texas, was still unbearably hot and dusty. Mitchell was glad Betty had remained with her parents in Detroit to give birth to their first child, while he managed the moving in of their furniture and the laying of new carpets.

Quarters Number 14 was not the best on the post, certainly not as fine as the accommodations usually given to generals. But it was comfortable. The house was built according to a two-story Italianate design, with limestone from the city's rock quarries. It had three bedrooms, a parlor, dining room, and servants' quarters in the back. Stables nearby housed three horses Mitchell had brought with him from Virginia: Eclipse, Boxwood, and Flood Tide. From the parlor's bay window, Mitchell had a beautiful view of a vast parade ground. He had to walk just several blocks to reach his office in the post's quadrangle. His old boss in Washington, Maj. Gen. Mason Patrick, had ordered that Mitchell's personal plane, the *Sea Gull 3rd*, be flown down to him.

Still, Fort Sam Houston, as Will Rogers saw it, was "Siberia." (The two had become fast friends after Mitchell took the famous humorist up for his first plane ride four months earlier.) Mitchell had been busted from brigadier general to colonel and banished to this "mosquito post in Texas," Rogers had written in one of his columns, because he had angered the brass in Washington.

But Texas was far from a backwater. Fort Sam Houston was the army's largest post in the United States. For decades it had guarded the country's strategically important southern flank against threats percolating up from Mexico. As the new air officer of the Eighth Army Corps, Mitchell had an area of responsibility that stretched from Texas to the West Coast. Elizabeth was thankful the army hadn't sent him farther away, to Panama. And though Mitchell had been reduced in rank, the army did not consider it a demotion. Colonel was his permanent rank, the highest he ever held during his career. Brigadier general had been his temporary rank during World War I, when officers were promoted rapidly as the army expanded for combat. After the war most reverted to their permanent peacetime ranks. Colonels went back to being captains, generals sank as low as major. The only reason Mitchell had been lucky enough to keep his star after the war was that his job as assistant director of the air service allowed for that rank while he held that position. When the job ended he stopped being a general.

But Mitchell felt humiliated by the reduction in rank. Elizabeth knew his feelings had been hurt "much more than he ever will say," she wrote to one of his sisters. John Weeks, Calvin Coolidge's secretary of war, had refused to reappoint him as air service assistant director the previous March, which meant that he returned to the rank of colonel. Mitchell had been so publicly critical of the War Department's management of air power—and so reckless with the facts, as far as Weeks was concerned—that he had practically been insubordinate. As far as Mitchell was concerned, he should have been named director of the army air service and promoted to major general a long time ago. He refused to accept the rank of colonel now. Soldiers on post still called him "general," and he never corrected them.

True, the Eighth Corps territory was vast, but its air arsenal was puny. In Washington, Mitchell had lorded over the entire air service, and his instant access to the national press and the city's powerful allowed him to push his cause for an air force independent of the army. Now he was relegated to a do-nothing job far away, the War Department hoped, from politicians and the media. In Washington. he had a platoon of air officers as loyal to him as disciples to a prophet. His staff now consisted of two clerks and a stenographer, Maydell Blackmon, whom he'd brought from Washington and who spent most of her days answering the hundreds of letters that poured in each week—most from admirers who thought he'd gotten a raw deal. It amused "Blackie" (the nickname Mitchell had given her) that he always dictated letters while walking in wide circles in his office. "The general," as Blackie always called him, had a good command of the language and always seemed to know what he wanted to say. He rarely went back and edited what he had dictated.

Mitchell had wrenched his right shoulder in the plane accident that morning. He had scratches on his hands and face, and a plaster cast was packed on his nose, which was probably broken when his head slammed into the cockpit's forward crash pad. He had sent Betty a quick telegram earlier that morning hoping it would reach her in Detroit before she read about the mishap in the afternoon newspapers. In fact, reporters had already phoned her shortly after his Western Union message arrived, asking her for a comment. "Thank heaven you are safe," she had wired back. Betty had given birth to their first child, Lucy, less than a month earlier. She did not need the extra worry, not with everything else going on in this turbulent year. "I wanted you to know ahead of any news items appearing that nothing had happened to your old man," Mitchell now wrote in the peace and calm of his parlor.

Flying was still dangerous in the 1920s. Planes were mostly contraptions made of wood, wire, and cloth. Equipment in open-air cockpits was crude: a stick to control ailerons, a wooden or metal bar on a pivot for rudders, a magnetic compass, drift meter, airspeed meter, fuel indicator, little else. Almost half the army's peacetime deaths were due to plane accidents. Air service pilots routinely made emergency landings on deserted roads or farm fields, shooing away cattle that liked to lick the varnishlike airplane dope applied to the fabric covering the wings and fuselage to make it airtight.

Shortly after 7:30 A.M., Mitchell had climbed into a Consolidated PT-1 biplane trainer at a nearby makeshift airfield that had once been a racetrack. Harry Short, his longtime mechanic, sat in the backseat. (Short's wife had accompanied him to San Antonio to keep house for Mitchell.) Before takeoff the two men had both thoroughly tested the aircraft's engine, landing gear, and shock absorbers. Though a couple of valves were leaking, the engine revved up to 1,650 rpm, which made it fit for flight. When all the cockpit controls seemed to work fine, Mitchell signaled the ground crewmen to turn the aircraft around so it faced the wind. They made eleven takeoffs and landings with no trouble, dazzling officers from the post's Second Division, who had come out to watch. On the twelfth takeoff, however, the engine suddenly went dead at an altitude of almost one hundred feet. The plane's right tank, they later discovered, had been empty; a faulty fuel indicator registered that it was half full.

Mitchell nosed the aircraft down to keep it from stalling, then leveled it out at fifteen feet so it wouldn't hit a clutch of laborers and mule teams just ahead. Once past them, he crash-landed at the corner of a fenced-in field. The landing gear collapsed, and the PT-1 flipped over on its nose. Upside down, Mitchell and Short quickly unbuckled their cockpit belts and crawled out. Mitchell stood up, grinning and waving to the officers running toward him. "It's all in a day's work," he told reporters later. The nonchalance wasn't false bravado. Mitchell had flown just about every model of aircraft in the army inventory and had walked away from several serious crack-ups. He rode Eclipse that afternoon. He may have had his faults as an officer, but as a pilot, forty-five-year-old William Mitchell was fearless.

He was a man of his times and a man far beyond his times. Born to a millionaire Midwestern family at the end of the 1870s, he was part of America's wealthy elite who built large mansions reflecting their enormous egos, who sailed to Europe for their educations and vacations, who took the train to Florida for their winters and to upstate New York for their summers, who ruled the country with their money, their influence, and a powerful sense of noblesse oblige. He joined the military—regarded by some in the upper class as a public service outlet—at the age of eighteen during the Spanish-American War, at the dawn of his country's emergence as a world power. Thus he became part of a small but growing group of energetic, ambitious, and innovative officers stuck in an army that was still trying to determine what style of saber its cavalry should carry. In World War I he led the largest armada of airplanes ever to attack an enemy force, returning as a dashing young general with a chest full of medals and the radical belief that airpower would be the only decisive instrument for future wars.

The United States turned inward after the Armistice and shrank its military as it had after previous conflicts, but Mitchell remained an apostle of empire, a committed internationalist both fascinated by and fearful of the turbulent geopolitics of Europe and the growing power of Asia. His greatest achievement came in 1921, when he led a brigade of airplanes that sank the surplus German battleship *Ostfriesland* off the Virginia coast, demonstrating for the first time the vulnerability of the world's mighty dreadnoughts to upstart airpower.

Mitchell was a trumpeter of ideas when the War Department had few new ones. By the time of his transfer to Texas, he had published numerous books and magazine articles with hundreds of predictions. Historians would later sniff that if you make enough of them, as Mitchell had, some are bound to come true. But Mitchell had an uncanny knack for forecasting the future. In the 1920s, when the average speed limit on roads was still thirty-five miles per hour and ocean liners were still the only means of transportation across the seas, he predicted that high-speed commercial airliners would one day carry passengers from New York to Europe in as little as six hours. Eighteen years before it actually happened, he detailed how Japan would launch a sneak attack on Pearl Harbor. He predicted that planes and space rockets would easily be hurtled over the oceans, making countries such as the United States vulnerable to strategic attack. He predicted that air forces would be able to strike targets from afar with munitions such as cruise missiles (fired seventy years later against Iraq) and unmanned aerial vehicles (used against Al Qaeda terrorists in Afghanistan eighty years later).

Some of his forecasts never materialized. He predicted that fleets of gas-filled dirigibles would transport commercial passengers and military hardware over vast distances. Today airships do little more than hover over football games. Other notions proved fanciful. Aircraft never scattered "minute grass seeds" over clouds to produce rain and "luxurious meadows" when the seeds "fall to earth." But he foresaw a day when gliding would be a popular sport, when aircraft would routinely be used for crop dusting, fire-fighting, medevacing the sick and wounded, photographing ter-rain, and spying on enemies. "A single explosion" well placed by aircraft into the heart of New York City, he once wrote, could wreck tall buildings, close the New York Stock Exchange, put communi-cation and transportation systems "completely out of order," and paralyze briefly "the financial center of the Western Hemisphere."

Mitchell was also a showman. The 1920s ushered in the era of mass communications: radio, movies, large-circulation newspa-pers and magazines. He understood their power and used them skillfully to press not only for a separate air force but also for a Department of Defense that would oversee it along with the army and navy. His enemies in the War and Navy Departments, who just as adamantly opposed such reorganization, grumbled that he manipulated the media too well. Mitchell became more of a propa-gandist than a reasoned advocate. The cause he championed—a radical reorganization of the defense establishment of his day— was a worthy one, but he lost whatever potential allies by behaving arrogantly and by playing fast and loose with the facts. As the years wore on he had become more strident in promoting his separate air force, more impatient with the slow pace of change, more disdain-ful of those who disagreed with him. Navy admirals sputtered with rage at the mere mention of his name because he so publicly deni-grated the value of their fleet.

In his private life Mitchell ran out of money often, drank heav-ily, and in 1922 went through a bitter divorce from his first wife, Caroline. His second wife, Betty, had been swept off her feet by this fiery air general who landed his plane on a beach near York Harbor, Maine, to court her at her family's vacation home. She had calmed down his personal life after they married in 1923, but his zeal for airpower still burned hot. By the time Mitchell reported to Fort Sam Houston on June 27, 1925, he had alienated practically every-one above him in the chain of command, including his commander in chief, President Calvin Coolidge.

Coolidge, who didn't think much of an officer using a government plane to visit his girlfriend, was still miffed that Mitchell had hoodwinked him the previous fall. The general, who had been under a War Department gag order not to publish any articles on aeronautics unless the army approved them, walked into the president's office with the editor of the *Saturday Evening Post* and asked the president for permission to write a series of bland pieces for the magazine. Coolidge saw no problem as long as he cleared it with his bosses in the War Department. Mitchell then went back to General Patrick, who as director of the air service was his immediate superior, and said the president had okayed the articles. "Very well, if you have the President's authority," Patrick recalled telling him. Mitchell conveniently didn't mention that Coolidge had conditioned it on the War Department's approval. Secretary of War Weeks was enraged when he opened the magazine and, to his surprise, found Mitchell's pieces warning about airplanes laying waste to nations in future wars and calling for an independent air force.

For Weeks the last straw came in January 1925, when Mitchell began appearing before a House investigative committee chaired by Florian Lampert, a portly, cigar-chomping Republican congressman from Wisconsin. Ignoring pleas from aides to tone down his testimony, Mitchell blasted the entire military establishment. America's air service, he charged, was woefully unprepared for a future war. Top admirals and generals, he claimed, had lied to Congress about the decrepit conditions in their services, and officers under them were muzzled or forced to give false statements when called before congressional committees. The army and navy hotly disputed his charges and the credibility of his evidence, but Mitchell remained defiant. To add insult to injury, at the end of August bookstores received Mitchell's latest unauthorized tome on airpower, *Winged Defense,* which contained political cartoons ridiculing Weeks, a popular secretary who happened to be ill and near resignation. Mitchell insisted that the publisher inserted the cartoons without his knowledge. But Betty knew that no one would believe it, and she feared that incident alone might be enough to get her husband court-martialed.

The press called Mitchell the "stormy petrel," for the seabird whose presence is supposed to warn of turbulent weather. Senior

army officers, in private, had dubbed him the "Kookaburra," for a
bird Australians called the "Laughing Jackass." He was—and continues to be—the object of extreme adulation or extreme vilifica-
tion. Even today officers at the nation's military schools argue
fiercely about him. Sen. John McCain, the maverick Republican
who ran for president in 2000, lists Mitchell as one of his heroes.
(McCain's grandfather, Adm. John Sidney McCain, opposed
Mitchell's campaign for a separate air force, though the admiral
told relatives privately that he liked the army man.) Mitchell's
admirers compare him to Socrates, Alexander, Napoleon, Robert E.
Lee—the greatest military prophet in centuries, a man who sacri-
ficed a promising career for a higher cause. His enemies accuse
him of being a scheming, mentally unbalanced, political opportunist—even a Bolshevik and the catalyst for the feuding we still see
among the army, navy, and air force. Both sides stretch the truth,
particularly with the charge that he was a Bolshevik or the father of
interservice rivalry. An intense patriot, Mitchell loathed commu-
nism. Service squabbling remains alive and well among generals
and admirals today who weren't born when he was in uniform.

What cannot be denied is the tremendous impact Mitchell had
on the modern U.S. Air Force. His ideas on how planes should be
used in combat became the fighting doctrine for World War II. Air
force officers are still immersed in his theories during their training. It was Mitchell who planted the intellectual seeds for what is
now America's global airpower.

But he was a far more complex man than black-and-white por-
traits suggest. He was only five feet nine inches, but seemed taller
because he stood so erect and kept his chin up. He was aggressive,
brash, and often contemptuous of superiors. He had a somewhat
high and twangy voice, almost dictatorial in tone, which could be
heard at a distance. Around children he could be bossy and intimi-
dating, treating them like privates, but some, like his niece Harriet,
stood up to him and he found it amusing. He quit smoking in his
twenties and never ate red meat. In Europe during World War I, he
designed his own flashy uniform. In civilian clothes he was a
dandy, sporting the latest expensive fashions from British tailors.
(His head was small, so he wore a small hat, always jauntily cocked
to the left.) He was handsome, and women were attracted to him.

He loved to hunt and play polo but hated card games and gambling. He kept three pairs of reading glasses in the house for the several books he was always reading.

Mitchell had many loyal followers or opponents or rivals, but he had few equals or close friends his age. An Episcopalian, he was deeply religious and fond of studying stars in the universe; he felt he was closer to God when flying. He spoke Spanish fluently, French fairly well, German poorly, and Tagalog, the language of the Philippines, slightly. A workaholic, he slept no more than five hours a night. Aides found him a difficult taskmaster. He often reduced Blackie to tears with his demands. After a grueling day of inspecting planes at an air base, he'd keep the exhausted pilots up half the night partying at the officers' club. Jimmy Doolittle, who later led the first U.S. bombing raid over Tokyo during World War II, was once assigned as Mitchell's temporary aide for a day. "The busiest day I ever had," he recalled.

On Tuesday morning Mitchell dropped the letter for Betty into a mailbox on his way to a nearby airfield. Though he ached all over from the accident the day before, he climbed into a De Havilland DH-4 biplane the mechanics had fixed up with a larger 110-gallon fuel tank and took it for a spin over the post. He spent the rest of the morning and afternoon in his office dictating to Blackie; then he set out for a nearby game preserve with a half dozen locals to hunt doves. They ended up shooting three armadillos, six skunks, and two buzzards.

Mitchell was intent on making the best of his exile. Two weeks after he arrived at Fort Sam Houston, driving onto the post in a new Packard the auto company had sold him at a discount, Mitchell had hopped into a plane and began touring his new domain with Harry Short in the backseat. The mechanic filmed the terrain below with a movie camera. Mitchell flew to Tucson, Arizona, where the Pueblo Club and Chamber of Commerce feted him at a banquet; then to Los Angeles, where he toured movie sets in Hollywood with Douglas Fairbanks Sr. and stayed overnight at Cecil B. DeMille's mansion. Flying in the open cockpit, with the hot wind beating against his face, invigorated him. He even slept late at times, and in a note to Betty said he was consuming "practically no drinks."

But how he longed to "get back to our little home in Virginia," he wrote to her in the same paragraph. The "little home" actually was a country estate in Middleburg, not far from Washington, which Betty's wealthy father had bought for them. It was a "perfectly ideal spot," Betty wrote, where she and Billy would one day "spend our old age happily." Blackie believed that Mitchell knew he would not be at Fort Sam Houston for long. Betty was to join him soon, but not all the furniture had been shipped from Middleburg, and the tip-off for Blackie was that he hadn't brought with him any of the model planes, charts, and paintings that had filled his Washington office.

Indeed, Mitchell was already quietly plotting his return to Middleburg and the bureaucratic battle he had left in Washington. "Either the War and Navy departments will have to listen or can me," he wrote Betty in July. His military career was probably over, he knew. He thought his allies in Congress might pass a bill by the winter retiring him at a general's rank. Business offers had poured in. Eddie Rickenbacker, the top American ace of World War I, wanted him to work for his automobile manufacturing company. Mitchell turned down most of the offers, although he did have Arthur Brisbane, one of the country's most powerful newspaper editors and an old pal from Washington, talk to Henry Ford about bankrolling a grand flying school for as many as ten thousand young Americans, which Mitchell might manage. If a business deal didn't pan out, his book, *Winged Defense,* might be a moneymaker. A friend had predicted that at least ten thousand copies would be sold in the San Antonio area. Politics was another possibility. A consultant in Washington had already outlined a plan for him to run for the presidency with just $25,000 in seed money.

All he needed was a spark to launch him back into the action. Returning from the game preserve late that afternoon, Mitchell did not know it would come in less than a week.

★ ★ ★ ★ ★ ★

2 Flight of the *Shenandoah*

Zachary Lansdowne stared at the dark skies out the wide windows of the airship's control car. The car hung by metal struts from the forward end of the airship and was crowded with equipment and men. The lieutenant commander had been bent over the plotting table in front of him for much of the night, marking the dirigible's course with his navigator. Over his head were the annunciators that telegraphed speed commands to operators of the five Packard engines that hung in gondolas from the underside of the airship. The crew had taken the engine out of the sixth gondola to lighten the ship and had put in its place a radio generator and gas stove for the cook. The USS *Shenandoah* rigid airship, which had left the Naval Air Station at Lakehurst, New Jersey, nine hours earlier on a westerly course, was flying at a speedy fifty-five miles per hour over the Allegheny Mountains.

The *Shenandoah* was a national treasure. Seventy-two Midwestern governors, mayors, and civic leaders had begged the Navy Department to have the dirigible fly over their towns and cities during this trip. As it now sailed west, thousands of people below rushed out of their homes to gaze up at the giant beast. Factory whistles blew. Car horns honked. The massive thirty-seven-ton airship, built two years earlier in Philadelphia based on a wartime German Zeppelin design, stretched 682 feet in length and had a width of 79 feet at its middle. By 1925 standards the navy had paid a fortune for the airship program: about $2.7 million for the

Shenandoah alone, plus $3 million for its hangar at Lakehurst, the largest in the world. From the beginning Mitchell and the army air service had schemed to get their hands on the program, insisting they were more qualified to operate the rigid airships. But the navy clung jealously to its monopoly.

Lansdowne, the *Shenandoah*'s skipper, had become a military celebrity, enjoying the same attention astronauts would receive two generations later. He had a young and glamorous second wife, and President Coolidge had written him glowing personal letters. The first lady, Grace Coolidge, had christened the *Shenandoah*'s sister airship, the USS *Los Angeles*. Reporters and navy bigwigs had flown on previous VIP flights. On this one Lansdowne had a photographer to chronicle the voyage.

Coolidge had begged off invitations to climb aboard the *Shenandoah* himself. Dirigibles also inspired fear because of their spectacular accidents in the past, often the result of defects in their structures or poor airmanship by their crews. Even the *Shenandoah* had had mishaps. A winter gale the previous year had torn the ship away from its mooring mast at Lakehurst, ripping apart its nose and casting it adrift over New Jersey and New York for about eight hours. Lansdowne had successfully flown it to the West Coast and back in 1924. But Coolidge had blocked a risky trip to the North Pole.

Lt. Joseph Anderson, the airship's weather officer, walked up from his desk in the rear of the control car and handed Lansdowne the radio report just in from Lakehurst. Thunderstorms loomed over the Great Lakes, he told the skipper. Lansdowne studied the weather map and nodded. He stood a trim but muscular six foot one, a descendant of the fiery Scottish Protestant reformer, John Knox, with high cheekbones and forehead, close-cropped hair, and dark eyes that could bore holes in his crew when he was angry. Lansdowne was a strict disciplinarian aboard the *Shenandoah*, but he was laid back when off duty, and that made him popular with his men. Still, the crew of forty-one was largely inexperienced at the complex job of flying a dirigible. Lansdowne was one of the most seasoned lighter-than-air officers in the fleet, but even so, he, and the entire navy for that matter, were still feeling their way around with these new giant airships.

The storms were too far north to bother them, the two officers agreed. "Don't call me unless something unusual comes up," Lansdowne said with a yawn and climbed up the control car's ladder into the hull of the airship for a nap. The ladder took him to the keel, a triangular tunnel twelve feet wide and nine feet high, running along the bottom of the hull from the nose to the tail. The keel housed tanks for gasoline and oil, water ballast bags, food lockers, and crew bunks that hung from wires. Pressing against the two top sides of the keel triangle were twenty gas cells, which looked like giant fat sausages and were made of fabric reinforced with the lining of steer intestines to keep them airtight. The gas cells were held in wire and twine nets attached to a skeleton of duralumin girders that made up the dirigible's rigid outer ribs. The hull's outer cover was cotton cloth treated with aluminized dope to seal it.

At the start of the trip each cell had been filled to about 91 percent capacity with helium. It did not have the lifting power of hydrogen, but the navy liked the inert gas because, unlike hydrogen, it wouldn't catch fire with a spark. When the ship went higher, the helium expanded in the gas cells. The cells were connected with a rubber hose so that when one reached capacity the helium could seep into another that was less full. When all the bags were 100 percent full, which occurred at about four thousand feet, automatic valves would open so that excess gas could escape out wicker chimneys to ventilators at the top of the ship. Otherwise the gas cells would burst. In addition to the automatic devices, the crew had backup manual valves it could operate by pulleys in the control car. Helium was scarce and expensive—fifty thousand dollars to fill all twenty cells—so the cash-strapped navy discouraged the crew from venting it except during emergencies. To cut back on weight, the crew had also removed ten of the eighteen automatic valves. This meant that the men would have to rely more on the manual valves if they had to vent gas quickly.

Lansdowne found his bunk in the forward part of the keel and climbed in. He had trouble falling asleep. This flight worried him. In fact, when the navy had sent these orders earlier in the summer, he had balked because it would be in the middle of the thunderstorm season along this Midwestern route. The dirigibles built at this time were not all-weather aircraft. German-modeled airships like the *Shenandoah* were designed for high-altitude flying in clear skies. What's more, the storms the German airships encountered in Europe and over the North Atlantic were far less violent than the ones in the middle United States. Finally the navy reluctantly agreed to postpone the trip until the first week of September, when the thunderstorm season usually ended, and Lansdowne just as reluctantly agreed to fly. But, he confided to his wife, Margaret, he was still fearful of thunderstorms that might linger into September.

Lansdowne recognized the political importance of this trip. His boss, Rear Adm. William Moffett, the head of naval aviation, was a feisty South Carolinian with an ego as large as Mitchell's. When it came to bureaucratic battles behind the scenes in Washington, Moffett was a savvier infighter than his army rival. But Moffett was steamed that Mitchell kept trumping him in the publicity department, particularly when army pilots became the first to complete an around-the-world flight in 1924. To upstage Mitchell—and to head off any momentum he had generated for a unified air force that might absorb the navy's aircraft—Moffett launched two navy seaplanes from the West Coast on August 31 to attempt a nonstop flight to Hawaii. He had also ordered the *Shenandoah* to begin a series of publicity junkets around the country (like the one Lansdowne was beginning now) before the new airship had been adequately flight-tested or even sent to sea, where other navy men thought it belonged.

For this run the navy had laid out a tightly packed itinerary for the *Shenandoah* to pass over twenty-seven cities en route from New Jersey to Iowa, at specific times so it would entertain spectators attending state fairs. Lansdowne could deviate from the planned route to avoid bad weather, but his orders pointedly warned him that the navy had sent out press releases with the times the airship would pass over each city. The admirals didn't want to disappoint the local politicians and their constituents.

At 3:00 A.M. a crewman shook Lansdowne's shoulder, rousing him out of a deep sleep. Storms were closing in on the *Shenandoah*, the skipper was told. He dressed quickly and climbed down to the control car. Lightning flashed east and northwest of the airship. And in front of him to the west, Lansdowne could see a very large, dark cloud. The airship was over Cambridge, Ohio, but barely crawling forward because of strong headwinds. With the distant storms starting to close in on them, Anderson, the weatherman, approached Lansdowne, who had been issuing rudder and engine speed directions in a soft voice so as not to worry the crew. "I think we need to turn south, sir," he said with an anxious look on his face. To the south the skies were clear. But turning in that direction would screw up the day's schedule of state fair appearances. "That storm's still a long way off," the skipper answered, shaking his head. "We've been ordered to fly over a certain course, and I want to keep that course as long as I can."

The decision proved fateful. An hour later Lansdowne was finally able to make some headway by flying his airship at a lower altitude of 2,100 feet. But as the *Shenandoah* reached Caldwell, Ohio, the skipper and his crew did not realize that one of the most dangerous weather conditions any aircraft could face was forming directly over them: a line squall. Today aircraft have ground controllers and sophisticated weather radar systems on board, which can track approaching storms and guide pilots around them. The *Shenandoah* crew had no instruments to warn them of the storm moving into the Ohio Valley or its severity. The airmen had only periodic radioed weather reports, such as the one from Lakehurst about bad weather over the Great Lakes.

A line squall is a line of intense thunderstorms forming at the head of a fast-moving cold front, where moist warm winds slam into dry cold air, creating violent up- and downdrafts. The squall now quickly lifted up the helpless airship to 6,300 feet, way past the pressure altitude when gas cells reached 100 percent capacity. Then it plunged in a matter of minutes down to 3,200 feet.

Lt. Cdr. Charles Rosendahl, the navigator, grabbed his ears, which ached from the sudden change in air pressure. But surprisingly, many of the crewmen remained asleep in their bunks through the pitching and rolling. Lansdowne, who kept issuing commands in a calm voice, inexplicably didn't sound orders for everyone to man his emergency station. The crewmen who were awake scrambled to vent gas from the swollen bags, dump water from ballasts, and rev up engines full speed to break free from the eye of the squall. But engines 1 and 2 overheated and conked out. Wires in the hull snapped under the strain as the wind and rain buf-

feted the *Shenandoah* in different directions. On the ground Caldwell residents just waking up to the storm watched the giant airship "swinging back and forth like a huge pendulum," as one put it.

The *Shenandoah*'s descent suddenly stopped, and the airship
leveled off. Lansdowne finally directed the rudderman to turn the
dirigible left toward clear weather in the south and ordered the
sleeping men to be awakened. But it was all too late. The wind
again whipped the *Shenandoah* upward to 6,200 feet, this time at a
faster rate than the first ascent. Rosendahl clambered up the control car's ladder to check on the dumping of fuel. When the airship
raced down after this second ascent, it would quickly have to be
made lighter to keep from crashing to the ground.

Rosendahl felt as if he were in a plane beginning a loop. The
Shenandoah was so long that one air current drove its nose up,
twisting it to the left, while another current at the same time
shoved its tail down, wrenching it to the right. The hull vibrated
fiercely. Rosendahl heard struts snapping, then "a terrific crashing
of metal," as he later recalled. The keel had broken like a tree limb,
cracking open the hull. Rosendahl realized, to his horror, that as
the girders tore, the control car with Lansdowne and seven other
crewmen separated from the airship and began falling more than a
mile to the ground. The forward section of the *Shenandoah*, with
some gas cells still full and its torn outer fabric flapping in the
breeze, eventually floated down in a wide circle with Rosendahl
and five other men inside it clinging to girders. The tail section of
the dirigible with twenty-five men inside it floated to a small valley,
breaking into two pieces just before hitting the ground.

Fourteen men, including Lansdowne and the seven who were
with him in the control car, died in the disaster. By midmorning,
thousands of sightseers and souvenir hunters swarmed over the
hillsides of Noble County, Ohio, where the *Shenandoah* wreckage
was scattered. They came in horse-drawn buggies and Model Ts
and carted away anything loose: flight instruments, logbooks, blan-
kets, steering wheels, girder sections, strips of fabric. Looters even
rifled through the clothes of the mangled bodies sprawled on the
ground. Among the personal items pilfered was the Naval Academy
class ring that had been on Lansdowne's finger.

3 "Criminal . . . Treasonable"

Mitchell sat in his office flipping through the *San Antonio Express*. He was pleased to see a one-column story on the front page about his new book, plus another item on the radio address he had given the night before on WOAI. A reporter from the Hearst newspaper chain also had just dropped by to interview him about the political hubbub over *Winged Defense* and to photograph him. "The book is going to sell like hotcakes," he predicted to Betty in a letter that day.

Several hours later officers from air service headquarters in Washington phoned him about the *Shenandoah* accident that morning. The next day banner headlines in newspapers from coast to coast announced that the dirigible had been destroyed. Friday's *New York Times* devoted half of its front page to the story, plus a full page inside with large black-and-white photos of the airship and profiles of Lansdowne and the other crewmen. Condolences poured in to the White House from foreign governments.

Mitchell was disgusted by the first report he received from Washington. The tragic accident came on the heels of another embarrassing mishap for the navy. The flight of its seaplanes to Hawaii, which had begun three days earlier, was snakebitten from the start. One of the flying boats scheduled to make the trip, a metal-hulled PB-1 biplane built by Boeing, damaged its engine mounts flying from Seattle to San Francisco and had to be scrubbed. A second biplane, the large PN-9 with two engines, plopped into the Pacific Ocean five hours into the flight because of motor failure. Its crew was rescued by a nearby destroyer, one of the warships the navy had placed at two-hundred-mile intervals along the entire route for just such emergencies. The third seaplane, another PN-9, flown by the leader of the mission, Cdr. John Rodgers, made it to within two hundred miles of Hawaii when it ran out of gas and was forced to land on the water. But rescue ships still had not been able to find Rodgers and the four other airmen on his plane.

Mitchell had inspected one of the PN-9s during his West Coast visit on July 15 and been unimpressed. Rodgers was a competent pilot, he thought. But the navy had rushed the preparations for the flight. The trip from San Francisco to Hawaii would take about thirty hours, whereas the PN-9 had flown in a test flight for only about twenty-eight and a half hours. The navy hoped that tweaks to the engines plus favorable winds would keep the planes in the air for the extra hour and a half.

Mitchell, however, had held his tongue as worry grew that Rodgers and his men had been lost at sea. During his WOAI address the previous night, he asked his audience to pray. "They are just as much martyrs to the progress of civilization as Columbus would have been had he perished in his voyage to America," he said respectfully.

Now, with news of the *Shenandoah* calamity just in, Mitchell didn't feel so respectful. He knew the game Moffett was playing. Mitchell had staged his share of publicity stunts for the air service, and he knew the navy was trying to turn the tables on him with the *Shenandoah* and the Hawaii flights. It was "just plain politics to try and disprove us," he wrote to Betty. "All have fallen flat." But the navy's gambit had gotten fourteen men in a dirigible killed and possibly five more drowned in the Pacific.

Still, Mitchell wasn't stirred enough yet to act. In fact, he seemed almost oblivious to the looming national crisis over the *Shenandoah*. After work he went to the range to shoot targets at two hundred yards, then home to ride two of his horses, Boxwood and Eclipse, and jump over fences in his backyard. That night he attended a Chamber of Commerce banquet at the Alamo Country Club, sitting with the mayor of San Antonio and the consul general of Mexico. A band played Spanish and American songs, and Mitchell had a wonderful time.

Friday morning, however, his mood changed. Newspapers in

San Antonio and the rest of the country blazed with the first horrifying accounts of the *Shenandoah* accident. Stories were already leaking that Lansdowne had had qualms about the flight and that the airship had had equipment problems. Anton Heinen, a former German dirigible pilot who had served as a technical adviser aboard the *Shenandoah,* told the Associated Press that the removal of ten of the dirigible's eighteen safety valves for the gas cells caused the accident. "I would not call it murder," he charged, but if the valves hadn't been removed, "the crash would not have occurred." Desperate to contain the political damage, Navy Secretary Curtis Wilbur insisted there was a bright side: The *Shenandoah* and Hawaii disasters proved the country was still safe from any hostile planes trying to cross the oceans to attack. No aircraft could make it.

Mitchell now seethed. And he saw his opportunity.

Summoning Maydell Blackmon to his office, he began dictating. As usual, he paced as she scribbled on a steno pad. Mitchell had a vast network of air officers in the United States and Europe who had sent him regular updates for the past three months on aviation conditions, much of it depressing news. He also had informants in the War Department and even sympathizers in the navy. Some of them began phoning with inside information on the *Shenandoah.* All morning long he dictated to Blackie, venting his anger and frustration over the military's handling of aviation. While she typed the first draft, he fielded phone calls from reporters looking for comment on the *Shenandoah.* Wait until tomorrow, he told them; he would release a statement then.

This time Mitchell edited what he had dictated. He took the draft and ran it by several friends and lawyers, who suggested changes. Then he sat up past 1:00 A.M. rewriting the statement with Harry Short, his mechanic, at his side.

Saturday morning at 6:00 A.M., Kenneth McCalla, a reporter for the *Houston Press,* and Harry McCleary from the *San Antonio Evening News* were camped out on the front lawn of Mitchell's quarters, waiting for him to emerge with his statement. Mitchell finally poked his head out the door and told them to meet him at his office in the quadrangle at 9:30 A.M. He'd have it for them then.

McCalla, McCleary, and four other newsmen showed up on time, but had to wait another two hours. Blackie had to type a new draft with all the changes her boss had penciled in the night before. Finally, at 11:30 A.M., Mitchell ushered the reporters into his office and handed each a carbon copy of what Blackie had typed: nine pages, single-spaced on canary yellow paper. It totaled 6,080 words.

"I have been asked from all parts of the country to give my opinion about the reasons for the frightful aeronautical accidents and loss of life," the statement began. "My opinion is as follows." Mitchell then delivered the blast that would lead news stories the next day: "These incidents are the direct result of the incompetency, criminal negligence and almost treasonable administration of the national defense by the Navy and War Departments."

Mitchell's indictment was far more sweeping than just a critique of the *Shenandoah* and Hawaii flights. Aviation policy, his statement continued, was "dictated by the non-flying officers of the army and navy who know practically nothing about it." Airmen had become "pawns," forced to fly antiquated biplanes like the De Havilland DH-4, which they nicknamed "the flaming coffin" because they claimed it easily caught fire when it crashed. "Our pilots know they are going to be killed if they stay in the service." The army and navy, forming "sort of a union to perpetuate their own existence," maintained "propaganda agencies" to sway public opinion. Senior officers who testified before Congress "almost always" gave "incomplete, misleading or false information about aeronautics" while "the airmen themselves are bluffed and bulldozed so that they dare not tell the truth." The "air fraternity" was fed up. In the past few years the army and navy had made any self-respecting pilot "ashamed of the cloth he wears."

As for the most recent accidents, Mitchell charged that the navy launched the Hawaiian flight only for publicity to "make a noise about what it was doing with aircraft." The PN-9 seaplane was a "good-for-nothing big, lumbering flying boat" that had "nothing novel in design" and was "untried for this kind of work." The navy should have spaced its guard ships much closer together than the two-hundred-mile intervals for an experimental flight with such "primitive flying machines." The "poor *Shenandoah*," he claimed, had manifold problems. It was an "experimental ship" overweight by 50 percent. Its structure was "badly strained" by its break from the mooring mast last year. Its girders were corroded by leaking radiator antifreeze. Safety valves that were removed made it even "more dangerous" for the crew. The airship, which didn't have a "modern" design, was clearly on a propaganda flight. "What business has the Navy over the mountains, anyway?" he demanded. "Their mission is out in the water."

Mitchell had a long list of other complaints. The navy staged elaborate Pacific maneuvers in the spring and joined the army in a mock invasion of Hawaii. Congressmen and reporters were "fed and entertained" aboard ships during the war games. The navy and army boasted that they took Hawaii, but in a real war Mitchell claimed that enemy subs would bottle up the fleet in San Francisco or sink warships in the Pacific. A navy flight to the Arctic in the summer, sponsored by the National Geographic Society and flown by the famed explorer Lt. Cdr. Richard Byrd, was badly managed, using planes borrowed from the army unsuited for the mission.

There was a dire shortage of weather stations around the country to supply meteorological information to air service planes. Meanwhile the navy was wasting hundreds of millions of dollars on a battleship fleet that "today is a useless element in the national defense." Antiaircraft tests the army conducted in the summer and fall were "laughable." The army issued glowing press releases, but its gunners couldn't hit targets towed by air service planes and couldn't find planes flying in the dark. Coastal antiaircraft defenses were "useless" against airpower. The only defense against a warplane was another warplane. Meanwhile "not one heavy bomb has been dropped by the Air Service line units in target practice for two years. . . .

"As far as I am personally concerned, I am looking for no advancement in any service," Mitchell concluded. "I have had the finest career that any man could have. . . . I owe the government everything. The government owes me nothing." But "as a patriotic American citizen, I can stand by no longer and see these disgusting performances by the Navy and War Departments."

The statement was incendiary. Mitchell had voiced many of these criticisms before—but never in such recklessly harsh language. Criminals ran the War and Navy Departments? Guilty not just of incompetence but of treason? By implication Mitchell was charging the president of the United States with high crimes. Coolidge was, after all, the commander in chief of the armed forces. In wartime

Mitchell would likely have been sent to the stockade for publicizing such mutinous thoughts. In peacetime he felt that officers were—or should be—freer to give their opinions, even sharply worded. But Mitchell was practically challenging the authority of his military superiors to lead, as well as the civilian control of the military—a constitutionally dangerous move for a senior American officer. The statement also raised a question of loyalty. His commanders would never forgive him for what they considered a betrayal of them and his service. Mitchell always believed he owed allegiance to a higher cause—making the nation secure with airpower.

Why had he said what he said? And with such inflammatory language? Relatives and friends have suggested many reasons. Mitchell's half-brother, David, believed he was still haunted by the memory of his younger brother, John, who died in a plane crash in World War I. His sister Ruth believed he broke ranks out of a sense of higher duty, inspired by his father, who had been a U.S. senator. Blackie wondered whether the bump on the head from the plane crash six days earlier had rattled his brain. Friends were sure that if Betty had been with him in San Antonio, she would have talked him into toning down the language. "The minute she left to go to Detroit, the newspapers just landed" on him, recalled Eleanor "Bee" Arnold, wife of Maj. Henry H. "Hap" Arnold, a Mitchell loyalist. "I guess he'd had a couple of Scotches." Perhaps Mitchell became more strident and impatient to get things done because he knew time was running out for him, historians have speculated. He knew he had a weak heart.

They were all factors. Mitchell *was* outraged over deplorable conditions in the air service and the needless deaths. He wanted his statement to rouse the country and its business titans, like Henry Ford, into pressuring Washington for improvements. Moreover, he'd become conspiratorial in his thinking, convinced that higher powers were colluding against him. Though in public he professed to be friendly with General Patrick and Admiral Moffett, in private he belittled them both for perpetuating what he considered a military monopoly that blocked progress. "Patrick and Moffett," he wrote to Betty, "were basking under the shadows of the edifice erected by the interlocking directories of the Army and Navy, supreme in their valor and ignorance and maintained by the willing hands of the professional office holders." Mitchell also had developed a grandiose, almost medieval, view of his own role as an agent of change. He was the one knight "equipped in armor from head to foot," he wrote Betty. "The people outside of the castle, fully stirred by what has transpired, grab anything within reach and rally to the lone man's support."

But there was another reason he released the statement: Money.

In letters to Betty that he told her not to let anyone else read, Mitchell predicted that his fiery words would drive up sales for *Winged Defense*. "Now people will buy our books and writings," he wrote. They could live comfortably back in Middleburg. Mitchell knew full well that what he had said could invite a court-martial, but he did not think that would happen. Instead the army would simply drum him out of the service, and that was fine with him. He expected to be summoned back to Washington for a grand set of congressional hearings by winter—with him as the star witness to air his charges. "They must have an investigation and they must show why my ideas of a department of national defense shall not be carried out," he wrote Betty.

In one letter Mitchell mapped out his public relations strategy, and told his wife to keep it "entirely confidential and secret." He would lobby papers like the *Chicago Tribune*, which had "been knocking us a little," to get them on his side. *Liberty* magazine planned to bestow on him its thousand-dollar hero award, given to the person showing the greatest physical and moral courage that year. He'd give the cash to widows and orphans of *Shenandoah*'s dead. He would also sign a contract with *Liberty* to write six articles for fifteen hundred dollars each. That total, nine thousand dollars, would pay for the African safari he had been considering "or anything else you might want to use it for." He might also write a syndicated series of news articles during the investigation of his charges, but only if he got "60% of the gross receipts."

"Now be very quiet, Rat, about these little things," he told Betty. (Mitchell liked to give nicknames to relatives. He called his sister Harriet "Arat" because he thought it rhymed with the last two syllables of her name and had begun calling Betty "Rat" and their baby daughter, Lucy, "the littlest ratlet" or "Snooks.")

They were about to make history, Mitchell was sure. But it would be history far different from what he ever imagined.

4 The Mitchell Problem

After Mitchell passed out his statement to the reporters, he climbed into a plane with Short and flew southeast to Port Aransas for a weekend of tarpon fishing in the Gulf of Mexico. Bobbing in a boat, he wore a broad-brimmed cowboy hat and a khaki private's uniform stripped of insignia. He pinned a large sunflower to his shirt. The six tarpon he caught he tossed back into the water.

Mitchell left a political firestorm behind him. His charges led the Sunday editions of newspapers all over the country. BRANDS AIR RULE 'CRIMINAL', screamed the giant headline on the front page of the *Chicago Tribune*. FLYERS KILLED BY STUPID CHIEFS' PROPAGANDA SCHEMES, COL. MITCHELL CHARGES, blared the *Washington Star*. Many printed the full text of his statement, which reverberated overseas where foreign governments questioned whether the United States was a paper tiger. "Is it really true that the Air Services of the War and Navy departments are in the condition he states?" a top Austrian officer asked the U.S. military attaché in Vienna.

Angry navy pilots griped that Mitchell was "showing damn poor taste," as one member of the Hawaiian mission put it. Sen. Hiram Bingham, a powerful member of the Military Affairs Committee and an air service leader during the World War, insisted that Mitchell's claims were "exaggerated." The *New York Times* editorialized that they "come pretty near breaking the back of what reputation [Mitchell] had left."

But those complaints were scattered and drowned out by a groundswell of grassroots support for the "flying general." In the

Roaring Twenties everyone was in love with the airplane. The country was bursting with automobiles, telephones, radios, and fancy new household appliances. The airplane was an even more wondrous innovation. Flying in these amazing machines, a man could have breakfast in Washington, lunch in Ohio, and "dinner the same night in Chicago," as Mitchell once wrote. Stunt flying became the rage, Hollywood idolized pilots, and publishers churned out story after story about their daring flights. Mitchell and war aces became cult figures. And readers devoured accounts of the bureaucratic battles they had with their superiors.

Telegrams poured into Fort Sam Houston congratulating Mitchell. Air service pilots vowed to reporters that they would "stand squarely" behind him. Poems were penned in his honor. Mothers named their newborns after him. Kiwanis and Optimists Clubs around the country passed resolutions backing his stand. Top American Legion officials called for a law creating a separate air force. William Randolph Hearst, the powerful newspaper magnate whom Mitchell assiduously cultivated, wrote that it was now an established fact that the army and navy chiefs "are incompetent with regard to aviation." There was also an ugly side to the groundswell, however. The Ku Klux Klan, still a politically powerful organization in 1925, seized on Mitchell's statement and charged that Roman Catholic generals in the War Department were the ones subverting U.S. national security.

Congressmen promised air investigations, and Arthur Brisbane warned in one of his columns that they had better "not be a whitewashing enterprise." Mitchell's disciples were gleeful over the pain he'd inflicted on the brass. "You shot them sitting," Maj. Horace Hickam, an air service officer, told him. Mitchell certainly believed it. "I have gassed these people out of their holes," he wrote triumphantly to his sister Katharine. "The holes are stuffed up behind them and they are forced to fight under great disadvantage. Things have broken almost perfectly so far and unless we make some bad mistake will go forward with constantly increased momentum."

On Sunday morning senior Army officers in Washington, reading the transcript of Mitchell's statement in their newspapers, were too stunned for words. Maj. Gen. John Hines, the army's chief of staff, rushed into the office and huddled with his deputy, Maj. Gen. Dennis Nolan. Both refused reporters' demands for a response. So did Mason Patrick, who privately thought that what Mitchell had said was "outrageous."

At the other end of the country William Moffett paced back and forth in his San Francisco hotel room with a copy of his newspaper. The admiral had been waiting there anxiously for word from rescuers that they had located Rodgers's seaplane in the Pacific. But now he was in a rage. "Did you read the morning papers?" he shouted to an aide. "That son of a bitch! What's he doing riding over the Navy's head to further his own interests? I am going back to Washington and I am going to put a stop to this!" He thought Mitchell had lost his mind.

Billy Moffett was as flamboyant as Billy Mitchell. The admiral was a fast talker who walked briskly and had a penchant for getting into an officer's face when he spoke to him. Like Mitchell, he sported the latest fashions in civilian clothes: British-styled double-breasted suits, which he wore often in Washington.

Moffett was the father of naval aviation and the aircraft carrier. He, too, had fought mossbacks in his service (the battleship admirals) and had carved out his own empire in the Bureau of Aeronautics. Mitchell was contemptuous of him because he was not a pilot but a naval aviation observer who rode in the backseat of planes. Moffett didn't pretend to know a lot about the mechanics of aviation, but his aides worshipped him. He also had powerful allies in Congress. Unlike Mitchell, however, he used gentle persuasion in public instead of a sledgehammer to get what he wanted.

The two men should have been allies. Instead they were bitter rivals. Moffett was constantly going to editors demanding equal space when Mitchell wrote articles in their publications. Moffett argued that Mitchell's plan to separate the navy from its air arm was a "foolish" idea he wanted no part of.

Moffett took the Sunday-morning train back to Washington to begin damage control and to assure a nervous Secretary Wilbur that the navy had nothing to be embarrassed about in ordering the *Shenandoah* and Hawaii flights. But it did. Moffett, who had become obsessed with the dirigible's strategic potential and political value for the navy, had personally brokered the compromise between Lansdowne and the chief of naval operations to launch the *Shenandoah* the first week in September, in time for many state fairs. His fingerprints were on the doomed flight.

Calvin Coolidge's eleven-week vacation was nearing its end, and he wasn't eager to return to Washington. White Court, the president's summer residence in Swampscott on the North Shore of Massachusetts, had been heaven. A No Trespassing sign and a marine guard at the entrance of the secluded estate kept sightseers out. The clear, cool New England air invigorated Coolidge. From the house's terrace he had a spectacular view of the blue waters of Massachusetts Bay. He indulged himself and had his pancakes with Vermont maple syrup at eight o'clock every morning instead of his seven o'clock breakfast time in the White House. Grace Coolidge loved her brisk walks around the grounds, often in her white linen dress, a Secret Service agent in a three-piece suit and straw boater always at her side.

Cabinet officers, ambassadors, and senior military men visited regularly for lunches and dinners, prepared by a Belgian cook brought from the White House. Coolidge put in several hours' work in the study during the morning and afternoon, but otherwise the schedule was kept light. In the evening a movie projector was set up in the living room, and the family, along with neighbors and their children, enjoyed the latest films shipped from Hollywood. A hundred million Americans now went to the movies each week. The hottest comedy that year was Charlie Chaplin's *The Gold Rush*, which lampooned "Coolidge prosperity."

The day after the *Shenandoah* accident, at 11:00 A.M. sharp, the half dozen or so White House correspondents who had accompanied the Coolidges to Swampscott were ushered into the study. The president's collie, Rob Roy, sniffed the reporters' trousers as they settled into their chairs. Coolidge was media savvy. He was the first president to use the radio effectively to push his agenda—he sounded conversational over the airwaves—and the first to hold twice-weekly press conferences.

Coolidge paid attention to his image and skillfully handled reporters, most of whom liked him. His ground rules for press conferences were that written questions had to be submitted in advance so aides could screen them. He also was never to be quoted directly. The session was always on background. No one in the White House press corps objected.

"I have a number of questions as to the reason why the *Shenandoah* was taking the trip," Coolidge said in his nasal, reedy voice as he flipped through the pieces of paper. "About that I haven't any information. Of course it is customary if there is a celebration anywhere for those who are having it to come to Washington and ask if the . . . *Shenandoah* [might] be sent." He claimed he didn't have any say in the dispatching of the airship; he assumed Wilbur left that up to the discretion of its commander. "My own observation has been that those who have been in command have not only been willing but anxious to take it out at any time that they thought was appropriate." Coolidge reminded them that he had canceled the *Shenandoah's* flight to the North Pole because he thought "it would be too dangerous."

Coolidge was spinning the reporters. The White House hadn't been as detached from the *Shenandoah's* itinerary as the president now said. For the past two years mayors around the country had flooded Coolidge with requests to have the *Shenandoah* fly over their cities, and his aides forwarded them all to the navy with memos asking if the department could satisfy them. Some states were feeling slighted that the dirigible hadn't visited, Republican officials warned Coolidge, and that was creating political problems for him. The White House never overruled the navy when it turned down a request. But the White House continued to send the admirals the requests, which increased the pressure to send the *Shenandoah* out on publicity trips like its last one. The accident now could become as embarrassing for Coolidge as it already was for the navy.

Historians have dismissed "silent Cal" as a do-nothing president. Franklin Roosevelt called him "a diffident little man." A friend once described him as "a stick" because he had no personality.

The caricatures weren't completely accurate, however. Ronald Reagan considered Coolidge a conservative hero and took down Harry Truman's portrait in the White House and replaced it with Coolidge's. Although he didn't enjoy bantering with friends and spoke little at Washington dinners because he found them boring, Coolidge did have a dry sense of humor and was a hard worker. If he didn't like a visitor, he sat him in a squeaky chair to make him feel ill at ease. But he regularly invited congressmen to breakfasts (though he said little at them), had many overnight guests, shook hands with about four hundred callers at lunchtime each day, introduced Christmas carol singing at the executive mansion, translated a page of Dante every day, and kept several dogs, a horse, a donkey, and a raccoon on the White House grounds.

Coolidge also was a hugely popular president. The economy was booming. Writers like Sinclair Lewis and Eugene O'Neill might be cynical or pessimistic, but Americans were conservative, probusiness, and isolationist like their president—and happy. The arts flourished. Jazz, Dixieland, and the Charleston were the rage. Irving Berlin, George and Ira Gershwin, Richard Rodgers and Lorenz Hart, and Cole Porter had begun turning out musical hits. Ouija boards, mah-jongg, flagpole sitting, yoga, and nudist colonies were popular. The country was beginning its love affair with sports heroes: Babe Ruth was belting out home runs, Jack Dempsey was putting boxers on the canvas, Red Grange was averaging 182 yards a football game, and Bobby Jones was winning nearly every golf tournament he entered.

A largely unremarkable governor of Massachusetts and a phantom vice president, Coolidge became president when Warren Harding died in 1923. Coolidge was a cautious manager rather than a bold leader, but that was all Americans wanted, and he was scrupulously honest, which was a relief from the scandals that had plagued the Harding administration. He handily won election in his own right in 1924 with the slogan Coolidge or Chaos.

But now he faced chaos within his military. A careful man who ran the executive branch tightly, Coolidge was still coping with such Harding administration scandals as Teapot Dome, which involved bribes Harding's interior secretary had received for leasing public lands to oil companies. The last thing Coolidge wanted was charges of impropriety in the handling of the nation's defenses, and the navy seemed to have a tin ear for public grief over the accident. The father of one of the *Shenandoah*'s dead complained to the White House—and to reporters—that the navy delivered his son's body to him COD, clad only in his underwear and "in an old black box."

Coolidge had occasionally met with Mitchell and had asked him to take his place at air functions around the country. The president recognized the importance of airpower, but he had never been impressed with flashy pilots or Mitchell's bravado. He had just two army officers assigned to his White House staff (they helped him with military public works projects), and he favored international arms limitations and modest defense budgets.

Mitchell and the president, in fact, could not have been more different. Mitchell was born to wealth and spent lavishly. Coolidge, whose father ran a country store in Vermont, lived frugally. Mitchell was an internationalist who had traveled the world. Coolidge cared little about foreign policy and up to that point had been out of the United States only once, to Montreal for his honeymoon. Mitchell was a technological visionary. Coolidge didn't ride in a car until he was thirty-two and didn't own one until he left the presidency.

Now, however, the president was furious with his rogue officer. Coolidge believed he had cut Mitchell a lot of slack with his past testimony before Congress, but these new charges were too serious for any commander in chief to ignore. The White House press corps at Swampscott reported that Coolidge refused to comment, but that "official circles here" were hinting that Mitchell would be court-martialed. Considering the ground rules the reporters followed, it was highly likely that Coolidge or his top aide, Everett Sanders, had leaked to the press that the White House didn't want Mitchell parading before a congressional hearing: It wanted him tried as a criminal.

Wednesday night, September 9, the Coolidges locked up White Court and were driven to Salem, where they boarded a special train headed for Washington. Thursday afternoon a small delegation, which included Secretary of Commerce Herbert Hoover and Secretary of State Frank Kellogg, greeted them when their train arrived at Union Station near the Senate side of the Capitol. The city was still sweltering in the summer heat.

Coolidge had a number of thorny issues awaiting him at the White House, which was being renovated in his absence. France and Italy still owed the United States war debts, and he wanted them repaid. Budget estimates had to be submitted to Congress. He had to decide whether to hike funding for the enforcement of Prohibition, which Americans by the millions ignored, and whether to settle on cuts in defense appropriations or allow an increase so the *Shenandoah* could be replaced.

And then there was the Billy Mitchell problem. The airman had powerful friends in Congress and the press. But so did Coolidge. The president had spent as much time wooing Brisbane and Hearst as Mitchell had. Coolidge had risen in politics because he was highly skilled in defusing crises or waiting them out. Dealing with Mitchell, his senior aides believed, would be a major test of his presidency.

FRIDAY NIGHT, SEPTEMBER 25, 1925

Mitchell's entry into Washington was far showier than Coolidge's two weeks earlier. His train from St. Louis pulled into Union Station at 7:00 P.M. Outside the station two hundred American Legionnaires carried placards and waved flags, with a fife-and-drum corps playing "The Stars and Stripes Forever." Joining them were several hundred others: delegates from foreign war veterans' organizations, tourists, gawkers, children, reporters, photographers.

Mitchell and Short had set out from San Antonio three days earlier in his Packard. But they got only as far as Muskogee, Oklahoma, when heavy rains made muddy roads impassable. So Mitchell left the car with Short in Muskogee and boarded a train to St. Louis, where he joined Betty for the trip east.

Stepping on to the railway platform in Washington, Mitchell looked like a traveling salesman. He wore a gray suit (rumpled from being on the train for more than a day), a bow tie, and a slouchy cowboy hat with a snakeskin band. He tapped the ground with a walking cane. (One of the many myths that had grown around him was that he used the cane because of a knee injury he suffered exploring the Alaska wilderness as a young officer. But his family knew the knee was fine. The cane, which had a special ruler inside it for measuring horses, gave him a jaunty air.)

When Mitchell stepped out of the entrance of the train shed, the cheering crowd broke through a line of policemen holding it back and surged in on him, jostling Betty and almost knocking her down. Hap Arnold, who had come out to meet the couple along with other air service officers, rescued her and guided her to the edge of the throng. Several husky Legionnaires, meanwhile, hoisted Mitchell onto their shoulders and began parading him down the concourse to the northeast gate.

"What's the matter with Billy Mitchell?" a cheerleader began shouting in a deep voice over the fife and drums.

"He's all right!" the crowd roared back.

"Who's all right?" shouted the cheerleader.

"Billy!" the crowd chanted. "Our Billy Mitchell!"

The black night lit up with popping flashbulbs from a dozen photographers, who almost got into a fight with police trying to control the mob. Mitchell, waving his cowboy hat and relishing every moment of it, pumped hands and posed for dozens of photos with men and boys and buglers and drummers, who all packed in around him.

"What I am here to do is to tell the truth," he shouted in response to reporters, "and to present irrefutable facts and figures which will awaken the people of the country to the breaking down of their national defense system."

White House aides reading about the spectacle in the next day's papers were furious. Mitchell was a U.S. Army officer ordered to Washington to explain the serious charges he had made, not a politician arriving at a rally.

Mitchell would not get the spectacular hearings before Congress that he would have preferred. Behind closed doors the War Department moved quickly to bring him before a court-martial. Maj. Gen. Ernest Hinds, Mitchell's immediate supervisor, who commanded the Eighth Corps at Fort Sam Houston, was enraged over the political tornado the celebrity pilot had brought to his quiet post. Hinds fired off a series of confidential cables to Washington demanding that he be allowed to relieve Mitchell immediately as the corps air chief. The general worried that this "violent and unjustifiable language," particularly coming from someone of Mitchell's "rank and prestige," could stir up insurrection among the air officers at nearby Kelly and Brooks Fields. The War Department approved Hinds's request.

After his fishing trip at Port Aransas, Mitchell kept busy the next two weeks in San Antonio. He answered the hundreds of letters and telegrams that still poured in, gave speeches to the junior Chamber of Commerce and a convention of insurance commissioners in town, attended the wedding of a colonel's daughter and graduation exercises for fliers at Kelly Field, and ducked out for afternoon hunting excursions.

Mitchell also began the public relations offensive he'd outlined for Betty. He signed the contract with *Liberty* magazine to produce six articles for nine thousand dollars and arranged for a clipping service to collect the news stories about him from around the country. He began conferring with influential reporters, like John Nevin of the *Washington Post*, who would cover him when he arrived back at the capital. He also churned out more public statements, all far milder than his first one. In them he outlined "a constructive policy for our national defense," defended his right to speak out, and hailed the rescue of Commander Rodgers and his crew. (The navy finally found the missing PN-9 seaplane on September 10.)

As the army began collecting evidence against him, Mitchell remained blasé—even downright cocky—about the legal trouble he was in. On September 17 a colonel named E. D. Scott, who worked for the Eighth Corps inspector general, walked into his office "with a very mysterious air," Mitchell thought. Scott had been ordered to obtain copies of the statements he had issued and to find out which reporters got them. But the newspapers refused to cooperate. Could Mitchell help him out? the officer asked sheepishly.

No problem, Mitchell told him. He had already signed a piece of paper for post headquarters acknowledging that what the newspapers printed was accurate. He had Blackie type up a list of the reporters and handed Scott copies of each statement. By the way, Mitchell said coyly, you've "forgotten to tell me, according to my constitutional right, that any statement that I made might be used against me." Embarrassed, Scott did so. Mitchell didn't really care. He took the colonel and two other post officers out for an afternoon of dove hunting and then for a cold supper at his quarters that night.

"We have accomplished exactly what we started out to do," he wrote Betty, brimming with confidence. Mitchell had already gotten permission from the army to ship to Washington eight hundred pounds of documents he had in San Antonio, which he would use to back up his claims. Lawyers from around the country had sent telegrams offering to defend him for free. "I shall handle my own case," Mitchell told Betty. He would merely explain to the court that a trial does not "fit a case of this kind and state that they must determine the case according to its merits. It does not make much difference which way they decide, as far as we are concerned. We shall come out on top."

Hap Arnold finally managed to extract Mitchell and Betty from the Union Station crowd and pile them into his car. The major drove the couple downtown to the New Willard hotel. Arnold would never forget the first time he met Mitchell. It was the summer of 1912 and this "eager young captain" from the army's general staff, who had never flown on a plane, walked into his office and said he wanted to write a research paper on the future of military aviation. Mitchell, however, was more interested in expounding on his own ideas about the potential of these new machines than in asking any questions, which Arnold found amusing. Arnold had been one of two army officers detailed the year before to learn how to fly planes at the Wright brothers' aircraft factory in Dayton, Ohio. His former commanding officer thought there was "no better way for a person to commit suicide." Arnold began to realize that, too. Flying was dangerous and exhausting work, demanding total concentration. He had been the first army airman to wear goggles, because of the bugs that kept hitting him in the eyes when he landed.

Arnold had been taken by the brashness—and brilliance—of this army captain who ran his mouth in his office. Six feet tall and elegantly handsome in his uniform, Arnold had an engaging smile and a dignified manner that exuded authority. He was also a lot like Mitchell—bold and headstrong, with a flair for public relations. The two men and their wives had become close friends over the years. Arnold, who was now chief of information for the air service, had already begun feeding Mitchell reports and memos to help with his case.

Mitchell's suite at the posh Willard was filled with air service officers and well-wishers. Betty, still radiant in a dark brown dress, managed to smile gamely at everyone even though she was exhausted from the long trip. She had left baby Lucy with her parents in Detroit.

The phone rang from the front desk. Some fifty reporters were in the lobby asking if Mitchell would come down for a press conference. "I won't talk now," he said. He had allowed only Charles Parmer with Universal Services, one of his confidants in the media, to come up to the room with him.

Mitchell slipped off his jacket and put on a dressing gown Betty had unpacked for him. He strolled over to the window in the suite, where he could see the Washington Monument in the distance. Aides had already begun stacking piles of reports and transcripts on coffee tables, and he would read them until late that night.

"General," one of the air officers finally called to him, "those Legion posts that greeted you tonight want you to go to a barbecue tomorrow night. Can I say yes?"

Mitchell spun around from the window. "That bunch that met me tonight—that played the drum for me?" he answered. "You bet I'll go." (And he would the next night, a noisy parade escorting him in a horse-drawn carriage to the barbecue on the Keane farm at Eighteenth Street and Benning Road.)

Mitchell turned back to the window and gazed again at the Washington Monument. The Union Station reception had invigorated him. When the army had returned him to the rank of colonel, he had wanted to be assigned to Chicago, which was closer to his family in Milwaukee and Betty's in Detroit. But San Antonio was not such a bad assignment. It gave him a sense of how Americans outside the fishbowl of Washington viewed the country.

He turned to Parmer, who had sidled up to him at the window. "They sent me to Texas, far away, but not so far that I couldn't come back and talk," he told the reporter. "Now I'm back in Washington.

"Say, it's great the way life turns out, isn't it?"

5 Tribunal

Mitchell leaped over the puddle of stagnant water in the narrow, dark corridor that led to the stairwell. He could see pools collecting in other rooms on the first floor and trash spread everywhere. Workmen, hurrying to clean the place, had tacked up signs to direct people. One had COURTROOM printed on it, with an arrow pointing up the stairs.

Mitchell climbed them, ducking his head at the top so he wouldn't bang it on a low-hanging crossbeam. The second-floor room where the trial would be held smelled dusty and dank. It looked like a dilapidated schoolroom. Thick posts broke up the cramped space. Bare lightbulbs under bowl-shaped, ribbed glass hung from the ceiling with long pull strings to turn them on. Dark shades hung over long windows that hadn't been cracked in years. Drab walls looked as if they had been covered with cardboard, pocked in places by ugly brown water stains. Scratched oak tables had been brought up for the lawyers and judges, along with uncomfortable hard-backed chairs. Makeshift signs hung over doorways to adjacent rooms to designate the jurors' chambers, witness room, press room, and conference rooms for the prosecution and defense teams.

Mitchell scowled as he looked around. He had wanted his trial to be held in one of the ornate caucus rooms of the U.S. House of Representatives. Instead, Dwight Davis, a Harvard man and law school graduate who had replaced the ailing Weeks as secretary of war on October 13, picked one of the army's seediest structures. The red-brick Emery Building was located at First and B Streets, at the foot of the Capitol on its northwest corner. A quarter century earlier the Census Bureau had been headquartered there. Now the War Department used it as a warehouse. Mitchell's trial was "[neither] a vaudeville show nor an advertising scheme," Davis answered testily when reporters questioned him about the shabby accommodations. This was "serious War Department business." Davis was a World War I veteran and a skilled tennis player, who had established the Davis Cup in 1900. Unlike Weeks, he was more willing to play hardball; Davis wasn't about to give Mitchell a dignified setting to air his charges.

Frank Reid followed Mitchell up the stairs to the courtroom. The Illinois Republican congressman was also unimpressed by what he saw. Not long after arriving in Washington, D.C., Mitchell realized that he needed a lawyer. The army had placed him practically under house arrest, refusing to allow him to travel to Omaha to speak at the American Legion convention or even to nearby Baltimore for a meeting of one of the local Legion posts. The service's judge advocate general had decided that Mitchell would be charged with violating the Ninety-sixth Article of War, which covered "all disorders and neglects to the prejudice of good order and military discipline" as well as "all conduct of a nature to bring discredit upon the military service." It was a catchall provision for anything the army found offensive. "Officers are tried under it for kicking a horse," Mitchell said sarcastically. But the punishment was left to the "discretion" of the court, which theoretically could mean anything from a slap on the wrist to jail. Betty had begun to worry about the latter possibility—her husband behind bars.

Mitchell had sent a wire to Reid in Aurora, Illinois, on October 3, asking if he would represent him. The representative wired back the same day accepting the job. And he would do it for free. The Mitchell trial would be a major press event. Reid was a largely unknown representative who was only in his second term, and he knew the trial would quickly make him a national figure. The two men had met when Mitchell testified before the House Aircraft Committee, chaired by Representative Lampert. Reid had been one of the panel's most aggressive members, scorching the government for mishandling the aircraft industry. The United States had spent close to a half billion dollars on aviation in the past five years with little to show for it, Reid charged, and any more money Congress appropriated would be "like pouring water into a leaky barrel" unless the country "enacted a national air policy." He fervently agreed with Mitchell's call for a unified air force.

Mitchell appreciated that. Reid, who was his age, had the qualities he was looking for in a civilian counsel. The congressman was a skilled politician who understood that this would ultimately be a political trial. Reid was a streetwise lawyer who wouldn't let the generals at the court-martial push him around. Born in Aurora, just outside Chicago, he was one of eleven children of an Irish grocery store owner. After graduating from the University of Chicago he had attended the Chicago College of Law. Reid knew nothing about military law and had only a beginner's knowledge of the War and Navy Departments from his service on the Lampert committee. But he had spent seven years in Chicago's hurly-burly criminal courts as a prosecutor before going into politics. In a trial he could be extremely persuasive.

Tall and lanky, with dark hair that curled at the ends, Reid was a complex man. His father had not given him a middle name, so he picked the letter *R* for his initial, somewhat like Harry Truman's *S*. He never appeared in public without a three-piece suit and a bow tie. In the winter he wore a derby and in the summer a boater. Fast-talking, with quick, darting movements, he could be brusque but witty. People meeting him the first time found him gregarious and generous. On the other hand, he could be distant with his own family and never gave friends his full attention for more than five minutes before he became bored and walked away from them.

Reid was smart and always came to congressional hearings well prepared. He loved words and scribbled the unusual ones he came across in a black notebook that he kept in his coat pocket. He didn't drink, smoke, swear, or gamble. For entertainment at dinner, he liked to challenge children and friends at the table to give the definitions of words from his notebook. He could listen to the radio for hours or, after dinner, relax with someone playing Irish songs on the piano in his parlor.

He was more moderate than the conservative Republicans in his district. The local unions supported him. And when he found a cause—like reform of the aircraft industry or Billy Mitchell—Frank R. Reid became passionate about it.

In the month since his return to Washington, Mitchell and the high command had been maneuvering intensely against each other. Reid had begun issuing press releases to whip up public support, promising to fight the War Department every step of the way at trial. Mitchell's statement had been an exercise of his First Amendment rights under the Constitution, the representative maintained. "The people want to know why Colonel Mitchell is to be denied the right to tell the truth," Reid told the *Washington Post*. Editorial pages of the *Chicago Evening American, Baltimore News,* and *New York Evening Journal* ran coupons that readers could clip and mail to Coolidge or the War Department, demanding a separate air force.

A pack of reporters followed Mitchell everywhere in the city. For them he feigned nonchalance, claiming that he was oiling his rifles and preparing for an African safari after the trial. Behind the scenes Mitchell was having old World War I buddies like Rickenbacker lobby powerful groups such as the American Legion on his behalf. Parmer, Mitchell's pal at Universal Services, wrote a story that the air hero might be a presidential candidate in 1928. "'Bosh!'" Mitchell responded in the Parmer piece, claiming he didn't even have a party affiliation. "'I'm a flier. That's the language I speak.'" (In fact, Mitchell was intrigued by the thought of a presidential run and, if he ran, he knew it would be as a Democrat.)

The nonstop press coverage eventually became too much even for Mitchell. He threw out photographers who had managed to work their way into the reception room of his hotel suite. "These are my private rooms," Mitchell snarled at them. "There's nothing doing on pictures." He was grumpy because one of the photographers had rung the doorbell before sunrise to take a shot of him.

The Coolidge administration also rolled out a formidable publicity campaign against the air officer. Refuting Mitchell's charge that there were too few weather stations to help pilots, the Agriculture Department issued a three-page press release on the fine work its weather bureau did "in aid of aviation interests." The War Department's Military Intelligence Division, which oversaw publicity for the army, gave reporters a Weekly Press Review of news stories around the country pro and con on Mitchell. But "they are always careful to pick out those that criticize you," an officer at air service headquarters wrote Mitchell in a confidential memo. Reid was incensed about an October 20 War Department press release, which gave biographical sketches and listed the military decorations of everyone who would participate in the trial except for one person—the defendant.

Moffett got permission from the navy to attack Mitchell in the press. "The most charitable way to regard" the army colonel's charges, the admiral said, "is that their author is of unsound mind and is suffering from delusions of grandeur." The navy had begun a formal inquiry into the *Shenandoah* accident and had summoned Mitchell to repeat his accusations before that investigative body. But Reid refused to let him testify, knowing full well that anything his client said before the decidedly hostile naval officers would be used against him in his court-martial.

Coolidge was a master at keeping his public distance from messy problems. His one exception in this case was a trip to Omaha to defend his administration's commitment to national security before the American Legion convention, whose delegates were still simmering because the War Department had refused to let Mitchell attend. No nation ever had an army large enough "to guarantee it against attack," Coolidge patiently explained. But he pointed out that in the United States, civilians decided how much defense was enough, not the generals. Coolidge didn't accuse Mitchell directly, but he made clear the constitutional threat posed by the officer. "Whenever the military power starts dictating to the civil authority, by whatever means adopted," he warned, "the liberties of the country are beginning to end."

Except for the Omaha speech, Coolidge stuck to the rule he followed during his presidential campaign: no one "ever injured himself very much by not talking." For the previous month he had busied himself with executive branch appointments, presidential pardons, a public buildings bill for the District of Columbia, plans for an international disarmament conference, and the French war debt. His only excitement came during one of his evening walks near the White House, when a car rounding a corner almost hit him as he stepped off the curb. A Secret Service agent grabbed his arm and yanked him back.

Coolidge closely tracked issues as mundane as whether Washington should construct "artificial pools" in the city for swimming. But when reporters asked him about the Mitchell case, he claimed to be detached and unaware of its details. The *Washington Post* bought that line, reporting confidently that "the President himself is not giving attention to the matter."

Of course that was not true. Coolidge had actually moved quickly to defuse the Mitchell crisis, or at least the blowback it could have on the White House. Six months before Mitchell made his September statement, Coolidge had been mulling over the idea of setting up a blue-ribbon panel to investigate the condition of the country's military and commercial aviation. Now the decision to form such a panel was easy. He quickly announced it and called on one of his classmates from Amherst College, Dwight W. Morrow, to be the board's chairman.

A high-powered New York lawyer, Morrow was a partner in one of the country's most successful banking houses, J.P. Morgan & Co. His daughter Anne would marry Charles Lindbergh five years later. Morrow maneuvered and cultivated influence well in the worlds of high finance, government, and politics. He had become wealthy on Wall Street. He arranged special loans from J.P. Morgan for Gen. John "Black Jack" Pershing, the famed leader of American forces in World War I, and gave him confidential advice on stocks to buy or sell. He also made a point of keeping in touch with his old classmate who was now in the White House, sending him occasional gifts, including six wild ducks one time for the Coolidge family to feast on.

Coolidge's political cronies, such us Frank Stearns, one of his campaign fundraisers, thought the formation of the Aircraft Board, with Morrow as its chair, was "one of [the President's] great strokes." The board's eight other members were as distinguished and politically reliable as Morrow: a retired general and admiral, an aviation industry consultant, Sen. Hiram Bingham (a Coolidge ally), Rep. Carl Vinson of the Naval Affairs Committee (a navy loyalist), Rep. James Parker of the Interstate and Foreign Commerce Committee, a federal appeals court judge, and a Stanford University engineer. None was an air service pilot, although there were several aviators on the technical committee advising the group.

Coolidge did not have to worry about the panel coming up with harebrained proposals that would embarrass the administration. Morrow came to the assignment with an open mind. But he didn't buy the argument that the United States had to have the world's best air force and he thought aviators like Mitchell tended "to exaggerate" the strength of foreign forces and to "belittle our own."

The War Department could not have been more delighted and quickly cozied up to Morrow. Davis, the new secretary of war, sent him two tickets to the Army-Navy football game, which was being played in New York that year. The Army assigned its aggressive assistant chief of staff, Brig. Gen. Hugh Drum, to provide Morrow anything he wanted: departmental reports, statistics, high-ranking witnesses. Drum, who hated Mitchell and realized that the influential Morrow could be important to his own military career, stuck to the banker like glue.

Ninety-nine witnesses came before the Morrow board. Drum and other top War Department generals testified on the army's view of airpower and its proper place inside that service. Moffett stoutly defended his position that the navy should keep its airplanes. But Morrow also summoned young airmen, who gave a bleaker picture of service conditions than did their superiors. Army pilots called for a separate air arm, and even naval aviators, who opposed breaking away from the fleet, complained of the admirals' stifling control. As he was about to testify, Hap Arnold had thirty-five planes roar over the House Office Building, where the Morrow board was holding its hearing (waking a grumpy Coolidge from his nap at the nearby White House). "You have just heard the noise of the entire air force of the United States—thirty-five planes," the major told the board. It was an exaggeration, but Arnold had made his point that the army had few modern aircraft.

Mitchell had his turn on September 29. Spectators overflowed into the hallway outside the hearing room, where many farther back stood on chairs to get a peek at the famous airman through the doorway. Betty sat behind him in a fashionable knee-length dress, wearing velvet gloves, taking notes.

Mitchell, however, proved to be a dismally dull witness. He had been writing and polishing drafts of his testimony as far back as the week before he left San Antonio. But inexplicably, he now began drily reciting from his *Winged Defense* book, which most of the board members had already read. "He sat there and opened this book and in a sing-song voice started to read paragraph after paragraph," recalled Bee Arnold, who was sitting behind Mitchell with her husband, Hap. "Betty got fidgety. Everybody got nervous." For a day and a half Mitchell droned on: "We, the air people, have had to develop a new and therefore unheard-of service. It has had to prove itself as it went along. . . . In our own country, the development of this important national asset has been slow and inefficient. . . . With our aeronautical condition growing worse, with our air service falling to pieces in material and personnel, we have appealed to the President and the American people to hear our cause."

Board members yawned and shifted in their seats. Women in the audience began flipping through magazines. Arnold muttered to himself at one point: "Come on, Billy. Put down that damn book. Answer their questions." Hap and Bee never figured out why Mitchell performed so horribly. He seemed nervous and worn out. There was none of the defiance or passion the airmen wanted for the hearing. "You could feel the coldness go through that Board," said Bee. "Oh, we were just sunk."

Morrow cleverly refused to cut Mitchell off or to be baited into arguments with him. He let him speak until he had talked himself out. Even sympathetic reporters had to admit that the stormy petrel had nothing new to say. His appearance, the *New York World* charitably concluded, "was disappointing."

Fortunately for Mitchell, he had a month after the Morrow board hearing to get ready for the next public test at his trial—even though it would be staged in the shabbiest setting the army could find. His inspection of the courtroom finished, Mitchell tugged at his overcoat. The Emery Building did not have heat, and repairmen didn't know if they could get a furnace working by the time of the court-martial. (They did.) The rough wood floor had splinters that jabbed into his shoes. Another army officer with them jumped up and down to see if the floor would give under extra weight. It creaked but seemed to hold. Mitchell and Reid walked out into the chilly fall day. Mitchell felt he deserved better than this dump for his tribunal.

9:00 A.M. WEDNESDAY, OCTOBER 28, 1925

Capt. Ken Fiedler rang the doorbell to an apartment at the Anchorage. The door swung open. Mitchell stood there in his white shirt, black tie, army jodhpurs, and boots, with a wide grin on his face. He and Betty had moved out of the expensive Willard and into the apartment at 1900 Q Street Northwest, which a friend had loaned them for two months.

"Well, well, hello there, Fiedler," Mitchell boomed, grabbing the nervous captain's hand and slapping him on the back. "Come on in and sit down. Glad to see you."

Fiedler, who was the acting adjutant for the army's Washington district, warily walked in. Betty and Maydell Blackmon sat on couches in the living room, along with several reporters scribbling notes. Mitchell's court-martial would begin in just an hour. All week Reid had kept issuing press releases defending his client's constitutional right to speak out. Even Josephus Daniels, long retired as navy secretary, argued against muzzling Mitchell with a court-martial. "Let him have his say," Daniels wrote in a newspaper column.

The military kept up its publicity campaign as well. The navy's lawyers drafted a three-page memo declaring that the *Shenandoah's* flight to state fairs was legal. The service sent out press releases and put its top officers on the radio the day before the trial to publicize the navy's 150th birthday and to repeat their opposition to a separate air force. Charles Rosendahl, the *Shenandoah's* navigator, who survived the crash, told a radio audience that the crew expected "good flying weather" on its last flight. Lansdowne and the others "set out with full confidence that we should accomplish this flight as satisfactorily as we had all others."

Fiedler settled into a couch. Mitchell had finished reading the morning papers and was in a jovial mood. Of course there were stories previewing his trial, and the sports pages had the latest gossip on Jack Dempsey's nose job. He got it to help his breathing, the fighter insisted to reporters, not for cosmetic reasons. Dempsey also revealed that he was worth a whopping $1.5 million.

"Have you had breakfast?" Mitchell asked the officer.

The captain said he was fine.

"Well, have a cup of coffee anyway," Mitchell said cheerily. Fiedler held up his hand to beg off, but Mitchell wouldn't take no for an answer. "Aw, come on," Mitchell said. Fiedler gave in, and Betty got him a cup. "That's the stuff," said the jaunty Mitchell.

The two men chatted about Washington's unusually cold weather for October. Fiedler finally realized he had forgotten to perform the duty for which he'd come. He set down his cup. "By the way," he said, pulling an envelope out of his coat pocket. "I've got these papers here. Court-martial papers, you know." The envelope contained a summons for Mitchell to appear at the Emery Building at 10:00 A.M. and a one-sentence letter announcing that he was formally under arrest and confined "to the city of Washington."

"Oh sure, let's have them, thanks," Mitchell said, unconcerned, stuffing the envelope in his pocket without looking at what was inside it. The two men had a few more minutes of chitchat until Fiedler found a graceful way to make his exit.

Betty fetched Mitchell's tunic with the rows of service ribbons over the left breast pocket and his Sam Browne pistol belt with its leather strap over the shoulder. The rest of the army wore stiff, high-collar tunics. But its pilots had finally managed to convince the service to allow them to wear coats with the collar and lapels turned down. The high collars chafed their necks during flights, when they had to keep their heads in a constant swivel.

Betty gathered up her coat. She and Mitchell, with Blackie and the reporters in tow, walked out the door to another apartment down the hall to fetch Mitchell's sister Harriet, who had rented it to be with them for the duration of the trial. Outside the Anchorage, Mitchell, his wife, sister, and Blackie climbed into a waiting car that would take them to the Emery Building.

6 The Challenge

The line of some five hundred people outside the Emery Building stretched for almost a block down B Street. Two army sergeants and a policeman stood at the doorway to keep the crowd from bunching. Many were Washington's political and social elite, who had arrived in chauffeur-driven cars. Some had been there since daybreak, hoping to get one of the few courtroom seats allotted for the audience. (Unless closed for security reasons, most courts-martial even today are open to the public.)

Mitchell's car pulled up at 9:45. Reid and the legal team had arrived ahead of them. So had the twelve generals assigned as jurors to consider Mitchell's case. The out-of-towners among them booked rooms at the downtown Army & Navy Club. Each was driven in a separate staff car—except for Maj. Gen. Douglas MacArthur. He and his wife, Louise, drove down in their personal car from Baltimore, where he commanded the Third Corps.

The crowd began applauding when Mitchell climbed out of his car, his briefcase in one hand, a Malacca walking stick in the other. He shook a few hands in the line, waved to others with his cane, then marched up the stairs with Betty clinging to his arm.

Inside the second-floor courtroom, the spectators, who numbered fewer than a hundred, sat on metal folding chairs they had grabbed at the doorway. A dozen more men and women, who had managed to talk the guards into letting them in, stood at the back. The press tables were jammed as well, with about forty reporters and photographers. The War Department had hoped for as little publicity as possible. But the trial was the biggest media event in the country. A telegraph operator in the nearby press room sat ready to type out bulletins to papers everywhere. A motion picture cameraman began filming as Mitchell and Betty walked in.

The courtroom seemed only a little more fixed up than when Mitchell had visited it four days earlier. There was the smell of fresh paint. The shades had been pulled up on the windows facing south and west so sunshine poured in to make it a bit more pleasant. But the walls still had large, ugly water marks and exposed electrical outlets. Dark oak tables had been arranged in an arc at the front of the room for the twelve generals who would hear the case along with the law member who would rule on legal questions. White porcelain water pitchers and glasses were placed on the jurors' tables, along with courts-martial procedure manuals, notepads, and pencils. Jutting from the center of the arc was a small table with two hard-backed chairs for the court stenographers. Mitchell's defense team crowded around two small tables on the right, facing the jurors. The prosecutors sat at tables to the left. Three phones had been installed for the court's jurors and the prosecution and defense teams. The army had assigned an officer and fifteen ser-geants and privates—some of them toting rifles—to serve as order-lies and bailiffs. Three of them were also assigned twenty-four-hour duty to guard the room and its safe, which held classified material.

Corinne Rich, a society reporter for Universal Services, cor-nered Betty, who wore a glamorous black dress, a black silk bro-cade coat trimmed with karakul lamb, a brightly colored Persian silk scarf, and a tam-o'-shanter on her head. "Am I for Col. Mitchell?" Betty answered one question breezily, her blue eyes beaming. "You bet I am. I'm for him through thick and thin." Rich scribbled notes. "But I'm awfully anxious to get [back] to Detroit," Betty added. "My baby is there with my mother. Little Lucy is only three months old." (Betty's father, Sidney Miller, a wealthy Detroit lawyer, had come to Washington and was not only advising Mitchell's defense team but also paying many of its expenses.)

Why hadn't she brought her daughter? Rich asked. "Well, she might have added some more color to this trial sitting here beside us," Betty answered with a laugh. "But you don't know Lucy. She has her father's big voice."

Meanwhile Mitchell had laid his cane and briefcase by the

defense table and begun bowing and glad-handing men and women among the spectators. He also slapped the backs of the generals who would hear his case, giving each one a hearty "Hello, there." The jurors (in military trials they are called "members of the court") were as resplendent as Mitchell in their beribboned service uniforms. Charles Summerall, the senior major general of the group, who had been designated to serve as president of the court, had ordered his colleagues to come without sidearms on their Sam Browne belts.

Mitchell acted as if he were attending a family reunion—and in many ways it was. This trial was unprecedented. The jury had been handpicked by Secretary of War Davis and General Hines, the army chief of staff. (There were unconfirmed rumors that Coolidge had had a hand in the selection as well.) The officer corps was small in the postwar army. Every man knew practically every other man personally or by reputation, and the thirteen officers of this court knew Mitchell well.

Brisbane, who branded the trial "preposterous" in one of his columns, would send the War Department into a tailspin when he wrote that the generals hearing Mitchell's case had been "loafing in the United States" while Mitchell was "fighting in France." Nothing could have been further from the truth. The twelve generals were drawn from the top leadership of the army. Summerall, a tough-talking artilleryman, was being mentioned as a future chief of staff. They were the service's best and brightest. Brig. Gen. Edward King was commandant of the prestigious General Services Schools at Fort Leavenworth, Kansas. They were decorated soldiers. Maj. Gen. Benjamin Poore, who commanded the Seventh Corps, had been awarded the Distinguished Service Cross, as Mitchell had. Maj. Gen. Robert Howze, commander of the Fifth Corps, had won the Congressional Medal of Honor. Most, like Maj. Gen. William Graves, were graduates of West Point (which Mitchell wasn't). Most had distinguished records (like Mitchell) in the World War. Brig. Gen. George Irwin had led artillery brigades in the Meuse-Argonne offensive.

As a jury, however, they could not have been less impartial. None was a pilot. Few were neutral; most either admired Mitchell or had little respect for him. Brig. Gen. Albert Bowley, another artilleryman, who commanded Fort Bragg in North Carolina, publicly stated his belief that Mitchell exaggerated the combat prowess of airplanes. Mitchell also suspected that Maj. Gen. Fred Sladen, the conservative superintendent of the U.S. Military Academy at West Point, was no friend.

Brig. Gen. Edwin Winans (who had fought in Cuba, the Philippines, and the World War) and Brig. Gen. Ewing Booth (a non–West Pointer like Mitchell, he commanded the Cavalry School at Fort Riley, Kansas) were considered two of the court's progressives who might side with Mitchell. So might Brig. Gen. Frank McCoy, who commanded the Third Infantry Brigade at Fort Sam Houston, to which Mitchell had been banished. McCoy was fond of the maverick airman. "Bill Mitchell has stirred up more agitation than anybody since war time," McCoy wrote to a friend. It was giving Coolidge, whom McCoy considered an immensely popular president, "an armful instead of a handful of trouble." McCoy would be a godparent to one of Mitchell's children. Another ally might be Col. Blanton Winship, the court's law member, who assisted on legal questions. Winship had been an occasional dinner guest of Mitchell and Caroline when they lived in Washington. That, of course, could just as well work against Mitchell. Winship may have sympathized with Caroline in the bitter divorce, although the army lawyer did become friendly with Mitchell and Betty afterward.

Then there was MacArthur, who had just been promoted to major general that year. Mitchell believed he was an unquestioned ally. He had greeted MacArthur warmly when he walked into the courtroom. The two had known each other since boyhood. MacArthur also came from a prominent Milwaukee family, although Mitchell had never liked to play with MacArthur when the parents got the two boys together because Mitchell thought MacArthur was a sissy. But as young men each remained close to the other's family. MacArthur dated one of Mitchell's sisters, Janet, although he was always fonder of Harriet. Mitchell had served in the Philippines under MacArthur's father, Gen. Arthur MacArthur, an outspoken officer like Mitchell who was eventually passed over for higher command by angry superiors.

Douglas MacArthur, like Mitchell, was close to his mother, could be prone to rhetorical flourishes, and fervently believed that America's destiny was to be a world power. Again like Mitchell, he had become one of the army's glamour generals, although MacArthur had risen higher than the older Mitchell and had ruffled far fewer feathers in getting to the top. During the World War he fought with the famed Rainbow Division, made up of National Guard units from around the country, and had returned a hero, twice wounded and gassed in combat. MacArthur, who had already begun sporting his trademark corncob pipe and crumpled service cap during the World War, had Mitchell's arrogant streak. MacArthur had clashed with Gen. John Pershing when MacArthur, as its superintendent, tried to liberalize West Point's curriculum. But his courtly, almost Victorian manner irritated fellow officers far less than Mitchell's rough edge did. At the trial Harriet found MacArthur far more somber than the rambunctious West Point cadet she had known when he came to see her.

Mitchell had kept in close touch with MacArthur over the years. MacArthur had invited Mitchell to speak to the West Point cadets. Mitchell warily accepted (he had no love for the academy, believing it produced closed-minded officers who looked down on men like him who hadn't graduated from it), but he ended up thoroughly enjoying his visit. Betty had befriended MacArthur's wife, Louise. The week before the trial, she had dropped by the Anchorage for lunch with Betty. Louise now had a seat in the audience to watch the spectacle. She would not leave it when court was in session.

MacArthur, however, would write later that the orders detailing him to the court were "the most distasteful" he had ever received. He was not looking forward to staring every day at a defendant he had known since boyhood. Although MacArthur had not yet bought in to Mitchell's vision of airpower, he believed that Mitchell had every right to speak out. MacArthur was as depressed as the defendant over the military's sorry state. "Conditions in the Army are more or less chaotic," he had written to a friend four months earlier. "A general sense of instability and lack of confidence in the higher command seems to permeate the rank and file. The War Department itself is a madhouse." But, not eager to jeopardize his own chances of becoming the army's chief of staff one day by siding too openly with Mitchell, MacArthur would try to stay as invisible as he could during the trial.

"Stand up!" a sergeant from the detail of orderlies finally bellowed. Conversations stopped. Everyone in the courtroom rose. The door of the anteroom, to which the generals had retreated, swung open. The twelve senior officers and their law member marched out silently and took their places behind chairs at the court's tables. They stood erect for several minutes to let photographers take their pictures. The only sounds in the room came from the whirring of the movie machine and the clicking of cameras.

Summerall finally motioned everyone to take his seat. Howze, who was second in seniority among the court members, pulled out the chair to his right. Winship, his legal adviser, sat at Summerall's left.

• The photographers turned around and began snapping shots of the prosecution and defense lawyers. Col. Sherman Moreland, the trial judge advocate, or lead prosecutor, flipped to page four of the fifteen-page script he had prepared to prompt him on what he should say at the convening of the tribunal. Stocky, balding, and bespectacled, Moreland looked every bit of his fifty-seven years. A New Yorker and a graduate of Cornell University Law School, he had had a distinguished career as a jurist, serving as an associate judge of the Supreme Court of the Philippines during the U.S. occupation and in the Office of the Judge Advocate General during the World War. He had been summoned to this trial from Ohio, where he served as judge advocate for the Fifth Corps. Moreland was a meticulous man, mild-mannered and polite to a fault in a courtroom. To his left sat his assistant, Lt. Col. Joseph McMullen, a Virginia lawyer with delicate features who enlisted in the army at twenty-two and won his commission five years later. Moreland also had sitting behind him an air service officer and, if he needed them, officers from the Navy Department to advise him on technical matters from their branches.

Reid jotted down on a piece of paper the seating arrangement of generals, from left to right, so he wouldn't forget their names. Mitchell sat to his left with just a notepad in front of him. Betty, her father, and Harriet had pulled their chairs as near as they could behind him. Betty would take copious notes throughout the trial.

Reid had dog-eared the *Manual for Courts-Martial* set to his right, which he had been reading each night. From it he had typed up thirty-three pages of crib sheets to help guide him through the strange procedures the military used for its trials. Reid also had a formidable defense team backing him up. Col. Herbert White, a soft-spoken Iowan, was a military lawyer from Fort Sam Houston, where Mitchell had last been stationed, and had been transferred to Washington to serve as Mitchell's military counsel. (Reid was designated his civilian counsel.) White, who had also rented a room at the Anchorage to be close to Mitchell, was a West Pointer and, like Moreland, a Columbia Law School graduate. Lt. Clayton Bissell, one of Mitchell's trusted pilots, served as his technical adviser on aeronautical matters. In addition to Betty's father, Mitchell was also getting legal advice from Joseph Davies, an old pal from the Wisconsin Democratic Party and former head of the Federal Trade Commission.

Reid had brought in Frank Plain, a judge he respected from his hometown of Aurora, to advise on constitutional issues. He also commandeered from one of his committees William Webb, a book-ish aide fresh out of law school, who did legal research and cataloged the thousands of pages of documents assembled for the case. This was his first trial, and Webb, who had served as a clerk for Pershing during World War I, would tell his children afterward that these had been the most exciting days of his life.

Moreland stood up and announced that he was ready to proceed "with the case of the United States versus Colonel William Mitchell." Reading from his script, he asked the generals a list of questions to determine if the prosecution had any objections to their serving as jurors. It was just a formality. Moreland was more than happy with this group.

"Will any member of the court be promoted" if Mitchell is found guilty? Moreland asked.

None of the generals answered.

"Is any member of the court related to the accused by blood or marriage?"

No one spoke up.

"Has any member of the court a declared enmity against the accused?"

Again silence.

"The prosecution does not desire to challenge any member of the court," Moreland said, turning to Reid.

Reid slowly rose from his chair. His left hand, which clutched several sheets of paper, trembled a bit. He cleared his throat and looked directly at Summerall. "If the court please," he said loudly. "I desire on behalf of the accused to challenge the right of Brig. Gen. Albert J. Bowley to sit as a member of this court-martial."

The courtroom went deathly silent. A faint smile crept across Bowley's face. He didn't seem surprised that Mitchell would object to his sitting on the court.

Reid read a newspaper account of a speech Bowley had given just eight days earlier to an American Legion meeting in North Carolina. "The backbone of every army is the infantry" with the artillery second in importance, Bowley had told the Legionnaires. Mitchell's vision of a single air force made no more sense than "a single medical corps or a single ordnance department."

It was "impossible" for Bowley not to show "bias and hostility" toward Mitchell, Reid argued.

"Has the challenged member any reply?" Summerall asked, turning to Bowley.

The news story was correct, Bowley said, keeping his composure. He had thick dark hair and wide expressive eyes. In the World War he had commanded artillery at the battles of Château-Thierry and Belleau Woods. "However, I have absolutely no prejudice or hostility toward the accused," Bowley insisted.

The other eleven generals and Winship retreated to their anteroom to debate Bowley's fate, leaving him looking a little ridiculous as he sat alone at the court tables while photographers practically blinded him with their flashbulbs.

Twelve minutes later the generals emerged from the anteroom. "The challenge is sustained," Summerall announced in a quiet voice. "General Bowley is relieved from further duty in this court."

Bowley stood up, smiled at Mitchell, and bowed deeply. Then he quickly walked out of the courtroom.

The rustling in the audience stopped. "Do you object to any other members of the court?" Summerall asked Reid, his tone betraying slightly his incredulity that this civilian had challenged such an outstanding fellow artilleryman as Bowley.

"Yes, sir," Reid said, standing up slowly once more. He again looked directly at Summerall. "On behalf of the accused, I desire to challenge the right of Maj. Gen. Charles P. Summerall to sit as a member of this court-martial on the grounds of his prejudice, hostility, bias and animosity against the accused."

Summerall was thunderstruck, and gasps were heard all over the courtroom. Before the trial he had made a point of being cordial to Mitchell, coming up to him and shaking his hand. Summerall was one of the most senior World War officers left on active duty. Considered one of the U.S. Army's best warriors, he was trim and still muscular at age fifty-eight, his hair gray only at the temples.

Summerall commanded the prestigious Second Corps, headquartered at Governors Island, New York. The son of a Florida plantation owner impoverished by the Civil War, he had fought in the Philippine insurrection and the Boxer Rebellion. Colorful and hard-charging on the battlefield, he had been the army's most innovative artillery tactician during the war. Pershing had promoted him rapidly and rewarded him first with command of the prized First Division then the army's Fifth Corps. Summerall was superb at motivating men and getting results. During the war, he threatened to fire any subordinate who wrote the word "stopped" in a dispatch to describe his unit's position. "There is no excuse for failure," he would lecture his soldiers. "No man is ever so tired that he cannot take one step forward."

Summerall sat stonily silent, his face flushed red with anger, as Reid ticked off the reasons he should be tossed from the jury. Summerall had shown the same public antipathy toward Mitchell's airpower theories that Bowley had. Air service officers had scoured Summerall's public statements and fed Mitchell the incriminating evidence. There was "no defect in our present military organization of the Air Service," the general had insisted, dismissing "the extravagant claims for a separate aviation arm or for replacing the other armed forces by airplanes." But there was a far more important reason Mitchell did not want Summerall to lead the other jurors: Two years earlier the two had had a run-in neither had forgotten.

It happened after Mitchell's and Betty's wedding in October 1923. The couple had taken an adventure-filled honeymoon through the Far East and Southwest Asia. They went tiger hunting in India as guests of a maharajah, visited the king of Siam, explored the islands of the Philippines, shopped in Singapore, and toured Java, Burma, China, Manchuria, Korea, and Japan. Mitchell had

arranged for it to be a working honeymoon, although it was sometimes hard to tell when he was on duty. He showed up in San Francisco before the voyage wearing a paisley tie and beige sweater with
his uniform, hardly regulation attire.

With the blessing of his air service boss, General Patrick (who
wanted to keep his maverick assistant away from the Washington
press corps), Mitchell decided to inspect the military assets the
United States had in the region and to collect intelligence on the
airpower capabilities of other nations, particularly potential rivals
like Japan and China. The War Department paid him six dollars a
day for expenses.

The couple's first stop was Honolulu and the army's Hawaiian
Department, commanded at the time by Charles Summerall. Though
the War Department recognized its importance, the army garrison
there had become a sleepy outpost. With budgets so stingy they
couldn't even practice firing cannons, commanders busied themselves with meaningless spit and polish drills. Schofield Barracks kept
a manicured polo field and some of the army's best ponies.

Summerall, however, had sent Washington glowing reports
about his army air units. Likewise, War Department inspectors had
visited Honolulu and left behind rosy—and superficial—evalua-
tions. One report, for example, noted how "well formed" the pilots
were when they lined up in front of their hangar and how smartly
they marched. Summerall thought he'd have an easy time with
Mitchell as well. He had an honor guard greet the couple when they
arrived on post, wined and dined them at his quarters, and put a
car and chauffeur at their disposal.

But Mitchell wasn't interested in watching parades. For almost a
month and a half, between fishing trips and sunbathing on the beach,
he carefully surveyed all the major islands and their airfields. He
grilled mechanics on the condition of their planes, reviewed rosters
and training schedules, inspected supply depots and pored over
finance records, had air commanders write him detailed memos on
deficiencies in their squadrons, ordered pilots into the skies to
demonstrate their flying skills, and watched them closely with his
binoculars. Summerall's staff, which had been prepared to keep
Mitchell busy with dog-and-pony-show briefings at headquarters,
hardly saw him because he spent all his time in the field with airmen.

Mitchell's eight-month tour of Asia produced a 340-page classified report on the region's importance to U.S. national security. It was a sweeping strategic survey. "Political conditions in the Pacific have changed greatly in the last ten years," Mitchell warned in his report. The Asia–Pacific Rim would one day rival Europe in world influence. The security of the United States would depend on the "foothold" it maintained there, along with such colonial powers as England and France. The security zone the United States must control—with airpower, as Mitchell envisioned it—could be thought of "as a huge isosceles triangle." Its northern vortex was the Bering Strait separating Alaska from Siberia. Its southern base stretched eleven thousand miles from the Panama Canal to the Philippines near the coast of Asia.

China, whose military power "was split" among three principal warlords "and a lot of smaller ones," exerted "little political influence outside of its own confines," Mitchell wrote. But with such a huge population, its commercial future "is tremendous and is being constantly extended," he correctly predicted. Japan, however, was the more immediate political and military rival. "Japan's power unquestionably is growing stronger constantly and her political, commercial, and territorial foothold upon the continent of Asia is becoming more secure," he wrote. It was aggressively looking for outside sources of iron and oil to feed its emerging industries. Its "total military strength is growing," he warned. It had a quarter million men under arms. The army's weapons were old, but "the navy appears in good condition," and its warplanes, copied from "the best European models," made it "probably the second air power in the world."

Mitchell also sketched out in detail how Japan would strike the United States in the Hawaiian Islands if there were war. The attack would begin at 7:30 A.M., he predicted. Sixty Japanese pursuit planes would swarm over the island of Oahu, destroying Schofield Barracks, hangars, and planes on the ground. One hundred bombers would bomb the naval base at Pearl Harbor and the city of Honolulu. In many respects his scenario was eerily similar to what actually happened eighteen years later.

Mitchell was not the first with this prediction. Since the end of the World War, army planners had envisioned a future conflict with

Japan, even a surprise attack on Pearl Harbor by Japanese warplanes. The army too was developing a healthy respect for Japanese military prowess, although its intelligence division felt Mitchell's aircraft estimates for the country were inflated.

Mitchell's crystal ball was also far from clear. He did not think the Japanese would use aircraft carriers, which they did. Instead Mitchell believed that ten Japanese submarines would transport the pursuit planes in crates to the northern Hawaiian island of Niihau, where they would be offloaded and assembled at an airfield for the attack. The other one hundred bombers would be flown to Niihau from Midway Island.

But at least Mitchell tried to envision how the Japanese might attack. Overall his report was a far more powerful and persuasive assessment of the Asia–Pacific Rim's strategic value than any written up to that point by an American officer. It was filled with details and intelligence he collected at every stop, rich in insights and historical analogies.

The report also revealed another side of Mitchell: He was a racist. Asia, as Mitchell saw it, was not just a future battleground for competing national powers. "The white and yellow races will be brought into armed conflict to determine which shall prevail," he wrote in his report. Before the war, "the white man dominated the Asia continent politically, commercially, and in a military way to a much greater extent than is the case at the present time." Whites could do so in the future. "Proportionately, the white people have better armies, better air forces, and better navies . . . than the Asiatics." But the white race suffered from "war tiredness" and the yellow races were demanding parity in the region with whites. "The policy of the United States and, in fact, of all the white countries having their shores washed by the waters of the Pacific Ocean, is to keep their soil, their institutions, and their manner of living free from the ownership, the domination and the customs of the Orientals," Mitchell maintained. "We are faced with a problem much greater than it appears on the surface: that of maintaining not only the political supremacy but also the very existence of the white race."

Mitchell's ideas weren't much different from mainstream thinking, however. Many reputable magazines and journals in the 1920s viewed Asian international tensions in the same racial terms. The

army also was a racist organization. Pershing and other senior officers did not believe African American officers had fought as well as
whites in the World War. But Mitchell wasn't shy about his racism,
and even some friends like Bee Arnold were embarrassed when he
ranted about black soldiers being cowards.

Summerall, whose opinions about Asians were just as racist,
didn't mind those derogatory references in the inspection report
Mitchell dropped on his desk when he departed Hawaii. What outraged him was Mitchell's evaluation of his command. It was a mess,
Mitchell concluded in his paper. The air assets of Summerall's
Hawaiian Department "would be almost useless" in repelling the
Japanese. The twenty-three Thomas Morse MB-3 pursuit planes on
the islands were poorly equipped, and their pilots "had very little
training." The fifteen Martin bombers on hand were "obsolescent"
and "hopelessly unable to ward off any decided attack." The air
supply depot was in a horrible state. Fewer than half the eighty-
eight De Havilland biplanes held in reserve were serviceable. The
command was poorly organized. Its defense plan was outdated.
There was no separate command to supervise the air assets and "no
plans for the employment of the air service in case of war."

For seventy pages Mitchell outlined an ambitious and detailed
defense plan for the islands, along with rigorous training to make
the Hawaiian Department war ready. Its air force should be beefed
up to 650 warplanes and organized under a single command, he
recommended. Airways and a radio network should be established
to interconnect defenses on all the islands. Instead of control being
divided between the army and navy, Summerall should command
all operations "within 200 miles of these islands."

Many officers privately agreed with Mitchell's diagnosis. The
War Department's defenses for the Pacific were largely illusory.
Only a fraction of the men and equipment needed to protect American interests was provided. The army and navy were constantly
feuding there. MacArthur thought the Pacific war plans were a
joke. George S. Patton Jr., a Mitchell friend who would serve as an
intelligence officer in the Hawaiian Department in the next decade,
envisioned a Japanese attack much like Mitchell's scenario.

To be fair, Summerall had begun putting together his own
aggressive defense plan for Hawaii in 1924, although its success

hinged on manpower he didn't have. Mitchell's defense plan like-wise depended on air capabilities the air service did not have at the time. Even so, the two men should have been allies in improving Hawaiian defenses. Instead Summerall thought Mitchell had stabbed him in the back.

Mitchell knew that, and it was the reason he wanted Summer-all off this jury. Reid read into the record the most pungent parts of Mitchell's Hawaii report. It clearly "indicated that General Sum-merall knew practically nothing about aviation," Reid said. There was no way Summerall could be "an unprejudiced member of the court."

Summerall struggled to keep his anger in check. "I did not regard his report at that time as made with hostile intent," he began defensively, pretending to have paid little attention to Mitchell's evaluation. "And I have learned at this moment for the first time of the personal enmity toward me as shown by Colonel Mitchell in that report. I had regarded his inspection as that of an official visit-ing a command with which he was friendly. I had not conceived any personal prejudice toward him on account of that report, although I regarded the report as untrue, unfair and . . ." Summerall paused for almost a minute, bit his lip and seemed to have trouble with his last words because of the fury boiling up inside him. ". . . and igno-rant," he finally said.

Summerall was lying. He had been furious about Mitchell's report, and he had fired off an angry letter to Patrick complaining about it. Summerall was a proud commander who didn't like out-siders second-guessing his operation and who closely watched his press clips. He also had a temper, other generals knew, as well as a vindictive streak—particularly when someone crossed him.

"In view of the bitter personal hostility shown toward me by Colonel Mitchell, I could not consent to sit as a member of this board," Summerall now said loudly and indignantly. "I shall ask the court to excuse me."

The ten remaining generals retreated to their anteroom. The audience buzzed. Summerall kept his seat and glared at Mitchell and Reid.

The generals returned in less than four minutes. Howze, the next senior officer on the court, was now their leader. "The challenge is sustained and the challenged member is accordingly excused," he announced. Summerall stood up, bowed to his fellow generals, and quickly walked out.

Harriet, who was sitting just behind Mitchell, could barely hide her glee. Her brother had told her about Summerall's "colossal egotism," as she wrote later, and she thought he marched off like a little boy kicked out of the clubhouse. Certainly not as gracious as Bowley had been.

Howze turned to Reid. "Do you object to any other member present?" he asked, not knowing what to expect now.

Reid leaned to his left, and Mitchell whispered into his ear. Reid stood up once more. "If the court please, I desire to challenge peremptorily, without stating any cause, General Sladen," he announced. Under the court-martial rules, Mitchell was allowed to disqualify one member of the court without giving a reason why.

There was no debating a peremptory challenge. "The challenged member is excused," Howze said.

Sladen, the West Point superintendent, looked almost as surprised as Summerall had. He sat in his seat for about a minute until he remembered it meant he had to leave.

"Do you object to any other member?" Howze asked again. The spectators grew silent and the judges tensed, as if waiting for another crime to be committed.

Reid stood up. "There are no more challenges," he announced. "The court is very satisfactory." Sighs could be heard in the audience.

Mitchell, in fact, had evened up the odds considerably. Two-thirds of the court, or seven of its ten members, had to find Mitchell guilty in order for him to be convicted. (Colonel Winship, the law member, also had a vote.) The number of hostile generals on the court had been reduced from seven to four: Graves, Poore, King, and Irwin. Mitchell believed he had five allies: MacArthur, McCoy, Winans, Booth, and Winship.

That left one undecided by Mitchell's count: Robert Lee Howze. A sixty-one-year-old Texan, he was built like a refrigerator, with a square face, almost slit eyes, and a thin mouth usually turned down in photographs taken of him. Howze was a legend in the army. He won the Congressional Medal of Honor in 1891 as a young lieutenant fighting Sioux Indians at Wounded Knee. He had distinguished himself as well in the Philippines, with a daring rescue of twenty-eight naval officers from Emilio Aguinaldo's insurrectionists. During Pershing's punitive expedition to Mexico, Howze and his cavalrymen had chased Pancho Villa's bandits relentlessly over some of the country's most hostile terrain.

Mitchell considered him an old friend. Two years earlier he had visited Howze and his cavalry division at Fort Bliss, near El Paso, Texas. The two had ridden horses around the post, and Howze had had Mitchell drop by his quarters to regale his son with stories of air battles. Mitchell thought Howze was a bit dense about aviation but at least willing to learn.

Howze was more neutral about the relationship. He had a much warmer friendship with Hines, the army's chief of staff, who wanted Mitchell convicted. Howze was also a no-nonsense officer. As a West Point commandant, he had banned women from wearing the cadets' military overcoats on school grounds, a measure that earned him a one-hundred-thousand-dollar lawsuit from one angry mother. Though Howze thought Mitchell could spin a good yarn about the airplane's potential, he didn't know how much of it was true.

Mitchell's formal arraignment came next, and it took almost two hours. The Article of War he was accused of violating, article ninety-six, had eight "specifications," four of which contained Mitchell's September 5 statement. McMullen, Moreland's assistant, read the specifications, repeating the 6,080-word statement four times in a monotone voice that had almost a hypnotic effect on the drowsy audience and generals. Mitchell insisted on standing through the entire reading of the charges. At one point Betty looked up at him and silently mouthed the words "Why don't you sit down?" Mitchell shook his head, whispering an impatient no. Betty unfolded a copy of the *Washington Times* and began reading as McMullen droned on.

After the arraignment Reid spent the rest of the afternoon arguing that the army had no legal grounds to try Mitchell. The charge against him was too vague. Even in uniform, Mitchell had a constitutional right to voice his opinions, particularly on such an important national issue, Reid contended. He hadn't committed a crime, hadn't libeled any individual, and hadn't disrupted army discipline. Reid pointed out that even Coolidge had said in a Naval Academy speech that officers "are given the fullest latitude in expressing their views before their fellow citizens."

But the day's story, as far as the reporters in the room were concerned, was Mitchell challenging the integrity of three of the army's most respected generals. MITCHELL PROTEST OUSTS THREE JUDGES AS HIS TRIAL BEGINS, headlined the front-page story in the next day's *New York Times*. The *Chicago Tribune* dubbed Reid the "Aurora avenger." Veterans who had served under the three excused generals sent angry letters to the army. Flabbergasted by what he read in the afternoon papers, General Nolan, the army's deputy chief of staff, ordered court stenographers to rush him a transcript of the trial's first day so he could see for himself what the defense had said about the senior officers.

After being excused Summerall had his driver take him to the War Department, which shared space with the State Department in an ornate building on Pennsylvania Avenue next to the White House. (It is now called the Dwight D. Eisenhower Executive Office Building and houses just the president's staff.) Inside Summerall ran into Robert McCormick, who published the *Chicago Tribune* and had served under him in the World War. Summerall erupted. "From now on, Mitchell and I are enemies," the general raged. "It cannot be otherwise after what he did at that court-martial."

Surely Summerall would try to get even. But Mitchell did not care. From the beginning he had always lived by his own rules.

7 Promise

For John Lendrum Mitchell, the voyage to Europe with his new bride was as much an escape as a honeymoon. Europe had always been his refuge, as it was for many of America's upper class. He had studied in Germany, Switzerland, and Great Britain as a teenager; was fluent in four languages besides English; and had developed a passion for Old World art and literature. He was a modest, softspoken man, to whom culture, good manners, and at least the appearance of proper etiquette were important. At thirty-five, he was setting out to rebuild a second life with a second wife, Harriet Danforth Becker, the youngest daughter of a prominent New York attorney. He had married her in a small private ceremony on July 11. Hattie—he called her "Hätchen" in his affectionate letters to her—was the calm antidote he needed. And Europe was the perfect place to recuperate.

John Lendrum had been born on October 19, 1842, in Milwaukee, the only son of Alexander Mitchell, one of the richest men in the Midwest. Alexander was a short, stocky, and ruddy-faced Scot who emigrated to Milwaukee in 1839 at the age of twenty-one with fifty thousand dollars in a tattered carpetbag that his boss, a financier back in Aberdeen, had given him to set up a wildcat bank in the Midwest. At the time banking was illegal in Wisconsin because earlier institutions had fleeced depositors, so the cover name Alexander used to set up his business was the Wisconsin Marine & Fire Insurance Company. Instead of banknotes customers received "certificates of deposit," engraved on silk paper.

Alexander Mitchell ran an honest operation, and over the next forty years he built his bank into one of the region's most respected financial institutions. He expanded his own investments as well, buying railroads, a steel plant, and a real estate insurance company. By the age of fifty, he was believed to be worth $20 million (which is more than $350 million by today's standards). He had married Martha Reed, a cultured Massachusetts beauty, who enjoyed entertaining visiting painters and authors. She founded Milwaukee's Museum of Fine Arts and helped organize the Mount Vernon Ladies Association to preserve George Washington's home. Together the couple built a magnificent mansion near downtown Milwaukee, as well as a palatial villa in Florida, to which they traveled during winter months in their personal rail car.

Father and son could not have been more different. Alexander was brusque and hardheaded in his determination to expand his financial empire. John Lendrum was an idealist and dreamer, more interested in public service and intellectual enrichment than in accumulating wealth. He became a Union Army officer during the Civil War and, according to his superiors, performed bravely the few times he saw combat. Alexander tried to use his political pull to get his son promoted and transferred to safer staff jobs; in any event John was mustered out early because of eye trouble.

In 1865 John married Bianca Cogswell, the daughter of a wealthy Milwaukee attorney, but it was a disastrous union. Bianca accused John of being an abusive alcoholic who slept with two of the household's female servants. John claimed Bianca was the "drunkard," who went out at all hours "with strange men." In 1877 Bianca filed for divorce. The lurid charges and countercharges from their court petitions quickly made their way into Milwaukee and Chicago newspapers in what became headlined as THE MITCHELL SCANDAL. Bianca was finally awarded two thousand dollars a year in alimony. One of the two sons from the marriage was diagnosed with a "feeble mind," and was packed off to a Massachusetts hospital. Alexander and Martha got custody of the other son, David, and raised him at their Florida villa, where they spoiled him.

John and Harriet settled in the southern French town of Nice, renting an apartment on Place Grimaldi called the Maison Corinaldi. On December 29, 1879, Harriet gave birth to a baby boy with dark brown eyes, whose name was registered in the town's civil office as

"William Mitchell." (Over the years the army, reporters, and historians would assign him different middle initials—from C to P to L—but his mother and father actually gave him no middle name.)

Willie, which was what his parents and siblings always called him, lived his first three years in France, speaking both English and French as first languages. In 1882, the family returned to Milwaukee, where John built a one-hundred-thousand-dollar country home on 480 acres of farmland outside the city. He called it Meadowmere.

For a little boy it was a wondrous place. The Queen Anne–styled mansion had an elaborate wraparound front porch, a gabled roof, and a pair of white marble Hungarian hunting dogs at its front entrance. The red oak woodwork of its rooms had been carved with jewel-like precision, inlaid with copper and mother-of-pearl. Many of its fourteen bedrooms had ornate fireplaces. (John and Harriet slept in separate rooms with a secret passageway connecting them.) A playroom was next to the apartments for the children the new couple would have. (Because he spent so little time in it, Willie's room on the third floor was small and austere, with only a desk and bed.) In addition to a billiards room, well-stocked library and upstairs study, John Mitchell had converted another chamber into a gallery for the expensive paintings he had collected around the world. Outside there were stables and a racetrack for the trotting horses he bred, plus a pond filled with fish. When the pond froze in the winter, there were skating parties.

John, who enjoyed puttering around the farm in a big straw hat, became more interested in politics and learning than he ever was in the family business. He was elected to Congress in 1890 as a Democrat and moved up to the U.S. Senate three years later. At the 1892 Democratic convention in Chicago, Wisconsin delegates even put his name up for nomination as vice president. But after one term in the Senate, he abruptly resigned and took his family to Europe for three years, where, in his late fifties, he studied French literature at the University of Grenoble.

John and Harriet ended up with a large family. Willie, the oldest, had five sisters—Martha, Janet, Harriet, Ruth, and Katharine—and one brother, John junior. They would be as different as any seven could be. Janet and Katharine married successful businessmen, Janet growing distant from Willie in later years. Katharine, an environmentalist, was elected to the New Hampshire state house and then the state senate. Ruth, a free spirit, would join Chetnik guerrillas in Yugoslavia during World War II. Martha, a troubled child, eventually ran away from home at twenty-one to be a painter in Greenwich Village. John tracked her down and had her committed to a mental asylum in New England, where she lived the rest of her life. The family never discussed her being in the institution.

Willie was closest to Harriet, who was eight years younger. The practical and frugal one among the children, Harriet was most like her mother. John, the youngest, whom the other children nicknamed "Little Pud," idolized Willie and followed him into the air service.

Willie was the leader of the youngsters at Meadowmere. He rode horses, fished in the pond, and at age five began hunting rabbits and squirrels with an air rifle his father gave him. His nanny, Mary Alexander, remembered years later that he was the worst kid she had ever cared for. He was small and wiry, always busy, always climbing things like the greenhouse, which terrified her because he might fall through its glass. "Very rarely—when he had been a good boy—Willie would be permitted to eat dinner with his father and mother and such guests as might be present," Mary recalled, and as often as not he was sent upstairs to finish his meal after he said something embarrassing.

When he was ten Willie was sent to Racine College, an Episcopal boarding school for upper-class children on the shores of Lake Michigan, south of Milwaukee. He adapted as well as any young boy did to living away from home. Set on ninety acres of woodland with plenty of places for exploring, the school had comfortable dormitories and classrooms, a gymnasium, a spacious dining hall, a well-supplied library, and a laboratory equipped with the latest scientific hardware. Racine also boasted an enlightened faculty, many of them trained at Ivy League schools, who tolerated no hazing among students—although the headmaster had to report to his mother that Willie did have "a little scrimmage" with another boy during his first few months there.

Willie wrote his mother almost every other day. His handwriting was horrible, his spelling poor, but he had a good sense of narrative, and his descriptions of life at the school were unusually detailed for someone so young. "The American Bobolink resembles somewhat the sky Lark of Europe," the ten-year-old wrote his mother of the birds he saw at Racine. "Its flight its song and the way it alights on the Meadow its nest also resembles the sky lark the only thing about its nest is that it doesn't have that little covering. . . . Sky Larks is a dirty white not souch [*sic*] a pretty white as the bobolink has that is tinged with pink just the least little." Willie also drew detailed pictures of the animals he saw.

He missed his parents terribly, however. He scolded his mother when he thought she had not written enough or when she couldn't visit him, and he begged to be sent home for holidays like Easter. Willie was a demanding child as well. Practically every letter had orders for items he wanted sent him—fishing gear for the nearby pond, stamps for more letters—plus instructions for taking care of his animals he had left behind at Meadowmere. "When you bring my typewriter, be sure not to turn it over, and please send me a knife as soon as you can . . . and please have my chicken coop papered with tar paper because that will keep out the cold better than building paper."

Early on he had problems with his eyes. They hurt when he studied late at night, and the printing in books appeared blurry. He recounted for his mother every ache and pain, hoping it would make her feel guilty and visit him.

Willie's grades were good but not spectacular. He scored high in history, English, and Latin, but often low in math, geography, and religion. Occasionally the headmaster had to send Harriet a letter explaining that her son's poor marks in conduct were "for talking before grace in the dining room," for being "boisterous" in his dorm room or "full of mischievous pranks." But his teachers were fond of him and found him unusually bright and inquisitive. Outside class Willie developed wide interests, singing in the glee club, acting in plays, and studying nature. He kept a garden, where he grew yellow violets and shooting stars. He made a record of the different birds he saw in the woods and bought a taxidermist kit from a mail order catalog so he could mount the ones he shot with his air rifle.

Harriet, who wasn't shy about sending notes to the school's administrators and meddling in the way courses were taught or rules were enforced, was sympathetic and loving with her precocious son. She tried to satisfy his many requests and tend to his pets at Meadowmere. "I could not sleep last night for thinking of you," she wrote Willie after one visit. "You seemed so fatigued when I left you that I fear you may become ill if you are not very careful. If the tired feeling continues you must begin taking iron." But Harriet did not bring him home on some holidays, such as Easter and even Thanksgiving, and that made her son sad.

Willie was never as close to his father as he was to his mother. John, who rarely interacted informally with his children, wrote his son far less frequently, and his letters tended to lecture. John would respond to some of Willie's notes in French to keep the young boy proficient in the language. When Willie was a teenager and wrote about the sports he was becoming good at, such as track, tennis, baseball, and particularly the latest "rage," football, his father sent back a sarcastic letter on Senate banking committee stationery: "Football, as played at present, is too savage and results in permanent injury. Your letter is silent as to your studies. This comes of over-modesty I suppose."

But John and Harriet had a right to be worried that Willie's class standing seemed to shoot up or down with every report card and that he spent a good deal of time in detention for minor infractions. In fact, John was a tenderhearted and kind man, who had a long soft beard that flowed almost midway down his chest and who missed his wife and children terribly when he had to be away in Washington for dreary sessions of Congress. Willie, likewise, was never more happy than when he went fishing or horseback riding with his father back at Meadowmere. The young boy also had his grandfather's personal drive to succeed. Willie was always intensely proud of what Alexander Mitchell had achieved in life and he wanted to do the same. But from his father he inherited an independent streak. Willie revered John Lendrum Mitchell, and in letters he would confide in him and ask for advice until the day his father died.

As a teenager Willie became increasingly irritated with the skimpy allowance his parents provided him at Racine: thirty-five cents a week if his grades did not drop and he had no detentions. He begged for more cash. "All the fellows here get money from home and I don't see why you can't give me some," he complained in one note. "I am sure Papa got it when he was away at school and you also. There are lots of fellows here who are a great deal poorer than we are and they get it."

But money had been hemorrhaging from the Mitchell family. The old adage that the first generation makes it and the second spends it was never more true than with Alexander and John Mitchell. John took over the bank and other financial interests after Alexander died in 1887, but he was not as energetic and attentive a businessman as his father, and the Senate kept him away from corporate concerns. He donated generously to civic causes and schools like Racine College. His daughters all studied abroad at pricey finishing schools, and the family vacationed in Europe almost every year. Meadowmere, where the family kept three cars, was expensive to maintain, along with a suite at the Congressional Hotel in Washington, which John used during Senate sessions. He dispensed quarterly allowances as well to various aunts and uncles. His mother, Martha, also spent freely at the family's Florida villa, where she now lived permanently. She and his son David badgered John to the point of threatening a lawsuit for a larger cut of the dwindling family fortune.

The heaviest blow came, however, with the panic of 1893, which closed banks, railroads, and thousands of businesses across the country. By that summer depositors began a run on Wisconsin Marine & Fire Insurance Company Bank, which was about $6 million short on covering its accounts. By law John and the bank's other major shareholders were liable for the amount. John remained at his Senate job in Washington, fearing that process servers from angry creditors might slap him with subpoenas to appear in civil court, or even before a grand jury, if he set foot in Wisconsin. After a good bit of haggling to get the bank's other major shareholders to contribute as well, John finally turned over about $1.3 million of his own assets—practically everything he had except for Meadowmere—to satisfy depositors who insisted on withdrawing their money. The bank eventually recovered and to some extent so did John. When he died in 1904, he was worth $505,847, a considerable sum in that day, but far less than the $20 million his father had accumulated.

After five years at Racine College, Willie was becoming irritably bored, and after much pestering, in 1896 he persuaded his father to let him transfer to Columbian University (now George Washington University) in Washington, D.C.

Willie spent his first year at Columbian in its preparatory school, then moved up to its college division. He was hardly a scholar. He excelled in sports and had an active social life. He had begun taking road trips to Rochester, New York, to visit Enoch and Caroline Stoddard, old family friends of the Mitchells, who had a pretty teenage daughter also named Caroline. By his junior year at Columbian, Willie had no better than an A in Latin, C's in logic and philosophy, and he'd flunked chemistry.

But by 1898 the eighteen-year-old had more on his mind than academics. The country was seized with the spirit of empire. America's continental frontiers had been conquered from coast to coast. Now expansionists wanted the nation to spread its democratic, Anglo-Saxon, Christian values—and exploit rich new markets along the way—to Latin America and the Asia–Pacific Rim. Old colonial powers, such as Britain, France, the Netherlands, and Spain, were already competing there for domination, as were emerging new powers like Germany and Japan. America needed a good war overseas.

It found one in the spring of 1898. Cuban guerrillas had been in revolt against Spanish rule for three years. Two powerful editors, William Randolph Hearst and Joseph Pulitzer, threw their newspapers into a circulation war to see which could print the most sensational accounts of Spanish atrocities. Expansionists saw an opportunity for American conquest, not only of Cuba but also in the Spanish Philippines, a gateway to more lucrative trade with the Asian coast. The USS *Maine*, the first modern battleship the navy had built, was dispatched to Havana to protect American property. On February 15, an explosion blew up the ship (the exact cause has never been determined), killing 260 of its crew. President William McKinley resisted military retaliation, and Spain had little stomach for a fight, but war fever among Americans—who rallied to the cry "Remember the *Maine!*"—became too hot. Congress passed a resolution on April 20 authorizing McKinley to use force to remove Spain from Cuba. Within a week the two powers had declared war on each other.

Willie had watched the noisy debate over the war resolution from the Senate gallery. His academic interests had been uneven, but history—particularly military history—had become a subject that intrigued him. His sister Ruth recalled that the other children were bored silly when John, a history buff himself, dragged the family to famous battlefields in Europe during vacations. But Willie was enthralled by the tours. "No dreariness could abate his vivid interest" as he walked over hallowed ground, she wrote later of her brother. He could picture a conflict "as if it were going on right then."

Willie was swept up by the expansionist rhetoric. He loved the outdoors and adventure. He could handle a horse and had become a fair shot with the many rifles his father had bought for him. Like most eighteen-year-olds, he had a romantic notion of war and chivalry on the battlefield. The night the debate ended and the Senate voted to declare war, he ran home and began packing his bags. When his father arrived after the vote, Willie announced that he was off to Wisconsin to join the same volunteer army regiment his father had served in during the Civil War.

John was not pleased. He'd had his fill of killing in the little combat he had seen. On Capitol Hill he had taken a number of enlightened stands unpopular with his constituents, such as supporting an income tax. He was also a pacifist. He had vigorously opposed war with Spain until the sinking of the *Maine*. After reluctantly voting for war, he opposed expanding American dominion to Hawaii and the Philippines, using his speeches to ridicule the popular catchwords of the hawks, such as "manifest destiny" and "mastery of the Pacific."

Nevertheless John did not stop Willie from joining the army. And as it was, his son never made it in time for the fight in Cuba. On May 19 Private William Mitchell, in "full marching uniform," a friend reported, with "a certain swing to his walk" and "the very worst" hat the friend had ever seen, climbed aboard a train with the First Wisconsin Voluntary Infantry and left Milwaukee, bound eventually for a staging area in Florida. There the unit languished on hardtack and corned beef in a stiflingly hot, typhoid-infested camp near Jacksonville, conditions that ended up killing scores of unfit soldiers. Mitchell himself was in excellent physical shape, however, and avoided the uncleanly habits of other men, who drank polluted water. His father used his political clout to get his son commissioned as a second lieutenant in the militia's Signal Corps, only seven days after he enlisted as a private. Mitchell

became the youngest officer in the army, and a college dropout at
that. (After prodding from his family he would return much later to
Columbian to finish his coursework for a bachelor's degree, partly
because he realized some of the finer clubs he was interested in
joining admitted only college graduates.)

It was not uncommon then for soldiers to use influential relatives or friends to win promotions in the army. Many of the officers
in Mitchell's regiment had gotten their commissions that way. John
Pershing had jumped from captain to brigadier general because he
was a superior officer, but it also didn't hurt that his father-in-law,
Francis E. Warren, chaired the Senate Military Affairs Committee.
Mitchell had no qualms about playing the same game. In letters to
his father he often asked him to speak to generals in Washington to
get him advanced in rank or to arrange for a commission in the
Regular Army instead of a state militia.

Unlike many of the junior officers in his regiment, Mitchell was
quite competent. From the moment he put on a uniform, he began
closely observing how armies were organized. He quickly grasped
the principles of military discipline and of commanding soldiers
fairly but firmly. Just as fast he learned the basics of electricity and
the battlefield use of communications. The initiative the eighteen-
year-old displayed impressed his superiors. They put him in command of a company that had both state volunteers and Regular
Army troopers.

The Signal Corps was the most technologically advanced
branch of the service, experimenting with such new hardware as
the telephone, telegraph, automobiles, cameras, blimps, and, eventually, the airplane. Careerwise it was not the best outfit to join.
Signal officers, particularly those like Mitchell, who had not
attended West Point, rarely rose high in rank. But Mitchell was an
energetic and inquisitive young man who liked gadgets and wasn't
afraid of something new. The Signal Corps was a perfect fit. After
little more than three months at "Camp Cuba Libre" (the name the
army had given to its Jacksonville cantonment), Mitchell was able
to supervise crews laying telephone and telegraph lines and had
mastered Morse code.

He thoroughly enjoyed military life. While other men turned
sickly, Mitchell gained weight and never felt better. He bought a

horse in St. Augustine for $125. He asked his mother to send him his college trigonometry and physics textbooks to bone up on sciences he would need for signal work, along with his trap gun and Winchester pump shotgun so he could hunt game in his spare time. "I like this kind of work very much," he wrote his mother toward the end of August, "and find that it is doing me as much good as college would have this fall."

Which was just as well, because the "splendid little war" with Spain was over by then. Commodore George Dewey led the American fleet into Manila Bay on April 30 and blasted ten Spanish warships out of the water the next day. Teddy Roosevelt's Rough Riders charged up San Juan Hill on July 1. The fighting in Cuba had ended by August 12, and American forces took Manila the next day.

Unlike many sons of influential fathers, Mitchell also lobbied John to pull strings in Washington to get him into the action. If his signal unit wasn't sailing to Cuba, maybe his father could help him with a transfer to the cavalry, which was sure to head to the island. When word spread that the regiment might be sent back to Wisconsin, Mitchell wrote his mother to "speak to Papa about it right away and have him do all he can to avert it. . . . We came down here to fight." Even though the shooting had stopped, Mitchell was still desperate to reach Cuba. He believed it would be disgraceful to return to Wisconsin having never set foot on the place where the battle had occurred.

Mitchell also had begun to notice things that were wrong with the army. The campaign against Spain had fortunately been easy, but the War Department had been woefully unprepared for it. Military equipment and supplies had been embarrassingly short. Training and discipline had been wanting. In Cuba only 379 of the 5,462 American deaths had come from combat; the others had been killed by disease or as the results of accidents. Mitchell was repulsed by junior officers who did not take care of their men. He was not shy—at least in letters to his family—about criticizing the high command. "The War Department does not seem to be backing us up," he complained in a note to his mother. The army had been badly mismanaged, Mitchell thought. "I really do believe that if we had been up against a first-rate power they would have whailed [*sic*] the mischief right out of us."

Mitchell and his signal company finally made it to Cuba in December. It was "a better Christmas Eve in one way than I expected," he wrote his father from the island on December 25. He was camped on a high bluff overlooking the Gulf of Mexico, about seven miles from Havana. There was no fighting. Spanish soldiers continued to slip away at night from the harbor wharf below, with Cubans throwing stones or shooting at them as they climbed aboard boats.

Mitchell walked to town on New Year's Day to watch the formal surrender at the Governor-General's Palace. A friend slipped him in to the closed ceremony in the courtyard, where Spanish officers lined up at the front of the palace and the American troops stood at attention in a hollow square around them. At precisely noon the Spanish flag came down, the American flag went up, a band played "The Star-Spangled Banner," and the Spanish commander was escorted to the wharf by two U.S. generals. Mitchell was overwhelmed. "This event, undoubtedly the most important in the history of our country since the surrender of Yorktown, has stamped itself on my mind and on the minds of everyone else that was there," he wrote to his father in breathless prose the next day.

Mitchell clearly had an exaggerated sense of what he'd witnessed. Nevertheless the Spanish- American War would profoundly shape his view of America's place in the world, as it did for many officers of his generation. The surrender in the Governor-General's Palace, he told his father, "marked the beginning of a new policy on the part of U.S., that of territorial expansion and showing himself to the world as one of the greatest nations."

The next eight months in Cuba were delightfully busy for Mitchell. With his signal company and a gang of Cuban laborers to cut poles and place them in holes, he laid sixty-six miles of telegraph line in twenty-six days, from Holguín to Las Tunas in the western part of the island. It was part of a larger east-west communications linkup between Havana and Santiago de Cuba. The work was grueling and at times dangerous. The terrain was mountainous, the rainy season had begun, and many men continued to drop from typhoid, smallpox, malaria, or yellow fever. Cuban insurgents and bandits roamed the jungles, attacking and robbing convoys, and Mitchell was never sure of loyalties among the general population. He kept his men heavily armed and ordered them to shoot anyone who acted suspiciously around the cable-laying teams.

Typical of Americans of his generation, and of future generations for that matter, Mitchell formed a colonialist view of the Third World nation his country had come to liberate. The Cubans were hard workers and "physically among the strongest I have ever seen," he acknowledged in letters to his family. But "they are no more capable of self-government than a lot of ten-year-old children. They are absolutely ignorant, filthy, untruthful and immoral. The Spaniards are as far superior to them as the Romans were to the Gauls. The only way to settle this thing is to annex the whole outfit, fight them until they dare fight no more." Although he did not recognize it at the time, Mitchell was discovering what soldiers, even liberators with the best of intentions, confront when they change from an invading to an occupying force. "When we first came they seemed to be glad to see us," he wrote in other letters. Now "these Cubans hate us more every day."

Mitchell's detachment laid a total of 137 miles of telegraph wire—more than any other company in the field, he proudly told his parents. It impressed his commanders, and Mitchell was made the assistant chief signal officer at headquarters in Havana, then a general's aide. Superiors marveled at how resourceful and articulate this teenage officer seemed. The chief signal officer of the army, after receiving a study Mitchell wrote on the condition of telegraph lines in the Department of Santiago, wrote back: "It is a very creditable report, and indicates [that] this officer, despite his youth, is a man of ability, energy and intelligence. I have seen few reports giving so much information in a clear-cut form on a technical subject of such range."

"I don't believe I have ever felt better in my life," Mitchell wrote his mother. He found the jungle fascinating, with "boas twelve feet long" and "a great many birds of brilliant plumage." On hunting trips he shot parrots, quail, pigeons, doves, guinea hens, deer, and wild boar. He worked hard and played hard. He was hospitalized for almost two weeks after a horse he was racing on a Havana track tripped and rolled onto him. He had his mother send him a finely tailored dress uniform with lieutenant's epaulets sewn on them. He even found time for parties. "Most of the young ladies here dance

pretty poorly," he wrote to his mother, "so I always make my card
out before I go and get good partners." Harriet had the names of
daughters of prominent Cuban families, which she mailed to her
son. But Mitchell was more interested in news from his mother
on the Stoddard family in Rochester, particularly their daughter,
Caroline.

He was a perpetually impatient young man. No sooner had Mitchell
unpacked his bags in Cuba than he began lobbying his father to get
him assigned to the Philippines, where fighting was still going on
between the Americans and Filipino guerrillas. Other young officers
were getting orders to the Far East, and he didn't want to miss out on
another war. John, who was critical of the U.S. war in the Philippines, had no interest in helping his son transfer there. Neither did
Harriet. But in the end it didn't matter. The War Department on its
own ordered Mitchell to report to the Philippines. John considered
trying to block the assignment but eventually decided not to. "Perhaps it is as well that he go," John wrote Hattie, who was in Europe
with the girls. Cuba was becoming increasingly dangerous due to
disease alone. The fighting would probably be over by the time Willie
reached the Philippines, John guessed. Then, after he had had his fill
of another jungle, "he can resign in the spring."

Besides, John's son seemed different when he stopped off in
Milwaukee for a short furlough in September on his way to the
West Coast. The impetuous youth who had run off to join the army
eighteen months earlier was now a lieutenant with a military bearing far beyond his nineteen years. Willie was in superb shape physically and mentally. He would survive the Philippines. "He stands
straight and talks straight and I may say entertainingly," John
wrote proudly to his wife. "The impression he has made here on
everybody is very favorable."

Indeed, Mitchell had women paying attention to him at the
country club lunches and parties he attended during his two weeks
in Milwaukee. One mother wrote Harriet to tell her "how handsome and fascinating all the girls found him."

But he seemed interested in impressing only one girl. When he
reached San Francisco, Mitchell wrote an uncle and asked him to
mail the photograph that had just been taken of him in his uniform to

a freshman at Vassar College. Her name was Miss Caroline Stoddard.

On November 2, 1899, Mitchell arrived in Manila, where the fighting was far from over. Filipino rebels, who considered U.S. annexation about as oppressive as Spanish rule, were waging a bloody guerrilla war against the American military occupation. Mitchell was assigned to the Second Division, commanded by Gen. Arthur MacArthur. That pleased John. He was sure that Arthur, a family friend whose son, Douglas, had played with Willie in Wisconsin, would look out for his son.

But within a week Mitchell was thrown into action, commanding a signal company as MacArthur's division launched a major offensive about eighty miles from Manila against five thousand heavily armed Filipino insurgents. Mitchell's signal company raced to string telegraph lines so MacArthur could communicate with the front and his flanks. Over the next several days and nights, Mitchell had his first taste of combat and was exhilarated by it. The Filipinos eventually retreated, but they had put up a ferocious fight, some attacking Mitchell's unit less than three hundred yards away. "I thought I could bring somebody [down] with my pistol they looked so near, but had to use my carbine," he wrote his father. "It was about the best target I ever saw."

Mitchell laid more than 150 miles of telegraph cable on the island of Luzon, trudging over rice fields in waist-deep water, through thickets of almost impenetrable bamboo, and across rivers with currents so swift they could sweep a man off a raft in an instant and drown him. Supplies were often scarce, and he and his men sometimes had "little or nothing to eat," only "pool water" to drink, and slept at night "with wet clothes." Mitchell caught malaria. In practically every province his company entered, they came under fire from insurgents who were "well armed, apparently well officered and with plenty of ammunition." But fortunately for him and his men, they were also "pitifully incompetent in marksmanship."

In skirmishes Mitchell's unit captured more than seventy insurgent flags. His most exciting adventure came in mid-May. For several days his camp had been fired on. Fed up, he had units from the Forty-eighth Regiment enter a nearby barrio and round up all its males. Mitchell, by now able to speak Tagalog, interrogated the

men who told him where the *insurrecto* camp was. Mitchell took
two soldiers with him on a night reconnaissance and found the
rebel position. He went back and asked for fifteen soldiers and an
officer from the Forty-eighth to help him raid it. "All this 48th Reg.
are niggers you know except the field officers and staff," Mitchell
wrote his father. But he set aside his prejudices for the moment and
took the black troopers. At half past midnight, with his forces
deployed around the *insurrectos,* Mitchell's raiders "charged up to
their camp across an open field," he wrote. "Their sentry was asleep
and very little firing occurred." Among the guerrillas Mitchell's men
had captured was a Captain Mendoza, the adjutant general of rebel
leader Aguinaldo. Mitchell kept Mendoza's .38-caliber pistol as a
souvenir.

Mitchell vividly described his adventures in letters to his family.
He wrote in detail about life in the tropics, going on for pages about
its flora, insects, reptiles, and animals. He mixed fact with fiction in
some of his notes, perhaps to entertain his family. He passed along
a tale the locals had told him that on a trip to northern Luzon, "I
shall see many different tribes of natives and among them the people who are said to have tails and have to make holes in their chairs
to sit down. It is also said that certain tribes have gills like fish
enabling them to swim great distances under water." Back at
Meadowmere, his excited sisters and brother read and reread every
letter that arrived and tried to reenact their stories in little plays.

The campaign in the Philippines, however, was not as splendid a
war as Cuba had been. It would take 200,000 American soldiers
three years to conquer the islands. More than 4,000 of them would
be killed in action or die from disease, and another 2,800 would be
wounded. Filipino casualties would be even more grievous: about
16,000 dead. Old American generals told Mitchell the Philippines
was "as hard and harder than the Civil War" and he believed them.
He had seen atrocities on both sides, although he rationalized the
American brutality as necessary to bring democracy to the islands.
War protests, however, erupted back home, where ratification of the
annexation treaty had squeaked by the Senate by only two votes.

Mitchell's opinion of the Philippines war was remarkably similar to the view many American officers would have of the war in
Vietnam two generations later. Mitchell and the other soldiers

called the rebels "gugus." (American officers would call the Vietnamese guerrillas "gooks.") "The stage is passed where these people can be treated with any consideration whatever," he wrote to his mother. The low-intensity conflict Americans were fighting was senseless. "I believe that the time has arrived for the fire and the sword," particularly for "the unsubmissive ones." But Washington was micromanaging the war and ordering the U.S. Army to "pat them on the back while they are plotting our destruction, while eating our food and receiving our money. . . . In short we are told to go and do with our hands tied behind our backs, our feet in a quagmire and our mouths sealed."

By the summer of 1900, Mitchell was miserable with bouts of malaria, and he began to map out his future. It did not include staying in the army. He believed that he had accomplished more in the service in the past two years than he had in his entire life. The army was a fine institution for making "a man of a person," he wrote to his father, but by Mitchell's calculation that took no more than six years. After that service life could be depressingly dull. Mitchell enjoyed combat or being in the field with his own unit to command and with little intrusion from higher-ups. But he was convinced he would languish in a peacetime garrison, shuffling papers in a staff job.

His new plan began in January 1901. He requested and received three months' leave from the army, during which he toured Asia and the Middle East, then joined his parents in Europe. The stops were important for his education, Mitchell believed. An expansionist America "seem[s] to be breaking to pieces the old bonds of conservatism and usage and making a more defiant bid for everything in sight in a commercial way, than ever before," he wrote to his father. Mitchell wanted to visit the places that one day might be part of the new American sphere of influence.

He returned to the United States that April and reported for duty at Fort Myer, Virginia, outside Washington. His plan was to use his father's help to win a commission in the Regular Army, then obtain a transfer, also with his father's help, to the cavalry, which offered an officer a better future because it was one of the army's combat arms branches. After three or four years in the cavalry, however, Mitchell would resign, enter the family business or law, and wait for the next war. There was bound to be another one, "probably with the very country in which you are now in," he wrote his mother presciently. (She was in Germany.) Then he would rejoin the army, which undoubtedly would be looking for officers with combat experience, and obtain a commission as a colonel, maybe even as a general.

The first piece fell into place on April 26. Mitchell finally obtained a commission in the Regular Army as a first lieutenant. John was now an ex-senator, but he asked a colleague still serving in Congress to write to Secretary of War Elihu Root and recommend his son for the appointment. Mitchell probably would have gotten it anyway. He was finally twenty-one and eligible for a Regular Army commission, and, more important, his superiors had begun to notice that he had potential. The army, which was still adjusting to being a global policeman, desperately needed aggressive young leaders who could think on their own in the field. Of the fourteen first lieutenants who had served in the Signal Corps during the Spanish-American War, Mitchell was ranked number six. He was a "bright, well-educated, zealous officer," a commander wrote in one of Mitchell's efficiency reports—an "excellent" prospect for the permanent service.

The next step Mitchell wanted to take—transferring to the cavalry—was derailed. But only because he got a better offer: Alaska. Gold in the upper Yukon had brought thousands of prospectors to the vast territory. The army wanted to lay telegraph lines that would link up Alaska's interior to its southern coast and then on to Seattle and the continental United States.

It was a daunting project: more than 2,500 miles of line across some of the most inhospitable land on earth. Arctic mosquitoes swarmed over wet tundra and swamps during the short hot summers, driving men and animals crazy. The long winters saw temperatures drop to seventy degrees below zero. Snow in some parts was sixty feet deep. Few officers were capable or even willing to tackle the assignment. Gen. Adolphus Greely, the chief of the army's Signal Corps who was quickly becoming Mitchell's mentor, talked him into accepting.

Over a two-year period Mitchell laid more than five hundred miles of the line from Fort Egbert on the Yukon River near the

Canadian border to the southern coastal town of Valdez. It was a huge job. There were no roads and few trails. Some three hundred tons of poles, wire, tents, and food had to be moved into the interior. A hundred pack animals and eighty dogs dragging sleds had to be rounded up for the transport. Mitchell eventually had fifty soldiers working for him, along with an assortment of Indian guides, lumberjacks, packers, mule skinners, and sled drivers, some of whom turned out to be unreliable. They surveyed routes, chopped down trees to clear paths, ran wires over snow, dug holes in the hard earth for telegraph poles, and then attached the wires to the poles with nails, brackets, and insulators.

Mitchell found the cold, clear climate a healthy break from the tropics. He gained nine pounds in the first three months and suffered no more relapses of malaria. But it was a harsh existence. Sometimes he slept in makeshift log cabins, but most of the time he lay under the stars. When the temperature dropped, he found it almost impossible to keep his feet from freezing in his heavy boots. He constantly froze his nose while "mushing" his dogsled through stiff winds, and he smashed his left kneecap when he fell off once. But Mitchell learned quickly to overcome the elements. When he had to sleep outdoors, he dug out a hole in a snowbank, then stacked up blazing logs on the opposite side so he could rest in the reflected heat. Or he would simply dig a hole in the snow, climb in, and have the sled dogs sleep on top of him.

The work could be dangerous. The enemy was always the cold. Horses and mules often froze, and he had to shoot them. Once Mitchell and his dogsled broke through the ice and into a frigid river. He and the dogs managed to climb out, and with his clothes instantly frozen into a sheet of ice he rushed to build a fire to stave off hypothermia.

But he loved the independence. General Greely gave him wide latitude to construct the telegraph network as he saw fit. "I don't believe that I could have been given such important work in any other place than the Signal Corps," he wrote his mother. Mitchell thrived under the heavy responsibility, and he wasn't afraid to bend the rules to get the job done. At one point he sent a message to Greely asking for extra cash to pay for supplies and salaries. Greely messaged back that he would send him all he had left under the

current congressional appropriation, $50,000, but it would take
months. Mitchell couldn't wait that long. Nothing would be accomplished during the winter months. He went ahead and bought the
goods and services on credit, which army officers were not supposed to do. The cash finally came, but because a zero had been
dropped in the paperwork it was only $5,000. The $45,000 short-
fall—a substantial sum in those days, which technically Mitchell
was liable for—did not seem to worry him. He knew the army
would never get the money out of him because he didn't have it.
"Had it been for $450 they probably would have taken it out of my
pay," he later recalled. But "if you get a large enough amount up
against you and it has been properly spent, you need not be
alarmed." Greely eventually sent him a check for the rest.

The many lonely nights on the trail had their advantages. They
gave Mitchell plenty of time to study for the examination the army
required him to pass to be promoted to captain. He would curl up
by candlelight at night with "Pointer," a large husky he'd grown
fond of, and read from the stack of Signal Corps manuals and
books he had brought with him. Among the engineering reports he
found interesting were the ones about balloons and gliders and
exotic experiments that were being conducted with machine-
powered planes.

Mitchell left Alaska in July 1903. The telegraph system he had
installed won him accolades from Greely and other top officers. At
twenty-three Mitchell became the youngest captain in the U.S.
Army. He was still conflicted about his professional future. One
month he wanted to remain in the Signal Corps, another month he
wanted to transfer to the cavalry, and the next month he was writing his father asking him if he wanted him to resign and return to
the family business. But one thing Willie was now sure of. He had
fallen in love with Caroline Stoddard, and by the time he had been
sent to Alaska two years earlier they were practically engaged. Now
he wanted to marry her.

8 "Not Guilty"

This was the second day the proceeding began late. Howze, who liked to be punctual, had been seven minutes tardy in convening the court on Thursday. Reporters noted that these military men weren't as punctilious as they made themselves out to be.

Braving chilly winds, long lines continued to form outside the Emery Building early in the morning before the doors opened. Some of Washington's luminaries, like Assistant Attorney General William "Wild Bill" Donovan (who would later head the Office of Strategic Services [OSS] in World War II) and Sen. Thomas Walsh, who investigated the Teapot Dome scandal, had managed to have seats reserved for them. Also in the front row sat an elderly woman from Georgia who had attended every federal investigative hearing in Washington since 1907 and who would continue her streak by showing up every day of the Mitchell trial. Several seats down from her was a little gray-haired man who also always seemed to be in the audience at congressional committee hearings and federal court trials.

The Mitchell trial came at a time when the United States was awakening to the modern age. The still largely agrarian country was becoming more industrial and technological by the day. Automobiles, radios, and household appliances were being produced and spread to the masses by the millions. The nation had come out of a wartime economy and survived a brutal recession in 1920. Now there was a boom in housing construction. Consumers were spending and prices had stabilized. In Washington, Breslau Gowns and Hats on G Street offered satin dresses for $9.90 and fur-trimmed coats for $19.95. At Old Dutch Grocery Store, a pound of porterhouse steak cost twenty-nine cents, and six pounds of cooking apples sold for a quarter.

A youth movement was emerging. College enrollments increased; the big men on campus drove top-down Model T's, wore Fair Isle sweaters, Argyle socks, and bell-bottom trousers, and pasted their hair down with Slikum. Radical politics and atheism became popular, as did bohemian lifestyles in cities. Among the icons for the young: airplanes and the pilots who flew the technological marvels. Older people were reluctant to climb into them.

High-profile trials also had become a favorite entertainment for the nation: Americans couldn't get enough of them. There had been the Leopold and Loeb murder trial in Chicago the year before. Nicola Sacco and Bartolomeo Vanzetti, two anarchists convicted of murder, were still fighting their death sentences. Earlier in the summer a Tennessee jury had found John Scopes guilty of teaching evolution in a trial that attracted worldwide attention because its legal combatants were famed lawyer Clarence Darrow and former presidential candidate William Jennings Bryan.

But Mitchell's trial was even more spectacular because the defendant wasn't a street criminal or a mousy high school teacher, but rather a handsome, dashing, and decorated army officer, who loved horses and fast planes, who had a glamorous rich wife, and who was standing up to the establishment.

The trial's other participants became media celebrities overnight. The *New York Sun* proclaimed Betty the "ideal Army woman as she sits beside her spectacular husband." Newspaper photos caught her flirting with Colonel Winship, the court's legal adviser. Reid, reported the *Baltimore Sun,* "looms as a national figure" for his brash defense. Most of the trial's spectators were women, many of them young and elegantly dressed in fur coats and stylish hats. They became Mitchell's court groupies.

Reid had spent all of Thursday attacking the court's right to try Mitchell. In fact he had seemed to go out of his way to deprecate the trial. Instead of addressing the generals hearing the case as "the honorable tribunal," as a military lawyer would, Reid had begun referring to them as "you people." Though Reid was a congressman and didn't feel he had to genuflect to the military, he wasn't doing his client any good by alienating these generals, who were insulted by such references.

The irony of the argument Reid was making, however, had been lost on reporters covering the case. Mitchell had told the press he did not fear a court-martial. In fact, he claimed, he welcomed it as a forum to expose the deplorable state of airpower in the country. But now his lawyer was trying to spring him from the trial on technicalities.

The jury, however, hadn't bought Reid's contention that this military court had no legal authority to try Mitchell and that his client had a higher constitutional right to speak his mind. Moreland had pointed out that even the Constitution recognized that while a civilian could say most anything he wanted, an army man couldn't, particularly if it disrupted military order and discipline. Winship had ruled that the court had jurisdiction to try Mitchell, and the jurors had backed him up.

Reid hadn't fared any better on his next motion: to throw out the case because Gen. Ernest Hinds, Mitchell's immediate commander at Fort Sam Houston, had not conducted a preliminary investigation of Mitchell's offense, as was normally done under military law, and Hinds had not recommended that charges be brought against him. Instead Moreland had revealed on Thursday that Coolidge had been the one who ordered the investigation and recommended the charges. Actually, there was no evidence that Coolidge had personally investigated the case or recommended the charges—they were done in his name by Secretary of War Dwight Davis—but it all had an odor to it. Reporters had bolted out of their chairs and rushed to the telegraph operator in the press room when Moreland made the startling disclosure, and Reid had jumped up, shouting: "I hesitate to believe what my ears convey to my mind!" At the very least the procedure used to bring Mitchell to trial created a conflict of interest. How could the generals sitting in judgment remain independent if their ultimate boss, the nation's commander in chief, had recommended that Mitchell be prosecuted? How could Coolidge, who by military law might one day be called on to review a verdict against Mitchell, be impartial if he was Mitchell's initial accuser?

Military law in 1925, however, was still somewhat primitive in its procedures. The legal code the American army used at the time dated back to the 1774 British Articles of War. It wasn't so much a code as a license for military commanders to discipline their men as they pleased without the interference of pesky attorneys. Until 1920 a soldier's commander, not a magistrate or grand jury, decided if there was enough evidence to prosecute him. The commander picked the officers who would sit as jurors in the case. The prosecutor, hardly a neutral party, also served as the court's legal adviser. The commander also picked the defendant's counsel, who often wasn't a lawyer; even in murder cases, he might be the post chaplain or a young second lieutenant totally ignorant of the law. There was no appeals court to review a case, and if the commander objected to an acquittal he could order the court to change its verdict.

In 1920 Congress enacted some reforms. A pretrial investigation now had to be conducted before a soldier could be charged. A lawyer from the Judge Advocate General's Corps had to sit with the court as its "law member" to rule on legal questions. And the judge advocate general was ordered to set up a board of officers to review the verdicts in serious cases. But the revised Articles of War still contained vague charges with unspecified sentences, like the one Mitchell faced. A soldier's defense counsel still didn't have to be a lawyer, the commander still picked the officers who served as jurors, and these legally untrained officers could still reverse the law member's rulings by majority vote. It wasn't until 1951 that Congress enacted the Uniform Code of Military Justice with more procedural reforms, such as an appeals court for military cases. But even today, commanding officers wield considerable power over who gets prosecuted, and they still pick the soldier's jury.

In 1925 the military court had wide authority to wing it. Winship had not been bothered by the way the trial had been convened. In a special case like this, Coolidge could have the secretary of war bring the charge against Mitchell. After all, Winship reasoned on Thursday, "the President of the United States, as Commander-in-chief of the Armies of the United States, is the commander of every officer in the Army and every soldier in the Army." Winship had overruled Reid's objections, and Howze and the other generals had quickly backed him up.

Friday morning Reid hoped that at least one of his requests would be granted. His last demand on Thursday was for the prosecution to provide him with a bill of particulars. The Ninety-sixth Article of War, which Mitchell was accused of violating, came with eight "specifications" that gave more details on the charge. But the specifications weren't good enough, Reid had complained. They were drafted so vaguely and worded so inaccurately, he claimed, that it was difficult to tell exactly what parts of Mitchell's lengthy statement had violated good order and military discipline. In a civilian court a bill of particulars was a more detailed statement of what one side was claiming against the other.

Thursday afternoon Moreland had seemed to Reid to be amenable to his request for a bill of particulars. This morning, however, the trial judge advocate was decidedly hostile to the idea. "There is no such thing in military law as a bill of particulars," Moreland pointed out. The eight specifications, not to mention Mitchell's own written statements, were detailed enough. What's more, the court "has no power" to order up anything extra like a bill of particulars, Moreland insisted.

Reid stood up. "It is rather peculiar that, within the short space of twenty-four hours, there should be shorn from this court every power in the world," he told the jurors indignantly. Yesterday Moreland "contended you had every power on earth and some that did not exist on earth." Yesterday the court ignored military law and allowed someone other than Mitchell's immediate commander to recommend the charge against him; today it had to follow military law.

"Now another strange thing has happened," Reid added, angry at what he considered backpedaling by Moreland. "In the first blush of this application, it appealed to the sense of justice of the trial judge advocate and he was going ahead last night to pick out the facts so as to comply with this simple, ordinary and just request. What has happened? Has the midnight oil burned so badly they have not been able to discover a way to grant this bill of particulars?"

Mitchell's September 5 statement was more than six thousand words long, and the specifications also refer to the follow-up statement he released September 9, which was far milder. How could any lawyer mount a defense on that much material? Did Moreland "contend that every paragraph of these statements violates or constitutes a disorder and disrespect and a breach of discipline?" Reid asked incredulously. "Surely he does not contend every paragraph is a violation of the specifications? I think it is simply a matter of justice that he point out [the offensive parts] so that we may prepare our defense."

Moreland was fed up with Reid's histrionics. The prosecutor had a miserable cold and should have been in bed nursing it. He jumped out of his seat, his face reddening. "Whose fault is it that these statements are so long?" he asked, turning to Reid with a furious look. "Is it mine? Is it the court's? Whose fault is it? And by what right does counsel for defense stand up here and ask me to correct the voluminosity of the statements of his own client?"

Reid stood up. "We evidently do not go to the same church, let alone sit in the same pew," he shouted to Moreland, sweeping his right arm like a swordfighter and moving closer to him. "May not the terrible length of the statement be due to the terrible state of our national defense? That does not mean you, as accuser, on behalf of the President of the United States and the people of the United States, can say that we must go to trial on a whole basket of things without your pointing out those things upon which you base your charge."

The two lawyers looked as if they were about to lunge at each other. The court was thrown into an uproar.

Howze banged his gavel on the table. "Please address the court, gentlemen," he said loudly, continuing to rap the table.

The two lawyers sat down to cool off.

Moreland collected his wits and finally stood up. "I hope the court will understand I meant no offense to the gentleman," he said apologetically. Moreland didn't like these kinds of courtroom confrontations.

"I understand that," Reid said, still pouting in his seat.

"I desire to say right now," Moreland continued magnanimously, "that if I had a son who was going to appear before the bar, I should be very glad if he was so able and gracious a lawyer as counsel for the accused."

Reid couldn't help but smile, and he stood up. "That overwhelms me," he responded, not to be outdone. "I might reciprocate by saying that if I wanted my son to be a great military lawyer, no greater thing could happen than to have him follow in the footsteps of learned trial judge advocate."

The Alphonse-and-Gaston routine was too much for the audience. Spectators laughed, and even the generals began chuckling.

Winship, however, rejected Reid's request for a bill of particulars. Reporters began keeping score. Reid might be an expert in trial tactics, but he didn't seem to them to be any match for Winship. Mitchell's attorney so far had not gotten the law member to grant a single one of his motions. "Representative Reid has proposed and Col. Winship has disposed," the *Washington Star* told its readers the next day.

Winship was not eager for this kind of notoriety. He and Mitchell had hunted and fished together. That certainly didn't bother Mitchell, who wanted as many friends on the court as he could get, but it made Winship nervous issuing legal rulings for a defendant he knew so well. A lifelong bachelor, still trim at age fifty-five, Winship had a thin face with dark hair combed to the side, and a mustache that was turning salt-and-pepper. He had sad gray eyes and seemed to Mitchell's sister Harriet to have grown considerably older since the last time she saw him.

Winship was both a warrior and a lawyer. A southerner, he had received his law degree from the University of Georgia. But he had spent almost as much time leading combat troops during his military career as he had practicing law. During the World War he had served briefly as judge advocate for the First Army. Then he led two infantry brigades in France, winning the Distinguished Service Cross, Silver Star, and French Legion of Honor for heroism under fire.

Winship had been judge advocate for the First Corps, headquartered in Boston, when the army ordered him to Washington to be the law member for the Mitchell court. He had told the War Department that he and Mitchell were old pals, but his superiors there didn't care. Winship was considered one of the best lawyers in the army.

Reid had no more pleadings before the court.

"If the accused will now stand," Moreland announced, turning to Mitchell, "I will ask him how he pleads."

Mitchell rose from his seat and snapped to attention. This began his formal arraignment on the charge of violating the Ninety-sixth Article of War.

"How does the accused plead on specification one of the charge?" Moreland asked.

"Not guilty," Mitchell answered in a firm, clear voice, his eyes looking straight ahead at the jury of generals.

"How does the accused plead upon specification two of the charge?" Moreland continued.

"Not guilty," Mitchell repeated. Sighs in the audience could be heard each time he answered.

"How does the accused plead upon specification three of the charge?"

"Not guilty."

"How does the accused plead upon specification four of the charge?"

"Not guilty."

According to reporters watching her closely, Betty appeared to crumple during the tedious arraignment. Mitchell tilted his chin up defiantly each time he responded, but Betty's face flushed and she bowed her head. The strain of the last two months now seemed to weigh her down.

"How does the accused plead upon specification five of the charge?"

"Not guilty."

"How does the accused plead on specification six of the charge?"

"Not guilty."

"How does the accused plead upon specification seven of the charge?"

"Not guilty."

"How does the accused plead upon specification eight of the charge?"

"Not guilty."

"And how does the accused plead to the charge?" Moreland finally asked.

"Not guilty."

Mitchell sat down, leaned toward Betty, and forced a broad grin that looked almost like a grimace.

Tears welled up in Betty's eyes. She had been scribbling down her observations in her notebook. At times she had studied the faces of the generals so intensely it made some of them nervous, and they looked away from her stare. Now she squeezed her husband's hand and managed to smile back.

Mitchell sat back in his chair. A grim look came over his face. His jaw clenched as he stared darkly in front of him at the generals. Saying "not guilty" nine times seemed to make him painfully aware that he was no longer an army officer of stature but rather a defendant in a criminal trial. Mitchell was a proud man. This was humiliating.

SATURDAY, OCTOBER 31, 1925

The presidential yacht *Mayflower* moved lazily down the Potomac River. A beautiful steam-powered vessel, 321 feet long and 36 feet wide at its beam, it looked almost like an ocean liner. Calvin Coolidge loved the yacht. He liked playing captain when he was aboard, pacing the bridge with a jaunty naval cap the ship's real skipper had bought for him at Brooks Brothers. He required a steward to stand at attention before him and request permission to strike the bells, and he returned salutes from the crew with an "Aye, aye."

Coolidge, however, was no sailor. He never ventured out into rough seas, and if the waters became choppy he put drops of liquid cocaine in his ears, believing they prevented seasickness. Though he thought the navy's officers were more cultivated than the army's, Coolidge was ignorant of nautical matters and hated attending naval ceremonies. He also thought the admirals could be devious, particularly when they inflated the threat from Japan in order to extract bigger budgets from him.

A large number of guests were on the *Mayflower* for this voyage, which was unusual. Grace wanted to throw many parties aboard the ship, but the unsociable Coolidge usually refused, so most of the time they sailed with no more than a few close aides. Today, however, Secretary of War Davis had joined them, along with three senators, a congressman, and several wives.

While Coolidge wandered around the ship, the passengers gathered on the main deck. The conversation soon turned to what had been plastered all over the front pages of the newspapers during the past week: the Mitchell trial. Washington was still buzzing over the revelation that Coolidge was Mitchell's accuser. After court ended Friday, Frank Reid had told reporters he might demand that the president of the United States be ordered to testify at the tribunal. The distance Coolidge wanted to keep from the trial was closing, and that irritated him. When newsmen asked him at their regular Friday press conference about Reid's threat to subpoena him, he snapped, "I don't care to comment on that while it is before the court of inquiry."

Reid quickly backed down. Even if he could subpoena Coolidge—which was doubtful because Moreland was the only one who had the authority to issue such an order and he wasn't about to—it was unclear whether a sitting president could be compelled to testify.

The *Mayflower* passengers all agreed that the trial was in danger of turning into an outrageous spectacle. Mitchell had much of the press behind him, but some papers were critical of him. One of the guests, Sen. Hiram Bingham, who was serving on Morrow's air inquiry board, told the others he had found Mitchell "utterly unreliable" in the discussions he'd had with him.

"Billy Mitchell's mentality should be questioned," Bingham concluded. The senator thought he was nuts.

9 Love

Capt. William Mitchell and Caroline Stoddard were married in an evening ceremony at Saint Luke's Episcopal Church in Rochester, New York. He was four weeks short of his twenty-fourth birthday. She had just turned twenty-three. Though they would not be thought so today, the bridal couple was old by turn-of-the-century standards. Children of the wealthy often did not marry early, however, and this was a decidedly upper-crust union. The cream of Rochester society filled the pews. Back in Milwaukee, the *Sentinel*, which had a stringer covering the important event in the East, noted the next day that "it was a most brilliant wedding."

Mitchell and his ushers, all of whom were army officers, wore their dress uniforms. Caroline looked stunning in a white satin gown trimmed with duchess lace. She had given each of her six bridesmaids, who carried tea roses in the procession, a gold ring set with pearls.

Mitchell had given his fiancé an expensive "crown" of diamonds and pearls, which his mother had paid for. Caroline's wedding gift to Mitchell was the finest trap gun money could buy. He treasured it. Instead of "darling" or "sweetheart," the two called each other "Kinnie" in their love letters.

The mothers of the bride and groom could not have been more delighted. Among the upper class, alliances between prominent families were serious business. The offspring of the rich married within a relatively small circle, so matches were chosen carefully. Caroline Sarah Butts Stoddard and Harriet Mitchell, in fact, had known each other since boarding school in New York and had talked often as young women of their children one day falling in love and marrying. Which is exactly what had happened. Though the marriage bordered on being an arranged one, Mitchell had actually fallen in love with the bright petite girl from Vassar whose gentle face, light auburn hair, and wide hazel eyes drew him like a magnet.

Caroline's mother was the daughter of a prominent New York editor and wealthy businessman. Her father, Dr. Enoch Vine Stoddard, was the descendant of a seventeenth-century New England governor. A Yale graduate and surgeon in the Union Army during the Civil War, Stoddard practiced medicine less and less as the years went by—his wife thought it unseemly for a man of his position to treat people for money—and instead busied himself heading charities, writing scholarly papers on science, and tending to the family fortune. They lived in a grand mansion on South Washington Street in Rochester's posh Third Ward (known then as the "Ruffled Shirt Ward") and were prominent members of the Browning Club, an exclusive literary society devoted to the poet Robert Browning. Stoddard would occasionally read one of his papers at its salons.

Caroline was proud of her blueblood line. Her parents provided her with everything, and a doting rich aunt named Lillie gave her a hefty allowance as well. She attended a finishing school in Rochester, shopped in New York City, and sailed to Europe to learn foreign languages. She was sent to Tours, France, because it was thought to be the place where a person could perfect the best French accent. As a young woman she became a talented artist, doing pen-and-ink drawings and making paper dolls of her favorite actors and actresses. In later years she wrote a few novels, although she never published any, and accumulated a large library of leatherbound books by the great writers she had read.

Caroline enrolled in Vassar College in 1899. In that day young women who attended college were considered independent and defiant. Caroline fitted that mold somewhat, though Vassar was considered a conservative school of standing for rich girls. Caroline flourished there. She acted in plays, joined the Eating Club, Drama Club, and Rochester Club, and was president of the French Club and a class leader. Reflecting the chauvinism of his time, Mitchell did not think a woman learned a great deal at a women's college, certainly not as much as a man who attended a university. But he had to admit that Caroline was unusually bright and had "learned a great deal" in her four years at Vassar. She was a quick study, he realized, adept at foreign languages, and she had "an extremely logical mind."

Vassar prepared Caroline for a role in society that required her to be educated. The polishing also made her the perfect wife for an army officer on his way to the top. Caroline recognized this, and wanted to become a person of influence and power. She wanted to throw elegant dinners, invite prominent people to them, and converse with guests on their level.

She graduated in 1902 with honors and an outgoing personality. Caroline spoke with a slight twang, as if she had been raised on Maryland's Eastern Shore, which her parents thought made her sound lower class for a New England woman of means. Her voice was not shrill or high, but it was authoritative. She was a take-charge woman who knew how to issue commands, especially to household servants, whom she thought rarely lived up to her standards. She could also be a control freak and vindictive. She had a temper, particularly when she felt wronged.

The Mitchell and Stoddard mothers had remained in close touch over the years. Caroline had traveled to Milwaukee occasionally as a little girl and loved to play at Meadowmere, where she saw Willie. "Caroline is the finest girl in every way," Mitchell now wrote to his mother. The two had fun together. They shared a love of horses, travel, and adventure. Caroline had had many suitors in Rochester and at Vassar, and she was a sought-after partner at college dances. But none of the boys she had dated were like "Will," which was what she called him. He was a young man who liked doing things and seeing new places. He played polo and hunted; he was clever, articulate, and engaging with his tales of combat in exotic places. And he craved even more excitement. She found it powerfully attractive. Doctor Stoddard was uneasy about his daughter marrying an army officer and following him from post to post. But Caroline, who knew she came from a decidedly sedate family in a town that could be boring for a young woman, was thrilled at the prospect.

Will had dated others but always found himself comparing them with his childhood friend from Rochester. "Caroline is the only girl that I have ever cared much about," he wrote his mother, "and I probably wouldn't ever care about anyone else in the same way, not for a long time at least. She has more sense and knows more and has more character than any girl I have ever seen."

In late July 1901 Mitchell wrote his mother that he and Caroline planned to marry. Caroline wrote her future mother-in-law several months later: "Will has often said that you know his every thought sometimes better than he himself—and so, as you say, it did not surprise you to hear of our engagement and I am still so little used to this new happiness." On August 2 Mitchell took the train to Rochester and asked Stoddard for his daughter's hand in marriage.

The overcautious doctor was less than enthusiastic. Caroline, he thought, was still too young to be formally engaged. He ordered that it not be announced until after Caroline had graduated. William grumbled, but as it was, not only the engagement but the wedding had to be put off for two years because of his assignment to Alaska. Caroline hated the thought of not seeing her boyfriend for so long. She threatened to take train and dogsled to the territory to join him.

She didn't. For two years they exchanged frequent long letters. Caroline wanted to hear everything about Alaska and what Will was doing there. She in turn became his cherished lifeline to the civilized world, writing him far more than the rest of the family about what was happening at Vassar, in Rochester, and with the Mitchell clan in Milwaukee. It strengthened their romance.

The newlyweds honeymooned first in Cuba, then Mexico City. Typical for Mitchell, he mixed in business and exploring. He inspected artillery emplacements outside Havana and Aztec ruins near Mexico City, recording in detail the topography and historic sites he saw along the way in letters sent back to Milwaukee. Caroline, who even tagged along with him on hunting trips, was excited by the adventure and this man, who seemed so comfortable in exotic places. From the hills near Mount Orizaba southeast of Mexico City, Caroline wrote enthusiastically to her mother-in-law: "Captain Mitchell, who has been around the world and in almost every coun-

try on the globe, thinks this is the prettiest and if such a connois-
seur holds this opinion, of course that settles it! I agree with him
heartily." People would laugh, she wrote Harriet, if they could "hear
the conversation between William and me when we finally reach
some rock or open place from which there is a beautiful view of the
valley and the mountains. I of course am as pleased as a child with
the flowers and cataracts and the things about us, while William
squints up his eyes and decides where the vantage position for a
battery would be, or how skillfully men could be deployed on the
slopes or if it is a historic spot." She marveled as her new husband
would "explain where the armies were stationed and tell us the
entire story of the place—he already seems to have the history of
Mexico at his tongue's end!"

After several temporary postings Caroline and William finally settled
into quarters 18-A at Fort Leavenworth, Kansas, in the fall of 1904.
It was a spacious two-story clapboard house with a long piazza in
the front. Mitchell commanded a signal company and instructed student officers at the post's signal school. Before settling in, he had to
cope with the death of his father on June 29, at age sixty-two. It was
a blow for Mitchell, who had leaned heavily on John for advice and
help in Washington. William now drew even closer to his mother,
whom he began to address as "Mummy" in letters.

The new couple was blissfully happy in Kansas. Mitchell was
not thrilled with garrison life, but Fort Leavenworth was "the intellectual center of the army," and he managed to stay busy experimenting with field radio stations and kites carrying cameras to
hover over troops. His superiors thought he was an energetic and
zealous officer, adept both at leading enlisted men in the field and
at instructing officers at the signal school.

Caroline also thrived. She took Spanish lessons and began
painting again, this time with watercolors. Their social life stayed
busy. She took long walks or drives with William or with other
wives in the afternoon, usually stopping at the quarters of other
officers to "make calls." Their quarters were filled in the evening
with callers as well. Mitchell's younger brother, John, who became
close to Caroline, visited them for long stretches and enjoyed himself thoroughly going out on field maneuvers with William. The

couple hosted large dinners and teas for other officers and their wives. Once Caroline gave a card party for fifty-four guests, serving strawberries, ice cream, cake, coffee, and candy. "Everyone seemed to have a fine time," she recorded proudly in her diary.

Mitchell continued to keep close track of world events. He worried that Japanese military expansion would one day be a strategic threat to the United States in Asia. Caroline became immersed as well in her husband's profession. She joined the post's 20th Century Club, whose members were required to write and present papers on world topics, such as "Russian Aggression in India, China and Manchuria," which one participant read. She studied military subjects with Mitchell in the evening and helped him edit his first article for *Cavalry Journal*, in which he predicted that future battles would be fought not only on land and the oceans, but also underwater in submarines and in the air in planes like the one the Wright brothers had recently flown.

Most times Caroline stayed home when William went on his frequent hunting trips. But she attended all his polo matches to cheer him on and went horseback riding and trapshooting with him. William was loving as well. He sent her violets on Valentine's Day, and the couple had romantic suppers cooked upstairs in their bedroom fireplace.

But Caroline, like most army wives, hated the long periods when her husband was away on a military assignment. When Mitchell and his company were dispatched to San Francisco to help reestablish communications after the great earthquake devastated the city in April 1906, Caroline "tried to be a brave Army woman," as she wrote in her diary. But depression and loneliness, fed no doubt by the fact that she was pregnant with their first child and that things in the house seemed to break down only when her husband was away, almost overwhelmed her. "It is growing so dismal that I cannot stand it much longer," she wrote on the eighteenth day he was away. When he finally returned from San Francisco on June 5, she was overjoyed beyond words.

Their first baby arrived on August 18, on an afternoon when it was an oppressive 104 degrees outside and not much cooler inside. She weighed nine pounds, and they named her Elizabeth. A "colored Mammy," as Caroline put it in her diary, was brought in to care for the baby. Mitchell was delighted, though he hoped for a boy the next time. Each afternoon after work and all day on weekends, he read to Caroline while she convalesced.

On October 1 Mitchell was again ordered to Cuba, this time as a brigade signal officer with the Army of Pacification. Caroline, with Elizabeth in tow, joined him about a month later. The living was crude, with the heat and humidity debilitating for foreigners unaccustomed to it. Their house in Havana was a drab, square cinderblock structure with no glass in the windows. Mitchell, who suffered a relapse of malaria, had a staff car assigned to him that spent as much time broken down on dusty roads as it did running. But Caroline thoroughly enjoyed Havana, for the house came with a pony, two Cuban servants to care for Elizabeth and clean and cook, plus an enclosed patio always filled with beautiful tropical flowers. Caroline had learned enough at Leavenworth to speak kitchen Spanish with the help. She and William took moonlight swims at the nearby beach and attended dances aboard the warships that docked in the harbor.

They returned to Fort Leavenworth at the end of August 1907, to their eighth home in two and a half years of marriage. Mitchell had been selected to attend the prestigious School of the Line, which accepted only the best officers for advanced training in such subjects as engineering, weapons and munitions, and tactics. It was a dreadful two years that wore both of them down. Mitchell studied practically every minute he wasn't in class. Most evenings Caroline corrected his papers or quizzed him for tests. Only occasionally would they take a break for a game of chess or to attend an evening lecture—once, for example, on "Air Ships." But he ended up a "distinguished graduate" not only from the School of the Line but also from the Army Staff College that came afterward.

His next assignment was to return in August 1909 to the Philippines, this time as the chief signal officer for the Department of Luzon. Caroline remained behind to give birth on November 14 to their second child, another daughter, whom they named Harriet. Caroline hated this separation more than the others. Sometimes she would cry all night out of loneliness. When letters from Mitchell arrived, she dropped everything to read and reread them for hours. Finally, this time coping with two young children for the long trip aboard the cruise ship *Manchuria,* she managed to join her husband in the Far East in March of the next year.

Though Mitchell had just turned thirty, Caroline thought he still acted like a little boy—energetic, inquisitive, always restless. Physical fitness became a passion for him. At five-foot-nine, he was broad chested and he made a point of keeping his weight at just under 140 pounds. He played polo for the American team at international matches in Hong Kong and China (Caroline began to find the games boring to watch). He made "confidential" spying trips to islands off Luzon and Formosa to sketch and photograph Japanese military activities. Still frustrated over the glacial pace of promotions in the army, he even began hatching a get-rich-quick scheme with Caroline's brother, Vine Stoddard, to buy a fleet of trawlers that would rake up sponges, pearl shells, and fish from Asian waters. The idea never went anywhere.

At the beginning of 1913, the advancement Mitchell so craved finally came. In fact Mitchell was moving up faster than many of his peers. At age thirty-three he became the youngest officer ever to join the general staff in Washington, D.C. "It is the most sought after position which a military man can aspire to," he wrote proudly to his mother. William and Caroline had both aggressively worked their political contacts to get it. Both had been "crushed" the previous year, as Caroline wrote, when it appeared that he had the assignment and the orders were postponed.

The general staff, headed by the army's top officer, who was called the chief of staff, had been created only ten years earlier to rein in the different branches of the service that had become fiefdoms and to bring some organizational sense to the way the army planned for the national defense. It was still a weak group that numbered less than two dozen officers, but only the best from each branch were selected for it. Mitchell was sure his polo playing in the international matches and his spy reports from Asia had cinched the job. An officer who served on the general staff rubbed shoulders with the army's top leaders and Washington's power brokers, he knew. "If fortunate," Mitchell wrote his mother, "I may be a general before many years have passed."

They bought a spacious and elegant three-story brick town

house at 2238 Q Street in northwest Washington. Its many rooms were filled with expensive antiques, paintings, velvet-covered couches with matching trimmed pillows, Tiffany lamps, dark cherry china chests, and a grand piano. One wide hallway had mounted on its walls hundreds of rifles, bows, arrows, and exotic spears Mitchell had collected in his world travels. On the mantel of practically every fireplace were silver riding cups he had won in competitions.

The Mitchells plunged into Washington's social scene. They became a favorite on the party circuit because both were so young compared to the other husbands and wives among the army's high command. Caroline bought an armful of etiquette books, such as *The Dinner Yearbook, The Habits of Good Society,* and *Social Usages at Washington*. "The social usages of Washington differ in many important respects from those of the rest of the country, because it is the seat of the Federal government and the home of a large official world," warned the last book. One "neglect or slight" and your "husband may be asked to resign his position" or, worse, it "may lead to great irritation or even to war" with another country. Caroline read them all from cover to cover.

They attended frequent receptions or teas at the Willard, the Army & Navy Club, Fort Myer, even the White House, mingling easily with senators, congressmen, generals, and top administration officials. Caroline lunched with the wives of cabinet officers, shopped at Woodward and Lothrop with girlfriends and snacked in its tearoom. She held dinner parties for up-and-coming officers like Capt. Douglas MacArthur, Maj. Blanton Winship, and Lt. George Patton, and for power couples in the capital's military circle, like the Summeralls and the Drums. Caroline kept a dinner record of each event with seating charts, so that next time she could be sure to partner her guests with someone different.

They did everything an ambitious officer and his wife needed to do to climb to the top. Mitchell, who thought it important for a general staff officer "to keep well mounted," had one horse for racing ("Highland Chief"), one horse for polo ("Brother"), and a third for the children to ride ("Kentucky"). Caroline played golf; William became a respectable tennis player. On weekends they rode together in Rock Creek Park or took the children to Glen Echo Park

for the merry-go-round. They attended operas that touring companies brought to town, like Puccini's *Madama Butterfly*, and were
regulars at the theater for such plays as *Ziegfeld Follies of 1914* or
Peg o' My Heart. Mitchell joined the Metropolitan Club. Caroline
took dance lessons, and they attended dances at the Chevy Chase
Country Club and Washington Barracks. Or they rolled up the rugs,
moved back the furniture, turned on the Victor phonograph and
packed their own house with partygoers.

For Caroline these early years in Washington were glorious
because the family was together in the United States, and they were
living in the closest they had come to a permanent home. There was
only one problem with their lifestyle: They could not afford it. Caroline joked privately that her husband's meager army pay covered
only the upkeep for the horses. She used all of her part of the Stoddard fortune—one uncle had recently left her $65,000 when he
died—to subsidize the household. Her aunt Lillie, whom Caroline
called her "fairy godmother," bought their bedroom furniture, dining room chairs, and Persian rugs. Her mother bought them the
phonograph.

Still, they ran short almost every month, by hundreds of dollars. Mitchell took out bank loans and struggled to stay a step
ahead of creditors. He sent his mother detailed lists of the family
expenses and begged for money. Mitchell's mother, who had
assumed the role of financial anchor for the family and was doing
better than her late husband in preserving the family fortune,
always sent checks to him—and to her other children. But it irritated her that even despite that generosity Willie never caught up
with his bills. Harriet knew her son did not live by her motto: Simple Living and High Thinking.

Mitchell was embarrassed about always being broke. He
rationalized to his mother that Washington was expensive, that
other officers had benefactors, that one had to entertain properly
and be seen in the finest places to advance one's career. "We keep
expenses down as far as they can be, and still keep up a decent
appearance," he insisted in letters to her. That was hardly the truth.
Neither he nor Caroline saw anything extravagant in keeping
horses and servants, running large tabs at pricey department
stores, sending their girls to dancing school, or having a country

club membership. They routinely traveled to New York with his horses for races, staying at the Waldorf-Astoria and dining at the Ritz, and they saw nothing wrong with borrowing from the bank for beach vacations in New London, Connecticut. Mitchell, whose attitude was typical of aristocrats who no longer have money, was anything but frugal.

He was, however, doing important work in Washington, as he always reminded Harriet in his letters. Mitchell put in fourteen-hour days at the office and became well versed in army organization and logistics. Congressmen began consulting him when they drafted military legislation. He was also put in charge of evaluating the intelligence military attachés cabled back on the widening conflict in Europe, and with keeping the War Department's map on troop movements there up to date. Just six months after joining the general staff, Mitchell appeared as a witness before a House committee investigating how European nations were using airplanes as weapons. He spent a week drafting his testimony and rehearsed it with Caroline at night. When he was asked at the hearing whether the army's aviation section, which was part of the Signal Corps, should be put under an independent organization, he stuck with the company line and told the congressmen it shouldn't.

Caroline became something of a policy wonk herself. Two days before Mitchell's testimony, for example, she went with a girlfriend to the House Rules Committee to hear humanitarian Jane Addams testify on behalf of a woman suffrage bill.

Mitchell seemed to be always working angles on the side. To pick up extra cash, he began writing articles on defense and international politics for *World's Work* magazine and the *Chicago Tribune*, using a pseudonym to hide his authorship from the army, whose regulations prohibited moonlighting. Caroline edited his pieces and helped draw maps for them. He dabbled with one scheme to make thousands of dollars importing ox hides from South America, and another to give up his Regular Army commission and organize a Wisconsin National Guard regiment that he would lead as a colonel if there was war with Mexico. Nothing came of either idea.

Mitchell's brash and independent streak had served him well in the field, but now it made his superiors on the general staff uneasy.

For the first time his efficiency reports contained negative comments. "Captain Mitchell is a careful and industrious officer," one
general concluded, "but I do not consider him specially qualified
for laborious and painstaking staff duties." Mitchell was mildly
rebuked by his superiors when a lecture he gave on American
unpreparedness for war leaked into the press. In an Army War College paper he wrote in the summer of 1915, titled "Our Faulty Military Policy," he offered another proposal his bosses did not appreciate, that the War and Navy Departments be reorganized with a
national defense council over them.

It may have been because he had been a precocious and
demanding child, because his upper-class background naturally
bred in him a sense of entitlement, or because he had his father's
independent streak, but Mitchell saw nothing wrong at this point
with speaking out as long as he kept it within the military family.
"When a decision has been arrived at by [the] number one of the
outfit we must conform," he had written to a fellow officer. But
"within our own council everyone should have ideas and if they
haven't we had better get rid of them." Among the army's top eche-
lon, the rap on Mitchell was that he was opinionated and better
suited for leading troops in the field than working behind a desk.

His staff work, in fact, began to take a backseat to a new interest—
airplanes. Mitchell was late in coming to them, a point his rivals in
the air community would always use against him. The Wright
brothers had taken their first flight in 1903 at Kitty Hawk, North
Carolina, and a tiny cadre of army officers had begun learning to
fly heavier-than-air machines in 1909. But Mitchell eventually
became as passionate about flying as the first pilots were.

It was a slow courtship, however, that began in August 1913. Lt.
Thomas DeWitt Milling, who had become somewhat of a celebrity
in Washington because he had been among the first army officers
to fly, began showing up at the Q Street town house for long dinners
with Mitchell and Caroline, regaling them with stories about his
exploits in the sky. The two men began taking horseback rides in
the afternoon to discuss aeronautics. Mitchell spent much of 1915
and the early part of 1916 in bed, first with a blood clot in his eye,
then with inflammatory rheumatism that damaged his heart. But

when he recovered, Milling took him up for his first plane ride. "He was crazy about it," Milling later recalled. On August 30, Caroline wrote in her diary, Mitchell marched into the house and announced, "he is going to learn to 'fly'!!!"

Milling didn't think it was a loony idea. At thirty-six Mitchell was a little old to become an army aviator. By now a major, he had been transferred from the general staff to the Signal Corps Aviation Section, which he headed temporarily. There were only about two dozen army officers trained as pilots, and most of them were young. Few seasoned officers were willing to climb into a cockpit. Milling thought late bloomers like Mitchell were needed to lead the force.

On September 2, forgetting it was Caroline's birthday, Mitchell showed up at the Curtis Aviation School in Newport News, Virginia, the nearest flying school to Washington and began his private lessons. From then on he would take a boat down the Potomac River to Newport News on Fridays or Saturdays when he got off work and spend the weekends in the air. Mitchell wasn't the best student at the controls, but his instructors felt he overcame this with his confidence. Though flying was dangerous business, Mitchell was never rattled. When he flipped his biplane over while trying to land it on a solo flight, the first words out of his mouth when the instructors rushed up to the wreck were: "What did I do wrong?"

By mid-January he had flown 1,470 minutes in thirty-six flights. It qualified him only as a rookie. At a dollar a minute, which is what the Curtis School charged, his final bill came to $1,470, which Mitchell had to pay out of his own pocket. The army refused to reimburse officers for private lessons.

Caroline showed remarkable spunk as well. On October 14 she joined her husband in Newport News and had an instructor take her up for a spin. "Words fail," she wrote afterward about the flight. "It was <u>glorious</u>." The next month she flew with an instructor again, this time up the Potomac River to the capital. "The first woman to fly over Washington," she proudly recorded in her diary.

It was late on the evening of March 20, 1917, when the launch sped Mitchell and Caroline from Havana's harbor out to the *Alfonso XIII*, a Spanish steamer weighing anchor and preparing to set sail. It had been a mad scramble for them to get to Cuba. Caroline was still weak from a lengthy illness, but she was determined to see her husband off. The World War in Europe was almost three years old, and Mitchell had been itching since the beginning of 1915 to land an assignment there. The Signal Corps had finally cut him orders a little more than two weeks earlier to travel to Europe and observe the state of British and French aviation. The army, which had no aviation force to speak of, realized it had a lot to learn from the Allies.

The Spanish envoy in Havana had held up the steamer's departure so Mitchell could board. The *Alfonso XIII* would take him to neutral Spain, where he would make his way as best he could to France. Caroline had debated whether she and the children should sail with Mitchell to Europe, but soon realized that would be too dangerous. She wrote later that the last words she spoke to her husband as he climbed up the ship's ladder were: "Good-bye, Billy. And God speed."

Old friends in Havana called at her hotel the next day to see if she would like to venture out for lunch or shopping. But Havana was the city of so many happy memories for her—their honeymoon, their first posting overseas. She was too depressed to see such familiar places. Caroline ordered meals in her room and went to bed early. But she did not sleep that night.

10 Insubordination and the Truth

Mitchell and Betty had spent the weekend at Boxwood. The army, which had ordered him confined to Washington while he was formally under arrest, expanded the limits so the couple could visit their country home in Middleburg. The court-martial remained topic number one in the capital and was becoming a tourist attraction as well, with out-of-towners now crowding into the morning line outside the Emery Building, hoping to get a seat. Local socialites who managed to get in to one of the sessions would hold lectures the next day to recount what they had witnessed. A newspaper published a poem, in the style of Rudyard Kipling's "Danny Deever," which hailed Billy Mitchell and flayed Navy Secretary Curtis Wilbur:

> "What are the bugles blowin' for?" said Wilbur on parade.
>   "To bring you out, to bring you out," the old press agent said.
> "What makes you look so pale, so pale?" said Wilbur on parade.
> "I'm thinking of the hell I'll catch," the old press agent said.
> "For they're hangin' Billy Mitchell, you can hear the trumpets
>   play;
> The staff has got its thumbs turned down, they're hanging him
>   today;
> They're chargin' of his service off, they'll cut his stars away,
>   They're hangin' Billy Mitchell in the morning."

The trial itself settled into a comfortable routine. Most of the courtroom guards who had stood at ramrod attention in the beginning now looked for window ledges to lean on when they became tired. Spectators, who had been warned at the outset that any peep from them would practically get *them* court-martialed, now wandered in and out, noisily scraping their metal chairs on the wood floors when they got up. They whispered and snickered when Reid or Moreland scored a debating point over the other.

Betty now brought a mailbag with her and set it next to her chair. Since the trial began, almost a thousand letters, postcards, and telegrams had been delivered to the Mitchells' apartment. During court breaks Betty busied herself reading and answering the mail. Two additional secretaries helped Blackie type responses.

Even the generals, who had been tense and stiff when they marched in on the first day, now ambled to their places in the morning and leaned back in their seats, stifling yawns as the attorneys droned on. Reporters also began to notice how chummy the jurors were with the defendant. Mitchell and the generals exchanged bows and waves before the court convened and chatted with one another during breaks in the proceedings.

For more than three days the lawyers had bickered. Finally the first witness was called to testify. Ironically, he wasn't a military man or an official from the War Department, but rather A. H. Yeager, a newspaper reporter.

Once all of Reid's motions to quash the charge had failed, the prosecution's case was fairly simple, at least as far as Moreland was concerned. All he had to prove, Moreland told the jury, was that Mitchell said what had been in the papers. The generals could decide for themselves whether it disrupted good order and discipline or brought discredit on the military. Just in case the senior officers had forgotten, Moreland again read them the most pungent parts of Mitchell's statement, in particular the sentences in which he accused the Navy and War Departments of "incompetency, criminal negligence and almost treasonable administration." The only thing Moreland now had to show was that Mitchell had given his statement to reporters and that it had been published in newspapers across the country.

That's where Yeager came in. The thirty-eight-year-old reporter for the *San Antonio Light* had been one of the newsmen who had been in Mitchell's office at Fort Sam Houston on September 5, when he passed out copies of his statement.

Wearing a new dark blue suit, Yeager settled into the witness chair. He had his hair slicked back for the occasion and looked freshly scrubbed.

"Did you see the accused on the fifth day of September, 1925?" Moreland began.

"I did," Yeager answered. Along with several other reporters, he had arrived at Mitchell's office in the quadrangle that morning.

"How did you come to be there?" Moreland continued.

Yeager said he had earlier asked Mitchell for a statement on the *Shenandoah* accident, "and he had promised to give it to me that morning."

"What was it to be furnished [to] you for?"

"For publication."

"Have you a copy of that statement with you?"

"I have."

"Will you produce it?"

Yeager pulled wrinkled sheets of paper out of his pocket and handed them to Moreland.

"I show the statement just referred to and ask you who handed it to you?" Moreland inquired.

"Colonel Mitchell handed it to me," Yeager answered.

That was all Moreland needed to establish. Reid, however, stood up and objected to it being entered as evidence because the sheets of paper Yeager produced had editing marks penciled all over them. "On its face it is not the same statement given to him by Colonel Mitchell," Reid argued.

Moreland stood up, exasperated. "It is quite astonishing to me," he said. For a man who once bragged "that he did not want any defense," Mitchell sure was lawyering this case to death. Now his attorney was objecting to entering into evidence the very statement he had once been so proud of. Winship gave Yeager's sheets of paper to the generals and instructed them to ignore the pencil marks.

Moreland called to the stand four more reporters who had been in Mitchell's office that day, and went through the same drill. Then

he summoned Henry Parsons, who was in charge of collecting newspapers from around the country for the Library of Congress. Parsons
produced four of the papers in which Mitchell's statement had been
reprinted: the *New York Times*, the *St. Louis Globe-Democrat*, the
Chicago Tribune, and the *New Orleans Times-Picayune*. Reid tried to
throw up one legal roadblock after another, but he succeeded only in
irritating Howze and the other impatient generals, who began to
think they were going to be trapped in this room for the rest of their
lives.

The only military man Moreland called to the stand was Lt. Col.
George Hicks, who had been the Eighth Corps adjutant general at
Fort Sam Houston when Mitchell was stationed there. Hicks gave
the court the letters he had exchanged with Mitchell the day his
statement appeared in the San Antonio newspaper. In the correspondence Mitchell wrote unabashedly that what had appeared in
the papers was "substantially as I gave it out, and I take full responsibility for it."

It made hash of all of Reid's objections to introducing the statements or the newspapers as evidence. His client, who hadn't had a
lawyer back in September, had dug his own hole. But Reid gamely
stood up and scored what would turn out to be an important point.

"You are Colonel Hicks, from Fort Sam Houston?" Reid began,
on cross-examination.

"Yes, sir," Hicks answered.

"And that is the same military organization to which the
accused belongs?"

"Yes, sir."

Then Reid asked Hicks what territory the Eighth Corps was
responsible for.

"It takes in five states, I believe," Hicks answered.

"Would you say that the issuing of this statement caused any
lack of discipline or insubordination by personnel in your entire
corps area?"

Moreland jumped to his feet: "I object to that as immaterial and
not proper cross-examination and irrelevant to the subject matter
in hand," he said loudly and quickly.

Reid pretended to be wounded and surprised. "It certainly cannot be that the government is objecting," he said, his voice rising.

Hicks had investigated the case at Fort Sam Houston and would know what effect Mitchell's statement had had on the men there. "I think I am entitled to have the question answered."

Moreland argued furiously to keep that from happening. The last thing he wanted was some lieutenant colonel—his own witness to boot—potentially punching a hole in his case by being the judge of whether Mitchell's statement had disrupted good order and discipline among the rank and file.

Winship, however, saw no reason why Hicks shouldn't be allowed to answer the question.

The court reporter reread it: "Would you say that the issuing of this statement caused any lack of discipline or insubordination by personnel in your entire corps area?"

Hicks paused for a moment, and the courtroom went silent.

"In my opinion," the lieutenant colonel finally said, "it did not."

"That is all," Reid said with a slight smile on his face. "No further cross-examination."

It was just after 3:30 P.M. when all of Moreland's witnesses had been heard and all of Reid's objections had been disposed of. Reid had drawn blood with Hicks's admission that Mitchell's statement hadn't caused a mutiny within the Eighth Corps, but otherwise Moreland had managed to establish clearly that Mitchell had made the statements, which was all the evidence Moreland thought he needed to convict him for violating the Ninety-sixth Article of War. Finally Moreland stood up, looking something like a schoolboy who had finished his homework early.

"The prosecution rests," he announced and sat down.

Reid stood up. "Of course we want to make a motion to strike out and dismiss the charges on the ground that up to this point there is no evidence to support the charges—"

Howze held up his hand to interrupt. "The members of the court have not thoroughly understood what you have said," he said, turning around to look behind him. "There is quite a bit of noise in back of us here." The large windows behind the jurors had been opened to let in fresh air, but the rattle of cars driving by on the street below and the honking of horns was making it almost impossible for the generals to hear.

Reid spoke up. "I make a motion that the charges now be

stricken out because the prosecution has failed to make any case under the counts as set up. And I want to argue that at some length."

Howze sagged in his chair. More hot air from the lawyers.

Reid, however, had another request. He asked to be allowed to argue his motion the next morning. Reid may have caught the same cold Moreland had. More likely he was just exhausted from the grueling schedule he had maintained since the trial began. Reid had had to forget about congressional business or the law practice he still kept up in Illinois. The trial had become all-consuming.

Debating Moreland from ten until four each day, when court was in session, was draining enough. But then he had to spend the rest of each afternoon and evening in his office huddled with his legal team on the next day's tactics. On top of that Mitchell, who was a night owl, liked to take an afternoon horseback ride, then a leisurely dinner, before showing up at Reid's office late. It was usually past midnight before Reid finished briefing his client on what he planned to do the next day. He hadn't gotten home until 2:00 A.M. the previous night.

"I do not want to stay here any longer than any of the rest of us," Reid said, begging for a recess. "I have got to practice law back home, and any time I spend here is away from my own business, so I want to hurry this thing as fast as I can."

"We are sure of that," Howze said, although he and the other generals had been trying to hurry the lawyers along as best they could.

"And I am sure," Reid continued, "[that] you people want to get back to your commands."

Again the "you people."

Howze, unimpressed, banged his gavel. "The court will stand adjourned until ten o'clock tomorrow morning."

10 A.M., TUESDAY, NOVEMBER 3, 1925

Reid stood up and shuffled his notes in front of him. He felt a little better than he had the day before, although Mitchell had again kept him up discussing the case until midnight.

Reid was about to speak, but he and the courtroom audience became distracted by what was happening behind the generals. The shades again had been pulled up, and the large windows had been lifted to let in the morning sunshine. But Tuesday was wash-day, at least for the lady on the roof of the building next door. Reid, Mitchell, the defense team, the prosecutors, reporters, and specta-tors all stared for a few moments transfixed as the determined washlady wrestled to get wet sheets pinned to the clothesline in the face of a stiff wind.

Reid finally began to speak, still distracted a little by the sound of sheets flapping in the breeze. "On behalf of the accused, I desire at this time to make a motion for a finding of not guilty . . . on the following grounds." Reid listed them: "There was no proof offered by the prosecution" that Mitchell made his statements "with intent to discredit" the War and Navy Departments. The prosecution, fur-thermore, offered no proof that Mitchell wanted "to prejudice good order and military discipline" or that he intended to be insubordi-nate or contemptuous of the way the military was run.

That last point was a stretch. Even by the kindest reading of his statements, Mitchell was clearly contemptuous of his bosses. But Reid, who had spent the night before rereading the court-martial manual and thought he had pretty decent grounds for his argu-ment, was just getting warmed up.

The charge and specifications listed all the ways Mitchell dis-credited the service and disrupted discipline, Reid continued. But Moreland had offered no proof that Mitchell had actually perpe-trated these evils or, just as important, that he even intended to do so. On the contrary, it was clear to Reid that his client spoke out "to benefit good order and military discipline by correcting the evils which are admittedly destroying it in the air service and in the War Department."

Moreland had proved that Mitchell had made the statements in the newspapers, Reid conceded. But "there is not a scintilla of evi-dence of any kind, there is no attempt to produce, and I do not think the prosecution will claim that they have produced, any evi-dence that would go to those other elements which must be proven. Not one syllable of evidence has the prosecution produced to prove that [the statements] were made, uttered and published with any

intent to bring discredit upon the military service, or to prejudice
good order and military discipline."

Reid's throat hurt and his nose was stuffed, but he was becoming more excited, and the more excited he became, the faster he
talked. Alexander Galt—a bespectacled, middle-aged man in a
three-piece suit and striped tie who was the court stenographer and
who happened to be Calvin Coolidge's brother-in-law—scribbled
furiously and flipped pages on his steno pad to keep up.

"How [could] any fair-minded, intelligent American citizen,
having his country's welfare at heart," Reid continued, waving the
notes he held in his left hand, contend that the statements

> were issued with any other intent whatever than the correc-
> tion of the evils they denounced in plain language, the arous-
> ing of the conscience of the American people to stop the
> wasteful extravagance of government money, the preventing
> of a continuance of the loss of life and treasure? . . . The peo-
> ple of this country, I may say to you frankly, regard the
> accused here on trial before you as one of the greatest patriots
> that this world has ever seen. His statements have been read
> by millions of people, and commented on in the street, press
> and public gatherings, yet never has anyone intimated that he
> thought that they had the deliberate intent to bring discredit
> upon the military service and to prejudice good order and
> military discipline. Yet the prosecution comes here and asks
> you to find that on their face, from the mere reading of them,
> with not one word of evidence to support the claim, they were
> issued with despicable motives and with this wicked intent. . . .
>
> The prosecution stands all alone on its claim, deserted by the
> world, and would have this court accept its interpretation of
> these statements as opposed to the opinion of nearly everyone in
> the country!

Reid pointed out that the only witness Moreland offered who
touched on the question of whether Mitchell had stirred up any
kind of mutiny was Hicks, who ended up saying "just the reverse."
He hadn't. Mitchell "attacks no individuals," Reid also pointed out,
and technically it was true. Mitchell had not named any names in

his statements. "He merely criticizes a system, and one which is entitled to no respect at the present time from any army officer."

Reid now slowly turned his head from left to right, looking at each general in front of him for a brief instant. They had each served in top jobs around the country and were "of course well informed of the state of good order and military discipline in their own commands," Reid pointed out.

> I venture to express the opinion that not one of [you] has ever stated in your official reports submitted from each corps area weekly to the War Department that good order and military discipline had been prejudiced or affected in his command by the issuance of these statements. And yet, the prosecution would have the court believe—with no proof offered and with their own witness testifying to the exact opposite—that good order and military discipline have been affected in the Eighth Corps and elsewhere in the army!
>
> For this reason, therefore, and upon the grounds enumerated in the formal motion, I move the court for a ruling of not guilty on each and every specification.

Reid fell into his chair and leaned back feeling totally spent. He had delivered a dramatic plea for acquittal—perhaps a little disingenuous with the facts here and there—but one that was soaring in its oratory and powerful in its political impact.

Moreland, who was a bland speaker, could not hope to match it, so he didn't try. He pointed out that Mitchell may not have named names in his statements, but, as the generals could plainly see, he was clearly attacking the army and navy, and that was enough to warrant a conviction. The notion Reid was trying to foist on the court, that the prosecution had no evidence that Mitchell intended his statements to be disrespectful or disruptive, was ludicrous. By any "reasonable interpretation" the judges should conclude they were insubordinate. "It is my opinion," Moreland argued politely, "that these attacks upon these two indispensable instrumentalities of government by a high-ranking officer of one of them constitute all of such offenses, and, I believe accordingly, that the motion should be denied."

Moreland's uninspired rebuttal was enough to convince the jury. Winship overruled Reid's motion to dismiss the charge, and the generals quickly backed him up.

But Moreland was a long, long way from declaring victory. The afternoon before, the defense had dropped a bombshell on the prosecution—a three-page list of seventy-three witnesses Mitchell wanted subpoenaed to testify for the defense. Many were Mitchell loyalists in the air service, along with friends among the retired pilots, in the aircraft industry, and other parts of the army and navy. Many were from Washington, but others would have to travel from New Jersey, Texas, and even as far away as Hawaii. Mitchell wanted to summon top Coolidge administration officials: Navy Secretary Curtis Wilbur; Secretary of War Dwight Davis; Coolidge's top White House aide, Everett Sanders; Dwight Morrow, who chaired the aircraft board, and Secretary of Agriculture William Jardine.

Mitchell also wanted to back a truck up to the War and Navy Departments and empty them of practically every document they had. He demanded budget papers, payroll records, air accident reports, antiaircraft test results, military intelligence files, army and navy press releases, the hundreds of letters he had exchanged with his bosses over controversial congressional testimony, reports from the1921 battleship bombing test off the Virginia coast, all the reports and correspondence from the last *Shenandoah* flight, all the documents from the failed Hawaiian flight, records from every other military operation or program Mitchell had criticized in his statement, practically everything the Morrow board had accumulated in its investigation, plus every scrap of paper that every top army commander in the United States and overseas had put out the past two years on the state of order and discipline in their units.

Moreland was floored by the request, which would keep a battalion of clerks in the War and Navy Departments busy for months collecting material. The travel costs to bring in all the defense witnesses would be huge for the cash-strapped army. Even as Reid handed Moreland the first list, the defense team was typing up lists of more material and more people for the trial. Moreland, who had the power to subpoena witnesses and documents, even for the defense, wanted to whittle down this massive request to a more manageable size.

And a very important legal question was left hanging in the air: For what purpose was Mitchell proving the truth of his statements?

He was accused of being insubordinate and disrespectful. It did not matter, at least as far as military law was concerned, whether or not what Mitchell said had been the truth. He could be convicted just for saying it if the generals thought he was insubordinate.

Moreland knew that, which was why he gulped when Reid demanded a train full of witnesses and documents to prove that Mitchell had told the truth. It was immaterial as far as settling the question of whether he was innocent or guilty. Moreland had told the jurors the day before that he had no objection to Reid offering evidence and calling defense witnesses to prove the truth of Mitchell's statement, if—and only if—it was "for the purpose of mitigation and extenuation, but not complete defense or partial defense."

In other words, the generals could weigh the truth of Mitchell's statements in deciding how severe his punishment should be *after* he was convicted. But Moreland objected to that same evidence being used to decide whether Mitchell was guilty or innocent in the first place. Reid, of course, wanted just the opposite, that evidence on the truth could be a defense in the case, and keep Mitchell from being convicted.

Winship, however, failed to rule on whether this evidence could be used for the purpose of mitigation and extenuation or as a defense on the merits. It was a puzzling slip for a lawyer as meticulous as Winship. Moreover, none of the generals sitting in the courtroom questioned why they were allowing all this material to be introduced in evidence.

The War Department knew what was up. In any other case what Reid wanted to do would likely not be allowed, and the generals would be in the jury room by now deciding the verdict. But Mitchell's court-martial had become a national political trial. Mitchell might be out for favor with the army brass, but he was a war hero and a celebrity with powerful friends in the press and Congress. Reid wasn't just a defense attorney but a congressman who could make trouble for the War Department after the court-martial, and, in fact, he had already begun hinting to reporters that that was exactly what he planned to do. Coolidge continued testily to refuse reporters' demands for comment on the case, but the army's Press Relations Section was playing the game, issuing daily news bulletins on the trial, which often tried to spin the journalists with the prosecution's side of the story. Moreover, the men hearing Mitchell's case were the army's rising stars, as ambitious as Mitchell. They knew the risks of angering Congress, whose Senate approved their nominations to higher ranks. They were now willing to give Mitchell extraordinary leeway in his defense.

But there was another problem. Neither Moreland nor Reid was prepared to take this next momentous step in the trial. Moreland had assumed that proving Mitchell had issued the statements was enough, and he had not planned much for the next move. Reid had genuinely thought he could get his client off on a technicality and had only just begun to assemble evidence to prove the truth.

Both men pleaded with Howze for time. Reid wanted the court to recess for almost a week so he could review his evidence. Moreland agreed it would take until next Monday for the government to gather up the thousands of pages of documents Reid demanded.

Howze approved the recess, but he and the other generals were angry that they would have to fritter away a week in Washington with nothing to do.

11 War

Mitchell flew his biplane as low as he safely could over the Saint-Mihiel salient, where in two days the American army would begin its first large offensive in the World War. The observation aircraft was a speedy French-made Spad two-seater. On the side of its fuselage he had painted his private insignia: a silver eagle on a scarlet field with a gold band around the circle. Maj. Paul Armengaud, a handsome French pilot with a thick black mustache, sat in the backseat of the plane, binoculars pressed to his eyes. Armengaud had been assigned to Mitchell's staff to help him coordinate operations with the French and to smooth the feathers that Mitchell had a habit of ruffling.

The salient was a narrow bulge in the German lines on the Western Front. It protruded around the French town of Saint-Mihiel and just across the Meuse River southeast of Verdun. Dug in with a labyrinth of barbed wire, trenches, and machine-gun nests, the Germans had stubbornly held it since the beginning of the war as a buffer to protect critical rail and supply lines at Metz. Black Jack Pershing, who so far had been parceling out his units to support European armies, now had a major attack under his control. It was the big test of the American Expeditionary Force (AEF). More than six hundred thousand U.S. and French soldiers, 3,010 artillery pieces, and 267 tanks (some under the command of George Patton) were massed on the northern and southern edges of the salient, ready to squeeze out the Germans inside the bulge.

Mitchell had assembled the largest concentration of aircraft ever put together in the war for one battle: 1,476 American, French, British, and Italian warplanes manned by thirty thousand pilots, staff officers, and mechanics. The Germans, he calculated, could launch nearly two thousand aircraft against the Allies by day three of the attack. So Mitchell proposed a bold plan that no air commander had ever attempted—a massive first strike behind enemy lines to knock out German supply points and air facilities. Waves of air brigades, with no fewer than four hundred in each of them, would cross the northern and southern borders of the salient and attack "just as a boxer gives a right hook and a left hook successively to his opponent," Mitchell wrote. He hoped the heavy blows in the beginning would stagger the enemy and give the Allies control of the skies for the first few days until the Germans managed to recover and counterattack.

Mitchell dispersed his planes over fourteen flying fields and set up three supply depots to feed them fuel and ammunition. To hide the buildup from the Germans, he camouflaged aerodromes, moved aircraft to them in secret, and had pursuit planes constantly patrolling the skies to shoot down enemy observation craft trying to watch his movements. He also had crews erect fake hangars at other locations, with dummy planes in front of them, to confuse the Germans if their observation aircraft did manage to take photographs.

Mitchell assembled around him the air service's most energetic and aggressive leaders—men like Tom Milling, who became his chief of staff, Maj. Lewis Brereton, who led an observation wing, and Maj. Harold Hartney, who commanded the First Pursuit Group. He set up his headquarters about fifteen miles from the front lines in a school building at Ligny-en-Barrois. A local wine merchant kept the mess stocked with the town's finest bottles. On the floor of one room of the schoolhouse, he built a twelve-by-twelve-foot relief map of the Saint-Mihiel salient, complete with hills, forests, roads, and model buildings so his pilots could picture the terrain that would be below them.

Mitchell was not particularly skilled as a combat pilot, but he was a superb air tactician. He wrote clear, concise battle plans for his pilots and watched meticulously to make sure they carried them out to the letter. It was a commander's fault if a unit did not follow his orders, Mitchell believed. "Either the orders had not been delivered or they were so [poorly] written that nobody could understand them," he said. To make sure the latter never happened to him, Mitchell had the dumbest officer on his staff read every order he sent out. "If he could understand them, anyone could," Mitchell said.

Flying over the Saint-Mihiel salient, Mitchell and Armengaud quickly realized the Germans had no intention of holding it. They knew the Americans would soon attack, and Mitchell could see that some of the German units were making preparations to move to the rear.

Mitchell had made a habit of flying over future battlefields so he could picture in his own mind the combat his men would fight. The flights, which were dangerous, had uncovered valuable intelligence in the past for ground commanders. When the Germans had launched their last thrust toward Paris in the spring and summer, Mitchell had been on such a personal reconnaissance mission, flying his Spad north up the Marne River, through fog and low clouds. "Suddenly as I rounded a turn of the river east of Dormans," he recalled, "I saw a great mass of artillery fire hitting the south bank and, spanning the river, five bridges with German troops marching over." Though he was flying just five hundred feet off the ground, none of the soldiers fired at him. He raced back to friendly airspace, evading German planes along the way, and delivered his intelligence to headquarters so Allied commanders, who were unaware of the threat, could counterattack.

Mitchell was contemptuous of how ignorant ground commanders and their staffs were of the value of aerial reconnaissance. The Saint-Mihiel offensive was the American army's most important operation in the war up to that point, and, save for one major brave enough to climb into a cockpit, not a single ground officer "had shown any inclination to go up in the air and see what was going on," he recalled. The evening of September 11 Pershing gathered his senior officers for a final review of the war plan. To Mitchell's horror, the chief engineer urged that the attack be delayed because heavy rain had bogged down supply convoys and "several of the old fossils there agreed with this foolish view," he later wrote. "I told them very plainly that I knew the Germans were withdrawing from the St. Mihiel salient as I had seen them personally." Now was the time "to jump on the Germans, and the quicker we did it, the better."

A dignified and somewhat remote general, Pershing had never warmed up to Mitchell. He was not a West Pointer, and Pershing had shown an affinity for putting academy buddies in key staff and command jobs. Mitchell also wasn't a team player, which the general prized in his officers. Pershing encouraged subordinates to speak freely, but Mitchell stretched the privilege. During one table-pounding session the two men had, Pershing threatened to ship him home if he didn't stop demanding changes in the air service organization. "If you do, you'll soon come after me!" Mitchell shouted back. He claimed that Pershing laughed at his impertinence.

Stupidity and vagueness in an officer (two attributes Mitchell certainly didn't possess) irritated Pershing more than anything else, however, and he could be a ruthless leader who didn't blink at firing even old classmates who proved incompetent in the field. He wanted his commanders to break out of the trench warfare mentality paralyzing the Europeans, and to take the battle to the Germans. Mitchell was arrogant and headstrong, but he was the best air warrior Pershing had to do just that. Rain or no, the general ordered the attack to begin the next day as planned.

Who knows if Mitchell was the one who actually persuaded Pershing not to delay the attack—as Mitchell later claimed. But the episode was typical for Pershing's air commander. He had not been shy the previous seventeen months.

The *Alfonso XIII* had deposited Mitchell at Corunna, Spain, and he had managed to reach Paris by April 10, 1917. The city was gloomy. The Allies were worn out, their military leaders squabbling among themselves after three years of fruitless fighting that had resulted in little more than a bloody stalemate. "What a foolish kind of war this seemed," Mitchell wrote upon his arrival, "where an army could not advance twenty or thirty miles for months."

Ten days later he loaded a gas mask, helmet, field glasses, and a typewriter into a car and set out for the front to view the carnage himself. He spent a Sunday afternoon wandering through the trenches of a French infantry division locked in a deadly artillery duel with the Germans fifteen miles north of Châlons.

Mitchell found the hell he witnessed almost "impossible [to describe] with the words we have in our language." Years of fighting over the same real estate had reduced the once lush countryside to a desolate moonscape. Elongated balloons, nicknamed "sausages" because that's what they looked like, hovered above, with tethers to the ground, spotting where artillery rounds fell. Formations of French warplanes swooped overhead, their pilots performing aerobatics that American aviators had not yet learned. One German flying machines, its fuselage painted menacingly black with white crosses on each side, buzzed low. Mitchell had come under artillery fire during the Philippines war, but it was nothing compared to the rapid, heavy barrages that now fell around him, shaking the earth in a deafening quake. Machine-gun fire and shrapnel kept the infantrymen huddled in gouges cut into the trenches, their muddied rifles stacked against the scarp. Pools of blood trailed from first-aid stations. Listening posts tried to detect German miners digging deep tunnels to fill them with explosives, which when detonated would cave in the Allied trenches above. The French commanders, who directed the war from dank underground *abris,* were shocked that any foreign officer would come of his own free will to visit them.

That night guests in Mitchell's hotel in Châlons were kept up late by the clicking noise of the typewriter coming from his room. "Truly this war was being waged under the ground and over the ground," he wrote. "The men on the surface did the least actual work. Life could not exist in the presence of the dreadful weapons of modern war, and men were forced to burrow in the ground like gophers. Above in the air our pilots could penetrate deep into the enemy's country. In other words, the immemorial battleground was being displaced, rendered obsolete." Over the ground with airplanes, under the sea with submarines, "war was being thrust beneath it or lifted above it." The French government later awarded Mitchell the Croix de Guerre for being the first American officer willing to come under fire.

Back in Paris Mitchell set up a makeshift office the American Radiator Company loaned him at 138 Boulevard Haussmann, manning it with French and American volunteers from the city. The War Department refused to pay for rent or a staff. He toured European aerodromes and flew in the backseat with French pilots over battlefields for a taste of the action they saw. He visited Britain's foremost air tactician, Gen. Hugh Trenchard, at his headquarters near Abbeville and told him he wanted to learn everything about his organization, then be taken up for a flight with a British pilot against the Germans. "Quite a big order," the taciturn Trenchard responded. How much time did he have? Two days ought to suffice, Mitchell said cockily. Did Mitchell think he had nothing else to do but show him around and tell him everything he knew? Trenchard asked incredulously. Trenchard "had such an excellent organization that it should not need his leadership for the space of a day or two," Mitchell recalled saying. The British general laughed and gave him the tour.

Mitchell soaked up information like a sponge. The French pilots had the best planes, he concluded, and had begun to fight effectively in large combat formations. British squadron commanders were less hidebound and more open to new equipment and tactics. The American army, Mitchell quickly realized, would be coming to Europe woefully unprepared for modern war. It was a "deplorable situation," Pershing had already concluded. The army could count only about two hundred thousand soldiers, including the National Guard, many who had never fired their rifles at a target. The force had just fifteen hundred machine guns, 150 heavy artillery pieces, and embarrassingly few bombs or grenades. Its Air Section was starting from scratch with only thirty-five officers who could fly, fifty-five training planes of questionable quality, and no concept of how to use aircraft in a war, except as spotters for the artillery.

Mitchell drafted ambitious plans for the organization of an American air force in Europe, which he cabled to the War Department along with long lists of the types of airplanes, engines, and flight instruments that would be needed. "No attention was paid by Washington to these suggestions from me, the person on the ground, familiar with the conditions in Europe," he wrote bitterly. The War Department, however, was being swamped with forty thousand messages like Mitchell's each day and didn't think that a major who had been in Europe only a few months should have the final word on planes. Congress threw $640 million at the aviation problem, but much of the money was wasted. The country's primitive aircraft industry was unable to assemble quickly the necessary raw materials, such as spruce for the wings and castor oil for the engines, or to produce in mass quantities planes that each had to be handcrafted like fine wooden yachts. War profiteering and contract disputes bogged things down further. In the end most American pilots flew into combat with European-made planes.

Because their own country could not teach them, most American pilots also were sent overseas for their instruction in combat flying. Among the thousands of prospective aviators at training centers in Europe was John Lendrum Mitchell, Jr. He had grown into a handsome and sturdy young man who desperately wanted to follow in his big brother's footsteps. John had become the mirror image of William. He preferred hunting, fast cars, and motorcycles over academics, and Harriet was always sending him checks because he ran out of money. After their father died William took John under his wing, and Caroline had begun treating him as a brother instead of a brother-in-law. The minute he graduated from the University of Wisconsin, John applied for the air service. During his entire time in the army he rarely told comrades he was related to Mitchell, not wanting to ride on his brother's coattails. But when John arrived in Paris, Mitchell showed him the sights and promised their mother he would look out for Little Pud and return him home safely after the war.

Whether it was because he was poorly trained as a pilot (many of them were) or his plane was faulty (they often were), no one could be sure. A little before five o'clock on the afternoon of May 27, 1918, John, piloting a Nieuport, approached the Colombey-les-Belles air depot south of Toul. The fighter plane had given him engine trouble earlier. Unfamiliar with the landing field at Colombey-les-Belles, John banged the Nieuport on the ground too far down the runway, forcing him to gun the engine and lift off for another pass. But the hard touch-and-go the first time had cracked the girders in the rear of the fuselage. When John circled his plane for another try, his controls gave way and he crash-landed. Thrown from the aircraft, he died on impact. The ambulance found him on the ground with the back of his head crushed.

Mitchell arrived at the accident scene within an hour. He buried his brother in a hospital cemetery north of Toul and hired a farmer to mow the grass around the grave regularly and keep flowers growing over it. He visited the site often to make sure the work was done. He shipped home all John's personal effects except for his mother-of-pearl cufflinks, which he wore for the rest of the war as a reminder. John's death "was the hardest thing that has ever happened to me," Mitchell wrote his mother. "He had every quality that

I wanted in a brother and admired in a man. I suppose he was very nearly the dearest living thing in the world to me."

War leaders under tremendous stress inevitably spend as much time fighting their friends as they do the enemy. Pershing had bitter feuds with generals back in Washington who tried to meddle in his operation, and he furiously battled Allied commanders who wanted to amalgamate his forces into theirs. His staff, top-heavy at first, bickered among themselves as well. Even so, Mitchell's turf wars within the AEF were titanic by any standard. He had one run-in after another with the senior officers around Pershing—men like Hugh Drum, James Harbord (Pershing's chief of staff), and Dennis Nolan (the intelligence chief), who would run the army after the war and had long memories.

The mutual antipathy was fed by the fact that Pershing's commanders had little idea how to use airpower in a war, while Mitchell did. Ground soldiers, who lived miserably in the field, also were naturally disposed to view pilots as prima donnas enjoying the high life in the rear. The picture wasn't completely true. But the airmen did tend to be quirky individualists, and Mitchell certainly did his part to feed the maverick image. He hunted wild boar in his free time, commandeered a Mercedes that he drove ninety miles per hour through the French countryside, and always managed to book fancy châteaus for his quarters near the front.

Mitchell deeply resented that Washington sent what he considered poorly trained carpetbaggers to run the AEF's air arm when the army should have turned to its officer with the most experience in European aviation matters at the time—which was him. Pershing did promote Mitchell rapidly and gave him extraordinary responsibilities for someone so young, but the general recognized correctly that to assemble and put into battle a large air force, he needed a seasoned manager with more administrative skills than Mitchell had.

Mitchell's biggest bureaucratic fight was with an officer who was a more experienced pilot than he. Benjamin Foulois had practically taught himself to fly and at one point in 1910 was the army's only aviator. He organized the service's first tactical squadron and impressed Pershing when he flew reconnaissance missions for him during the 1916 punitive expedition into Mexico. Foulois was as headstrong and opinionated as Mitchell, but otherwise the two men could not have been more different. Foulois came from humble beginnings, preferred getting his hands greasy with the mechanics, and was shy in public.

Foulois arrived in Europe with a brigadier general's star recently pinned to his uniform and a healthy contempt for Billy Mitchell. Foulois had known Mitchell for almost ten years and considered him an incompetent grandstander who bungled staff work and created more problems for the air service than he solved. Mitchell despised him in return. When Pershing appointed Foulois chief of the air service over Mitchell, Mitchell declared war. The two men fought like children, and Mitchell acted the most childish. When Foulois moved into the headquarters that Mitchell was supposed to turn over to him at Toul, Mitchell tried to clear out the furniture so Foulois would have nowhere to sit.

Foulois eventually tried to fire Mitchell and have him sent home. Pershing refused. Mitchell, he knew, was the better combat commander. Pershing also soon realized that Foulois was not a particularly strong administrator. With his air force in bureaucratic gridlock and consuming an inordinate amount of his precious time, a frustrated Pershing finally turned to Mason Patrick. A West Virginian whose father had been a Civil War surgeon, Patrick was another classmate of Pershing's at West Point, where Patrick had graduated second in the class. Patrick was more than happy serving as a commander of engineers in the AEF, but Pershing pleaded with him to take over the air arm. These were good men, Pershing told him, but they were "running around in circles." The engineer reluctantly accepted the assignment.

Patrick restored order. He had known Mitchell since the two had served together in Cuba fifteen years before. He found him "very likeable," as he would later write, but with a "highly developed" ego. A talented administrator, Patrick brought order to what had become a complex air organization. He also quickly realized that Mitchell's place was at the front leading the airmen rather than back in headquarters, where his highhanded manner would get him into trouble. Mitchell was the ideal combat commander, while Patrick made sure planes and supplies got to the fight. Mitchell "is aggressive, courageous, and fearless," the major general would later tell Pershing. "He possesses, I think, exceptional qualifications for leadership." Foulois, in a surprising burst of magnanimity considering how much he hated his rival, eventually agreed and stepped aside to let Mitchell run the air war at the front while Foulois became Patrick's assistant. Mitchell had won the bureaucratic battle—he would emerge the heroic air leader of the Great War—but it had cost him dearly with the army's senior officers, who never forgot his bitter feud with Benny Foulois.

"The battle of St. Mihiel was really over on the first day," Mitchell wrote, which was true. Heavy rains and high winds limited the massive air strike he planned at the outset, but Mitchell, who slept only about three hours a night for most of the war, drove his pilots relentlessly to get into the air, and some managed to strafe enemy troops and bomb supply dumps in the German rear.

It was exceedingly stressful and dangerous work. Only volunteers were recruited for the air services of most countries, and they had to be unmarried and young. Most carried lucky charms with them in the cockpit, such as medallions, horseshoes, or cloth dolls, to ward off death. Hastily manufactured biplanes were unreliable. Aviators learned to be good glider pilots because engine failure was common. Wooden airframes caught fire easily, a horrifying experience for men without parachutes, or they literally broke apart in the air during stressful maneuvers. Bombing was inaccurate, machine guns mounted on fuselages jammed often, and even when they didn't, airmen still had difficulty hitting enemy planes with them. In open cockpits the engine noise could be deafening. Sitting in stiff wicker seats, pilots often had to manhandle balky controls, their faces blasted by wind, motor exhaust, and spraying oil. In cold weather their cheeks blackened from frostbite. Aerial dogfights were mentally and physically exhausting. Necks were rubbed raw, and eyes were filled with tears from heads twisting and turning constantly to look for the enemy. About three hours of flying was the most even the strongest could handle in a day.

By day three of the Saint-Mihiel offensive, the Germans managed to send some planes over Allied lines, but Mitchell's strategy of overwhelming force kept most of the enemy aircraft pinned down or defending their rear echelons. Pershing was delighted to have the skies over his troops cleared of hostile planes. He promoted Mitchell to brigadier general.

Caroline counted each day of the two years her husband was away, like a prisoner scratching marks on a cell wall. After packers hauled the furniture to a nearby warehouse on May 2, 1917, she closed the Q Street town house in Washington and moved with the children to Rochester to live with her mother. (Her father had died of throat cancer in 1908, which had devastated her.)

Caroline tried to keep family life normal, though Rochester, like other communities, went on a war footing. The shoes she bought for the girls often had thick paper soles because the army consumed most of the country's leather. Gasoline was short and, to conserve it, automobiles could not be driven on Sundays. But she managed to drive the children to most of Douglas Fairbanks's new movies, like *Wild and Woolly*. Adults didn't exchange presents for the War Christmas, but she bought gifts for the children, and they stood outside her bedroom door Christmas morning, as they always did when Mitchell was home, singing carols to wake her up. There were other occasional splurges. She took outings with Aunt Lillie to New York City, staying at the Waldorf, and even joined another seminar group, this one called the Wednesday Morning Club. The subject of her paper for the club: the White House in wartime.

Caroline was also determined to do her part for the war effort. Feeling guilty about not being at her husband's side, she tried at one point to get a passport to go to France, but Mitchell ordered her not to come. So Caroline settled for long days at the Red Cross House in Rochester, though she considered the work trivial compared to the great campaign her husband was fighting in Europe. She cut gauze, assembled "first-trench packets" for the troops, and gave French lessons to soldiers who would soon be sent overseas. She took a crash course in first aid and became an operating room nurse's assistant at Rochester General Hospital. She joined the Red Cross's Motor Corps, driving U.S. marshals around the state to hunt for draft dodgers. She also got behind the wheel of an ambulance to transport tuberculosis patients and victims of the influenza epidemic that swept the country in 1918. When her ambulance kept breaking down, leaving her stranded on the road, she enrolled in a motor mechanic's class to learn how to fix it.

The work kept Caroline's mind off the deep loneliness and sense of desertion she felt. She followed the war closely from newspaper reports and the infrequent letters from Mitchell that reached her mother's house. (One disadvantage of leaving Washington was that there were no air service officers nearby to pass along news that came to headquarters from her husband.) The City Hall bell in Rochester rang each time there was word of an American advance on the Germans, and Caroline was thrilled when she learned of Mitchell's rapid battlefield promotions: from lieutenant colonel to colonel, and then to brigadier general. But at times she felt almost suicidal. Attending horse shows made her homesick for Mitchell and their horses. She refused to go to church on Sunday, December 2, 1917. It was their fourteenth wedding anniversary, and she could not bear to sit in the church where they had been married. On March 20, 1918, the one-year anniversary of the last time she had seen her husband, Caroline had friends come to the mansion "to help me live through this day," she noted in her diary. "It does not seem," she wrote on another day, "as if this war would ever end!"

The final American offensive, to punch through German lines on the Western Front between the Meuse River and the Argonne Forest, proved extremely difficult for Pershing's ground soldiers and Mitchell's aviators. More than a million Americans were thrown into the costly battle, which took six and a half weeks for Pershing to win. The weather stayed miserable. This time the Germans put more planes into the fight. To teach infantrymen how to use air cover in battle, Mitchell had his pilots take their officers up in planes to show them what aircraft could do. They even dropped leaflets on the doughboys, with instructions on how to call in air strikes. Mitchell continued to employ large concentrations of airpower to attack the enemy. It sometimes made him unpopular with ground commanders when he refused infantry requests for help because it would spread his forces too thinly. But the strategy of overwhelming force had worked at Saint-Mihiel, and it succeeded again in helping block some German advances during the Meuse-Argonne offensive.

What did Mitchell's pilots end up accomplishing in the war? They dropped 138 tons of bombs on 150 targets and shot down twice

as many German planes as the Germans did of theirs. (The air service's death rate also was higher than the American infantry's.) But
contrary to the pilots' boasts, the airplane was not the decisive
weapon of the war. The artillery was. The heavy gun was the great
killer, made more accurate, incidentally, by the observation planes
that spotted targets for them. Aerial bombing did more psychological than actual damage; troops felt helpless when the flying
machines dumped ordnance on them. Aviation technology simply
had not caught up with the war the pilots envisioned or promised.
Mitchell had grand plans for air raids deep into Germany if the conflict lasted longer. He had already suggested to Pershing that
infantrymen strapped into parachutes should be dropped behind
enemy lines. Both ideas would have to wait for the next world war.

Pershing, however, left Europe pleased with his pilots. He
awarded Mitchell the Distinguished Service Cross for valor. Senior
officers around Black Jack privately griped that Mitchell should
not be given such an important medal just for doing his job. But
none of them had climbed into a cockpit. Mitchell had in fact
risked his life often by flying over war zones to watch his pilots
work. Behind the scenes he lobbied intensely to keep the citation
from being derailed until Pershing finally approved it.

Mitchell handwrote copies of the congratulatory notes Pershing
and other foreign commanders had sent him after battles and
mailed them to his mother. Such letters "are seldom written," he
proudly told her. It wasn't true, but a son could be forgiven for
wanting to impress his mother. Harriet treasured them and had
Wisconsin newspapers reprint Pershing's letters.

More than nine million soldiers and five million civilians had died
over the four cruel years of war. Though they had joined the fighting
late and their casualties (a little more than fifty thousand killed in battle and fewer than two hundred thousand wounded) were light compared to what the Europeans suffered, Americans had still paid a
heavy price. And they had learned painfully there was no gallantry in
these new weapons that brought senseless slaughter on a mass scale,
no honor in victories measured in body counts or inches on the battlefield. For the one and a half million Americans who had fought in
it, the Great War had been a shocking and sobering experience. For
Billy Mitchell it had been a glorious adventure.

12 Preparing for Battle

Court had recessed ten minutes before noon, giving Betty just enough time for a quick lunch before Blackie took her to Union Station, where she boarded a train for Detroit. It had been at least two weeks since she had seen Lucy, who was staying with Betty's parents in Michigan, and she missed her daughter terribly. Mitchell, who remained in Washington with his defense team, still had his sister Harriet to look after him while Betty was gone.

Harriet sat in on many of the lawyers' strategy sessions that week, and she and Mitchell went horseback riding in the afternoons. In the evenings they dined with other officers or by themselves at the Occidental Restaurant on Pennsylvania Avenue, next to the Willard. Next to Betty, Harriet was William Mitchell's closest confidant. The three had become inseparable during the trial. Harriet came to adore Betty. If Mitchell had something he could not tell his wife, such as not to wear a particular dress for an evening, he told Harriet, who passed it along to Betty. Harriet, in turn, was fiercely proud and protective of her brother.

Harriet had been at Mitchell's side for every step of the proceedings. She found the court-martial, even the dreary legal arguments, fascinating, and was excited by the military circles her brother ran in, with their dashing young officers. She had married Arthur Young, a kindly Brit much older than she, seventeen years earlier. It had been an arranged marriage, and by the time of the trial, the two were practically living separate lives.

Harriet had a plain face. She wore little makeup but always dressed stylishly and kept a star sapphire ring on her finger. Harriet had an inner strength men found attractive. She had been the pet of the family. After her early formal schooling, all in Europe, she returned to Milwaukee and attended Downer College. She was skilled in foreign languages but did poorly in math. Harriet, however, had a good head for money, and she invested and protected her part of the family fortune far more wisely than did the other children. She was always making loans to her siblings, particularly Willie, who spent freely. Harriet believed that her mission in life was to take care of everyone else in the family. She was bossy and got what she wanted, which probably explains why Willie adored her: He was the same way.

The week was hectic as Reid prepared for the defense he would offer on Monday. Mitchell spent most mornings at his apartment in the Anchorage huddled with Joe Davies, the former Federal Trade Commission chairman who was an old family friend and political adviser. At midday, Lieutenant Bissell, Mitchell's technical adviser, usually brought other air service pilots to the Anchorage for conferences. These were men passionately loyal to Mitchell—men like Arnold and Lt. Corley McDarment and Capt. Robert Oldys—and they had their own bitter experiences with the air service's horrible state and could advise the defense team on what documents to demand from the War Department. Mitchell also had moles in the navy who were slipping him inside information on material he should request from the sea service on the *Shenandoah* accident and other embarrassments. Late afternoons and evenings, Mitchell drove to Reid's office on Capitol Hill for strategy meetings with the congressman, Colonel White, Judge Plain, and Webb.

The War and Navy Departments worked day and night to dig out the thousands of pages of documents Mitchell had requested. The services balked at supplying secret material—especially intelligence reports Mitchell might use to compare the military strength of the United States with that of other countries. The prosecution and defense also were still arguing over the number of witnesses to be called. Reid had trimmed nine people from the original list of seventy-three that he had first handed Moreland on Monday. He would end up not calling any top administration officials. But within days of giving Moreland the first list, Reid sent him another one with more people he wanted called, which brought the total back up to eighty-eight. And more than half of them lived in twenty different states. Angry army finance officers had calculated that it would cost a staggering $6,832.83 to transport all of them to the capital and put them up in hotels.

The defense team had already begun interviewing the witnesses who lived in or around Washington. Reid organized a detailed battle plan for how he would prove that Mitchell had spoken the truth. The 6,080-word statement his client had given on September 5 was divided into sixteen parts. Reid then divided up the defense witnesses so that several could take the stand for each category and vouch for what Mitchell had said. Reid even tried to game out what officers the army and navy might call to the stand to contradict what his witnesses would say.

Moreland, in fact, was already thinking along those same lines. One of the reasons the army took so long to cough up the documents was because staff officers were carefully reading every file before it was delivered to the defense team, in order to determine whether the file was "favorable" or "unfavorable" to the War Department. The screening provided Moreland with valuable intelligence on Reid's plan of attack. General Drum, the army's aggressive assistant chief of staff, who was feeding material to the Morrow board, also began passing memos to Moreland's team. Drum expected Mitchell to make accusations that he had given false testimony on behalf of the army to congressional committees, and he wanted to fend those off before they could get anywhere.

Hap Arnold also suspected that the army had begun to snoop around for dirt on Mitchell. Weapons procurement programs tended to be controversial, and Mitchell had come under fire for some of the planes he had ordered purchased for the air service. And like a lot of senior officers of that day, Mitchell had not been careful enough when it came to accepting favors from businesses or using government property for personal benefit. The Cadillac Motor Car Company loaned him their best automobile when he visited Detroit for aviation races (Mitchell liked to gun the touring car to seventy miles per hour). On another trip to Michigan, he arranged to have three soldiers and an army veterinarian fix up a stable and tend to the six horses he was shipping in for a hunt club competition. Arnold worried that if auditors looked hard enough they would also find problems in the expense vouchers Mitchell submitted for his Asia trip the year before when he mixed official business with a honeymoon.

9:00 A.M., SATURDAY, NOVEMBER 11, 1925

Betty arrived at Union Station on the overnight train from Detroit. The trial would not resume until Monday, and she could have stayed in Michigan another day—every moment with Lucy had been precious. But Betty had an appointment today that she didn't want to miss. Blackie had picked her up at the station and driven her back to the Anchorage so she could freshen up first.

At noon Betty left the apartment for a luncheon engagement with Margaret Lansdowne, whose husband, Zachary, had been the skipper of the *Shenandoah* and had died on its last flight. Mrs. Lansdowne had a bombshell to drop on the Mitchell trial, and Betty had been quietly working behind the scenes to help arrange it. This meeting was one of many she would have with the angry widow to prep her for her day in court.

It was hardly surprising that Betty was on such an important errand for her husband. Women had been an important part of Billy Mitchell's life. They could make or break his career.

13 Triumph

Caroline and Mitchell's sister Harriet stood anxiously at the New York City pier. It had taken the *Aquitania* all day to dock, and the wait had driven them crazy.

The war had finally ended. The City Hall bell had awakened Caroline and the other residents of Rochester at 3:25 A.M. on November 11, 1918, to herald the signing of the Armistice agreement in France. Mitchell returned to the United States almost as big a celebrity as General Pershing, who had led the American forces. Just turned thirty-nine, Mitchell was now one of the army's youngest generals, and a flying one at that, who had commanded thousands of planes in battle and had won many medals for his heroics. On his victory lap through Europe after the war, foreign generals lined up to meet him. Pilots idolized him. The French government gave him an automobile. He took the Prince of Wales (the future king Edward VIII and Duke of Windsor) up in one of his personal planes (Caroline had read about the flight in the New York papers) and had met King George V and Winston Churchill (Secretary of State for War and Air in Lloyd George's coalition government). On the *Aquitania's* voyage home, he strutted around, inspecting the other troops on board in a uniform he'd designed himself—tunic with outsize pockets, British pink breeches, and gleaming cordovan leather boots. To welcome the "Prince of the Air," army planes from a nearby field circled over the liner as it steamed into New York Harbor. "Billy Mitchell," recalled Hap Arnold, "was on top of the world."

For a long time Mitchell hugged Caroline and Harriet at the pier. Peace was so wonderful, Caroline thought. Mitchell's absence was a trauma she never wanted repeated. The countless sleepless nights—gripped by what she described as a "horrible chilled scared feeling" worrying if he was safe—had left her emotionally and physically drained. "All life will be anti-climax after that," she wrote in her diary.

She could not have been more wrong.

Mitchell returned out of sync with his country. American doughboys, who had seen enough killing to last them a lifetime, could not wait to be home and shed their uniforms. But Mitchell, like a lot of senior officers of his day, had mixed feelings about the war's end. The German government had been defeated, but its army certainly "marched back in good order," he noted in a letter to his mother. The Germans would return to fight another day, he was sure. The Armistice, Mitchell also was convinced, had interrupted the war just as airpower was about to prove itself as the decisive force on the battlefield. He came home thinking about the next war, his head filled with ambitious plans for a large and independent air force to win it.

But Woodrow Wilson had sailed to Europe with just the opposite in mind: a League of Nations so there would never again be a war like the last one. The Senate would reject the League, but the country was in a pacifist mood. Americans were fascinated by airplanes, but they wanted no part of a military the size Mitchell envisioned. Congressmen and the press clamored for drastic cuts in defense. Army officers were under orders to process men out of the service as fast as they could.

Though the United States would soon experience profound changes, they had not yet come in 1919. Soldiers returning from the front wore wristwatches instead of pocket watches, used safety razors instead of straight razors, and had zippers on their pants instead of buttons. But the nation was in an antiliquor, antilabor, antigovernment, and antiforeign frame of mind. Women had just begun to look different, with shorter hair and skirts, but few yet smoked cigarettes in public or wore heavy makeup, knowing they would be labeled "fast" if they did. Mitchell returned from the war convinced that the world was entering a new age of mass communications and aviation. But there was still no commercial radio network in the country, and airplane technology, which had not yet lived up to its promise on the battlefield, was still primitive.

Mitchell believed that the War Department, the U.S. government, and the American people would quickly catch up to his ideas. He would be sorely disappointed when they did not.

The family moved temporarily into a town house Caroline had rented for them at 1509 20th Street in northwest Washington. Eleven months later Caroline, who had gotten pregnant shortly after his return, delivered their third child. This time it was the son Mitchell wanted. He named him John Lendrum, after his father.

Mitchell also believed that his war record had earned him the right to lead the army air service. He was backed by a cadre of loyal aviators like Arnold and Milling, who were just as enthusiastic about the potential of airpower and who were in a rebellious mood over the way aircraft procurement had been mismanaged during the war. But Mitchell had clashed with too many senior officers in Europe. The ground commanders considered Mitchell and his pilots undisciplined, unmilitary, and, with some justification, still too inexperienced to manage large organizations. The men who led the AEF in Europe now ran the peacetime army in the United States, and many were powerful enemies of Mitchell. Maj. Gen. Charles Menoher was picked to lead the air service; Mitchell was made his deputy.

An artilleryman who had ably commanded the Rainbow Division during the war, Menoher was a genial-enough fellow who had also been a classmate of Pershing's at West Point. But he knew nothing about airplanes and had never even flown in one before taking this job.

However, Menoher was a bright officer who began to warm to aviation the more he studied it. He recognized that the air service was in a dismal state. It retained only thirteen hundred of its twenty thousand wartime pilots after the army shrank, and he knew that the planes were rapidly becoming obsolete. Still, Menoher was hopelessly out of his element when it came to putting together an air organization to fix the problems and harnessing Mitchell's talents. About the only direction he gave Mitchell was not to hire too many office workers. Otherwise Menoher left his ambitious deputy free to do mostly as he pleased.

Mitchell took the freedom and ran with it. He filled Menoher's in box with recommendations for new equipment or programs: bombers to cross the Atlantic, army aircraft carriers to transport planes overseas, dirigibles for offensive operations, amphibious planes for search and rescue over the ocean, air raid shelters for cities. Most were ignored. But Mitchell had many other accomplishments: He drafted training manuals for the service, sponsored the first aerial forest fire patrol, promoted planes for crop dusting and mapping the country, set up the first airways system in the United States, equipped planes with skis for arctic flights, organized an air race from New York to San Francisco to generate publicity for his pilots, and wrote his first book on aeronautics, *Our Air Force,* in 1921.

Mitchell also was in the air practically every week. He flew everywhere—to aircraft plants and airfields around the country, to horse shows in Detroit and World Series games in New York. He took up practically every newly designed plane himself for test runs. He held the world speed record for a day, flying an army Curtiss racer in Detroit more than 224 miles per hour (although even some of his aviators grumbled that he'd hogged the limelight from a younger officer who flew the plane faster the next day). Like most pilots then, Mitchell also had his share of engine trouble and stormy weather in the air, which sometimes forced him to land in makeshift fields such as East Potomac Park near Washington, or gave him scarier moments with crashes.

Mitchell became one of the most flamboyant generals in the army. His large office on the second floor of the Munitions Building near the White House was practically a museum to his eclectic interests. On the walls hung watercolors, maps, aircraft blueprints, photos of bombing tests, a piece of a Breguet plane he'd flown over enemy lines during the war, the wheel of the first German Zeppelin shot down, and a tiger skull from Siam (now Thailand). Model airplanes hung from the ceiling. In front of his desk, which was always piled high with paper, lay a twisted piece of metal, part of the first two-thousand-pound bomb ever dropped. To one side stood a large globe that Mitchell used to plot routes for around-the-world flights. In a corner stood a cabinet stuffed with secret documents on the operating status of army planes. In another corner fishing boots hung from a coat tree. Mitchell usually dressed in a mufti during office hours. Sometimes he received visitors in a green golf suit with knickerbockers, and wearing buckskin shoes.

Everyone who dealt with him had a story to tell. When aircraft manufacturer Donald Douglas showed him a new design, Mitchell, beating his boot with a swagger stick, always had the same response: "Now, that's fine, but you fellows ought to do better than that." After one late-night party, Mitchell organized a formation of cars—his own in the lead—that raced through downtown Dayton at sixty miles per hour. Fortunately no one was killed. When Maj. Reed Chambers considered resigning from the air service, Mitchell took him down to the basement of his house where he kept a still, dripping out sour mash. "Now look, Chambers, I got your resignation," Mitchell said after the pilot was sufficiently liquored up. "You can't do it. Too many of the old-timers have left, and we need you in the service. I'll give you command of the First Pursuit Group." Chambers stayed.

The Mitchell treatment wasn't always pleasant, though. Navy Lt. Eugene Wilson remembered a lunch hosted for Mitchell by the commandant of the Great Lakes Naval Station north of Chicago. The lunch was scheduled for 1:00 P.M. and Wilson discovered to his horror that at noon Mitchell was still in Chicago, an hour-and-a-half drive away. "Don't worry about it," Mitchell told the aide when he phoned to remind the general that it wouldn't be polite to show up late.

At 1:00 P.M. a Stutz Bearcat screeched to a stop in a cloud of dust at the naval station's front gate, Mitchell himself at the wheel. His terrified driver, who thought it would be only a matter of time before Mitchell killed them both, had a white-knuckle grip on the door.

At lunch in the commandant's house Mitchell "was really arrogant and thoroughly disrespectful," Wilson recalled. Later the general strutted through the station's machine shops "blustering around and criticizing this, that and the other." At the gate "I gave him my washerwoman's salute," Wilson said. "He clicked his heels together, and gave this military, highly Continental salute of his, behind the ear, with a wide sweep. He said to me, 'Well, Wilson, keep going, keep going. Maybe someday you can catch up with Chanute Field,'" an army facility. As Mitchell gunned the Bearcat's engine and sped away, Wilson thought to himself: What kind of bird is that?

Early on Mitchell was low-keyed in his crusade for a new air force. His proposals stayed mostly inside military and congressional circles. He wanted the air arms of the army and navy and planes from other civilian agencies such as the Post Office consolidated into one cabinet-level department of aeronautics, which would field a huge force of five thousand planes, almost two dozen dirigibles, and twenty aircraft carriers. The army, navy and this new air force would be coequal services, operating under a Department of Defense.

But the army by the early 1920s had become a hollow force of fewer than 140,000 men, crippled by inefficiency and dissatisfaction among its junior officers. The air service fared better than other branches, but still had only 880 pilots. The nation's aircraft industry withered on the vine after the war, and the air service could count fewer than two thousand planes, three-fourths of which were obsolescent. Pershing and other top generals, who presided over the military largely as caretakers, adamantly opposed separating the air service from the army. So did Menoher, who believed a pilot's mission was to serve the infantryman.

Mitchell took his fight to the people, believing that the military establishment would change only when public opinion forced it to. He began giving speeches and writing articles in newspapers and magazines (using his own name now rather than a pseudonym), calling for an independent air force. He openly criticized the way the War Department was run, particularly the fact that decisions affecting pilots' lives were being made by men like Menoher who didn't know how to fly planes. By the beginning of 1920, Hap Arnold began to notice that Mitchell seemed more impatient and angry with those who disagreed with him: "He seemed to brush aside the possibility that a lot of people still might not understand his theories," Arnold later wrote.

But Arnold and the other disciples overlooked Mitchell's failings—and he would soon give airpower its finest moment.

2:11 P.M., WEDNESDAY, JULY 20, 1921

Mitchell's biplane had just passed over the lighthouse at the southern tip of Cape Charles, Virginia. He banked it slightly to the right and put it on an eighty-degree course east out into the Atlantic Ocean. The biplane, nicknamed *Osprey*, was a two-seat De Havilland DH-4 with his personal insignia from World War I painted on the fuselage and a blue pennant flapping from the tail. Its fuel tank had enough gas for five hundred miles. His observer, Lt. St. Clair

Street, was in the backseat scribbling notes on the flight and helping plot his course.

It had been a miserable rainy morning, with rough seas and
winds gusting to twenty miles per hour, typical for Chesapeake Bay
in the summer. By noontime, however, the winds had died down.
There were broken clouds only to the northwest and southwest.

Six minutes later, Street spotted destroyer number four three
thousand feet below. He tapped Mitchell on the shoulder, pointed
down, then marked the position in his notebook. (The navy had
spaced nine destroyers in a line to guide the planes to the target
area, about fifty miles east of the Virginia Capes.) Another three
minutes passed when Mitchell and Street approached five Martin
MB-2 bombers flying below them in a V formation. The heavy twin-
engine biplanes, each loaded with three six-hundred-pound
bombs, traveled low to the ocean to take advantage of the extra
cushion of air that was created when their wings were close to the
water, a technique seagulls and pelicans use to save energy.

Mitchell had been impatiently radioing the navy all morning to
give his bombers permission to launch. But the navy, which had
been close to canceling the test earlier in the day because of the
stormy weather, kept putting him off. Irritated with the delays, he
finally ordered the army planes to take off without the navy giving
the go-ahead.

At 2:41 P.M., Mitchell saw the target just ahead of him—the German battleship *Ostfriesland*. He had flown his plane over the mon-
ster vessel three days earlier to check it out. It sat still, anchored to
the ocean bottom. Concentric red, white, and blue circles had been
painted fore and aft on its deck.

Practically all of the U.S. Navy's Atlantic fleet—cruisers, destroyers, tenders, and eight battleships—surrounded the German vessel
to watch the spectacle. Also nearby sailed the USS *Henderson*, a
cruise ship converted to a troop transport, which was packed with
three hundred VIPs, including Pershing, Secretary of War Weeks,
Secretary of the Navy Daniels, top admirals and generals, Moffett,
the dirigible skipper Zachary Lansdowne, eighteen senators and
congressmen, foreign diplomats, and about fifty reporters. Army
observation planes and airships hovered above, with photographers and motion picture crews aboard, their film rolling. The navy

had wanted the results of these tests kept secret. Mitchell had no intention of doing that.

The newspapers, in fact, had been full of stories on the tests, which had begun earlier in June. Army and navy attack planes had already sent a surplus German submarine (the *U-117*), destroyer (the *G-102*), and cruiser (the *Frankfurt*) to the bottom of the ocean in the exercises, proving that those types of vessels were vulnerable to airpower. (Navy pilots who joined the army aviators in the exercises were eager to demonstrate to their hidebound admirals that planes could be powerful weapons in naval warfare.) But the end of these lesser vessels mattered little if warplanes could not dispose of the queen of the seas, the mighty battleship. Sinking the *Ostfriesland* was the ultimate prize. Mitchell's claims of airpower superiority—and probably his military career—hung in the balance.

The *Ostfriesland* was considered unsinkable. It had withstood a pounding during the World War I Battle of Jutland in the North Sea and had just finished undergoing repairs when Germany surrendered and turned it over to the Allies. It weighed 27,000 tons, was almost two football fields long, and more than ninety-three feet wide at the beam. It had three giant smokestacks, a dozen twelve-inch guns, many watertight compartments, and was covered in armored plating. Krupp steel almost a foot thick shielded its sides. The navy had one of its battleships, the USS *Pennsylvania,* nearby to fire its fourteen-inch guns at the behemoth if the planes couldn't sink it. The admirals doubted that even the *Pennsylvania* could do the job, so they also had a wrecking party standing by with depth charges.

But Mitchell was just as convinced that the *Pennsylvania* and the wrecking party wouldn't be needed. The battleship fleet had been in his sights since the end of 1919. Mitchell's argument that airpower would be the supreme offensive weapon had gone nowhere in the military establishment. Now he had begun fervently to believe that control of the seas lay in airpower. In future conflicts warships would play less of a role unless protected by planes from aircraft carriers. The most powerful weapon in the country's defense, the modern dreadnought, was "just as helpless as the armored knight was when the firearm was brought against him," Mitchell told Congress in January 1921. Airpower would make navies practically "useless."

The admirals were beside themselves. Secretary of the Navy

Daniels, a North Carolina newspaper editor who became famous in naval history for banning liquor from ships, complained bitterly to the War Department. One reporter who had been out with the fleet told Mitchell that battleship captains "tremble with rage at the mention of your name."

The navy was already under siege. The service wanted to build the world's largest fleet, but it was in a fierce budget war with the army for money. Moreover, disarmament fever was intensifying by 1920. The battleship became the symbol of a growing arms race. In February 1921 Harding called for an international disarmament conference. Ten months later, diplomats from nine nations attended the Washington Naval Conference and agreed to scrap nearly seventy warships sailing or being built, a staggering two million tons.

The War Department tried to rein Mitchell in, but he refused to stay quiet. Capitalizing on the country's budget-cutting mood, he touted aviation's cost-effectiveness. For the price of a battleship, you could build a thousand warplanes, he told congressmen and reporters. A forty-thousand-dollar plane dropping a single thousand-pound bomb could cripple a forty-five-million-dollar battleship. The money estimates were shaky, and it was questionable whether a single bomb could actually dispatch a battleship. But reporters knocked over chairs in hearing rooms and rushed to file stories whenever Mitchell made such claims.

Many of the navy's more innovative officers, particularly its aviators, who wanted to see the development of aircraft carriers, privately admired Mitchell for challenging the battleship mind-set. Even a few admirals had been sending the air general private letters encouraging him to continue pressing his case. But Mitchell's brash tactics made enemies of others in the sea service who could have been allies. Hap Arnold worried that he almost seemed to enjoy taunting the navy. When reporters, for example, asked him to comment on a flight of twenty-four navy planes scattered by bad weather on their way to San Francisco, Mitchell answered sarcastically, "What more can you expect from the Navy than that?" The admirals, said Eugene Wilson, were "so completely outraged by his breach of the most elementary principles of playing the game" that they "closed their minds" to his ideas.

By the fall of 1920 Mitchell had begun using congressional tes-

timony and speeches to demand that the navy give the army a surplus battleship so he could demonstrate that planes could sink it.
The navy balked. It even resisted army requests for technical information on aerial torpedoes, suspicious that giving it would only aid
the air service's war against ships.

Instead the navy conducted its own ordnance test on the Spanish-American War–era battleship USS *Indiana*. Daniels, who hoped
to keep the results secret, would only say afterward that the test
proved that aerial bombing could not put an old and defenseless
battleship out of action. But the results soon leaked. (Mitchell was
suspected of being the leaker, but it was never proved.) Navy pilots
had not been able to sink the ship during the test, but that was
because they had dropped only dummy bombs.

The navy brass remained absolutely convinced that their ships
could withstand an air attack with real munitions. If Mitchell "ever
tries laying bombs on the deck of naval vessels . . . he will be blown
to atoms long before he gets near enough to drop salt upon the tail
of the navy," Daniels bragged. Newspaper reporters claimed that
the navy secretary told them he was so confident of the dreadnought's invulnerability he would stand bareheaded on deck and let
Mitchell's planes take their best shot. It's open to question whether
Daniels actually issued that challenge or, if he did, whether he
really meant it. An air service aide had slipped Mitchell what purported to be a copy of a private letter Daniels had written four years
earlier, admitting that "no nation can confidently look for victory
because it is mistress of the sea or master of the land. Both may be
made impotent by the nation which commands the air."

By the end of January 1921, the navy was under intense public
pressure to give the air service a battleship to bomb. Mitchell, then
a national figure, had powerful friends in Congress who threatened
legislation to force the navy to turn over a ship.

The admirals finally relented. Mitchell's air service would be
allowed to join the sea service's planes in bombing the *Ostfriesland*
and the surplus German sub, destroyer, and cruiser. But the navy
would be in charge of the tests. Mitchell found it galling that the
naval officer who would be giving him orders during the bombings,
Capt. Alfred Johnson, was junior to him in rank and not a pilot.

The navy also set the ground rules for the trials and made it as difficult as possible for Mitchell to sink the *Ostfriesland*. The navy insisted that all the warships be parked at least fifty miles from the Virginia Capes. This meant that Mitchell's planes, which were based twenty-five miles inland at Langley Field near Hampton, had a two-hour round trip to and from the target, giving them less time for bombing. Mitchell's planes couldn't use aerial torpedoes, which would likely have sent the *Ostfriesland* to the bottom quickly. An inspection party also would board the battleship after each heavy bomb struck to survey the damage. Air service pilots would also be allowed only two hits with their heaviest bomb, a two-thousand-pounder. Mitchell could not mount a mass attack.

The two sides could not have been more starkly opposite in their objectives. The navy wanted this to be strictly an ordnance test to measure the damage the *Ostfriesland* could withstand. Mitchell wanted to sink the damn ship.

But he had another problem even bigger than the rules being stacked against him. His air service did not really know how to destroy a battleship. Most of its veteran bombardiers from World War I had left the service. Mitchell's pilots knew little about dropping bombs and had no experience flying over water. He had few suitable bombers for the mission, their bombsights were primitive, and the largest weapon in the army inventory weighed only eleven hundred pounds.

Mitchell launched a crash program to put together an attack force. It was code-named Project B. One hundred and fifty planes were flown to Langley Field. Ten thousand bombs were offloaded from rail cars and barges. Spare parts were cannibalized off aircraft the army had in Texas and from surplus warplanes the U. S. Post Office had in Chicago. Radios were installed in aircraft, along with special bomb racks, reinforced with extra pipes and steel cable, for the heavy munitions. The Ordnance Department rushed to build two-thousand-pound bombs, shipping them to Langley packed in ice so the molten TNT that had been poured into their casings would cool in time for the tests.

Poor Thurman Bane had the most thankless job in the air service. Bane was in charge of developing new aircraft at McCook Field's engineering division in Dayton. For more than a year, Mitchell had been badgering Bane to renovate the Martin bombers for the battleship test. "Get those Martin airplanes," Mitchell demanded in a typical letter to Bane on March 1. "Have them work and be delivered." The engineers were under the gun. Rolling out Martins and "getting them to Langley in the shortest possible time," Mitchell wrote Bane in another letter, ". . . is the most important thing there is today." The two men developed a love-hate relationship.

A First Provisional Air Brigade was formed at Langley with Mitchell as its commander. He scoured the country for the best air service pilots. One thousand officers and enlisted men were eventually summoned. Jimmy Doolittle, who flew the De Havilland, was pulled from duty along the Mexican border. The brigade took over empty hangars and an airfield overgrown with grass. A message center with three cars, two motorcycles, and one bicycle was set up to handle ten thousand communications during the exercise. By May, Mitchell had assembled the largest air command in the United States. Always one to travel in style, he also had a Cadillac touring car sent to Langley for his personal use.

Mitchell drove his men and himself relentlessly. His sister Harriet came to Langley to care for him. At times she even sat in the backseat of his plane on flights. But he would skip meals for days, living only on coffee as he put his men through a brutal training schedule. The outline of the deck of a battleship was drawn on a marshy field near Langley, and pilots spent days hitting it with concrete-filled bombs to simulate the weight of the actual weapons. For striking the ship's deck, the airmen practiced a form of dive-bombing: pointing their planes toward the ship at a sixty-degree angle, dropping one or two bombs with a manual release when they got to within a hundred feet of the vessel, then pulling the plane up.

The practice wasn't always well coordinated. Doolittle's unit of De Havillands used live ammunition to bomb a bonfire his sergeant was supposed to have lit on an uninhabited island in the Chesapeake Bay. But the day after, Doolittle discovered to his horror that the sergeant had not done his duty. The De Havillands had attacked a bonfire apparently lit by poachers who had sneaked onto the island. A search party never found anybody afterward.

Mitchell decided that his pilots would have a better chance of sinking the *Ostfriesland* if their bombs did not actually hit it. The thick sides of the German battleship, where it might be rammed or struck by naval artillery shells, were nearly impenetrable. But the underside of the hull wasn't so heavily armored. Mitchell was convinced that bombs with delayed fuses, which landed near the *Ostfriesland* and exploded underwater, would create a "water hammer" effect whose shock wave would cave in the ship's bottom.

Just before the tests began, the brigade's pilots gathered in a hangar. Mitchell stepped up onto a toolbox to give them a pep talk. Perhaps it was the long hours and lack of sleep, but his emotions had begun to well up inside him lately. He had been deeply moved by the history surrounding Langley Field. Just north, John Smith had established his colony at Jamestown, and Cornwallis had surrendered to Washington at Yorktown. The *Monitor* and *Merrimac* had fought their epic naval battle nearby. The sinking of the *Ostfriesland* could be an event just as historic, he was convinced. "The modern battleship is the strongest vessel ever to sail the world's seas," Mitchell told his men in the hangar. It was the culmination of generations of engineering to make a ship that naval men firmly believed was unsinkable: "The question upon which hangs the whole future of our force—and the future of each one of us—is whether that belief is correct."

As the *Ostfriesland* came into his view Wednesday afternoon on July 20, Mitchell could see that the battleship listed slightly to port. Eleven marine De Havillands and navy seaplanes, which had begun dropping 230-pound bombs just before noon, had slightly wounded it. Nine of the thirty-three bombs they dropped had actually struck the *Ostfriesland*. But seven of the nine that hit turned out to be duds.

Mitchell and his five Martin bombers arrived at the target as the navy seaplanes were finishing their work. When the navy aircraft were through, the Martins, which were commanded by Lieutenant Bissell, formed into a line to begin the army's first attack on the *Ostfriesland*.

But the radios crackled in Bissell's bomber and Mitchell's command plane: "Do not attack until ordered. Observers have to go on board."

Mitchell was incensed. His bombers would now have to loiter over the *Ostfriesland*, wasting precious fuel, while a navy ordnance team climbed into a boat, motored out to the German battleship and took their sweet time wandering through the holds to record the bomb damage. Mitchell ordered Street to radio an urgent message to the USS *Shawmut,* a navy tender with the umpires controlling the exercise: "Must attack in 40 minutes. Fuel limited." Mitchell swooped the *Osprey* low over the *Ostfriesland* to check the damage himself. It was minimal, he could plainly see. The navy did not need to waste critical time nosing around the ship.

Aboard the *Shawmut,* Captain Johnson was just as irritated, but for a different reason. He had radioed explicit orders to Langley that the army's bombers not take off until 2:05 P.M. But Mitchell had jumped the gun and sent them into the air at 1:56 P.M., nine minutes early. Johnson was getting fed up with Mitchell's impatience to bomb the ships. The army pilots had showed up early to attack the German cruiser *Frankfurt* two days before. As far as Johnson was concerned, Mitchell had no one to blame but himself for their gas problem now. "Return to base if fuel is short," he radioed back to Mitchell. "Observers have to go on board."

For forty-seven frustrating minutes, the five army bombers circled the *Ostfriesland* while navy inspectors wandered through the battleship. The team noted that the seven duds that had struck the ship poked holes in the deck, while the two hits that had detonated created fiery openings in deck planking. But the light bombs that had exploded near the *Ostfriesland* did act like mines and had apparently done enough damage to cause it to list to port.

Meanwhile Langley radioed Mitchell that another "terrific thunderstorm" was "raging" there and seemed headed out to sea. His bombers didn't have much time left.

Finally, at 3:35 P.M., Bissell got the signal to attack. Circling army airships, which also had rescue equipment and first-aid kits for planes that crashed into the water, radioed him last-minute information on wind velocity and direction. Bissell formed the Martins into a line at an altitude of fifteen hundred feet to begin their assault on the battleship with their 600-pound bombs. Because the storm was creeping closer, Johnson ordered another six navy seaplanes, which had been loitering with a dozen 550-pound bombs, to begin their strike as well. Each plane swooped down, dropping one or, in some cases, two bombs at a time. The army planes were spaced two hundred feet apart so the pilot just behind the one diving down on the ship could adjust his aim based on where the bomb in front of him dropped. Mitchell believed that a succession of bombs dropping from a line of planes would have a more powerful impact on a battleship, even one trying to maneuver out of the way in wartime.

The impact of the heavier ordnance in this case was certainly more powerful. Fourteen bombs struck the water near the *Ostfriesland,* sending huge geysers of white foam hundreds of feet into the air that showered the ship. Five bombs hit the dreadnought, four of which were duds. But the blast from the one six-hundred-pounder that did detonate on the *Ostfriesland's* main deck sent fragments sailing out for hundreds of feet and created a shock wave that knocked back a movie cameraman filming from a nearby observation plane.

Shortly before 4:00 P.M., however, Johnson halted the attack. The winds had begun to pick up, and the storm from the coast was closing in on the target area. Much of the fleet and all aircraft were ordered back to shore.

By 4:30 P.M., Mitchell's De Havilland was a little more than twenty miles from the Virginia coast when the storm and lightning became too much to fly through. A navy seaplane had already been forced down and was being towed to shore by a destroyer. Mitchell turned his aircraft south to see if he could fly around the bad weather. Another De Havilland and an army seaplane soon followed him. As the three crossed Currituck Sound just south of Virginia Beach, however, the winds buffeted them even harder, and the seaplane found a smooth patch of water to land on between Knatt's Island and the coast. The other De Havilland reached the coast, but the high winds forced the crew to land in a small bean patch.

Mitchell struggled to stay aloft, pointing his De Havilland north after he had crossed the coast. But the storm had become even more violent, so he was finally forced to land on a triangular patch of uncultivated field just across the Virginia state line near the village of Creeds. He had almost brought the De Havilland to a stop when the plane ran into a three-foot ditch, sinking its propeller and landing gear into the soft dirt.

Street climbed out and walked to Creeds, returning with two mules, ropes, and most of the villagers. They all grunted and pulled for about two hours. Finally they were able to drag the plane out of the ditch and get it pointed in the right direction so Mitchell could manage a takeoff from the field, which was full of ruts and holes and covered with three-foot-high weeds.

At a quarter to eight Mitchell's De Havilland touched down at Langley, its landing strip partly lit by flaming gas cans. He and Street were exhausted. The other pilots, or at least the ones who hadn't been forced down on the way back, were celebrating the day's bombing. Mitchell slept very little that night as mechanics worked to attach even bigger bombs to the planes, and he pored over field orders for the next day. Tomorrow would be his last chance to prove that he could sink the battleship.

As the rain began to pelt down, the *Ostfriesland* not only listed to port but the stern also had sunk about three feet. Yet it was still afloat. Admirals aboard the *Henderson* snickered on the trip back to shore. The battleship had survived. The airmen had barely injured it, they boasted to reporters, many of whom had become seasick from the pitching ship. Pershing and Secretary of War Weeks decided not to return Thursday for the next round of bombing because it seemed obvious that the planes would not be able to sink the ship.

But the navy inspectors who boarded the *Ostfriesland* after the second attack realized that it had suffered more than a flesh wound. The one six-hundred-pound bomb that had struck the ship and detonated tore a four-by-five-foot hole into the starboard side of the main deck and demolished equipment in the gun deck below. The shock wave damage from bombs exploding near the ship and below the waterline was even more severe. Some of the engine rooms were a mess, and water was rushing into compartments because of pipe joints and hull seams that had ruptured.

The USS *Delaware* remained at the target area, keeping a lonely vigil over the *Ostfriesland*. Sailors pointed a searchlight at the German dreadnought throughout the night to watch for any change in its draft.

Thursday morning Mitchell's plane was flying over the *Ostfriesland* by a quarter past eight. Its stern seemed to be even lower in the water than when he had left the previous afternoon. Bissell's formation of eight Martin bombers, each loaded with two eleven-hundred-pound bombs, circled above. Mitchell had already radioed a message to the *Shawmut* that morning asking that his bombers "be not interfered with by Naval aircraft." Johnson considered it an insolent request. The navy had five of its Martin bombers over the target, and according to the rules both sides had agreed to, they were also supposed to drop their eleven-hundred-pounders in the attack.

At 8:32 A.M. the *Shawmut* signaled the attack to begin. Bissell led off with an eleven-hundred-pound bomb that slammed into the starboard side of the forward deck with an ear-shattering explosion that opened up an eight-foot-wide hole. Four other army planes followed his, dropping bombs about a minute apart and scoring two more hits.

Aboard the *Shawmut* Johnson and the other umpires were furiously flipping through pages of the test rules. They found the section they were looking for and reread the orders that had been sent to the army. They could not be more clear. After each hit with an eleven-hundred-pound bomb, the attack was supposed to stop and the inspection team was supposed to board the ship to view the damage.

The *Shawmut* crew had taken down the all-clear flag to signal the bombers to stop. Johnson grabbed his radio telephone and shouted into it: "Cease bombing! Observers going aboard. Acknowledge." Mitchell radioed back. His bombers "will let you know when it's safe to board the target." (He and Bissell would later insist the one-hit rule was ambiguous and that they halted the attack as soon as they could after seeing the signal from the *Shawmut*.)

Johnson was livid. Finally, at 8:50 A.M., the *Shawmut* received a message from Mitchell: "Safe to go aboard target now." The inspectors motorboated to the battleship. There was no vital damage, they concluded, but in wartime the ship's fighting ability may have ended. The navy and army bombers were ordered back to their bases.

Shortly after noon, with a haze creeping in from the southeast that made visibility poor, the army flew to the *Ostfriesland* with its most powerful sortie: eight Martin and two Handley Page twin-engine biplanes, each loaded with new two-thousand-pound bombs. (Three Handley Pages had actually taken off from Langley, but one had engine trouble on the way out and crashed into the Atlantic about 150 feet from a guard destroyer, whose crew plucked the airmen out of the water.) Mitchell's final orders to the pilots: Aim for close misses to maximize the water hammer effect.

Capt. Walter Lawson, who commanded the formation, banked away from it and pushed the stick in his cockpit forward to point his

Martin down toward the *Ostfriesland*'s bow. He released a hundred-pound sighting bomb, which the pilots behind him watched to gauge the likely effect of the winds on their projectiles. It landed 150 feet short. Three minutes later the Martin bomber behind Lawson roared down, releasing the first two-thousand-pound bomb, which exploded 225 feet off the starboard bow. Two Martins dove in minutes later: one dropping another sighting shot, the other holding up on releasing the big bomb. Lawson circled around and came in for another attack. His two-thousand-pounder glanced off the port bow and exploded 25 feet away, puncturing large holes in the hull. Navy observers on the *Shawmut* scored it as a hit.

The next two bombs, one of which grazed the ship, came at one-minute intervals and detonated in the water close to the port side. They sent tons of the ocean over the deck and likely blew a hole near the stern. Another Martin dropped its bomb 200 feet off the starboard side just aft of the smokestacks.

Johnson and the other umpires on the *Shawmut* again angrily turned pages in their rulebooks. Mitchell technically had not violated the two-hit rule. The four other bombs had missed, although they likely did as much damage because of their mining effect. But Johnson had also ordered that the Martins drop no more than a total of three two-thousand-pound bombs; then the ordnance team was to board the battleship to inspect damage. The army had dropped six bombs. Mitchell later complained that Johnson had tossed in that three-bomb rule at the last minute—as a last-gasp ploy to keep the army from sinking the ship.

The squabble became a moot point in a few minutes. The helpless *Ostfriesland* began to list more to port, and the stern became flush with the water. Slowly and silently it turned completely over while at the same time the stern sank into the ocean. The bow pointed up in one last gasp for life, then fell back and slipped into the sea. A Handley Page bomber swooped down and dropped a final two-thousand-pounder that exploded near the large pool of white foam the battleship had left on the water, as if to tamp down the dirt over its grave.

St. Clair Street, who had been taking notes in the backseat of Mitchell's plane, unclipped his safety belt, stood up, and began waving his arms and cheering at the top of his lungs. On the

Henderson mouths of the VIPs gaped open. No one spoke. Politicians, many of whom had staked their careers on funding the battleships, looked as if they had just witnessed a murder. Some admirals sobbed like babies.

Mitchell banked his De Havilland down and flew just a few feet over the white pool that still marked where the dreadnought had sunk. He had tears in his eyes. A powerful mix of emotions churned inside him. He saw the *Ostfriesland* as a "grim old bulldog, with the vicious scars of the Battle of Jutland still on her," he wrote later. "We wanted to destroy her from the air but when it was actually accomplished, it was a very serious and awesome sight." He felt anger as well—at all the roadblocks the navy had thrown up to keep him from proving his point—and absolute joy at the final triumph. Mitchell turned his De Havilland and buzzed the *Henderson,* where sailors had climbed its rigging to wave at him. Many of the VIPs, finally recovered from the shock, rushed out to the deck railing and cheered him.

Planes circled Langley to greet Mitchell and Street when they returned in the *Osprey.* Cannons boomed, and signs were hung from hangars proclaiming the sinking. Officers, mechanics, and their families lined the airfield. They rushed to Mitchell's plane when it finally came to a stop on the runway. A band had been playing when he landed, but the musicians dropped their instruments and ran to his plane leaving only one bandsman banging a bass drum.

As the mob pulled him from his cockpit, Mitchell struggled to rip off his goggles and helmet and give a speech, but he couldn't be heard over the bass drum and the cheering pilots who carried him on their shoulders. That night, huge bonfires were lit around the base and discipline disappeared. The pilots, their wives and girlfriends danced around the blazes all night and got roaring drunk.

The navy complained loudly afterward that Mitchell had cheated. "Bombing a vessel under way at sea" that's fighting back, Daniels also maintained, "is an entirely different and far more difficult task than dropping projectiles upon a stationary target," particularly with guide ships and bull's-eyes helping the planes to their prey. Mitchell argued that a fighting warship would suffer even more from bombs that set off live ammunition in its stores. Air strikes would cripple its war-fighting ability long before it sank.

But the complaints could not obscure this remarkable achievement. Mitchell had proved conclusively that planes could sink a battleship. Overnight he became an international hero. Congratulatory letters poured in from politicians, business leaders, and military men. Air enthusiasts now claimed that the test proved that battleships were obsolete. Mitchell boasted that the air brigade he had assembled at Langley could wipe out "the entire Atlantic Fleet in a single attack." After the tests he staged mock attacks with his planes over New York and other East Coast cities to demonstrate how vulnerable they would be to airpower. It created near hysteria in the press. Calmer editorials chastised Mitchell for exaggerating. Aerial-bombing technology was still relatively new and crude.

Naval leaders, who felt they'd been victimized by Mitchell's publicity stunts, resisted giving the army any more surplus battleships for target practice. (Eventually they were forced to.) The sinking of the *Ostfriesland* marked the beginning of what would be a slow end for these giant vessels. A board of naval officers who had observed the bombing concluded the next day that the test proved that "the airplane is a powerful weapon of offense." One could quibble over the test rules and the fact that the ships were anchored, but the fact remained that they all "were eventually sunk and by airplanes with bombs alone." Ironically Mitchell ended up being the godfather of modern naval aviation. The navy's pilots used the trials off the Virginia Capes to press for aircraft carriers, arguing that if the sea service didn't develop this capability, Mitchell's air service would steal it from them. Farsighted naval thinkers, such as retired admiral William Fullam, agreed that aircraft carriers would become the new powers of the sea; "the fleet with superior air forces will no doubt win the next naval battle."

For Billy Mitchell the day his men sunk the *Ostfriesland* was the greatest of his life.

But his joy was short-lived. Mitchell became more convinced that entrenched interests in the military were conspiring against him. He fought back by taking bigger swipes at the navy and sprinkling his congressional testimony with claims—exaggerated for that time—about the potential of airpower. "Keep cool and use good judgment," his worried mother cabled him. But her son remained defiant. When Pershing and the navy concluded after the sinking of the *Ostfriesland* that battleships were still the backbone of the fleet, Mitchell drafted his own lengthy report contradicting them. It leaked to the press and the air general had to deny army accusations that he had given it to reporters.

It was inevitable that Mitchell and Menoher would clash. Menoher tried to clamp down on his deputy's public campaign, particularly against the navy. But by the time Mitchell began preparing for the battleship bombing test in the Spring of 1921, Menoher had lost control of his subordinate. The air service was in a state of chaos. As the bombing tests began, Menoher demanded that the army fire Mitchell from the deputy's job.

Menoher had no hope of winning the showdown, which was soon splashed all over the newspapers. Weeks, the secretary of war, only reprimanded Mitchell. Humiliated, Menoher was allowed to transfer to a troop unit.

Hoping to generate momentum for him, Mitchell's cadre of loyal aides began leaking to reporters that he would finally be named the next air service chief. But there was no chance that Pershing, who knew Mitchell's limits as an administrator and logistician, would allow that to happen. Instead he gave the job to a man who didn't want it: Mason Patrick.

Pershing asked the engineer to rescue the air service once more. Looking forward to retirement, Patrick loathed the thought of again having to manage the unruly pilots. But Pershing wouldn't take no for an answer. He knew from the war that Patrick was the only one who could control Billy Mitchell.

When he learned that Patrick again would lead the air service, Mitchell tried a power play. He sent the major general a five-page memo outlining what he thought his duties should be as Patrick's deputy. Mitchell wanted to run everything, with Patrick as a figurehead.

Patrick was no dummy. He promptly returned the memo to Mitchell "disapproved," curtly informing him that he "proposed to be Chief of the Air Service in fact as well as in name."

Thinking he could bulldoze Patrick the way he had Menoher, Mitchell threatened to resign from the army. Patrick, however, was made of sterner stuff and had many admirers in the War Department. He hauled Mitchell before Maj. Gen. James Harbord—the army's deputy chief of staff, who also knew how difficult Mitchell was to deal with from their days together in France—and announced that Mitchell has "found it impossible to serve under me." "Well, are you going to offer your resignation?" Harbord asked Mitchell gruffly. "If so, it will be accepted."

Mitchell backed down. He never challenged Patrick again.

The airmen gave Patrick mixed reviews. Rickenbacker thought that installing him as air chief was about "as sensible as making Pershing admiral of the Swiss Navy." Mitchell privately agreed, although he maintained cordial relations with his boss the next four years. Arnold found Patrick to be a morose and temperamental man who liked to drink by himself and had an irritating habit of interrupting subordinates who were trying to explain things to him with, "Yes, I know, I know." He once threw a paperweight at Arnold in a fit of anger. Patrick could be a prig with subordinates, sending them nasty notes if they didn't show up promptly at receptions.

He also had a vain streak. He liked riding in fancy cars and enjoyed the celebrity status of being connected with the air service. Patrick hit the speaking circuit on behalf of aviation as avidly as Mitchell did and made the cover of *Time* magazine, which Mitchell never did. Patrick also sported a toupee, which the pilots thought looked ridiculous, particularly when he insisted on wearing it under his helmet when he flew. One day, when he climbed out of a cockpit and removed his headgear, the plane's prop wash blew the wig off. Mechanics found it down the runway and returned what looked like a dead rat to him. The story spread like wildfire through the air ranks.

But Patrick had his own loyalists in the air service. He learned to fly at age fifty-nine. He was rated only a junior aviator and never flew solo. Mitchell never thought much of the gesture. But it impressed other airmen. They bought him a Lincoln automobile when he retired.

Indeed, some military historians believe that Patrick, and not Mitchell, is the unrecognized father of the Air Force because he was a builder, not an agitator. Unlike Menoher, Patrick shared Mitchell's futuristic vision of what airpower could accomplish, and he agreed that it ultimately should be independent. But he favored a more gradual approach to achieving that independence. Patrick believed the air service should first become an air corps in the army, semiautonomous (as the Marines were within the Navy Department); then it could eventually break off as an independent air force—which is exactly what would happen. Though top army commanders thought Patrick's air corps idea was about as much nonsense as Mitchell's independent air force, the low-key Patrick didn't alienate his superiors the way Mitchell had, and he knew how to work the system.

Patrick also knew how to channel Mitchell's creative energy to make it a productive force for the air service. He kept Mitchell away from the Washington hothouse, putting him on the road inspecting air facilities and suggesting improvements.

By the end of 1921, it became even more imperative for Patrick to get his deputy out of town—for the sake of the air service and of Mitchell himself.

The marital bliss Caroline so desperately wanted after her husband returned from the war lasted less than a year. Mitchell had come back a changed man, driven now to make his airpower theories a reality. Nearly forty, he feared that time was running out for him to succeed in the military or, if he got out, in politics or business. As he threw himself into his work, Mitchell spent less and less time at home. The loneliness that had tormented Caroline during the war years returned. She also had a rough pregnancy with John, and William was away on air service business for a lot of it, which made her angry.

Money became a source of friction. They both continued to be extravagant in their spending, racking up thirty thousand dollars in bills annually, which was far beyond Mitchell's military salary, which amounted to no more than twelve thousand dollars. His mother was now matching that with as much as twelve thousand dollars each year, and Caroline dipped into her family fortune. But Mitchell still had merchants, such as his tailors in London and Paris, hounding him for unpaid bills. Caroline began complaining in her diary that a general's wife shouldn't have to sew her own dresses to make ends meet.

Exactly when the marriage began falling apart was a matter of dispute between them. According to Mitchell, they started quarreling several years before he left for Europe. Caroline said the fights began after John was born. Mitchell had been under enormous

pressure to succeed in the battleship-bombing test, while bureaucratic enemies in the War and Navy Departments were constantly
attacking him. To Caroline he always seemed to be nervous and agi-
tated, unable to spend a relaxing evening at home or to sit through
an entire play at the theater. Mitchell said that Caroline was the one
who became unhinged, constantly nagging and throwing scissors,
bottles, and even chairs at him when they argued.

Their domestic turmoil turned even more violent on September 2,
1920. It was Caroline's birthday, and Mitchell again had not remembered it. They had gone to the theater, but he had rushed out in the
middle of the first act. At home they had a huge row. Caroline was
shot in the chest with a .38-caliber revolver. It was only a flesh wound,
which healed quickly. The police never knew of the incident. Mitchell
claimed that Caroline had inflicted it on herself in a suicidal rage; Caroline, that her husband had been drunk and accidentally shot her.

When army investigators later learned of the shooting, they
didn't know whom to believe. Mitchell, however, had begun drinking heavily. Caroline was furious about the reports she heard of
wild parties he had attended out of town during inspection trips
and at Langley during the battleship bombing. She suspected that
her husband had had affairs in Europe during the war and that
he continued to play around when he returned to Washington.
Mitchell adamantly insisted that he had always been faithful. Caroline, he maintained, was insanely jealous over his innocent flirting
with other women, who flocked to him at social events.

The two had another ugly scene about a month before the *Ostfriesland* was bombed. Mitchell had taken Helen Brereton and her
sick child to be examined by a doctor in Maryland. Helen was the
wife of Lewis Brereton, an air service pilot and one of Mitchell's
loyal friends. But after they finished with the doctor, Mitchell and
Mrs. Brereton left the child in a Baltimore hotel room with a
matron while they went out for an evening of dinner, drinking, and
dancing. The Brereton marriage was already strained, and each
spouse had cheated on the other.

Suspicious, Caroline drove to the hotel and waited in the room
until the two finally showed up after midnight. Caroline and
Mitchell had another of their shouting matches, which brought the
hotel detective up to the room. The general gave him a generous tip

to keep quiet. Mitchell pleaded innocence and Caroline claimed she never accused him of planning to sleep with Helen. But it looked awfully suspicious.

By the time of the *Ostfriesland* test, the two were unofficially separated. Caroline had sailed to Europe for two months in the spring with her brother, Vine, to sort out her marriage in her mind. Mitchell had moved out of the house. Gossip about his turbulent home life was already spreading through the army and navy. By November 1921 the seamy story was in danger of being made public.

Caroline became convinced that her husband was going crazy. She paid a visit to Harbord, the army's deputy chief of staff, and asked him to have Mitchell committed to a hospital. Caroline and Harbord were old friends. She and Mitchell had socialized with the general and his wife during their first posting in Washington, and Harbord had later agreed to be one of John's godparents. Harbord alerted Pershing, who in turn alerted Weeks that they had a potential scandal on their hands. Caroline was not being particularly discreet about who heard her story. She had unloaded it to Sen. James Wadsworth, a genteel, conservative Republican from New York. He was another family friend who had eventually been turned off by what he considered Mitchell's political opportunism. Wadsworth, who served on the Military Affairs Committee, told Caroline "the Senate could do nothing in the way of intervening in a domestic situation."

On November 25 Weeks grounded Mitchell so he couldn't fly and ordered him to report to Walter Reed Hospital for a psychiatric exam. Mitchell was outraged. If anyone should be institutionalized, it should be Caroline, he thought. He decided to sue her for divorce and gain custody of two of the children, Harriet and John. He had grown distant from his oldest daughter, fifteen-year-old Elizabeth, who was more like her mother than the rest. Later, however, he decided he would seek custody of Elizabeth as well, perhaps to punish Caroline. His wife had turned over most of their household receipts to the army's inspector general (IG) to show how reckless he had been in his spending. Confidential IG documents also were circulating among top generals at the War Department with the accounts Caroline had given investigators of the shooting and the Baltimore episode. Furious, Mitchell considered suing her for slander or even trying to have her imprisoned.

The Mitchell family rallied around him. "I have got to stand by Willie," his mother wrote her daughter Katharine. "He mustn't break during this ordeal." She found Caroline's "bravado . . . perfectly astonishing. She seems to have no refinement of feelings." Mitchell's sister Harriet rushed to Washington to be at her brother's side. Together they made the rounds to Harbord, Weeks, Pershing, and even Wadsworth, complaining at each stop that Caroline was trying to frame him with lies. Mitchell was convinced that his wife and Harbord were now in league against him. His other sister, Ruth, wrote later that Caroline had even conspired with Mitchell's enemies to try to block the *Ostfriesland* test, though she offered no proof. Harriet wrote her mother that Willie might even demand "a senatorial investigation" of the way Harbord was handling the case. "Our little general has put it over the old men again and they are afraid of him," Harriet bragged.

It was an empty boast. Mitchell would never get a Senate investigation. Wadsworth had made that clear enough to Caroline. But the old men in the War Department knew that Mitchell could make trouble for them, and they wanted this embarrassing problem to go away.

Mitchell pleaded with Weeks to have the medical examination take place at his apartment instead of Walter Reed. He worried that a hospital visit would surely leak to the press and destroy his career. Weeks agreed. On November 29 two army doctors knocked on his door to begin the exam.

Was Mitchell mentally unbalanced? Some powerful people in Washington thought so, but that was only because he had a haughty manner and his ideas about airpower seemed so farfetched to them. There had been and would be traces of mental illness in the Mitchell family, however. Mitchell's father, according to his first wife, Bianca, had an alcohol problem. Mitchell's sister Martha had been institutionalized, although it was unclear whether that was because of mental illness or the unconventional life she had been living in Greenwich Village. The second son Mitchell would have with Betty would later suffer from manic-depressive illness. If the symptoms Caroline said her husband exhibited were true—nervousness, erratic behavior, heavy drinking—they might be indicators, by today's standards, that he needed help. But in 1921 the medical profession was just beginning to understand and treat mental illness. There was no indication in the army records that the two medical officers who showed up at Mitchell's apartment had psychiatric training.

After six days of reviewing Mitchell's medical history, giving him a thorough physical, and intensively interviewing both him and Caroline, the two doctors concluded that the general was perfectly sane. Mitchell admitted to them that he enjoyed a good party and sometimes drank too much, but insisted that he wasn't an alcoholic. He was also trying to cut back on expenses. The trouble he and Caroline had was no different from any couple breaking up, he claimed.

The doctors agreed. Mitchell was in fine shape physically and "oriented in all spheres," they wrote in a seven-page report, stamped CONFIDENTIAL. In their conversations with him the doctors found the general to be bright, coherent, alert, and able to recall the past in detail. His "attention is easy to gain and to hold. No questions have to be repeated. There is no disorder of apprehension or apperception. Emotionally at time of examination patient appears neither depressed nor elated." The doctors did note that Mitchell had an outsize ego. "He believes that he has done much toward the advancement of aviation and that he is one of the few whose foresight and aggressiveness have made possible a great future for the Army Air Service." But considering how rapidly Mitchell had advanced in the military, the doctors saw nothing unusual with his vision of grandeur.

Ironically the medical officers thought that Caroline was the one who needed help. "She gives the impression of being nervous, emotionally unstable, and of hysterical temperament," they wrote in their report. As for Mitchell, he was pronounced "fit for full military duty."

On December 10 the ocean liner *Rotterdam* set sail for Europe with Mitchell aboard. The ship's captain gave him the best stateroom and allowed him free access to the bridge. Mason Patrick, who had sided with his deputy during the Caroline crisis, now wisely sent him on a European inspection trip so he wouldn't stir up any more trouble in Washington. Clayton Bissell, who accompanied Mitchell and would later serve as his technical adviser during the trial, thought it was just the tonic his boss needed. For four months the general toured the capitals of Europe, inspecting air facilities, conferring with pilots and plane designers, and, at one point, a German scientist who had been researching the idea of rocket-propelled bombs and jet engines for planes. The trip reinforced Mitchell's conviction that dramatic changes were needed in "our organization for national defense."

Patrick ordered Mitchell to stay away from the European press. To make sure he did, the War Department's intelligence division had its military attachés in the U.S. embassies monitor Mitchell and report if his name appeared in the papers. The spies all cabled back that the general, for the most part, behaved himself. The attaché in Paris did complain, however, that Mitchell wore out the embassy staff with his demands. His chauffeur thought he was going to die of exhaustion driving him around until 4:00 A.M. each night.

When he returned from Europe in the spring of 1922, Mitchell had his lawyers in Milwaukee file a divorce petition there, accusing his wife of being the one who broke up the family with her jealous rages and violent behavior. Caroline felt stung when a process server showed up at the Rhode Island Avenue town house in Washington, where she now lived with the children, handing her the papers on March 29. Though far from liberated, women of the 1920s were enjoying more freedom to break the bonds of child bearing and failed marriages. Birth control became more popular. The more promiscuous girls, who smoked and wore skimpy clothes in public, were called "flappers." The country's divorce rate had begun to soar. But Caroline, who remained a status-conscious Victorian in her thinking, did not believe in divorce. Or at least she didn't when she first went to Harbord. Now she had a battery of lawyers from Washington and Rochester file a counterpetition accusing Mitchell of desertion.

On September 27 Caroline, Mitchell, and their lawyers gathered in a Milwaukee courtroom for a trial both sides had kept secret up to that point. When the judge learned that Mitchell had in fact been absent from the household since the battleship-bombing test, it took him only a half hour to decide in Caroline's favor. He awarded her custody of the children and ordered Mitchell to pay four hundred dollars a month in child support. That afternoon Caroline took the train to Chicago, checked into a hotel, and went to dinner and then the theater with friends to celebrate.

She was livid, however, when she picked up a copy of the *Washington Times* on November 4 and found a front-page story on the divorce. Caroline suspected that Mitchell had leaked it. The article gave mostly his side of the story.

In mid-December, Mitchell's mother visited him in the Washington town house he now occupied by himself on Phelps Place. Harriet, then seventy years old, had come to die, and she wanted to be near her son when it happened. Pleurisy racked her body, and her heart grew weaker by the day. Mitchell summoned a full-time nurse and sat by her bed for hours, holding her hand and trying to soothe her pain. She seemed to him to improve slightly on Christmas Eve, but it didn't last. Shortly after 4:00 A.M. on December 28, Harriet, with almost her last ounce of strength, reached for a little bell on the bedside table and rang it. Mitchell and the nurse rushed in. She asked her son to take off the two rings she had on her fingers and keep them. Those were her last words.

Mitchell was grief stricken. It was "as if the great supporting and impelling force behind me has been shattered," he wrote. "As if the castle with its great moats, high walls and secure drawbridges, to which I could always repair in case of need and find absolute shelter and protection, has vanished into the earth. I felt that way when father went, but I feel even more so now and I am just as much a little boy with mother as I was when I ran around with my little dogs and ponies years ago."

He now looked to another woman to take her place.

4:00 P.M., THURSDAY, OCTOBER 11, 1923

Brig. Gen. William Mitchell and Elizabeth Trumbull Miller were married in a quaint little Protestant church in Grosse Point near Detroit. Only family members and a handful of special guests—a White House aide, a wing commander from the British Embassy, the conductor of the Detroit symphony, several senior pilots—could fit inside. Newspapers around the country carried stories on the event. Instead of a bouquet, Betty held a white prayer book that had belonged to Mitchell's grandmother as she walked down the aisle. His dress uniform draped with medals and a gleaming saber hanging from his belt, Mitchell had Joseph Davies as his best man. When the ceremony ended a dozen air service planes flew low over the church to salute the newlyweds. "Everything faded into insignificance this week when compared with the Miller-Mitchell wedding," gushed one Detroit society writer.

They had met at a Grosse Point Hunt Club horse show in the summer of 1922. In town for air races at nearby Selfridge Field, Mitchell was competing in the horse show. Betty had also entered it. (She always rode sidesaddle.) Mitchell was instantly smitten with this glamorous, mature woman, who was a crack shot and handled horses as ably as he did. Mitchell's daring captivated her as well. Betty was not afraid to take risks. She liked jumping her horse higher, driving her car faster. After the club competition ended, he took her up in his personal plane to show off.

In portrait photographs, Elizabeth has almost a haunting look with high cheekbones, sad blue eyes, and light brown hair. But "Pat," which was a nickname many called her in addition to Betty, was vivacious and outgoing. She tilted her head back, as Mitchell did, when she laughed. She had Mitchell's sense of flair. She also bore an uncanny resemblance to Caroline.

Certainly the two women came from similar backgrounds. Elizabeth was a descendant of one of Detroit's old-money families— although Caroline, who began tracking the romance in the society pages, considered her lower class because she was not East Coast bred. Betty's father, Sidney Miller, was a Detroit attorney heavily involved in banking and a partner in one of the city's prominent law firms. Her mother, Lucy Trumbull Robinson, had been a Hartford, Connecticut, blueblood, whose own father had been a friend of Mark Twain's. The Miller family kept a town house in Detroit and a larger country home in an exclusive section of Grosse Point. Their summers were spent at Cove Cottage, a huge house they owned in York Harbor, Maine, which was a haven for the well off.

When she met Mitchell, Elizabeth was thirty-one, nearly a spinster for that day. She had had a traditional upbringing for a rich girl. Society pages described her as "one of the most popular debutantes of her set." She had attended an exclusive finishing school, had joined the Junior League in her twenties, and was active in local charities. But Elizabeth was also considered somewhat avant-garde for her day, always a little outside the bounds of what was deemed proper by her father's Victorian standards. Her family said she was the first woman in Grosse Point to drive a car.

Elizabeth never went to college, but she was well read and could hold her own in almost any conversation. She was a direct person who, like Mitchell, was not afraid to speak her mind or join in spirited discussions at the dinner table. She was still a proper lady. She held a lorgnette to her eyes for reading and the theater and always showed up for dinner in a tea gown. She was proud of her Yankee roots from her mother's side of the family (after Elizabeth settled with Mitchell in Middleburg, she found the pretensions of the First Families of Virginia–types silly). She could manage servants but didn't know how to boil water in the kitchen and shunned housework. She could not balance a checkbook and didn't like to handle money, which was why her father set up a trust to manage her part of the family fortune. But though she had the wherewithal to dress lavishly, which she often did, she did not mind shopping for bargain clothes.

During the war Elizabeth sailed to France, working as a Red Cross volunteer in YMCA canteens for servicemen. She did not cross paths with her future husband there, but lonely doughboys fell in love with her, sending her poems and long letters pouring out their hearts. "Why couldn't the other American soldiers be as lucky as I was last Thursday night for that short time with you?" one corporal wrote her. "Do you know that there are tens of thousands of American men—good men—who have not heard an American woman's voice for over six months?" She smiled and listened to all their war stories but never became romantically involved. In Detroit as well, she had dated a lot but never found the right man. "I've been out with every lawyer and banker around," she once told her parents. "And they're all boring."

Mitchell was anything but boring. Rumors spread quickly in Detroit that there might be a budding romance. Mitchell was taking an unusual number of flights to Michigan, and the two were spotted together at air races at Selfridge Field.

The general acted like a giddy teenager with his first case of puppy love. "How I love, love, love you," he wrote her in one of his many passionate letters that fall. "Every waking moment that I have, you are a part or the whole of it, whether I am in the air, on the land, or in the water. . . . Betty, my love for you is so far above any little thing on this earth that it transcends whatever little understanding I have ever had. It grows with the seconds, the minutes, the hours and the days."

Sidney Miller was anything but pleased. Elizabeth was his darling, and she was now dating a forty-two-year-old man with the ink barely dry on his divorce papers. Miller had begun to pick up the private gossip in Detroit social circles that a potential scandal was brewing in his family. He refused to allow his daughter and Mitchell to announce their engagement until a decent interval had passed after the divorce, and he ordered them to put their courtship under cover. Elizabeth abided by her father's wishes, and by October 1922 she had told her ardent lover they would have to meet less often and then only in private places where they could not be seen by others. Mitchell was devastated, but he accepted the ground rules. "I naturally would not embarrass you or your family in any way," he wrote her. "I shall never push in where there are not willing hands not only to receive me but to pull me in also. I know full well as I told you that 'there are no bells on me,' that I have been divorced, which I agree is a very reprehensible thing."

Finally, in August 1923, the Millers announced their daughter's engagement. Even then the society reporters noted disapprovingly that it came less than a year after the general had formally ended his first marriage.

Elizabeth was a calming influence on Mitchell, which he desperately needed. Betty was not a partier or a heavier drinker. She enjoyed cocktails before dinner, but preferred quiet nights with a few friends. After he started dating her, Mitchell had no interest in dancing the night away at wild parties. The only social functions he would now attend without her were the ones required by his job, and even at them he would look for the first chance to slip out early. Betty had also begun to lecture him about not being so rebellious at work. "I shall do all in my power to carry out your wishes," he assured her in one letter, "just because I adore you so absolutely."

14 Tables Turned

"This, then, is a fair statement of what we intend to prove," Reid finally said, taking off his reading glasses and laying them on the defense table. His voice had grown raspy, and his throat felt dry. Howze gave him a fifteen-minute recess to recover. It had taken an hour and a half for the defense attorney to read to the judges the case his client intended to make before the court. Mitchell had packed the 6,080-word statement he had made on September 5 with practically all the complaints he had. Reid's defense team had used every waking minute during the week's recess to cull thousands of pages of documents, and they had interviewed scores of witnesses in order to assemble the evidence they hoped would prove that everything Mitchell had said was true.

It was an ambitious undertaking, to put it mildly. Mitchell's September 5 statement contained a staggering total of 129 allegations. Beginning at 10:00 A.M., Reid reviewed each one in detail. To help reporters follow along, the defense team had passed out press releases ahead of time, with Reid's description of each point. When he finished with the first list, Reid also read each recommendation that Mitchell had made during the past seven years to improve the air service. Bissell and a half dozen air service pilots had scoured the official records and by their count, Mitchell had made a total of 163 recommendations. The airmen concluded that only a tiny fraction of them had ever been approved or implemented; most had been ignored or disapproved.

Reid's opening presentation had been the equivalent in the military of an artillery barrage at the dawn of a battle. It mattered little that not all of the 129 allegations could be proven or that the War Department, from its own search of the records, had a difficult time verifying that Mitchell had actually made all 163 recommendations. The fact that Mitchell could fire so many charges at the army and navy rocked the prosecutors back on their heels. The reporters were certainly impressed. Such a long list of complaints meant that something had to be seriously wrong with the armed forces. ARMY AIR FORCE FACING COLLAPSE, the headline in one Washington paper warned. "To the surprise of civilian as well as military Washington," the *New York Times* reported the next day, the Mitchell case has been "thrown wide open." The flying colonel "at once took the offensive and sensation followed sensation with bewildering rapidity." To the *Times* it looked "as if the whole air service wrangle may be thrashed out before the court-martial."

Reid used his first witness to strike a sharp blow at one of the War Department's top officers. The witness was Amos Fries, a handsome young brigadier general with wavy black hair parted down the middle and a dark mustache. The army's foremost expert on chemical weapons, Fries had been chief of its gas service during the World War, and he now headed the peacetime research and production of toxic agents.

Fries and Mitchell were kindred spirits. The army's chemical warfare service was about as new as its air service, and Fries was convinced that chemical weapons would be as powerful a force in future wars as Mitchell believed planes would be. Fries also was as frustrated as Mitchell; out of every dollar the army spent, only a quarter of a cent now went to the chemical warfare service.

"From your observation and study, are you able to tell the amount of gas necessary . . . to gas areas of different sizes?" Reid asked.

"Yes, sir," Fries answered. Knowing the conditions of the atmosphere and terrain, Fries could easily calculate the amount.

Howze ordered the courtroom guards to open the windows. The radiators had only one setting—high—and the courtroom was becoming stuffy, making everyone drowsy. Reporters chuckled. All this talk about chemical weapons must have spooked Howze and made him want to breathe some fresh air. But the open windows again let in the traffic noise, and everyone had to speak up.

"Now, can you tell us what amount of gas would be necessary to effectively gas an area the size of the District of Columbia, under peacetime and not wartime conditions?" Reid asked.

Before Fries could open his mouth, Moreland jumped up. "I object to that," he said firmly. "It is not shown in what way the gas would be administered . . . and the witness has not been shown competent to testify on that subject."

Fries was more than competent to answer the question. But Reid decided to rephrase it to get to the point he wanted to make more quickly. He picked up a piece of paper from the defense table. "I read you a statement," he began, looking up at Fries. "'In order to effectively gas an area the size of the District of Columbia, about 60 square miles, it would require 3,439,150 pounds of mustard gas for a concentration which would have a material effect, or 9,573,850 pounds of mustard gas to cause evacuation of the area.' Is that statement correct or incorrect?"

"I object," Moreland shouted, jumping up again.

Winship overruled him.

"Is that correct?" Reid asked again.

"It is not correct, whether it would be against a civilian population or an army," Fries responded confidently.

"Now, as to this question," Reid continued, reading from the same sheet of paper. Delivering these huge amounts of chemical munitions would take "'about 2,000 heavy bombing planes in the first case and 5,830 in the second case, each carrying 1,700 pounds of gas or 2,000 pounds of gas bombs.' State whether or not that is correct."

"That is not correct," Fries answered.

"That is all," Reid said, turning to Moreland and sitting down.

Reid was dealing with a ticklish subject. Tons of chlorine, phosgene, and mustard gas had been used during World War I, and although they hadn't decided the outcome and hadn't caused nearly as many casualties as bombs and bullets, the soldiers in the trenches thought the chemicals were horrifying weapons. Most Americans considered them inhumane as well. Just five months earlier the United States had joined twenty-eight other countries in signing a protocol in Geneva that committed them to not be the first to use chemical or biological weapons in the next war.

For a long time Mitchell had tried to stay quiet, at least in public, about the possibility of airplanes delivering these kinds of weapons of mass destruction, particularly against population centers. He believed they could and should be used. Strategic attacks on civilians, Mitchell argued, were the best way to destroy a country's fighting capability and end the next war quickly. But the politicians of his day considered such warfare almost criminal, so the War Department treated it as a taboo subject. Only recently had Mitchell broached it in his speeches and writings.

But Reid wasn't trying to start a theoretical debate on strategic warfare. He had another reason for raising the question. Moreland knew what he was up to, which was why he tried so hard to stop Fries from answering. Reid was going after Brig. Gen. Hugh Drum, the army's assistant chief of staff and the officer the War Department often used to deliver its official position at congressional hearings. Drum had told a House committee that it would take 1,720 to 4,787 tons of chemical munitions to gas the District of Columbia, and up to five thousand planes to carry them. He had thrown out the numbers to demonstrate the limitations of airpower in crippling a large city, but they were wildly inflated. Fries calculated that about twenty tons of tear gas carried by twenty bombers would be enough to force an evacuation of Washington.

In the early 1920s Congress was touchy about the testimony that War Department witnesses gave. Too often top army officers trooped up to Capitol Hill unprepared and delivered inaccurate, imprecise, or sometimes deceitful testimony. In his September 5 statement, Mitchell had blasted the War Department for its arrogance in misleading Congress. Air service aides had slipped him a fifty-three-page memo that cited instances in which Drum and other senior officers had been less than truthful when they testified about airpower. Of course Mitchell was also guilty of being cavalier with the facts when he testified. But Reid was interested only in the erroneous statements Mitchell's enemies had made.

Reid also had to prove that the air service was in terrible shape. To do that, which lay at the heart of Mitchell's statement, he called to the stand Mitchell's most loyal pilots.

Carl "Tooey" Spaatz used few words to get to the point and, except for a sarcastic wit that sometimes flared, he kept his emotions to himself. He had a round face, thinning red hair, and a mustache cropped no wider than his nose. Spaatz had gotten the nick-name Tooey at West Point.

Tooey had been a hero during the World War, winning the Distin-guished Service Cross for shooting down two German planes on one patrol before he had to make a forced landing after running out of gas. When Spaatz returned to the United States, he took command of the West Flying Circus, which staged aerobatics and dogfighting exhi-bitions across the country to generate publicity for the air service. Spaatz once talked a San Francisco chef into taking a flight with him, holding a hen in the open cockpit, which would also carry an electric grill. The idea was to have the hen lay an egg, the chef fry it on the grill, then serve it on the ground before news photographers, demon-strating the first in-flight meal from chicken to plate. Of course it didn't work. The terrified hen not only didn't lay the egg, it managed to escape the cockpit and plunged into San Francisco Bay.

Now a major and working in Washington, Spaatz oversaw the training and equipment for the air service's tactical squadrons. He was painfully aware of their problems and had been helping Mitchell prepare his defense.

"Will you tell the court the condition of the equipment at the present time that the air service is supplied with?" Reid asked.

"The equipment in the air service has reached the condition where it is very difficult to figure out how we are going to continue flying," Spaatz answered bluntly. Reid handed him a stack of status reports that air units from around the country had sent Washing-ton in September, and Spaatz began flipping through them. They showed that all the De Havilland planes the air service had were built during the war, except for a few, Spaatz said, that had "new fuselages."

"What is the fuselage?" Reid asked.

"The fuselage?" Spaatz answered, somewhat perplexed. Reid was either showing his ignorance of basic airplane terminology, or he thought the generals didn't know it. Either way the question did not impress the pilots sitting behind Mitchell.

"Is that what we call the chassis on an automobile?" Reid con-tinued, unfazed.

"It would probably amount to the chassis on an automobile," Spaatz patiently answered.

The major then recited some of the more depressing numbers from the reports. The air service had only twenty-six bombers and thirty-nine observation planes that had been built or remodeled since the war, and no modern attack aircraft that could be used for bombing and strafing troops. All told, of the 1,820 planes listed in the reports, Spaatz could count only 400 that were postwar models. At its strategically important facility in Hawaii, the army had only seventeen pursuit aircraft used to fight other planes, and just ten bombers. And many of them were missing equipment like radios or bomb racks for heavy ordnance.

"What percent of the total aircraft of the United States air service do you figure as standard aircraft fit for service?" Reid asked.

"Slightly over twenty-two percent," Spaatz said. The shortage of air service officers was just as severe. Spaatz could count 147 in the squadrons when there should have been 613.

"Do you believe the organization of the tactical units of the air service is being retarded by the War Department?" Reid asked.

Moreland jumped up, but before he could say, "I object," Spaatz had quickly answered: "I do." Laughter broke out in the audience. Spaatz, Hap Arnold, and the other airmen who planned to testify for Mitchell had agreed among themselves that whenever Reid asked a loaded question they would blurt out the answer before Moreland could stop them.

Some of the generals on the jury, such as William Graves, were beginning to feel defensive about the bleak picture Spaatz painted. But Reid pressed on.

"Do you know of any bombing practice with 2,000-pound bombs in the last year?"

"I know of none," Spaatz answered.

Had there been any major exercise staged by the air service in the past two years? Reid asked. "There has not been," Spaatz said. During a machine gun and bombing competition the previous fall at Langley Field, only a few units had "competent" gunners and "airplanes equipped for shooting," he added.

"Are the officers of the General Staff qualified by training or experience to lay down principles for military aviation?"

"I object!" Moreland shouted. This time he got it in before Spaatz could answer.

"I will withdraw the question," Reid said, but asked it another way: "Do you know whether any officer of the General Staff, either by training or experience, has had any connection with the flying or direction of flying units?"

"I object to that on the ground that the witness has not been shown competent to answer it," Moreland interrupted.

Winship overruled him.

Only two general staff officers had "had air service training," Spaatz answered.

"You may cross-examine," Reid said, turning to Moreland.

The prosecutor stood up.

"What is your age?" Moreland began.

"Thirty-four and a half years."

"You have been in the military since when?"

"Since 1910 at West Point."

"Do you know what proportion of the British planes are of wartime construction?"

"I do not."

"Or the French?"

"I do not."

"Or the Italian?"

"I do not."

"You do not know what part of them are obsolete."

"I do not."

"That is all," Moreland said and sat down. He was obviously trying to make Spaatz look like a rookie unqualified to speak on weighty subjects. But it was a weak cross-examination.

Howze decided to do the prosecutor's job for him.

"Did you serve in any arm of the service prior to going into the air service?" the president of the court asked.

"I served in the infantry one year," Spaatz answered.

"Who is responsible for the lack of gunnery training in the air service?" Howze demanded. He was determined to make a point Moreland hadn't: If there were problems in the air service, they were the pilots' fault, not the War Department's.

"That would be a very difficult questions to answer, sir," Spaatz hedged. But he was forced to admit that the chief of the air service oversaw all training and the officer who commanded, for example, a pursuit group was directly responsible for the gunnery instruction his pilots received.

"This officer is an air officer?" Howze asked brusquely.

"This officer is an air officer," Spaatz conceded.

"Is there anybody higher up than the commander of this unit who is responsible for the gunnery work?" Howze continued. That gave Spaatz an opening.

In the case of the First Pursuit Group, which Spaatz had led up until four months ago, "the commander of the Sixth Corps Area has charge of it," he answered.

In civilian courts jurors mostly remain silent, and judges usually confine themselves to ruling on points of law. But the rules are far more relaxed in military courts, where the officers who sit as jurors will often ask witnesses questions. Even so, the jurors in this court-martial were close to stepping over whatever line there was by playing prosecutor. It was easy to understand why they were becoming hostile to the defense. Mitchell was attacking the system these generals led. Privately Howze thought most of the airmen's complaints were unjustified. The United States might not have the best air service in the world, but Howze did not think it was as bad as the whiners made it out to be.

General Graves now perked up because of Spaatz's last answer. He was commander of the Sixth Corps, which was headquartered in Chicago.

Had any recommendations from the Sixth Corps airmen "ever been disapproved by the War Department or the Corps area commander in reference to the training in gunnery?" Graves asked testily. He was a stout man with a professorial look to him.

The gunnery training was delayed once, Spaatz said, when it seemed to take forever to get the War Department to pay the town of Oscota, Michigan, for the use of one of its airfields. The rent was one dollar a year.

The audience laughed again. Howze banged his gavel to restore order. To Graves's relief, Spaatz admitted that he did not know exactly who was responsible for holding up the dollar.

The witness Reid offered up the next morning did not make Howze any happier. Capt. Robert Oldys had a boyish face that made him look barely old enough to drive, much less fly planes, which he had been doing the past eight years. Oldys worked in the air service's war-planning division, which prepared mobilization plans for combat. He also watched over any special projects the service had in the United States or overseas. Oldys was proud to be a pilot and intensely loyal to Mitchell. He brought his little son, Robert junior, with him to court, dressed in an airman's uniform. Mitchell eagerly posed with the child for newspaper photographers.

"What is the Lassiter Board report?" Reid asked the captain after he had settled into the witness chair. It was a sore subject, not only for Mitchell, but also for Mason Patrick. Two years earlier, John Weeks had convened a military board, chaired by Maj. Gen. William Lassiter, to consider Patrick's plan to rebuild the air service. The board concluded that the rebuilding was desperately needed. Lassiter recommended an ambitious ten-year program to expand the air service to 29,000 men. Weeks endorsed the report but nothing happened. The navy opposed it, fearing that the army would hog all the extra money, and the War Department never pushed Congress to put the plan into effect. It infuriated Patrick and convinced Mitchell even more that the only way to get things done in Washington was to raise the political pressure.

"Has the Lassiter board report ever been carried into effect?" Reid asked Oldys, knowing the answer full well.

"To that I object," Moreland interrupted; Reid was just rehashing old news. "The prosecution concedes that the Lassiter report is the policy of the War Department but has not been fully carried into effect. I reserve the right, however, to establish the reason why it has not been carried out."

Reid turned to another subject. "Were you ever stationed in Hawaii?" he asked Oldys.

"I was, sir," the captain answered.

"Did you know Major S. H. Wheeler?"

"I did very well. He was my group commander."

"How was he killed?"

"He was killed in an airplane crash."

"And just before he was killed, did you have a conversation with him in regard to the orders of his commander?"

"I object to that as incompetent, immaterial and irrelevant," Moreland said standing up.

It was relevant as far as Reid was concerned. Mitchell had complained that nonflying officers, who were clueless about the dangers of air operations, were giving orders to pilots that were getting them killed, and that Sheldon Harley Wheeler's death was the best example of it.

Winship, who was becoming irritated with Moreland's constant objections, allowed Oldys to tell the court what Wheeler had told him twenty minutes before he died.

"We were going down to our headquarters to get our flying equipment," Oldys began. The courtroom grew quiet. The Hawaiian Department's chief of staff, who was not a pilot, had just demanded that Wheeler explain why the aviators were having so many forced landings with the De Havilland airplanes. "The chief of staff bawled him out," Oldys said. The forced landings were damaging planes and costing money. Wheeler "would be subject to disciplinary action if the forced landings did not cease." What's more, the pilots would have to pay out of their own pockets "for the damage done to the planes." It was a ridiculous edict, but Wheeler told Oldys "that it worried him considerably," the captain recalled. "He did not know what he was going to do. Twenty minutes later he took off and his motor quit two hundred feet over the field."

Wheeler had always told his pilots that in case of engine failure they should glide straight ahead and look for a place to land. Even if an emergency landing banged up the plane, they "should save themselves," Oldys said. But with all the pressure headquarters had heaped on him, Wheeler tried to "turn back into the field and save his plane. He fell into a spin, crashed, and by the time I got to the wreck, which was approximately forty-five seconds, he had been burned up with his sergeant observer."

"Now, is there any air force at the present time on the Pacific Coast?" Reid asked, taking up another safety issue.

"There is not, sir," Oldys answered.

"Was there ever any recommendation by the air service to the War Department that an air force be put on the Pacific Coast?"

"The chief of the air service has recommended on several occasions that the Third Attack Group, now stationed at Kelly Field, Texas, be transferred to the West Coast." Patrick wanted the unit moved because flying conditions were safer in California.

"What was done with that recommendation by the War Department?" Reid asked.

"Disapproved," Oldys answered.

"Did General Patrick ever recommend to the War Department a separate air corps?"

"He has, sir," Oldys said. Patrick had done so eleven months ago.

"Was any action taken on that?"

The War Department hadn't yet responded, Oldys said.

"No further direct examination," Reid said and sat down.

"How old are you, captain?" Moreland asked contemptuously.

"Twenty-nine, sir."

"And what position do you occupy in the air service now?"

"I am next to the senior officer in rank in the war planning section."

"How long have you been in that position?"

"Since May 1923, sir."

"That is all," Moreland said and sat down. The generals were dumbstruck. Moreland obviously did not know enough about the air service to challenge these pilots beyond the fact that they were young. Reid was having a field day with the prosecution.

Howze began grilling Oldys. He knew that a board of officers was always convened to investigate every serious air accident. "What was the finding of the investigation board in the Wheeler case?" he asked Oldys.

"The finding was that he had attempted to turn back into the field and had been crashed, sir, in the attempt."

"Was his death reported by that investigating board as being in the line of duty?"

"It was, sir."

Did the board hold the chief of staff responsible for Wheeler's death? Howze asked, staring steely eyed at Oldys. He had a pretty good idea what the answer was.

"As I remember the final draft of the finding, sir, it did not," Oldys said softly.

Edward King, the burly general who commanded the service schools at Fort Leavenworth, jumped in. On the recommendation that the Third Attack Group be transferred from Texas to California, did the pilots "take into consideration the border situation?" he asked. Mexico was always a potential threat.

"They did, sir," Oldys answered.

"Is it not in the realm of reason to believe that the higher command considers that the air service was needed on the border rather than on the Pacific Coast at the time the recommendation was made?" King asked sarcastically.

"It is within the realm of reason," Oldys answered coolly.

General Graves joined in. The War Department wasn't at fault because the Lassiter board's recommendations were not implemented, he contended. "No funds had ever been provided by Congress for this purpose."

"They have never been asked for," Oldys shot back.

Howze took another swing at the young captain. "Do you think that the general staff should always accept your recommendations as to the part to be played by the air service in the major defense problems of the United States?"

"As the general staff is at present constituted, I do, sir," Oldys said defiantly.

"What branch of the service have you served in other than the air service?" Gen. Ewing Booth, the Cavalry School commandant, asked mockingly.

"None, sir," Oldys calmly answered, trying to contain the fury he felt inside.

"Are you a graduate of any school that teaches tactics, strategy, or logistics?" Booth asked with relish.

"Not any school since the war."

"Have you ever made a study of the organization of the armies for war?"

"I have, sir, as far as I have been able to see them."

"Keeping that in mind," Booth continued condescendingly, "from your studies of the organization of armies for war, how would you organize the general staff?"

"As recommended by General Mitchell," Oldys fired back. That got the courtroom audience on his side. But Oldys could take small comfort. He left the witness chair and lit a cigarette. Being put on the griddle by a bunch of generals was an unnerving experience for any young captain. Oldys had held his own, but Howze and the other jurors had scored an important point for the prosecution. Save for a few like Fries, most of Mitchell's witnesses were junior officers. He did not have the senior, more experienced leaders on his side.

There was, in fact, a yawning generational gulf in the United States military at the time. Younger members of the officer corps were disgruntled over how their seniors were running the service. It was a reason Mitchell became popular with so many of the young men in uniform; he was one of the few in the upper ranks giving public voice to their frustrations. The airmen weren't the only ones who were angry; the army as a whole was a depressing place to be for officers with energy and ideas, such as Dwight D. Eisenhower, George S. Patton, and George C. Marshall. Military housing was substandard; slow promotions sapped morale. Officers in the field began complaining that the general staff, which advised the senior leaders, no longer attracted the best and brightest from their branches.

It was not that the men at the top were incompetent. The generals had been given a poor hand to play—a Congress always whittling down their budgets, a public that preferred to see their force locked away in a closet until the next war. It created a conservative mind-set in the senior ranks. With little to spend, they became nearsighted. Many, such as Pershing (still a revered figure among them), were relics of the "old army," who had difficulty grasping the realities of modern warfare. Form became more important than innovation. The service pampered its polo team but disbanded its tank corps. Officers who questioned conventional wisdom were shunned. Eisenhower, who kept getting assignments to coach the soldiers' football team, was warned that he and Patton might be court-martialed if they continued agitating for a separate armored branch. The army was in a rut.

The next witness, Hap Arnold, took the stand. He was now in charge of the air service's information division, which collected and distributed any material it could find on aeronautics. Arnold was more seasoned than Oldys. He had seen his share of scrapes with generals, and he wasn't about to be pushed around by the ones in this courtroom.

"Now, do you keep the records of fatal accidents happening in the air service?" Reid asked.

"I do," Arnold responded. He read the numbers from the reports sitting on his lap. During the past six years 517 airmen in the army, navy, marine corps, and post office had died in accidents. Arnold read grisly details from thirty-six of the accident reports. They showed that in a number of wrecks the De Havillands, whose pilots were sandwiched between the engine and gas tank in earlier models, caught fire and exploded when they crash-landed. Mitchell had never liked these British-designed planes.

"Now, have you in your official records information in regard to the English, French, Italian and Swedish air services?" Reid asked.

Arnold had the reports from U.S. military attachés in each country. The British Royal Air Force, which was twice as large as the U.S. Air Service, was coequal with the Royal Army and Royal Navy. The French, whose force was also larger, were consolidating their air assets. The Italians were close to having an air ministry. And the air arms of the Swedish army and navy would soon be united. "Can you state from your records there whether or not the tendency of foreign countries is toward a unified air service?" Reid asked.

"Yes, sir," Arnold answered, they were moving in that direction. Reid wanted this evidence in because Drum and other high-ranking officers had told Congress otherwise.

Reid next had Arnold pull out an organizational chart for the army's military intelligence division. "Does the War Department maintain a propaganda section?" the congressman asked.

"Yes, it does," Arnold answered, explaining that the MI 3 Section had four army press officers to handle the media, censor stories in wartime and distribute propaganda.

Moreland showed a little more life in his cross-examination. The large number of air deaths was spread out over many years, he pointed out. European countries that had larger air forces did not have an ocean separating them from enemies, as the United States had. "France is close to a power that has just spent all its energies trying to conquer [it]," Moreland challenged.

"I think that makes no difference in an aerial war, where time is annihilated to a few hours," Arnold countered.

"Is 3,500 miles of salt water annihilated?" Moreland asked skeptically.

"Yes, sir, it is today."

Howze and the other generals picked up the questioning. Didn't the air service have a publicity section just like the War Department's? Arnold had to admit that it did. How many air accidents were due to pilot error? More than half for 1925, Arnold acknowledged. How did America's air accident rate compare to Europe's? It was about the same, Arnold said. Whose responsibility was it to make flying less dangerous? The air service's, he answered. Were the De Havillands forced on the air service by the general staff? "No, sir." What forced you to use them? During the war "we had to produce something in quantity and as quickly as possible." Was flying planes in combat more dangerous than fighting in the infantry? During the war it was. "Do you know how many individuals were killed in the United States in automobile accidents?" "No, sir, I do not." Do the Japanese have an independent air service? "No, sir." Did you know that the person who heads the Italian air ministry, and who's taken over their war and navy ministries as well, is a dictator named Mussolini? "Yes, sir."

Mitchell was delighted with the turn the trial had taken. After court recessed he had a leisurely horseback ride in Rock Creek Park. Then he paid a visit to an old friend at the British Embassy, and ate a long and hearty dinner before dropping by Reid's office. Betty felt more relaxed as well. During court breaks she had passed around photos taken of little Lucy during her Michigan visit the previous week.

Arnold, Oldys, and the other defense witnesses had taken punches from the generals. But the headline in the next morning's *Washington Post* said it all, as far as Mitchell and Reid were concerned: ARMY HIGH COMMAND ON TRIAL IN MASS OF MITCHELL DATA.

15 Pearl Harbor

Repairmen still had not been able to adjust the radiators so that they wouldn't cook the courtroom and make the air uncomfortably stuffy. Howze's wife, Anne, took her seat in the audience, which she had occupied every day the tribunal had been in session. The heat now, however, made her clammy and her face felt flushed. Her husband had been under tremendous pressure managing these proceedings, what with the entire nation watching them. The strain was also beginning to tell on her.

Before Howze gaveled the court to order, reporters noticed that one person was missing from the room: Betty Mitchell. She had been at her husband's side every minute of the trial. It wasn't like her to be absent. Newspapermen cornered Mitchell to find out what was wrong.

Betty was fine, he told them. She would be there by noon. Satisfied, the reporters returned to their seats. What Mitchell didn't tell them was that Betty wasn't in court because she was doing some private business for him—making sure that the witness who would drop a bombshell on the trial the next day wasn't getting cold feet.

The generals were restless that morning. They had been uneasy about the headlines in the morning papers. Mitchell was supposed to be on trial, not the War Department. Why did they have to sit here day after day, the jurors now wondered, listening to Reid's witnesses disparage the army and vouch for what the air colonel had said? It got back to the question that hadn't been answered earlier. Was this evidence being offered to prove that Mitchell was innocent of the charge? Or was it offered for extenuation and mitigation when the

jury considered a punishment? Before court convened, the generals
had huddled with Winship and told him they wanted that question
answered this morning. Winship did as he was told.

After Howze gaveled the session to order, the law member
announced: "At this point it is appropriate to raise a question with
reference to these witnesses and as to the evidence that they are to
give." Was the evidence Reid now offered intended for mitigation, as
Moreland said it should be, or for absolute defense of the charge?

Reid stood up. Moreland might believe it should be considered
only in deciding the severity of a sentence, but "we expect to prove as
an absolute defense in this case each and every charge in the statement issued by Colonel Mitchell," the defense attorney insisted.

"The court wants to decide that question this morning," Winship told Reid.

That was the last thing Reid wanted. If Winship and the generals made their decision today, Reid worried they might just rule
that the evidence could be used only in considering the sentence,
which would mean that all the witnesses Reid planned to call to the
stand would be of no use as far as proving his client innocent. Better for Reid to pile up his evidence first and then have the jurors
decide how it should be treated. That would put more pressure on
the generals to rule that it could be used as an absolute defense.

"Do you not think this is an appropriate time to settle that question?" Winship pressed.

"No," Reid said emphatically. "I do not think it is a proper question now."

"Very well," Winship said. "Then we will put that aside now."

Winship was making a mistake. He was the one who should
decide when legal questions were settled, not Reid. And this one
should have been settled at the outset. The prosecution and the
defense had a right to know how the evidence would be treated; so
did the jury. But Winship and the generals continued to be overly
deferential to Mitchell. They did not want to be accused of treating
him unfairly. But they were in danger of losing control of the trial.

Reid's first witness of the day was Maj. Gerald Brandt, one of
the few pilots serving on the general staff. Brandt had been sent to
the Hawaiian maneuvers.

They were called the Hawaiian Grand Joint Exercises, and they had been staged the previous April with all the fanfare the army and navy could muster. The largest fleet the U.S. Navy had ever assembled in the Pacific—127 warships, including the sea service's only aircraft carrier, the USS *Langley*—had set sail from San Francisco for Hawaii. Fifty reporters, editors, and congressmen had been on board to watch the spectacle. The goal of the "Blue Force," as this mighty armada was called, had been to capture the Island of Oahu and its strategically important naval base at Pearl Harbor. The some fourteen thousand soldiers garrisoned at Oahu had been designated the "Black Force," which would defend the island. For months, the War and Navy Departments had been priming reporters. The critically important maneuvers would test the ability of the two services to work together. Afterwards the army and navy proclaimed the exercise a smashing success. Both sides won, the judges ruled; the Blue Force had captured the island's north coast while the Black Force had held the west coast. "Everyone was on the qui vive," boasted Hines, the army's chief of staff.

Mitchell thought the exercise was a fiasco. He ridiculed it in his September 5 statement. Enemy submarines in a real war would have sunk much of the Pacific Fleet before it got out of San Francisco Harbor, he had claimed, and the rest "would be sent to the bottom" by aircraft as the ships crossed the ocean. Ironically Hines and other top army officers privately agreed with Mitchell that the exercise had exposed severe weaknesses in the Pacific defenses. The Hawaiian garrison was woefully inadequate, Hines realized. The antiquated planes the army had on Oahu would be quickly wiped out in war. Hines also knew that the army and navy were still not cooperating. If there was a silver lining, senior army officers thought the exercise's dismal results would prod Coolidge to put more money into the Hawaiian defenses. But this was a view that was kept within the military family, and the brass was furious that Mitchell had aired their dirty linen.

The general staff had sent Brandt to the Hawaiian exercise to command the ninety-two planes the army had on Oahu.

"Did you have sufficient equipment there?" Reid asked.

"No, absolutely not," Brandt answered, almost with a chuckle. "We had about half of the equipment and personnel that would have been necessary if this had been actual war."

"Did any question of the command of all the air forces come up, and what was done there?" Reid continued.

"I recommended when I first got out there that there should be one officer put in command of the combined air force, army and navy," Brandt said. But the admiral in charge nixed that idea. "He would not consider for a minute any naval units being placed under any other command." Army orders to the navy planes on the island had to come through him.

"What did this result in, in giving orders to the air forces?" Reid asked.

"It resulted in a very roundabout way of conducting operations," Brandt responded.

The major had just begun to trace the bureaucratic maze an army order had to go through in order to reach a navy squadron when Howze halted the proceedings and stood up. The generals on each side of him rose from their chairs as well. Everyone else in the courtroom quickly followed and stood at attention.

It was 10:57 A.M. Eleven o'clock would mark the seventh anniversary of the signing of the Armistice. (The day would not become a federal holiday until 1938.)

"Seven years ago there came to an end the greatest war the world has ever seen," Howze said solemnly. "And I am sure that all persons in this room agree with me that we should pay tribute to the heroic dead of both the military and naval forces of the United States who gave their lives to their country and thereby joined the choir invisible—those immortal dead who live again in minds which are made better by their presence."

Howze turned to his right. The generals did as well. The audience turned also so that everyone faced east, toward a far-off land where America's young had fought valiantly on hallowed ground now consecrated by their blood. For two minutes they all stood silent in the courtroom, deep in their individual thoughts, the only sound coming from the clicking of the telegraph machines in the adjoining room and the faint echo of cannons booming at nearby Fort Myer.

At 11:00 A.M., the men and women in the room sat down. "The court will come to order," Howze said and turned to Reid. "Proceed."

Reid returned to the convoluted chain of command the army and navy had had during the Hawaiian maneuvers. "What effect did it have on your air operations there?" he asked Brandt, who had settled back into the witness seat.

"Of course it slowed them down considerably," the major answered. "I think in time of war it would have been fatal." The best example of this problem occurred on the first day of the war game, he explained. The invading Blue Force seized the island of Molokai and set up an air base there to launch attacks against Pearl Harbor, seventy miles away. "I endeavored to get the navy to agree to a joint attack on this air base at dawn the next morning, but they refused to consider the project. They said they considered that their prime duty was the discovery of the whereabouts of the main fleet, and pointed out that the presence of the *Langley* had not yet been determined. The *Langley* was the airplane carrier with the fleet, which of course was the enemy's main striking force."

In wartime what would have happened if an enemy was allowed to use Molokai as a staging base for its planes? Reid asked.

"It undoubtedly, if uninterrupted, would have resulted in the capture of Pearl Harbor," Brandt said. Senior army commanders like Hines privately agreed that the navy's refusal to join the army in a counterattack on Molokai was a serious blunder, and it demonstrated that the current command arrangements were not working.

"Were things supposed to be done in the maneuvers as in time of war?" Reid continued.

"Absolutely," Brandt answered.

"There was no one head in charge of the entire air force?"

"No, and not a unified command. That is really what you need."

"Were the aircraft utilized to the maximum effectiveness in the defense of Hawaii?"

"They could not be under the circumstances."

"Did the navy capture the Hawaiian Islands in that maneuver?" Reid asked.

Brandt considered the question for a moment. "Of course that is a theoretical proposition. I should say that the air force was quite confident that no landing would ever have been made in time of war under those conditions, even with the inadequate force that we had. The conditions were entirely favorable to the defense."

"What do you mean by that?"

"We were fortunate to discover their approach in ample time to have seriously discommoded their landing, to say the least." Most newspapers reported that Oahu had been captured, but that would not have happened in a real war with this invading force, Brandt contended.

"There was never any conclusive finding given out to the world as to the results of the Hawaiian maneuvers, was there?" Reid asked.

"No, sir," Brandt answered. Hines also wasn't sure that this invading force would have succeeded in a real war.

"Was there a report by Colonel Mitchell recommending certain changes in the Hawaiian Islands?" Reid asked.

"If the court please," Moreland interrupted, "I object to that on the grounds that it is confidential."

"I am not asking what was in it," Reid responded. "I am asking him whether a report was made by Colonel Mitchell on the Hawaiian Islands."

"General Mitchell made a report on the conditions in the personnel, which included the Hawaiian Islands," Brandt answered. When Mitchell's report, which recommended a beefed-up force and a unified command at Hawaii, finally reached Brandt the previous Saturday, it had attached to it a lengthy comment from the general staff's war plans division.

What did the war plans division say about the recommendations Mitchell had made in his report? Reid asked.

"It stated that these recommendations were based on General Mitchell's personal opinions and therefore no consideration need be given them," Brandt answered.

Why was it necessary to send a general staff officer like you to Hawaii to command the army planes during the exercise? Reid asked Brandt.

"I think it was because they had no war plans," Brandt answered.

"Whose duty was it to draw up those war plans?"

"The duty of the staff of the commanding general."

"Were those plans available at Hawaii when you went there for the maneuvers?"

"No."

"Were the deficiencies pointed out by General Mitchell in his report verified by your actual experience during these maneuvers?"

Moreland jumped up. Brandt's testimony was becoming a problem. The major had accused the army of having no defense plan for Hawaii. Moreland was sure that the next words out of Brandt's mouth would be to say that Mitchell had exposed this. "I object to that as incompetent and not the best evidence, and irrelevant and immaterial!" the prosecutor shouted.

Brandt was there, Reid heatedly argued. He'd know if the deficiencies Mitchell pointed out in his report were true.

But Mitchell's Hawaii report hadn't even been entered into evidence, Moreland argued back. How could the jurors determine whether Brandt's statements about the report's conclusions were true if they hadn't seen the document?

"I think we have a stipulation covering it," Reid said. To speed up a trial, lawyers for both sides often sign stipulations, in which they agree ahead of time on certain pieces of evidence to be introduced.

"If it is not ready yet, I wish you people would get those stipulations so that I may know," Reid said to Moreland angrily. Anyone in uniform had now become "you people" to Reid. He turned around to Mitchell's military lawyer, Colonel White, who was in charge of negotiating the stipulations with the prosecution. "That was part of the stipulation, as I understood, was it not, colonel?" he asked White menacingly.

"No," White answered, looking up at him, mystified.

The left hand didn't know what the right hand was doing on the defense team—a situation that was not uncommon for military trials. Soldiers often hired civilian lawyers to represent them because they did not trust that the military counsel assigned to them would defend their case vigorously. The army lawyer, after all, was part of the same service prosecuting the soldier. Civilian attorneys usually kept the military lawyer on the defense team, as Reid had, because he could be helpful in deciphering military procedures. But often civilian lawyers also didn't trust their military colleagues, so it was easy for coordination between the two to break down.

Mitchell liked White, and the colonel had sat in on most all of the important strategy sessions Reid held. But this embarrassing stumble showed that the military wasn't the only organization having a problem with unity of command.

"Are you an advocate of the separate air service idea?" Moreland asked on cross-examination.

"No," Brandt replied, exposing that not all the army pilots were in lockstep with Mitchell.

"As I remember, you spoke about the difficulty in Hawaii resulting from the lack of unity of command," Moreland continued. "In command of what?"

"In command of the air forces. I am talking simply from having to operate with other troops."

"So, you are not yourself in favor of a separate air service?"

"Not at this time."

Howze was about to begin his questioning of Brandt when he was interrupted by a commotion in the courtroom audience. Howze's wife had fainted. The tension, the hot stuffy air, the fact that she had not felt well coming into the courtroom had all become too much for Anne.

Howze shouted "recess" and rushed to her side. The guards threw open the windows to let in some cool air. Mitchell grabbed a glass of ice water from the defense table and elbowed his way through the crowd surrounding the woman to give it to her. When Anne was revived, the guards helped her out of the courtroom, and her husband continued the trial.

"Did you testify that, in your opinion, Oahu was not captured?" Howze asked Brandt.

"There is no question in my mind but what the expedition as carried out and the landing as attempted met with absolute failure," Brandt answered. "I have photographs that bear out that contention."

"Then, if so, was not the air force stationed at Honolulu sufficient for its defense?"

"No, sir, because our operations were attended with a great deal of luck and the conditions were entirely favorable to the defense. Under war conditions, where operations would extend over a much greater length of time, the small air force now stationed at Oahu would have been completely worn out."

Were the infantry and artillery as short of equipment as the air service had been during the Hawaii exercise? Howze asked. Brandt admitted they were. Howze believed that Congress had starved all the branches of the army, not just the air service. During the exercise, "were you given all the support and assistance that was practicable?" Howze followed up.

"Absolutely," Brandt answered. He was not helping Mitchell's case.

Was the War Department unbiased when it came to dealing with the air service? another general asked.

"Yes, I think so," Brandt admitted. "I think the general staff, as a rule, tries to look upon any subject that is presented in an unbiased light." The defense took another bullet.

When the court reassembled after lunch, Mitchell and Reid noticed something suspicious over at the prosecution table—new faces.

"Might I ask who the gentlemen are sitting as counsel at the table with the trial judge advocate?" Reid asked.

"They are from the Navy Department," Moreland said, feigning innocence. The two services may not have cooperated in military maneuvers but they were now working together to convict Mitchell.

"I should like to know their names for the record," Reid demanded.

"Captain A. W. Johnson; Captain M. G. Cook," Moreland answered. Admiral Moffett, Mitchell's bitter rival in the naval air force, had sent the men to whisper questions into Moreland's ear when he was cross-examining Reid's witnesses on the sea service. Mitchell knew the first officer well. Alfred Johnson had been his nemesis during the *Ostfriesland* bombing. He would not be giving Moreland friendly questions.

The defense might call Johnson as a witness, Reid now announced. "I do not think he ought to be allowed to assist the prosecution at this time," he said.

Johnson gathered his overcoat and left. When Moffet found out about it, he replaced Johnson with another officer. Moreland would now always have at least two navy men with him as advisers.

Reid's next witness was Col. O. C. Pierce, the air service's personnel chief. Pierce had depressing numbers for the court. Of the 960 officers in the air service, only 32 were rated as "superior pilots." (Mitchell was one of them, Pierce said, because "he flies anything.") Based on the current annual rate of deaths from airplane accidents, which was 2.6 percent, Pierce calculated that practically all the pilots now in the air service would be killed if they stayed in the army. He was stretching the math to make a point, but Pierce was as convinced as Mitchell that too many aviators were dying—or quitting because "the air service had nothing to offer them," he told the court.

Reid then tried to prove that Mason Patrick and Theodore Roosevelt, Jr., the oldest son of former president Teddy Roosevelt, had hatched a sleazy deal to fix an air race. He called Maj. Hubert Harmon to the stand. Harmon was Hap Arnold's assistant in the air service's information division. He also did duty at the White House as a junior aide.

"Now, have you a letter containing the agreement between the army and navy as to the airplane races?" Reid asked Harmon.

The major had a batch of letters, and he began reading them. They were correspondence that Patrick had in 1923 with Roosevelt, who was then assistant secretary of the navy. Mitchell claimed the letters showed that the two men had agreed to divide up the Pulitzer speed races, and their propaganda value, so an army plane would win the race one year and a navy plane would win it the next.

It was an explosive accusation. Each year the Pulitzer Trophy was awarded to the fastest plane in an international competition that attracted not only the army and navy but foreign entries as well. The races, however, had become controversial recently because of two spectacular crashes that had occurred at them when the pilots pushed their aircraft beyond their structural limits. Critics in the press had begun questioning whether the competition was worth getting people killed just for the sake of publicity. Mitchell claimed that because of the deal Patrick and Roosevelt had struck, the navy did not enter the Pulitzer race in October 1924. With no competition from the other service, he charged, the army gave its pilots older-model planes for the contest instead of spending money to build newer and safer racers. The result: The wings broke off "the two old crates" when Lt. Alexander Pearson and

Capt. Burt Skeel flew them at "terrific speeds," Mitchell complained. Pearson and Skeel died in the crashes.

Reid let the letters speak for themselves after Harmon read them.

"That is all," the defense attorney said and sat down.

Howze turned to Moreland. "No questions," the prosecutor said. Moreland was becoming comatose in the trial. Reid was running circles around him. The generals, who had been doing most of the heavy lifting in cross-examination, this time could not think of any questions to ask about these potentially incendiary letters.

But Mitchell was taking a cheap shot at Patrick, and Reid should have known better than to raise this allegation at the trial. For starters, it wasn't clear from a careful reading of the letters that Patrick and Roosevelt *had* agreed to divide up the races. The two men adamantly insisted later that they were dividing up only their planes for the races—and the correspondence could just as easily back up that story. If that was the case, if the army and navy simply were pooling the aircraft they had for the competition, then it was an example of interservice cooperation, not corruption.

Reid had made a tactical blunder. Even if Patrick and Roosevelt had been fixing the races, why alienate Mitchell's old boss for the sake of a few headlines in the next day's papers? Patrick was sure to testify at the trial, and in the past he had generally agreed with Mitchell on aviation matters. Reid had correctly calculated that this case was being tried in the court of public opinion. But in this instance he was thinking too much like his client and not enough as a lawyer.

The three hundred Legionnaires who gathered at New York City's Roosevelt Hotel for a Wednesday-night Armistice Day dinner were in an ugly mood. They had invited Mitchell to be their guest speaker. One of the city's American Legion posts had even sent two telegrams to Coolidge begging that the airman be released from house arrest that one night so he could be honored at the banquet. The White House sent the telegrams to the War Department, but the generals had no intention of giving Mitchell another platform, and Coolidge did not overrule them.

When a telegram from the army's adjutant general was read in the banquet hall, explaining that Mitchell could not be released because his "physical presence" was "necessary at the court-martial," the veterans booed and hissed. It was not the reaction the White House wanted, particularly with WRNY radio broadcasting the ruckus live to the city's listeners.

Instead of Mitchell, Fiorello H. La Guardia, the fiery Italian American congressman who had flown combat planes in the World War and would later become mayor of New York City, spoke to the vets. "Billy Mitchell is not being judged by his peers," La Guardia thundered. "He is being judged by nine dog robbers of the General Staff!" "Dog robber" was slang of the day for an officer's orderly.

16 Bombshell

The carnival atmosphere the courtroom had fallen into was beginning to irritate Howze. There was entirely too much chatter and laughter coming from the audience. The guards had started snickering when the lawyers argued. Spectators were lolling back in their chairs reading the comics pages during dull parts of the proceedings, the rustling newspapers becoming so loud that Reid had begun to complain that he couldn't hear himself think. Reporters at the press table had even begun bringing in bags of peanuts to crack open and munch.

Howze took the lieutenant of the guards aside and chewed him out for not maintaining order. The guards now snatched newspapers from spectators—"This isn't a reading room," they snarled—and rapped their knuckles on the press table when reporters became rowdy.

Mitchell had also adopted a carefree mood. After the previous day's session, he took a long horseback ride on one of the bridle paths in Rock Creek Park. It was becoming his habit after court ended, and he'd even ridden sometimes in the morning before the proceedings began. After yesterday's ride he met with a reporter, then attended the opening of a local veterans' hospital, visiting soldiers in the new wards.

The officers around Mitchell began to worry that he was riding his horse too much and spending too much time at publicity events. Each evening Arnold, Spaatz, Oldys, and the other airmen loyal to Mitchell gathered at the Anchorage with their wives to brainstorm strategy for the next day's trial. But they were becoming increasingly annoyed that Mitchell did not seem to be taking the court-martial seriously. These men were risking their careers meeting like this. Patrick had warned them all not to get too cozy with Mitchell; it could have repercussions for them later. But Mitchell was treating the trial like a lark, walking into court each day gaily greeting the jury of generals, then wasting his time after the sessions socializing when he should have been closeted with his lawyers. "For goodness sakes, this is a serious thing!" Arnold began warning him. Mitchell couldn't bring himself to believe it was.

The officers also began to grumble about Reid, who also was becoming frustrated with Mitchell's lackadaisical attitude. Bee Arnold, reflecting her husband's view, thought Reid "was a big mistake—a very brilliant man, but he didn't know the service." His flubs with basic military terms were becoming embarrassing, and the army men knew he was alienating the jurors with his insensitivity toward military custom. Bee thought Reid should have enforced discipline and kept his client focused on the trial. But "I don't think he knew how to handle Billy," she said.

Mitchell, however, was happy with his lawyer. The trial, both men realized, was far more than a legal proceeding. It was political theater and, so far, Reid was triumphing handily. His next witness would offer even more drama.

Mitchell and his wife had picked up Margaret Lansdowne that morning at an M Street town house in northwest Washington, where she was staying with relatives, and had driven her to the Emery Building. Mitchell had known Margaret and Zachary Lansdowne for four years. The previous morning Betty had been sipping tea with the widow and prepping her for her testimony today. She stayed close by Margaret's side as they walked into the Emery Building.

The generals rose from their seats when Margaret entered the room. So did the others in the courtroom, to pay homage. "Good morning," Howze said with a bow. Margaret smiled shyly to the generals.

"Mrs. Lansdowne," Reid finally said, motioning her to the witness chair.

Margaret walked to the seat slowly. She raised her right hand, which trembled slightly, to be sworn in.

She looked stunning. Just twenty-three years old, Margaret was tall and slim, with an angelic face, creamy white skin, large blue-gray eyes, and long black lashes. Her thick brown hair was cut short in the latest bob, the bangs brushed neatly over her forehead. For the trial she wore all black, but it could have been out of a fashion magazine: A long string of pearls hung low over her dress, a thin overcoat with a thick fur collar draped over that, a smart black felt hat was pulled low, close to her alluring eyes.

The granddaughter of a navy admiral, Margaret had met and married Lansdowne when she was only nineteen. It was his second marriage. She had been in Washington since October in order to testify at the naval board investigating the dirigible accident. She would soon become a darling of the capital's press corps. Reporters spotted her on lonely walks in Washington parks with her three-year-old daughter, Peggy, and the family's white English bulldog, Barney—the brave young widow of the *Shenandoah*'s fallen skipper, who "should inspire pity and sympathy," as one correspondent wrote. Her story became even more of a tearjerker for newspaper readers when they learned that shortly after Zachary's death, little Peggy had to undergo an operation. Papers ran portrait photos of Margaret with her smiling daughter and noted how remarkable it was that "she showed no sign of the terrific strain she has gone through."

Reporters had been tipped off that she would testify for Mitchell today, and the press section was jammed. Photographers crowded behind the jurors, angering the generals with the noise of their clicking cameras and popping flashbulbs.

"Your name, please," began Moreland, who as the judge advocate had to introduce each witness to the court formally.

"Margaret Ross Lansdowne," she answered in a low but clear voice.

"Do you know Colonel Mitchell, the accused in this case?"

"I do."

Reid now stood up.

"What was your husband's name?" he began.

"Zachary Lansdowne," she answered, with a slight quaver that always came to her voice each time she now said his name, "Lieutenant Commander, United States Navy, commanding the USS *Shenandoah*."

"Do you remember the occasion of the court of inquiry of the navy, regarding the *Shenandoah* accident?" he asked.

"Yes, I do remember it," Margaret said, looking not at Reid but at Howze. She had testified before the naval court on October 9.

"Was there a communication delivered to you purporting to come from Captain Foley, the judge advocate of the *Shenandoah* court of inquiry?" Reid asked. An aide to Navy Secretary Curtis Wilbur, Paul Foley was in charge of managing the board's investigation into the dirigible accident.

The communication, Mrs. Lansdowne told Reid, was delivered to her the day before she was to testify before the court of inquiry.

Moreland stood up as she had begun to answer.

"When you see the trial judge advocate get up," Reid instructed Margaret, "he is going to object, and do not make the answer until he has an opportunity to object."

"I did not intend to object," Moreland said, at least not to that question. He was getting ready for what he knew would be the next question.

"Then you threw us off," Reid said, chuckling. He turned to Margaret and continued: "Can you state in substance to the court here what was in that communication?"

Now Moreland objected. He had done his homework on the widow, and he intended to do his utmost to keep the generals from hearing what she had to say. Foley had given this purported communication to Mrs. Lansdowne a month after Mitchell made his September 5 statement, Moreland pointed out. It "therefore could have had no influence upon his mind in making the statement," Moreland said emphatically. It was immaterial to the case. Reid could only introduce into the trial "the facts [Mitchell] knew at the time he made the statement."

"May it please the court," Reid said, turning to Winship. "The trial judge advocate evidently does not understand the purpose of this testimony. Colonel Mitchell, in his statement, for which he is now on trial, charged that the navy board would proceed to whitewash the *Shenandoah* accident, and pursuant to that, would do certain things. We expect to show that they absolutely did that by trying to get this witness to give false testimony in regard to the accident."

For twenty-five minutes Moreland hauled out every argument he could think of to keep Mrs. Lansdowne from testifying. His assistants had prepared a nine-page single-spaced legal memo for him as ammunition. But Winship was not about to stifle the beautiful young widow. He overruled Moreland's objections and let Margaret Lansdowne tell her story.

It began the night of October 7, two days before her scheduled testimony before the *Shenandoah* court of inquiry, when Captain Foley paid a visit to the widow at her uncle's town house on M Street. "He sought to impress me first with the importance of the court," Margaret recalled. "He then asked me what it was I was going to say to the court and I answered him that I preferred to make my statement to the court."

Foley persisted. "He wanted to find out what I had on my mind," she said, quoting the captain as telling her: "Let's rehearse the statement you are going to make to the court." Margaret said she refused. She would say nothing until she testified. Foley, the widow claimed, wanted to know "what was my reason for appearing and I told him my reason was I wanted to lay emphasis on the fact that the court had failed to develop the fact that my husband had been sent on this trip for a political purpose."

Foley argued with her, Margaret testified. "He told me I had no right to say that the flight was a political flight, as taxpayers in the Middle West had a perfect right to see their property." Margaret still refused to divulge what she would say at the inquiry.

The next day at noon, the wife of another naval officer and good friend of Margaret's visited the town house and handed her a typewritten sheet of paper from Foley, with what he wanted her to say at the inquiry.

"Tell the court what was in that statement," Reid said.

"It began with the remark that when I at first accepted the invitation to appear at the *Shenandoah* court and testify in my husband's behalf, I had done so with the idea my husband was in need of defense," Margaret testified, "but at the present time my opinion had been changed and I was appearing simply because I said I would and that I thought the court was absolutely capable of handling the situation and was entirely willing to leave it in their hands." The statement also said "that my husband always considered the *Shenandoah* a ship of war, and did not care to take the ship on political flights, but any time the flight was for military purposes, regardless of the landing facilities and the weather conditions, he was absolutely willing and ready to take the ship."

"Was that statement false?" Reid asked.

"False," Margaret said firmly. The audience buzzed. Reporters scribbled to take down every word, and photographers kept shooting.

How was the statement incorrect? Reid asked.

It said "my husband was willing, in the case of a military flight, to take the *Shenandoah* anywhere at any time regardless of weather conditions," Margaret answered. "It was an insult to his memory to insinuate he would do such a thing."

Over Moreland's strenuous objections, Reid then had Mrs. Lansdowne repeat the statement she actually delivered to the *Shenandoah* court. It was far less complimentary. Her husband believed that "the flight was made solely for political purposes," she had told the naval inquiry, but he was ordered to make it over his protests. Margaret had read from an August 15 letter Lieutenant Commander Lansdowne had sent to the chief of naval operations asking that the flight be postponed until the second week in September, but the navy chief refused because the state fairs along the route occurred the first week of that month. Because they would be flying over the Midwest during the thunderstorm season, "my husband was very much opposed to this flight, and protested as vigorously as any officer is allowed to do to his superiors," Margaret had claimed. "Everyone knows that in military or naval services, orders are given to be obeyed and no officer cares to earn the stigma of cowardice or insubordination by refusing outright, after his protest has been overruled, to do what he is told." Her husband, however, felt that the *Shenandoah* "should not be taken on commercial trips inland simply to give the taxpayers a look at their property," Margaret had said.

A man sitting next to Moreland, whom Reid had never seen before, whispered into the prosecutor's ear and passed him memos.

"May I ask who the new adviser is?" Reid said impishly as Moreland stood up to cross-examine Mrs. Lansdowne.

"This is not Captain Johnson," Moreland assured him. "This is Captain Marshall." Albert Marshall was another navy officer.

"I thought he would be in uniform the same as everybody else so that I would know him," Reid said, needling the prosecutor. The navy captain wore a business suit, giving him a somewhat furtive air. Next to him was Captain Cook from the previous day, also in civilian attire.

Marshall wasn't representing the navy, Moreland claimed defensively. "He is here at my request to advise me on certain of these matters."

"That is all right," Reid said. He enjoyed getting under Moreland's skin. "I have a large galaxy myself."

What Moreland's two naval advisers had shoved under his nose was a memo from Capt. Walter Gherardi, another one of Wilbur's aides, which, if true, undercut Margaret's testimony. Gherardi had paid the grieving widow a visit the morning after the *Shenandoah* accident. He claimed that Mrs. Lansdowne had told him that an Associated Press story quoting her as attacking Wilbur and the navy was a lie and that she had issued a denial to the AP. Mrs. Lansdowne, the naval aide wrote, said "she would not for the world have it thought that she would criticize the Secretary or the Department." Furthermore, Gherardi said, he later eavesdropped on an interview Mrs. Lansdowne was having with another reporter, who asked her if Lansdowne "had any premonitions that anything was going to happen to him or if he objected to going. To which Mrs. Lansdowne said he had not."

"Did you have a conversation with Captain Gherardi of the navy on or about the 4th day of September, 1925, at Lakehurst, New Jersey?" Moreland now asked Margaret.

"I did," she answered.

"Did you say to him at that time and place . . . that the statements in the papers, which quoted you as having attacked the Secretary of the Navy Department, were lies?"

"No," Margaret insisted. She had only told Gherardi that one part of the AP story was incorrect, which claimed she had accused Wilbur "personally of the murder of my husband." Margaret had not gone that far.

Didn't she say, Moreland challenged, "that you would not for the world have it thought that you would criticize the Secretary or the Navy Department?"

"I did not."

Didn't she tell another reporter that Lansdowne had no premonitions about the flight and didn't protest taking it? Moreland pressed. He hovered over her, the Gherardi memo in his hands.

"I said he made an official protest over his going, but he had no premonitions."

"You did not make the statement or statements I have read to you?"

"No," Margaret said sharply, turning her head to Howze.

"That is all," Moreland said resignedly. It could be suicidal for his case to continue trying to impeach the glamorous widow's testimony.

General Graves asked her gently: "Was that Foley letter signed by anyone?"

"It was not signed."

"Were any marks or anything on that letter to identify it as coming from Captain Foley?"

"Absolutely none, not even the letterhead of the Navy Department—only the government watermark." But the friend who brought it to her said it was from Foley, Margaret told the generals.

Moreland stood up and demanded to know the name of the friend.

"I would rather not give that," Margaret said anxiously, looking at the generals.

"I insist upon it," Moreland said huffily.

"Tell him," Reid told her quietly. Margaret took a deep breath.

"Mrs. George W. Steele," she finally said slowly. Murmuring in the audience increased. Mrs. Steele was another glamorous wife of a prominent naval officer, who was well known in Washington social circles. George Steele, Jr., was commandant of the Lakehurst Naval Air Station, the *Shenandoah's* home base, and the skipper of the navy's other dirigible, the USS *Los Angeles*.

Margaret Lansdowne was excused. The generals rose again and bowed as she stood up and left the courtroom.

17 Reinforcements

LATE MORNING, FRIDAY, NOVEMBER 13, 1925

Margaret Lansdowne's testimony created a political firestorm in Washington. She had accused the U.S. Navy and one of its top aides of trying to induce her to commit perjury in the *Shenandoah* investigation. The *Washington Post* called for Navy Secretary Wilbur's resignation, and editorial cartoons lambasted the service for ganging up on the poor widow. Moreland walked into court that morning and tried to have everything Mrs. Lansdowne had said the previous day stricken from the record. Foley also appeared at the trial, demanding that he be allowed to take the stand and rebut the charges. Reid objected, and Winship backed him up, denying both requests. Foley stalked out of the courtroom and resigned as the *Shenandoah* inquiry's judge advocate, acknowledging that the cloud now over him made it impossible for him to carry out that duty.

For the next couple of weeks, the capital's newspapers carried every detail of the battle that erupted in naval social circles, as officers and their wives lined up on both sides in the juicy scandal. Foley, who quickly hired a lawyer to defend him, insisted he was only doing his job screening witnesses before they testified, and denied that he had pressured Mrs. Lansdowne to change her statement. Mrs. Steele claimed the paper she had passed along to Margaret from Foley contained only "suggestions" to help her prepare her testimony, which the widow could use as she pleased. Mrs. Lansdowne was called back to the *Shenandoah* court to explain herself. Mitchell arranged for his pal, Joe Davies, to represent her, and she stuck by her story. Her aunt and uncle, who were also in the room when Foley visited, backed her up. The navy eventually cleared Foley of any wrongdoing. But Arthur Brisbane, with the Hearst chain, claimed in a column that Lansdowne had also told him before the flight "that sending the *Shenandoah* across the country in the thunderstorm season would be highly dangerous and, in case a thunderstorm were encountered, probably would result in disaster."

Mitchell was becoming the hottest celebrity in the capital. Crowds quickly gathered around him when he appeared in public. Movie audiences cheered when his handsome face appeared on newsreels shown at local theaters. Society ladies flooded the Anchorage with party invitations for the couple. The *Washington Star* reported that even "another class of Mitchell worshippers" had surfaced in the city—"the tens of thousands of government department clerks" who'd love to tell their own bosses how lousily they did their jobs. "Washington has been wanting a hero for a long time," the *Star* enthused, "and Col. Billy Mitchell appears to have filled the more or less aching void."

Some newspapers did try to step back from the spectacle with a little objectivity. The *Baltimore Sun* noted that Mitchell was winning his case only because of "dramatic but calculated publicity and a darned smart lawyer." Even the *Washington Post* conceded that he was "guilty of a breach of discipline." But the brass was guilty as well, the *Post* editorialized. In addition to firing Wilbur, the paper said Coolidge should "clean out" the army's general staff.

The army was feeling the heat. Hines and the service's other senior officers realized that Moreland was hopelessly outmatched. The general staff decided to take over the prosecution. Drum, who was feeding material to the Morrow aircraft board, had also been closely monitoring the Mitchell trial, particularly as Reid kept offering more evidence alleging that the assistant chief of staff had lied to Congress. Drum dispatched his best aide, Maj. Francis Wilby, to the Emery Building to sit at Moreland's side and begin managing the prosecution.

Balding, with beady eyes and thin lips, Francis Bowditch Wilby wasn't a lawyer. But he was a brilliant officer and an expert debater. Born in Detroit, he had dropped out of Harvard to enroll in West Point. Wilby had been stationed all over the world, and during the Great War he had received the Distinguished Service Medal and the French Croix de Guerre as an engineer at the front. He would eventually rise to the rank of major general and become the U.S. Military Academy's superintendent during World War II. Unlike Moreland, Wilby had an encyclopedic knowledge of the army. He could spot the holes in Reid's evidence.

Reid stood up to launch another attack on the War Department. Reporters had begun to notice something peculiar about the defense attorney. While his client came to court always nattily dressed—often wearing military riding breeches, boots, and spurs—Reid had shown up every day in the same mousy gray suit and wine-colored bow tie. When reporters asked why he at least didn't change his neckwear, Reid deadpanned: "If I put on a new tie, somebody would accuse me of taking a fee."

Maj. Herbert Dargue settled into the witness chair. As one of General Patrick's senior aides, Dargue supervised the preparations of war plans for the air service. He also handled other special projects for Patrick, such as working with other branches of the army on military exercises and looking out for the extra pay airmen received for flying.

"Do you have anything to do with antiaircraft gun tests?" Reid asked.

"I do," Dargue answered. It was one of his special projects. "I was designated by General Patrick as his assistant to handle the antiaircraft work from his end."

It was not a particularly pleasant chore for Dargue. The air service and the army's coast artillery branch had been locked in a raging debate over the value of antiaircraft guns. Mitchell and most pilots believed they were worthless. The best defense against an airplane, they argued, was another airplane, which could more easily shoot down hostile aircraft in a dogfight or, even better, penetrate deep into enemy territory and bomb airfields so the other side's planes could never get into the sky. World War I airmen bragged that the only aircraft downed by ground fire were the ones the antiaircraft guns accidentally hit—a claim disputed by antiaircraft battery commanders. Since the war the army had poured hundreds of millions of dollars into improving its antiaircraft weapons and ringing the country with coast artillery stations, but Patrick and Mitchell thought it was largely a waste of money. Airplanes still held the overwhelming advantage, they argued, and would continue to do so for many decades.

The army, and particularly its coast artillery commanders, didn't buy it and were just as determined to prove the airmen wrong. The debate was not simply an academic one. With army budgets so small, all the branches competed fiercely for a larger chunk of what little there was to spend. For the air service and coast artillery, future appropriations hung on the question of whose weapons worked best. In the summer the War Department had held a nationwide test of its antiaircraft guns that cost more than a quarter of a million dollars to stage—a princely sum for the service, which outraged the pilots who thought the money could have been far better spent buying them new planes. The two most publicized tests occurred at Fort Tilden, in New York City's borough of Queens, and at Camp Dix in New Jersey, both of which were part of the Army's Second Corps now commanded by Summerall, the court's ousted president.

The army arranged for trains to take senators, representatives, and Washington reporters north to watch the important tests. Air service planes towed large, cone-shaped cloth bags from a 2,100-foot-long wire while antiaircraft gunners on the ground at Fort Tilden fired at them. The hits were recorded by two observers, one standing on the ground, the other poor fellow lying perilously on top of the plane's fuselage, facing to the rear, with one arm wrapped around a strut to keep him from being blown away as he marked down the scores on a pad strung around his neck.

Hines, the army chief of staff, gave reporters glowing accounts of the tests. During one ten-day period, artillery and machine guns hit the target 372 times, results that Hines proudly pronounced "gratifying to those responsible for the development of antiaircraft fire."

Mitchell, however, ridiculed the exercise in his September 5 statement, calling the results "laughable." The pilots hated the boring and exhausting duty. Spaatz had complained to the court that the airmen were forced to tow targets all summer when they should have been practicing dropping bombs. Also the tests were hardly stressful for the artillery, other pilots told the court-martial. The planes towing the targets were required to fly in a straight line, at a set speed and altitude, and the artillerymen were overly liberal in what they scored as a hit. Even if the 372 hits were legitimate, the pilots did not consider the number particularly impressive; the gunners had to fire 88,005 rounds to make them!

The Camp Dix exercise was held at night to test how well their searchlights and listening devices could pick out planes in darkness. Air service bombers were ordered to fly toward Camp Dix with their navigation lights turned off and to drop flares, to simulate bombs, on a target below. The listening posts and searchlights on the ground were supposed to pick out the planes before they dropped the flares. The pilots complained that night flying over Camp Dix was dangerous because it was surrounded by heavily wooded terrain, which meant they would crash into trees if they had to make a forced landing. The War Department regulations for the test also required the pilots to fly to the targets in two-plane formations, which was also dangerous with their navigation lights turned off. But airmen told the court-martial jury that Summerall refused to move the test to another post or to change the two-plane regulation.

Dargue eagerly told the generals how the airmen ended up fooling the soldiers on the ground. The pilots turned off their engines as they approached Camp Dix and glided silently to the target.

"Were the listening devices able to follow the planes?" Reid asked.

"Not at all, except when the motors were on," Dargue said. The searchlights did not pick out a single bomber before it dropped its flare. The coast artillerymen were enraged by the trick played on them.

The dispute was hardly as black and white as the airmen made it out to be. The reason the army required the pilots to tow the targets along a predetermined path was for their own safety, so the planes weren't accidentally hit by rounds. The Fort Tilden results—about 237 shots fired for every hit—weren't all that bad and far better than the ratio in World War I. The prosecutors in Mitchell's court-martial pointed out that air service officers had been part of the teams that selected Camp Dix and established the two-plane formation rule. The generals hearing the case also thought the flyboys weren't so special that they couldn't help out by towing targets.

What was the War Department's policy on publicity for the antiaircraft tests? Reid asked Dargue. This was another sore subject for the army. Mitchell had angered the generals in the past by attending antiaircraft tests and then calling reporters aside afterward to give them his version of what happened. For the Fort Tilden and Camp Dix exercises, Dargue said the air service had received a War

Department directive ordering that publicity "be avoided." But when Dargue and Patrick arrived at the Camp Dix exercise, they found a gaggle of reporters covering it. The War Department, he charged, had gone behind Patrick's back and given Summerall the green light to summon reporters and pass out press releases.

"Was the lid ever taken off the air service" so it was "allowed to give out information in regard to the antiaircraft matter?" Reid asked.

"No, sir," Dargue answered.

Reid now turned to a sore subject for the pilots: their flight pay. But Moreland, who had Wilby passing him notes and leaning over to whisper instructions into his ear, suddenly came to life.

"During the summer, were you called upon to take any part or do any part in the studying of flying pay of officers?" Reid asked.

Dargue answered that the War Department had designated him to be the air service representative at a meeting with the navy, the post office, and the Veterans Bureau "to consider the matter of additional insurance for flying personnel."

"Did you receive any instructions when you attended this meeting?"

"I received instructions a half an hour after the meeting opened."

Moreland stood up and objected. Why was this relevant?

Reid pointed out that in his September 5 statement, Mitchell had charged that the War Department was studying "how the flyers' pay could be reduced or taken away from them." Dargue had a stack of papers on his lap that contained his instructions for the meeting on insurance and flight pay, but when he tried to read them, Moreland began objecting again. Dargue did not have all the War Department records on this subject, the prosecutor argued, just selected copies that he had collected in his work. "I believe that the witness should not be permitted to give testimony upon incomplete records," Moreland adamantly maintained. Instead all the original documents on the insurance and flight pay question should be offered as evidence "in fairness when the War Department is being charged." This time Winship sustained his objection.

Reid stood up, furious. For more than an hour the two lawyers argued back and forth in a bitter wrangle. Reid complained that he had been put in an impossible situation. He had subpoenaed all the documents in the flight pay case, along with the complete set of records for other charges Mitchell was making against the army. But over the last couple days, he claimed, the War Department had suddenly gone into slow motion sending him papers. What's more, Moreland was refusing to sign practically all the stipulations the defense team had drafted to avoid flooding the court with so much evidence. Now the prosecutor was blocking Reid's witnesses from testifying because they didn't have all the army records with them. "I have not been treated fairly in any way by the other side of this case," the congressman said loudly.

Reid knew what was up with the army and navy. He knew they were sending in reinforcements and beginning to play hardball. "Since they have had some new members sitting over there, Major Wilby and other people," Reid declared, pointing to the prosecution table, "we do not get anything! We did not have a bit of trouble in regard to these records until the general staff was introduced into this case."

"If the court please," Moreland responded, exasperated with Reid's theatrics, "I think exception ought to be taken to the charge that the counsel for the accused has not been treated fairly in any respect by this court."

"I did not say that," Reid shot back. "I said you over there. You have not produced me a single paper!"

Winship agreed that Reid was in an untenable position. If the prosecution was going to object to defense witnesses who had incomplete records, then Moreland had to provide Reid all the War and Navy Department documents that dealt with each of Mitchell's charges. But the volume of material Reid demanded was tremendous and covered a vast number of subjects, Moreland explained. It was taking the services quite a while to collect everything and turn it over.

The strain of spending long hours in court and reading material late into the night was beginning to tell on both lawyers. They walked into each day's session perpetually exhausted. Both now realized the enormity of this exercise. The trial had ballooned into something far bigger than either of them had ever expected. It was "perhaps one of the most difficult cases that has ever been tried before a court-martial in this country," Moreland said. Reid agreed. The two attorneys asked for another break so they could sift through the new material the army and navy would eventually release.

Howze agreed to recess the court until Tuesday. But before he did, Dargue was allowed to continue his testimony. While the lawyers had been bickering, a messenger had been sent to the War Department to retrieve all the records in the insurance and flight pay case. Dargue now had everything before him. Moreland kept throwing out objections, but Reid managed to fend them off so Dargue could tell his story. Reading from the correspondence, the major told the generals that the War Department had sent him to the meeting with the navy, post office, and Veterans Bureau with orders to say that if the group agreed to pay for life insurance for pilots, they should then cut back on the flight pay the airmen received. Many ground commanders weren't terribly fond of flight pay. All army work was risky, they argued. Why should pilots get special treatment?

The instructions Dargue had received from the War Department, however, were 180 degrees opposite from what Patrick had ordered him to say at the meeting. Patrick took the view held by all his pilots—that flight pay was sacrosanct. The aviators received it because of the dangerous work they did and if they didn't get the extra money they'd probably leave the air service in droves, Patrick warned. Flight pay should not be trimmed to provide life insurance. When the air service chief learned of Dargue's instructions, he tried to get the War Department to reconsider.

Did they? Reid asked.

"I have heard nothing more of it," Dargue answered. "Apparently it has been dropped."

This time Moreland scored more points with his cross-examination. Wilby fed him tougher questions to throw at Dargue. The general staff major also had been busily reading the documents the War Department had sent over on flight insurance and discovered a later memo on the subject from the army to the navy, which Dargue had never read. The note said that the War Department had eventually decided not to tamper with flight pay and that the services should consider only the question of providing life insurance. In other words, Mitchell's charge was out of date. "Thank you," Moreland said smugly, after an embarrassed Dargue had read the final memo to the court.

Dargue left many of the court's generals about as unimpressed as Mitchell's other witnesses had, particularly after the major admitted in an answer to one of their questions that he personally had not joined the air service for the flight pay and that he would not necessarily leave the air service if he didn't receive the extra cash. But at this point it was hard to tell which way the jurors were leaning as a group. Winship was trying to be fair in his legal rulings. Clearly Howze was no longer undecided, not with the hostile questions he had been asking the airmen. Jurors like Graves, who began the trial not particularly impressed with Mitchell, didn't appear to have changed their minds. On the other side Mitchell's allies still seemed favorably disposed toward him. Douglas MacArthur so far had kept silent during the trial, but his wife, Louise, accompanied by one of MacArthur's aides, had sat through all the sessions and chatted pleasantly with Betty during breaks. When court recessed that day for lunch, a smiling Gen. Ewing Booth posed for photographers outside with Mitchell, Reid, and their wives as the group prepared to head off to a restaurant—not a particularly appropriate position for a juror to be in with a defendant. Gen. Frank McCoy was so far impressed with the evidence Reid had presented. Mitchell, the general wrote a friend, "has handled himself so well. . . . The War Department is on trial instead of the festive Bill."

While the defense lawyers pored over the piles of government documents that came in from the army and navy, Mitchell and Betty drove to Middleburg for a relaxing weekend. On Monday evening, they returned to the capital and Mitchell delivered a radio address for the *Washington Post Hour* on WCAP. His arrest order kept him from making speeches outside Washington, but it didn't prevent him from talking to the nation from inside the city. Mitchell toned down the invective he'd become famous for lately and tried to deliver a more dignified discourse on the political war he was waging.

"For centuries," he told his listeners,

we have been accustomed to entrust the national defense to armies and navies and sometimes to regard them more as institutions than as agencies of the people for protecting the country from all enemies, both without and within. So long have these agencies been supreme in their particular field that any change from the ancient and fixed systems of an army on the land and a fleet in the sea [has] been looked on with real alarm and misgiving by these forces. The traditional military mind is notoriously sensitive to any breath of criticism, and any attempt to tear away the veil of its mystery is apt to be greeted by the cry of sacrilege.

But he maintained that a new reality was dawning. The nation victorious in future wars will be the nation commanding the skies. Aircraft will be able to strike at the enemy's nerve centers, to spread panic, cripple industries, collapse governments. "It is therefore impossible for people to put their trust in armies or navies alone," Mitchell insisted.

> Airpower must be given a place of equal importance. It must not be muzzled, gagged or belittled. By burrowing our heads in the sand on the advice of our armies and navies, we cannot escape the danger of airpower by shutting it out of our sight.
>
> We have brought these matters to the attention of the American people as it has been impossible in this country through our existing governmental agencies to organize our defense in a modern manner in accordance with the methods of our present civilization. We want every American to take a patriotic interest in these matters which concern us all.

After he finished Mitchell and Betty made a brief drop-by on Capitol Hill at a party hosted by the Secretaries Association. Then they headed to the Washington Auditorium to see the city's opera company perform Puccini's *Tosca*. Like most of high society they arrived fashionably late for the opening night. The performers on stage practically had to compete for the audience's attention as the couple settled into box seats, reserved for them by the American Legion.

18 Prelude

The good news Caroline had been anxiously awaiting for more than a year finally arrived. The Wisconsin State Supreme Court had ruled that Mitchell had to increase his annual child support payments for Elizabeth, Harriet, and John by $2,000, for a total of $6,800 a year. Caroline had originally asked for $12,000 annually when she filed a petition with the Milwaukee court in August 1924. A judge had cut that by almost half, but even so Mitchell had fought the new order all the way up to the state's highest court. His army salary had not been paying the bills for his life with Betty as it was, and he told the court his share of his late mother's estate was bringing in only $4,665 annually. Caroline, on the other hand, had inherited $172,837 from her family.

But the justices ruled that $6,800 was fair. There was no higher court to appeal to, and even if there had been, Mitchell did not want to pursue it. He had enough on his mind at that moment, and it was not the time for publicity that he was a stingy father. He began sending Caroline more each month.

Mitchell in effect divorced his first three children along with his first wife. The court had given him visitation rights, but Caroline resisted it. She told the children she would disown them if she ever caught them seeing their father. Mitchell showed no interest in challenging her. On Christmas Day 1922 he phoned Caroline and said he would be at the house in an hour to see the children. Caroline noted acidly in her diary that he arrived an hour and a half late and stayed for only "18 minutes." (Mitchell never phoned again on holidays or birthdays.) Three days later he phoned the children to let them know that their grandmother had died. After that all contact ended, except for one last time. Many years later Elizabeth and Harriet ran into their father at a horse show in Middleburg. The divorce had been especially devastating for Harriet, who adored her father and loved to go horseback riding with him.

Caroline moved quickly to rebuild her life. She remained in Washington, renting a town house on Massachusetts Avenue off Sheridan Circle, and became something of a party girl. She spent most weekends at dances or elegant dinners. A long line of boyfriends came into the picture. One day in 1924 she had three dates with three different men. "Several suitors are pleading for Mrs. Mitchell's hand," a gossip columnist noted around the time her first husband was getting remarried, "but so far she is nice to them all [and] does not particularly favor any."

Caroline also did not shy away from the military circles she once shared with Mitchell. She lunched regularly with air service pilots, sipped tea with Mason Patrick, and socialized with top army figures like Hines and his wife. During the court-martial she even mingled at cocktail parties and dinners with such jurors as General Winans and General Irwin. No record remains on whether she discussed her ex-husband's case with them. Caroline never mentioned the court-martial in her diary.

The War Department formally appointed Clayton Bissell as an "assistant defense counsel" to help Mitchell at the trial. He had informally been doing the job since the court-martial began. The beefing up of the defense team, however, paled in comparison to what was happening on the prosecution side. Four naval officers were now assigned to assist Moreland, and another army officer, this one a lawyer named Allen Gullion, was ordered to join Wilby as an assistant trial judge advocate.

The army also began to hunt even more earnestly for chinks in Mitchell's armor. Moreland sent Drum and other general staff officers copies of the trial transcript and a large pile of press clippings he had accumulated on Mitchell and asked the officers to scour them for any weak points the prosecutors might exploit. War Department aides began sifting through the records they had of all the recommendations Mitchell had made, to determine what exactly happened to them. The military intelligence division sent reporters weekly press reviews that contained more anti-Mitchell news stories the division had collected around the country. Moreland asked the adjutant general's office to send him Mitchell's personal military file, which contained not only his job efficiency reports but also his psychiatric report and court records from his divorce. The War Department even checked out a tip passed on by one of Moreland's naval advisers that defense contractors might secretly be paying for his legal expenses. The prosecution found no evidence they were; Mitchell's father-in-law, Sidney Miller, was bankrolling the defense.

Winship again asked Reid if he could rule on whether the evidence he was offering was for mitigation or an absolute defense. The generals had been nagging him about it earlier that morning, and Winship realized he probably should have issued a ruling before the defense ever began its case.

Reid asked to have until at least the end of the week, when he expected to wrap up his evidence. The judges excused themselves to huddle privately on that request. "The case will proceed," Howze announced when they returned. It wouldn't kill the jurors to sit through another week of Mitchell's evidence—even if they weren't exactly sure why.

For the next four days Reid had an assembly line of seventeen witnesses take the stand to back up other parts of Mitchell's September 5 statement. But Wilby and Gullion did not plan to give them the free ride they felt Moreland had.

11:00 A.M., TUESDAY, NOVEMBER 17, 1925

"What do your duties consist of?" Reid asked.

"My duties consist of development of model airways," Donald Duke answered. The air service had begun the model airways program in 1922 to set up a network of air routes in the United States connecting the army's airfields to one another. For Lieutenant Duke it had been a frustrating job. So far the model airways consisted of routes stretching only from New York to Langley, Virginia, and from Washington to air service fields in the Midwest and Southwest.

Duke's frustration, shared by Mitchell, was compounded by the fact that at a number of critical points along the air routes the army had no meteorological stations to warn pilots of bad weather. The situation was "exceptionally hazardous," Duke told the court, along a stretch of the route that went from Cumberland, Maryland, over the Allegheny Mountains to Uniontown, Pennsylvania. It always had erratic weather. The lieutenant had flown over the mountainous terrain many times. The day would be beautiful when he took off at Bolling Field in Washington, and he would receive a report from his destination in Dayton, Ohio, that the weather was also fine there, but when he hit the Cumberland-to-Uniontown leg over the Alleghenies, "I would encounter snowstorms or rainstorms and winds." Sometimes he had to turn back, other times he was "forced to land in the mountains."

"Have you any stations at Cumberland, Maryland, and Uniontown, Pennsylvania?" Reid asked.

"We have had no meteorological facilities at either of those stations for some time," said Duke. The air service had been pestering the War Department to send army meteorological units not only to Cumberland, but also to three other critical points along the model airways at Kansas City, Missouri; Dallas, and Muskogee, Oklahoma. But the department refused, claiming it didn't have the $1.95 a day needed for the travel expenses of each weatherman. Patrick had fired off an angry memo, complaining that "economy is being practiced at the expense of safety." Lack of accurate and timely weather information was becoming a vexing problem. Aviators were taking off from airfields and dying in crashes because they ran into unexpected storms or heavy winds along their flight paths—just as the *Shenandoah* had. Reid had raised the issue before the jury because in Mitchell's September 5 statement he had charged that "the lives of the airmen are being used merely as pawns." Army stinginess over weather stations was the best example of it.

Wilby stood up to ask questions. There was no rule in the manual for courts-martial that a nonlawyer could not act as a prosecutor and interrogate a witness.

"Are the model airways safe?" he asked curtly.

"Are they safe?" Duke asked back.

"Yes."

William Mitchell, bedecked in medals, sat for a portrait photo when he held the rank of brigadier general. Arrogant, opinionated, and highly controversial, Mitchell was a bold combat leader and airpower theorist, whose harsh criticism of the army and navy eventually led to his downfall. *(Tom Gilpin Collection)*

John Lendrum Mitchell, shown with two of his seven children, was a tender yet distant father, whom Billy Mitchell revered. *(Bass Family Collection)*

Mitchell's mother, Harriet, was an emotional as well as financial anchor in his life. *(Bass Family Collection)*

His governess remembered him as the worst child she had ever tended. Inquisitive, energetic, and demanding, "Willie," as his parents called him, is photographed here at age ten, when he was packed off to Racine College, an Episcopal boarding school for the sons of wealthy families. *(University of Wisconsin—Milwaukee)*

Eager to fight in the Spanish-American War, nineteen-year-old Mitchell joined a Wisconsin Volunteer Army regiment as a private. Within a week Mitchell's father had used political connections to get his son commissioned as the youngest second lieutenant in the Signal Corps. Mitchell, standing far left with other officers at a Jacksonville, Florida, camp, proved to be a bright, energetic leader. *(National Archives)*

After a combat tour in the Philippines, First Lieutenant Mitchell went to Alaska, where he supervised the laying of more than five hundred miles of telegraph line over some of the most inhospitable land on earth. Mitchell, at Fort Egbert in 1903, prepares to set out in winter, when temperatures dropped to seventy degrees below zero. *(Library of Congress)*

The army's youngest captain and one of its rising stars, Mitchell made a name for himself as a zealous and hard-working officer. He was assigned to the army's prestigious general staff. But superiors soon concluded that his brash and independent streak made him more suited for leading men in the field than staff work. *(Library of Congress)*

In 1903 Mitchell married Caroline Stoddard, a Vassar-educated blue-blood from Rochester whose intellect and polish made her the perfect wife for an army officer on his way up. Though it had been practically an arranged marriage, Mitchell had fallen in love with the captivating young woman. Caroline found Mitchell exciting. *(Cicely Banfield Collection)*

Caroline followed Mitchell from post to post. When he learned to fly in 1916, she climbed into a plane to experience the thrill. But his long absences from home depressed her. After World War I the marriage soured, with bitter fights. Caroline tried to have Mitchell committed for mental treatment. They divorced in 1922. *(Cicely Banfield Collection)*

Mitchell, standing in a French trench in spring 1917, was the first U.S. Army officer to witness World War I combat at the front. His tour of French lines convinced him of the futility of trench warfare and the importance of breaking the stalemate with an offensive weapon like the airplane. *(Library of Congress)*

Mitchell, by his plane, with his personal seal painted on it, during World War I. He braved danger, flying over battlefields to scout where his men would fight, and commanded the largest air armada ever assembled in the war to attack the Germans. But Mitchell clashed with fellow officers in fierce turf battles. *(Library of Congress)*

In 1921 Mitchell led an aerial force off the Virginia coast to prove that planes could sink a battleship. Here he flies over the target area directing the attack from his command plane. The sinking of the German battleship *Ostfriesland* (left over from World War I) was one of Mitchell's finest moments. *(Library of Congress)*

An aerial bomb explodes near the *Ostfriesland*. Navy men considered the mighty German dreadnought unsinkable. When Mitchell's planes sent it to the bottom of the ocean, admirals aboard an observation vessel wept. *(Library of Congress)*

After the war the army picked Maj. Gen. Mason Patrick (*left*), to lead the air service instead of Mitchell. Patrick, who shared many of Mitchell's airpower views, was able to control Mitchell as his deputy. With Patrick is Brig. Gen. James Fechet, who succeeded Mitchell as assistant director of the air service. (*National Archives*)

Gen. John Pershing (*left*), who led American forces during World War I, never warmed to Mitchell but recognized that he was a superb combat leader. After the war, Pershing became army chief of staff and, with his deputy, Maj. Gen. James Harbord (*right*), had to deal with Mitchell's rebellious nature and his marital strife. (*National Archives*)

In 1923, a year after his divorce, Mitchell married Elizabeth Trumbull Miller, the daughter of a wealthy Detroit family. As accomplished an equestrian as Mitchell, Betty was considered avant-garde for her day. Mitchell worshipped her, and Betty became a calming influence on his turbulent life. *(Tom Gilpin Collection)*

Mitchell and Betty display the skins of game they shot during their honeymoon in the Far East and Southwest Asia. Inspecting military facilities and gathering intelligence during the trip, Mitchell wrote an exhaustive report on Asia's strategic importance. He criticized U.S. defenses in Hawaii, predicting a Japanese attack on Pearl Harbor eighteen years before it occurred. *(Tom Gilpin Collection)*

Lt. Cdr. Zachary Lansdowne became a military celebrity as skipper of the *Shenandoah*. Americans were shocked by his death in the dirigible accident. *(National Archives)*

Emerging from its hangar at Lakehurst, New Jersey, the USS *Shenandoah* was a national treasure and the pride and joy of the navy. The rigid airship was considered the aerial transportation of the future, and the navy was anxious to show it off to politicians and Americans across the country. *(National Archives)*

After a line squall downed the *Shenandoah* over Ohio in 1925, hundreds flocked to the wreckage to gawk and scavenge for souvenirs. Mitchell then blasted the navy's handling of the airship, accusing the sea service and the army of "criminal negligence" in running national defense. His charges precipitated the court-martial. *(National Archives)*

Though a pariah in the army by the time of his trial, Mitchell had powerful friends in Washington and was popular across the country. After he befriended Will Rogers by taking him for a plane ride in April 1925, the famous humorist began poking fun at the War Department. *(Library of Congress)*

A popular and politically savvy president, Calvin Coolidge *(right)*, was outraged by Mitchell's attacks on the military, which challenged his authority as commander in chief. His secretary of war, Dwight Davis *(left)*, wasn't afraid to play hardball in bringing Mitchell to trial and cracking down on other disgruntled army pilots. *(National Archives)*

For months Washington and the nation were captivated by the upcoming high-profile court-martial. Mitchell became a media star the press followed everywhere he went. Here he stops with Betty and two aides for photographers and movie cameramen staked out to cover his testimony at an aircraft hearing before his trial began. *(Library of Congress)*

On the first day of Mitchell's court-martial, some five hundred people lined up outside the Emery Building for a chance at the few spectator seats inside. The seven-week trial became a major Washington attraction with politicians, society ladies, and tourists flocking to the court each day. *(Library of Congress)*

Maj. Gen. Charles Summerall, the court-martial's first president, was challenged by Mitchell for bias and dismissed. Angry, Summerall plotted to get even. *(National Archives)*

Maj. Gen. Robert Howze succeeded Summerall as court president. A war hero, Howze had been a Mitchell friend but turned against him as the trial progressed. *(National Archives)*

The jurors in the Mitchell court-martial (*left to right*): Generals Ewing Booth, Frank McCoy, Benjamin Poore, Douglas MacArthur, Robert Howze, Col. Blanton Winship (law member), Generals William Graves, Edward King, Edwin Winans, and George Irwin. They were among the army's best and brightest but did not come to the trial unbiased. All knew Mitchell well. *(Library of Congress)*

Col. Sherman Moreland (*left*), was the trial judge advocate. Lt. Col. Joseph McMullen (*right*), was his assistant. Polite to a fault, Moreland was a lackluster prosecutor, whom the defense team ran circles around at the trial's beginning. (*Library of Congress*)

Maj. Allen Gullion, a skilled lawyer and debater (shown here after the trial, when he was a colonel), was also brought in to take over much of the prosecution from Moreland. (*Gullion Family Collection*)

Though a nonlawyer, Maj. Francis Wilby was a brilliant officer the General Staff dispatched to the trial to beef up the flagging prosecution. (*National Air and Space Museum, Smithsonian Institution [SI 2003–31625]*)

Mitchell with his defense team (*left to right*): William Webb, Col. Herbert White, Representative Frank Reid, and Judge Frank Plain. Reid, the colorful and combative lead counsel, knew little about the military and made tactical mistakes in the trial. But he recognized that it was a political trial and won his case in the court of public opinion. (*Library of Congress*)

Mitchell standing the first day of the trial as Lieutenant Colonel McMullen read the lengthy charge and specifications against him. He was accused of violating the Ninety-sixth Article of War, a catchall provision covering prejudice to "good order and military discipline" and conduct that brought "discredit" on the service. *(Library of Congress)*

Betty *(left)* with her father, Sidney Miller, and Mitchell's sister Harriet. A wealthy Detroit lawyer, Miller advised Mitchell during the trial and paid for the defense expenses. Harriet fiercely defended her brother in his political battles in Washington and was also at his side during the trial. *(Library of Congress)*

Maj. Henry "Hap" Arnold, a Mitchell loyalist who testified for the defense, was banished to Kansas after the trial. He later led the air force during World War II. *(National Archives)*

Carl "Tooey" Spaatz as a young lieutenant before World War I. The jury dismissed his testimony for Mitchell as naive. Spaatz became the first chief of staff of the U.S. Air Force. *(National Archives)*

Margaret Lansdowne, the glamorous widow of Lieutenant Commander Lansdowne, dropped a bombshell at the Mitchell trial. She claimed that a navy officer had tried to get her to give false testimony at the navy's court of inquiry into the *Shenandoah* accident. *(Library of Congress)*

The army, which often stumbled in its public relations war with Mitchell, refused to let him travel to Detroit to visit his baby daughter during breaks in the trial. So Betty, with the strain of the court-martial showing on her face, brought little Lucy to Washington, where they posed for eager photographers. *(Bass Family Collection)*

Mitchell with Betty and hunting dogs on their country estate in Middleburg, Virginia. Betty's father had bought the home for them. Mitchell always lived beyond his means. He stayed a step ahead of creditors, borrowing from banks and relatives to maintain his upper-class lifestyle. *(Library of Congress)*

"They are as safe as we can make them without further assistance."

"You stated, if I'm not mistaken, in your testimony that it was your individual responsibility to see that the airways were safe before you permitted any flights. Is that correct?"

"I did not state it that way."

Wilby had the court reporter reread what Duke had said. You "implied it is your responsibility to establish the model airways and see they are safe," he challenged Duke.

"I object to that," Reid interrupted. "The answer stands for itself." Wilby couldn't be asking what the witness implied.

"I am not a lawyer and I am at a disadvantage with the distinguished counsel for the defense," Wilby said disingenuously, "but I understood there was a great deal of latitude on cross-examination."

There was. "Do you object to the question?" Winship asked Reid, knowing that Wilby had put one over on the lawyer.

"No, I withdraw the objection," Reid said grumpily and sat down.

Duke explained that he wasn't solely responsible for the model airways' safety. Ultimately, it rested with Patrick. "The chief of the air service gets the blame if anything happens."

"Then the chief of the air service is responsible for the model airways," Wilby continued.

"He has so been held," Duke answered.

"When a flight is about to take off from Bolling Field for the West, who is in command of it?"

"The pilot is in command."

"Has he any discretion as to whether he takes to the air or not?"

"He has."

"Then the flight is actually initiated by a flying officer?"

"The flight is authorized by higher authority and the pilot is directed to proceed on his mission."

And the mission is "usually authorized by the chief of air service?" Wilby asked.

"Yes, sir," Duke answered.

"Is the chief of air service a flying officer?"

"He is."

This wasn't going well for the defense claim that non–flying officers made life-or-death decisions for the air service. Wilby continued to circle his quarry. Did the War Department refuse to set up the meteorological stations at Cumberland and the other three cities "for any other reason than for lack of funds?" he asked Duke.

"That would appear to be the reason," Duke acknowledged. But the War Department could have moved funds from other accounts to pay for it, he argued.

Could it? The War Department's budget has been cut to the bone so "any request for shifting personnel from one activity to another," Wilby pointed out, "is a very difficult request to carry out. Would you, for instance, like to have some of your personnel and funds transferred from one of your activities to some other activity?"

Duke wouldn't, but he tried to deflect the question. "It depends entirely on the value that that soldier can give to the service," the lieutenant answered.

And "that is a question which can only be determined by someone who is familiar with the needs of all activities," Wilby followed up.

"Yes, sir," Duke conceded.

On the subject of travel expenses for soldiers going to new assignments, did he know how much was "available for the whole army for the fiscal year 1925?" Wilby asked.

"I cannot answer that question," Duke said.

"Would you be surprised to learn that the total amount . . . was $9,000?" Wilby said. If the War Department doled out what the air service wanted for its one project, there would be hardly any money left for moving other soldiers around the country.

"I believe in your direct examination the fact that airmen are being used merely as pawns was mentioned by counsel for the defense," Wilby continued. "Is it not a fact that practically every flight made by the army air service is . . . actually ordered by the chief of the air service or one of his subordinates?"

"That is true," Duke answered.

"They are all flying officers?"

"They are."

"Then you charge the chief of air service or his subordinates with using fliers as pawns?"

"I do not place the responsibility on the chief of air service," Duke retorted.

"You just now said that they ordered every flight in the air service."

"The flights are ordered by the chief of air service, but he is not responsible."

Mitchell looked as if he were sitting in the theater enjoying a good movie. He munched on candy from a paper bag much of the day, chuckling whenever Wilby made a misstep because he didn't know trial procedures.

The defendant should not have been so nonchalant. Wilby had made the points he wanted to make with Duke, and they all supported the prosecution's case. The War Department was not mean-spirited; it just didn't have the money to give the pilots everything they wanted. If there had been casualties, Mitchell and his airmen were responsible for them. Of course the truth lay somewhere in between, but Wilby was bringing out the evidence the generals wanted to hear. They had no questions this time. Wilby had sliced up the witness nicely.

10:20 A.M., WEDNESDAY, NOVEMBER 18, 1925

"Captain, when did you first go into the lighter-than-air work?" Reid asked.

"In the beginning of the year 1911," Anton Heinen answered in his thick Prussian accent. If there was such a thing as an archetypal German Zeppelin commander, Heinen was it. A short and compact man, he had red hair that had begun receding considerably and a mustache and goatee that accentuated his sunken cheeks. During the war Heinen had test-flown Zeppelins and trained crews in how to operate the airships. He had emigrated to the United States in 1921 to advise the navy in its construction of the *Shenandoah*, which was patterned after the World War I–model Zeppelin.

From the beginning his relations with the navy had been stormy. The service ended up firing him from his job at Lakehurst before the *Shenandoah*'s fatal flight. Heinen was a hothead who did not suffer fools lightly and brooked no questions—especially from green U.S. Navy officers—when he issued orders on a dirigible. But without a doubt he was the most experienced rigid airship pilot living in the United States. Heinen had been aboard the *Shenandoah* when it broke away from its mooring mast in the gale at Lakehurst. He had

abruptly taken charge of flying the wounded dirigible back to the air
station, angering naval officers on board who resented taking orders
from the temperamental instructor. But airship operators in the
army air service admired him and thought their navy counterparts—
including Lansdowne—had arrogantly and unwisely ignored the
sound advice Heinen and other German instructors had given on
building and flying dirigibles.

Reid had called the Prussian to the witness stand to begin his
defense of the most controversial aspect of Mitchell's September 5
statement, which had sparked his court-martial in the first place—
the navy's "criminal negligence" in handling the USS *Shenandoah*.

"Was the *Shenandoah* an experimental ship?" Reid asked
Heinen.

"It was an experimental ship, by all means," he said authoritatively. That was an important answer for Reid. Mitchell had
claimed the *Shenandoah* was experimental and not war ready. He
had also charged that it was built from an outdated design and was
poorly equipped and operated.

The navy denied the allegations, but they were true. The
Shenandoah design, in fact, was eleven years old, based on a German dirigible the Allies had captured in 1914. Its long, thin shape
made it vulnerable to being broken apart when a thunderstorm's
winds battered it from different directions. It also was not speedy
enough to outrun bad weather. Since 1914 the Zeppelin Airship
Company had replaced that model with new designs that flew
faster and farther, had better lift, and were more sturdily built to
survive the buffeting of storms.

Aircraft procurement procedures in the 1920s were not particularly sophisticated. The Pentagon today requires that a new plane
and all its hardware be thoroughly tested before being sent to the
squadrons. The *Shenandoah*, however, was a work in progress. Her
crew was constantly tinkering with her design and equipment even
as the men were learning how to fly the airship. And Reid was
about to expose the most glaring example of this.

"Tell the court what the purpose of the automatic valves are on
a lighter-than-air ship," he said to Heinen.

The *Shenandoah's* gas bags had automatic valves fitted to them,
which vented helium to prevent the expanding bags from bursting

when the dirigible rose above four thousand feet, Heinen explained. "These automatic valves were installed as a primary safety device in a rigid airship."

"How many automatic valves did the *Shenandoah* originally have?" Reid asked.

"Eighteen valves," Heinen answered.

How many valves were on the airship when it crashed? Reid asked.

"I found ten valves in the valve system of the *Shenandoah* were removed from the ship and only eight valves remained," Heinen said.

"What was the effect on the safety of the ship by the reduction of the automatic valves from eighteen to eight?" Reid asked.

"It reduced the safety of the ship against inner pressure from one hundred percent to zero," Heinen declared.

"You mean it was absolutely unsafe then?"

"Absolutely unsafe—nil."

If the dirigible flew only in normal weather, the automatic valves wouldn't be needed, so reducing their number from eighteen to eight would make little difference. But the Germans had put eighteen in their design for just such emergencies as the one the *Shenandoah* faced when the thunderstorm's violent updrafts forced it high into the sky quickly.

"If she had to rise rapidly," would the *Shenandoah* have been able to vent gas quickly enough with ten fewer valves? Reid asked.

"Certainly not," Heinen said gruffly.

Satisfied, Reid motioned to the prosecutors that they could begin their cross-examination. Gullion, who had crowded out Moreland at the prosecution table, rose from his chair. More than six feet tall and lean, he was a handsome man who stood erect with a patrician air. His uniform was immaculately tailored. Women found him attractive, and in later years, after his wife died, Gullion enjoyed being seen with glamorous movie starlets on his arm.

But Mitchell thought he looked like a lizard, his tongue always flicking out to lick his lips. The two men had crossed paths in their previous assignments, and by the time of the trial they were contemptuous of each other. That was fine with the army, which ordered Gullion to the court-martial because he was one of the most skilled and aggressive prosecutors the service had.

Gullion was from Northern Irish stock, his family having settled in the hardscrabble town of Carrollton, Kentucky, near
Louisville in the mid-1800s. Gullion's father had been editor of the
county's newspaper and had scraped together enough money to
send his son to Centre College in Danville, where he excelled in
Latin, Greek, and oratory. At Centre, Gullion read the classics with
a passion and won the school's declamation prize for public speaking. Like Reid, he enjoyed the English language immensely and
would constantly correct his children's grammar.

After graduation Gullion got an appointment to West Point,
where the cadets gave him the nickname "Slum." He was commissioned in 1905 as an infantry lieutenant. But he found garrison life
insufferably dull and eventually returned to his native state to earn
a law degree at the University of Kentucky.

Gullion was a bit of an eccentric. Though he played polo and
enjoyed watching boxing matches, he smoked heavily (always with a
cigarette holder) and thought exercise could be bad for his health. He
read the newspaper in bed wearing white gloves so the print wouldn't
soil his hands. On car trips from Washington back to Kentucky, he
would stop at each railroad crossing and order his son out to inspect
the track both ways and then signal him to pass over it.

Gullion also expected others to live their lives with the sense of
dignity and propriety that he had. Like many officers of his day, he
never voted in an election the entire time he was in uniform, believing that military men should not in any way be involved in politics.
Officers who acted in an ungentlemanly or unprincipled manner
deeply offended him. He came down hard on them in court—something he would do now with Mitchell.

"Captain, you say you came to America in 1921?" Gullion asked
with just a trace of a southern accent.

"Yes, sir," Heinen answered.

"Why did you leave Germany?" Gullion asked.

"Because I had an offer from the American navy to enter the
service in order to organize and train and help in the construction
of the *Shenandoah,*" Heinen answered warily.

"Did your last business connection in Germany terminate of
your own—"

"I object!" Reid shouted before Gullion could finish his sentence and shot up from his chair. That wasn't proper cross-examination, he argued.

"It is eminently proper, the prosecution submits," Gullion said calmly. "The witness has been offered as an expert by Mr. Reid. It is certainly proper to ask him about his former business connections . . . how they terminated."

Winship agreed and overruled Reid.

"How did your . . . business connection in Germany terminate?" Gullion repeated the question. "Of your own accord or by request or direction of your employers? Please answer yes or no, captain."

"There is no yes or no answer possible," Heinen said, ruffled by the question.

"It is a simple question," Gullion insisted innocently, but Winship let the Prussian elaborate.

The German government "kicked me out of the service" because of "political differences," Heinen said rapidly, his accent becoming thicker. The Treaty of Versailles required Germany to turn its wartime dirigibles over to the Allies, and "I was kicked out of the service" for advocating the transfer.

"Do you know who recommended the change in the valve system?" Gullion asked, turning to the automatic valves that had been cut back.

"I might say I know who did," Heinen answered. "It was the crew." Lansdowne and his men, in fact, had recommended that ten of the valves be removed. The navy's air bureau had been reluctant to do it, but the *Shenandoah* crew argued that it would save 136 pounds of weight that they needed for other purposes. Altering the valve system, however, was a mistake. So were other changes the crew made in the airship's mechanics, like installing jam pot covers over the automatic valves so the expensive helium would not leak from them. In an emergency the crew would have to waste precious time removing the covers before the automatic valves could vent gas.

Gullion, however, was having Heinen make a critically important point for the prosecution. The *Shenandoah*'s safety problems were the crew's fault, not the navy's. In fact, army air service officers had warned Mitchell that Lansdowne and his men were far too confident about their ability to handle emergencies than they had a right to be, considering their limited experience with dirigibles. But acknowledging that in open court would put Reid and Mitchell in a tactical bind, and Gullion knew it. Reid could not very well accuse Lansdowne and the crew of incompetence, not after putting Margaret on the stand and siding so openly with her defense of her dead husband.

Gullion prepared for another strike. Cutting back on the automatic valves was a big mistake, but it wasn't clear whether that move resulted in the *Shenandoah*'s gas bags exploding and breaking apart the airship. Just after the disaster, Heinen had confidently declared that the removal of the automatic valves had caused the wreck. Since then, however, he had begun to hedge. The Prussian was trying to persuade a consortium of financial backers to put up millions of dollars to build a fleet of commercial airships, but all this publicity about the *Shenandoah* accident was scaring them off. So Heinen started to tone down his comments about structural flaws in dirigibles.

"Do you know . . . what caused the wreck of the *Shenandoah*?" Gullion asked.

"Nobody has any knowledge of what caused the wreck of the *Shenandoah*," Heinen said. "It is a question that nobody in this world can answer."

It was not the response Reid or Mitchell wanted to hear from the Prussian. But Gullion saved the defense by committing the same error Reid had made in the past—asking one too many questions.

"No, it is a simple question whether you do know or do not know," Gullion said haughtily. "Please answer if you do not know or do know."

That got Heinen's back up. "I am proud to say I do know," he announced defiantly.

"Do you know of your own knowledge, or is it based upon your theory?" Gullion asked, trying to recover.

"Of my own knowledge."

"Are you confident, captain, in all your conclusions?"

"I am, as far as—"

"On every matter then you have positive knowledge," Gullion interrupted testily, "and you are willing to back it as against everybody else?"

"No, sir," Heinen protested.

"That is what you said," Gullion challenged, raising his voice.

"No, sir!" Heinen said angrily. "I did not say that, not by any means."

Howze tapped his gavel to cool both men down. "Do not let us have a personal argument here," he admonished Gullion. "Just proceed with the case."

"I will not pursue that," Gullion agreed, regaining his composure. He did not want to risk another mistake and ask Heinen what he knew to be the cause of the accident. Gullion didn't know what the unpredictable Prussian would say. Neither did Reid. So both lawyers let him step down from the witness chair with that question unanswered.

Many army airship officers were contemptuous of the way the navy ran its dirigible program, some out of jealousy because the navy, and not the army, had been given control of the rigid airships. The army flew only observation balloons and airships not surrounded by metal frames. But many of the army complaints were valid. Unlike most army aviators who remained in the lighter-than-air service their entire careers, naval airship officers were considered seamen first and routinely rotated back to the fleet, which degraded their piloting skills. (Being routinely sent to nonflying jobs is a problem navy pilots face even today.) As a result, the navy men were amateurish in the way they handled the dirigibles, the army complained. Some of the navy's senior airship skippers took command of the complex craft with relatively little experience in operating them. Naval officers also were just as snooty about accepting advice from experienced army airship operators as they were from the Germans. Air service pilots sent to Lakehurst on temporary duty got the distinct impression from the navy men that they were to be seen not heard.

Reid now had four of the army's top airship men, all of them close friends of Mitchell's, take the stand to unload on the way the sea service handled the *Shenandoah*.

Maj. Frank Kennedy, who headed up the air service's lighter-than-air section at McCook Field near Dayton, hopped into a plane when he learned of the *Shenandoah* disaster and flew to the accident scene.

"How soon were you there after the accident?" Reid asked him.

"I arrived approximately 8:30 in the morning," Kennedy replied, not exactly answering Reid's question.

Gullion stood up to demand a clarification. "We would like to know how soon he did get there," he interrupted.

Reid decided to rough up the newcomer to the trial. Didn't Gullion know he had to wait until cross-examination before he could ask his questions? Reid complained to Winship. "I do not mind this from a beginner," he snapped, looking at Wilby, but a real lawyer like Gullion "should handle his case in a proper way. If he wants to explain away anything, he can do that when it comes to his turn."

Chastened, Gullion said he wasn't trying to do Reid's job for him.

When Kennedy arrived at the accident scene, "tell the court what you saw," Reid continued.

"I saw the main part of the wreck from the air," Kennedy said. "The stern half of the ship was lying in a small valley with the bow slightly uphill. And the wreckage was rather complete, so there was nothing that could be salvaged from it."

"Tell the court what you found about the gas cells," Reid said.

"Completely destroyed, deflated and torn to pieces," Kennedy said. This lent credence to Mitchell's charge that gasbags had exploded at high altitudes when the fewer number of automatic valves couldn't vent them.

Gullion had no questions.

Capt. Charles Clark was one of those army airship officers who had been sent to Lakehurst as an observer.

"Did you examine the designs and specifications of the *Shenandoah*?" Reid asked him.

"Yes, sir," Clark answered.

"Are you able to tell whether or not the *Shenandoah* was overweight in her structure?" Reid asked. Mitchell had charged that it was, which strained its metal frame.

"Yes, sir," Clark answered. "It was overweight."

Gullion had questions this time when it was his turn to cross-examine. "Do you know whether this added weight was put on to increase the safety factor?" he asked Clark.

"There was some weight put on to increase the safety factor," the army captain conceded, which didn't help Mitchell's case. "But the main increase in weight was due to the metal" in the *Shenan-doah's* airframe, "which was over-size."

"How much did you estimate this extra weight to be?" Gullion asked. Mitchell had said the airship was "fifty percent overweight in her structure," but he seems to have pulled that number out of a hat. The navy insisted that the dirigible was no more than 3 percent overweight.

"I never figured it out," Clark admitted.

Gullion perked up. How did he know it was overweight "if you cannot give any estimate of the weight?" he asked.

"Because I took the word of people who had something to do with the design," Clark said.

"How much of your testimony is based upon other people's words and how much on your knowledge?" Gullion asked sarcastically.

"You will have to go over it before I can tell you that," Clark retorted.

Lt. Col. John Paegelow had been flying observation balloons since the war, when he served under Mitchell.

"Would you tell the court which has the greater lifting power, hydrogen or helium?" Reid asked.

"Hydrogen," Paegelow answered. "If you take the lifting power of hydrogen as one hundred percent, helium has a lifting power of about ninety-two percent."

The German design for the *Shenandoah* called for hydrogen. Filling it with the more expensive helium gave it less lift, another criticism Mitchell had of the dirigible. "If the *Shenandoah* was inflated with helium, would her buoyancy be as great as if she were inflated with hydrogen?" Reid asked the lieutenant colonel.

"No," Paegelow answered.

"Should parachutes be carried on airships?" Reid asked. There had been none aboard the *Shenandoah* and Mitchell found that outrageous.

"Absolutely," Paegelow insisted.

"Are parachutes being carried on all ships at your station?"

"I would try any man for disobedience of orders if he did not carry a parachute."

"You may cross-examine," Reid said, turning to Gullion.

"Do you know, colonel, why the navy changed from hydrogen to helium?" Gullion asked.

"I do not, sir," Paegelow said, but he did. Even Paegelow preferred to use helium in an airship, for an obvious reason. Hydrogen might provide better lift, but it was explosive. A spark could set it off. Helium was an inert gas. "It was for safety," Gullion pointed out.

"Now about parachutes," Gullion said. "The navy, upon the recommendation of their crews, has recommended against the use of parachutes on rigid airships." The crewmen found it difficult to walk along the narrow runways inside the dirigible wearing the bulky chutes. If the airship broke apart, the men would be better off remaining inside and free-ballooning to the ground. If they jumped out with the parachute, the heavier airship would "very likely fall on top of them," Gullion maintained. And if an airman were under a dirigible, "would he not be killed?"

"He would not be under it," Paegelow said calmly.

"How can that be?"

"If he has any sense, he will not be under it."

Reid stood up for another question after Gullion finished. During World War I, "where a lighter-than-air aircraft has fallen in France," he asked, hadn't the men wearing parachutes "escaped readily from the airship?"

"All the time," Paegelow answered.

Another army observer, Lt. Orville Anderson, was at Lakehurst the day the gale ripped the *Shenandoah* from its mooring mast. Mitchell claimed that that accident "badly strained" the dirigible's structure, making it dangerously weak on its final flight.

"What damage was done to the ship?" Reid asked.

"The upper vertical fin was the first part to give away [*sic*]," Anderson recalled. "It was crushed. Then the ship was torn loose from the mast, leaving the mooring mast attachment and a small portion of the longitudinal brace with the mast. . . . The actual length of these tears was anywhere from two to five or six feet." Anderson was convinced the accident "did weaken the structure."

"This is your opinion," Gullion challenged when it was his turn to cross-examine.

"No, sir," Anderson maintained. "That is my knowledge."

"Are you familiar with the inspection and repairs, which the

Navy Department made on the *Shenandoah* following this break-away, and that the aircraft was subsequently pronounced ready for the fleet?" Gullion asked.

"Yes, sir," Anderson answered.

"Did it make a successful flight following that breakaway?" Gullion pressed.

"Yes, sir," Anderson conceded. He still believed it remained a weaker ship.

Reid had no naval officer who could or would back up what the army men alleged. In fact he had only one naval officer willing to testify for Mitchell, and he was retired.

William Sowden Sims was a lot like Mitchell and even more popular with the press. SCHOLAR, OFFICER, GENTLEMAN, read the headline for the *Time* magazine cover on the admiral. An innovator, he had commanded the navy's European fleet during the war, becoming famous for improving ship gunnery and pushing the use of convoys to protect merchant vessels. Tough and ambitious, Sims had never been afraid to challenge his military and civilian bosses when he disagreed with them. A former president of the naval War College, he ridiculed narrow-minded admirals whom he felt had no vision, and he sneered at the service's hidebound traditions. Sims was one of a handful of top naval officers who believed that aircraft carriers, not the old battlewagons, were the capital ships of the future. He had been feeding Mitchell inside information on the navy to bolster the army aviator's case.

What was the navy's aircraft policy? Reid asked the admiral.

"As I understand it, the Navy Department has not any defined policy," Sims answered. Retired since 1922, he looked distin-guished in his three-piece suit with his snow-white beard neatly cut. "It is going along from day to day, more or less in a higgledy-piggledy way."

"Tell the court whether or not you have encountered any offi-cers or members of the navy who have told you they were afraid to testify before committees of Congress," Reid asked. Mitchell claimed both services intimidated officers to not stray from the party line when they testified, but he didn't have any witnesses so far willing to risk their careers and say so publicly.

"If the Navy Department has a certain opinion and an officer testifies before a court in such a manner as to be markedly critical of that opinion," Sims said, "he endangers his promotion the next time the selection board meets."

"Will you tell the court, in a general way, about the naval War College?" Reid asked.

"The naval War College has been established now for approximately twenty-five or thirty years and, until comparatively recently, it has been there against the opposition of the senior officers of the service." The school, located in Newport, Rhode Island, was the only place a seagoing officer was taught broad war-fighting strategy, but the navy hierarchy gave it only "lip service," Sims testified. None of the service's top admirals were graduates of the college, "and that is what is the matter with the Navy Department today."

"What effect has this action had on the efficiency and morale of the service?" Reid asked.

"All history shows that it has had a bad effect on the morale of the service," Sims answered gravely. "It is hard, or almost impossible, to prove just exactly how, but for instance, in the *Shenandoah* case, I venture to say that any properly educated and trained officer would not have conducted the *Shenandoah* the way it was conducted." The problems with the *Shenandoah* program were endemic throughout the navy, Sims argued. The admirals "are good men and friends of mine and honest men, but they are uneducated men."

This was vintage Sims, but it wasn't necessarily helping Mitchell's case. Gullion immediately knew what holes to poke in the testimony.

So Sims believed that the navy should have a military education system like the army's, which required a War College degree as a prerequisite "for the high command in the army?" he asked the admiral.

"Yes, sir," Sims answered—not bolstering Mitchell's complaints about the army.

"Now you stated that the navy is controlled by uneducated and untrained officers," Gullion continued. "Do you mean officers [who are] not graduates of the War College?"

"Yes, officers not graduates of the War College," Sims said.

"Do you not regard it as entirely possible for an officer of great native ability and combat experience to so equip himself by his own energies and study that he is fitted for command?"

"Just about as much as a man who makes a thorough study of all the books he can find on golf and never takes a club in his hand."

Abraham Lincoln and Andrew Jackson were self-taught, Gullion challenged.

"They are not parallel cases," Sims argued. "A naval officer must be educated to make his decisions instantaneously."

"Admiral, you stated, I believe, that the navy had no well-defined policy. Is that correct?"

"That is what I understand. Yes."

But when Sims was president of the War College, he had been an ex-officio member of the navy's General Board, which deliberated service policy on a number of issues. Gullion recited more than a half dozen times when that board considered important aviation matters. Sims couldn't remember any of them.

Gullion knew why. Sims had skipped many of the board's meetings. "Is it not a fact that the Secretary of the Navy found it necessary on two occasions to give a positive order for your presence before the General Board, in order to formulate what you now call this indefinite naval policy?" Gullion asked accusingly.

"No, I do not remember any order at all," Sims said unconvincingly.

Howze wasn't impressed. When it came time for the court to ask its questions, he shattered what little value the admiral had left for Mitchell.

"Do you believe from your experience and study that the air service of the navy should be an independent service?" Howze asked.

"Independent from the navy?"

"Yes."

"No, sir," Sims answered. He disagreed with Mitchell on that point.

"Were you in actual combat at any time during the World War?" asked the general, who had been shot at quite a bit during his thirty-seven years in the army and didn't think much of people who propounded that he hadn't learned from it.

"No," Sims said quietly, understanding full well the insult.

"In spite of your . . . outspoken attitude toward the Navy

Department for some years, have you not arrived at the highest rank in the navy in the World War?" Howze asked, getting in one last dig at Sims's claim that officers who tell the truth are punished.

"I did it by a process of promotion by seniority," Sims said, nettled, his face reddening, "except when I was selected at the very last."

11:20 A.M., THURSDAY, NOVEMBER 19, 1925

Eddie Rickenbacker first met Mitchell on a hill near Pont Saint-Vincent in France during the war. Mitchell's car had stalled. A staff officer in another automobile pulled up and offered to lend him his chauffeur "to see what he could do," Mitchell later recalled. "This man took the carburetor off the engine, adjusted the needle valve and had the car running in ten minutes. It was one of the best and quickest jobs I ever saw."

Mitchell sent him to flying school, which turned out to be a wise move. The chauffeur was Rickenbacker, a race-car champion from the United States who had sailed over with Pershing as a driver. At twenty-seven Rickenbacker was old to become an aviator, but from his experience as an auto racer he had all the attributes great pilots need—a keen sense of speeds and distances, superb hands on the controls, quick reflexes, a burning competitive streak, and a lust for adventure. He became the "Ace of Aces" during the war for shooting down more enemy aircraft than any other American aviator: twenty-six planes and balloons. A national hero back home, Rickenbacker hung up his uniform and became a wealthy man starting up his own motorcar company. He remained close to his old mentor during the postwar years and had been a Mitchell ambassador to the aircraft industry and to powerful veterans' groups like the American Legion, which revered the air ace. Rickenbacker would later become president of Eastern Air Lines.

"How many hours were you in the air over there?" Reid began.

"Approximately three hundred," Rickenbacker answered. He had dark brooding eyes, thick eyebrows that nearly met, and a hawklike nose.

"How many hours over enemy lines?"

"Approximately three hundred."

"How many hours exposed to enemy aircraft fire?"

"Approximately three hundred."

"Did the enemy antiaircraft gunfire ever keep you from carrying out your mission?"

"No."

Reid had paraded other World War I vets before the court who had said the same. They could not have been more disdainful of the antiaircraft guns.

"How low an altitude did you fly at times?" Reid continued.

"At the surface, practically, at times," Rickenbacker said, his answers always clipped and confident, as if he were still in the cockpit, "hedge-hopping, as low as practicable to fly at times, investigating troop movements, balloon strafing, which demanded 5,000- or 7,500-foot altitude."

"Did you ever come down as low as twenty-five or fifty feet?"

"Yes, at times. It was difficult to judge exactly."

"Did you consider antiaircraft guns protection against aircraft?"

"No, sir."

"Were any of your planes shot down by antiaircraft gunfire?"

"No, sir." Then Rickenbacker thought about it for a moment. "I might inject there that there was one brought down a few days before the Argonne offensive." The plane had been hit by friendly fire.

"Do you know of any enemy aircraft shot down by our antiaircraft gunfire?"

"One."

This time Wilby stood up to cross-examine. Rickenbacker might be America's greatest war pilot, but Wilby believed he was as guilty of exaggerating as the other airmen who took the stand. Antiaircraft artillery officers had been feeding him memos with a far different story.

"Major Rickenbacker, we have all been very interested in your record," Wilby began in an oily voice. "As I understand it, you flew a pursuit plane?"

"Yes, sir," the Ace of Aces answered.

"You never flew a bombardment plane over the front?"

"No, sir."

"Are you aware of the fact that no one makes any claim that antiaircraft defense is an effective defense against pursuit planes?"

"No, I have not heard that as a positive fact, or any claim of that nature." But it was true. Antiaircraft gunners tried to target slower-moving bombers and had better kill rates against them than the speedy pursuit fighters that Rickenbacker flew.

"Have you heard of the German ace by the name of Baron von Richthofen?" Wilby asked.

Rickenbacker had. Everyone knew about the "Red Baron," who had shot down eighty Allied aircraft.

"He was one of their best fliers," Wilby said.

"He was exceptionally good," Rickenbacker agreed. "Their best."

"How did he come to his death?"

"My understanding is he was brought down by machine-gun fire on the ground in trench strafing during the advance on Paris," Rickenbacker answered—although there has been considerable controversy over the years whether ground soldiers or a Canadian pilot flying a Sopwith Camel fighter shot down the Red Baron.

"He was not as fortunate as you in avoiding machine-gun fire," Wilby said with a sly smile. He also believed the ground-fire story.

"No, sir," Rickenbacker said, giving him a dark look.

"Are you aware that our 23rd Anti-Aircraft Battery . . . brought down officially nine planes" in a four-month period during the war "with only 5,092 shots?" Wilby asked. That averaged out to one plane for every 566 shots—a pretty good kill rate, as far as the jurors were concerned.

"Not as a positive fact," Rickenbacker said defensively. But he wasn't about to win the argument. Wilby had after-action reports from other antiaircraft batteries during the war with similar results. The jury could see that Rickenbacker and the other war pilots disdainful of the antiaircraft guns had only anecdotes.

4:00 P.M., FRIDAY, NOVEMBER 20, 1925

Gullion saved his cross-examination of Hiram W. Sheridan for Friday. An air service flight instructor, Lt. Sheridan had been aboard the USS *Langley* when it sailed to the Hawaiian maneuvers the previous spring. He had taken the stand on Thursday to tell horror stories about the aircraft carrier. Sheridan testified that it nearly collided with another warship as the fleet steamed out of San Francisco Harbor. The carrier crept along at just twelve knots. Its deck could hold only a dozen planes, all obsolete, with poorly trained pilots. Four of the aircraft crashed when they landed on the carrier. And even if they had been modern aircraft, the admiral in command of the fleet didn't have a clue how to use them.

Many of Sheridan's complaints were valid; even the navy acknowledged that its planes were old and the *Langley* was a crude, slow-moving ship that could carry only a small number of them. But to have an army officer, who was a guest aboard the ship, air those problems made navy men apoplectic. Gullion and Wilby had been so incensed with the testimony that at one point they both jumped up at the same time to object. "I object to this tandem objection," Reid shouted back, and the audience laughed.

Gullion had postponed his cross-examination of Sheridan so he could spend the night reading a scathing seventy-page memo the lieutenant had written on the voyage. Now the Kentucky lawyer was loaded for bear.

"Are you a graduate of the Naval War College?" Gullion asked Sheridan, his voice rising.

"I am not," Sheridan answered, a bit startled by the question. He had been sitting in a back room with other witnesses most of the day, playing cards, and thinking he'd have as easy a time on the stand the second day as he had the first. He straightened up in his chair quickly after Gullion's opening salvo.

"Do you know that the defense has placed a witness on this stand who has testified that no one can be a worthwhile commander of a ship or of high command unless he is a graduate of the Naval War College?"

"I have no high command, sir."

Yet in testifying the previous day about the *Langley*'s near collision, Sheridan was passing himself off as an expert on how a large fleet of navy warships should sail, Gullion charged. "You were talking about the passage of some one hundred ships out of San Francisco Harbor," the prosecutor said accusingly. "Is that not so?"

"Yes, sir," Sheridan said. He had seen the ships sail out.

"What?" Gullion demanded.

"The passage of some one hundred ships," Sheridan said.

"Anybody could see it."

"Yes, sir."

"A blackamoor could see it!"

Sheridan's face reddened, and he pushed himself up from the chair as if he were going to take a punch at Gullion. He sat back down quickly and turned to the generals. "May it please the court," the lieutenant said angrily, "am I being called a blackamoor?" *Blackamoor* was a racist term used then for a dark-skinned person considered not particularly bright. Murmuring grew loud in the audience.

"I certainly do not want the witness to think I would do any such thing as that," Gullion protested. "He says that he could see it and I mean that the most ignorant person could see it."

Reid jumped into the fray demanding that Gullion not be allowed to badger the witness with his favorite "Kentucky phrase."

Gullion tried to calm everyone. "Do you know anything about the sovereign State of Illinois?" he asked Sheridan.

"A very fine state," Sheridan answered, regaining his composure.

"Do you know that Kentucky is proud to be a neighbor of Illinois?"

"It should be."

"Do you know that Kentucky is proud to be a neighboring state that gives to the United States such representatives as Mr. Reid?"

"They should be."

"Well, they are. Now, with that understanding, are you ready to proceed?"

"Yes, sir," Sheridan said, leaning back in his chair—warily.

Gullion returned to the attack. "How much sea service have you had with this fleet?" he asked.

"I have never had actual sea service with the fleet, but I was with them as an observer," Sheridan answered.

"How long as an observer?"

"Twelve days."

"You still believe yourself qualified as a critic of fleet maneuvers and tactics?"

"I certainly can tell when I am about to be collided with!"

Did Sheridan know that the near collision he saw resulted from an equipment breakdown with one of the lead vessels in the sortie, which forced other warships in the rear, like the *Langley,* to stop abruptly to avoid hitting it? Gullion asked. Did he know that the *Langley*'s captain was praised for his quick thinking in avoiding the accident?

Sheridan did not.

"You spoke of four planes being damaged on the *Langley* on landing," Gullion said. "How many landings have you observed on the *Langley* or any other aircraft carrier?"

"Well," Sheridan said, thinking for a moment, "about seventeen or eighteen."

"Have you ever landed an airplane on the deck of an aircraft carrier?"

"No, sir."

Did Sheridan know "that 700 landings have been made" on the *Langley* "in which no material failures of any sort occurred?" Gullion asked. (The navy was proud of that number, even though an accident rate of four in 700 would be considered appallingly high by today's standards. Modern navy aircraft carriers have four or fewer mishaps for about every 175,000 landings.)

But Sheridan had no idea what the accident rate was in 1925.

"Do you know that the *Langley* is only an experimental carrier for the purpose of developing desirable equipment for the *Lexington* and *Saratoga,* which are the two aircraft carriers under construction?" Gullion continued. It was not intended to be a war-capable vessel.

"Yes, sir, I realize they are very much handicapped on the *Langley*," Sheridan conceded.

Gullion turned to Winship. "I move that the entire testimony given in direct examination by this witness be stricken out!" he announced with a flourish. Sheridan, he charged, was so unqualified to speak on naval matters "that his testimony should not be in the record."

Winship quickly rejected it. But the one and only question from the generals made clear what they thought. "What is your age, lieutenant?" Howze asked.

"Twenty-eight years old, sir."

SATURDAY EVENING, NOVEMBER 21, 1925

Hiram Sheridan was walking toward the Willard hotel when he noticed a man following him. Sheridan ducked into the Willard and sat down in the lobby to read a newspaper.

Soon he looked up and saw the man from outside staring at him in the lobby. The man walked up to Sheridan and asked him how he thought the Mitchell trial would end. The army lieutenant shrugged his shoulders not wanting to talk to him, but the stranger kept talking.

Did Sheridan know he was in danger? the man finally asked.

"What?" Sheridan said, folding his paper.

He would pay for the statements he made in court about the navy, the man warned. It might "cost [him his] job" or other serious consequences if he didn't retract what he said.

Would it cost him bodily harm? Sheridan asked, annoyed.

"You never can guess to what length they will go," the stranger said, refusing to identify himself.

"You don't know what you're talking about," Sheridan said.

"I ought to know something about it," the stranger would only say. "I was connected with the navy for years."

Sheridan laughed and walked off. But the encounter unnerved him, and he reported it to Reid. The next week Sheridan returned to the Emery Building to see if he could spot the man who had delivered the threat, but he never saw his face.

After his usual afternoon horseback ride Friday, Mitchell dictated to Blackie his next article for *Liberty* magazine. He skipped driving to Middleburg and instead spent the weekend on Capitol Hill in Reid's office. They decided that Mitchell would finally take the stand on Monday. The two men closeted themselves, writing drafts of what Mitchell would say. But after Gullion's performance on Friday, they should have spent more time thinking about what he would be asked.

19 Cross-Examination

The spectators' section had been filled long before Howze gaveled the court to order. This was the big day of the trial. After four weeks of squabbling attorneys, on-again-off-again sessions, and testimony by his allies, Mitchell was finally about to speak on his own behalf. Washington's society ladies made up most of the audience. MacArthur's mother-in-law had come for the dramatic event, sitting next to his wife. The standing-room-only crowd began to creep forward from the spectators' section so it practically hovered over the attorneys' tables and even the jurors. The press section was so jammed that reporters had to elbow their way to the telegraph room to file stories. Photographers jostled for positions behind the generals to take the best shots of Mitchell on the stand. General King had developed a loathing for the cameramen during the proceedings, becoming ever more irritated by their constant rustling behind him. Later in the day he would angrily order all the photographers thrown out of the courtroom.

Reid stood up from the defense table. "The first witness today is Colonel Mitchell," he announced. His client rose.

"Colonel Mitchell, it is my duty to explain to you your rights at this time," Winship said. Mitchell could remain silent, he could make a statement to the court not under oath, or he could testify under oath as a witness, "in which case you will be subject to cross-examination," the law member explained. "Do you understand those rights?"

"I do," Mitchell said firmly.

Reid announced that his client would testify. Notwithstanding that "we think we have proved every material fact one hundred percent," he declared, "we tender the witness for such things that are essential to a full understanding of the case and for cross-examination."

Mitchell took the witness chair. For the next hour and twenty minutes, however, he said little that was controversial. Instead of rehashing evidence, Reid had his client recite his military credentials. Mitchell told his life story beginning when he enlisted in the army in 1898 and ending with his last duty station in Texas twenty-seven years later. He told of the combat he had seen, the medals he had been awarded, the glowing letters he'd received from Pershing. He recounted his triumph in sinking the *Ostfriesland*. He explained his theories on airpower and its future in the nation's defense. He offered some of the many technological predictions he had made over the years. He detailed more than forty of his recommendations to his superiors to improve military aviation. He talked about some of the more adventurous flights he had taken in planes, and the one time he had broken the world's speed record.

"How many hours have you had in the air?" Reid asked.

Mitchell didn't know. "I imagine between a thousand and two thousand hours," he said.

Reid turned to the prosecutors. "Take the witness," he said.

Gullion stood up and paused for a moment to arrange a pile of papers on the table in front of him. They contained the questions he planned to ask.

"Colonel Mitchell," he finally said, looking up at the defendant. "Have you any idea of the estimated wealth of the United States?"

"No," Mitchell answered, somewhat taken aback.

It was $302,803,862,000, according to the *World Almanac*, Gullion told him. "Now I would be much obliged if you would keep that figure in solution, and the relevancy of questions will appear later," the prosecutor said.

Gullion next read from Mitchell's September 5 statement on the navy fleet leaving San Francisco Harbor for the Hawaiian maneuvers. Mitchell had claimed that in a real war a "Pacific power's submarines would have planted all entrances to the harbor with mines, would have covered all the approaches with these death-dealing engines."

"Would you mind telling us what Pacific power you had in mind when you made that statement?" Guillion asked.

"Japan," Mitchell answered.

"Aside from the United States, has Japan the greatest number of submarines?"

"That I do not know."

"Do you know what nation other than the United States has submarines in the Pacific?"

"Japan has submarines in the Pacific."

"Do you know how many mine-laying submarines Japan has completed?" Guillion asked, several questions later.

"No," Mitchell answered.

Did Mitchell know how many planes the navy had with its fleet assembled at San Francisco Harbor? Guillion asked.

"I do not remember the exact number," Mitchell said, testiness beginning to creep into his voice. "It does not make any difference how many."

They had ninety planes, Guillion told him. "Do you know how many submarines were assembled with the fleet?"

"No, I do not," Mitchell answered. "I do not carry those figures in my head."

"Do you know how many minesweepers were there?"

"No. That is all a matter of record, and I can find it, if you want it."

"Well, do you know whether or not the fleet had assembled with it an adequate number of minesweepers to sweep the channel before it?"

"No."

"Do you know how fleets protect themselves against mines?"

"No."

"Do you know what paravanes are?" Guillion asked. They were torpedolike devices with sharp teeth around them that ships towed to cut the mooring cables for mines.

"No," Mitchell answered, becoming more irritated with the test Guillion was giving him, which he was flunking.

"Do you know whether aircraft are valuable in locating mine-fields?" Guillion continued.

"Under certain conditions," Mitchell acknowledged.

The fleet steaming out of San Francisco Harbor for Hawaii had aircraft practicing searches for minefields, it had minesweepers simulating the sweeping of mines, and even "the battleships actually streamed their paravanes," Gullion pointed out.

"Those features are of a kindergarten nature," Mitchell said dismissively.

"How do you know this is of a kindergarten nature if you do not know what paravanes are?" Gullion asked, enjoying himself.

"That has nothing to do with it," Mitchell snapped.

Gullion read another part of Mitchell's September 5 statement. If the fleet had managed to slip through the cordon of enemy mines around San Francisco Harbor, Mitchell predicted, "the whole Pacific Ocean would be districted off into squares and to each of these districts submarines would be assigned for the purpose of tracking the surface ships and attacking them."

"About how many miles would these districts cover?" Gullion asked.

"I do not know," Mitchell answered.

Gullion did. According to the navy, a submarine could cover about nine hundred square miles. The area U.S. warships would use to sail to the Far East takes in over ten million square miles. That would require about 12,500 submarines. Gullion claimed that Admiral Sims, Mitchell's witness, had written that during the World War, Germany was able to keep about one-tenth of its subs deployed at sea at any given time. So, using that percentage, Gullion calculated Japan would have to build 124,946 submarines to conduct the war Mitchell envisioned. At $5 million a sub, "that would cost about $624,713,000,000," he declared.

"No," Mitchell said, scoffing at him.

"Now, I believe we stated for your edification and instruction that the wealth of the United States was $302,803,862,000," Gullion continued. "To carry out your plan, which you heralded to the world on September 5, it would cost twice as much as the total wealth of the United States!"

"I object!" Reid shouted.

"Well—" Mitchell began, wanting to jump into the argument, but Reid cut him off.

"When I object, you stop," he told his client curtly. This wasn't going well. Like a basketball coach seeing the other team try to run up the score at the beginning of a game, Reid called a time out. "I object to the assistant trial judge advocate making an argument instead of asking a question."

But the pause didn't help Mitchell, who was woefully unprepared for such a skilled debater. Gullion continued the attack. Mitchell had also claimed that submarines could not only destroy the navy's fleet from underwater, they also could easily sink warships from the surface firing the guns they had on their decks. Any navy man could have told him that a tiny sub was no match for a battleship on the surface, but Mitchell had insisted in his statement that the surface warships "would be under constant attack by gunfire from the submarines that can carry any size cannon and use projectiles containing gas, high explosives or armor-piercing" rounds.

Mitchell, however, didn't have any earthly idea what size gun a submarine would have to carry for this kind of fight. "They may have them carry a twenty-inch gun," he testfied, throwing out a number.

"But you do not know," Gullion challenged.

"No," Mitchell admitted.

"Then if you do not know, why did you say in your statement of September 5 that they could carry any size?"

"I say that was my opinion."

There are few times in a lawyer's life when a hostile witness utters the golden answer that will sink him. Gullion had just experienced that rapturous moment.

"It is your opinion?" he asked.

"That is my opinion," Mitchell insisted.

"Is that your opinion now?"

"Yes."

"Then . . . there is no statement of fact in your whole paper?"

"The paper is an expression of opinion."

"There is no statement of fact in the whole paper?" Gullion repeated.

"No," Mitchell answered testily.

"Any statement of fact in your whole paper?"

"No."

Reid showed no expression from the defense table. But he knew that Mitchell had just sucked all the air out of his case.

Now every time Gullion asked a question about Mitchell's September 5 statement he snidely referred to it as the one that "does not contain any facts," until Reid finally objected and Winship ordered him "to stop that." Gullion apologized and moved on to another subject. If Mitchell had not read any of the navy reports on the Hawaiian maneuvers, how did he conclude they were a worthless exercise?

"From what I saw in the newspapers," Mitchell answered, digging himself deeper into his hole.

"Is that your usual source of information?" Gullion asked.

"Usually, respecting the navy, because I cannot get any statements from the navy."

Gullion then began payback for Mitchell's claim that senior army officers like Hugh Drum had misled Congress. The prosecutor grilled the airman on instances when his congressional testimony had been inaccurate. Reid, however, began to trip up Gullion with objections so his points became muddled.

Mitchell appeared revived after the lunch break and began to fight back. Gullion made no headway attacking his claim that the navy seaplanes that attempted the nonstop flight to Hawaii the previous August were "good-for-nothing big, lumbering" aircraft unsuited for the mission. Mitchell knew a lot more about planes that he did submarines or minesweepers. He was far more convincing in arguing that the mission was a botched publicity stunt. After all, none of the planes had made it to Hawaii.

Reid had obviously warned his client over the lunch break that he also had to clean up his horrible testimony about the September 5 statement being a collection of opinions, not facts. The first chance he got, Mitchell explained to the jury that the past events he had cited in the statement were based on facts, but "those in the future," such as his prediction on how Japanese subs would attack U.S. warships, "are opinions." It was an important point, although Mitchell did not make it articulately, and it's unlikely that the generals appreciated the distinction.

On all the recommendations Mitchell had made, Gullion next asked, were they "carefully worded or just general suggestions?" The prosecutor suspected the latter was more the case.

"They were sufficiently worded to allow the organization which we have in the air service to take them up, look into them and solve them," Mitchell maintained.

If the air service and every other branch of the army got everything on their wish lists, "have you any idea how much it could cost?" Gullion asked.

"That has nothing to do with the proposition," Mitchell said, tilting his head back. "This is the development of air power."

Mitchell had accused the army and navy of "criminal negligence and almost treasonable administration of the national defense." Was he saying that the men who ran those departments were traitors who should be locked up for crimes? Gullion asked.

"There are two definitions of treason," Mitchell argued. One was the constitutional definition of "levying war against the United States, or giving aid or comfort to its enemies," he said. The other form of treason—the one Mitchell was talking about—was the betrayal of public trust by the army and navy in not giving "a proper place to air power in organizing the defense of this country," he explained. "That is what I believe. It is a question of the system and not the individuals, entirely."

Mitchell had charged that the army and navy had been so "disgusting" in their conduct that any "self-respecting" officer was "ashamed of the cloth he wears."

"Do you mean that is to be taken literally?" Gullion asked, incredulously.

"Yes," Mitchell said.

"Do you think that any self-respecting person, any officer of the army, should be ashamed of his uniform?"

"No, not any officer of the army, but I think officers in the air service who are subjected to the command of people who know absolutely nothing about aviation, who come and inspect their outfits without knowing anything about them whatever and ask foolish questions—"

"Please answer the question," Gullion interrupted peevishly. He was growing weary of these speeches.

"I think that is repugnant in every way to a man who gives up his life to his duty and is constantly exposed to danger in the air in that way," Mitchell continued, ignoring Gullion. "It is the worst example of that sort of command I have ever known in any nation in aviation."

Gullion complained to Winship that Mitchell was getting signals from Reid to filibuster the questions.

Reid bolted out of his chair. "You are liable to encounter considerable trouble if you make that accusation," he said angrily. "I have made no signals to the witness and do not intend to and do not have to!"

"Go ahead with the questions," Winship said wearily to Gullion.

Turning to the *Shenandoah* accident, did Mitchell have "any experience in the design or construction of rigid airships?" the prosecutor asked.

Balloon units had been under Mitchell's command during the war. He had inspected German airships and had reviewed the designs of dirigibles. "I do not consider myself a technical man, but I have studied them as far as I could," he said, which was true. He was far more than just a layman on the subject.

"You would not qualify yourself as a designer of airships?" Gullion pressed.

"No," Mitchell conceded.

"Are you a free balloon pilot?"

"No."

"A rigid airship pilot?"

"No."

"Have you taken much training in the operation of the rigid airships?"

"No, sir."

"Have you ever flown in a rigid airship?"

"I do not think so."

It was after four o'clock in the afternoon. Howze decided that Gullion should continue his cross-examination in the morning, which was fine with Mitchell. He was exhausted from his day on the stand.

The minute Mitchell finished dinner that evening, Reid had him in his congressional office, where the defense team brainstormed the next round of questions Gullion might fire at him. They did not want a repeat of that day's disaster.

Fortunately for Mitchell the reporters covering the trial gave him a free ride in their stories. They wrote mostly about the charges he had repeated on the stand instead of the devastating points Gullion had scored in cross-examination. Mitchell had been wounded, but it wasn't fatal. The press was still on his side. Speaking requests continued to pour in from around the country, which he had to decline because of his arrest order. The army also did not help its public relations case any when word leaked that it had denied Mitchell permission to visit poor little Lucy in Detroit during Thanksgiving.

Not everyone on the prosecution side thought Mitchell had taken a serious beating. Captain Cook, one of Moreland's naval advisers, wrote to his superiors "it is not apparent" from the first day of cross-examination "that the accused contradicted himself on any material point." When Mitchell was "obliged to confess his ignorance of details or when confronted with the facts in the case," he "took refuge" in the explanation that his September 5 statement was a mixture of fact and opinion.

Cook's job was not only to advise Moreland. He was also supposed to report back to the navy on everything happening to Mitchell in the trial. The question of whether someone was spying on Mitchell had become a sensitive one. Rumors had been circulating around Washington that mysterious agents were following him and reporting his movements to the War Department. Mitchell believed them. So did Rickenbacker, who claimed that military intelligence snoops were listening in on the phone calls of air service officers. But neither man offered proof. And there are no records of spying in the War Department's military intelligence division files, except for when army attachés were ordered to monitor Mitchell during his European tour four years earlier. But the airmen were convinced that the men from G-2, another name for the department's intelligence wing, were on the prowl. They even circulated a poem about it:

G-2 has—Shsss—spies about,
G-2 has—Shsss—spies about,
G-2 will get you, for they do not want to let you
Talk about the Air Service needs.

10 A.M. TUESDAY, NOVEMBER 24, 1925

The guards had stretched a thick hemp rope in front of the spectators' section to keep the audience from crowding in on the attorneys and the jurors again. Mitchell settled back into the witness chair, and Gullion resumed his cross-examination.

"Colonel Mitchell, in your statement of September 5, and in your direct examination, you referred to accidents that had taken place in the army air service," Gullion began. "Do you know the number of flying hours per fatality in the army service for the calendar year 1921?"

"I do not remember what they are, but I have the records of them here," Mitchell answered, looking toward the defense table.

Gullion had it: 955. "Do you know the number of flying hours per fatality in the army air service during the fiscal year 1925?" he asked.

"I do not remember what it was," Mitchell answered.

Gullion had that as well: 5,269. In other words "the safety of flying has increased 550 percent in that time," he proudly announced. The 1925 number was not much to brag about; the modern U.S. Air Force averages about one fatality for every 200,000 hours of flying. Mitchell, of course, didn't have the benefit of that comparison. So all he could do was argue that Gullion's statistics were "very misleading." The air service, he explained, had been doing more tactical flying in 1921, and there had been fewer restrictions then on the type of flights student pilots could make. Aviators were also better trained now. Even so, flying was still unnecessarily dangerous, he insisted, adding that "there is a decrease in safety."

Didn't the statistics show that it was "almost twice as safe to fly in the American air service" as it was in the English or French service? Gullion asked.

"It is not a fact," Mitchell insisted.

"Do you base that opinion upon talking to the officers in the club or on newspapers?" Gullion asked sarcastically.

"I object!" Reid angrily shouted.

"I base that [on] personal observations in the countries," Mitchell answered coldly, "[on] the organization of airways, meteorological service and the people who fly."

Gullion turned to Mitchell's charge that the De Havilland planes were "old flaming coffins." Studies have shown that the plane was as safe as other aircraft, particularly after the position of the gas tank had been changed. But the evidence Gullion now trotted out ended up demonstrating just the opposite. The prosecutor read the accident reports from five De Havilland mishaps to try to show that they were the result of pilot error. But the reports also showed that in each case the aircraft stalled on takeoff and then burned when it crashed—two problems Mitchell claimed the De Havillands had.

"Col. Mitchell, you stated in paragraph four of your statement of September 5 . . . 'the airmen themselves are bluffed and bulldozed so that they dare not tell the truth in a majority of cases,'" Gullion said, changing subjects again.

"I refer to myself principally," Mitchell responded.

"You dare not tell the truth?" Gullion asked.

"Not that I dare not tell the truth," Mitchell explained, "but that I am bluffed and bulldozed." Maybe not actually bluffed and bulldozed, he clarified later, but "it has been attempted." The best example was his transfer to a backwater post in San Antonio.

"Do you consider San Antonio a most out-of-the-way place to which any officer can be sent?" Gullion asked.

"I certainly consider it an out-of-the-way place so far as influencing air service development is concerned," Mitchell testily replied.

Gullion was getting nowhere, so he tried a cheap shot. He picked up a copy of Mitchell's new book, *Winged Defense,* from the prosecution table and opened it almost midway.

"Did you write pages 102 to 105?" he asked quietly, looking at them.

"I did," Mitchell answered.

Gullion also pointed out that Mitchell had boasted in the press release he sent out on September 9 that "whenever I make a statement, it is authentic."

"Is that a question or is that a tirade?" Reid interrupted.

"That is preliminary to this question," Gullion said calmly, handing Mitchell a copy of his book. "Now, colonel . . . will you read to the court the marked places consecutively."

"No," Reid objected, "if you want to read it, all right." His client wouldn't.

"All right, I will read it," Gullion said pleasantly.

The passages dealt with the value of submarines in warfare. "'Existing records show that during the war the Germans maintained only about thirty submarines at sea,'" Gullion read. "'They started the war with a total of forty submarines, counting all sizes. That was a small number but they had a good start in their design and development work.'"

"Do you want to see this?" Gullion said to Reid, offering him the book.

"Yes," Reid said warily, taking it.

Gullion lifted a typed report from the prosecution table and turned to Mitchell. "This is a confidential document, but for pertinent and evident reasons it is no longer confidential, and I am authorized to introduce it to the court," Gullion began, as murmurs could be heard in the audience. "It is a lecture delivered at the General Staff College by Captain Hart, United States Navy."

"What are you trying to do?" Reid stood up and interrupted, his voice showing alarm.

"I am going to show," Gullion announced excitedly, practically shouting because the crowd noise had grown, "that the accused cribbed page after page of this book from which he is making money."

"Oh, is that it?" Reid roared.

"Yes!" Gullion shouted back.

Mitchell gripped the arms of the witness chair. He was almost trembling with rage. Loud hisses and even boos came from the audience.

"I certainly object to this testimony for this purpose!" Reid shouted indignantly over the noise.

Gullion demanded to introduce into evidence Mitchell's book and Hart's lecture, which, he argued, were "in deadly parallel."

"Nothing is deadly except in your mind," Reid shot back. "I object to it because it is not proper in this case. If you want to try a copyright suit or a libel suit, that is a different thing."

The evidence was indeed irrelevant to the case. But it was true. Mitchell was guilty of plagiarism. He had lifted a number of paragraphs from a lecture Thomas Hart had given at the General Staff College in 1919, and he had reprinted them verbatim with no attribution in his book. (*Winged Defense* had been slapped together hurriedly.) Hart had noticed it and had complained to the army, particularly because the lecture had been classified.

Mitchell had become famous for predicting the exotic and unconventional. But he had never been "an original thinker," as one air historian has put it. He borrowed heavily from airpower theorists such as Hugh Trenchard in England and Giulio Douhet of Italy, who was court-martialed and jailed for a year for being critical of his army's leadership during World War I. Mitchell's gift was in synthesizing and articulating the ideas he vacuumed up from around the world and in forcing his superiors to confront them. But he did have sticky fingers when it came to borrowing the words of others. Hart had first come across the lifted material in a *Saturday Evening Post* article Mitchell had written on planes and submarines. Gullion suspected that even parts of the colonel's radio address the previous week had been cribbed.

Winship intervened to keep the trial from spinning out of control. He sustained Reid's objection. "If we bring collateral issues of this character in about any matter," the court "will never get through" this case, the law member said.

Unfazed that the audience appeared ready to lynch him, Gullion resumed his attack. He brought up several recommendations Mitchell had made to buy airplanes that ended up having performance problems. That was not uncommon in the world of military procurement, where contractors often don't deliver on their promises. Mitchell was no different from a long list of senior officers who have made, and continue to make, bad choices.

"Now, Colonel Mitchell, in one of your statements you speak of 'we in the air fraternity.' Do you recall that expression?" Gullion asked.

"Yes," Mitchell answered. He had claimed that the air fraternity had decided to "put the issue" of airplane safety "squarely up to Congress and the people."

"Is this 'we in the air fraternity' an incorporated organization?" Gullion asked, implying that Mitchell was the leader of a group of one.

"Unquestionably, it is not."

"What does this air fraternity consist of?"

"It means the people who fly in the air."

So how did this amorphous group decide to "put the issue squarely up to Congress and the people?" Gullion asked.

"We talked it over together and discussed what had gone on and decided we would stand that sort of stuff no longer," Mitchell insisted.

Gullion reached back to 1913, when Mitchell as a young officer had a different view about a separate air force and had testified before Congress that aviation should remain a part of the Signal Corps.

"Yes, I was a member of the general staff then, and I never made a worse statement, I think, anywhere," Michell said with a laugh. "I remember that very well." The audience also laughed.

It was past three o'clock in the afternoon when Gullion finally gave up and sat down.

"Colonel," Howze began with Mitchell, "you testified on direct examination, in substance, that you made many recommendations relating to the air service through proper military channels to the proper authorities. Were there any restrictions placed on you as to the number, character, subject or contents of these recommendations?"

"No, general," Mitchell conceded, "never." He was free to recommend. The army was free to ignore.

"Will you give the court specific instances of officers of the air service being bulldozed and bluffed in giving their statements before various investigating bodies?"

"You wish me to give their names."

"You do not have to give the names," Howze said, "but instances."

"One naval officer came to me and told me he had a family," Mitchell recalled. "He was in Washington, and he wanted to give the information, but knew if he did he would be ordered away to some place, and could not afford it. Another officer told me he was taking a law course here and if he gave the information the chances were he would be ordered away. Another officer came to me and told me if he gave information, that his duties would be interfered with. . . . A great many other instances have occurred that could be specified."

Mitchell and Betty celebrated his surviving the second day of cross-examination with a dinner that night at the Occidental. The Washington papers would ridicule Gullion the next day for accusing Mitchell of plagiarism. But later, publications like the *New York Sun* would print side-by-sides of Mitchell's book and the Hart lecture to show that he definitely was guilty of it. The press only intermittently gave the other side of the story. But Gullion, Wilby, and the War Department planned to—with a vengeance.

20 "Crushing"

Mitchell's second round of testimony had been the newspaper headline for Tuesday's proceedings, but Reid followed with still more witnesses. Randolph Perkins, a New Jersey representative who had been on the Lampert committee investigating the air service, joined Admiral Sims in vouching for Mitchell's claim that airmen were being bluffed and bulldozed. Perkins had seen the problem from his end as a legislator trying to pry information loose from the military, and it had been frustrating. "Three lieutenants in the navy were brought before me for a preliminary examination as to what they would testify to," Perkins recalled for the jury. "They told me about their views and the spokesman of the three said, 'Don't call me. If you call me I will not tell you what I think.'" The other two said the same. Why? Perkins asked. "'Because it is a long way to Guam,'" Perkins said the leader of the three told him.

Reid also called Alfred Johnson, the navy captain who ran the *Ostfriesland* test, as a hostile witness. He was definitely hostile, but Reid managed to drag out of him the fact the navy had waged a robust propaganda campaign to discredit Mitchell and his air-power theories, distributing, for example, a film entitled *Eyes of the Fleet,* which showed only misses from bombs that planes dropped on battleships. The navy's publicity campaign, of course, rivaled Mitchell's.

A second representative testified for the defense—Fiorello La Guardia, the "Little Flower" from New York. La Guardia didn't have much to say beyond what Rickenbacker and other former pilots had testified to: that antiaircraft guns from the World War were worthless, and that the planes in the current inventory were obsolete. But he did entertain the courtroom.

Did you really say that Mitchell is being tried "by nine beribboned dog robbers of the general staff?" Gullion asked. He had read the New York press reports about the congressman's Armistice Day speech.

"I did not say beribboned," La Guardia corrected him, and the audience laughed. Several of the jurors grinned. Howze was one of them.

"The court would like to have you explain what was meant by your characterization of the members of this court?" Howze asked with mock formality. He had also read the news article and found it mildly amusing.

La Guardia said he hadn't known that Douglas MacArthur was a juror. He would not have put him on the list of dog robbers. The audience tittered. "From my experience as a member of Congress and from my contact with the general staff," La Guardia explained also with mock seriousness, "I am convinced the training, the background, the experience and the attitude of officers of high rank of the army are all conducive to carrying out the wishes and desires of the general staff." (And to becoming members of the dog-robbing class.)

"How high a rank does an officer have to get before he comes within your characterization?" asked Graves, who was not amused.

It happened by the time they were majors, La Guardia answered authoritatively. Sitting on the Military Affairs Committee, he'd suffered through many hearings with them. "I had one case where a quartermaster officer came up and testified about some patent [for a] self-greasing axle," La Guardia recalled. "It was the most ridiculous thing I ever heard of, and I asked him about it afterwards, and he said, 'We had to testify to this.' I have had hundreds of such instances in my congressional life, which has been very short."

Col. White, Mitchell's military counsel, spent the rest of Tuesday and all day Wednesday laboriously reading into the record hundreds of pages of documents the defense had extracted from the army and navy, the most explosive of which was a lengthy letter Patrick, the air service chief, had written to his superiors in 1924.

The general, who was widely admired throughout the War Department, agreed with Mitchell that conditions in the air service were "unsatisfactory." Aviation was stagnating under the thumb of the army, Patrick warned. The death rate among pilots was, in fact, too high, he had concluded. A "united air force" eventually must break away from the army, Patrick wrote. It must have an "equal footing" with the land and sea commands.

On Wednesday afternoon Reid finally stood up and announced: "As far as we are concerned, we are absolutely through."

The generals were anxious to speed up the proceedings. It was all the weary lawyers could do to keep them from convening a session on Thanksgiving. Howze reluctantly agreed to take the day off. But there would be no long weekend. He ordered the attorneys to be ready to resume promptly at 10:00 A.M. on Friday.

THANKSGIVING, NOVEMBER 26, 1925

The War Department would not allow Mitchell to travel to Detroit, but it did let him drive to Middleburg for the holiday. Mitchell found it humiliating that he had to ask for permission every time he wanted to visit his country home. He and Betty left early Thursday morning. The trip took three hours by car on Highway 50 from Washington, although Mitchell usually made it in less time (he terrified passengers by driving sixty miles per hour on the country road). Before his banishment to Texas, Mitchell had also flown his personal plane there sometimes, landing at a strip a mile and a half from Boxwood.

The couple attended Middleburg's Thanksgiving foxhunt, which had become an annual event. Mitchell was decked out in full equestrian regalia: shiny black riding boots, breeches, dark jacket with suede collar and carnation pinned to the lapel, white silk ascot, and top hat. Betty wore the new riding hat her sister-in-law Harriet had just sent her. She still had weepy moments thinking about baby Lucy being so far away and Mitchell unable to see her. But they made the best of the day. A group of cowboys from Texas had sent them a live turkey. The cowboys had thought about taking the train to Washington and standing behind Mitchell in court with their

Winchester rifles loaded and cocked, but instead settled on the gobbler. The couple decided to save the bird for a party the following week.

Mitchell loved Middleburg and the rolling country around it. Though a Midwesterner, he worked hard to become a Virginia patrician, chasing foxes on the weekends, entering his horses in its Hunt Cup races, joining the local tennis club, even taking the first aerial photo of the town. Middleburg today is a haven for the Virginia horse set, for first ladies and Georgetown doyennes seeking rural refuge, for movie stars prowling its trendy shops, and millionaires with money to pour into its lavish estates. In the 1920s, however, Middleburg was in transition, changing from a quaint village of old southern families to a more cosmopolitan retreat for the society and sporting set. Yankees from New York and New England had begun buying up tracts of still inexpensive land, where they built neocolonial mansions with stables. Washington's elite had begun to recognize the town as a convenient getaway. *Fortune* magazine would soon proclaim it the mecca for the nation's smart set, "the Valhalla of the young married Valkyries."

Mitchell turned his car left on Plains Road, which intersected the main street running through Middleburg. Boxwood was on the right about a half-mile up, straddling the Fauquier and Loudoun County line. Betty's father had bought it for them as a wedding present. The estate had 115 acres of woods and pastures with a small stream running through it and two springs. Built in 1826 of Virginia fieldstone, the house sat on a terraced hill, shaded by large elms, maples, oaks and beech trees, with a spectacular view of the Blue Ridge Mountains from the backyard. Because it faced west the sun warmed it in the winter and a breeze drifting in from Ashby Gap cooled it in the summer. The estate also had a caretaker's cottage, a henhouse, pig house, and machine shed, plus a stable with a dozen stalls, a tack room, and a feed room.

Betty was still refurbishing the main home, adding a wing to its southern side. Electricity had only recently come to Middleburg, and a line had not yet been strung to Boxwood. A large veranda with Doric-styled columns stretched out from the front, opening into a grand entrance hall inside, with a large drawing room on the left and the dining room on the right. Mantels were filled with riding trophies. A dumbwaiter enabled meals to be brought up from a basement kitchen. Spacious family bedrooms were on the second floor, and smaller rooms for servants occupied the third floor. Over the kitchen and to the right of the dining room, Mitchell had set up a small and cluttered study, whose tall windows allowed him to watch his horses grazing on the rich green pasture.

Mitchell had just begun buying and selling horses as a business. He also rented out part of his land to a local sharecropper named Isaac Waddell. The two men fought constantly for the next three years. Waddell complained that Mitchell never paid the seed bills on time, and Mitchell claimed Waddell took more than his agreed-to share of the crops he grew.

After the Middleburg hunt, Mitchell and Betty made the long drive back to Washington, where they had a quiet Thanksgiving dinner at the Anchorage. Afterward Mitchell went to Reid's office. The two men were spending practically every late night and early morning together there.

The prosecutors were grateful for the one day off. They did not spend it relaxing over a turkey dinner. It was now their turn to introduce their rebuttal evidence, and the prosecution planned to bring the full weight of the War Department down on Mitchell. It would be "an orderly crushing presentation," Moreland wrote in a strategy memo to Gullion, Wilby, and McMullen. Gullion would take the navy's case against Mitchell, Wilby and Moreland the army's, and McMullen would assemble the mass of material needed for the job. The War and Navy Departments, which had taken their time on Reid's requests for documents, now promised to speed up the process for Moreland.

Long lists were drawn up of every claim the defense had made. Rebuttal witnesses were assigned to each point, and counterarguments were prepared. The testimony of every defense witness was carefully analyzed for errors or inconsistencies that might be exploited. The army searched for evidence, for example, to contradict Hap Arnold's claim that the American air service was inferior to European air forces. Moreland had aides root through World War I records that might show that Rickenbacker's plane was hit by antiaircraft fire. The prosecutors also decided they would no longer cede the media war to Reid. Copies would be made of all major statements Gullion or Wilby gave at the trial and distributed to reporters.

Mitchell's image had to be remade from national hero to public enemy, the prosecutors decided. Pershing was the most revered military figure in United States. "We must bring out whenever possible the fact that ninety percent of Mitchell's attack is directed against the administration and actions of Gen. J. J. Pershing," Wilby wrote in a note to Gullion. Army officers who'd had run-ins with Mitchell during World War I were tracked down. Moreland had the adjutant general's office check records for any airfield Mitchell may have visited when a plane crash occurred to see if he could be blamed for the accident.

The Judge Advocate General's Office assigned one of its lieutenant colonels, Kyle Rucker, to locate army witnesses who might testify against Mitchell and to bring them to Washington. The navy eagerly offered more than forty of its officers as witnesses. All told Moreland sent out summonses to about one hundred men to take the stand.

The prosecution team divided up the witnesses and began interviewing them. A "Steering Committee" was set up to evaluate each interviewee and a color-coding system was used to designate interrogatories that were good or bad for the prosecution's case. Blue marked by an answer meant it was "okay." Red meant "not good." Maj. B. Q. Jones, one of the air service's best pilots, got a blue mark because he didn't find the De Havillands extraordinarily dangerous to fly. Maj. Gen. Charles Saltzman, the army's chief signal officer, got a red mark; he agreed with Mitchell that there were too few weather stations and the War Department had been stingy in paying for them.

Drum became the prosecution's chairman of the board. He kept a close watch over the witness list Moreland compiled. He sent the lawyers suggestions on other officers to call and wrote them long notes on subjects they should raise in rebuttal. Drum also had his aides draft for him talking points to refute what the defense witnesses had said about him during the trial and to fire some of his own charges at Mitchell when the assistant chief of staff took the stand. And Drum definitely planned to take the stand. He had ordered that his name be placed on the prosecution's witness list. It was get-even time.

Charles Summerall felt the same way. The ousted president of the court-martial sent the prosecutors letters as well, demanding that other witnesses be summoned, particularly those who would disparage Mitchell's report on the Hawaiian defenses Summerall had commanded. It was highly improper for the general to be doing this. As a former juror—and one who complained loudly that he'd been unfairly accused of bias—Summerall had no business helping the prosecution. It confirmed once more that Mitchell had been right to get him off the court. In a modern military tribunal Summerall's action would be considered subversive to the legal process and deeply frowned upon by the army. Most officers dismissed from a court-martial jury are happy to be freed from the onerous duty and never look back—as Bowley and Sladen had been when Reid had them dismissed. Summerall, however, could not wait to return to the Emery Building and take the witness chair.

A long line of senior officers wanted to settle scores with Billy Mitchell.

21 "Damned Rot"

Frank Reid had a trap to spring on Sherman Moreland.

The prosecution began its rebuttal case with an army general, LeRoy Eltinge, who commanded Fort McPherson in Georgia. But no sooner had Moreland sworn him in than Reid stood up to object.

"For what purpose is this testimony about to be offered?" Mitchell's lawyer demanded.

"If the court please," Moreland said. "That will appear in due season."

"You did not understand my question," Reid said, setting his trap. "Are you abandoning your original proposition that our defense was only in mitigation?" If Moreland was still sticking to the mitigation defense, then the rebuttal evidence he was now so anxious to offer "is not admissible." But if Moreland had abandoned his original position and now accepted Mitchell's evidence as an absolute defense, then "go as far as you like," Reid said, with a sweep of his hand.

Moreland was taken aback. "Evidence of mitigation can be rebutted the same way as any other evidence in the case," he sputtered.

"If the court please," Reid said with all the authority he could muster. "This is the first time in the history of the world that I have heard that mitigation . . . could either be rebutted, contradicted or doubted." Moreland could only present rebuttal evidence if the prosecution now acknowledged that Mitchell's evidence was for absolute defense. "As everyone knows, mitigation is a request for mercy and leniency," Reid pointed out. You introduce it and the jury decides the sentence. Never in the history of jurisprudence has mitigation evidence "become a subject of rebuttal testimony," Reid declared.

It was as clear as the nose on his face.

What was clear was that Reid was trying to pull a fast one on the court. There was no rule that said the prosecution couldn't dispute evidence the defense offered, be it for mitigation or proving guilt. Reid was trying to trick Moreland into accepting Mitchell's evidence as absolute defense. Moreland didn't bite. Neither did Winship. He overruled Reid's objection and asked both lawyers again if he could finally settle this thorny question of mitigation or absolute defense. But Reid again got Winship to put off a decision. Moreland, who was eager to begin the War Department's assault, didn't object. The lawyers were starting to run the trial.

Distinguished looking with wire-rimmed glasses and his hair graying on the sides, LeRoy Eltinge was a decorated officer with a long career in the army, so long that Howze and the other jurors griped to Wilby that they did not want to sit through an endless recitation of his résumé. The only thing important in Eltinge's background for the prosecution was the fact that he was considered an expert on army war plans. It also didn't hurt that Eltinge had flown as a passenger in planes. Wilby had called him to the stand to refute the testimony of Maj. Gerald Brandt, a Mitchell witness the prosecution considered a know-nothing upstart, who had testified that the general staff had sent him to command the air units in the Hawaiian maneuvers because the defenders had no war plans. That wasn't entirely true, Wilby pointed out. Brandt was sent to Hawaii because the air officer on the island had been fired for incompetence.

And Eltinge insisted that there were certainly war plans to defend Hawaii: He had helped draft them. But the more the general explained the war plans, the clearer it became that they were not actually fighting plans to defend the islands. Rather the plans were a collection of ideas on how Hawaii might be protected, along with army projects to supply the department there with men and arms. In peacetime, Eltinge explained, it was not customary to have a "tactical plan" for how the Hawaii defenders would actually hold off an enemy force. Today the Pentagon and its regional commanders draw up elaborate and detailed war plans to fight in most any part of the world, but the army of the 1920s was a force in waiting. The War Department did not draw up plans to fight unless there was an actual war.

To prove that the army and navy did cooperate on aviation matters, Wilby had Eltinge describe the Joint Army and Navy Board, on which he sat. The esteemed panel was supposed to study ways the two services could work together, and it had a Joint Aeronautical Board under it that made recommendations. In reality the navy used it to veto any air service encroachment on its turf. The board's members usually agreed only on mundane matters. The most important aviation question it had settled in the past year and a half was the new meeting time for the aeronautical panel.

This wasn't a compelling launch of the prosecution's rebuttal, but Wilby had to run a gauntlet to get the testimony out of Eltinge. Reid had decided to give the prosecutors a taste of their own medicine. The representative objected to practically everything that came out of the general's mouth unless Wilby had an official army document to back it up. It got to the point where Eltinge began looking to Reid after each question to see if he would be allowed to speak.

Moreland finally stood up, totally exasperated. "I am surprised now that at the time the witness was put on the stand, the learned counsel did not object to his stating his name and rank until we produced the order," he complained, as the audience laughed.

"That is entirely uncalled for," snapped Reid, who didn't find it funny. He had every right to demand that the government produce "the best evidence." That's what the prosecutors demanded of the defense. "I object to any comment that we are trying to make horse-play out of this, even if he does talk about horsemeat."

But if Reid demanded a piece of paper to back up everything a witness says, "there [would] not be any records left in the War Department," Wilby declared. "If a man cannot be asked a simple question, as for instance who is President of the United States, without getting the election returns to prove it, then the situation has reached a sad pass."

Winship pleaded with the two sides to cooperate and move the trial along. But Reid continued throwing out objections. The way he saw it, Gullion and Wilby had ridiculed his witnesses as unqualified. So now, when it was his turn to cross-examine, Reid decided to knock the general down a peg.

Eltinge, who had served as an umpire at the Hawaiian maneuvers, had pronounced them "a success" in helping the army and navy understand each other better—a questionable conclusion. "How long before this time had you been in official service in the Hawaiian Islands?" Reid asked.

"Never," Eltinge answered. He had passed through Oahu but had never been stationed there.

When Eltinge passed through, did he have any "official business of any kind?" Reid asked.

Of course, Eltinge testified. He would stop by the army's headquarters, and the staff would bring out the war plans for him to review.

"Did you examine them so that you could now state what was in them?" Reid asked.

"No," Eltinge admitted. The last time he had seen the plans was four years earlier.

"Could you state what they stated in regard to the air service?" Reid asked.

"No," the general answered. He couldn't remember if the department had a plan for using planes to defend the islands.

Wilby's next witness was fresher on the subject of Hawaii's defenses. Jarvis Bain, a stocky middle-aged major on the general staff, had inspected the island's war plans last spring when he attended the Hawaii maneuvers as an umpire, and he found them adequate. Moreover, cooperation between the army and navy during the Hawaiian maneuvers had been generally satisfactory, Bain testified.

"Was there unity of command" among the army and navy forces defending the island in the exercise? Wilby asked. Mitchell and his disciples believed there should have been.

"There was not," Bain answered.

"Was it ever contemplated?" Wilby asked.

"Not by those who drew up the problem, sir," Bain said, as if stating the obvious. And to Bain and most military leaders then it *was* obvious. Unity of command was a concept largely foreign to them. The army and the navy had always operated separately and always would, they believed. There would never be one commander over both forces except for the president. Mitchell recognized that the old notion of the army and navy keeping their operations neatly separated in battle had become outdated. Planes could fly over land and water. The wall between warfare on land and at sea was crumbling. In the future there would have to be a commander over the ground, maritime, and air forces. But the generals and admirals of the 1920s could not see past the spot on which they were standing.

Instead the army and navy had worked out a complicated arrangement where they would cooperate when they had to fight together in exercises like the Hawaiian maneuvers. The cooperation was based on a principle called "paramount interest," which Bain now tried to explain to Reid.

"The method of cooperation by paramount interest means that the service which has the lesser interest will cooperate in combined operations with the service which has the paramount interest," Bain told Reid, when it was the congressman's turn to cross-examine. For the forces defending the Hawaiian Islands, the army was considered to have the paramount interest since the big prize for the enemy—the naval base at Pearl Harbor and its army garrison—was on land. The navy was deemed to have the lesser interest since its job was to keep the enemy from the shore.

"Well, who will run the show?" Reid asked. This was the first he had heard of "paramount interest."

"The person who has the paramount interest leads in the operation and the others are supposed to cooperate," Bain explained. But the important word was "cooperate," not follow. The navy did not have to take orders from the army. The admiral in Hawaii only agreed to cooperate with the general there.

"The navy refused to cooperate with the army in trying to prevent the enemy establishing an air base at Molokai," Reid pointed out.

"They did, sir," Bain agreed.

So shouldn't somebody have been "given command over the army planes and the navy planes" in Hawaii? Reid asked.

"Not if it was against the law," Bain said.

"Is it against the law?" Reid asked.

"There is no provision in law for" unity of command, "so far as I know," Bain said.

Reid's jaw dropped. "You do not mean that?" he asked, astounded. "You do not mean to say it is against the law for the army and navy to work together and that the one having the paramount interest at that time should not take command? You do not mean that?"

"I do mean that," Bain said. "That is my understanding."

"You mean it is against the law?" Reid repeated, not believing what he'd just heard.

"It is not against the law, perhaps, but it is not provided for in the law," Bain clarified.

"Is it considered against common sense even by military and naval men?"

"There is a difference of opinion about that."

"I'm asking your opinion. You are the expert on war plans and maneuvers and everything else on this subject."

"I am not an expert."

"You are not an expert?"

"No, sir."

This was going horribly for the prosecutors. They were supposed to be calling to the stand the War Department's best experts on these subjects, and here their second witness said he wasn't one.

Bain, however, still had Reid thoroughly confused over how the army and navy operated under paramount interest during the Hawaiian exercise. The more the amiable major tried to explain it, the more bewildered Reid became, which was understandable. Only a military mind could fathom its logic.

Couldn't the Joint Army and Navy Board that Eltinge mentioned write up rules—ones that, for example, allowed the navy to "direct army aviation?" Reid asked.

"Only in the method of cooperation," Bain answered.

"Has the sister service ever cooperated with the brother service?" Reid asked.

"Yes, sir," Bain said.

"In what way?"

"In many ways," Bain said. "The Hawaiian maneuvers [are] a case in point."

"Did the army and navy aviation have one commander?" Reid asked.

"No, sir."

"How did they work together, then?"

"On this system or method of cooperation, when the service that did not have paramount interest was supposed to coordinate its activities with the service that did have."

So "the army should have been able to control the navy planes" just by asking since "the army had paramount interest and command at that time," Reid said, thinking he'd finally figured it out. "They should have been able to direct the navy aviation. Is that correct?"

"No, sir," Bain answered patiently. Paramount interest had its loopholes. The navy was supposed to cooperate with the army in the Hawaiian exercise. But it didn't necessarily have to.

Edward King was becoming crankier and fidgetier by the minute. The general was beginning to hate everything about this trial—the reporters, the photographers, the endless arguing by the lawyers, the fact that it was costing him more than $12 a day to stay in Washington, and now this congressman who couldn't get into his thick head a concept as simple as paramount interest. King had a nervous habit of chewing on a rubber band all the time and pulling it from his teeth as a child does with chewing gum. Reporters expected to see rubber bands flying from the juror at any time.

King now leaned over to Winship and said in a voice loud enough that Reid and the other lawyers could hear it: "This is damned rot and ought to be stopped."

Reid whipped around and began shaking his finger only a few feet from King's nose.

"I overheard that and I object to that!" the representative shouted in a rage. "This is not damned rot in your mind or anybody else's and I object to it!"

"I wasn't speaking to you," King, his face flushed, snarled back. "I was speaking to the law member of the court!"

"I know, but I heard it!" Reid yelled, still furious.

"Go ahead with your questions," Winship told Reid, trying to restore calm and order.

"I have kept within every rule in regard to this proceeding," Reid thundered, ignoring Winship, "and I certainly do not want any member of the court making such a remark!" Indeed, King had no business uttering a comment like that. He should have been thrown off the jury. It could even have been grounds for declaring a mistrial, but Reid held off demanding that. There was dead silence in the courtroom. The representative and the general stared angrily at each other, not saying a word, each one waiting for the other to blink.

King finally did. "I am sorry, Mr. Reid," the general said quietly.

"This may be a little tedious to you," Reid said, still steaming. "But I have a mission to perform in my cross-examination of this witness, and it is not being unnecessarily prolonged."

King let Reid have the last word. The general sat silent.

It was only a little after two in the afternoon, but Howze decided that the court definitely needed an early recess for the weekend. King huddled afterward with several other generals in an anteroom to ask them what he should do after this embarrassing gaffe.

They must have told him that he had to make amends, because he emerged from the anteroom and caught Reid as the latter was picking up his briefcase to leave. "I am very sorry about this matter," he said loudly enough so the reporters who remained could hear him. He wrapped his beefy arm around Reid's shoulder and said with a broad laugh: "I'll see that I keep things to myself hereafter."

Reid gave him a thin smile but said nothing. While King had been sequestered, the representative had asked the court reporter to read back the general's "damned rot" remark. That left the newsmen wondering if Reid planned to ask for King's expulsion on Monday, or even for a mistrial.

2:00 P.M., MONDAY, NOVEMBER 30, 1925

Wilby and Gullion could not have imagined a worse beginning for their rebuttal. Whatever value their opening witnesses had on Friday—and it ended up being not much—was completely destroyed by General King's outburst. Every news story on the Friday proceedings led with what King said and on the sensational confrontation it had sparked with Reid.

Reid milked the incident for all it was worth. He wisely calculated that it was far better to keep King on the jury than demand that he be thrown off. The contrite general had been neutered. He wouldn't be blurting out any more "damned rots"—not after the tongue-lashing he'd received from Reid and the press. On Friday evening, Reid released a statement to reporters. "It is an unfortunate episode, and I regret its occurrence," the congressman said magnanimously. Some might think that King had already found Mitchell guilty, but not Reid. "This court is an impartial tribunal," he said, although he knew it wasn't. There was little chance that Howze would declare a mistrial, and even less chance that Mitchell would be acquitted. So for Reid it was far better to keep King on the jury and the public perception of bias alive. Reid announced in his press release that on Monday morning he would move to strike what King had said from the record, claiming he would "take no advantage of the incident—although, as every lawyer knows, were this a civil procedure the jury immediately would have been dismissed." Insisting that he wouldn't accuse a jury of being biased was as good as saying that it was, Reid knew.

The prosecutors decided to skip the Army-Navy game in New York on Saturday. (Army won 10 to 3.) Instead they remained in Washington, to deliberate on how they could recover from Friday, which the press had concluded was a debacle for them. "America, acknowledged leader of the world in many respects, now leads in its funny army and navy courts," chided the *Philadelphia Inquirer,* lumping the *Shenandoah* probe with the Mitchell trial. Trying to distance the president from the mess, White House aides told reporters that while the army and navy would have to tighten their belts once more, Coolidge would soon ask Congress to increase the air service's budget.

Mitchell had spent the weekend tromping around the chilly fields of Middleburg, and he had a nasty cold by the time he arrived at court Monday morning. The Chamber of Commerce of Phoenix, Arizona, had sent him a box with a large Ponderosa lemon inside and instructions to give it to the sour prosecutors. Mitchell told reporters he'd use the lemon to nurse his cold.

During Monday morning's session Gullion managed to lay out a credible case that airplanes like the De Havilland were not as dangerous and decrepit as Mitchell and his witnesses had claimed. The prosecutors had decided to have at least one big name testify each day, someone who would be the center of attention for the reporters covering the trial. Gullion called his celebrity to the stand Monday afternoon.

Cdr. John Rodgers and his four crewmen of the PN-9 seaplane

became national heroes after a navy sub rescued them from waters off the Hawaiian Islands. A cheering crowd, honor guard, and dozens of navy dignitaries met the tanned and weather-beaten airmen when they arrived at San Francisco the end of September. They were paraded to City Hall, feted at luncheons and banquets, given testimonials by local politicians, sung to by opera stars, and pinned with medals from adoring admirals. Readers thrilled to the gripping accounts the crew wrote in the *New York Times* of their heroic attempt to fly nonstop from San Francisco to Hawaii and their nine harrowing days lost at sea when their seaplane landed in the water short of the islands. When Rodgers and his men reached Washington in early October, movie cameras filmed their arrival at Union Station, and a navy car whisked them to the Willard, where they were put up in the suite Coolidge and his wife had used before moving into the White House.

Rodgers settled into the witness chair as photographers snapped their last shots of him before scurrying away for fear that King might erupt. The general didn't.

Tall and stern looking, Rodgers had a distinguished military pedigree, which Gullion made him recite. His great-grandfather had been a sea captain during the War of 1812, a great-uncle had been a Union naval officer during the Civil War, and his father was still on active duty as an admiral. Rodgers was even a descendant of Commodore Matthew Perry, who opened the ports of Japan to the world.

"Are you ashamed of the cloth you wear?" Gullion asked, taking a pointed jab at Mitchell.

"No," Rodgers said quietly.

"Who made the preparations for the Hawaiian flight as far as the planes are concerned?" Gullion asked.

"I was in charge of all preparations," Rodgers answered.

"Were those preparations adequate?" Gullion asked.

Reid objected. Mitchell had complained in his statement that they were far from adequate. But Winship allowed the navy commander to answer the question.

"I consider them adequate," Rodgers said.

He went on to explain how the flight had been organized. Rodgers decided five men would be aboard his seaplane instead of two. It meant extra weight so there would be less gasoline for the trip, but the other men were needed for the long flight. The navy had consulted him on the two-hundred-mile interval for guard ships along the flight path to Hawaii. Mitchell had claimed that interval was far too wide, but Rodgers believed it "was a proper distance under the circumstances."

The navy commander slowly recounted the flight. There had been unexpected crosswinds the afternoon of August 31 so the seaplane did not get aloft until its second try, which consumed more fuel than they planned for at the start. There had been minor problems during the trip. An inductor compass jammed, and they had to resort to a backup magnetic compass, but they flew through the night at five hundred to six hundred feet off the sea and "picked up all the ships on our course without difficulty," Rodgers testified. Yet the favorable trade winds they hoped would give them the extra lift to Hawaii never arrived.

By the morning Rodgers realized they were two hours behind schedule, and they would not have the gas to make it to Hawaii. "It was part of the plan that in case we should run short of gasoline we would refuel from one of the station ships," he told the jurors. Rodgers pointed the seaplane to the ninth ship in the line, the USS *Aroostook*, an airplane tender he knew was "experienced in that work." But either the *Aroostook* radioed him the wrong bearings for its location or Rodgers made a mistake in his navigation—he admitted he didn't know which was the case—but the seaplane ended up fifty miles north of the tender and plopped into the water with its tanks dry. "The searching ships didn't know our position," the commander explained, and he had no way of sending it to them because the radio was powered by the engines, which now had no gas.

Compared to other aircraft, "what is your opinion" of the seaplane you were flying? Gullion asked.

"Well," Rodgers said, thinking for a moment, "she is the best flying thing that has ever been gotten out in the line of a boat as far as I know."

"Is it a great, big, 'good-for-nothing, lumbering flying boat'?" Gullion asked. That is what Mitchell had called it. He had also complained that the flight was poorly planned.

"Well," Rodgers said, pausing again, "it is a big flying boat, but I do not think it is good for nothing."

"In view of your experience and the hardships undergone, have you any criticism to make of personnel or material supplied to you by the Navy Department?"

"No."

"Have you any criticism to make of the preparations for your flight?"

"No, I made them all myself."

Mitchell's moles in the navy had been sending him questions to trash Rodgers. If the commander was so confident of the preparations for the flight, why did he have a still put aboard the plane to make fresh water from seawater? Did he suspect he wouldn't reach Hawaii and would spend some time floating around the ocean until a ship found him? Why didn't he land on the water before his gas ran out so he would have enough left to power the radio and give a rescue ship his position? Rodgers was an intrepid airman, but had his tours at sea interfered with maintaining his proficiency as a pilot?

Rodgers's strength as a witness, however, was that he never overstated his case, and he deliberated carefully before giving any answer. It gave him an aura of authority difficult for Reid to puncture.

How many times before the Hawaii trip have you "engaged in a nonstop flight over 100 or 200 miles?" Reid asked.

"I suppose about ten," Rodgers said, most of them flying around the Hawaiian Islands when he was stationed there. Not an impressive record.

"Do you consider it more dangerous to fly over water than you do over land?" Reid asked.

"Yes," he answered. There were no landmarks over water to guide a pilot, but Rodgers did not consider the flight to Hawaii unusually hazardous. (Though he did admit later that he had put the still on board.)

So "you did not pay any particular attention to the preparations that were made for this trip more than the ordinary trip?" Reid asked, trying to bait him.

"I paid very great attention to it," Rodgers answered testily.

"Did you save any gasoline of any kind for an emergency?" Reid asked.

"I did not," Rodgers replied. He expected to find the *Aroostook* with his remaining gas, so he used it all instead of saving some to power the radio later.

"Is that good naval aviationship?" Reid asked, with a mocking tone.

"I object," Gullion interrupted. Reid had no business "trying to attack Cdr. Rodgers."

"Oh, nobody tried to do that," Reid scoffed. "I think he did wonders." Although Reid really didn't believe he had.

"What naval mission were you to perform?" Reid asked, turning to another charge Mitchell had made—that the flight was just a publicity stunt.

"You mean what was the object of the flight?" Rodgers asked.

"Yes, what was the object of the flight?"

"Well, the object of the flight was primarily to test the practicality of sending planes from the West Coast to the Hawaiian Islands with a view to transporting them in that way in time of war."

It was not a terribly convincing answer, particularly when Rodgers had to admit that that mission was never specifically stated in his orders. But the press didn't believe Reid had drawn any blood. The commander left the witness stand with his hero status still intact from his adventure at sea. He did not deserve to be armchair quarterbacked by an army colonel on land.

For the next day's session Gullion had a celebrity as well known as Rodgers. Lt. Cdr. Richard Evelyn Byrd was becoming world renowned as a naval aviator and navigator. A scion of the famous Virginia Byrds (his brother would become the state's governor, then senator), Richard Byrd had as great a flair for publicity and adventure as Mitchell. He also had powerful friends in Washington. Byrd would go down in history as the man who opened up exploration of Antarctica. He had begun his adventures in the Arctic the previous June leading three navy amphibian planes on a flight over Greenland and Ellesmere Island. The expedition had been financed by the National Geographic Society, and the navy had hailed it as "the last of the great adventurous voyages into the unknown."

But Mitchell had ridiculed it in his September 5 statement as a publicity joyride that "got nowhere and did nothing." The three Loening Amphibian planes, which could touch down on water or land, had been borrowed from the army and were not built to be flown in Arctic waters filled with chunks of ice, he charged. Reid had paraded three army airmen before the court to back up Mitchell and to point out that the amphibians were untested aircraft the navy unwisely rushed into service. "The little jitneys," as Mitchell called the planes, had no hope of reaching the North Pole.

The navy strongly disputed him. Grover Loening, the plane's designer, who was livid with Mitchell because his wisecrack had cost him future contracts, also adamantly insisted that his plane was suited for the Arctic. The designer would testify later that Mitchell had seen the amphibian perform and had told him he thought the aircraft could land in icy waters. During his cross-examination Mitchell denied he ever said that, but Loening claimed he had proof to back up his story—a photograph of Mitchell standing with him next to the amphibian, just after it had landed on a snowy day.

Byrd was outraged by the potshot the colonel had taken at his expedition.

"How many miles did you cover" on the trip? Gullion asked him.

"We covered over a thousand miles in the Arctic," Byrd answered.

"Did you return with the three planes that you set out with?" Gullion asked.

"Yes, we brought three planes back to the States," Byrd said, adding that the three returned "in excellent condition."

"As a result of your experience in the Arctic with these planes," Gullion continued, were they suitable for that region?

"Well, the proof of the pudding is in the eating of it," Byrd said. "We gave the planes a good trial and they did very well. No other plane . . . could have flown as many miles as we did." But under cross-examination Byrd admitted that they did have to bail water out of the plane's pontoons "once a day" because of leaks.

Mitchell also suspected the expedition had been hatched so that *National Geographic* could sell subscriptions, and the Zenith Corporation, which supplied the communications gear, could peddle radios. Zenith's president had been on the expedition.

"Was not this a trip to boost the Zenith radio?" Reid challenged.

"Oh, no," Byrd replied firmly.

Didn't Zenith's president "say he would not go unless he could take his radio up there?" Reid asked.

"Not that I know of," Byrd insisted.

But Reid did get the explorer to acknowledge that the team never reached the North Pole. Byrd insisted he wasn't looking for it but rather for unexplored "land in the Polar Sea."

The navy, however, had expected Byrd to reach the top of the world. So "did you fail in your mission on the Arctic flight?" Reid pressed.

"We failed in the main mission," Byrd admitted.

"That is all," Reid said, satisfied, and sat down.

Gullion had far better witnesses on Monday and Tuesday. But the prosecutors were still stepping on their message. Monday morning, before they called their first officer to the stand, Gullion had stood up and announced that he wanted to deliver a speech on what the prosecution planned to prove with its rebuttal evidence. Reid predictably objected. The time for making an opening statement was at the beginning of the trial, not in the middle of it. But then Moreland stood up and stunned everyone in the courtroom by announcing that his associate had not consulted him on this ploy. Moreland agreed with Reid. The rules would be "violated" if Gullion were allowed to deliver a statement now.

Considering that they had spent the entire weekend together, Moreland and Gullion should have ironed this out earlier. The reporters had their leads for the next edition. PROSECUTION RIFT CAUSES SENSATION IN MITCHELL TRIAL, read the headline in the *Washington Star*.

The next day, what progress Gullion had made discrediting Mitchell was wiped out again by a disruptive juror. As Reid was alternately arguing with Gullion and grilling one of his witnesses, General Graves leaned over to Winship and snapped: "All this bickering is disgraceful and ought to be stopped!"

"I have a right to conduct this cross-examination as I see fit," complained Reid, who again had heard the remark, "and I object to your saying it should be stopped!"

This time Reid demanded that Graves be thrown off the jury. Throughout the trial, Reid claimed, Graves had been making snide comments to King and Winship when the defense questioned a witness.

Gullion thought Reid was blowing the matter way out of proportion.

"You can cross-examine all you want," Reid told Gullion angrily. "Everybody is for you! But when I attempt to bring the truth out of the witness, certain members of the court interfere with me."

Graves, who commanded the Sixth Corps in Chicago, was a handsome and fastidious man. He was just as fed up as King with the expenses he was piling up in Washington, but unlike King he wasn't going to let a lawyer push him around, even if the lawyer was a congressman. Graves refused to apologize. "I claim the right to express my opinion to the law member of this court without criticism from you!" he said, glaring at Reid.

The generals, however, decided to keep Graves on the jury. As Howze saw it, Graves had been complaining about the bickering by both lawyers, not just Reid.

Instead of recounting Byrd's testimony, the *Washington Post* led its story the next day with Graves being challenged "for prejudice."

Mitchell could not have been more delighted with the prosecution's misfortune. Tuesday night he hosted a dinner party at the Anchorage for some of the witnesses in the trial. Betty served the Texas turkey the cowboys had sent. Even Grover Loening, who was still nursing a grudge over what Mitchell had said about his amphibian, showed up. Mitchell presented him with the Ponderosa lemon as a peace offering.

22 Siege

The celebration at the Anchorage was premature. The day after Mitchell and his guests feasted on turkey, Dwight Morrow released the final report of the President's Aircraft Board, and it did not contain what Mitchell wanted to hear. Morrow and the eight other members of the panel had spent a month listening to ninety-nine witnesses, half of them pilots. Much of the testimony had been confusing or wildly contradictory—no one could agree on how many good planes the army had—but one thing was crystal clear to the men on that board: The United States was in no danger of enemy attack by air. Nor, they wrote, "is there any apparent probability of such an invasion in any future which can be foreseen." The nations of Europe may have to build large armies and air forces to protect themselves, but vast oceans "freed" the United States "from the heavy burden of armament."

The airmen had grand visions of the plane being the decisive weapon in the future, but "we do not consider that air power, as an arm of the national defense, has yet demonstrated its value," the board concluded. "The next war may well start in the air but in all probability will wind up, as the last war did, in the mud." Aviation technology was still too new and unproved to justify having a separate air force, as Mitchell advocated. The Morrow board also could not see how establishing a "super-organization" like a defense department over an army, navy, and air force "would make for economy in time of peace or efficiency in time of war." The panel instead recommended a semiautonomous air corps within the army as Mason Patrick advocated; there would be assistant secretaries for aviation in the War and Navy Departments. The panel did recommend that air budgets be increased, but much more modestly than what Mitchell wanted.

The aircraft board had produced a sober and judicious report. The wise men had correctly summed up the country's defense needs at the moment—and to the horizon that they could see. They recommended what blue ribbon panels typically recommend—compromises that the powers in Washington were already prepared to accept. Senior air officers like Patrick thought the recommendations were a good start. The White House quickly endorsed them. A copy of the report was put in the next diplomatic pouch for Pershing, whom Coolidge had sent to South America to settle a boundary dispute between Chile and Peru. The retired General of the Armies had kept close tabs on the court-martial from his hotel in Chile. He had grown increasingly irritated with Mitchell and his extravagant proposals for aviation (although Pershing wasn't adverse now to investing in commercial aviation ventures if he could make money from them). Black Jack was delighted when he finished reading the Morrow report. "It will settle many questions in the minds of the public which had been stirred up by some of the air service enthusiasts," he wrote to the board's secretary.

Mitchell considered the Morrow report a terrible blow. It was a public rebuke of his call for a unified air force, delivered by a panel of the nation's most distinguished leaders.

On Wednesday Howze served notice on the attorneys that the court would no longer tolerate witnesses being subjected to "irrelevant, insulting and improper questions." Reid took it as a slap at him, because he was the only one asking tough questions during cross-examination. (The generals asked few questions of Gullion's witnesses, and when they did they were softballs.) But Howze and the jurors had become just as irritated with Gullion's hardball tactics, which were slowing down a trial that they already thought was moving at a crawl. Howze began to feel that the Emery Building had become his permanent home. He had started the trial sitting ramrod straight in his chair, making rulings. Now he slumped back with his feet stretched out under the table much of the time.

The general staff moved to tighten up the prosecution's operation and to keep closer tabs on the rollout of evidence against

Mitchell. Most evenings after court, Moreland and his assistants were now summoned to the War Department to deliver progress reports. Senior officers screened the witnesses that the team planned to call each day and continued to send telegrams to commanders in the field looking for better witnesses to testify against Mitchell.

The prosecutors now had the wind at their backs. The Morrow report had served them well, painting Mitchell's ideas as too far outside mainstream thinking. Over the next five days of the trial, Gullion methodically chipped away at Reid's case. One naval officer after another took the stand to ridicule many of the claims the colonel had made. Mitchell's prediction that an Asiatic power could send its planes across the Bering Strait and over Alaska to attack the United States from the north was deemed outlandish; no country's bombers could fly such long distances and through such cold weather. Likewise, no enemy force could sail across the Pacific and instantly mine all the sea entrances to San Francisco, as Mitchell envisioned, without the U.S. Navy finding out and destroying it first. Mitchell also was delusional, the navy men testified, if he thought a submarine could successfully sink a battleship with gunfire or could carry an airplane to a distant island for an attack. (Actually, Mitchell's notion of a sub transporting a plane, which he predicted in his Hawaii report, was not so fanciful. Naval intelligence agents found evidence that the Germans had been experimenting with submarine airplane carriers toward the end of World War I.)

The most important offensive Gullion mounted, however, was against Mitchell's criticism of the *Shenandoah*. On Wednesday afternoon the prosecutor called to the stand his best witness on the accident.

Lt. Cdr. Charles Rosendahl had been the dirigible's navigator and was its senior surviving officer. Rosendahl had been at sea for most of his first nine years in the navy. It wasn't until 1923 that he began duty with airships at the Lakehurst Naval Station. In the navy's aviation community, the lieutenant commander was considered a rising star. Mitchell liked him. Rosendahl had turned into a passionate advocate for dirigibles, and he had become just as fierce in defending Lansdowne and the other crewmen from second-guessers who questioned their performance during that final flight. Army air officers who had observed Rosendahl aboard the *Shenan-*

doah, however, had told Mitchell that they considered him a rookie, only marginally competent to handle the complex dirigible.

Rosendahl began by reading the report he had written for the navy on the crew's final harrowing hours on the dirigible. The courtroom became totally silent as he recounted in clinical detail the *Shenandoah* flying into the line squall over Ohio the morning of September 3, its being blown up and down by violent wind drafts, the crew's frantic efforts to save the airship, the sickening sounds of snapping struts and tearing metal, and the chaos on the ground as he collected bodies and hunted for survivors.

"Are you familiar with the arrangement of gas valves on the *Shenandoah?*" Gullion asked, addressing Mitchell's charge that the reduction of the valves from eighteen to eight resulted in gasbags exploding when the airship ascended, which broke apart the dirigible.

"I am," Rosendahl answered.

Why were the valves cut back? Gullion asked.

"For the purpose of saving weight," Rosendahl said. Lansdowne and the airship's officers persuaded the navy to approve the change, and the ten valves were taken out.

Did the *Shenandoah* encounter any difficulties with "the revised arrangement of the valves?" Gullion asked.

"None," Rosendahl answered, adding that the airship made a number of uneventful flights with just eight valves. Rosendahl conveniently didn't mention that the airship's navy designer, Cdr. Jerome Hunsicker, had already told the *Shenandoah* inquiry he opposed removing the valves because it did make the dirigible less safe. But Hunsicker would never be able to say that at Mitchell's trial. In a move some might consider open to question, the navy had transferred the commander to the U.S. Embassy in London the previous week.

"What is your opinion as to the cause of the breakup of the ship?" Gullion asked.

Rosendahl's opinion was the same as that of the *Shenandoah* inquiry, the other officers aboard the dirigible, Hunsicker, and the top navy leadership. "The *Shenandoah* was destroyed by the aerodynamic stresses imposed upon it by the vertical currents of a line squall to which the ship was subjected," the lieutenant commander testified. In other words the squall's violent updrafts and downdrafts had broken the airship apart.

"Did gas pressure have anything to do with the destruction of the ship?" Gullion asked.

"It did not," Rosendahl said emphatically.

"Speaking as operating officer and from your experience on the *Shenandoah* on the last flight, will you state whether or not the gas system operated satisfactorily?" Gullion asked.

"It did operate satisfactorily," Rosendahl answered.

The testimony was damaging for Mitchell, who had said that exploding bags had broken up the ship. Clearly Mitchell had rushed to judgment when he made this charge in his September 5 statement. Removing the gas valves had certainly been an unsafe move. It could one day have resulted in a mishap for the airship. But it didn't cause the accident on September 3. It was clear from the testimony given by other naval experts at the trial, who either were aboard the dirigible or who investigated the accident afterwards, that the *Shenandoah's* gasbags had not exploded. Even an army observer who happened to be on board the airship during its last flight told the jury that removing the valves did not cause this accident. Mitchell had his facts wrong.

"Please state what was in the radiator to prevent freezing, if anything, at the time of the last flight," Gullion said. He was turning to another instance where Mitchell had erred. The colonel had claimed that calcium chloride, a nonfreezing liquid used in the dirigible's engine radiators, had spilled onto the airship's duralumin girders, which corroded and weakened them. Mitchell had the right problem but the wrong airship. Calcium chloride had been used in the radiators of the other dirigible, the *Los Angeles*, against the advice of the German technicians, and it had indeed corroded its girders. But the *Shenandoah* was a different story.

"There was no anti-freezing mixture used in the radiators on the last flight," Rosendahl revealed.

"Why was that?" Gullion asked.

"Because we did not expect to encounter any freezing temperatures," Rosendahl said.

"When anti-freezing compounds were used in the radiator, what was the main ingredient to prevent the freezing?" Gullion asked.

"A mixture of alcohol and glycerin," said Rosendahl. It wasn't corrosive.

"What other kind of anti-freezing compounds were used in the *Shenandoah*, if any?"

"A solution of calcium chloride was used for a short period in the ballast bags of the *Shenandoah*."

"Was there any evidence of rust or deterioration in the vicinity of those bags?"

"There was not," Rosendahl insisted. The crew was careful about making sure no calcium chloride spilled, and if it did, the liquid was wiped up quickly so no damage was done.

That pretty well buried Mitchell's second allegation. Gullion moved on to a third one, that when the *Shenandoah* broke away from its mooring mast the previous year, the tear permanently weakened its structure.

"After the *Shenandoah* broke away from her mast, was she repaired?" Gullion asked.

"She was," said Rosendahl, adding that her structure afterward "was just as good as it had ever been." Navy repair records introduced by Gullion corroborated the lieutenant commander.

"Would it have been practicable for members of the crew to wear continuously any of the existing types of parachutes on the *Shenandoah*?" Gullion asked, turning to another subject.

"Wait a moment, I object," Reid interrupted.

But Rosendahl answered anyway. "It would not," he said.

"When I object, I wish you would not answer," Reid told him, irritated.

"I beg your pardon," Rosendahl said politely.

"Do you want that stricken?" Winship asked.

"I will let it stand," Reid said grudgingly. The answer was already out. Reid's objection probably would have been overruled anyway. The defense was taking heavy blows.

Gullion now set up Rosendahl to deliver the heaviest. "Do you know whether Cdr. Lansdowne undertook the Midwest flight under protest?" the prosecutor asked. (Like most naval officers in his position, Lansdowne was referred to by three titles: Lieutenant Commander Lansdowne, which was his official rank; Commander Lansdowne, which is the way lieutenant commanders are sometimes addressed as a matter of courtesy, dropping the "lieutenant"; or Captain Lansdowne, because he was captain of the airship.)

"He did not undertake the Midwest flight under protest," Rosendahl said firmly. It undercut Margaret Lansdowne's testimony that her husband had objected to the flight. Rosendahl added that Lansdowne's orders from the navy always gave him some discretion on when the *Shenandoah* would fly and what route it would take.

"Do you know whether any member of the *Shenandoah* crew considered the *Shenandoah* unsafe after the valve change?" Gullion asked.

"As far as I know, no member did," Rosendahl said, which was true—although the crewmen had worried about the safety of the airship under Lansdowne's predecessor because they did not consider him qualified.

"No further questions," Gullion said, satisfied he had punctured the defense.

Reid, however, opened with a set of powerful questions.

"Did the *Shenandoah* withstand the last storm?" he began asking, rapid fire.

"Did she withstand it?" Rosendahl asked, caught a little off guard.

"Yes," Reid said.

"No, sir," Rosendahl answered, "she did not."

"She was destroyed, was she not?"

"She was."

"How many men were killed?"

"Fourteen men were killed."

"Including Capt. Lansdowne."

"Yes, sir."

"Tell the court what scouting mission she was on with the fleet at the time of the disaster."

"She was not operating on a scouting mission at the time."

"What time was the first time you found the ship in danger?" Reid asked.

"Four thirty-five," Rosendahl answered. It was early morning. An hour and ten minutes later, the dirigible had crashed.

"Would it have been possible for anybody to have put a parachute on, if they had been there, in the hour and ten minutes?" Reid asked. It was a good question. If the chutes had been too bulky to wear during operations, they could have at least been nearby so the men could grab them in an emergency.

"Certainly," Rosendahl conceded.

It was an excellent beginning for Reid's cross-examination. Focus on bottom lines—the airship was destroyed, men died. Mitchell may not have all his details correct, but something went terribly wrong on the last flight. Reid, however, became overconfident and stumbled.

"You are sure that the gas valves had nothing to do with the destruction of this ship?" he asked. Reid should have left this issue alone.

"Yes, sir," Rosendahl said confidently. None of the gasbags exploded. Rosendahl, in fact, was supervising the venting of gas using manual valves that were connected to the bags in addition to the automatic valves. He said the officers always intended to use the manual valves to help the automatic ones in an emergency. Crewmen could open the manual devices by moving a handwheel hooked to wires stretching as far as 450 feet to the valves on the bags. Rosendahl used a stopwatch to time how much gas was released as the airship rose.

But was Rosendahl standing at the gasbags 450 feet away to verify that valves were actually venting properly? Reid asked.

"No," Rosendahl admitted.

So those long wires could have snapped in all the twisting and turning of the airship and failed to open the valves, Reid pointed out.

The congressman should have ended his questions there, to leave a flicker of doubt remaining over whether the valves—automatic or manual—vented adequately. But he didn't.

"Then in your opinion, whether the valves actually let out gas or not is merely an opinion," Reid challenged.

"It is a well-founded opinion," Rosendahl insisted.

"Well-founded on what?"

"From the fact that if the control wires had been separated from the valves when we let go of the hand wheel, the wire would have remained in a constant position rather than going back to the original position," Rosendahl explained. Because the wire connected to the handwheel snapped back taut, it showed that the manual valves opened and closed properly. Reid ended up burying any reasonable doubt.

"Now, you stated . . . that Captain Lansdowne never protested against making this trip," Reid asked. He was on firmer footing with this line of questioning. The defense had subpoenaed all the correspondence between Lansdowne and the navy on the flight, and the memos tended to back up Margaret's story more than Rosendahl's.

"Yes, sir," Rosendahl said, adding that Lansdowne did not protest the flight "as finally ordered." It was an important caveat the lieutenant commander left out when Gullion questioned him, and Reid intended to exploit it now.

"Did he protest before the final order?" Reid asked.

"He protested when the trip was suggested to be made in June," Rosendahl acknowledged.

Indeed, the navy was anxious to have one of its two dirigibles make the Midwest flight before July 5. The *Los Angeles* had originally been picked for the mission, but it ran into equipment trouble so its helium was transferred to the *Shenandoah* to make the journey. (The navy owned only enough to fill one dirigible.) Lansdowne, however, fired off a memo to Adm. Edward Eberle, the chief of naval operations, warning that the airship would be flying through dangerous thunderstorms that occurred along the Midwest route during the summer months. George Steele, who commanded the *Los Angeles*, also sent Eberle a memo backing up the warning his fellow skipper had given. Lansdowne told Eberle a Midwest trip was far safer "in the season after the thunderstorm season has passed (September)."

But putting September in parentheses created some confusion in Lansdowne's memo. Was he saying that it was safer to fly in September or after September had passed? Reid interpreted the note to mean that Lansdowne did not want to fly even in September. Eberle fired back an angry memo to Lansdowne complaining that if the weather conditions were as dangerous as the *Shenandoah* and *Los Angeles* captains claimed, then there was never any safe time to fly, and "our airships are of little military and commercial value." Eberle thought his two skippers were being alarmists. Thunderstorms could occur any time from June through September along the Midwest route, but there were a lot of days with clear weather. Eberle was correct up to a point. The most severe storms did occur before September, and a good dirigible captain should be able to fly earlier in the summer simply by maneuvering around the bad weather.

The correspondence showed that Moffett, who headed the navy's aeronautics bureau and was eager to keep the flight on track, finally intervened to broker a compromise. Eberle agreed to postpone the flight until September 2. The airship could still reach some two dozen state fairs along the route.

Lansdowne followed up with another memo asking that the trip be postponed again until the second week of September. He also asked that the airship be allowed to make a preliminary flight to Detroit to check out a mooring mast Henry Ford had erected there so the *Shenandoah* could dock and refuel. But this time the admiral refused. The airship would miss five state fairs if it flew the second week. Eberle believed the *Shenandoah* crew had enough experience docking at mooring masts so that it did not need to practice at Detroit.

The correspondence was potent proof of one of Mitchell's most important charges. Eberle, a nonflier, was making decisions better left to the airmen. He was also putting considerable pressure on Lansdowne to make a publicity flight the skipper wasn't eager to undertake. Every memo from Eberle did have an escape clause, to protect the navy. Lansdowne could deviate from the route for safety reasons. But Eberle also told the dirigible captain that he wanted the route the navy had mapped out to be followed "as closely as possible." And even after Lansdowne finally agreed to leave on September 2, the navy kept packing his itinerary with more state fairs until he had to plead with the service to stop.

"There were thunderstorms at this time you made the trip," Reid finally pointed out.

"Yes, sir," Rosendahl acknowledged.

"So Commander Lansdowne was right when he said they were liable to encounter thunderstorms on this trip?"

"Yes, sir."

Reid next turned to the question of Rosendahl's experience with dirigibles. "How many hours did you ever have on any airship before you went to Lakehurst?" he asked, already knowing the answer.

"I had never been in aviation until I went to Lakehurst," Rosendahl said.

"The entire experience you had in rigid airships was from April 1923 to September 1925—is that correct?" Reid asked.

"Correct," Rosendahl acknowledged.

"And you claim to be expert on all these matters you testified to, and that is all the experience you have had?" Reid asked skeptically.

"I have made no claim to expertness on anything except to mooring masts," Rosendahl answered defensively. He had been the officer in charge of docking the *Shenandoah* to the masts.

Gullion stood up to continue questioning his witness. The prosecution interpreted Lansdowne's initial letter to be the opposite of what Reid claimed it meant; the dirigible skipper had written that it was safe to fly in September. "Do you know at what time Commander Lansdowne wanted to make this flight?" Gullion asked the navigator.

"He wanted to make it either in the latter part of August or early in September," Rosendahl said.

"Did he confer with you as to when the trip was to be made?" Reid asked, standing up to cross-examine again.

"Yes," Rosendahl insisted. As navigator, he had plotted the route.

Did Lansdowne take Rosendahl into "his confidence" and share with him all his thoughts on the trip? Reid asked.

"Yes, sir."

"And you say he never made any protest [about] visiting these state fairs on this trip?"

"He did not."

Could any airship have been built strong enough to withstand the thunderstorm the *Shenandoah* encountered? the generals finally asked.

"From my meager knowledge, I do not think so," Rosendahl answered, although if he really believed that, his knowledge of airship construction was meager indeed. The *Shenandoah* had not been built to withstand the strongest updrafts and downdrafts that Midwest storms produced, and the navy knew that. There were also

newer designs for dirigibles that could withstand those strong air
currents. Even if the *Shenandoah* had escaped the storm over Ohio,
it might have been only a matter of time before disaster befell it.

On Saturday, Gullion put on the stand the other important witness in the *Shenandoah* affair: Edward W. Eberle, the chief of naval
operations and the man who issued all the orders sending the
Shenandoah on its fateful flight. Ironically Eberle, who had held
the top sea job for only two years, liked navy pilots and was sympathetic to their needs. The admiral now proceeded to tell the generals a story completely different from what the defense attorneys
alleged.

Eberle testified that Lansdowne had absolutely no qualms
about making the Midwest trip in June or July as long as he had
wide discretion on when his airship would leave Lakehurst and on
what route she would take so she could avoid thunderstorms. The
navy chief claimed that on June 30 he had given Lansdowne that
latitude. "With that liberty of action, it is perfectly safe to go out
now," Eberle claimed Lansdowne told him.

The Midwest flight, the admiral insisted, had been postponed
until September 2 not because of worries about thunderstorms but
so that the *Shenandoah* could first train with warships off the
Atlantic Coast in scouting targets for the fleet. Eberle also claimed
that in a second meeting he had with Lansdowne on August 15, the
Shenandoah captain agreed there was no longer any need for a preliminary flight to Detroit—Rosendahl had inspected the mooring
mast there and found it satisfactory—so the airship could leave the
first week of September instead of the second.

Lansdowne "seemed very much pleased" with the final itinerary for the trip, Eberle told the jurors, "and said he was looking forward to the flight with a great deal of pleasure." The admiral
claimed that the only regret Lansdowne voiced was that "this was
his last flight" before transferring to a new assignment. "I may say
here that Lieutenant Commander Lansdowne always talked to me
very freely. I had known him since he was a young ensign and every
time he came to Washington, he came to see me."

"What was the reason for the flight of the *Shenandoah* on September 2?" Gullion asked.

To develop commercial air routes for dirigibles flying to the

Midwest and to train the crewmen in "flying over land as well as over water, in case we should wish to transfer airships from one coast to another in an emergency," Eberle answered. He said nothing about the state fairs, and Gullion didn't ask.

The admiral was the navy's final word on the *Shenandoah* accident. To listen to Eberle tell it, how could anyone doubt that he and the service had acted with the utmost propriety? Every order had been issued with the goal of improving the airship's military capability, including the last one. The navy chief had looked out for Lansdowne as a father would a son, but accidents happen in the service, and the *Shenandoah* crewmen who perished had died in the line of duty.

Reid thought it was the biggest cock-and-bull story he had ever heard.

"Have you anything in your files or anything in writing that Captain Lansdowne said that it was satisfactory to make this flight the second of September?" the congressman asked.

"It was not the custom," the admiral answered stiffly.

"I am not asking you for the custom, I am asking if you can answer the question," Reid said sharply.

"I think I have answered it," Eberle protested.

"I submit he can answer it," Reid said, turning to Winship for help.

"I will answer it the way I like to," Eberle said indignantly. "I am under oath as a witness here. It is not the custom of officers to write to say that they accept a thing or [to] say they were not satisfied with it."

"Is that what you want to tell the court?" Reid asked incredulously. "They never say they are not satisfied after they once receive their orders?"

Well, not never, Eberle backpedaled. An officer could write to protest an order after it was issued.

"I ask you now," Reid repeatedly loudly, "if you have any scrap of paper in the Navy Department, Bureau of Operations, or any place in the world, which shows in writing that Captain Lansdowne said that he was satisfied to take the trip on September 2?"

"No, not that I know of," Eberle said gruffly. But, he added quickly, Lansdowne had told him "in the presence of others" that he approved of the flight. Those aides, of course, corroborated their boss's story.

Did the navy consider the state fairs when it was making out the *Shenandoah*'s itinerary? Reid asked.

"Yes," Eberle said, trying to put the best gloss on it. "After we had mapped the schedule out we found she could pass over certain state fairs along about those dates and we had her do it."

Why? Reid asked.

"Because millions of people [had] requested to see the ship that belonged to the government," Eberle answered brusquely.

"All right, do I understand you to state that this flight was taken to satisfy the American people?" Reid countered.

"No, I did not!" Eberle snapped. "I told you what the flight was undertaken for." It was to train the crew in operating over land. "And, incidentally, we like to fly over as many places as possible to let the people see it."

Eberle was lying. The *Shenandoah*'s final flight was a publicity trip, first and foremost. Eberle knew it and so did his top officers. The navy was obsessed with having the airship pass over as many state fairs as it could. Yes, the crew would be trained in flying over land, but that mission ran a distant second in priority compared to showing off the dirigible.

"From the lessons you learned on this flight of the *Shenandoah* over these cities," Reid asked pointedly, "would you order that again next year under the same conditions for training of the personnel?"

"I don't think that is a question I could answer," the admiral said.

"Captain Lansdowne would be alive today if he had not gone on the trip . . . under your direction?" Reid asked.

"I do not care to answer any such question," Eberle said dismissively.

The jury sympathized with the admiral. The navy had as much right to generate publicity as the army, the generals believed, and Americans had a right to see the *Shenandoah* in flight.

Betty had taken the train to Detroit on Thursday to fetch baby Lucy and bring her back to Washington. Mitchell ached at not being able to see his daughter, and there was no reason for Betty to sit through these few days of the trial, particularly with the prosecution laying out its unpleasant rebuttal.

Betty returned with Lucy on Monday morning. Mitchell proudly cuddled his daughter before photographers. He needed the lift. The media coverage had begun to turn slightly against him. Most of it was still biased in his favor, but there were more passages in news stories and more lines in headlines acknowledging that he had erred in some instances. The Morrow report had demonstrated that Mitchell and the other airmen had "magnified their grievances into a national danger," noted the *New Republic* magazine, but "there is no national danger." Fortunately for Mitchell the trial coverage had moved to the inside pages of most newspapers. The flying colonel's charges had always been the big story. The prosecution's rebuttal would never be able to match it.

But the prosecutors were determined to continue their siege, even if the press paid no attention.

23 "Lawless"

10:00 A.M., TUESDAY, DECEMBER 8, 1925

While Gullion delivered the navy's attack on Mitchell, the other prosecutors were preparing the army's offensive. It looked more like total war. Moreland, Wilby, and five assistants had spent practically every minute court had not been in session during the previous two weeks taking statements from potential witnesses. They had pared down their list for the army, but it was still staggering. Moreland and Wilby wanted to call more than forty officers to the stand to defend their service.

When the generals hearing the case got wind of that number, they were aghast. The Mitchell trial had been relegated to the back pages, but it was still news and it could easily become hot news again. Washington's winter political season had just begun. Congress had reconvened the previous day and lawmakers were bitterly divided over how to deal with the country's aviation problems. Returning representatives and senators told the *Wall Street Journal* they'd had an earful from constituents on two subjects during the recess: Mitchell and tax cuts. Former airmen like Rickenbacker continued to fan the flames. Taunting the court-martial, the Ace of Aces told the Executives Club in Chicago he hoped the flying colonel "is found guilty because of the public wrath it will arouse and the storm of disapproval that will result. Mitchell will be a sacrifice, but a willing one, to the future of aerial transportation." The jury was becoming fed up with the marathon trial. The generals began demanding that Moreland and his assistants condense the testimony of witnesses.

There was another practical reason for speeding up the trial. It

was becoming expensive for the army. The people who came from
out of town had to be paid five cents a mile for their travel costs, in
addition to the $1.50 a day they got as a witness fee. The court ste-
nographer billed at $5.00 a day, plus another fifty cents for each
hour he actually sat in court taking notes. Transcribing those notes
cost twenty cents for every one hundred words, and the trial transcript already numbered 2,776 pages. Since the trial began, the
Quartermaster Corps had delivered to the Emery Building 174
blotters, two large boxes of paper clips, four pints of ink, 125
scratch pads, 324 pencils, eighteen erasers, two boxes of pens,
forty-eight cork-tipped penholders, 118 rolls of toilet paper, and
1,028 bars of soap, all of which cost $51.92. And people in the court
gulped down water; sixteen hundred pounds of ice had been consumed in the month of November alone, costing $3.36. Totaled up,
the trial was expected to cost more than twelve thousand dollars.
Army finance officers had already warned the prosecutors they had
better have receipts for everything. Congress was sure to investigate such a large expense.

Moreland had a half dozen officers testify on Tuesday. They
strongly defended the army's treatment of the air service, arguing
that any problems in aviation were the result of too little money
from Congress or poor management by the airmen themselves. The
most distinguished among the first six witnesses: Maj. Gen. Hanson Ely, the commander of the prestigious Army War College. A
hulking six-footer, Ely was a pugnacious leader never afraid to
speak his mind, who had spent most of his thirty-nine years in the
army commanding troops in the field. During the World War he
had been under fire 111 days, some of it the most intense fighting
any American officer saw. Ely was now considered the army's
authority on leadership and training.

He was also a hard-line conservative when it came to the air
service. Ely thought the aviators were a bunch of complainers and
Mitchell the biggest crybaby of them all. What the air service
needed, the general liked to tell anyone who would listen, was
about seventy infantry, cavalry, and artillery officers brought in to
teach these pilots something about discipline and loyalty. Likewise,
every new airman should be sent to ground units for at least two
years to learn how to be part of a team. Ely believed fervently in

unity of command, but to him it meant that squadrons followed the orders of the generals on the ground.

Moreland's team thought he would be one of their most impressive witnesses. The jurors revered Ely. The prosecutors had only one worry: Ely's son had been washed out of the air service during training because his instructors considered him unfit to be a pilot. The defense might accuse the general of holding a grudge against the airmen. But Reid either didn't know about Ely's son or, if he did, considered it unimportant because he never raised the subject.

Ely told the jury that the army's nonfliers were not as ignorant of aviation as Mitchell made them out to be. Young combat officers attending the infantry school at Fort Benning, Georgia, received instruction on what airplanes could do for them in the field. At the army's advanced school at Fort Leavenworth, students spent more time learning about aviation than any other subject besides the infantry. The War College also had a faculty member teaching aviation.

"Based on your long experience, general," Moreland asked as if he were consulting an oracle, ". . . what is your opinion as to whether a separate air force would or would not benefit national defense?"

"I am opposed to a separate air force," Ely said firmly. "It is with me more than a theory. I am convinced it is a fact indisputable that it would take away from the power of the commander of the whole the very important element that he needs to accomplish the best results."

Moreland, who had not questioned a witness in weeks, seemed energized. "Is there, in your opinion, any difference in the principles of leadership in the air service as distinguished from other arms of the service?" he asked the veteran general.

"No," Ely answered, as if stating the obvious. "Leadership in command is the same in all services." There was nothing special about the air service.

"Have you ever heard, general, of the doctrine with reference to command that mob psychology is the principle upon which the infantry fights?" Moreland asked. Mitchell liked to spout that theory in his writings. Ground soldiers had to be herded into battle, while the airman was a lone sky warrior fighting on his own initiative. It won him no friends among infantrymen.

Ely didn't think much of the idea either. Airmen did operate independently, but "the same is true today with the infantryman," he argued. No one massed troops anymore for grand charges. The infantryman must have the will to fight on his own. "The discipline has got to be instilled beforehand."

"So, I understand the result of your opinion is that the same purposes that underlie an efficient infantryman underlies an efficient air service?" Moreland asked.

"Undoubtedly," Ely said. There was nothing wrong with the army commanding the air service. In fact it made good sense.

Reid began his cross-examination by asking, "Are you friendly with the air service?" He didn't think the general was.

"Yes, very," Ely maintained.

"Do you think they are very important in the scheme of national defense?"

"Extremely so."

"Do you realize the importance of flying officers?"

"I certainly do."

Ely seemed downright chummy, so Reid tried to push further. Didn't the pilot always perform his mission well in battle? he asked.

Most of the time, Ely hedged, seeing where Reid was leading him. "The difficulty I found with [them] is that they are a little too independent of the commander," he said.

Reid quoted from a statement Ely had made before the Morrow board that a ground commander did not have to be a flier in order to send a pilot on a mission any more than a man had to be "a chauffeur in order to send an automobile anywhere." Did Ely consider an aviator nothing more than a chauffeur? Reid asked.

"That is a general statement," Ely protested.

"That is your general idea?"

"No, I have not said that—"

"Do you believe that," Reid asked, interrupting him.

"Wait a minute, I am talking!" Ely snapped. "I do not intend to infer at all that an aviator is merely a chauffeur."

"You think they are absolutely necessary to military defense?" Reid asked.

"I would not use it quite that way," Ely answered, "but practically, yes. They are very necessary." But he did not believe that "the air service alone can win a war."

Reid read Ely another statement, which had been made by someone else: "The development of aircraft indicates that our national defense must be supplemented, if not dominated, by aviation." Ely agreed with the first part, that the national defense must be supplemented by aviation.

"Do you believe that the development of aircraft indicates that our national defense must be dominated by aviation?" Reid asked.

"No," Ely answered.

"You think that is absolutely absurd?"

"Yes."

"That is the statement of President Coolidge," Reid revealed with a smile.

"I do not care [whose] it is," Ely said huffily.

2:00 P.M., WEDNESDAY, DECEMBER 9, 1925

The enemies Mitchell made during the World War were not just among Pershing's senior officers. Some of the pilots who served under him resented his high-handed manner and his demanding leadership. Howard Rath was one of them. The prosecutors were delighted when they found the airman. Not only was Rath willing to trash Mitchell, he also gave them the names of comrades who also had beefs with the air commander.

Rath took the stand to cast doubt on Mitchell's leadership in combat, which up to this point no one had questioned. An investment banker in Los Angeles, Rath still held the rank of captain in the air service reserve. During the war he had been a bomber pilot and had received the Distinguished Service Cross for leading three of his planes through a formation of fifteen German fighters in order to attack enemy targets during the battle of Saint-Mihiel. It was during that offensive that Rath parted company with Mitchell.

"What weather conditions are necessary for successful bombing?" Wilby asked him.

"Clear weather, clear visibility," Rath answered, ". . . with very few clouds, if any."

"What was your experience if you were sent out in bad weather with clouds?" Wilby asked.

"It was very disastrous," Rath said.

Mitchell could see where the questions were going. His back stiffened, and he leaned forward in his chair.

"Can you state to the court your experiences under bad weather conditions?" Wilby continued.

"At Saint-Mihiel the attack opened up with very bad weather—cloudy, rainy and windy," Rath said in a quiet voice. "It was practically impossible flying conditions some days. . . . Nevertheless we got orders to go out on those days."

Mitchell indeed had given the orders to fly. The whole point of his air campaign during Saint-Mihiel was to strike the enemy first with overwhelming force, and he had pushed his pilots hard to get into the air despite miserable weather. But Rath now complained that half of his squadron's bombing missions had to be scrubbed, and many of the ones that were launched should never have been sent. Rath claimed that the British, the French, and even the Germans thought it foolish to fly bombers in that bad weather, and they never did. But Mitchell insisted that his pilots take to the air.

The results, Rath testified, were horrible. Missions failed, and pilots were needlessly killed. On the first day of the offensive, one of the squadron's bombers was shot down. On the next attempt to launch that day, nine bombers got aloft but never reached their targets. His squadron commander protested making a third attempt in the evening, but Mitchell, who was at the field, countermanded him.

"He said, 'Yes, you can make it. They should go,'" Rath recalled.

Five bombers eventually managed to take off from the muddy field, but the sun was setting and the aviators were not trained for night flying. "It was pitch dark when they came back, and they didn't have any proper illumination for the field," Rath testified. "They all came back, but they all crashed. One pilot ran into the ground with his engines on and was killed."

Mitchell was seething. He gripped the defense table as if it would keep him from launching himself at Rath. At times he leaned over to Reid, angrily whispering into his ear. Other times he turned around to the reporters sitting just behind him and in a low hoarse voice uttered insults about Rath. Betty nervously patted his shoulder, trying to calm him down.

Rath refused to be intimidated. The weather was just as bad for the beginning of the Argonne offensive, he testified, but Mitchell continued to send men on death missions.

"What effect did the antiaircraft fire have on your bombing operations?" Wilby asked.

"It had three effects," said Rath, who had far more respect for antiaircraft gunners than did Rickenbacker. "It injured or killed personnel, it confused the formation or prevented the formation [flying] through the barrage and smoke . . . and indirectly it was one of the biggest menaces we had."

"Was it only the bombers who felt this way about antiaircraft [fire]?" Wilby asked.

"No, sir," Rath answered forcefully. The pilots in the faster-moving pursuit planes feared it as well. "Captain Rickenbacker speaks about it in his book," Rath said, holding up a copy.

Wilby had Rath read a dozen passages from Rickenbacker's *Fighting the Flying Circus,* which acknowledged the dangers of "Archy," the pilots' nickname for antiaircraft fire.

"You may cross-examine," Wilby told Reid after Rath had finished.

Mitchell had been able to ignore, even laugh off, most of the barbs thrown at him during the trial. But to have one of his airmen accuse him of incompetent and reckless leadership in combat enraged him. It was the ultimate betrayal, as far as he was concerned. Reid was just as angry, which was a mistake. As Mitchell's attorney, he needed to keep his cool.

"You say you got a Distinguished Service Medal?" Reid asked, almost contemptuously.

"Yes, sir," Rath said calmly.

"What for?" Reid asked, as if he didn't believe it.

"A Distinguished Service Cross," Howze interrupted Reid. A Distinguished Service Cross was an award for heroism in battle, much more important than a Distinguished Service Medal. The president of the court was not impressed that the representative didn't know the difference.

"What for?" Reid, unfazed, asked again.

"I don't like to answer that question," Rath said modestly.

"Do you know what you got it for?" Reid asked, sounding annoyed.

"I know what it was given to me for," Rath said.

"Tell the court," Reid commanded, as if Rath was having to admit a sin.

Rath read his citation for the bombing raid he had led.

"Did any enemy antiaircraft fire ever keep you from carrying out your mission?" Reid asked.

"Yes, sir," Rath said.

"Now, tell the court the number of times that you were kept from your mission in your airplane on account of being afraid of antiaircraft gunfire?" Reid asked, as Mitchell began bending back and forth in his chair with nervous energy.

"I didn't say I was afraid, sir," Rath responded angrily.

"You are not afraid?" Reid challenged. "You are never afraid of antiaircraft gunfire?"

"Well, I think any soldier may be—"

"No, are you?" Reid interrupted, shouting. "Were you ever afraid of antiaircraft gunfire?"

Wilby jumped out of his chair. "I don't think he has a right to charge him with being afraid until he has got some foundation for it," Wilby said angrily.

"I think his direct testimony makes me believe that he was very much afraid," Reid retorted.

Groans could be heard in the audience. Then hisses. For the first time in the trial, the crowd was angry at the defense.

"Has he a right to charge him with being afraid?" an outraged Wilby asked Winship.

"He is not charging him with being afraid," Winship explained, trying to remain neutral. "He is asking him if he was afraid of enemy gunfire. I think that is proper cross-examination."

"No, I am not afraid of enemy gunfire," Rath spoke up loudly and angrily, interrupting everyone.

"Were you during the war?" Reid continued to press. He was determined to portray Rath's complaints as those of a coward.

"No, sir."

"Did it keep you from doing anything you otherwise would have done if it had not been there?"

"No, sir, not as far as being afraid is concerned."

"Well, what kept you from doing it?"

"You perhaps don't understand about bombing raids," Rath tried to explain. Reid, in fact, did not understand. He had never spent a day of his life under fire. "If you have got a smoke cloud underneath you just at the instant you have got to pull your bombs, you can't see to pull, can you?"

* "Oh," Reid interrupted. "Now you claim that you are only afraid of antiaircraft gunfire."

"I am not afraid of antiaircraft gunfire," Rath repeated, frustrated.

"Then it never interfered with you?"

"It did interfere, but not because I or anybody else was afraid!"

General King couldn't stand any more of this. He didn't care if he'd be dressed down again for speaking out of turn. He wasn't going to let a U.S. representative humiliate a brave soldier. "I would like to ask the president of the court . . . to inform defense counsel that a man may do things even if he is afraid!" he shouted, almost sputtering with rage. "I certainly object to the insinuation, as I get it, that this witness was a coward. I don't think his testimony shows it!"

The audience began clapping and cheering loudly for Rath. Their hostility stunned Reid and Mitchell. Howze banged his gavel and shouted over the noise for the courtroom guards to move in and quiet the rowdy ones.

Realizing that his questions had seriously backfired, Reid protested that he agreed with King that a man can fight even if he is afraid. But King wasn't finished. "Any soldier who says he is not afraid is saying something that I personally think he is mistaken about," the general continued emotionally. "Many men do things when they are afraid, but they do their duty in spite of the physical fear."

Graves, who sat next to King, put his arm around his fellow general's shoulder and squeezed it.

Winship intervened to explain again that the defense attorney had every right to cross-examine Rath this way. "I think that this witness is taking very good care of himself," the law member said.

Reid tried to recover with a different set of questions. Rath was forced to admit that military leaders often had to ask their men to do the impossible in battle. Reid also pointed out that Pershing wanted the planes in the air as much as Mitchell did. The pilot also did not grasp the bigger picture; his squadron may have fared poorly, but overall Mitchell had scored a resounding victory in the air. Reid, however, had touched a raw nerve among the combat veterans on the jury.

It was finally time for the chief of the army air service to take the stand. Mason Patrick could not have been put in a more difficult spot. A majority of his pilots sided with Mitchell. Many of them had been openly helping the air colonel with his defense, doing it against Patrick's wishes. Patrick had an organization to run and to hold together. He could not do that without the loyalty of his airmen. He had become as committed a proponent of airpower as Mitchell, albeit with far more finesse and diplomacy. But he was now testifying for the prosecution. Patrick was also just as loyal to his superiors in the army. And Mitchell had become an unmitigated pain.

The prosecutors were nervous about Patrick. They weren't blind to his divided loyalties. Four days earlier Wilby had sat down with the air chief to rehearse his testimony. Patrick was cooperative, willing to help the prosecutors with questions they should ask him. He agreed that some of Mitchell's charges—for example, that airmen were being used merely as pawns—were "perfectly foolish." Wilby tried his best to coach the general on the type of answers that would be the most helpful. But Patrick supported many of Mitchell's proposals, such as eventually establishing an independent air force, and he let Wilby know that he didn't intend to back away from those positions on the stand. They would have to avoid some subjects.

The low-key Moreland decided to question him. Who selects the planes the air service will fly? the judge advocate began.

"I have selected them and the entire responsibility for the equipment in the air service is mine," Patrick said, explaining that he depended heavily on a team of aviators to advise him in making those decisions. And he had consulted closely with Mitchell when he was his deputy.

"Of what type of plane have you the greatest number at the present time?" Moreland asked.

"I think we have more of the DH type than of any other one type," Patrick answered. DH was the acronym the airmen used for the De Havilland, which were all built during the war.

How have the De Havillands been rebuilt "since their original construction?" Moreland asked.

"Every DH plane which has been put in service has been carefully examined and has been repaired, reconditioned or entirely rebuilt before they have been flown," Patrick testified.

"Do you consider the DH plane inherently dangerous?" Moreland asked. Mitchell did.

"No airplane is absolutely safe," Patrick said. But "with that understanding, I do not consider the DH plane as inherently unsafe." A harmful answer for Mitchell.

"General, have you ever heard the DH planes referred to as 'flaming coffins?'" Moreland asked.

"Yes," Patrick said. But it was an old wives' tale among airmen. The De Havillands "have no greater tendency to burn than other types of planes."

"Are pilots forced or permitted to fly in planes that are known to be dangerous?" Moreland asked.

"Not with my knowledge," Patrick said emphatically.

This was no help to Mitchell. But Patrick did acknowledge there was "a decided shortage" in fighter planes and bombers. He blamed it, however, on tight budgets rather than willful neglect by the army.

Were the air service bombers "fully equipped?" Moreland asked.

"They are not," Patrick answered.

"Why not?"

"It is not customary anywhere, I think, to have military planes, all of them fully equipped in time of peace."

Moreland tried to dance around topics on which he knew Patrick and Mitchell shared the same view, but he wasn't entirely successful. Patrick was able to tell the jury that he agreed with Mitchell that towing the targets the previous summer for the antiaircraft batteries "did interfere decidedly" with the training of bomber pilots, although he was more diplomatic about it than Mitchell. He did not dismiss out of hand the value of antiaircraft defenses.

Reid stood up and gently tried to nudge Patrick into admitting other things that he and Mitchell were in accord on. "Has the United States any real air force at the present time?" he asked the general.

"Yes," Patrick said.

"What is it?" Reid asked.

"A very small one," Patrick answered—no more than twenty pursuit planes that could be called modern, plus another twenty bombers, and all of them were "obsolescent." It was just what Reid wanted the jury to hear.

"Have you any real air policy, military or commercial, in this country?" Reid asked.

"It is very difficult to say whether there is any—military or commercial," Patrick answered candidly. He had tried to establish such a policy but hadn't made much headway with the powers that be. Another Mitchell point.

Was it possible to build better-performing planes now than during the World War? Reid asked.

"It certainly is," Patrick said.

Does a war-built plane remodeled in 1925 remain "aerodynamically a 1917 plane?" Reid asked.

"Practically so, yes," Patrick agreed.

"The remodeled war planes used at the present time are substitutes for modern equipment, are they not?" Reid asked.

"I should not put it that way," Patrick said. He didn't completely agree with Mitchell on this point. "I should say we are using the rebuilt war planes instead of more modern types for reasons which seem to me good." The arithmetic was simple, Patrick explained. It cost less than two thousand dollars to remodel a war-vintage De Havilland compared with as much as sixteen thousand dollars for a brand-new plane. With tight budgets it was far wiser to rebuild the old De Havillands, so pilots would have at least something to fly, while better planes were being developed. That's what Patrick had done the last four years, and none of his advisers, including Mitchell, had questioned the policy.

"All right, general, I will ask you this question," Reid said. He felt as if he were pulling teeth. "Rebuilt wartime planes do not fully meet the requirements of a sound, modern air service, do they?"

"No, they do not," Patrick conceded. He and Mitchell both agreed the De Havillands "should be done away with just as soon as possible."

Reid then blundered by raising the subject of the Pulitzer races. Patrick, who was still steamed at Mitchell for insinuating that he conspired with the navy to fix the competition, set the record straight. He and Roosevelt, the navy's assistant secretary, had agreed to divide up the racers, not the races. The correspondence may have said "races" at one point but it was "a typographical error," Patrick said.

"If you will let me interject," Patrick interrupted his own story. As long as he had the floor, there was something else he wanted to get off his chest—about this tale Mitchell was peddling that he had made more than a hundred recommendations as assistant air chief, most of which were ignored. "General Mitchell made a great many recommendations," Patrick testified. "I took them all into consideration. Many were very fine and very good." Others may have ignored his deputy's suggestions, but Patrick said he didn't. He recalled "74 specific recommendations" that Mitchell had made. "I practically approved and put into force 59. There were fifteen I did not think I could, and therefore I took no action on them."

Reid quickly shifted to friendlier territory. Patrick agreed with Mitchell that the meteorological information provided to pilots was "far from satisfactory."

Has the War Department "ever interfered with you in the performance of your duties?" Reid asked.

"No," Patrick answered.

"Have they helped you as much as they should?" Reid asked.

"I object to that," Moreland said quickly. He knew what Patrick's answer would be, and he didn't want the jury hearing it.

"The objection is not sustained," Winship ruled.

"I do not think I have received as much assistance from the War Department as it could have given, and as I should have liked to have," Patrick said, choosing his words carefully.

"That is all," Reid said. At least Patrick's last answer was one the defense wanted to hear.

But it troubled Howze. "Has your treatment from the War Department differed markedly from that accorded any other chief of a . . . branch?" the president of the court asked.

"I think not," Patrick said thoughtfully.

"Explain wherein the War Department has not helped you as much as they should?" Howze asked.

"I said the War Department has not helped me as much as I desired," Patrick clarified. "I think there has been a lack of understanding on the part of the War Department of the air service problems."

Patrick had carefully walked a tightrope with his testimony. Neither side got everything it wanted from him. The general had slapped down his former deputy on many points. But the *Washington Star*'s headline concluded, PATRICK UPHOLDS MITCHELL IN PART, which was the charitable view of most reporters. Wilby thought the air chief had done more damage to the prosecution's case than to Mitchell's, so he began plotting how other witnesses might repair it with their testimony. Dennis Nolan, the army's deputy chief of staff, was pleased, however. He sat down later in the evening and wrote a note to his boss, General Hines. The chief of staff of the army was on a golfing vacation in St. Augustine, Florida. Hines saw no need to return to Washington. The prosecutors now had the case well in hand.

Nolan agreed. Patrick did fine on the stand, the deputy believed. "I think I can say that the accused is having a bad week so far," Nolan wrote Hines, "and I am sure you will be glad to know that."

3:10 P.M., FRIDAY, DECEMBER 11, 1925

Gen. Frank Coe had just been excused from the witness chair when a commotion erupted in the back of the courtroom. Will Rogers had slipped in and slumped into one of the seats there, hoping no one would notice him.

That would never happen. The humorist was one of the biggest celebrities in the United States. The nation's powerful fell over themselves to stay on his good side. A comic dart from this homespun entertainer could make or break a politician. His satirical column appeared in more than 350 newspapers. Ever since Mitchell took him up for his first plane ride the previous spring, Rogers had been poking fun at the War Department.

Spectators began pushing up from their seats and leaning over to get a peek at him. Mitchell soon twisted around in his chair to see what the hubbub was about and spotted Rogers. He smiled and winked; Rogers winked back. At the same time, Howze saw who he had in his courtroom. He quickly declared a recess and motioned the famous man to come forward.

"Now I know they are going to hang me," Rogers mumbled good-naturedly to the spectators around him, and they began laughing. One of the guards escorted him up to the front, and the members of the audience applauded as if they were in a theater. Howze may have spent most of his time in the field, but he knew a good photo op when he saw one. So did the other generals. They all crowded around Rogers and took him back into their anteroom for a private chat, Howze arm in arm with the star as they walked out.

When the beaming generals returned, Rogers was placed in a seat up front with the lawyers so he could have a better view of the proceedings.

The prosecutors would have gladly had Will Rogers's appearance be the lead story in the newspapers instead of the one they got. Frank Coe, the general who had just left the stand, ended up being a disaster for them.

As the army's chief of coast artillery, Coe was such a widely recognized expert on antiaircraft defenses that Reid told Wilby he needn't bother having the general recite his credentials. Coe, who had drawn up the plans for the antiaircraft tests at Fort Tilden and the searchlight tests at Camp Dix the previous summer, started out a stellar witness for the prosecution. He shredded many of the complaints the airmen had about the exercises. The antiaircraft batteries at Fort Tilden, Coe testified, performed much better than the pilots gave them credit for. The searchlights at Camp Dix even picked up some of the aircraft gliding in; the umpires said they hadn't, but that was only because the observers were standing at the wrong spot to see them, Coe's artillery officers claimed.

Reid was getting nowhere cross-examining Coe until the end, when he asked the general about congressional testimony Hugh Drum had given. Drum had boasted in a hearing that with just a dozen antiaircraft guns he could keep any bomber from "doing serious destruction" to a target. Mitchell had raised this as an example of Drum misleading Congress. But Coe cautioned that Drum's offhand remark was so vague it "did not mean anything." One bomber might be kept at bay with twelve antiaircraft guns, but certainly not a formation of bombers, Coe said.

So no matter how fast the bombers "could go or what they

could carry, your twelve guns could protect the city of Washington?" Reid asked.

"I never said anything about the protection of the city of Washington," Coe said, surprised, because he hadn't.

"You did not say anything about it at all?" Reid asked and began looking for a hearing transcript on the defense table. He thought he recalled someone making such a statement.

"No, sir," Coe said emphatically as Reid continued to root around the papers on the table. "I will go farther and state that ten thousand antiaircraft guns cannot protect the city of Washington."

Reid looked up as if a voice from heaven had delivered a divine revelation.

"That is all," he said with a broad smile and sat down. He was not going to spoil this golden moment with another question.

The next day a front-page headline in the *Washington Post* screamed: CITY DEFENSELESS AGAINST BOMBERS, GEN. COE DECLARES. The *New York Times* proclaimed: MITCHELL SCORES ON GROUND DEFENSE: GEN. COE TESTIFIES THAT 10,000 ANTI-AIRCRAFT GUNS COULD NOT PROTECT THE CAPITAL.

The prosecution was thunderstruck. With one sentence Coe had wiped out the entire day for them—and nearly panicked the capital's residents at the same time. A mystified Nolan wrote Hines another letter. "I have not yet found a satisfactory explanation of General Coe's testimony," he told his boss. War Department officers raced all over town to track down Coe after he left the Emery Building and find out if he really meant to say what he had said. Wilby hauled him back to the stand the next week, but by then the general had his back up and refused to recant his testimony. The only thing a frustrated Wilby could do was try to impeach his own witness, which made the prosecution look silly.

SATURDAY EVENING, DECEMBER 12, 1925

Washington was getting into the Christmas mood early this year. Cabbies seemed more polite at intersections, laying off their horns and allowing pedestrians to pass. Despite the court-martial and dreary news out of Congress, people seemed happier on the streets. Shoppers jammed downtown stores to scoop up holiday specials. The Young Men's Shop on F Street had imported English broadcloth shirts for $1.95, Homer L. Kitt Company on G Street offered baby grand pianos for $485, and the new Studebaker Country Club Coupe was on sale in Georgetown for $1,295. President Coolidge had just signed an executive order giving federal workers the Saturday after Christmas off so they would have a three-day holiday. He warned them, however, not to expect him to do this every year.

Betty headed for a night out with the girls to see *What Price Glory?* at Poli's Theater. Maxwell Anderson's antiwar play about the Great War had just come to Washington after a triumphal run on Broadway. The court had recessed early, and Mitchell had spent the afternoon at a second sitting for a British artist drawing a charcoal portrait of him. Betty and Blackie thought it a good likeness. Afterward he suited up in his dress uniform for the annual Gridiron Club dinner, a tribal ritual in Washington at which reporters skewer the city's powerful with jokes and comedy skits.

Four hundred and twenty men gathered in the banquet hall of the Willard. Coolidge and most of his cabinet sat at the head table along with celebrities like Orville Wright, composer Irving Berlin, and Prince Bismarck, grandson of the former German chancellor. Mitchell was at the head table as well. He sat next to Coolidge's top aide, Everett Sanders. Several seats down were other military stars like John Rodgers, the Hawaiian flight commander, and Richard Byrd, the Arctic explorer.

Jokes were made about Coolidge and such presidential aspirants as Nicholas Longworth, the new Speaker of the House. One club member gave a hilarious impersonation of Vice President Charles Dawes as an anguished Macbeth, hamstrung by his do-nothing job. Curtis Wilbur, the navy secretary, sat uncomfortably as one skit lampooned him over Mitchell's charge that officers were muzzled. Reporters dressed up in sailor suits sang:

And now Wilbur's bedtime stories
Are the anthem of the sea.
But the sailor men are silent.
For they don't like Guam, you see.

But if you like bedtime stories,
Then you'll sleep safe and sound every night.
For no doubt you read
Mister Wilbur said.
That the navy is all right.
Pos-i-tively!

As waiters served dinner, a mock world court of judges in black robes convened to decide Mitchell's case. He was charged with violating the Ninety-sixth Article of War for "parking overtime in the newspapers." Mitchell and the other men in the hall roared with laughter. Everyone knew he was one of the biggest press hogs in town. If Coolidge stood up and said anything funny during the evening, or said anything at all, no reporter wrote it down. He usually consumed his meals in silence then spent the rest of the evening grimacing because of chronic indigestion. Asked once why he went to so many of these banquets, the president answered curtly, "Gotta eat somewhere."

11:00 A.M., TUESDAY, DECEMBER 15, 1925

For the last week of the trial the prosecution brought in some of the army's top generals to finish off Mitchell. On Monday, Summerall took the stand to settle scores. The Hawaiian Department had war plans when he commanded it, Summerall told the jury, and he had been aggressively improving the island's defenses. When Mitchell conducted his 1923 inspection he never once sat down with Summerall to discuss those defense plans, the general complained. Summerall also vigorously defended his oversight of the antiaircraft tests at Fort Tilden and Camp Dix, producing a stack of paperwork to show that he had not ignored the pilots' safety concerns, as some of Mitchell's witnesses charged. Reid grilled Summerall for more than an hour, but it ended up a draw. The representative finally decided to question whether the general's testimony was tainted—which he certainly had a right to do.

"Did you make this statement, 'From now on, Mitchell and I are enemies,' after you were challenged as president of this court?" Reid asked.

"I have no recollection of ever having made that statement, and I am quite sure I have never made that statement," Summerall answered. The press table's reporters, who believed the quote was accurate, looked up suspiciously.

"Were you not interviewed by certain newspaper reporters after being removed as president of this court on the 28th of October, 1925?" Reid asked, trying to pin him down.

"I had some conversation in one of the offices of the War Department and some newspaper reporters were present," Summerall conceded.

"Now I ask you again," Reid said, in the voice he reserved for witnesses who were lying. "Did you ever make this statement to anybody: 'From now on Mitchell and I are enemies?'"

"I do not recall making that statement."

"Are you now friendly with the accused?"

"I am indifferent towards the accused," Summerall said, his face expressionless.

On Tuesday it was finally Hugh Drum's turn, and the brigadier general could not wait to take his best shot at the defendant. Drum hated Mitchell. It was ironic, because the two men's career paths were somewhat similar. They were the same age. Drum had been born into an army family, his father a Civil War veteran who had died at San Juan Hill during the Spanish-American War.

Like Mitchell, Drum had dropped out of college and had taken an army commission two days after his nineteenth birthday. He had won a Silver Star for gallantry in the Philippines but afterward had made his name in the army as a brilliant staff officer. Drum had sailed with Pershing to Europe, and by the end of the war he was the First Army's chief of staff, drawing up the attack plans for the Saint-Mihiel and Argonne offensives. Mitchell considered him a paper pusher, not a true fighter, but the World War had propelled both men up the promotion ladder. Drum had arrived in Europe a captain and, like Mitchell, left as a brigadier general.

Drum was also as egotistical and nakedly ambitious as

Mitchell, perhaps even more so. He was outraged and bitter when he had been forced to revert to his peacetime rank of major after the Armistice, while other officers like Mitchell got to keep their generalships immediately after the war. Drum spent the next three years maneuvering and clawing to retrieve his star. He watched the promotion lists like a hawk for anyone who jumped ahead of him and carefully cultivated powerful men such as Hines and Morrow who might help him advance. Even Drum's wife lobbied fiercely for her husband. "Poor little Drummie has had so much of bitter disappointments and is so crushed by it all," she wrote Pershing when Drum thought he wasn't returning to brigadier general fast enough. "His nerves are at the breaking point."

Drum now believed he deserved a second star. He had loyally carried the War Department's water the past year. He had willingly been the point man for the army's opposition to a separate air force. He had worked aggressively behind the scenes to make sure the Morrow board produced a report the service could live with. He had managed the general staff's operation to destroy Billy Mitchell at his court-martial. Drum would make sure he got his just reward after this trial.

And he did not intend to have his future tripped up by the scurrilous charges Mitchell had tossed out at the court-martial that he had lied to Congress in testimony. Meticulous and always well prepared, Drum had aides compile a mountain of memos for him on his past testimony to demonstrate that he had been accurate. Then, over the weekend, he sat down with the prosecutors for a careful dress rehearsal of what he would say. Drum settled into the witness chair midmorning on Tuesday, armed with so many documents that a War Department officer was sent over to help McMullen keep track of them.

For more than three hours Drum carefully detailed his role as the general staff's point man on air policy. McMullen, Moreland's original assistant trial judge advocate, who had remained silent during most sessions, had been assigned to question Drum. But Drum already knew what he wanted to say, so McMullen's job was mainly to prompt him. Though he insisted that he was "in sympathy with aviation and its development," Drum explained to the jury he had been designated by the War Department to be its spokesman in opposition to a separate air force. All his statements before congressional committees had been reviewed by his bosses, "and they approved them," Drum claimed. He never acted as a free agent.

Who was "primarily responsible" for the principles, doctrines, and regulations that governed the army's relationship with its air service? McMullen asked. It was time to bring in the closest thing to God in the service.

"I know at the time these fundamental regulations were issued, that General Pershing was Chief of Staff of the Army," Drum answered. "Therefore, he must be responsible."

So were criticisms of the organization of the armed forces, like the ones Mitchell had voiced, "a direct attack on General Pershing?" McMullen asked, just as Drum wanted him to.

"Wait a minute!" Reid shouted. "I object."

Winship sustained the objection. It was up to the jury to decide if the airman had violated God's will.

Before defending his statements that Mitchell claimed were misleading, Drum trotted out examples where the flying colonel had played fast and loose with the facts—such as when he boasted to a congressional hearing that he had had indirect command over American antiaircraft units during the World War (he hadn't) and that Pershing had never given him "a single order as to what to do with the air forces" during the Argonne offensive (he had). As for Drum's own alleged misstatements, the general claimed that when he told Congress it would take more than nine million pounds of mustard gas and five thousand planes to clear out Washington, he hadn't pulled those numbers out of thin air. They were based on calculations taken from one of the Chemical Warfare Service's textbooks. Mitchell also had taken out of context what he had said about a dozen antiaircraft guns holding off bombers. He read the jury his entire testimony, insisting that he was talking about only one bomber moving at a slow speed and low altitude.

"Was this your personal opinion or a statement of fact?" McMullen asked about the antiaircraft testimony.

"My personal opinion," Drum answered, taking a page from Mitchell.

Reid stood up. Mitchell, who loathed Drum as much as Drum

loathed him, had been waiting for this day as well. Reid had in front of him more than seventy pointed questions typed out on legal paper that Mitchell had prepared for him. He spent the rest of Tuesday and Wednesday morning firing them at Drum.

"In all your statements before congressional committees, did you fully and fairly present every argument to show the full effect of the air force with relation to national defense?" Reid began.

"In my statements before the congressional committees, I expressed the viewpoint of the War Department," Drum said.

"Were you sent before those committees to oppose a separate or unified air service?" Reid asked.

"I was sent before the committees—"

"Can you answer that question yes or no?" Reid cut him off.

"I was sent before the committees to carry out the instructions of the Secretary of War," Drum continued, ignoring Reid. And War Department policy "was against the united air service."

"You tried to carry those [instructions] out faithfully, did you not?" Reid asked. Mitchell and his allies thought Drum had been too enthusiastic in following his orders.

"I did," Drum answered, making no apologies.

Reid tried to punch holes in Drum's explanations for his controversial congressional testimony—the general used the wrong chemical service tables to cook up his numbers for gassing Washington, the representative charged—but Drum refused to back down. As the cross-examination dragged into Wednesday morning, Reid became increasingly irritated that Drum kept answering each question with a long "dissertation" instead of a simple yes or no. Drum refused to be bullied and gave yet another windy explanation about his testimony on the dozen antiaircraft guns holding off a bomber.

What kind of experience did Drum have with bombers in the World War to make such a statement? Reid finally asked, fed up with the general's weasel-worded answers.

"Tell me what your war experience was!" Drum shouted defiantly, sticking his chin out and his Roman nose up. Drum had already had his aides look up Reid's draft record. He'd gotten a deferment because he was married with children.

"Sure, my war experience was just as much in my line as yours is in yours!" Reid shouted back. "I was not chief clerk of the General Staff, and I was not a handy boy either!"

The two men were about to come to blows. Spectators stood up, ready to roll up their sleeves. Graves interrupted and had Howze recess the court and clear everyone from the room before there was a brawl. When the trial resumed a few minutes later, Howze said he hoped "these proceedings will be continued with proper decorum." But when Reid asked what Drum's duties had been during the war, to see if he was qualified to speak about anti-aircraft defenses, Drum began reciting a week-by-week account of his jobs in France.

Reid could not get Drum to shut up. He had made a mistake by asking such an open-ended question, but he shouldn't have had to pay for it with Drum talking endlessly. Winship should have put a stop to the filibuster. A witness had a right to answer a question fully, even if it was an answer the lawyer didn't want to hear, but the cross-examiner also had a right not to be talked to death. But Winship did not halt Drum. The law member either was afraid to cut off the powerful general or he had decided to pay back Reid for all his posturing during the trial. Reid finally gave up. In view of Drum's "refusal to answer the questions I have propounded to him, I refuse to examine him further," the representative said angrily and sat down.

The prosecutors decided to cut back their witness list. They believed they had the case won. Moreland ended his side's rebuttal with Nolan, the army's deputy chief of staff who at the moment was the service's senior officer in Washington because Hines was on vacation. A former West Point football player who now looked owlish with his wire-rimmed glasses, Dennis Nolan was considered a military genius by his peers. During the war he had turned the army's amateurish intelligence division into a first-class collection operation against the Germans.

In the witness chair, Nolan pointed out that while Congress was shrinking the army, the generals had been increasing the manpower of the air service "at the expense of other branches." The aviators were a privileged lot, not downtrodden, he argued.

But Nolan had taken the stand for a more important purpose—to make public the private letter Weeks had sent to Coolidge the previous March explaining why he was firing Mitchell as assistant air chief. Nolan's aides passed out copies of the letter to reporters after he read aloud every word of it in court. "General Mitchell has not only attacked the Navy Department and the active officers in that Department, but his own Department and the officers who are largely responsible for its administrative policies," the former secretary of war had written. The army officers he criticized were the ones who had been victorious in Europe. It was "unconscionable," Weeks declared.

> General Mitchell's whole course has been so lawless, so contrary to the building up of an efficient organization, so lacking in reasonable team work, so indicative of a personal desire for publicity at the expense of everyone with whom he is associated that his actions render him unfit for a high administrative position such as he now occupies. I write this with great regret because he is a gallant officer with an excellent war record, but his record since the war has been such that he has forfeited the good opinion of those who are familiar with the facts and who desire to promote the best interests of national defense.

It was a deadly blow for Mitchell. John Weeks, who had been a popular war secretary, had accused Mitchell of being criminal in his behavior. Reid tried to prove that Weeks hadn't really written the letter, that Nolan and his conspirators on the general staff had, but it wasn't true. Weeks had been the author.

The jury of generals then let Nolan know how they felt.

"If there was any marked inefficiency in the War Department, would it come to your attention?" Howze asked.

"It would," Nolan said.

Among the officers of the War Department, "do you find any great amount of disloyalty?" Howze asked.

"No," Nolan answered. He could not believe the court was giving him this chance to twist the knife he'd just stuck into Mitchell. And he couldn't believe that Reid wasn't objecting. But there was not much Mitchell's attorney could do now to stop the president of the court.

"Is there prevailing in the War Department a negligence or inattention to duty?" Howze continued.

"There is not," Nolan answered. "It has not come to my attention."

"Do you find a patriotic devotion to duty" among the men of the War Department or are they "given to acts bordering on treasonable conduct or criminal negligence?" Howze asked.

"There is a great devotion to duty," Nolan said gravely. "I have noticed nothing that bordered on criminal negligence or treasonable conduct on the part of any officer of the War Department. I would add . . . that such an accusation is absolutely false and without foundation."

After Moreland announced that the prosecution was finished, Reid stood up and finally asked for a ruling from the court on whether the evidence he had introduced would be considered as absolute defense or only for mitigation in deciding a sentence. Reid had succeeded in stalling the decision for the entire trial. Now he wanted it. If the jury agreed with him that his evidence was for absolute defense, then he planned to call more witnesses to rebut the prosecution's rebuttal. The trial that never ends—the generals found it about as appealing as life in prison. But if the jury decided the evidence was good only for mitigation, "we are through," Reid told them. Any more witnesses "would be a waste of time."

The generals retired to their anteroom to mull the question in private. They returned shortly.

"The court decides that it will not give a decision on the question at this time and the case will proceed," Howze announced. He gave no reason. The jury would simply settle this legal issue along with everything else when it finally retired to reach a verdict. Reid and Mitchell took it as a clear signal that the generals had already decided the evidence would be considered only for mitigation, but they did not want to acknowledge that in public.

"In view of the refusal of the court to determine that question," Reid declared, "we have no further evidence."

On Thursday morning the lawyers would deliver their final arguments.

24 The Verdict

For the last day of the trial the courtroom was crowded with almost as many army and navy officers as it was with civilian spectators. They were all there to witness what they believed would be history. As far as War Department historians could determine, the Mitchell court-martial had been the longest ever in the U.S. Army for a senior officer. Forty-one witnesses had testified for the defense. The prosecution had called fifty-eight. Court had been in session for thirty-four days, over more than seven weeks.

Sidney Miller, Betty's father, had returned to Washington with her mother to be at their son-in-law's side for the last day. Betty looked gaunt and haggard, with dark shadows under her eyes, but she still smiled gaily when news photographers shot her. In private she was bitter and emotionally drained. The trial, Betty believed, was an army vendetta against her husband and was totally unwarranted and unfair.

"The court will come to order," Howze announced, rapping his gavel. "In advance of the arguments which are to be presented, the court desires to announce that it is its wish that there be no interruption on the part of opposing counsel during the argument." Reid grumped that he didn't think it was fair, but the jury was adamant. No more bickering lawyers.

Gullion stood up as if he was about to say something, but Mitchell jumped up as well to preempt him.

"May it please the court," Mitchell said loudly. "I desire at this time to make a statement to the court as provided for in the Manual for Courts-Martial."

"I should like to know under what paragraph [of the manual] that statement is to be made?" Gullion asked, a little taken aback.

"Shall I proceed?" Mitchell continued looking at Winship and not at Gullion. He could not stand the prosecutor.

Reid had prepared a final argument for the jury. So had White, who had planned to talk about discipline and truth as an absolute defense, and Judge Plain, who had written an even longer discourse on Mitchell's First Amendment rights. But the night before, Mitchell had decided he would deliver the closing statement instead of his lawyers. It was generally unwise for a defendant to do this. But Reid hadn't put up a fight. This was, after all, a political trial, and an excruciatingly long one. Legal arguments probably would add little at this point.

Winship warned Mitchell of his rights. He could speak for himself now "or you may have the defense counsel present your statement to the court for you," the law member said. "Do you understand these . . . rights?"

"I do," Mitchell said.

"And knowing these rights," Winship continued, "will you take time to consult with your counsel and then let the court know what you choose to do?"

"I have already decided what I desire to do," Mitchell answered firmly.

"Very well," Winship said quietly.

Mitchell looked down and picked up one sheet of legal paper. The defense team had made copies of it to pass out to reporters.

"May it please the court," he began in the staccato voice he used to lecture people. "My trial before this court-martial is the culmination of the efforts of the general staff of the army and the general board of the navy to deprecate the value of air power and keep it in an auxiliary position, which absolutely compromises our whole system of national defense. These efforts to keep down our air power were begun as soon as the sound of the cannon had ceased on the Western Front in 1919." When his bombers sank the *Ostfriesland* in 1921, their pilots had "proved to the world that airpower had revolutionized all schemes of national defense. . . . The truth of every statement which I have made has been proved by good and sufficient evidence before this court, not by men who gain their knowledge of aviation by staying on the ground and having their statements prepared by numerous staff to bolster up their predetermined ideas but by actual fliers who have gained their knowledge first-hand in war and in peace."

Mitchell insisted that his congressional statements had not been lies, as Weeks had portrayed them in his letter to Coolidge. "The evidence before this court bears out these facts in their entirety. . . . Secretary Weeks and indirectly the President were wrongly and untruthfully informed as to the condition of our aviation and our national defense by the persons furnishing the data on which his letter was based."

Mitchell wrapped it up. "This court has refrained from ruling whether the truth in this case constitutes an absolute defense or not. To proceed further with the case would serve no useful purpose. I have therefore directed my counsel to entirely close our part of the proceedings without argument."

Mitchell remained standing as the silent court took in what he had said. It was not a particularly forceful speech. Typical of Mitchell, it read as if only a fool would not accept his arguments. He sounded disdainful of the prosecution's case, which he shouldn't have been. Mitchell had proved many of his claims during the trial, but certainly not all of them. The statement may have been good propaganda for the press, which reprinted it in full, but it did not impress the jury.

Gullion stood up. "May I ask if the accused wants that to go in as a sworn or unsworn statement?" he said coyly, looking at Winship and not Mitchell. If the statement was a sworn one, under the court-martial rules, Gullion had a right to cross-examine him, which he would dearly have loved to do.

"That is an unsworn statement," Winship announced before Mitchell had a chance to answer. The law member wanted no more cross-examination.

Gullion, who was far and away the best orator on the prosecution team, arranged his papers to begin his side's closing statement. He also had copies of his speech ready to pass out to reporters.

"It is with diffidence that I now address you," Gullion began his argument to the generals fawningly. "Throughout this long and tedious trial your patient attention has been remarkable. The searching questions you have asked have revealed the incisiveness of your minds and demonstrated your thorough grasp of the evidence and its bearing on the issues presented—"

Moreland suddenly stood up. "I do not like to interrupt counsel," he said politely, "but I think, under the circumstances of the case, if the defense counsel does not desire to address the court, I do not believe we should take the time of the court in addressing it from the standpoint of the prosecution."

Gullion looked at Moreland as if his colleague had just taken off all his clothes in the room. Moreland's sense of propriety bordered on the incredible. Howze knew it was ridiculous for the prosecution to forgo its closing statement just because the defense attorneys had. "I think it is the sense of the court," Howze said looking to his left and right for nods of approval, "that the proceedings should go ahead in this case." Moreland sat down.

"As I was just saying," Gullion continued, ". . . never in the United States has there been a jury in a criminal case with the high intelligence and the appropriate experience which you possess. . . . You have been the Gamaliels at whose feet I have sat in acquiring what knowledge of my profession I now have." Likening the nine generals to the Jewish scholar who taught the Apostle Paul was a bit much, but Gullion wasn't finished spreading the butter. He had served with many of the men on the court, and "the careers of all of you are known in every club and barracks in the service, inspiring your juniors and forever forming part of the cherished records of our glorious army."

Mitchell's attorney had accused this of being a kangaroo court, but the generals should not fear that they might be voting against the will of the people if they returned a guilty verdict, Gullion argued. "Who are the people?" he asked rhetorically, looking at each juror. "Are you not the people? Does not the distinguished soldier who presides over this trial represent the people of Texas and the United States as truly as the Honorable Frank Reid represents the people of Illinois and the United States? Does not the courtly law member, whose decisions throughout this trial have been so eminently fair, represent the people of Georgia?" Didn't MacArthur, "the brilliant leader," represent Wisconsin? "Does not General McCoy, whose intellectual powers have shown so clearly in this trial, represent the people more fairly than any editor who would write an editorial?"

"The real will of the people is that justice be done," Gullion declared, his voice rising. Do not be swayed by the heat of the moment. "We the people are always, finally, right," but it often takes time. "Our sober second thought is always right. Our hysterical first impulses are, very often, wrong."

Gullion ticked off the witnesses Mitchell had summoned for his defense. He had nothing but scorn for them. "There is the opinionated, narrow-minded, hobby-riding, egomaniacal Adm. Sims type," he ridiculed. "The pseudo-expert type" like Lt. Orville Anderson, the army aviator who claimed the *Shenandoah* had been seriously weakened when a gale ripped it from its mooring mast; Maj. Gerald Brandt, "the gay, gallant, lovable type," who fell under Mitchell's "evil influence" and ridiculed the Hawaiian exercise. "There is the congressional expert," LaGuardia, "with fifteen or twenty hours in the air. He is beyond my powers of description. Thank heaven he is sui generis."

Mitchell's disciples were not trying to be dishonest on the stand with their "casualness to the facts," Gullion maintained. Mitchell had become a Svengali warping their minds "with his grandiose schemes." But "compare the defense witnesses with those of the prosecution and note the exactness of knowledge which the latter possess."

Gullion spent the next hour repeating point by point the highlights of the rebuttal evidence. His assignment had been to defend the sea service, whose officers Mitchell had maligned for flying the *Shenandoah* and trying to explore the Arctic or reach Hawaii by plane. "Do the vision, the courage and the hardship of these fundamental efforts mean nothing to him?" Gullion asked, outraged. "Does not the virile Robert Browning sing the value of 'each rebuff / That turns the earth's smoothness rough' and hold that 'not failure but low aim is crime' and that 'a man's reach should exceed his grasp else what's heaven for?'" (Guillon was guilty of some minor misquotes here, but he was making his point.) The navy "is a gallant service . . . this service of John Paul Jones, of Decatur, of Bainbridge, of Farragut, of Dewey, of Lansdowne. Do you think that this proud service would stoop to defend itself against such mouthings as filled the statement of September 5?"

Mitchell's words from San Antonio were not the product of "mature deliberation," Gullion railed, but rather a hysterical outburst.

> Rarely has a cause so confidently asserted been found in the acid test of a trial to be so absolutely groundless . . . Is such a man a safe guide? Is he a constructive person or is he a loose-talking imaginative megalomaniac, cheered by the adulation of his juniors, who see promotion under his banner, and intoxicated by the ephemeral applause of the people whose fancy he has for the moment caught?
>
> Is this man a Moses, fitted to lead the people out of a wilderness which is his own creation, only? Is he of the George Washington type, as counsel would have you believe? Is he not rather of the all too familiar charlatan and demagogue type—like Alcibiades, Catiline, and . . . Aaron Burr? He is a good flier, a fair rider, a good shot, flamboyant, self-advertising, wildly imaginative, destructive, never constructive except in wild non-feasible schemes, and never overly careful as to the ethics of his methods!

Gullion was back at Centre College winning a declamation prize. It was soaring oratory, full of historical and literary allusions. It was brilliant in organization, passionate in delivery. It also stretched the truth, which didn't bother Gullion. He was reflecting the blinding hatred many of the top officers in the army and navy had for the maverick airman. Mitchell sat stoically through most of it. Occasionally he smiled when the prosecutor got wound up.

Noon had arrived. Gullion's throat was dry, and his voice was becoming hoarse. But he had one more important point to make to the court: Mitchell's sentence. A reprimand or reduction in rank "would hardly be a punishment at all" for the crime the defendant had committed. A corporation or religious organization would not "tolerate such conduct as the accused's," Gullion argued. Neither should the military, whose survival depends on "loyalty and subordination." A lowly private "with only a sixth-grade education" would be splitting rocks in prison for such an offense. "How can this unrepentant accused with all his advantages of education and position be let off with less than dismissal?" Gullion asked loudly.

Mitchell had to be thrown out of the army. "Every trooper in Fort Huachuca as he smokes his cigarette with his bunkie after mess is talking about this case." Soldiers from Governors Island in New York to Schofield Barracks in Hawaii were waiting for the verdict. "If the accused is not dismissed," Gullion concluded, "the good trooper will be dismayed and the malcontent and sorehead will be encouraged in his own insubordination."

During the noon recess Mitchell and Betty went home for a quiet lunch with her parents. When the court reconvened at two o'clock, Moreland stood up and gave his summation for the next hour and a half, but he was only piling on. Gullion had already inflicted the damage.

At three-thirty Winship and the nine generals filed into the anteroom to begin their deliberations. The audience sat quiet for a moment, then a few spectators began talking in low voices. But not for long. Less than ten minutes after they had excused themselves, the door to the anteroom swung open and the generals returned to their seats in the courtroom.

"The court desires to know from the trial judge advocate whether he has any record of previous convictions of the case of Colonel Mitchell?" Howze asked the prosecutors.

Moreland stood up somewhat flustered and began to make a speech, but Howze cut him off. Just "answer directly," Howze demanded testily. Yes or no?

No, Moreland said.

The generals got up from their seats again and marched back into the anteroom, closing the door behind them.

Immediately spectators began talking in hushed and urgent tones. A slight bitter smile crept across Mitchell's face. He leaned over to tell his in-laws what this meant. The generals would not have come out and asked if he had any prior convictions unless they had already decided he was guilty. It certainly hadn't taken them long to reach a verdict. They must now be deciding his sentence.

Everyone waited. Slowly the hours crept by. Spectators, some of whom had sat through every day of court, stretched and milled around. Mitchell stayed with a clutch of family and friends in one corner, chatting pleasantly, sometimes laughing. Reid and the other defense lawyers mingled with the prosecutors. Reporters at the press tables leaned back in their chairs and read the papers. The Senate was debating whether the United States should be a member of the World Court. Rudolph Valentino announced from Paris that he and his second wife, designer Natacha Rambova, were divorcing. The U.S. attorney for New York complained in a speech that if Prohibition wasn't going to be strenuously enforced then the law should be repealed. A dispatch from Tokyo announced that Japanese troops had captured the capital of Manchuria.

After about an hour a Marine Corps major arrived with a subpoena for Mitchell to appear before the *Shenandoah* investigative board on Monday. The navy wasn't through with him yet. Mitchell, who had refused to speak before the board while his trial was in progress, told the major he would show up on Monday morning.

Around six o'clock Mitchell suggested that Sidney and Lucy Miller go back to their hotel. The jurors might remain sequestered late into the night, and he knew his in-laws were tired and hungry. They decided to leave, but Betty refused to go with her parents. She would stay with her husband until the jury returned.

At 6:35 P.M., everyone in the courtroom was jolted to attention from a loud thump they heard at the door of the jury room.

The door swung open, and the generals walked out, their uniforms rumpled from almost four hours of deliberation. Spectators rushed back to their seats and reporters flipped open notepads. The room grew deathly silent. A cloud of smoke hovered near the ceiling, from all the people who had been puffing cigarettes. It had grown darker, and the hanging lamps cast harsh shadows on the stained walls.

Howze took his usual seat in the center. MacArthur sat to his right, then Poore. On Howze's left sat Winship, then Graves. Instead of taking their chairs, Booth, McCoy, King, Winans, and Irwin stood behind the seated men so the photographers could get everyone in one shot. None of the generals smiled for the cameras. MacArthur looked wan and exhausted.

"The court wishes to make an announcement that there must be no demonstration of any kind in the room," Howze finally said when everyone was in his right place.

Mitchell stood at attention.

Howze nervously lifted up a sheet of paper on which he had scribbled what he wanted to read. "Upon a secret written ballot," he announced in a tense voice, two-thirds of the court (the number needed to convict) "finds the accused guilty of all specifications and of the charge."

Howze paused for a brief second to let that sink in. Betty pressed her hands to her lips. Howze continued: "Upon secret written ballot the court sentences the accused to be suspended from rank, command and duty with the forfeiture of all pay and allowances for five years. The court is thus lenient because of the military record of the accused during the World War."

Howze looked up from his notes. "This court will now stand adjourned," he said loudly.

There were no outbursts as a result of the verdict. A hush fell over the crowd, like the silence just after a cease-fire has been declared. Betty stood up, patted her husband's hand, and leaned over to whisper something into his ear. He smiled and shook his head. Some reporters thought they heard him say: "Why, these men are my friends."

The courtroom audience was quiet, partly because everyone was trying to digest the sentence the generals had just handed down. It didn't make sense. The army and navy officers in the crowd scratched their heads. Mitchell was being sentenced to what amounted to five years of peonage. He would be allowed to remain in the army, but he would have no rank, command nobody, do no job, and be paid nothing. Even Gullion thought it was screwy.

Mitchell walked around the defense table and shook the hand of each general. They all wore strained smiles now. The spectators rose from their chairs and finally began talking. Reporters and airmen from the audience crowded around Mitchell when he returned to the defense table. "We are still with you," some of the pilots said, reaching out to pat him on the back. The reporters fired questions but Mitchell said nothing as he gathered up his files and stuffed them in his briefcase. In the confusion after adjournment, souvenir hunters lifted five desk pads and any scraps of paper they could find from the tables.

Seven of the ten court members had to find Mitchell guilty for him to be convicted. The generals were under strict orders not to reveal how they voted, and they all refused to talk to the press after the trial. Newsmen assumed that the verdict had been unanimous and the generals had spent all their time behind closed doors arguing over the sentence. Howze, however, revealed to Betty much later that "the guilty finding was the result of a split decision," but he never told her how each general voted.

How had Douglas MacArthur voted? The question lingered for decades. There were unconfirmed reports that one of the newsmen rooting through a trashcan in the jury room found a slip of paper with MacArthur's handwriting on it that indicated he had voted not guilty. Much later, as MacArthur was considering a run for the presidency, his political enemies began spreading rumors that he had betrayed his boyhood friend during the trial. MacArthur adamantly denied it, insisting to friends that he had cast the lone vote to acquit and had then lobbied the other generals not to dismiss Mitchell from the service. The air colonel needed a few more years in uniform to be eligible to collect his retirement pension. Mitchell guessed that the generals gave him the weird sentence because they thought he was wealthy enough to survive five years without his army pay. He wasn't.

MacArthur would follow Mitchell's lead twenty-six years later. Harry Truman would fire him for publicly criticizing administration policy in the Korean War. MacArthur later wrote about Mitchell and the trial in his memoirs: "That he was wrong in the violence of his language is self-evident." Nevertheless "a senior officer should not be silenced for being at variance with his superiors in rank and with accepted doctrine. I have always felt that the country's interest was paramount, and that when a ranking officer, out of purely patriotic motives, risked his own personal future in such opposition, he should not be summarily suppressed." But doubts remained within the Mitchell family: Betty was never convinced that MacArthur had voted not guilty.

When Mitchell walked down the steps of the Emery Building for the last time, he felt dazed, particularly by the weird sentence, which was "such a shock of cold water," Betty wrote later, that it "left us in a kind of haze." It was dark outside, but photographers' flashbulbs lit up the night. The temperature had dipped to just below freezing, so Mitchell buttoned his thick overcoat and slipped on his gloves. Howze had walked out with him. The general didn't wear an overcoat. The two men stood together at the foot of the steps for a few minutes so photographers could get their last shots. Reid soon came down the steps to Mitchell's right and reached across him to shake Howze's hand. The two men held the grip for the photographers, though neither had much use for the other.

After Reid left, Howze finally turned to Mitchell. "Good-bye, Billy," he said with a smile. The general walked away to a waiting staff car.

Late into the night the phone rang nonstop at the townhouse at 1632 19th Street. The Mitchells had moved there at the beginning of December because the two-month loan of the Anchorage apartment was up. Airmen, old friends, representatives, senators, and reporters called. "Everything will work out all right," Mitchell told them all. "This is only the beginning of the fight."

25 Resignation

Four men with movie cameras, six still photographers, and even more reporters staked out Mitchell's town house on 19th Street, hoping to catch the defendant the day after the trial. Finally Mitchell emerged briefly with Betty and little Lucy so they could take pictures, but he gave no interviews. He was too exhausted from the ordeal, physically and mentally, to answer questions from the press. "Both our brains kind of went flat after the trial," Betty recalled. The morning after, the phone began ringing again at first light with newsmen and well-wishers. A line of messenger boys also formed at the front door, punching the doorbell every few minutes for a chance to see the famous colonel and hand him the latest batch of telegrams.

Cables and letters "began pouring in like they did at the first statement," Mitchell's secretary, Maydell Blackmon, noted in her diary. The *St. Petersburg Daily News* telegraphed him with a job offer to be an editorial writer for ten thousand dollars a year. The Tucson City Council delivered him its resolution condemning the "injustice being done to a patriotic and gallant officer." World War airmen wrote with messages like "the old crowd is with you as it always has been." A representative mailed him an acrostic his wife had penned in his honor. His brother-in-law William Jackson, who was Katharine's husband and an executive with the United Fruit Company, wrote him that if he could hold out with no pay there were "distinct advantages in your staying in the army until you can be retired." He couldn't. His sister Harriet, depressed after the verdict, wrote that she would contact his Milwaukee attorneys, now that he wasn't distracted by the trial, to see about filing a counter-suit to contest again the new support payments Caroline had won. Mitchell never did this.

The War Department received its share of letters, but they were fewer and many were hostile. A guilty verdict "was the only thing you could do to save your own face," an angry Pennsylvania man wrote Howze. Please "soften . . . the harsh treatment meted out to [Mitchell] in his latest court-martial," a California doctor wrote Secretary of War Davis.

Some foreign governments were not impressed with what the American army had just been through. The *Baltimore Sun's* London correspondent reported that British military officials now dismissed Mitchell as a lightweight on defense. Austrian and Czech officers approached their American counterparts at embassy parties with puzzled looks on their faces. How could a U.S. soldier get away with such an insubordinate attitude? they asked. In Moscow the Communist Party newspaper, *Pravda,* warned that militarists like Mitchell wanted America to become "boss of the world's air."

Congress reacted as it always did to a passion of the moment. Representatives trooped to the House floor to demand that Mitchell's conviction be reversed, that congressional investigations be launched into the conduct of the trial, that he be restored to his old rank of general. Fiorello La Guardia, who didn't appreciate what Gullion had said about him and was even more furious that the prosecutor had given the press copies of his final statement with those wisecracks, introduced a bill to prevent the military from sentencing a soldier to more than thirty days without pay for violating the Ninety-sixth Article of War. A Texas representative even offered a resolution to abolish peacetime courts-martial altogether. "Col. William Mitchell is a 1925 John Brown," declared Reid, who had been busy cranking out press releases with his spin on the trial's outcome. "They may think they have him silenced but his ideas will go marching on." The Senate, where Mitchell never had many allies, remained silent, however. Even in the House, the anger soon died down. Nothing ultimately happened with the Mitchell bills.

Arthur Brisbane excoriated the War Department. "Colonel Mitchell's career is just beginning," he wrote in one of his columns. "The people will not forget a man of courage, who has refused to join the lickspittle brigade of officers that say whatever they are expected to say." But while most reporters had sided with Mitchell during the trial, most editorial pages now concluded the verdict was proper. "An army exists and functions by the enforcement of discipline," the *New York Times* pointed out. "Colonel Mitchell broke the bonds of discipline defiantly. The effect upon the morale of the army would have been disastrous if he had not been called to account." Even Mitchell's hometown paper, the *Milwaukee Journal*, believed he was guilty: "The extreme charges that Colonel Mitchell made were not justified by the evidence before the court."

The trial left deep wounds in the military. Many airmen were angry and in a rebellious mood. Secretary of War Dwight Davis moved quickly to quell dissent, not only among the pilots but also from officers in other branches who were disgruntled with the army's leadership. Davis ordered Patrick to clamp down on aviators still publicly criticizing administration policy or making end runs to Congress. "I am in a disciplinary mood," Davis wrote Morrow. Senior army officials leaked to reporters that Davis meant business. He would convene more courts-martial if he had to. There were rumors that even Patrick's head might roll if he and the air service didn't act more like team players.

Patrick got the message. He ordered his officers who had testified for Mitchell or helped him with his defense to lie low. When he caught Hap Arnold lobbying Congress behind his back on behalf of a bill to set up an air corps, Patrick banished the major to Fort Riley, Kansas, and put a letter of reprimand in his personnel file. Arnold was clearly guilty of violating War Department rules that barred officers from trying to influence legislation without the top brass's approval. But he never forgave Patrick, and his exile to what was considered the worst post for an air service officer sent a powerful message to the other pilots that the old freewheeling days were over.

General Pershing welcomed this kind of housecleaning. "There seems to be a Bolshevik bug in the air," he wrote from Chile to a friend. The general could not have uttered a more serious charge against Mitchell and his disciples. The country was gripped by paranoia over Bolshevism. "What is needed," Pershing wrote, ". . . is a good big club with a few dismissals and other salutary forms of military punishment."

But what to do about Mitchell's punishment? Pershing wrote another friend that he hoped there would be "no political clap-trap about giving him his medicine without sugar coating." Mitchell wasn't the first to be suspended from duty without pay. Other soldiers had received similar punishments in the past. But even the army realized that the sentence was impractical. What would they do with a senior officer who could not perform any military function and could not take an outside job while he wasn't being paid for five years? Army regulations prevented moonlighting.

As president, Calvin Coolidge was the last man to review the case, and he had the authority to reverse the verdict or change the sentence. He announced his decision on January 25.

Coolidge didn't touch the verdict. He had no doubt that Mitchell was guilty. Coolidge thought it outrageous that two days after the *Shenandoah* accident a senior U.S. military officer, whom Americans looked up to, would take advantage of the country's horror stricken state of mind and violently assail the War and Navy Departments. Coolidge believed it was demagoguery at its worst, and there wasn't a shred of truth in what Mitchell had charged. But he knew that preventing the colonel from supporting himself and his family was more than the political market would bear. Coolidge ordered that during Mitchell's purgatory he could draw half of his pay with a subsistence allowance, which would amount to $397.67 a month. The army agreed to the change, although it would have preferred the president to have given Mitchell less money. "The theory of government implies that every official so long as he retains his office shall deport himself with respect towards his superiors," Coolidge said in announcing his decision. Without discipline the army and navy "would not only be without value as a means of defense but would become actually a menace to society."

Reid complained that, even amended, "it is the most un-American sentence ever pronounced." But White House aides moved quickly to have friendly representatives praise Coolidge on the House floor and key senators like Hiram Bingham thought the president had been more than generous with the airman.

Betty had a portrait photographer take her picture with Lucy on the morning of January 25. Mitchell, who had stayed busy since the trial ended answering correspondence, meeting with politicians, and tending to his Middleburg farm, had visited the ophthalmologist that day and then had dropped in on Reid at his office. They had heard that Coolidge was reviewing the case but the White House had been secretive about it. John Nevin of the *Washington Post* finally phoned to alert Mitchell that he had learned from his sources that Coolidge planned to issue a decision on the sentence later in the day.

Hours later wire service reporters called asking for comment on the White House announcement. Mitchell said nothing.

The next day he phoned Arnold and other trusted lieutenants, asking their advice on what he should do. Then Mitchell drove to Capitol Hill and conferred with Reid and other representatives. Remaining in the army was impossible, he decided. Even at half pay, he couldn't afford it. Though the army was not prepared to block him from testifying before Congress in the future if the committees demanded it, Mitchell found the five-year suspension from command and duties not only vindictive and unjust but insulting. He refused to accept the legitimacy of his trial, or its verdict, or even his demotion. Until the day he died, he had Blackie refer to him as "General" in all correspondence she typed for him. In fact, he had a right to be called that. Though Mitchell had left the service officially a colonel, he was allowed by law to use "General" as his title after resigning because that was the rank he had achieved during the war.

At noon he returned to his town house on 19th Street for lunch. An army captain arrived in the evening and served him with the court-martial order with Coolidge's amended sentence. The phone rang constantly, with reporters pleading for a statement. Mitchell found a quiet place in the house and took out a sheet of paper to write a letter to the adjutant general. "I hereby tender my resignation as an officer in the United States Army, to take effect February 1, 1926," was all he wrote, and then he signed his name.

Mitchell delivered the letter to the War Department the next morning. By that night, as he and Betty attended a ball at the Mayflower Hotel, the note had made its way through the army chain of command and was over at the White House for review. The next day at noon Davis announced that the War Department had accepted Mitchell's resignation.

As a final parting shot army finance officers docked his last paycheck by $393.67 for a leather coat, moleskin trousers, Kodak camera, field case, three sets of goggles, seven flight suits, and two general's flags he didn't return when he processed out.

Mitchell, however, had already trumped them. Before he resigned, he had driven out to Bolling Field in Washington, climbed into a plane, and had taken off and landed thirty-seven times in just one day. The thirty-seven flights he recorded, to make up for the ones he'd missed during the past three months, made him eligible for an extra $1,027.08 on his last check. The finance officers howled, but the comptroller general of the United States ruled that he could not be denied the flight pay.

26 Periphery

The taxi raced Mitchell and Blackie to Union Station. It had been a busy day for him, consumed by meetings with friends and airmen. Joe Davies, an adviser during the trial and his unofficial political consultant, was the first to drop by the town house that day. After the court-martial Davies had secretly raised money for Mitchell from wealthy contributors the lawyer knew, and had turned the checks over to Betty to cover expenses. Mitchell made several phone calls to his book publisher and to the Pond Bureau in New York, which was still putting the finishing touches on his speaking tour. Pond had already set up twenty-five paid lectures for him across the country. Mitchell was late now because his last meeting with Brig. Gen. James Fechet had run over its allotted time. Fechet, who had taken over Mitchell's job as assistant air chief after he had been fired the previous spring, dropped by the town house for a chat with his old friend.

Mitchell and Blackie practically ran through the station with their bags. They climbed aboard the afternoon train to Boston with only three minutes to spare. They were beginning the New England swing of his speaking tour. Blackie went along to handle travel arrangements and dictation on the road. Betty had decided to remain in Washington with Lucy. She took over Blackie's job answering the large volume of mail that still arrived each day, and, when she could, she drove to Middleburg to supervise the renovations at Boxwood. Betty liked the secretarial chores but hated having to manage the household finances.

Sunday night Mitchell spoke at Mechanics Hall in Worcester,

Massachusetts. The crowd, however, was disappointing. Only five hundred showed up. Blackie thought the snowstorm that night kept many away. James Pond had taken the train from New York to watch his celebrity client, and realized that Mitchell was not a terrific public speaker. He had suggested changes in the airman's delivery to make it more interesting for the audience, and Mitchell had agreed. But the poor showing at Worcester was an omen.

The fame and fortune that Billy Mitchell had predicted in his confidential letters to Betty after he delivered his blast from Texas never came. Perhaps if he had been summoned to Washington to account for his charges at a quick set of high-profile congressional hearings, maybe that would have been enough to launch a successful writing and speaking career. But the court-martial took almost three months of his time away from producing articles or giving speeches around the country to hawk his new book. By the time the trial was over, the issues he wanted to market had been talked to death in the newspapers. Sales of *Winged Defense* slumped. His publisher, George Putnam, reported the company had moved only 4,454 copies by the end of January. "I can't remember a non-fiction book which in one way or another stirred up so much attention and at the same time sold so disappointingly," he wrote Mitchell. But Putnam should have realized why. The public had had its fill of the subject.

Also, Americans were always more in love with the man than the message. Mitchell was popular because he was a brave, handsome officer who was not afraid to challenge his superiors. What he had to say was listened to because he dared to say it while in uniform. Coolidge and the War Department correctly calculated that the excitement over Billy Mitchell would fade rapidly after he left the service, which was one reason they approved his resignation request so quickly. Once he took off his uniform, Mitchell became just another civilian with an opinion.

The lecture tour stretched into May and took Mitchell to more than twenty-four states. He returned to Washington exhausted but nevertheless buoyed by the money that he did make and the people who had come out to hear him warn that airplanes could one day level their communities in minutes. There had been large turnouts in many cities. A sell-out crowd heard him speak in Chicago, 1,500 listened to him in Dayton, and 3,000 packed a hall in Cincinnati.

But Mitchell spoke to half empty rooms in other places. Only 250 showed up in Buffalo, and he was even snubbed at some stops. The local military authorities in Duluth, Minnesota, refused to allow him to speak in the armory for fear it would anger the War Department. Detroit newspapers reported that Everett Sanders, Coolidge's top aide, had pressured the city's Union League Club to rescind an invitation to Mitchell to speak. Sanders denied it. J. Edgar Hoover, the director of the Justice Department's Bureau of Investigation (it was not designated the FBI until 1935), dispatched one of his agents to check out whether Sanders had acted improperly. The agent reported back that the story was bogus. Hoover dutifully passed the findings on to the attorney general.

Mitchell went on tour again in 1927 and 1928, but not nearly to as many stops as before, and before smaller audiences. He turned in the articles *Liberty* magazine had contracted for after the trial and collected his nine thousand dollars. He churned out a batch of columns on the court-martial for the Bell newspaper syndicate and branched out to other magazines, such as *Popular Science* and *Field and Stream*. But soon editors, even those from the friendly Hearst chain, began paying less for his pieces or rejecting them altogether. The problem: After railing against the army and navy, after calling for a separate air force and warning of foreign threats, Mitchell didn't have much new to say. His writing became repetitive. The *New York American,* a Hearst paper, began paying him as little as fifty dollars for each article. "It really does not seem to contain any NEWS," a *Liberty* editor complained to Mitchell in 1935 after reviewing a manuscript he had submitted, entitled "Throwing Our Aeronautics to the Dogs."

Mitchell nevertheless persevered, and he wasn't entirely unsuccessful. He found publishers for another book on aeronautics, titled *Skyways*, and for a biography he wrote of Gen. Adolphus Greely, his mentor in the Signal Corps. Both received favorable reviews in the *New York Times*.

Editors were nervous, however, about another problem with Mitchell's writing. He became even more strident in his views. "These poor people in the army and navy are still in the kindergarten of national defense," he stated in a letter to one friend. The land and sea services were still engaged in an "orgy of killing fliers," he wrote to an editor. He even accused the American Legion of becoming "a Communist organization" for backing the "Bonus Army" of World War I veterans who marched on Washington demanding benefits. The Hearst chain rejected one series of articles, calling them "scathing editorials." Mitchell, who could be prickly about the editing of his pieces, rarely toned them down. "Most of the magazines and newspapers now are afraid to say anything," he complained in 1935.

He began to see conspiracies around every corner. The navy, he charged in 1929, maintained a "pernicious lobby" that corrupted Washington, with her admirals obeying the orders of the steel industry and oil companies that fed the fleet. The aircraft industry, he now believed, had been "thrown to the profiteers." By 1934 he was convinced that a cabal of stock market manipulators, manufacturers who controlled aircraft patents, and influential Washington lobbyists (including President Franklin Roosevelt's own son Elliott) had conspired to milk the industry of profits and retard aviation's technological progress. When he publicly accused the Curtiss-Wright Corporation that year of being among those profiteers, the aircraft manufacturer slapped him with a two-hundred-thousand-dollar libel suit. The suit was eventually dropped but Mitchell's legal fees became so high that he asked his old pal, columnist Arthur Brisbane, if the Hearst chain could run a series of articles on the case and solicit money for his defense.

Mitchell clung to the belief or, better yet, the delusion, that he alone had been responsible for progress in aviation. "I am the only one of prominence in aeronautics who has consistently tried to educate our people about what we should have," he wrote Arthur Brisbane in 1934, "and who has insisted on honesty in aircraft transactions and in the development of our aeronautics as a great national asset." But by the mid-1930s just the opposite was the case. Mitchell was isolated and largely ignored. Charles Lindbergh was the nation's air hero for his historic transatlantic flight. The War Department continued to shun Mitchell. Even members of the influential National Aeronautical Association blocked his bid to become president of their organization, fearing he had become too radical.

Within months of the trial's end, Mitchell began testing the political waters. The mayor of Dayton tried to launch a "Mitchell for President Club." Another friend proposed an "Aviation Party," with the colonel as its standard bearer, a notion Mitchell eagerly endorsed. A Washington attorney organized "Billy Mitchell Volunteers" to put his name in nomination for president when Democrats held their 1928 convention in Houston, hoping it would give him enough lift to be seriously considered for the second spot on the ticket. Wisconsin politicians began talking him up as a possible candidate for the U.S. Senate from their state. Mitchell believed he had a better chance at a Senate seat, so he fanned that speculation even more. He studied Wisconsin's political landscape closely and sent Joe Davies to Milwaukee to investigate if a campaign was feasible.

It was not unusual for generals of his day to consider running for office. In fact it had become common practice. Pershing was mentioned as a possible running mate for Coolidge in 1924. Mitchell thought Black Jack would have trouble connecting with the voters on the stump. During the war Pershing "never endeared himself to the private soldier," he wrote.

Mitchell, who planned to campaign as a Democrat, told his sister Harriet he would need at least $25,000 to enter the Wisconsin primary and win the nomination. "The Republican Party," he complained, "has become the symbol for conservatism, monopoly, backsliding, selfishness and dishonesty in government." He probably couldn't have run as a Republican even if he had wanted to, considering the enemies he had made in the GOP by attacking the Coolidge administration's defense policy.

Mitchell had opinions on issues other than national security. The lecture tour had given him the opportunity to become acquainted with his country, and the long train rides had provided many hours to think about the direction the nation should take. Mitchell considered himself a liberal, although the label meant different things then than it does today. He wrote that Prohibition was a "dismal failure." He favored "conservation of our historic places, wildlife, streams and forests." He thought taxes were too high, government spending out of control, and the federal bureaucracy bloated; the ten cabinet departments should be shrunk to six, eliminating such Republican "citadels" as the Commerce Department. He also backed tariffs to protect industry and tighter immigration quotas so as to "not flood us with cheap labor and incompetent people from the lower strata of the world's millions."

None of Mitchell's political forays went anywhere. The Democrats never considered him even a serious vice-presidential possibility during their Houston convention. A Wisconsin senatorial candidacy also fizzled. Some party leaders there feared the maverick officer would be too uncontrollable. Mitchell eventually lost interest in a run and contented himself with following Virginia politics and doing favors for state officials. He did campaign across the country for Al Smith, the Democratic presidential candidate in 1928. His sister Harriet hosted an elaborate party for the candidate in Milwaukee. Mitchell considered Herbert Hoover, Smith's Republican opponent, a "large puffball." But Smith, a progressive New York governor, had no hope of winning with "Coolidge prosperity" still alive; Hoover trounced him.

Four years later Mitchell attended another Democratic convention to push fellow Virginian Harry Byrd for vice president. When it was over he enthusiastically hit the campaign trail once more, this time for Franklin Roosevelt. The New York governor "will go down in history as one of our greatest presidents," Mitchell predicted to a Milwaukee journalist. He was sure FDR would create a separate air force under a new department of defense. He also hoped that Roosevelt would give him a job. Mitchell worked aggressively behind the scenes to have political friends lobby Roosevelt to appoint him as his air secretary, either in the War Department or a newly created defense department.

Roosevelt had probably not forgotten his days as a navy assistant secretary during the Wilson administration, when Mitchell had accused him and the admirals of trying to dismember naval aviation and Roosevelt had angrily dismissed Mitchell as a know-nothing. FDR also probably got an earful from War Department officials, horrified at the idea of Mitchell returning as a top civilian leader. So Roosevelt did what any president-elect does with an important campaign supporter whom he does not want to alienate but doesn't want in his administration: He strung him along. Roosevelt met with Mitchell several times before taking office. He read the half dozen letters Mitchell sent and answered them personally with friendly but noncommittal notes. And he gave him a ceremonial job on his inaugural committee.

But Roosevelt never made Mitchell his air secretary, never

appointed him to an air commission he set up later, and never created a defense department with a separate air force. As FDR
became immersed in the New Deal, aides began answering
Mitchell's letters and running interference for the busy president
when the colonel asked for meetings with him at the White House.
Gradually Mitchell became disillusioned with Roosevelt. "It seems
to me that FDR will have to do something about aviation," he wrote
a friend in the spring of 1935. "He is getting it in a worse mess every
day. I am getting pretty much fed up with him." Mitchell told his
friend that he had already warned Postmaster General James Farley that he "was going to open up on" the president, "and I think I
shall write FDR to that effect." If Farley ever bothered to pass the
threat on to Roosevelt, it's hard to imagine that Roosevelt would
have been worried.

Despite the disappointments Billy and Betty made a comfortable
life for themselves in Middleburg. In 1928 Betty gave birth again,
this time to a boy, whom Mitchell proudly named William junior.
Betty spoiled Billy junior, but Mitchell tended to be a stricter disciplinarian. One day when Lucy was about ten, she leaned over a
banister in the house and called out to Mitchell: "Billy, would you
come up here?" Mitchell marched up the stairs and gave her a
spanking. "Don't ever call me that," he told her sternly. Mitchell also
treated nephews and nieces as if they were his own children, correcting their grammar and shushing them when they became too
loud at the table. He also wasn't shy about giving his sisters advice
on how to raise their kids. After his sister Katharine's son Danny
had come for a visit, Mitchell wrote her: "He needs polishing up—
language, manners, and more care about his clothes." Both Betty
and Billy believed that children should be seen and not heard. On
most evenings the cocktail hour was five to six for adults only, and
most nights, particularly if guests were over for dinner, the children
ate with the servants. But on weekends the couple always had
breakfast with Lucy and Billy junior in the sitting room off their
bedroom as a special time.

Mitchell could also be a doting father and uncle. When Lucy
balked at wearing glasses to help correct crossed eyes, Mitchell
bought spectacles for himself and everyone else in the family to put

on so his daughter wouldn't feel out of place. Nephews and nieces called him Uncle Willie and loved coming to Boxwood, where he kept them busy from dawn until dusk. They rode horses, waded through streams, and played croquet. They feasted on roast lamb and chicken at barbecues and stuffed themselves with ice cream, cake, and apples picked off the tree. Mitchell also took them on sailing trips off the Virginia coast, where they fished and crabbed and put up tents for overnight camping at the shore. When his niece Harriett made him a birthday cake that fell flat and tasted awful, Mitchell ate it and praised her profusely.

Lucy and Billy junior never took to horses, which Mitchell accepted but could never understand. He once mused to a friend about what made a son a good pilot: "The men who make the best pilots are horsemen, people who play polo and ride to hounds," he wrote. "Next to that, the men who are accustomed to athletic competition, such as football, baseball and things of that kind which require quick action of the reflexes."

Mitchell became a country gentleman, earning tens of thousands of dollars each year breeding horses and hunting dogs. He was a canine expert as well as an equestrian, writing a number of articles on both subjects. At any time Boxwood Farms, as it came to be known, had for sale almost twenty horses for foxhunts, polo, or races. Mitchell rode his thoroughbreds in most all the area horse shows, often collecting prizes, and was a regular on the foxhunt circuit, with friends like George Patton.

During the summers the couple often vacationed abroad. In 1927 they sailed first class to Paris. Mitchell visited his birthplace in Nice. Military attachés from the American embassies kept a close watch on him when he passed through their countries and filed detailed reports on his movements back to the War Department. "General Mitchell's visit to Berlin brought about a situation of a certain amount of embarrassment," the attaché there wrote. The U.S. embassy did not want to associate itself with so controversial an officer, but German aviation officials pestered American diplomats to set up meetings with the famous airman. The Germans hosted a luncheon in his honor, took him on a tour of Tempelhof Airfield, and flew him over the city in a Junker passenger plane. Mitchell had a grand time. On the return voyage he befriended a gang of World War I vets in a second-class barroom.

Back home Mitchell paid $25,000 for a fifty-six-foot cabin cruiser, which he christened the *Canvas Back* for a duck he liked to hunt, and sailed it thousands of miles up and down the East Coast. He loved to take the children or nephews and nieces for sails. The Capital Yacht Club in Washington unanimously elected him its vice-commodore.

His family budget would have been less strained if he'd bought a rowboat. Boxwood Farms provided enough income to make up for the drop-off in writing fees. When Mitchell's mother died she left an estate worth $744,331.39, which was more than her husband had left and provided Mitchell an annual income of $14,593.89 as of 1928. By November 1933 his support payments to Caroline were down to $166.67 a month because two of his first three children had reached adulthood. But Mitchell still spent beyond his means. In addition to Blackie, who continued as his personal secretary, there were servants at Boxwood and a nanny for the children. Mitchell bought his clothes from tailors overseas, stocked his cellar with fine wines and liquors, stayed at pricey hotels when traveling, sent his children to private schools, and practically every year traded in his car for a new one through a friend from the Packard Company in Detroit.

Mitchell, who fancied himself an expert on the stock market, loved to trade tips with Arthur Brisbane and other friends. But even in bull years he often lost money, and when the stock market crashed in 1929 his portfolio was nearly wiped out. Creditors hounded him constantly. The Virginia Chamber of Commerce even received a complaint from an Italian saddler angry that Mitchell hadn't paid a two-year-old $165 bill. Mitchell tried to skate by each year making partial payments on many bills or taking out loans with Riggs Bank or Milwaukee relatives who ran the family's financial institutions. His more frugal sister Harriet, who had invested wisely, lent him money. Betty's family also helped. But Mitchell always came up short. In 1927, for example, he earned more than $53,000, a substantial sum in that day. But he spent more than $56,000.

Mitchell was sensitive about his money troubles. He became

testy with creditors who weren't polite with their past due letters. (But he would get just as angry when he wasn't paid quickly for his articles or speeches.) Mitchell tried to keep it a secret from friends that he needed his wife's money to make ends meet. To scrimp, Betty went to a five-and-dime store in nearby Warrenton for many of her clothes. When Harriet visited, however, she would take Betty shopping at the more expensive stores in Washington and pay for what they bought.

Mitchell could also be peculiar about how he earned money. He scraped up cash from a variety of sources, badgering the Veterans Administration, for example, until it finally agreed to pay him a pension of thirty-five dollars a month for his service in the Spanish-American War, and agreeing to appear in an educational film about aviation for three thousand dollars and a new Chevrolet sedan. But Mitchell turned down lucrative offers to be an executive with an airline company or plane manufacturer. And he refused to allow his name or photo to be used in advertisements for such products as Lucky Strike cigarettes and Elgin watches.

Middleburg continued to thrive, even through the depression. By the early 1930s the town had the area's first air-conditioned theater, to which Blackie took the children on Saturdays. Middleburg also boasted a tearoom, hardware store, undertaker, and several restaurants. Eating establishments began to prosper after the town voted by a wide margin to repeal Prohibition in 1933. Millionaire William Ziegler Jr.'s grand barbecue and horse race down the road from Mitchell's estate attracted some 10,000 people in 1931. Thousands of society's finest turned out for the horse show at John Hay Whitney's estate in nearby Upperville.

"General Billy" and his fashionable wife were among Middleburg's resident celebrities. Boxwood became a magnet for parties. In 1933 Mitchell gave the opening speech for the Daughters of the Confederacy's centennial celebration of John Mosby's birth. Betty delivered a ringing speech in 1934 to keep Middleburg School from closing. Mitchell helped the town hire a flamboyant police sergeant, named E. W. Bosher, who terrified tourists by firing his pistol into the air. When a state trooper stumbled onto a driver illegally bringing in beer from Pennsylvania, Mitchell was called to adjudicate. He decided the hauler should pay a small "import fine," then deliver the beer to its customers.

Mitchell also became Middleburg's unofficial spokesman, and he often aroused controversy. On a wintry January night in 1932, Agnes Boeing Isley, a popular Middleburg society lady, was brutally bludgeoned to death in her cottage, which was near Mitchell's estate. The body of Isley's maid was also found beaten to death in the home. Mitchell, who had been good friends with the matron, was the first to arrive at the crime scene. A year later a black man, an ex-convict named George Crawford, who had worked for Mrs. Isley, was arrested in Boston on a petty thievery charge, and police there allegedly got him to confess to the Middleburg slayings.

The National Association for the Advancement of Colored People, which believed the confession was coerced, took up Crawford's case. The NAACP persuaded a Massachusetts judge not to extradite Crawford to Virginia on the grounds that the grand jury that had indicted him excluded blacks, that he would never receive a fair trial in Loudoun County, and, even worse, that he might be lynched. They were all legitimate concerns for an African American defendant accused of killing a white woman in 1932.

Outraged, Mitchell led a public drive not only to have the extradition decision reversed but also to get Congress to impeach the Massachusetts judge. If he'd had his way, Mitchell would have had the judge extradited to Virginia to be "strung up" with Crawford, he wrote his sister Katharine. Crawford was eventually sent back to Virginia. An NAACP investigator who ventured into Middleburg to gauge the mood of the community claimed that Mitchell told her that if the town police had caught Crawford the year before "there would have been a burning." Mitchell denied he ever said it, but even if he hadn't, he certainly believed it. Mitchell was a segregationist. The NAACP, he once wrote a friend, was "a communist organization financed to some extent from abroad."

Crawford entered a courtroom in nearby Leesburg ringed by police armed with submachine guns, gas grenades, and gas masks. Mitchell testified during the high-profile trial, recounting how he saw the iron bootjack used to kill Agnes Isley lying near her in her room. After a number of witnesses disputed Crawford's alibi, he eventually changed his plea to guilty and was sentenced to life in prison. Even the *African American* newspaper acknowledged that he had received a fair trial. But blacks had been excluded from the jury that heard his case. The State of Virginia had nothing to be proud of, and neither did Mitchell.

Mitchell was never completely separated from larger issues of the nation. Though he became more peripheral to aviation as the years passed, he still kept a small but loyal following. He stayed in close touch with Arthur Brisbane about world events and corresponded regularly with old air comrades like Clayton Bissell, Tom Milling, and Thurman Bane to catch up on army news. Sometimes he sent cash to friends who had fallen on hard times. Mitchell and Betty even wrote Pershing frequently, begging him to visit Boxwood for a weekend. Pershing always declined.

Mitchell wrote his correspondence in his cluttered office over the kitchen, sitting at a rolltop desk with the head of a young deer buck mounted on the wall to his left. Blackie would squeeze in to the cramped room to take dictation. During office hours Mitchell was not to be disturbed by children: Any youngster who dared enter received a stern tongue-lashing.

Mitchell enjoyed writing long notes to friends. If the subject was national defense, his letters usually became tirades. But on other issues his correspondence showed a fertile mind. In the Middle East, Palestine was the historical "center of the European, Asiatic and African world," he wrote a friend in 1929. "Someday it will regain its importance." In Europe "it looks very much to me like war," he wrote plane designer Alfred Verville in 1933, six years before war began. "The Germans are not going to stand being relegated to the background the way they have been." He was impressed with the way Hermann Göring was building up the country's airpower. In the next conflict, Mitchell warned in another essay, Germany "might be able to bring about one of the greatest military surprises of history with her air force."

By the 1930s Mitchell was convinced that Asia was "now the center of world politics." Though he remained obsessed with Japan as the next enemy of the United States, by 1935 he was painting fantastic war scenarios. Mitchell now believed that the Japanese air force—instead of attacking Hawaii, as he had predicted twelve years earlier—would strike Alaska first to establish a beachhead on the North American continent. From there Japanese planes would attack San Francisco or "seize . . . islands in our Great Lakes," using them as staging bases for raids on Chicago and New York.

The one blank spot in Mitchell's writings after he left the army was the trial. His articles for the Bell syndicate on the court-martial were largely superficial, mostly his spin and bromides. ("My trial was a necessary cog in the wheel of progress.") Though the court-martial held the nation's attention for almost two months, Mitchell never considered it to be a momentous event in his life. His experience in World War I and the bombing of the *Ostfriesland* were far more important, he believed, and he returned to those subjects frequently in his letters and articles. To Mitchell the trial represented nothing more than a bitter episode in his life.

This was understandable: Instead of exoneration he had received a guilty verdict, instead of redemption a black mark on his legacy. He wrote about the court-martial in its immediate aftermath. Then he moved on—and never looked back.

27 The End

Alfred Verville wandered through the rooms of Washington's Metropolitan Club looking for Mitchell. The colonel had phoned him three days earlier and asked Verville to meet him there. The airplane designer, who had accompanied Mitchell on his European tour after his divorce from Caroline, finally found his old boss in the club's barbershop, getting a haircut. He looked awful. Face pasty. Flesh on his cheeks sagging. Eyes glistening and dead-like. A friend had told Verville that Mitchell did not appear well. In fact Mitchell had sensed as early as two years before that his body was wearing down. He watched his weight and continued to try to climb mountains and tromp through woods hunting grouse, but "it will not last so many years," he wrote his sister Katharine. Just before his fifty-fifth birthday, he wrote to a journalist: "It is difficult for me to realize that I am beginning to be an old man." Mitchell's hair had grayed quickly after the trial. Blackie thought he had been in a serious decline since the summer. By late fall 1935 Mitchell knew that his heart was weakening and, for the first time in his life, that he had to slow down. "Well, one can't expect to be perfect forever and I have had a pretty good run," he wrote Katharine on December 14. Verville was stunned by how different Mitchell looked from when he had seen him a month earlier.

Mitchell spotted the designer as he walked into the barbershop and called out his last name. (He always pronounced it *Vervee*, as the French did.)

Verville walked up to the barber chair to shake his hand. "How are you?" Mitchell asked, and Verville finally detected a twinkle in his eye.

"I'm fine, general," the designer said, still holding the general's hand.

"Well, Bissell and you ought to be happy now," Mitchell said with a chuckle. "I just had nine ulcerated teeth taken out." Mitchell had chronic dental problems; Bissell and Verville had been nagging him to go to the dentist. He liked to put up a macho front before other airmen, always claiming he didn't need medical attention for ailments, but in private he watched himself carefully and visited the doctor and dentist often. He told Verville now that Betty had finally ordered him to take care of the bad teeth, which again wasn't completely true.

Mitchell saw a waiter pass by the barbershop and motioned to him. "Bring over two brandy and sodas," he ordered.

"No, general, I don't think you should have one," Verville protested. Mitchell moved stiffly from the barber chair, and he had a vacant stare. Verville guessed he'd had "a mortal blow to his system," as he recalled later. In fact, Mitchell had recently suffered a heart seizure, and a chauffeur had had to drive him to the club. Tears began to well up in Verville's eyes. Mitchell was obviously in pain.

"The doctor said it was quite all right for me to have a brandy," Mitchell said assuredly. "It's good for me. You go into the library and I'll be right in."

The two men found comfortable chairs in the library, and the waiter brought them their drinks. "You know," Mitchell said, turning to Verville, "the doctors tell me my valves are all shot, my bearings are worn out. But you know, I've lived three lives."

That was certainly true. Mitchell had driven himself all his life. He was constantly on the go, working hard, playing hard, sleeping little. People around him couldn't keep up. Neither could his own body.

Mitchell had always been a magnet for various illnesses. He had had trouble with his eyes as a child and scarlet fever when he was seven. During his first tour in the Philippines he contracted malaria. In 1908 he developed rheumatic arthritis in his right hip and left knee. Off and on for ten years he suffered painful neuralgia on the left side of his face, which was relieved somewhat when an abscessed tooth was pulled from his upper jaw. He was hospitalized for a serious case of influenza in 1924.

Five decades of riding, living in the field, and flying had left his bones battered. He smashed his knee in Alaska. He fractured two of his left ribs in 1922. Falling from horses three different times, he seriously injured an eye once and broke his nose twice, which left his frontal sinuses "practically obliterated," according to one of his medical reports.

His heart had always been a problem. His family had a history of heart disease. By age thirty-five, Mitchell was diagnosed with a heart murmur. From winter 1915 until early 1916, he suffered another punishing bout of rheumatism that attacked his ankles, knees, wrists, elbows, shoulders, and, more critically, his heart. It put him flat on his back in a hospital for six weeks and left him feeble for another three months. By his forties and fifties, too, Mitchell had high blood pressure.

Now, barely a month after his fifty-sixth birthday, he sensed that he would soon die. But Mitchell was not ready for it. He had three more books he wanted to write, he told Verville as they sipped their drinks, and he dearly wanted "to be around for the next big show."

"What do you mean, general?" Verville asked.

"I mean the real airpower war," Mitchell said. It would start again in Europe, he told his friend, "only this is going to be a war in everybody's backyard. This is going to be the real world war. . . . I'd like to be around here to see the color of the faces of those who opposed our military aircraft program."

The two men reminisced about the pilots they had both known. Mitchell was sure Jimmy Doolittle, one of the airmen who had bombed the ships off the Virginia coast in 1921, would make a name for himself in the next war. "You're going to hear a lot about him," Mitchell predicted. The same with Hap Arnold; he was a forward thinker. "Arnold is going to be a great leader for airpower," the general said.

After about two hours they parted. Verville would later be heartbroken that this was the last time he saw his dear friend.

On Saturday night, January 25, Betty piled her husband onto a train bound for New York. Once there she checked him into Doctors Hospital on Tuesday and had Dr. Samuel Lambert, a heart specialist who was her cousin, begin examining him. Mitchell told friends that he went to New York just to make his wife happy, and Lambert told reporters he was there for "merely a rest." But his condition soon worsened. Clogged arteries were squeezing off the flow of blood to his heart. His systolic blood pressure hovered between 165 and 200. A kidney developed "complications," according to Betty. The bone in his mouth was no longer infected from the ulcerated teeth that had been removed, but a nurse had to replace the dressing every day, which was excruciatingly painful for Mitchell. The only way he could have a restful night was with morphine, but he resisted having the injections and tried to fight their effect when he was doped up. "If he could only get some decent sleep and relax," Betty wrote to Katharine. "I think he'd get better more quickly, but his mind keeps rampaging around and around and they don't seem to be able to quiet it." Finally Mitchell came down with influenza and nurses placed him in an oxygen tent to help treat the weak heart.

Betty was "so desperately worried," she told Katharine. Not only was her husband gravely ill, but she had no idea how she was going to pay for this expensive hospital stay. They had no savings to speak of, and she couldn't go once more to her father, who had become financially strapped himself because of the Great Depression. She asked Mitchell family members for money. Mitchell's sister Harriet, who knew that Betty was largely clueless about how her husband juggled accounts to make ends meet, mailed her a check. But Betty knew enough to realize she had to begin cutting expenses at Boxwood.

Within a week, however, her husband looked better to her. He was very tired, but Betty cabled Harriet in Milwaukee that he was improving.

Harriet didn't believe it. When a heart patient looks as if he's improving in the hospital, she was convinced, that's when he goes. Mitchell's sister packed her bags for New York. It turned out to be a daunting journey. The temperature outside was seventeen below zero, and tall snowdrifts covered the farmland where she lived north of Milwaukee. A horse-drawn sleigh took Harriet as far as it could; then, wearing snowshoes she trudged to an open road, from which a brother-in-law drove her to a station, where a train took her to Chicago, from which a plane took her to New York. A stewardess helped her change clothes in flight so she would be presentable when they landed.

Her brother *did* appear to her to be happy and revived when she finally walked into his hospital room—though she had to climb into the oxygen tent to speak to him. Mitchell laughed when she told him of her ordeal in getting there. For the next two weeks, Betty and Harriet remained at his side almost constantly. Katharine came for a visit as well. As snow fell outside, they all had many days to talk. Mitchell wanted to know everything that was happening to their children, who remained in Middleburg with friends. He quizzed Harriet about her daughter, Harriet, a favorite niece who was now seventeen. For hours he talked about his mother.

As his vital signs showed some improvement, Mitchell began to think that he might have another chance at life. He began talking more animatedly about future plans and the things he still hoped to accomplish. He seemed to Harriet like his old enthusiastic self. Doctors removed the oxygen tent, and Mitchell slept soundly for long periods. On Wednesday morning, February 19, he even managed to get out of his bed and walk around a bit.

By the afternoon, however, he had grown weary and crawled back under the covers to sleep. Harriet sat silently at the foot of the bed, and Betty sat at his side, watching as he lay there peacefully. He never awoke. The influenza had weakened him far more than the doctors realized, and his clogged arteries finally stilled his heart. Mitchell died at 4:45 P.M.

A police detail escorted the hearse to New York's Pennsylvania Station. Eddie Rickenbacker supervised the loading of Mitchell's flag-draped casket onto the baggage car of a train bound for Wisconsin. Several dozen city officials, World War I veterans, and Legionnaires stood around a color guard as an army bugler sounded taps. Betty had a private car for the trip, which she shared with Harriet; Mitchell's sister Katharine, who had come down from Boston; a Mitchell family cousin named Sherman Becker; and Doctor Lambert. At Chicago the party and the casket were transferred to a rail line founded by Mitchell's grandfather. They made the final ride to Milwaukee through high banks of snow on each side of the track.

Even in death Mitchell stirred controversy. Boake Carter, a radio commentator for WCAU in Philadelphia, told his listeners nationwide that the army had refused to allow Mitchell to be buried at Arlington Cemetery with his war comrades. It was an irresponsible and inaccurate broadcast, which upset Betty and enraged the War Department. The army had no problems with Mitchell being buried at Arlington, but the family didn't request it. Mitchell had left explicit instructions with Betty that his final resting place be with his family in Wisconsin.

The funeral service was held Saturday afternoon in Milwaukee's St. Paul's Episcopal Church, where three generations of Mitchells had prayed. More than 175 mourners crowded into the main sanctuary, which was festooned with lilies, roses, orchids, and ferns. Along with family and old friends from Wisconsin, there were scores of American Legion officials as well as Army Reserve and National Guard officers. In a front pew sat four representatives from Washington still recovering from their harrowing trip. The military transport plane flying them to the funeral developed engine trouble just outside D.C. and had to make an emergency landing in a farm field near Winchester, Virginia. The rough landing damaged the aircraft and terrified the representatives, but after repairs they took off again and eventually reached Milwaukee.

Mitchell was buried in Forest Home Cemetery next to his father and grandfather. Gen. Frank McCoy, who had served on the court-martial, was one of his pallbearers, along with Col. George C. Marshall, who was stationed in Chicago at the time. Florists had fashioned white carnations into a large pair of wings that stood at the head of the gravesite. At the other end, a general from President Roosevelt's staff laid a wreath the president had sent with a picture of the White House attached to it. Taps were played once more after a rifle team from the American Legion fired three volleys into the wintry sky.

Shortly after the funeral Betty returned with Harriet to Middleburg, where Blackie and a nurse were taking care of Lucy, Billy junior, and Harriet's daughter Harriet. The townsfolk had known for a while that General Billy had been ill, but his sudden death had shocked them all. They rallied around Betty now, giving her advice on how to dispose of her husband's affairs. More than a thousand letters poured in from well-wishers. Betty answered each one personally—the letters to her had been written "from the heart," she said, and they deserved more than a "printed acknowledgment"—but the task took her months to complete.

Betty began sorting through her husband's military and financial papers. She wasted no time sounding out friends and relatives on a suitable author to write his biography. Mitchell had been a careful record keeper. He had saved and cataloged thousands of documents from his army career, dating back to the day he joined the service, and had packed them in boxes stored in the attic and basement.

Newspapers reported at the time that Mitchell left a personal estate worth only about $15,000 with an assessed value of just $5,765. That fit neatly into the Everyman myth he liked to project, and previous biographers have never questioned the number. Actually he ended up worth a bit more. Betty owned Boxwood, but Mitchell still had stocks and income from family real estate and financial interests in Milwaukee. That, combined with the cash he had in Riggs Bank and the sale of his personal property, brought his total estate to $56,454.27, according to the final executrix report filed in a Warrenton, Virginia, courthouse. Betty had a lot of expenses to pay out of that amount. The final medical bills totaled $1,427.08. Blackie was due $150.00 in back wages. Abercrombie & Fitch, Brooks Brothers, and other pricey clothing stores had to be paid. Mitchell owed small amounts to practically every business in Middleburg. Larrimer's Wine Store had an unsettled bill for $190.73. The $15,092.00 in loans he had taken out with Riggs and family institutions in Milwaukee also had to be paid off. But after everything was finally deducted, Betty had $32,998.66 left.

She remained exhausted during the cold dreary weeks after the funeral. The combination of visitors who streamed to the estate every day to pay their respects, the hundreds of details that had to be attended to, and the crushing grief she felt over his death became almost too much for her. It seemed as if she was in "a tailspin," she wrote Katharine a month after her husband's death. "I still feel as though it all were a nightmare, which must disappear, and that my beloved Willy must come dashing in from some trip or other, full of something new. It is just impossible to realize that he never will." Young Harriet slept with her in her bed for comfort. But most nights Betty couldn't sleep because of what she called a "dead loneliness" in her heart, so she roamed the house that she and her husband had so treasured. Harriet lay awake in Uncle Willie's bed by herself. It felt spooky being there. She was sure his ghost was walking around in the room.

Epilogue

SPRING 1964

Neighbors in Alexandria, Virginia, began noticing clouds of smoke billowing up from a backyard on North Washington Street. Caroline stood in front of an incinerator in the yard tossing letters into the fire inside it. She was burning her past with Billy Mitchell.

A maid carted the heavy boxes to the yard for her. Caroline was eighty-three years old and too frail to lift them herself. A large closet in the house had been packed to the ceiling with the boxes. They contained all her correspondence with Mitchell, plus personal papers from their nineteen years of marriage. Caroline always kept the closet locked. Nobody was ever allowed inside it.

Five years earlier her granddaughter Felicity had asked a friend from the Library of Congress to pay Caroline a visit and plead with her to preserve the valuable papers. Caroline said not a word as Felicity's friend tried politely but emphatically to convince the old woman of the historical importance of what was stored in her closet. Finally, when he had finished, Caroline stood up and shook his hand. "Thank you so much. I appreciate your coming over to have tea with us," was all she said. Felicity prayed that her grandmother had paid attention.

It took Caroline a couple of weeks to burn all the papers. She slowly and carefully tossed small handfuls into the incinerator. But she set aside the diaries she had kept from 1906 to 1925. They contained sixteen of her nineteen years of marriage to Mitchell, told through her eyes. She decided not to burn them.

Ten years after the divorce, Caroline married Franklin Frederick Korell, a former Republican representative from Oregon who became a Treasury Department lawyer after the people of his district voted him out of office. Fritz Korell was a soft-spoken, gentle man, almost boring, whom Caroline's children and grandchildren came to love. He was just the respite Caroline wanted from the turbulent life she had lived with Mitchell. Korell, for his part, was proud that he was marrying the ex-wife of such a famous airman. He admired Mitchell, although the general's name was never mentioned in their new household.

Caroline and Fritz settled into a quiet routine. As a side business they renovated historic homes in Alexandria. Their own three-story house at 428 North Washington Street had once been owned by Edmund Jennings Lee, an uncle of Robert E. Lee. Every day after Fritz returned from work, they would fix old-fashioneds for the cocktail hour, listen to the news on the radio, then have dinner served promptly at 7:05 P.M. Caroline always dined in a stylish dress, high heels, and jewelry. Grandsons always came to the table wearing a coat and tie, granddaughters always in skirts. Though the couple became less and less connected to Washington social circles, they still managed to entertain out-of-town celebrities like Eddie Rickenbacker and Charles Lindbergh.

Caroline was generous to a fault with her children and grandchildren, but she demanded their loyalty and unquestioned obedience. Cross "Mema," as the grandchildren called her, and you got your allowance cut off. Caroline wanted to control every part of her life—including when it would end.

Toward the latter part of July 1964, after she had finished burning all her papers, Caroline took the next step in a plan she had thought through carefully. She decided to die. She suffered from coronary insufficiency, a limited blood flow to her heart. Though she had trouble breathing, she was not seriously ill. But she told a servant she had had enough. Caroline stopped taking her digitalis (used to strengthen and regulate her heart contractions). She lay down on a sofa in her living room and died on July 31.

After Mitchell died Betty opened a tearoom in Middleburg so she could earn money to pay off his debts. One of Lucy's most vivid memories of that dreadful year was of the men coming to take the horses away from Boxwood's stables. Her mother sold the nineteen mounts to raise cash. Betty tried for a while to hold on to Boxwood. The children desperately wanted to remain there and so did Betty, even though reminders of the life she and Billy had so enjoyed in Virginia hunt country often overwhelmed her. During a horse show in nearby Upperville the summer after Mitchell's death, Betty sent the children to sit in the grandstand by themselves while she remained crouched low in the car alone. She couldn't bring herself to mingle at an event her husband had so enjoyed.

In 1939 Betty married Tom Byrd, a widower and the little-known son among the Virginia Byrds. His oldest brother, Harry, was the famous senator, then governor; his middle brother, Richard, was the world-renowned explorer, who had testified against Mitchell at his trial. Tom Byrd was content to run his apple orchard in Timberville, Virginia. A tall, hardy, self-assured man, he had a contagious laugh and a quiet, laid-back manner. Tom enjoyed playing poker and hunting with the boys or skinny-dipping in his pool after a hot day in the orchard. He never raised his voice, and if there was a ruckus on Betty's side of the family, he never stepped in, preferring to wander off to another room and take a nap.

Betty had deliberated and prayed for many weeks before accepting Tom's proposal. She wrote Mitchell's sisters to ask their permission, telling them she'd turn Tom down if they objected to the marriage. "It has been an awful decision to make for Bill so absolutely filled my whole life and consciousness that no one can ever take his place," she wrote Katharine. The sisters urged her to accept. Tom also was just what Betty needed after Mitchell's high-energy life. Billy had worn her out. Tom, who had seen combat in World War I, was no more intimidated by Mitchell's memory than he was by his two brothers. Mitchell and Tom had, in fact, been friends when Mitchell was alive. Betty kept framed photos of Mitchell in the library of her new house with Tom. During dinner parties she would often stand up and propose a toast to her first husband. Tom never seemed to mind. Betty sold Boxwood in 1943 and together with Tom built a comfortable home in Boyce, Virginia, which is near Middleburg. She died in 1963 at the age of seventy-two.

The War Department would have preferred that the painful memory of Mitchell's court-martial be locked away forever. It was almost forty years before the army allowed outside historians and biographers to read the trial transcript, which consisted of 3,781 pages. Like Mitchell, the other men involved in the case went on with their lives and told their children and grandchildren little of what happened during those thirty-four days in the Emery Building.

Gen. Robert Howze died nine months after the court-martial after undergoing a gall-bladder operation. He was only sixty-two years old. His son, Hamilton, who also became a general in the army, believed as his father did that Mitchell was justly convicted not for what he advocated but because of his "disgraceful charges against senior officers."

Blanton Winship rose to the rank of major general. Franklin Roosevelt appointed him governor of Puerto Rico in 1934. Eight years later he served on a military commission trying eight Nazi saboteurs who infiltrated into the United States during World War II. He remained friends with Betty and Billy after the trial, becoming a godfather to their children. At seventy-seven, stricken with a heart attack, he fell over a table, and died.

Sherman Moreland was never promoted past colonel. He retired from the army four years after the trial. Though he'd had a varied career in law, politics, and the military, he would forever be known as the chief prosecutor in the Billy Mitchell trial. He died in 1951 at the age of eighty-three.

Allen Gullion had many promotions after the trial. He ended up a major general and the judge advocate general and provost marshal of the army. During World War II he helped begin the internment of Japanese Americans. Toward the end of the war he went to Europe to supervise the handling of displaced persons and POWs in areas liberated by the Allies, but was forced to return to Washington in December 1944 because of heart trouble. Eighteen months later, he dropped dead in his apartment while listening to the Joe Louis–Billy Conn fight on the radio. He was sixty-five years old.

Ironically, Gullion's youngest son and a son-in-law joined the Army Air Corps. Around pilots both kept quiet about the fact that they were related to the man who had prosecuted the patron saint of airpower. One of his grandsons, Gen. Thomas S. Moorman, Jr., became vice-chief of staff of the air force. Moorman recalls once being introduced to an audience of airmen as the grandson of Allen Gullion and hearing boos in the crowd.

Frank Reid never achieved the national prominence some reporters thought he would from being Billy Mitchell's lawyer. But he did compile a respectable record in Congress. In 1927, after floods ravaged the Mississippi River Valley, he chaired the House Flood Control Committee and held a number of high-profile hearings on the problem of flooding rivers. After six terms he decided to quit the House and resume his lucrative law practice back in Aurora. He kept in occasional touch with Mitchell after the trial, but eventually the two men went their separate ways. Reid rarely discussed the court-martial with his family. He died of a heart attack in 1945 at age sixty-five.

The other important woman in Mitchell's life, his sister Harriet, remained a financial anchor for the surviving siblings. Harriet divorced her first husband, Arthur Young, in 1930 and two years later married a tall Norwegian named Martin Fladoes. They lived in a country home north of Milwaukee, which she called Little Meadowmere. The original estate had been sold in 1925. Until the day she died in 1968 at age eighty-two, Harriet led the family's fight to have her brother officially vindicated by the U.S. military.

For two decades after Mitchell's death, bills rattled around Congress to either exonerate him, to restore him to the rank of general, or even to award his survivors thousands of dollars in back pay because he was forced out of the service. The War Department opposed most of the measures, and none went anywhere. The army also battled senators who pushed legislation in 1941 posthumously to award Mitchell the Congressional Medal of Honor. The nation's highest military award should be reserved only for soldiers who performed extraordinary acts of heroism, Roosevelt's war secretary, Henry L. Stimson, argued. Mitchell, he insisted, had "been adequately rewarded" for his bravery with the Distinguished Service Cross. Congress eventually compromised and voted to give Mitchell a special medal of honor. Because it was not the real Congressional Medal of Honor, the Mitchell family viewed the award as little more than a consolation prize. Instead of putting it on display in his house, Billy Mitchell Jr. ended up dumping the medal in a desk drawer.

In 1956 the Air Force Association, a powerful private group that lobbies for the air force in Washington, convinced Billy junior to make one last stab at official vindication. He filed a petition with the secretary of the air force to have his father's court-martial conviction reversed. Top army officials fiercely fought it, insisting that Mitchell had been tried by the army and that his conviction had been upheld by a President of the United States, and a secretary from another service had no business trying to reverse that thirty years after the fact. The air force secretary, James Douglas, decided not to step into the thick of it. He did not try to change the conviction.

But with the public Mitchell remained a hero. His popularity as a prophet grew as Nazi Germany combined massive airpower with highly mobile divisions on the ground in a blitzkrieg to conquer much of Europe. After the Japanese attacked Pearl Harbor on December 7, 1941, reporters remembered that Mitchell had predicted it, and they wrote scores of he-told-us-so stories. Japanese planes began bombing the naval fleet shortly before 8:00 A.M.—only about twenty minutes later than the time his 1923 report said they would strike. Of course the time of the attack was easy to predict: Military forces usually begin them early in the morning. Mitchell, moreover, was wrong in predicting that the Japanese would seize an island as a staging base for planes instead of launching them from aircraft carriers. Toward the end of his life, Mitchell also believed that Japan would consider Alaska far more strategically important to seize than the Philippines. The Japanese seized the Philippines but took only two of the Aleutian Islands off Alaska.

But Mitchell did predict a Japanese attack on Pearl Harbor. More important, he did warn that American forces were woefully unprepared for that attack, which was certainly the case. An Army Air Corps was created in 1926, but airpower remained under the War Department's control and badly underfunded through much of the 1930s. By 1941 cooperation between the army and navy in Hawaii was still about as poor as what Mitchell had found when he inspected the islands in 1923.

When the United States joined the battle, the conservatives who had presided over the interwar years were, by and large, put out to pasture. The innovative officers who had languished during that stifling period—men like George Marshall, Dwight Eisenhower, and George Patton—became the army's World War II leaders. Mitchell's disciples took charge of airpower. Hap Arnold, whom Patrick had banished to Kansas, became commanding general of the Army Air Forces during the war. Tooey Spaatz, whom Mitchell's jurors had dismissed as a naive junior officer, led U.S. strategic bombing forces in the European theater and later became the first chief of staff of the new independent air force.

The "Mitchellites," as they were often called, put the theories of their intellectual father into practice. Mitchell's ideas had a profound effect on World War II strategy. Airplane technology had improved dramatically, with all-metal monoplanes, more powerful engines, retracting landing gears, and closed cockpits. Gallant British pilots became a powerful air defense against German raids. Tactical air attacks over the battlefield were a godsend for soldiers slogging their way across Europe. Paratroopers by the thousands dropped from the skies, as Mitchell had envisioned for the First World War. In the Pacific, airpower proved critical to capturing Japanese-held islands and defeating the Japanese fleet. The aircraft carrier replaced the battleship as queen of the sea. Independent strategic bombing, which Mitchell advocated, reduced much of Germany to rubble and delivered the atomic bombs that resulted in Japan's surrender. Though they were far more diplomatic than Mitchell, his acolytes were able to carve out the autonomy Mitchell had preached in order to wage a largely independent strategic bombing campaign against Germany and Japan. "Had he lived through World War II, [Mitchell] would have seen the fulfillment of many of his prophecies of air warfare," concluded Douglas MacArthur, who led American forces in the Southwest Pacific.

Afterward the jet age brought far-flung countries together within hours, as Mitchell had forecast. And airpower, in the form of planes and rockets carrying nuclear weapons and the threat of mutual assured destruction, forced an uneasy peace between superpowers during the Cold War.

Not all of what Mitchell prophesized proved true. Airpower was critical in World War II, but it did not win the war alone, as he believed it would. Armies on the ground and ships at sea played equally important parts. Antiaircraft defenses proved far more troublesome for aviators in the next war than the jaunty pilots at Mitchell's trial envisioned. Though the Japanese demonstrated at Pearl Harbor that battleships sitting still could be sent to the bottom, they became much more difficult for World War II pilots to sink when they were underway and fighting back. The Mitchellites went into the next battle believing that strategic bombing was the key to victory. As things turned out close air support for American ground units was far more valuable to winning the war, at least as far as the army was concerned. Ground commanders grumbled that there never were enough planes carrying soldiers and supplies or hitting the enemy in front of them because the air generals were so fixated on flying deep into enemy country to strike cities and industries. Strategic bombing ended up not causing German civilians to rise up and stop the war or to overthrow Hitler. (Mitchell had predicted such a scenario for any country so attacked.) In the case of Great Britain, strategic bombing did just the opposite, strengthening the resolve of civilians to resist.

In the next two wars airpower could not break the stalemate that evolved in Korea nor block the flow of communist guerrillas and supplies coursing through the jungles of Vietnam. But since the Desert Storm war of 1991, bombing accuracy has been improving by leaps and bounds. By the time of the second American war with Iraq twelve years later, Mitchell's ideas about airpower winning battles almost single-handedly did not seem so far-fetched. Cruise missiles can now be launched from distant countries to topple individual buildings in a city. Sophisticated sensors and high-speed computers can almost instantly feed pilots accurate information on what to hit. Radar-evading jets can fire smart bombs from miles and miles away and have them laser-guided to even smaller targets by satellites in space, observation drones flying over the battlefield, or spotters on the ground.

Futurists envision a day not far off when wars will be won by planes and missiles armed with even more accurate precision-guided munitions. Instead of large heavy armored divisions, ground commanders will send in small special operations units to guide aerial bombs to their targets. Infantrymen will follow to mop up pockets of resistance and the POWs. Battles will be shorter, neater, cleaner, with less unwanted damage and fewer civilian casualties.

Army men are understandably still skeptical. A surgical air strike will always remain an oxymoron, they argue. There will always be collateral damage and innocent civilians will suffer. Targets will still be missed, or the wrong targets will be hit. Planes and their fancy gizmos may be able to blow up any building they choose or reduce any tank to a burning hulk. But it will always take soldiers on the ground to finally win a war, and to enforce the peace.

In 1947 Harry Truman made Mitchell's dream a reality and created a Department of Defense with an independent air force coequal with the army and navy. But Mitchell would not have been completely happy with the way the organization turned out. Instead of one unified air force, as he advocated, there are now five. In addition to the regular air force, the army has its own air force, a vast fleet of helicopters. The navy, which fought the formation of a Defense Department from the beginning, has kept its planes aboard carriers. Even the marines and the coast guard have their own air arms. It also took another forty years after the Defense Department was created for the admirals and generals finally to put into practice Mitchell's ideas about unity of command. In 1986, Congress forced the balky services to shift war-fighting powers to the chairman of the Joint Chiefs of Staff and the regional commanders in chief who lead the troops.

But much of what Mitchell envisioned or dreamed of did come to pass. Over the years honors sprouted across the country. The American Legion post in Detroit became the General William Mitchell Post. During World War II a plane manufacturer named its bomber for him, and a senator tried but failed to have the Aleutian Islands renamed the Billy Mitchell Islands because he had so forcefully warned of their strategic importance. In Washington the Smithsonian Institution unveiled a bronze statue in his honor. The U.S. Postal Service issued a stamp in his honor in 1999. In 2003 another bill was passed in the House to promote Mitchell posthumously to major general, this one introduced by Rep. Charles Bass, who is also a grandnephew of the airman. Milwaukee named its airport after him. Inside the terminal there is the Mitchell Gallery of Flight with a small collection of his medals, papers, and photos. The terminal's food court is also called the "General's Court" with a "Mitchell's Café" and "Billy's Pub." The general would have been furious with those establishments, considering how much he opposed the commercialization of his name.

Among aviators Mitchell's stature has grown to mythic proportions. Air generals in the Pentagon still speak of him in tones reserved for deities. At the Air Force Academy in Colorado, a bust of Mitchell sits in the cadet honor court adjacent to the administration building, and a large portrait of him hangs in the academy's dining facility, which is named Mitchell Hall. Among the young cadets he is still revered for his flamboyance and rebellious nature. The academy's class of 2001 selected Mitchell as the man they most wanted to emulate.

Even Hollywood got in on the act. In 1955, Warner Brothers released *The Court-Martial of Billy Mitchell*. The film was directed by the highly respected Otto Preminger. It had big-name stars like Gary Cooper, Rod Steiger, and Ralph Bellamy. It was also one of the worst docudramas ever produced. Facts were distorted, events were fabricated, and characters were invented who never appeared in the trial. An army lawyer who reviewed the script complained in a memo that the court-martial was depicted as an "almost surreptitious Star Chamber proceeding."

Even the Mitchell family hated the movie. The taciturn and sedate Cooper was totally miscast as Mitchell. The family thought it should have been someone with more overt spunk, like Jimmy Cagney. Billy junior approached Cooper at one point just before the shooting started and asked him what he knew about his father.

"Well, son, I read the script coming in on the plane," the famous actor answered.

"Well, do you think you can play my father?" Billy asked.

"They pay me to play myself," Cooper told him.

Billy walked away, irritated. Cooper was like a lot of people who saw Mitchell the way they wanted to see him, not the way he was.

How should Mitchell be viewed? His court-martial had been reasonably fair by 1925 standards, although certainly not by today's. His jury was far from unbiased. But with such a small senior officer corps, it probably would have been impossible to find a jury of peers who did not know Mitchell well. The generals gave him the widest of latitude to present his case—even though a majority of them were predisposed to convict him anyway. Mitchell spoke the truth in much of what he said on September 5, 1925. His jurors dismissed many of his claims because they could not see as far into the future as he could. But not every paragraph of his statement was correct. Mitchell did have a tendency to exaggerate, and in some cases he did not have his facts straight. In the end he had been insubordinate. A constitutional democracy cannot tolerate a challenge to military and civilian authority as harsh as Mitchell's. Even as ardent a disciple as Hap Arnold realized that the jury had no choice but to convict him. "In accordance with the army code," Arnold wrote many years after the verdict, "Billy had had it coming."

What place should he have in history? Mitchell could be vain, egotistical, power hungry, and a self-promoter. He was outspoken when he should have been prudent, opinionated when he should have been objective, confrontational when he should have been accommodating, self-centered when he should have been a team player. He saw evil in many who simply had honest disagreements with him, made enemies of men who could have been valuable allies. Friends like Jimmy Doolittle, who won the real Congressional Medal of Honor for his bombing raid over Tokyo, worried that Mitchell ended up doing more harm than good for his cause. "He was ahead of his time," Doolittle concluded. But "the methods he used were so stringent that they destroyed him, and probably delayed the development of airpower for a period of time." Arnold had similar feelings. "He was a hard man to make peace with," Arnold wrote. "He was a fighter, the public was on his side, he was righter than hell and he knew it, and whoever wasn't with him a hundred percent was against him." But the trial left the army so bitter toward Mitchell the generals "seemed to set their mouths tighter, draw more into their shell, and, if anything, take an even narrower point of view of aviation as an offensive power in warfare."

Yet even his friends may have been too hard on him. Great leaders, particularly those in wartime, have outsized egos. Institutional mavericks, whistle-blowers, critics who press for reform in bureaucracies all tend to be abrasive, outspoken, hard to get along with.

Prophets by nature are opinionated and overconfident. Agents of change break china, make people angry and uncomfortable, leave enemies in their wake. Did Mitchell retard progress in airpower? It's a weak case to make. More likely, progress would have been much slower if Mitchell had not been there. As an institution the military reforms at a glacial pace if left to its own. Men like Mason Patrick who work the system from the inside can rarely do it alone. Lightning rods must galvanize public opinion and prod politicians to force the bureaucracy to change. Mitchell was a needed spark.

He deserves a place in history. Mitchell had his personal flaws, to be sure. But he was a brilliant and innovative officer. In combat he was a brave and daring commander. During their dismal interwar years he was an inspiration to his men. He was a visionary willing to challenge the status quo. He may have been an opportunist, but ultimately Mitchell did lay his military career and his reputation on the line for what he believed in. He had the courage of his convictions.

Source Notes

ABBREVIATIONS USED

ACL   Archives and Special Collec-
tions, Amherst College Library
DM   Dwight Morrow Papers
AWC   U.S. Army Military History
Institute, Army War College
CB   Charles L. Bolte Papers
DN   Dennis Nolan Papers
HD   Hugh Drum Papers
HH   Hamilton Howze Papers
IE   Ira C. Eaker Papers
SF   Sladen Family Papers
BA   Bass Family Papers
BF   Banfield Family Papers
CCP   Calvin Coolidge Presidential
Library and Museum at Forbes
Library
GF   Gilpin Family Papers
HP   Harriet Pillsbury Family Papers
LOC   Library of Congress
CC   Calvin Coolidge Papers
CS   Charles P. Summerall Papers
ES   Everett Sanders Papers
FM   Frank McCoy Papers
GG   George S. Gibbs Papers
GM   George Van Horn Moseley
Papers
GP   George Patton Papers
HA   Henry Arnold Papers
IE   Ira Eaker Papers
JB   Dr. Joel T. Boone Papers
JH   John L. Hines Papers
JP   John J. Pershing Papers

LW   Leonard Wood Papers
SP   Carl Spaatz Papers
WM   William Mitchell Papers
WF   William F. Fullam Papers
MHS   Milwaukee County Historical
Society
MB   Maydell Blackmon Diary,
William Mitchell Papers
WMP   William Mitchell Papers
NA   National Archives
HAW   Record Group 18, Hawaiian
Department
IG   Record Group 159, Office of
Inspector General Correspon-
dence 1917–34
MID   Record Group 165, Military
Intelligence Division Corre-
spondence
MT   Mitchell trial records in Record
Group 153, Records of the
Office of the Judge Advocate
General, Entry no. 40
NAV   Record Group 80, General
Records of the Department of
Navy, General Correspondence
WP   Record Group 165, War Plans
Division General Correspon-
dence
NASM   National Air Space Museum,
Smithsonian Institution
WMC   William Mitchell Court-Martial
Collection

NPRC	National Personnel Records Center	UWM	University of Wisconsin–Milwaukee, Golda Meir Library
201	Mitchell 201 File	GH	George Hardie Collection
OHC	Oral History Collection of Columbia University	JLM	John L. Mitchell and Mitchell Family Papers
TF	Trueblood Family Papers	WHS	Wisconsin Historical Society,
CS	Caroline Stoddard Diaries		Writers' Program. Madison,
UNC	Southern Historical Collection, Wilson Library, University of North Carolina at Chapel Hill		Wisconsin
		AM	Alexander, John, and William Mitchell Papers
BD	Burke Davis Papers		

(In many instances a source note covers several paragraphs. Unless otherwise indicated, each source note lists material cited up to the previous source note. Mitchell also saved hundreds of newspaper clippings on himself and the trial, which can be found in the Mitchell Papers at the Library of Congress, National Archives, and University of Wisconsin–Madison. William Webb, one of his attorneys, also collected hundreds of news clippings on the trial, which can be found in scrapbooks with the Mitchell Papers at the National Air and Space Museum. I have referred frequently to the newspaper articles in these collections. Most of these news stories had notations for the name of the paper and the date the article appeared, but no page number. When a news article is cited in the source notes with no page number, the article came from those collections, unless otherwise noted.)

CHAPTER 1   EXILE

Page

1   *down to him:* "A Pocket Guide to Staff Post: Fort Sam Houston Museum, 1991, pp. 1–68; "A Pocket Guide to Historic Fort Sam Houston," Fort Sam Houston Museum, 2000 Edition; Elizabeth Mitchell letter to Katharine Jackson, July 25, 1925, BA; J. E. Fechet letter to William Mitchell, June 18, 1925, box 11, WM, LOC.

2   *in Washington:* Will Rogers, "Up in the Air with a Flying General," *Washington Post,* May 10, 1925, p. 2; Will Rogers, "Mitchell Is Back from Siberia," *Washington Post,* Sept. 27, 1925, p. 2.

3   *he had dictated:* Elizabeth Mitchell letter to Katharine Jackson, June 27, 1925, BA; Maydell McDarment letter to Burke Davis, June 10, 1966, box 56, BD, UNC.

3   *of his parlor:* diary entry, Aug. 31, 1925, box 1, MB, MHS; Mitchell letter to Elizabeth Mitchell, Aug. 31, 1925, GF; Elizabeth Mitchell telegram to Mitchell, Aug. 31, 1925, box 11, WM, LOC.

3   *airtight:* Mauer Mauer, *Aviation in the U.S. Army, 1919–1939* (Washington, D.C.: U.S. Government Printing Office, 1986), pp. 22, 153–55; Phillip S. Meilinger, ed., *The Paths of Heaven: The Evolution of Airpower Theory* (Maxwell Air Force Base, Ala.: Air University Press, 1997), p. 107.

4   *was fearless:* Mitchell letter to Elizabeth Mitchell, Aug. 31, 1925, GF; Associated Press dispatch, San Antonio, Tex., Aug. 31, 1925, box 58, WM, LOC; Elizabeth Mitchell letter to Katharine Jackson, July 25, 1925, BA.

5   *future wars:* Author interview with Felicity Trueblood, July 13–14, 2002;
       Edward M. Coffman, *The War to End All Wars: The American Experience in
       World War I* (Lexington: University Press of Kentucky, 1998), pp. 12–13.

6   *"Western Hemisphere":* Russell F. Weigley, *History of the United States Army*
       (New York: Macmillan, 1967), p. 413; Frederick Lewis Allen, *Only Yesterday*
       (New York: Bantam, 1959), p. 5; Alfred F. Hurley, *Billy Mitchell: Crusader for Air
       Power* (New York: Franklin Watts, 1964), p. 121; William Mitchell, *Our Air
       Force: The Keystone of National Defense* (New York: Dutton, 1921), pp.
       xxiii–xxiv, 102–3, 151, 154, 156–57, 220–22; William Mitchell, *Winged Defense:
       The Development and Possibilities of Modern Air Power—Economic and Military*
       (New York: Putnam, 1925), pp. 6, 79–82, 89–92, 156, 165.

6   *Calvin Coolidge:* Author interview with Kenneth Gilpin, Sept. 16, 2002.

7   *independent air force:* Isaac Don Levine, *Mitchell: Pioneer of Air Power* (New
       York: Duell, Sloan and Pearce, 1943), p. 287; Mitchell letter to Select Commit-
       tee on Aviation, March 2, 1925, box 46, WM, LOC; Coolidge letter to Mitchell,
       Nov. 12, 1924, reel 35, CC, LOC; Mason Patrick press release (undated), box 38,
       WM, LOC.

7   *husband court-martialed:* Memo from A. E. Saxton (Adjutant General) to
       Patrick, Jan. 29, 1925, box 6, MT, NA; Mitchell and Patrick memos, "SUBJECT:
       Testimony of Brigadier General Mitchell," Feb. 5, 1925, box 37, WM, LOC; cor-
       respondence Feb. 7, 1925, among Saxton, Mitchell, and Patrick, box 37, WM,
       LOC; War Department press release by John W. Weeks, Feb. 28, 1925, box 16,
       MT, NA; Elizabeth Mitchell letter to Mitchell, Sept. 3, 1925, with Sept. 1, 1925,
       Associated Press dispatch, box 11, WM, LOC.

8   *in uniform:* "Battle Hymn of the Kookaburra," box 22, HD,AWC; Roger
       Burlingame, *General Billy Mitchell: Champion of Air Defense* (New York:
       McGraw-Hill, 1952), p. 151; Ruth Mitchell, *My Brother Bill: The Life of General
       "Billy" Mitchell* (New York: Harcourt, Brace, 1953), pp. 9–10; Nicholas Lemann,
       "The McCain Code" *New Yorker,* Feb. 4, 2002, p. 53; author interview with John
       McCain, Sept. 10, 2003.

9   *he recalled:* Author interview with Harriet Pillsbury, June 1–2, 2002; interview
       with Richard Jackson, Sept. 17, 2003; Burke Davis, *The Billy Mitchell Affair*
       (New York: Random House, 1967), p. 146; James J. Cooke, *Billy Mitchell* (Boul-
       der, Colo.: Lynne Rienner Publishers, 2002), p. xi.; reminiscences of Gen. James
       Doolittle, no. 1085, p. 71, OHC.

9   *two buzzards:* diary entry, Sept. 1, 1925, MB, MHS.

9   *"no drinks":* Diary entries, July 11 and 15, 1925, MB, MHS; Mitchell letters to
       Elizabeth Mitchell, July 15 and 21, 1925, GF.

10   *Washington office:* Mitchell letter to Elizabeth Mitchell, July 21, 1925, GF; Eliz-
       abeth Mitchell letter to Katharine Jackson, June, 27, 1925, BA; Maydell
       McDarment letter to Burke Davis, June 10, 1966, box 56, BD, UNC.

10   *in seed money:* Mitchell letters to Elizabeth Mitchell, July 27 and Sept. 3, 1925,
       GF; John W. Chappell letter to Mitchell, Feb. 20, 1925, box 11, WM, LOC; Eddie
       Rickenbacker telegram to Mitchell, Feb. 19, 1925, box 2, WM, LOC; Mitchell's
       response to Rickenbacker, Feb. 19, 1925, box 20, WM, LOC; Arthur Brisbane
       letter to Mitchell, March 6, 1925, box 11, WM, LOC; Mitchell letter to Charles
       C. Grey, March 20, 1925, box 11, WM, LOC; D.C.; Hodgkin letter to Mitchell,
       March 20, 1925, box 11, WM, LOC.

CHAPTER 2 FLIGHT OF THE *SHENANDOAH*

Page

11 *the Allegheny Mountains:* John Toland, *The Great Dirigibles: Their Triumphs & Disasters* (New York: Dover Publications, 1972), pp. 105–6.

12 *to its monopoly:* Navy report on "requests for the Shenandoah to visit State Fairs," Defense Exhibit A-52, box 8, MT, NA; "Intricate and Scientific Construction of the Shenandoah," *New York Times*, Sept. 4, 1925, p. 3; "memorandum re cost of Shenandoah," Nov. 23, 1925, file no. 6000–1424, NAV, NA; Toland, *The Great Dirigibles*, pp. 63, 78, 81; Mitchell memo to Chief of Staff, Jan. 31, 1920, and Chief of Naval Operations memo Feb. 19, 1920, box 8, WM, LOC; Patrick memo to Adjutant General, Feb. 12, 1923, box 9, WM, LOC.

12 *chronicle the voyage*: Coolidge letter to Lansdowne Nov. 1, 1925, reel 24, CC, LOC; Toland, *The Great Dirigibles*, p. 102.

12 *the North Pole:* Charles Glidden letter to Coolidge Oct. 4, 1923, and White House response Oct. 5, 1923, reel 24, CC, LOC; Toland, *The Great Dirigibles*, pp. 81–87, 91–101; "The Shenandoah Bubble," *The Standard Union*, March 21, 1924, reel 24, CC, LOC; "Guarding the Shenandoah Against Disaster," *Outlook* 136, Sept. 19, 1924, p. 36.

12 *new giant airships:* Toland, *The Great Dirigibles*, pp. 90, 107; William F. Trimble, *Admiral William A. Moffett: Architect of Naval Aviation* (Washington, D.C.: Smithsonian Institution Press, 1994), pp. 133–34; technical paper on the USS *Shenandoah* and meteorology in the Midwest, prepared for the author Feb. 26, 2003, by Capt. John Cooper, USNR (Ret.).

13 *to seal it:* Toland, *The Great Dirigibles*, pp. 94–95, 108; "Intricate and Scientific Construction of the Shenandoah," *New York Times*, Sept. 4, 1925, p. 3.

13 *gas quickly:* Toland, *The Great Dirigibles*, p. 102; trial transcript, p. 2367, MT, NA; memo from Moffett to Lansdowne, Sept. 1, 1925, on "shortage of helium," box 8, MT, NA.

14 *into September:* Two memos from Chief of Naval Operations to Lansdowne, Aug. 12, 1925, memo from Chief of Naval Operations to Lansdowne, Aug. 15, 1925, confidential memo from Lansdowne to Chief of Naval Operations, Aug. 17, 1925, box 8, MT, NA; Cooper technical paper.

14 *their constituents:* Trimble, *Admiral William A. Moffett*, pp. 13, 127–33, 154–56; memo from Chief of Naval Operations to Lansdowne, Aug. 12, 1925, box 8, MT, NA; navy memo for the press, Aug. 17, 1925, file 6000–1424, NAV, NA; reminiscences of Eugene Edward Wilson, no. 480, p. 201, OHC.

15 *"long as I can":* Toland, *The Great Dirigibles*, pp. 109–11; trial transcript, pp. 2347–49, MT, NA.

15 *the Great Lakes:* Cooper technical paper.

15 *to 3,200 feet:* Toland, *The Great Dirigibles*, pp. 112–26; Cooper technical paper.

16 *as one put it:* Toland, *The Great Dirigibles*, pp. 118–21; trial transcript, p. 2350, MT, NA.

16 *to the ground:* Toland, *The Great Dirigibles*, pp. 126–27; trial transcript, p. 2351, MT, NA.

16 *hitting the ground:* Toland, *The Great Dirigibles*, pp. 130–41; Cooper technical paper; trial transcript, pp. 2351–59, MT, NA; "Shenandoah Wrecked in Ohio

Storm; Breaks in Three and Falls 7,000 Feet; 14 Dead, Including Commander, 2 Hurt," *New York Times*, Sept. 4, 1925, pp. 1, 2.

16   *Lansdowne's finger:* Toland, *The Great Dirigibles*, pp. 146–47. "Souvenir Hunters Cripple Inquiry into Cause of the Shenandoah Crash; Coolidge Would Build New Dirigible," *New York Times*, Sept. 5, 1925, p. 1.

CHAPTER 3   "CRIMINAL . . . TREASONABLE"

Page

17   *letter that day:* diary entry, Sept. 3, 1925, box 1, MB, MHS; Letter from Mitchell to Elizabeth Mitchell, Sept. 3, 1925, GF.

17   *foreign governments:* "Shenandoah Wrecked in Ohio Storm; Breaks in Three and Falls 7,000 Feet; 14 Dead, Including Commander, 2 Hurt," *New York Times*, Sept. 4, 1925, pp. 1, 2; Sept. 10, 1925, letters to the White House, reel 24, CC, LOC.

18   *on his plane:* Trimble, *Admiral William A. Moffett*, pp. 157–59; Navy Department press releases, Aug. 25 and 26, 1925, box 18, MT, NA; Chief of Naval Operations memo on ship movements, Nov. 12, 1925, box 13, MT, NA.

18   *and a half:* Mitchell letter to Elizabeth Mitchell, July 15, 1925, GF; Trimble, p. 156.

18   *said respectfully:* "Sea and Air Armada Vainly Hunts Plane Lost Near Hawaii," *New York Times*, Sept. 3, 1925, p. 1; Davis, *Billy Mitchell Affair*, p. 214.

18   *in the Pacific:* Mitchell letter to Elizabeth Mitchell, Sept. 3, 1925, GF.

18   *wonderful time:* diary entry, Sept. 3, 1925, MB, MHS; Mitchell letter to Elizabeth Mitchell, Sept. 3, 1925, GF.

19   *make it:* "Heinen Lays Crash to Valve Removals," *New York Times*, Sept. 5, 1925, p. 1; "Flight Ordered Over Protest, Is Charged," *New York World*, Sept. 4, 1925, p. 1; "Policy Unchanged, Wilbur Declares," *New York World*, Sept. 4, 1925, p. 2.

19   *statement then:* Mitchell letter to Gen. A. C. Dalton, April 25, 1925, and Charles Grey letter to Mitchell, June 11, 1925, box 11, WM, LOC; Maydell McDarment letter to Burke Davis, June 10, 1966, BD, UNC.

19   *at his side:* diary entry, Sept. 4, 1925, box 1, MB, MHS; Davis, p. 218.

20   *6,080 words:* Trial transcript, pp. 173–229, MT, NA; diary entry, Sept. 5, 1925, MB, MHS.

20–22   from *"I have"* to *with airpower:* "The Statement of William Mitchell Concerning the Recent Air Accidents, Sept. 5, 1925," Prosecution Exhibit A, box 18, MT, NA.

22   *weak heart:* "Brother's Death Goads Mitchell to Air Attack," undated newspaper article, box 56, WM, LOC; Ruth Mitchell, p. 305–6; Maydell McDarment letter to Burke Davis, June 10, 1966, BD, UNC; reminiscences of Eleanor P. Arnold, no. 384-A, p. 57, OHC; Michael Grumelli, Ph.D., *Trial of Faith: The Dissent And Court-Martial of Billy Mitchell*, Rutgers University, 1991, pp. 25, 84; Ruth Mitchell, *My Brother Bill*, p. 275.

23   *"lone man's support":* Mitchell letters to Elizabeth Mitchell, Sept. 10 and 12, 1925, GF.

23   *he wrote Betty:* Mitchell letters to Elizabeth Mitchell, Sept. 4, 10 and 12, 1925, GF.

23   *"gross receipts":* Mitchell letter to Elizabeth Mitchell, Sept. 12, 1925, GF; Mitchell letter to Col. Kenyon A. Joyce, Dec. 10, 1924, box 10, WM, LOC.

23   *or "Snooks":* Mitchell letter to Elizabeth Mitchell, Sept. 12, 1925, GF; Harriet Pillsbury interview.

CHAPTER 4   THE MITCHELL PROBLEM

Page

24   *into the water:* diary entry, Sept. 6 and 7, 1925, MB, MHS; Associated Press dispatch from Port Aransas, Tex., Sept. 6, 1925, box 57, WM, LOC.

24   *in Vienna:* BRANDS AIR RULE 'CRIMINAL': Mitchell Lays Air Disaster To War Chiefs," *Chicago Tribune,* Sept. 6, 1925, p. 1; "Flyers Killed by Stupid Chiefs' Propaganda Schemes, Col. Mitchell Charges," *Washington Star,* Sept. 6, 1925, p. 1; memo from American Legation, Office of the Military Attache Vienna to G-2, Washington, Sept. 25, 1925, box 1659, file 2657-FF-126, MID, NA.

25   *with their superiors:* "Mitchell Talk Angers PB-1 Crew," undated newspaper article, box 57, WM, LOC; "Mitchell Unfair to Air Services, Says Bingham," *New York Herald Tribune,* Sept. 7, 1925; "Both Insubordination and Folly," *New York Times,* Sept. 7, 1925; Robert H. Ferrell, *The Presidency of Calvin Coolidge* (Lawrence, Kans.: University Press of Kansas, 1998), pp. 32–34; Mitchell *Winged Defense,* p. 143; Al Wilson, "Stunt Flying," *Saturday Evening Post,* Sept. 19, 1925, pp. 17–39; Lee Kennett, *The First Air War* (New York: Free Press, 1991), pp. 165–66, 228; Grumelli, *Trial of Faith,* pp. 38–45.

25   *national security:* Fan mail in box 11, WM, LOC; "Houston Air Service Officers Unite In Praising Mitchell's Denunciation of Non-Flyers," undated newspaper article, box 57, WM, LOC; "'Billy' Mitchell" and "Here's to You Billy Mitchell" poems in box 37, WM, LOC; "Mitchell Name Given to Newest Duncan Arrival," *San Antonio Evening News,* Sept. 17, 1925; "Kiwanians Back Col. Mitchell in Air Row," and "Optimists Approve Mitchell Stand," undated newspaper articles in box 56, WM, LOC; Associated Press dispatch, El Dorado, Ark., Sept. 8, 1925, box 56, WM, LOC; William Randolph Hearst, "Mr. Hearst Urges Independent and United Air Force," *New York American,* Sept. 7, 1925; "Defense Is in Hands of Roman Generals," *Fellowship Forum,* Sept. 26, 1925, p. 1.

25   *"increased momentum":* "Oldfield Pledges Demos Aid for Mitchell," Sept. 10, 1925, newspaper article in box 56, WM, LOC; Arthur Brisbane, "Col. Mitchell's Case. The Joy of Work. Gold in the Arctic. Deep Plowing," *Chicago Herald Examiner,* Sept. 8, 1925; Mitchell letter to Elizabeth Mitchell, Sept. 9, 1925, GF; Mitchell letter to Katharine Jackson, Sept. 22, 1925, BA.

26   *was "outrageous":* "Col. Mitchell Must Pay This Time, Army Men Say," *Washington Star,* Sept. 6, 1925; Mason Patrick, *The United States in the Air* (New York: Doubleday, 1928), p. 181.

26   *lost his mind:* reminiscences of Adm. Joseph J. Clark, vol. 1, part 1, p. 157, OHC; Trimble, *Admiral William A. Moffett,* p. 161.

26   *in Washington:* Clark reminiscences, p. 157, OHC; Eugene Wilson reminiscences, pp. 363–64, OHC.

26   *he wanted:* Trimble, pp. 4–12; Mitchell letter to Alfred Verville, April 17, 1933, WM, LOC; Clark reminiscences, pp. 157a, 206, OHC; Eugene Wilson reminiscences, p. 364, OHC.

26   *no part of:* Eugene Wilson reminiscences, pp. 206–9, 365, OHC.

27   *doomed flight:* Trimble, *Admiral William A. Moffett,* pp. 13–14, 159–61; Clark reminiscences, p. 157, OHC; Eugene Wilson reminiscences, pp. 200–203, OHC; memo from Moffett to Adm. E.W. Eberle, CNO, June 24, 1925, box 8, MT, NA.

27   *"Coolidge prosperity":* Virginia Pope, "Mrs. Coolidge Returns to Simple Life," undated newspaper article in press clipping files, CCP; "President's Stay at

White Court," *Daily Hampshire Gazette*, Sept. 9, 1925, p. 11; Geoffrey Perrett, *America in the Twenties: A History* (New York: Simon & Schuster, 1982), pp. 224, 228–29.

28   *press corps objected:* "Mrs. Coolidge Returns to Simple Life," Virginia Pope, undated newspaper article in press clipping files, CCP; Robert Sobel, *Coolidge: An American Enigma* (Washington: Regnery, 1998), pp. 19, 27, 236, 239–40, 301–30; Perrett, *America in the Twenties*, p. 193; Ferrell, *The Presidency*, pp. 9–10, 23.

28   *"too dangerous":* Coolidge Press Conference Sept. 4, 1925, transcript no. 2, vol. 4–7, CCP.

28   *for the navy:* Letters sent to White House requesting *Shenandoah* flights over cities and states, 1923–25, reel 24, CC, LOC.

28   *no personality:* Sobel, *Coolidge*, pp. 3–5, 149, 236; Ferrell, *The Presidency*, p. 9.

29   *White House grounds:* Sobel, *Coolidge*, pp. 11–14, 56, 217, 236; Ferrell, *The Presidency*, pp. 19, 23, 41, 204–5; Perrett, pp. 180, 287; author interview with Lu Knox, curator Calvin Coolidge Presidential Library and Museum, Sept. 23, 2002.

29   *he entered:* Bruce Bliven, "The Great Coolidge Mystery," *Harpers*, December 1925, pp. 145–53; Sobel, *Coolidge*, p. 278; Ferrell, *The Presidency*, p. 140; Perrett, *America in the Twenties*, pp. 149–50, 208–22, 231–37, 276.

29   *Coolidge or Chaos:* Ferrell, *The Presidency*, p. 40; Sobel, *Coolidge*, pp. 6, 156, 227–28; Perrett, *America in the Twenties* pp. 190–91.

29   *"old black box":* Sobel, p. 243; Correspondence between White House and Navy on William Spratley's complaint, Sept. 6–11, 1925, reel 24, CC, LOC.

30   *defense budgets:* Coolidge letter to Frederick Patterson, Sept. 27, 1925, reel 109, and Porter Adams telegram to White House, Oct. 13, 1924, reel 34, CC, LOC; War Department press release: "New Military Aide to the President," April 4, 1925, box 16, MT, NA; Robert P. White, *Mason Patrick and the Fight for Air Service Independence* (Washington, D.C.: Smithsonian Institution Press, 2001), pp. 87–92; Ferrell, *The Presidency*, pp. 26, 146; Hurley, *Billy Mitchell*, p. 99.

30   *the presidency:* Ferrell, *The Presidency*, pp. 9–10, 101; Sobel, *Coolidge*, pp. 21–22, 28, 59, 339; Perrett, *America in the Twenties*, p. 179.

30   *as a criminal:* "Serious View by Coolidge," *New York Times*, Sept. 6, 1925, p. 6.

30   *summer heat:* "Coolidges Visit Aunt in Hub—Will Leave White Court Tonight," *Daily Hampshire Gazette*, Sept. 9, 1925, p. 1; John Edward Nevin, "President Is Returning Silent on Mitchell Case," *Washington Post*, Sept. 10, 1925; "President at Desk Within Hour After Return to Capitol," *Washington Star*, Sept. 9, 1925.

31   *be replaced:* "Big Issues Await Coolidge's Return," *New York Times*, Sept. 6, 1925, p. 3; Ferrell, *The Presidency*, pp. 74–75; Sobel, *Coolidge*, pp. 340–43.

31   *his presidency:* Ferrell, p. 205; Everett Sanders letter to William Allen White on "Outstanding Features of the Coolidge Regime," Feb. 18, 1935, ES, LOC.

31   *reporters, photographers:* Charles B. Parmer dispatch for Universal Service, Sept. 25, 1925, box 55, WM, LOC; "Mitchell Arrives; to Prove, He Says, Every Allegation," *Washington Post*, Sept. 26, 1925, p. 1.

31   *the trip east:* Diary entries, Sept. 22–25, box 1, MB, MHS.

31–32 from *Stepping on to* to *"national defense system":* Parmer dispatch, Sept. 25, 1925; *Washington Post*, Sept. 26, 1925, p. 1; "Mitchell Draws Ovation in Capital," *Philadelphia Evening Bulletin*, Sept. 26, 1925; "Mitchell Is Hailed by Capital Throng," *New York Times*, Sept. 26, 1925, p. 1; Harriet Pillsbury interview.

32   *at a rally:* Sept. 26, 1925, entry, Boone diaries, box 40, *JB*, LOC.

33   *Hinds's request:* Hinds memo and confidential telegram to Adjutant General's
      Office, Washington, Sept. 13 and 19, 1925, Adjutant General's Office confiden-
      tial telegram to Hinds Sept. 18, 1925, Eighth Corps General Orders no. 25
      relieving Mitchell, Sept. 19, 1925, box 20, MT, NA.

33   *hunting excursions:* Diary entries, Sept. 8–22, 1925, box 1, MB, MHS.

33   *on September 10:* Mitchell letter to John N. Wheeler, Sept. 14, 1925, box 11,
      WM, LOC; Walter Hyams & Company memorandum to Mitchell, Sept. 7, 1925,
      box 57, WM, LOC; diary entry, Sept. 14, 1925, box 1, MB, MHS; "What a Con-
      structive Pol-
      icy for Our National Defense Should Consist Of," Mitchell statement Sept. 8,
      1925, "Mitchell's Statement on Disciplinary Action," Sept. 9, 1925, statement
      on Sept. 12, 1925, Prosecution Exhibits B, C, and D, boxes 9 and 19, MT, NA.

33   *quarters that night:* Col. E. D. Scott memo to Commanding General, Eighth
      Corps, Sept. 18, 1925, box 20, MT, NA; Lt. Col. George Hicks Eighth Corps
      memos to Mitchell, Sept. 6 and 11, 1925, and Mitchell's response, box 9, MT,
      NA; Mitchell letter to Elizabeth Mitchell, Sept. 17, 1925, GF.

34   *"out on top":* Mitchell letter to Elizabeth Mitchell, Sept. 17, 1925, GF; War
      Department telegram to Mitchell Sept. 23, 1925, box 11, WM, LOC; telegram
      from H. A. Toulmin Jr., Sept. 6, 1925, box 11, WM, LOC.

34   *when he landed:* H. H. Arnold, *Global Mission* (New York: Harper & Brothers,
      1949), pp. 21, 37, 42–43; Thomas M. Coffey, *Hap: The Story of the U.S. Air Force
      and the Man Who Built It, General Henry H. "Hap" Arnold* (New York: Viking
      Press, 1982), pp. 7–9, 40, 51, 57–58.

34   *with his case:* Coffey, *Hap,* p. 96, 123; Arnold, *Global Mission,* p. 119; DeWitt S.
      Copp, *A Few Great Captains: The Men and Events That Shaped the Development
      of U.S. Air Power* (McLean, Va.: EPM Publications, Inc: 1980), p. 29.

35   *"isn't it?":* Parmer dispatch, Sept. 25, 1925; "Mitchell Is Guest of Overseas
      Men," *Washington Star,* Sept. 27, 1925; diary entry, Sept. 25, 1925, MB, MHS;
      Mitchell letter to Elizabeth Mitchell, Sept. 17, 1925, GF.

CHAPTER 5   TRIBUNAL

Page

36   *defense teams:* Dispatch by William J. McEvoy, United Press, Oct. 24, 1925, box
      55, WM, LOC; Frederic J. Haskin, "The Mitchell Court-Martial," unidentified
      newspaper article, photos of inside of courtroom, William Mitchell Scrap-
      books, WMC, NASM.

37   *air his charges:* Arthur Sears Henning, "Weeks Resigns; Davis Named as War
      Secretary," *Chicago Tribune,* Oct. 14, 1925, p. 1; "Not a Show, Says Davis, Pick-
      ing Site of Mitchell Trial," *Washington Post,* Oct. 23, 1925; War Department
      press release, box 16, MT, NA; Cooke, *Billy Mitchell,* pp. 180–181.

37   *behind bars: A Manual for Courts-Martial: U.S. Army* (Washington, D.C.: U.S. Gov-
      ernment Printing Office, 1943), pp. 187, 225; *United States Army Officer's Hand-
      book of Military Law and Court-Martial Procedure* (Washington, D.C.: National
      Law Book Company, 1942), pp. 27–28; Levine, *Mitchell,* p. 343; Mitchell letter to
      Adjutant General and response, Oct. 9, 1925, box 11, WM, LOC; "Mitchell Ordered
      to Report Monday to Confront Charges," *Washington Star,* Oct. 2, 1925; Elizabeth
      Mitchell letter to Katharine Mitchell, October 7, 1925, BA.

38   *air force:* diary entry, Oct. 3, 1925, MB, MHS; press release: "Remarks by Con-

gressman Frank R. Reid, of Illinois, in Connection with Air Service Items of Army Appropriation Bill, Jan. 7, 1925," and Reid press release to New York Tribune–Universal Service, undated, box 1, WMC, NASM.

38   *extremely persuasive:* Drafts of articles 3 and 5 by Mitchell on his trial, box 28, WM, LOC; author interview with Charlotte T. Reid, Nov. 22, 2002.

38   *about it:* Charlotte T. Reid interview, Nov. 22, 2002; Bettie Larimore, "Director of Mitchell's Defense Is Full of Pep," *Boston Post,* Nov. 1, 1925.

39   *separate air force:* "'Bombshells If I'm Tried'—Mitchell," *New York American,* Oct. 6, 1925; "Mitchell Defense to Be Free Speech," *New York Times,* Oct. 25, 1925, p. 7; "Mitchell's First Defense Act May Challenge Court,' John Edwin Nevin, *Washington Post,* October 24, 1925; 420 "Separate Air Force" coupons, Record Group 457, package no. 448, 201–Mitchell, Wm. Col. A.S., Office of the Adjutant General Correspondence File, NA.

39   *a Democrat:* Charles B. Parmer, "Mitchell Oils Guns for Hunt in Dark Africa," unidentified newspaper, Oct. 20, 1925, box 54, WM, LOC; Mitchell letter to Rickenbacker, Oct. 1, 1925, box 20, WM, LOC.

39   *shot of him:* "Mitchell Gives Camera Men 'the Air,'" *Washington Times,* unknown date in October 1925, box 55, WM, LOC.

40   *the defendant:* Agriculture Department press release: "How the Weather Bureau Helps the Flyer," Sept. 17, 1925, box 38, WM, LOC; Weekly Press Review, Military Intelligence Division, G-2, Oct. 23, 1925 with McDarment memo attached, box 38, WM, LOC; War Department press release: "Trial of Colonel Mitchell," Oct. 20, 1925, MT, NA.

40   *court-martial:* "Moffett Hotly Assails Charges Mitchell Makes," *Washington Post,* Sept. 14, 1925; "Mitchell Refuses to Appear Before Naval Air Board," *Washington Star,* Oct. 8, 1925.

40   *"beginning to end":* "America After the War: The President's Omaha Address," *Outlook* 141, Oct. 14, 1925, p. 219.

41   *"to the matter":* Coolidge Press Conferences, Sept. 8–Oct. 20, 1925, transcript no. 2, vol. 4–7, CCP; Sobel, *Coolidge,* p. 304; "Coolidge Barely Escapes Being Hit by Auto; Pulled Back by His Guard; Driver Arrested," *New York Times,* Sept. 21, 1925, p. 1; Ferrell, *The Presidency,* p. 12; "White House Will Support the Army in Mitchell Case," *Washington Post,* Sept. 12, 1925, p. 1.

41   *feast on:* Coolidge letter to Morrow, March 11, 24, PPF 900, CCP; Morrow memorandum for Private Files, Jan. 31, 1925, Pershing letter to Morrow, June 10, 1926, Pershing letter to Morrow, Nov. 2, 1926, series 1, box 38, folder 55, DM, ACL; Morrow exchange of letters with N. Dean Jay, Oct. 13-Nov. 5, 1926, series 1, box 38, folder 55, DM, ACL; Mary Randolph letter to Morrow, Nov. 4, 1925, series 1, box 13, folder 31, DM, ACL.

42   *"belittle our own":* Stearns letter to Morrow, Sept. 18, 1925, series 9, box 1, file 3, DM, ACL; Coolidge letter to Morrow board, Sept. 12, 1925, reel 109, CC, LOC; Morrow letter to William Adams Brown, Dec. 22, 1925, series 9, box 1, file 2, DM, ACL.

42   *like glue:* Exchange of letters between Morrow and Davis, Nov. 14 and 20, 1925, series 1, box 17, folder 39, DM, ACL; Drum letters to Morrow, Sept. 29, Nov. 14, and Dec. 4, 1925, series 9, box 1, folder 2, DM, ACL; Sobel, p. 175.

42   *modern aircraft:* John Edwin Nevin, "Air Service Must Be Reformed, Naval Aviators Testify," *Washington Post,* Sept. 2, 1925, p. 1; Coffey, *Hap,* p. 123–25.

43   *"hear our cause":* Morrow Board photo, box 10, GH, UWM; Elizabeth Mitchell photo, family scrapbook, box 11, GH, UWM; Carter Field, "U.S. at Mercy of

Foes in Air, Says Mitchell," *New York Herald,* Sept. 30, 1925, p. 1; Arthur N. Chamberlin, "U.S. Wide Open to Air Foes, Says Mitchell, Blaming Army; Foulois Does Same," *New York World,* Sept. 30, 1925, p. 1; Eleanor Arnold reminiscences, p. 58, OHC.

43   *"was disappointing":* Arnold, *Global Mission,*pp. 119–120; Hurley, *Billy Mitchell,* p. 103; Arthur N. Chamberlin, "U.S. Wide Open to Air Foes, Says Mitchell, Blaming Army; Foulois Does Same," *New York World,* Sept. 30, 1925, p. 1.

43   *his tribunal:* Dispatch by William J. McEvoy, United Press, Oct. 24, 1925, box 55, WM, LOC.

44   *"to see you":* "Trial of Mitchell Is Dramatic Scene," *Washington Star,* Oct. 28, 1925; Elizabeth Mitchell letter to Katharine Mitchell, Oct. 7, 1925, BA.

44   *newspaper column:* Josephus Daniels, "Can Anybody or Everybody Muzzle Mitchell?" unidentified newspaper, box 58, WM, LOC; diary entry, Oct. 28, 1925, MB, MHS.

44   *"all others":* Reid press release for morning papers, Oct. 25, 1925, box 1, WMC, NASM; Department of Naval Judge Advocate General memorandum, Oct. 1, 1925, box 8, MT, NA; Navy Department press release Oct. 27, 1921; "Balanced Fleet Needs Own Air Force, Says Moffett," *Washington Post,* Oct. 28, 1925; Navy press release on Lt. Cdr. C. E. Rosendahl's radio address, Oct. 27, 1925, box 37, WM, LOC.

44   *$1.5 million:* "Dempsey Insists His Nose Is Real," *New York Times,* Oct. 28, 1925, p. 22.

45   *Emery Building:* Lt. Col. Sherman Moreland summons letter to Mitchell, Oct. 27, 1925, box 16, MT, NA; Brig. Gen. S. D. Rockenbash letter to Mitchell, Oct. 27, 1925, box 11, WM, LOC; "Trial of Mitchell Is Dramatic Scene," *Washington Star,* Oct. 28, 1925; diary entry, Oct. 25 and 26, 1925, MB, MHS.

CHAPTER 6   THE CHALLENGE

Page
46   *the public:* Photos in the *Washington Star,* Oct. 28, 1925, and *Washington Daily News,* Oct. 29, 1925; "Mitchell Protest Ousts Three Judges as His Trial Begins," *New York Times,* Oct. 29, 1925, p. 1.

46   *to his arm:* Correspondence on motor transportation for members of the Mitchell court, Oct. 28 and Nov. 18, 1925, box 16, MT, NA; Harriet Mitchell notes on the trial, family scrapbook, box 11, GH, UWM; "Mitchell Attacks Powers of the Court After He Forces Three to Retire," *Washington Star,* Oct. 28, 1925, p. 1.

47   *classified material:* "Mitchell Protest Ousts Three Judges As His Trial Begins," *New York Times,* Oct. 29, 1925, p. 1; "Mitchell Attacks Powers of the Court After He Forces Three to Retire," *Washington Star,* Oct. 28, 1925, p. 1; "President Of Court Loses Post," *Washington Times,* Oct. 28, 1925, p. 1; Harriet Mitchell notes on the trial, family scrapbook, box 11, GH, UWM; Lt. Col. A. B. Cox memo to Col. McMullen on guard detail, Oct. 27, 1925, box 16, MT, NA; Adjutant General's Office memo on temporary phone service for the Emory Building, Oct. 28, 1925, file 333.9 Col. William Mitchell, box 910, IG, NA.

47   *"father's big voice":* "'Mrs. Billy' to Back Mate 'Tooth and Nail' in Trial," Corinne Rich, *Washington Herald,* Oct. 29, 1925.

48   *Sam Browne belts:* "President of Court Loses Post," *Washington Times,* Oct. 28,

1925, p. 1; "Mitchell Attacks Powers of the Court After He Forces Three to Retire," *Washington Star*, Oct. 28, 1925, p. 1; Moreland memo to court members on uniforms, Oct. 27, 1925, box 16, MT, NA.

48–49   from *Brisbane* to *Betty afterward:* Undated column by Arthur Brisbane, Mitchell Scrapbooks, WMC, NASM; memos of 1st Lt. J. A. O'Neill, Maj. Henry C. Rexach, and Lt. Col. Walter O. Boswell, Nov. 1–10, 1925, box 369, file 290–11, MID, NA; War Department press release, "Trial of Colonel Mitchell," with biographies of court members, Oct. 20, 1925, box 16, MT, NA; "May Protest on Court Member," *New York Times*, Oct. 25, 1925; "Case Is Unusual, Mitchell Shows," *Washington Star*, Oct. 30, 1925; Frank McCoy letters to Gen. Leonard Wood, Sept. 30 and Oct. 8, 1925, box 177, LW, LOC; diary entry, Jan. 12, 1913, CS, TF.

49–50   from *Then there was* to *during the trial:* Harriet Pillsbury interview; Clive Lee and Richard Henschel, *Douglas MacArthur* (New York: Henry Holt, 1952), pp. 7–39, 43–47; Douglas MacArthur, *Reminiscences* (Greenwich, Conn.: Fawcett Publications, 1964), pp. 84–88, 92–93; Donald Smythe, *Pershing: General of The Armies* (Bloomington, Ind.: Indiana University Press, 1986), pp. 276–78; William Mitchell, *Memoirs of World War I* (New York: Random House, 1960), p. 305; Davis, *Billy Mitchell Affair*, p. 146; Levine, *Mitchell*, p. 194–197; diary entry, Oct. 24, 1925, MB, MHS; MacArthur letter to Leonard Wood, June 30, 1925, box 177, LW, LOC.

51   *their branches:* "President of Court Loses Post," *Washington Times*, Oct. 28, 1925, p. 1; "Mitchell Attacks Powers of the Court After He Forces Three to Retire," *Washington Star*, Oct. 28, 1925, p. 1; "Mitchell Protest Ousts Three Judges as His Trial Begins," *New York Times*, Oct. 29, 1925, p. 1; court-martial procedure notes for Colonel Moreland, box 12, MT, NA; War Department press release, "Trial of Colonel Mitchell," with biographies of court members, Oct. 20, 1925, box 16, MT, NA; Cooke, *Billy Mitchell,* p. 189.

52   *days of his life:* Reid notes on court members, box 1, WMC, NASM; Reid's court-martial procedure guide, box 1, WMC, NASM; Draft of Mitchell articles on the trial, part 5, box 28, WM, LOC; Author interview with William Webb, Jr., June 26, 2002; "Wizard of Legal Research Helps Reid Defend Mitchell, *Baltimore Sun*, Nov. 3, 1925; William H. Webb, "Why General Douglas MacArthur Voted 'Not Guilty' in the Court-Martial of 'Billy' Mitchell," draft article, Nov. 29, 1972, given to author by William Webb, Jr.

53   *the courtroom:* Mitchell court-martial trial transcript, pp. 1–7, MT, NA. (In the interests of readability, the dialogue from the courtroom has been considerably condensed from what appeared in the court transcript, which is 3,781 pages long. As in any lengthy trial, the questions from the attorneys and the answers from the witnesses are often long, repetitive, and rambling. I have condensed many of these quotes or paraphrased them. None of the quoted words has been altered in any way from the original transcript, but in some instances the sentences in quotes have been shortened to get to the point of what the lawyers and witnesses were saying. The prosecution and defense attorneys also often called witnesses out of what might be considered logical narrative order. In order to make the story more understandable for the reader, in a few instances the witnesses appear in the book not in the same order that they took the stand in the trial.)

54   *"step forward":* Biographies of Army Figures, U.S. Army Center of Military History, pp. 1077–80; Coffey, *Hap*, pp. 235–36, 348–54; Smythe, pp. 152, 157, and

225; trial transcript, pp. 8–9, MT, NA; report of interviews with Gen. Hamilton Howze, April 12, 1973, box 1, HH, AWC.

54 *had forgotten:* trial transcript, pp. 8–9, MT, NA; Maj. H. R. Harmon memo to Mitchell, Oct. 26, 1925, box 11, WM, LOC.

55 *for expenses:* "Bride Shoots Big Game on Honeymoon," *Wisconsin News and Evening Sentinel,* July 14, 1924; photo of Mitchell and wife, *Washington Post,* Oct. 28, 1923; undated *Philippines Herald* article, box 58, WM, LOC; "Brig. Gen. Mitchell and Bride Leave For Hawaii," unidentified article, box 56, WM, LOC; "Report of Inspection of United States Possessions in the Pacific and Java, Singapore, India, Siam, China & Japan," by Brigadier General William Mitchell, Assistant Chief of Air Service, Oct. 24, 1924, p. 1, folder 4, 201, NPRC; War Department orders for the Pacific trip, Sept. 29, 1923, box 10, WM, LOC; Undated Patrick letter to Mitchell in Hawaii on his inspection of the Philippine Garrison, box 11, WM, LOC.

55 *best ponies:* Brian McAllister Linn, *Guardians of Empire: The U.S. Army and the Pacific, 1902–1940* (Chapel Hill: University of North Carolina Press, 1997), pp. 120, 194, 200–202.

55 *at their disposal:* Summerall letter to Patrick, May 28, 1923, box 3016, file 333.1, HAW, NA; Letter from Major General Eli A. Helmick, Inspector General, to Patrick, March 20, 1923, box 3016, file 333.1, HAW, NA; memo by Maj. W. G. Kilner on Helmick's inspection, July 11, 1925, box 3016, file 333.1, HAW, NA; Extracts of Helmick inspection, April 9, 1923, box 4, CS, LOC; Summerall radiogram to Mitchell, Sept. 27, 1923, box 10, WM, LOC; trial transcript, p. 18; Preliminary Report of Inspection of Air Service Activities in the Hawaiian Department," by Brigadier General William Mitchell, Dec. 10, 1923, box 42, WM, LOC; "President of Court Loses Post," *Washington Times,* Oct. 28, 1925, p. 1.

55 *with airmen:* "Preliminary Report of Inspection," Dec. 10, 1923, pp. 43–47, 121–70, WM, LOC.

56 *"in the world":* "Report of Inspection," Oct. 24, 1924, pp. 1–40, 201, NPRC.

56 *years later:* "Report of Inspection," Oct. 24, 1924, pp. 50–59, 201, NPRC.

57 *were inflated:* Linn, *Guardians,* xi-xii, 170–177, 207–208, 251; Brig. Gen. George Van Horn Moseley letter to Maj. Gen. William R. Smith, June 17, 1925, box 3, GM, LOC; memo Col. James H. Reeves, G-2, to Assistant Chief of Staff, WPD, box 84, file 2050, WP,NA.

57 *Midway Island:* "Report of Inspection," Oct. 24, 1924, pp. 50–54, 201, NPRC.

57 *"white race":* "Report of Inspection," Oct. 24, 1924, pp. 1–3, 26–29, 201, NPRC.

58 *being cowards:* Sir Philip Gibbs, "The World in Peril," *Collier's* 75, Feb. 21, 1925, pp. 8–9; Lothrop Stoddard, "The Japanese Issue in California," *World's Work,* 4 October 1920, pp. 585–99; John Bakeless, "Contemporary Voices Prophesying War," *Outlook* 142, March 10, 1926, pp. 370–372; Smythe, pp. 72, 142; Coffman, pp. 317–320; Eleanor Arnold reminiscences, p. 59, OHC.

58 *"these islands":* Linn, pp. 152–55; "Preliminary Report of Inspection," Dec. 10, 1923, WM, LOC.

58 *Mitchell's scenario:* Linn, pp. xii–xiv, 146–47, 167–69, 175–76, 183, 210–13; George Patton memo to Chief of Staff, Hawaiian Department, June 3, 1937, box 71, GP, LOC.

59 *in the back:* Linn, *Guardians,* pp. 153, 195, 203–14, 251.

59 *he finally said:* trial transcript, pp. 14–18, MT, NA; "President of Court Loses Post," *Washington Times,* Oct. 28, 1925, p. 1.

59   *crossed him:* Summerall letter to Patrick, Dec. 27, 1923, box 10, WM, LOC; unsigned memo on Summerall in "Summerall File," box 10, HD, AWC.

60   *Bowley had been:* Trial transcript, pp. 18–19, MT, NA; "President of Court Loses Post," *Washington Times,* Oct. 28, 1925, p. 1; Harriet Mitchell notes on the trial, family scrapbook, box 11, GH, UWM; "Mitchell Protest Ousts Three Judges as His Trial Begins," *New York Times,* Oct. 29, 1925, p. 1.

60   *and Winship:* trial transcript, p. 19; "President of Court Loses Post," *Washington Times,* Oct. 28, 1925, p. 1; F. Granville Munson and Walter H. E. Jaeger, *United States Army Officer's Handbook of Military Law and Court-Martial Procedure* (Washington, D.C.: National Law Book Co.: 1942), pp. 49, 97.

61   *it was true:* Bettie Larimore, "Head of Mitchell Air Court Inquiry Is 'Stormy Petrel': Maj. Gen. Robert Lee Howze Has Medals for Bravery," unidentified newspaper article, Mitchell Scrapbooks, WMC, NASM; "Gen. R. L. Howze, Noted Fighter, Dies," *New York Times,* Sept. 20, 1926; Herbert Molloy Mason, Jr., *The Great Pursuit* (New York: Random House, 1970), pp. 160–67; Mitchell letter to Patrick, Feb. 17, 1923, box 11, WM, LOC; Feb. 11–13, 1923, entries, Daily Journal of Brig. Gen. William Mitchell, box 5, WM, LOC; report of Interviews with Gen. Hamilton H. Howze, Apr. 12, 1973, box 1, HH, AWC; Mitchell letter to Commander Reams, March 4, 1926, box 12, WM, LOC; Howze letter to John L. Hines, Sept. 18, 1922, JH, LOC.

62   *"fellow citizens":* trial transcript, pp. 23-(1)-48, MT, NA; "Intoning of Mitchell Charges Lulls Courtroom in a Doze," *Washington Star,* Oct. 29, 1925; *Address of President Coolidge before the Graduating Class U.S. Naval Academy Annapolis, Md., June 3, 1925* (Washington, D.C.: U.S. Government Printing Office, 1925), p. 4.

62   *senior officers:* "Mitchell Protest Ousts Three Judges as His Trial Begins," *New York Times,* Oct. 29, 1925, p. 1; James O'Donnell Bennett, "Ousts 3 Judges as Mitchell's Defense Opens," *Chicago Tribune,* Oct. 29, 1925, p. 1; Harry Johnson letter to Gen. Fred Sladen, Oct. 28, 1925, box 5, SF,AWC; War Department letter to Gen. J. A. Hull, box 16, WM, LOC.

62   *own rules:* "Summerall Hits Mitchell's Stand," Washington Star, Oct. 28, 1925, p. 4; "President of Court Loses Post," *Washington Times,* Oct. 28, 1925, p. 1; "Let the Public Pass on My Army Record, Summerall Asks," *Chicago Tribune,* Oct. 29, 1925.

CHAPTER 7   PROMISE

Page

63   *to recuperate: In Memoriam: John Lendrum Mitchell, 1842–1904,* Milwaukee, Wis., 1925, pp. 1, 19, HP; Mitchell-Becker wedding announcement, box 1, JLM, UWM; John Mitchell letter to Harriet Mitchell, Mar. 13, 1886, box 1, JLM, UWM.

64   *personal rail car:* Charles H. Buford, *Alexander Mitchell: Banker, Industrialist, Builder of Railroads, Pioneer of the Great West!* (New York: Newcomen Society in North America, 1950), pp. 7–20; George Reardon, "Alexander Mitchell: A Wheeler Dealer par Excellence," *Exclusively Yours,* Mar. 1989, pp. 26–97; Alexander Mitchell biography, pp. 1–17, box 27, AM, WHS; "A Short History of the Wisconsin Club," Wisconsin Club brochure, 900 West Wisconsin Ave., Milwaukee; "The Croesus of the West," article from unidentified newspaper, box 18, JLM, UWM; "The Milwaukee Story: The Magnificent Mitchells," article

from unidentified newspaper, box 8, GH, UWM; "A Loss to the West," *New York Times,* Apr. 20, 1887, p. 1; Alexander Mitchell letter to John Mitchell, Feb. 3, 1887, JLM, UWM.

64   *eye trouble:* Nicholas Greusel letter to Alexander Mitchell, Jan. 9, 1863, and James S. Brown letter to Secretary of War E. M. Stanton, Feb. 23, 1863, box 1, AM, WHS; Alexander Mitchell letter to Martha Mitchell, Mar. 18, 1862, box 1, JLM, UWM.

64   *spoiled him:* Interview with Harriet Pillsbury, June 1–2, 2002; "The John Lendrum Mitchell Residence/'Meadowmere,'" script prepared by Traci E. Schnell, Historic Milwaukee, Inc., Spaces & Traces Neighborhood Tour 2002, West Allis, HP; "The Mitchell Scandal," *Milwaukee Sentinel,* Aug. 20, 1877, p. 3; "The Great Scandal," *Milwaukee Sentinel,* Aug. 21, 1887, p. 2; "Habeas Corpus," *Milwaukee Sentinel,* Aug. 30, 1877, p. 3; "The Mitchell Scandal," *Milwaukee Sentinel,* Sept. 3, 1877, p. 4; "Milwaukee's Ulcer," *Milwaukee Sentinel,* Sept. 3, 1877, p. 3; "Shadows of City Life," *Republican-Sentinel,* Nov. 4, 1882, p. 10.

65   *middle name:* "A Niçois Who Has Made His Mark," Box 54, WM, LOC; Harriet Pillsbury interview; Mitchell letter to Army Adjutant General, Apr. 27, 1901, box 10, GH, UWM.

65   *skating parties:* "The John Lendrum Mitchell Residence/'Meadowmere,'" script, HP; "Meadowmere, a Monument to Regal Living," *Milwaukee Journal,* Nov. 11, 1955, p. 16; "Historic Farm to Be Lots," *Wisconsin News,* Sept. 12, 1925, p. 1; author visit to Meadowmere, June 7, 2002; photos of Meadowmere, box 3, WMP, MHS; photos of Meadowmere, box 7, GH, UWM.

65   *University of Grenoble:* John Lendrum Mitchell memoriam, pp. 1, 59–67, HP.

66   *air service:* Harriet Pillsbury interview; "Billy Mitchell's Sister, Mrs. Jones, Dies at 81," article from unidentified newspaper, July 28, 1966, box 8, GH, UWM; "Gen. Billy Mitchell's Sister Joins Yugoslav Band to Fight Nazis," article from unidentified newspaper, box 54, WM, LOC; "Mitchell Kin's Release Uged," *Los Angeles Examiner,* Jan. 4, 1942; author interview with Charles Bass, Sept. 17, 2003.

66   *something embarrassing:* "Col. Mitchell Was 'Awful' Boy, Says Former Nurse," article from unidentified newspaper, box 11, GH, UWM; Mitchell letter to Katharine Jackson, Jan. 9, 1923, BA.

66   *few months there:* "Peep at Racine College," *Daily Journal: Milwaukee,* Dec. 17, 1891; Racine College letter to Harriet Mitchell, Feb. 7, 1890, box 19A, WM, LOC.

67   *animals he saw:* Mitchell letter to mother, Feb. 17 and Mar. 29, 1890, box 19A, WM, LOC.

67   *"building paper":* Mitchell letters to mother, Jan. 31, Feb. 2, Mar. 17, and circa April, 1890, box 19A, WM, LOC.

67   *visit him:* Mitchell letters to mother, Feb. 1 and 5, 1890, box 19A, WM, LOC.

67   *air rifle:* Mitchell report cards from Racine College, Mar. 1890–February 1891, Racine College letter to Harriet Mitchell, Dec. 23, 1890, H. D. Robinson letter to Harriet Mitchell, Oct. 24, 1892, box 19A, M. L. Brown letters to Harriet Mitchell, Jan. 12 and Feb. 26, 1891, box 19A, and Mitchell letters to mother, Mar. 16, June 1, and Nov. 8 or 9, 1890, box 19A, WM, LOC; unidentified news clipping on Racine play, June 6, 1894, box 1, JLM, UWM.

68   *her son sad:* Harriett Mitchell letters to William Mitchell, Sept. 12 and 26, and Nov. 11, 1890, box 1, WMP, MHS; Mitchell letter to mother, Apr. 3, 1890, box

19B, WM, LOC; Sarah Schmall letter to Harriet Mitchell, Apr. 8, 1890, and H. D. Robinson letter to Harriett Mitchell, box 19A, WM, LOC.

68   *"I suppose":* John Mitchell letter to William Mitchell, Sept. 1, 1884, box 1, JLM, UWM; John Mitchell letter to William Mitchell, Nov. 18, 1893, box 19A, WM, LOC; Charles Bass interview.

68   *father died:* Harriet Pillsbury interview; John Mitchell letter to Harriet Mitchell, Mar. 20, 1886, box 1, JLM, UWM; Mitchell letter to mother, Mar. 27, 1902, box 19B, WM, LOC; John Mitchell letter to Harriet Mitchell, July 18, 1884, box 1, JLM, UWM; Harriet Mitchell letter to William Mitchell, May 22, 1891, box 1, WMP, MHS.

68   *"they get it":* Mitchell letter to mother, Apr. 27, 1894, box 19A, WM, LOC.

69   *family fortune:* Harrison Reed letter to John Mitchell, May 24, 1889, box 2, AM, WHS; David Mitchell letter to father, Sept. 29, 1893, box 1, AM, WHS; John Mitchell letters to Harriet Mitchell, Sept. 27 and Oct. 7, 1893, Bill to Harriet Mitchell for German boarding school, Oct. 31, 1901, John Mitchell letter to Harriet Mitchell, May 16, 1894, and Martha Mitchell letter to Washington Becker, no date, box 1, JLM, UWM; Arthur Piper letter to Harriet Mitchell, box 19A, WM, LOC.

69   *had accumulated:* John Lendrum Mitchell memoriam, pp. 173–75, HP; John Mitchell letter to Harriet Mitchell, Oct. 2, 1893, box 1, JLM, UWM; Washington Becker letter to creditors of Wisconsin marine and Fire Insurance Company Bank, Dec. 20, 1893, box 1, JLM, UWM; John Mitchell letter to Harriet Mitchell, Oct. 5 and 7, 1893, box 1, JLM, UWM; Washington Becker letter to John Mitchell, Nov. 4, 1893, box 1, AM, WHS; Alfred Cary letters to John Mitchell, Nov. 4 and 10, 1893, box 1, AM, WHS; Wisconsin Marine and Fire Insurance Co. Bank letter to John Mitchell, Nov. 9, 1893, box 1, AM, WHS; John Mitchell letter to Harriet Mitchell, July 6, 1896, box 1, JLM, UWM; Probate documents for John L. Mitchell, Envelopes 1–3, file 18679, Milwaukee County Register in Probate.

69   *Washington, D.C.:* Mitchell letter to mother, Nov. 17, 1893, and Feb. 20, 1894, Mitchell letter to father May 23, 1895, box 19A, WM, LOC.

70   *flunked chemistry:* Mitchell letter to mother circa 1897, box 19A, WM, LOC; Mitchell report card from Columbian College, May 27, 1897, box 1, JLM, UWM.

71   *"on right then":* Ruth Mitchell, *My Brother Bill*, pp. 30–32; John Lendrum Mitchell Memoriam, p. 19.

71   *Civil War:* Ruth Mitchell, pp. 32–33; Davis, pp. 16–17.

71   *"of the Pacific":* John Lendrum Mitchell Memoriam, pp. 59–63, 83–85.

72   *college graduates:* Lucy Mercein letter to Harriet Mitchell, May 19, 1898, and Mitchell letters to mother, May 21 and Aug. 3, 1898, box 19A, WM, LOC; letter to Katharine Jackson from her mother, Feb. 15, 1917, BA; Caroline Mitchell letter to her mother-in-law, Harriet, Feb. 15, 1917, BA.

72   *state militia:* Mitchell letter to mother, July 22, 1898, box 19A, WM, LOC; Meilinger, p. 82; Smythe, p. 2.

72   *Morse code:* Mitchell letter to mother, Aug. 9, 1898, Mitchell letter to father, Dec. 9, 1899, box 19A, WM, LOC; Hurley, *Billy Mitchell*, p. 10; Mitchell letters to Uncle Doc, Sept. 3 and 14, 1898, box 19A, WM, LOC.

73   *"have this fall":* Mitchell letters to mother, July 11, Aug. 9, 14 and 29, 1898, box 19A, WM, LOC.

73   *had occurred;* Mitchell letters to mother, Aug. 20 and 23, Sept. 13, 1898, and Mitchell letter to father, Sept. 20, 1898, box 19A, WM, LOC.

73   *"out of us":* Mitchell letters to mother, Sept. 6, 1898, Mitchell letter to Uncle Doc, Sept. 3, 1898, box 19A, WM, LOC.

74   *aboard boats:* Mitchell letter to father, Dec. 24, 1898, Mitchell letter to mother, Dec. 27, 1898, box 19A, WM, LOC; War Department Efficiency Report for William Mitchell, July 2, 1901, box 10, GH, UWM.

74   *"greatest nations":* Mitchell letter to mother, Jan. 2, 1899, box 7, GH, UWM; Felicity Trueblood interview.

75   *cable-laying teams:* Letter from Col. H. H. C. Dunwoody to Mitchell, Feb. 2, 1899, letter to Col. Dunwoody, Feb. 11, 1899, Mitchell letter to father, Jan. 27, 1899, and Mitchell letter to mother, Mar. 28, 1899, box 19A, WM, LOC.

75   *"every day":* Mitchell letters to mother Feb. 19, Apr. 6 and June 14, 1899, and Mitchell letter to father Feb. 14, 1899, box 19A, WM, LOC.

75   *"such range":* Mitchell letter to father, Jan. 27, 1899, Mitchell letters to mother, May 10, May 17, and June 7, 1899, and Lt. N. W. Stamford letters to Mitchell, June 1 and June 14, 1899, box 19A, WM, LOC.

76   *daughter, Caroline:* Mitchell letters to father, June 4, 12, and 16, 1899, and Mitchell letters to mother, Mar. 4, Apr. 6, and June 23, 1899, box 19A, WM, LOC.

76   *"in the spring":* Mitchell letters to mother, Jan. 5, Feb. 7, July 23 and 29,and Aug. 28, 1899, Mitchell letters to father, Jan. 10 and 14, Mar. 31, June 24, and July 12 and 13, 1899, Harriet Mitchell letter to William Mitchell, Apr. 16, 1899, and John Mitchell letter to Harriet Mitchell, Aug. 25, 1899, box 19A, WM, LOC.

76   *"very favorable":* John Mitchell letter to Harriet Mitchell, Sept. 25, 1899, box 19A, WM, LOC.

77   *Caroline Stoddard:* Mitchell letter to mother, Sept. 21, 1899, Lucy Mercein letter to Harriet Mitchell, Dec. 16, 1899, and Mitchell letter to Uncle Doc, Oct. 4, 1899, box 19A, WM, LOC.

77   *"I ever saw":* Mitchell letter to Uncle Doc, Nov. 1, 1899, and Mitchell letters to father, Nov. 4 and Dec. 9, 1899, box 19A, WM, LOC; War Department Efficiency Report for William Mitchell, July 2, 1901, box 10, GH, UWM; Summaries of Efficiency Reports for William Mitchell, 201, NPRC; letter from Capt. D. J. Carr to 2nd Division Adjutant General, Feb. 1900, 201, NPRC.

77   *"in marksmanship":* Summaries of Efficiency Reports for William Mitchell, 201, NPRC; Mitchell letter to mother, Jan. 25, 1900, and Mitchell letter to Uncle Doc, Dec. 14, 1899, box 19B, WM, LOC; Ruth Mitchell, *My Brother Bill*, p. 46.

78   *as a souvenir:* Mitchell letters to mother, May 15 and June 1, 1900, box 19B, WM, LOC.

78   *little plays:* Mitchell letter to mother Mar. 4, 1900, and Mitchell letter to father, Apr. 20, 1900, box 19B, WM, LOC; Ruth Mitchell, p. 44.

78   *two votes:* Mitchell letter to father, Dec. 9, 1899, and Mitchell letter to mother, Dec. 21, 1899, box 19B, WM, LOC.

79   *"mouths sealed":* Mitchell letter to Uncle Doc, Dec. 14, 1899, Mitchell letter to Father, Jan. 28, 1900, and Mitchell letter to mother, June 1, 1900, box 19B, WM, LOC.

79   *a staff job:* Mitchell letters to father, Dec. 9, 1899, box 19A, and Mar. 18, 1900, box 19B, WM, LOC.

79   *of influence:* War Department Efficiency Report for William Mitchell, July 2, 1901, box 10, GH, UWM; Mitchell letter to father, June 26, 1900, box 1, JLM, UWM.

80 *as a general:* War Department Efficiency Report for William Mitchell, July 2, 1901, box 10, GH, UWM; Mitchell letter to mother, June 1, 1900, box 19B, WM, LOC: Mitchell letters to father, Jan. 3 and 7, 1900, box 1, JLM, UWM.

80 *permanent service:* John Mitchell letter to Harriet Mitchell, June 25, 1900, box 1, JLM, UWM; Chronology extract from William Mitchell's military service, 1901–1905, 201, NPRC; Summaries of Efficiency Reports for William Mitchell, 201, NPRC; Sen. John Spooner letter to Elihu Root, Feb. 23, 1901, Elihu Root letter to Sen. Spooner, Feb. 27, 1901, and War Department Adjutant General letter to Sen. Spooner, Apr. 17, 1901, box 10, GH, UWM; Grumelli, *Trial of Faith,* pp. 1–2; Cooke, *Billy Mitchell,* p. 31.

80 *into accepting:* "Hitching Up to Alaska," *Dearborn Independent,* Oct. 24, 1925, pp. 6, 30; William Mitchell, "Building the Alaskan Telegraph System," *National Geographic* 15, Sept. 1904, pp. 359–61.

81 *and insulators:* "Mount Billy Mitchell," J. C. Hicks, unidentified magazine, December 1969, HP; letter from Elva R. Scott to Harriet Pillsbury, Apr. 12, 1999, HP; Mitchell letters to mother, Mar. 27, Aug. 6 and Nov. 6, 1902, box 19B, WM, LOC; "Building the Alaskan Telegraph System," William Mitchell, *National Geographic,* Sept. 1904, vol. 15, pp. 359–61.

81 *top of him:* Mitchell letters to mother, Oct. 24, 1901, and Jan. 4, 1902, and Mitchell letter to father, Jan. 21, 1903, box 19B, WM, LOC; "Building the Alaskan Telegraph System," William Mitchell, *National Geographic,* pp. 359–361; Ruth Mitchell, p. 100.

81 *off hypothermia:* Mitchell letter to mother, Feb. 21, 1902, box 19B, WM, LOC; Ruth Mitchell, *My Brother Bill,* pp. 100–101.

82 *for the rest:* Mitchell letter to mother, Dec. 13, 1901, box 19B, WM, LOC; Ruth Mitchell, pp. 105–6.

82 *machine-powered planes:* Mitchell letter to mother, Feb. 3, 1902, box 19B, WM, LOC; Ruth Mitchell, *My Brother Bill,* pp. 87, 97.

82 *marry her:* Summaries of Efficiency Reports for William Mitchell, 201, NPRC; Telegram from Evans, Adjt. Gen., to Mitchell, Aug. 26, 1902, box 19B, WM, LOC; Mitchell letters to father, Jan. 17 and May 20, 1902, and Mitchell letter to mother, Apr. 26, 1902, box 19B, WM, LOC.

CHAPTER 8 "NOT GUILTY"

Page

83 *out to be:* "Call for Coolidge and Davis to Face Mitchell in Court Proposed by Reid," *Washington Star,* Oct. 31, 1925, p. 1; "Trial of Mitchell Ruled Legal; Reid Flays Procedure as Law Violation," *Washington Star,* Oct. 29, 1925, p. 1.

83 *federal court trials:* "The Intense Drama of the Mitchell Trial," *New York Times,* Nov. 15, 1925, p. 3.

84 *for a quarter:* David R. Mets, *The Air Campaign: John Warden and the Classical Airpower Theorists* (Maxwell Air Force Base, Ala.: Air University Press, 1999), p. 6; Perrett, *America in the Twenties,* pp. 31–50, 117, 229–51, 337; Sobel, *Coolidge,* p. 7; Ferrell, *The Presidency,* pp. 32, 96–101; advertisement in the *Washington Star,* Oct. 29, 1925, p. 5.

84 *into them:* Perrett, pp. 151–55; Kennett, *The First Air War,* pp. 227–28; Grumelli, *Trial of Faith,* p. 63; Patrick, *United States in the Air,* pp. 135–136.

84 *court groupies:* "Mrs. Mitchell Ideal Army Woman," *New York Sun,* Oct. 29,

1925, p. 2; photo of Mrs. Mitchell and Winship from unidentified paper, Oct. 30, 1925, box 58, WM, LOC; "Reid, Mitchell's Counsel, Looms as National Figure," *Baltimore Sun*, Oct. 30, 1925; "Colorful Audience of Women Present at Court-Martial," *Washington Star*, Oct. 29, 1925, p. 1.

84–85   from *Reid had spent* to *initial accuser:* Trial transcript, pp. 49–93, MT, NA; "War Dept. Charges Illegal, He Said," W. K. Hutchinson, *Washington Times*, Oct. 29, 1925, p. 1; John Edwin Nevin, "Coolidge Revealed as Actual Accuser of Col. Mitchell," *Washington Post*, Oct. 30, 1925, p. 1; Reid notes on Motion to Strike Out the Charge, box 20, MT, NA; "Colorful Audience of Women Present at Court-Martial," *Washington Star*, Oct. 29, 1925, p. 1; author interview with Eugene Fidell, May 8, 2002.

86   *soldier's jury:* Samuel T. Ansell, "Military Justice and Injustice," *The Nation*, Dec. 27, 1919, pp. 828–29; Jonathan Lurie, *Military Justice in America: The U.S. Court of Appeals for the Armed Forces, 1775–1980* (Lawrence, Kan.: University Press of Kansas, 2001), pp. 28–75; Frederick B. Wiener, "The Seamy Side Of The World War I Court-Martial Controversy," *Military Law Review* 12, 3 1989, pp. 109–23; "The Court Martial on Trial," *The Nation* 108, May 3, 1919, p. 679; *The Army Lawyer: A History Of the Judge Advocate General's Corps, 1775–1975* (Washington: U.S. Government Printing Office, 1976), pp. 113–57; Beth Hillman, "Chains of Command," *Legal Affairs*, May/June 2002, pp. 50–52; "Unequal Justice," Edward T. Pound, *U.S. News & World Report*, Dec. 16, 2002, pp. 19–30.

86   *backed him up:* Trial transcript, pp. 92–130, MT, NA.

88–89   from *Friday morning* to *began chuckling:* Trial transcript, pp. 131–38, MT, NA; "Counsel's Flowery Apologies Bring Roars in Mitchell Case," *Washington Star*, Oct. 30, 1925.

89   from *Winship, however* to *in the army:* Trial transcript, p. 144, MT, NA; "Mitchell's Court-Martial Proves Battle of Keen Wits," Robert T. Small, *Washington Star*, Oct. 31, 1925; Biography of Blanton Winship, Biography File, AWC; "Maj. Gen. Winship Dies at Age 77," *New York Times*, Oct. 10, 1947, p. 25; Article titled "National Whirligig" from an unidentified newspaper, box 54, WM, LOC; Harriet Mitchell notes on the trial, family scrapbook, box 11, GH, UWM.

89–91   from *Reid had no* to *was humiliating:* Trial transcript, pp. 144–46, MT, NA; "Mitchell's Wife at His Side," *New York Times*, Oct. 31, 1925; "Mrs. Mitchell Ideal Army Woman," *New York Sun*, Oct. 29, 1925, p. 2; "Coolidge Immune from Testifying in Mitchell Case," *Public Ledger and North American*, Oct. 31, 1925, p. 1.

91   *budgets from him:* Joel T. Boone memoirs, pp. xxi–101, 466, box 46, JB, LOC; Ferrell, pp. 152–53.

91   *several wives:* Joel T. Boone Diaries, entry for Oct. 31, 1925, box 40, JB, LOC; Joel T. Boone memoirs, pp. xxi–482, box 46, JB, LOC.

92   *to testify:* "Mitchell's Actual Court-Martial To Begin Next Monday," John Edwin Nevin, *Washington Post*, Oct. 31, 1925; "Congress to Hear Flyer's Case," *Washington News*, Oct. 30, 1925; "Mitchell Seeks Missing Letter," William J. McEvoy, *Washington News*, Oct. 31, 1925; Coolidge Press Conference, Oct. 30, 1925, transcript no. 2, vol. 4–7, CCP.

92   *was nuts:* Joel T. Boone memoirs, pp. xxi–475, xxi–476, xxi–482, box 46, JB, LOC.

CHAPTER 9   LOVE

Page

93   *love letters:* Stoddard wedding invitation for Caroline, box 9, GH, UWM; "Capt. Mitchell Takes a Bride," *Milwaukee Sentinel,* Dec. 3, 1903, p. 5; Mitchell letter to mother, November 1903, box 19B, WM, LOC; Felicity Trueblood interview.

94   *like a magnet:* Felicity Trueblood interview; author interview with Cicely Banfield, June 17, 2002.

94   *its salons: John Butts: His Ancestors and Some of His Descendants* (Poughkeepsie, N.Y.: Press of A. V. Haight), pp. 102–4, TF; Isaac Butts, *Protection and Free Trade,* (New York: Putnam, 1875), pp. 5–8, TF; Enoch Vine Stoddard family history papers, TF; Charles E. Fitch, "The History of the Browning Club: 1884–1910," pp. 5–27, TF; Hamilton B. Allen, "Billy Mitchell's 1st Wife Was Local Society Girl," article from unidentified Rochester newspaper, BF.

94   *she had read:* Felicity Trueblood interview; Cicely Banfield interview.

95   *on their level:* Vassar College Biographical Records Questionnaire for Caroline Stoddard; Perrett, *America in the Twenties,* pp. 155, 158; *Vassarian* yearbook, 1900, BF; Mitchell letters to mother, May 24 and June 25, 1902, box 19B, WM, LOC; Felicity Trueblood interview; Cicely Banfield interview.

95   *felt wronged:* Felicity Trueblood interview; Cicely Banfield interview.

95   *the prospect:* Mitchell letters to mother, June 30, July 14, and 30, 1901, box 19B, WM, LOC; Felicity Trueblood interview.

96   *"ever seen":* Mitchell letter to mother, Sept. 19, 1901, box 19B, WM, LOC.

96   *to join him:* Mitchell letters to mother, July 20, Nov. 1 and 22, 1901, box 19B, WM, LOC; Caroline Stoddard letter to Harriet Mitchell, Dec. 2, 1901, box 7, GH, UWM; diary entry Aug. 2, 1907, CS, TF.

96   *their romance:* Mitchell letters to mother, Nov. 5 and 29, Dec. 1, 1901, box 19B, WM, LOC.

97   *"tongue's end":* Caroline Stoddard letter to Harriet Mitchell, January 1904, Mitchell letter to father, Jan. 7, 1904, Mitchell letters to mother, Dec. 13, 1903, Jan. 11, 1904, box 19B, WM, LOC; Caroline Stoddard letter to Harriet Mitchell, Jan. 2, 1904, box 7, GH, UWM.

97   *in letters:* Efficiency Record of William Mitchell, Account of Services, 201, NPRC; Caroline Stoddard scrapbooks, BF; Cooke, *Billy Mitchell,* p. 39; Mitchell letter to mother, Aug. 23, 1905, box 19B, WM, LOC.

97   *signal school:* William Mitchell Summary of Efficiency Reports, 201, NPRC; Davis, *Billy Mitchell Affair,* p. 19; Cooke, *Billy Mitchell,* p. 43.

98   *in her diary:* Diary entries, Jan. 1, 10, and 25, Feb. 18 and 29, June 27–29, July 22, 1906, CS, TF.

98   *recently flown:* Diary entries, Jan. 18 and 23, Mar. 8 and 12, 1906, CS, TF; Mitchell letter to father, May 1, 1904, box 1, WMP, MHS; Davis, *Billy Mitchell Affair,* 19–20.

98   *bedroom fireplace:* Diary entries, Feb. 3, 13, 25 and 26, Apr. 7 and 10, Aug. 4, 1906, CS, TF.

98   *beyond words:* Diary entries, Apr. 19–27, May 18 and 25, June 5, 1906, CS, FT.

99   *she convalesced:* Diary entries, Aug. 18, 26 and 30, Sept. 19, 1906, CS, FT; Mitchell letter to George Gibbs, Saturday 1909 [*sic*], box 2, GG, LOC.

99   *the harbor:* Diary entries, Nov. 22–24, Dec. 8 and 14, 1906, Feb. 14 and Mar. 30, 1907, CS, TF; Caroline Stoddard scrapbooks, BF; Felicity Trueblood interview.

99   *came afterward:* Diary entries, Sept. 3, 1907, Mar. 25, 1908, May 5 and 13, 1908, CS, TF.

100   *next year:* Diary entries, Aug. 22 and 30, 1909, Feb. 2, 1910, CS, TF.

100   *went anywhere:* Summary of Efficiency Record of William Mitchell, 201, NPRC; diary entries, Dec. 5 and 29, 1907, CS, TF; Mitchell letters to George Gibbs, Feb. 28 and Mar. 13, 1912, box 2, GG, LOC.

100   *"have passed":* Diary entries, Dec. 15, 1912, Jan. 2 and 16, 1913, CS, TF; Mitchell letters to mother, Mar. 6 and May 9, 1912, box 19B, WM, LOC; Coffman, *War to End All Wars*, pp. 12, 31–33, 49–52; James R. Locher III, *Victory on the Potomac: The Goldwater-Nichols Act Unifies the Pentagon* (College Station: Texas A&M University Press, 2002), pp. 16–17.

101   *in competitions:* Caroline Stoddard scrapbooks, BF; diary entry, Feb. 17, 1913, CS, TF.

101   *to cover:* Marion Harland, *The Dinner Year-Book,* (New York: Scribner's, 1901), TF; *The Habits of Good Society: A Handbook for Ladies and Gentlemen* (New York: Rudd & Carlton), TF; Florence Howe Hall, *Social Usages at Washington,* (New York: Harper & Brothers, 1906), pp. v–ix, TF.

101   *someone different:* Diary entries, Feb. 22, Mar. 15 and 22, Apr. 9 and 16, May 12 and 14, Nov. 12 and 22, Dec. 10, 1913, CS, TF; dinner record for Caroline Mitchell, TF.

102   *with partygoers:* Diary entries, Feb. 2, Apr. 21 and 29, May 7, 26 and 28, June 27, Oct. 14, Nov. 19 and 21, 1913, Nov. 20–21, 1914, Jan. 16, Sept. 24, 1915, CS, TF; Caroline Mitchell letter to her mother-in-law, Harriet, Feb. 15, 1917, BA.

102   *the phonograph:* Diary entries, Mar. 17–18, 20–21, May 10, 1913, CS, TF; Felicity Trueblood interview; undated letter from Harriet Mitchell to Katharine Jackson, BA.

103   *but frugal:* Diary entries, June 1, 1913, June 10, July 28, 1914, CS, TF; Mitchell letters to mother, Feb. 10, 1913, undated 1914, Jan. 4 and 13, Feb. 2, Apr. 1, July 23, July 18, 1914, box 19B, WM, LOC; Harriet Mitchell letters to Katharine Jackson, Feb. 10 and Oct. 5, 1917, BA.

103   *it shouldn't:* Mitchell letters to mother, Mar. 16 and Sept. 1, 1914, box 19B, WM, LOC; diary entries, Aug. 14–16, 1913, CS, TF; Mitchell, *Memoirs of World War I,* p. 10; Davis, pp. 23–24.

103   *suffrage bill:* Diary entry, Aug. 14, 1913, CS, TF.

103   *either idea:* Mitchell letters to mother, Oct. 29 and Nov. 12, 1913, Jan. 22, 26, and 29, May 9 and Dec. 1, 1914, box 19B, WM, LOC; diary entries, Nov. 16, 1913, Oct. 11, 1914, Mar. 8 and 20, May 25, July 15, 1915, CS, TF.

104   *behind a desk:* William Mitchell Summary of Efficiency Reports, 201, NPRC; Mitchell letter to George Gibbs, Mar. 13, 1912, GG, LOC; Mitchell letter to mother, Sept. 1 or 8, 1914, box 19B, WM, LOC; Davis, pp. 25–26, Levine, *Mitchell,* p. 85.

104   *first pilots were:* History of U.S. Army Air Service: 1862–1920, box 32, WM, LOC; Benjamin D. Foulois with C. V. Glines, *From the Wright Brothers to the Astronauts: The Memoirs of Major General Benjamin D. Foulois* (New York: McGraw-Hill, 1968), pp. 125, 140–141.

105   *"to 'fly'!!!":* Diary entries, Aug. 12–13, 17, and 30, 1913, Apr. 25, 1915 to Jan. 17, 1916, CS, TF; Thomas D. Milling reminiscences, p. 83, OHC.

105   *lead the force:* Diary entry, June 14, 1916, CS, TF; Mitchell letter to mother, circa Apr. 1915, box 19B, WM, LOC; Thomas D. Milling reminiscences, p. 83–84, OHC.

105   *"do wrong":* Diary entry, Sept. 2, 1916, CS, TF; Davis, pp. 24–27; Cooke, pp. 48, 50–51; Mitchell, *Memoirs of World War I*, p. 10.

105   *private lessons:* Curtiss Aviation School invoice, Mar. 1, 1917, Capt. A. G. Gutensohn letter to Mitchell, Apr. 13, 1917, box 6, Mitchell receipts for flying lessons, box 45, WM, LOC.

105   *in her diary:* Diary entries, Oct. 14 and Nov. 28, 1916, CS, TF.

106   *that night:* Diary entries, Mar. 3–21, 1917, CS, TF; Harriet Mitchell letter to Katharine Jackson, Mar. 12, 1917, BA.

CHAPTER 10   INSUBORDINATION AND THE TRUTH

Page

107   *"the morning":* "Mitchell Allowed to Visit Homestead at Middleburg, Va.," *Washington Post*, Nov. 1, 1925; letter from Adjutant General to Commanding General, District of Washington, Oct. 30, 1925, box 16, MT, NA; diary entry, Oct. 31, 1925, MB, MHS; unidentified news clipping, box 57, WM, LOC; "'Billy' Mitchell" poem, unidentified news clipping, box 52, WM, LOC.

108   *the proceedings:* Rex Collier, "Hard-Boiled Court-Martial Tradition Is Upset at Trial," *Washington Star*, Nov. 4, 1925; Dixie Tighe, "Windy Wash Day Next Door Only Spice at Army Trial," *Washington Herald*, Nov. 4, 1925.

108–112   from *For more than* to *"tomorrow morning":* Trial transcript, pp. 160–263, MT, NA; "Newspapermen Witnesses at Mitchell Trial" photo, *Chicago Journal*, Nov. 2, 1925; "Army Rests Case Against Mitchell After Warm Row," *Washington Star*, Nov. 2, 1925; "Papers Admitted in Mitchell Case," *Washington Star*, Nov. 3, 1925, p. 4; diary entries, Oct. 28 and 29, 1925, MB, MHS; letter from Lt. Col. George Hicks to Mitchell and Mitchell's response, Sept. 6, 1925, box 9, MT, NA.

113   *stiff wind:* Diary entry, Nov. 2, 1925, MB, MHS; Dixie Tighe, "Windy Wash Day Next Door Only Spice at Army Trial," *Washington Herald*, Nov. 4, 1925.

113-16   from *Reid finally* to *backed him up:* Trial transcript, pp. 264–86, MT, NA; photo and caption of Alexander H. Galt from unidentified newspaper, Nov. 5, 1925, box 56, WM, LOC.

116   *their units:* Trial transcript, pp. 259–261, MT, NA; Reid's witness list, memorandum for Mr. Fisher on documents to secure, defense memo on lighter than air and heavier than air witnesses to call, box 38, WM, LOC; defense indexes of request for subpoenas duces tecum, box 12, MT, NA; "Mass of Confidential Navy Data Asked in Mitchell Case," *Washington Star*, Nov. 2, 1925.

116   *manageable size:* Trial transcript, pp. 287–88, MT, NA; "Mitchell Is Given Right to Summon Long Witness List," *Washington Star*, Nov. 11, 1925, p. 1; War Department Press Release: Trial of Colonel Mitchell, Oct. 20, 1925, box 1, WMC, NASM.

117–18   from *And a very* to *in his defense:* Trial transcript, pp. 168–69, MT, NA; "Precedent Broken in Mitchell Trial," *Washington Star*, Nov. 3, 1925; Coolidge Press Conference Nov. 3, 1925, transcript no. 2, vol. 4–7, CCP; Press Relations Section G-2 release, Colonel Mitchell #2, Nov. 2, 1925, box 7, MT, NA.

118   *nothing to do:* Trial transcript, pp. 289–93, MT, NA; James O'Donnell Bennett, "Mitchell Case Delays Get On Court's Nerves," *Chicago Tribune*, Nov. 4, 1925.

CHAPTER 11   WAR

Page

119   *of ruffling:* Mitchell, *Memories of World War I*, p. 243; photo of Mitchell's Spad

in World War I with December 1918 note from Mitchell, box 19B, WM, LOC; Coffman, *War to End All Wars*, pp. 5–6.

119   *the bulge:* Coffman, *War to End All Wars*, pp. 179–181.

120   *counterattack:* Mitchell, *Memoirs of World War I*, pp. 238–41; "General Principles Underlying the Use of the Air Service in the Zone of the Advance, A.E.F.," SECRET no. 229, Oct. 3, 1917, box 45A, WM, LOC; Mitchell memo to Commanding General, First Army, Aug. 20, 1918, box 45A, WM, LOC.

120   *take photographs:* Mitchell, *Memoirs of World War I*, pp. 238, 242–43.

120   *below them:* Mitchell, *Memoirs of World War I*, pp. 234, 237; Cooke, *Billy Mitchell*, pp. 85–86; Mitchell diary, p. 272, box. 2,WM, LOC.

121   *Mitchell said:* Mitchell, *Memoirs of World War I*, pp. 234–37; Cooke, *Billy Mitchell*, p. 87.

121   *to the rear:* Mitchell, *Memoirs of World War I*, pp. 243–44.

121   *counterattack:* Mitchell, *Memoirs of World War I*, pp. 219–23; Mitchell letter to mother, July 9, 1918, box 19B, WM, LOC; Patrick memo to Mitchell, Nov. 7, 1918, box 6, WM, LOC.

121   *"the better":* Mitchell, *Memoirs of World War I*, pp. 239, 243–244.

122   *as planned:* Smythe, *Pershing*, pp. 17, 21, 26, 72, 238–44; Coffman, *War to End All Wars*, p. 138; Mitchell, *Memoirs of World War I*, p. 195, 244.

122   *"for months":* Mitchell, *Memoirs of World War I*, pp. 11–15.

122-23   from *Ten days* to *under fire:* Ibid., pp. 20–47.

124   *him the tour:* Mitchell, Ibid., pp. 16–20, 97–99, 103–5.

124   *the artillery:* Mitchell, Ibid., pp. 23–26; John J. Pershing, *My Experiences in the First World War, Volume I* (New York: Da Capo Press, 1995), pp. 26–27, 159; James W. Rainey, "The Questionable Training of the AEF in World War 1," *Parameters*, Winter 1992–93, pp. 89–102; Coffman, *War to End All Wars*, pp. 18, 60–66; Mitchell, *Winged Defense*, pp. 33–34; Arnold, *Global Mission*, p. 52.

124   *European-made planes:* Mitchell, *Memoirs of World War I*, pp. 16–17, 122–25, 143, 150–57; Pershing, *My Experiences*, pp. 160, 324–325; Hurley, *Billy Mitchell*, p. 23; Roger E. Bilstein, *The American Aerospace Industry*, (New York: Twayne Publishers, 1996), pp. 16–19.

125   *after the war:* John L. Mitchell Jr. letters to mother, Apr. 21 and Nov. 10, 1910, Jan. 16, 1911, July 17 and 27, Aug. 18, Sept. 23, and Dec. 17, 1917, and University of Wisconsin letter to John L. Mitchell Jr., June 5, 1917, box 1, WMP, MHS; Mitchell letter to mother, July 30, 1914, box 19B, WM, LOC; Harriet Pillsbury interview; Harriet Mitchell letter to Katharine Jackson, June 25, 1917, BA.

125   *head crushed:* Mitchell letter to mother after John's death, undated, box 7, GH, UWM.

126   *"world to me":* Mitchell letters to mother, June 26, Aug. 20, Oct. 7 and 26, 1918, box 19B, WM, LOC.

126   *long memories:* Smythe, pp. 49, 65, 70–71, 82–83, 162–64; Coffman, *War to End All War*, pp. 159, 167–86; Cooke, *Billy Mitchell*, pp. 21–22, 64, 73–74; Mitchell memo to General Brewster, July 21, 1918, box 6, WM, LOC.

126   *the front:* Mitchell, *Memoirs of World War I*, pp. 157–58, 167–68; Coffman, *War to End All War*, pp. 256; Kennett, *First Air War*, pp. 77, 143, 225–226.

126   *Mitchell had:* Mitchell, *Memoirs of World War I*, pp. 194–98; Cooke, *Billy Mitchell*, p. 100.

127   *to sit:* John F. Shiner, *Foulois and the U.S. Army Air Corps 1931–1935* (Washington, D.C.: U.S. Government Printing Office, 1983), pp. 1–11; Foulois memo to Pershing on Relief of Colonel William Mitchell, Air Service, June 4, 1918, box 77, *JP,* LOC; Foulois, *From the Wright Brothers,* pp. 111, 124–25, 138–44, 156–58, 166–74.

127–28 from *Foulois eventually* to *Benny Foulois:* Foulois memo to Pershing on Relief of Colonel William Mitchell, Air Service, June 4, 1918, AEF Officer of the Chief of Staff letter to Foulois, June 8, 1918, and Fox Conner memo to Pershing, Oct. 22, 1919, box 77, JP, LOC; Harry S. Aldrich letter to Francis Wilby, Nov. 30, 1925, box 15, MT, NA; Pershing, pp. 284–85, 333–34; Patrick, pp. 15–16, 73, 82–86; White, pp. 3, 15–19; Patrick memo to Pershing on Mitchell, Jan. 17, 1919, 201, NPRC; Foulois, *From the Wright Brothers,* pp. 175–76.

128   *German rear:* Mitchell, *Memoirs of World War I,* pp. 249–50, 290.

128   *in a day:* Kennett, pp. 50–51, 79–82, 99–115, 146–49, 168, 170; Mitchell, *Memoirs of World War I,* pp. 172–73; Cooke, pp. 99–100.

129   *brigadier general:* Lt. Clayton Bissell, "Brief History of the Air Service and Its Late Development," pp. 81–90, box 32, WM, LOC; Pershing letter to Mitchell, Sept. 16, 1918, box 19B, WM, LOC; Coffman, p. 208; Mitchell, *Memoirs of World War I,* pp. 249–250.

129   *devastated her:* Diary entries, June 9, 17–19, 21, 1917, CS, TF; Felicity Trueblood interview.

129   *in wartime:* Diary entries, Sept. 17, Dec. 13, 21–22 and 25, 1917, Feb. 10, 13 and 27, Apr. 3, 1918, CS, TF.

130   *to fix it:* Diary entries: July 11 and 21, Aug. 29, Dec. 17, 1917, Apr. 24, May 11 and 16, June 12, 19 and 26, July 11 and 21, Aug. 27, Sept. 3–5 and 10, Oct. 7, 13, 15, and 18, 1918, *CS* TF; Vassar College Questionnaire for Biographical–Address Register for Caroline Stoddard, May 10, 1919; Harriet Mitchell letter to Katharine Jackson, June 17, 1917, BA.

130   *"ever end":* Diary entries, May 25, June 24, July 4, Sept. 4, Dec. 2 and 6, 1917, Feb. 2, Mar. 20 and 23, July 17 and 20, Oct. 4, 1918, *CS* , TF; Harriet Mitchell letter to Katharine Jackson, June 17, 1917, BA.

130   *Meuse-Argonne offensive:* Lt. Clayton Bissell, "Brief History of The Air Service and Its Late Development," pp. 91–104, box 32, WM, LOC; Mitchell, *Memories of World War I,* pp. 250–63; Mitchell letter to Gen. Duncan, Oct. 19, 1918, box 6, WM, LOC; Coffman, pp. 208–9, 299–351; Smythe, pp. 190–230.

131   *World War:* Kennett, *First Air War,* pp. 209–220; Patrick, *United States in the Air,* pp. 49–51; White, *Mason Patrick,* p. 23; Lt. Clayton Bissell, "Brief History Of The Air Service And Its Late Development," pp. 105–6, box 32, WM, LOC; Mitchell, *Memories of World War I,* pp. 267–68, 291–92.

131   *approved it:* War Department General Orders no. 120, Dec. 4, 1918, folder 9, 201, NPRC; reminiscences of Leroy Prinz, no. 388, pp. 24–28, OHC.

131   *Pershing's letters:* Mitchell letter to mother, Sept. 18, 1918, with copies of news clippings, Pershing's letter and other letters, box 11, GH, UWM.

131   *glorious adventure:* Martin Gilbert, *The First World War: A Complete History* (New York: Henry Holt, 1994), pp. xv, 400; Coffman, *War to End All Wars,* p. 363; Smythe, *Pershing,* p. 233.

CHAPTER 12   PREPARING FOR BATTLE

Page

132   *of her brother:* Diary entries, Nov. 3–6, 1925, MB, MHS.

132   *same way:* Harriet Pillsbury interview; author interview with Rebecca McCoy, July 6, 2002.

133   *and Webb:* Diary entries, Nov. 4–8, MB, MHS; defense indexes of request for subpoenas duces tecum, box 12, MT, NA.

134   *in hotels:* Col. H. A. White letter to Col. Sherman Moreland, Nov. 5, 1925, box 16, MT, NA: correspondence between the War and Navy Departments on requests for documents in the Mitchell trial, Nov. 4–23, 1925, file 6000–1424, *NAV,* NA; defense request for documents from the War Department, Nov. 4–10, 1925, box 16, MT, NA; prosecution memo on defense witness list, box 15, MT, NA; unsigned memorandum to Colonel Moreland on right of the executive to withhold secret documents, box 16, MT, NA; partial list of witnesses desired by counsel for the defense and supplemental list of witnesses to be called, with travel costs, Col. A. H. White, memo to Colonel Moreland from the Office, Chief of Finance, box 12, MT, NA.

134   *would say:* Partial List of Witnesses Desired by Counsel for the Defense, Nov. 10, 1925, box 12, MT, NA; Defense breakdown of Mitchell's Sept. 5 statement into 16 parts, and list of defense witnesses assigned to testify on the 16 parts, box 37, WM, LOC; list of contradictory witnesses, box 1, *WMC,* NASM.

134   *get anywhere:* memorandum to Colonel Moreland, Subject: U.S. vs. Mitchell, Nov. 5, 1925, box 18, MT, NA; Brig. Gen. H. A. Drum memo to Lt. Col. Joseph McMullen, Nov. 6, 1926, box 6, MT, NA.

135   *a honeymoon:* Maj. W. G. Kilner memo to Division and Section Chiefs, with note by Maj. H. A. Arnold, Nov. 6, 1925, box 37, WM, LOC; letter from Cadillac Motor Car Company to Mitchell, Oct. 20, 1922, box 9, WM, LOC; Mitchell letter to Carl Spaatz, June 1, 1925, and Spaatz's response to Mitchell, June 4, 1925, Grosse Pointe Hunt Club letter to Mitchell, May 31, 1925, box 3, SP, LOC.

135   *day in court:* Diary entry, Nov. 7, 1925, MB, MHS.

CHAPTER 13   TRIUMPH

Page

136   *them crazy:* Diary entry, Feb. 28, 1919, CS, TF.

136   *"the world":* Perrett, *America in the Twenties,* pp. 19–20; Levine, *Mitchell,* pp. 164–65; Arch Whitehouse, *Billy Mitchell: America's Eagle of Air Power* (New York: Putnam, 1962), p. 108; Mitchell, *Memoirs of World War I,* pp. 307–10; Davis, *Billy Mitchell Affair,* pp. 3, 7, 46–48; Arnold, *Global Mission,* p. 85.

137   *her diary:* Diary entries, Nov. 12, 1918, Feb. 28, 1919, CS, TF; Mitchell letter to mother, Dec. 13, 1918, box 19B, Dec. 13, 1918, WM, LOC; undated Caroline Mitchell letter to Harriet Mitchell, BA.

137   *to win it:* Mitchell, *Memoirs of World War I,* pp. 4, 10, 289, 302–3; Mitchell, *Our Air Force,* p. 1; Levine, *Mitchell,* pp. 150–53; Hurley, *Billy Mitchell,* pp. 39–40; Arnold, *Global Mission,* p. 86; Smythe, *Pershing,* pp. 230–33, 248–249; reminiscences of Gill Robb Wilson, no. 388, p. 75, OHC.

137   *they could:* "What Congress Did" and "Our Future Army," *The Nation* 109, Nov. 29, 1919, pp. 675–76; James B. Connolly, "The Flying Sailor," *Colliers* 64, Aug. 9, 1919,

pp. 12–13; Joseph G. Cannon, "The National Budget," *Harper's* 139, Oct. 1919, pp. 617–28; "The Progress of the World," *Review of Reviews* 59, May 1919, p. 465; Arnold, *Global Mission*, pp. 86–89, Perrett, *America in the Twenties* pp. 123–24.

138   *they did not:* Allen, *Only Yesterday*, pp. 1–2, 9–10; Perrett, *America in the Twenties*, pp. 19, 28; Mitchell letter to mother, Dec. 18, 1919, box 19B, WM, LOC.

138   *his deputy:* Diary entry, Feb. 10, 1919, CS, TF: Copp, *A Few Great Captains*, pp. xvii, 25; Grumelli, *Billy Mitchell*, pp. 142–43; Levine, *Mitchell*, p. 167; Kennett, *First Air War*, pp. 157, 225.

138   *he pleased:* Menoher memo to Mitchell, Dec. 4, 1920, box 8, WM, LOC; Menoher memo to Mitchell, Mar. 8, 1919, box 7, WM, LOC; Patrick, *The United States in the Air*, pp. 74–76; Coffman, *War to End All Wars*, p. 150; Cooke, *Billy Mitchell*, pp. 106, 109.

139   *in 1921:* Hurley, *Billy Mitchell*, pp. 52, 89; Levine, *Mitchell*, p. 191–94, 282; Davis, *Billy Mitchell Affair*, p. 53; Copp, *A Few Great Captains*, pp. 28–29.

139   *with crashes:* Daily journals of General William Mitchell, Aug. 23 and Dec. 13, 1919, Apr. 24, 1920, Oct. 4, 1921, box 4, WM, LOC; "Mitchell Air 'Record' Opens New Wrangle," *Detroit Free Press*, Oct. 24, 1922.

139   *buckskin shoes:* Oscar Cesare, "Mitchell, the Tireless Flying General," *New York Times Magazine*, Mar. 8, 1925, p. 5.

140   *Chambers stayed:* Reminiscences of Gen. Delos C. Emmons, no. 388, p. 8, OHC; reminiscences of Donald Douglas, no. 384, p. 59, OHC; reminiscences of Reed M. Chambers, no. 388, p. 56, OHC.

140   *bird is that:* Eugene E. Wilson reminiscences, pp. 176–78, OHC.

141   *of Defense:* Mitchell memo to Menoher, July 15, 1919, Mitchell memo to Pershing, Oct. 27, 1919, box 7, WM, LOC; William Mitchell, "Why We Need a Department of Air," Dec. 21, 1919, draft article, box 31, WM, LOC; Mitchell, *Our Air Force*, pp. 199–203, 210–11.

141   *the infantryman:* Shiner, pp. 17–18; Grumelli, *Trial of Faith*, p. 20; Smythe, pp. 275–280; Frank E. Vandiver, *Black Jack: The Life and Times of John J. Pershing*, vol. *II*, (College Station: Texas A&M University Press), pp. 1059–60; Hurley, pp. 46–49.

141   *later wrote:* Mitchell, *Our Air Force*, pp. 110–11, 114–15, 127–28; Mitchell, *Winged Defense*, pp. xviii, 159–61; Arnold, *Global Mission*, p. 96; Hurley, *Billy Mitchell*, pp. 58, 60; Cooke, *Billy Mitchell*, pp. 108, 113.

142   *save energy:* First and second reports by Lt. St. Claire Fleet of Mitchell flight to the *Ostfriesland*, July 20, 1921, box 40, WM, LOC; Mitchell, *Winged Defense*, pp. 53–55, 60.

143   *of doing that:* First report by Lt. St. Claire Fleet of Mitchell flight to the *Ostfriesland*, July 20, 1921, box 40, WM, LOC; Report by Lt. St. Claire Fleet of Mitchell flight to the *Frankfurt*, July 18, 1921, box 40, WM, LOC; Mitchell, *Winged Defense*, p. 56: Levine, *Mitchell*, pp. 238–40; Vice Adm. Alfred W. Johnson (Ret.), "The Naval Bombing Experiments Off the Virginia Capes, June and July 1921, Their Technological and Psychological Aspects," for the Naval Historical Foundation, Washington, D.C., May 31, 1959, pp. 22–24; memo from Adjutant General of the Army to Chief of Air Service, May 9, 1921, box 9, WM, LOC.

143   *depth charges:* Report of the First Provisional Air Brigade in ordnance tests, pp. 146, 338, box 40, WM, LOC; First Provisional Air Brigade Information Bulletin: Identification of the ex-German Battleship "Ostfriesland," July 19, 1921, box 40, WM, LOC; Navy news bureau release, Mar. 1, 1921, box 40, WM, LOC.

143   *practically "useless":* Mitchell, *Winged Defense,* pp. 67–68, 110, 159, 163, 169–71; Davis, *Billy Mitchell Affairs,* p. 65; Cooke, *Billy Mitchell,* p. 116; "An Airman's Opinion of Naval Dreadnaughts [*sic*]," *Boston America,* Jan. 28, 1921; "Would Scrap Sea Fleet for Airplanes," *Boston American,* Jan. 29, 1921.

144   *"your name":* Herbert Corey letter to Mitchell, undated, box 9, WM, LOC; Hurley, p. 60.

144   *two million tons:* Hurley, *Billy Mitchell,* pp. 57–58, 64; Sobel, *Coolidge,* pp. 221,353–54; Levine, *Mitchell,* pp. 207, 274; Perrett, *America in the Twenties,* p. 124.

144   *such claims:* "An Airman's Opinion of Naval Dreadnaughts [*sic*]," *Boston America,* Jan. 28, 1921; Arnold, *Global Mission,* p. 100; Hurley, *Billy Mitchell,* pp. 60–61; Davis, *Global Mission,* p. 67; Ruth Mitchell, *My Brother Bill,* p. 228.

144   *to his ideas:* Cooke, *Billy Mitchell,* p. 112; Arnold, *Global Mission,* p. 99; Eugene E. Wilson reminiscences, pp. 332, 456, OHC; Clark reminiscences, pp. 204–5, OHC.

145   *against ships:* S. W. Fitzgerald memo to Air Officer, 9th Corps Area, Feb. 21, 1921, box 48, WM, LOC.

145   *dummy bombs:* Davis, *Billy Mitchell Affair,* p. 68; Levine, *Mitchell,* pp. 207–9.

145   *"commands the air":* "Daniels Scores Air Chief Stand on U.S. Warships," *Washington Herald,* Feb. 1, 1921; Patrick, *United States in the Air,* pp. 79–80; Levine, *Mitchell,* p. 215; Arthur Christie memo to Mitchell with Daniels, June 19, 1917, letter, box 10, WM, LOC.

145   *over a ship:* "New Demands Air Bomb Test," *New York Sun,* Jan. 31, 1921; Arnold, pp. 102–3; Hurley, pp. 61–62.

145   *not a pilot:* W. G. Kilner memo to Mitchell, May 14, 1921, and Mitchell memo on Exercises of Aircraft vs. Ex-*Iowa* and Ex-German Ships, box 40, WM, LOC; Navy Office of Information biography of Vice Admiral Alfred W. Johnson, Aug. 15, 1963.

146   *the damn ship:* Johnson report, pp. 1–28; Henry B. Wilson memo to Chief of Naval Operations, May 24, 1921, box 40, WM, LOC; Minutes of the Pre-Bombing Conference, May 10 an 18, 1921, with Johnson report; Patrick, pp. 78–79; Mitchell, *Winged Defense,* pp. 43–44.

146   *for the tests:* Davis, pp. 75–77; W. G. Kilner memos to Mitchell, Apr. 28 and May 10, 1921, box 40, WM, LOC; St. Clair Street memo to Mitchell, May 11, 1921, box 40, WM, LOC; Ruth Mitchell, *My Brother Bill,* p. 238; Mitchell, *Winged Defense,* pp. 50–51; First Provisional Air Brigade report, pp. 138–56, 88–101, WM, LOC.

147   *love-hate relationship:* Mitchell letters to Thurman Bane, Mar. 1 and 4, 1921, box 6, GH, UWM.

147   *personal use:* First Provisional Air Brigade report, pp. 6–32, 392–95, 399–04, WM, LOC; Doolittle reminiscences, pp. 71–72, OHC; Chief of the Air Service memo to Quartermaster General on Cadillac car for Langley, June 9, 1921, box 40, WM, LOC.

147   *the plane up:* Ruth Mitchell, *My Brother Bill,* pp. 237, 240–41,257; Harriett Mitchell Fladoes letter to Burke Davis, Apr. 2, 1966, BD, UNC; reminiscences of Gen. James D. Milling, no. 385, pp. 96–97; First Provisional Air Brigade report, pp. 1–5, WM, LOC.

147   *anybody afterward:* Doolittle reminiscences, p. 73, OHC.

148   *ship's bottom:* Mitchell, *Winged Defense,* pp. 141–42; Doolittle reminiscences, p. 73, OHC.

148   *"is correct"*: Mitchell, *Winged Defense*, pp. 44–45; Ruth Mitchell, *My Brother Bill*, pp. 234–35.

148   *out to be duds*: Second report by Lt. St. Claire Fleet of Mitchell flight to the *Ostfriesland*, July 20, 1921, box 40, WM, LOC; Johnson report, pp. 20–27; First Provisional Air Brigade report, pp. 61–65,WM, LOC; memo from A. M. Merrill, Asst. Chief Draftsman to the Construction Officer, Aug. 2, 1921, pp. 10–11, in the Johnson report.

148–50 from *Mitchell and his five* to *nearby observation plane*: Second report by Lt. St. Claire Fleet of Mitchell flight to the *Ostfriesland*, July 20, 1921, box 40, WM, LOC; Johnson report, pp. 20–27; First Provisional Air Brigade report, pp. 61–67, WM, LOC; Mitchell, *Winged Defense*, pp. 66–69; memo from A.M. Merrill, Asst. Chief Draftsman to the Construction Officer, Aug. 2, 1921, pp. 11–12, in the Johnson report; Field Order no. 14 for First Provisional Air Brigade, July 21, 1921, box 40, WM, LOC.

151   *the battleship*: Second report by Lt. St. Claire Fleet of Mitchell flight to the *Ostfriesland*, July 20, 1921, box 40, WM, LOC; Mitchell, *Winged Defense*, pp. 69–71.

151   *in its draft*: memo from A. M. Merrill, Asst. Chief Draftsman to the Construction Officer, Aug. 2, 1921, pp. 11–12, in the Johnson report; Johnson report, pp. 26–27.

151–53 from *Thursday morning* to *over its grave*: First Provisional Air Brigade report, pp. 68–73, 169–72, WM, LOC; Johnson report, pp. 29–39; first and second reports by Lt. St. Claire Fleet of Mitchell flights to the *Ostfriesland*, July 21, 1921, box 40, WM, LOC; Information Bulletin no. 25, First Provisional Air Brigade, Sinking of the "Ostfriesland," July 22, 1921; Field Order no. 14 for First Provisional Air Brigade, July 21, 1921, box 40, WM, LOC; Mitchell memo to Commander-in-Chief, Atlantic Fleet, May 17, 1921, box 40, WM, LOC; memo from A. M. Merrill, Asst. Chief Draftsman to the Construction Officer, Aug. 2, 1921, pp. 13–14, in the Johnson report; letter from Commander Air Force to Commander in Chief, U.S. Atlantic Fleet on Bombing Experiments off the Virginia Capes, July 29, 1921, in the Johnson report; H. T. Bartlett memo to Base Commander, July 22, 1921, on Chronological Report in connection with the *Ostfriesland*, in the Johnson report; "Gen. Mitchell Denies That He Disobeyed Orders In Bombing Tests Off Virginia Capes In 1921," unidentified newspaper, Feb. 14, 1921, box 10, GH, UWM; Levine, pp. 248–51; Davis, pp. 105–7; Film of Aerial Bombing Tests of Watercraft, June 21-Sept. 26, 1921, 342-USAF-1546, NA.

154   *cheered him*: Ruth Mitchell, *My Brother Bill*,. 265; Mitchell, *Winged Defense*, pp. 72–73; Milling reminiscences, p. 96, OHC; Davis, *Billy Mitchell Affair*, p. 108–9.

154   *roaring drunk*: Ruth Mitchell, *My Brother Bill*, pp. 267–68.

154   *before she sank*: unidentified news article on Daniels, box 53, WM, LOC; Levine, *Mitchell*, p. 226; First Provisional Air Brigade report, pp. 74–75, WM, LOC.

155   *new and crude*: Congratulatory letters in Box 9, WM, LOC; "City in Theoretical Ruins from Air Raid," *New York Herald*, July 30, 1921; St. Claire Street report of Mitchell flight over New York, First Provisional Air Brigade, box 40, WM, LOC; Patrick, p. 81; Mitchell memo to Chief of Air Service, Aug. 29, 1921, box 40, WM, LOC; "The Battleship and The Bomb," *The Outlook* 128, Aug. 3, 1921, p. 530.

155   *"naval battle"*: Examples of Navy stalling can be found in correspondence among Gen. Mason Patrick, Gen. J. L. Hines and the Secretary of the Navy, Aug. to Sept. 1925, box 38, WM, LOC; General Conclusion of the Naval Board on

USS Delaware, July 22, 1921, pp. 44–45, in the Johnson report; draft of Adm. W. F. Fullam statement, box 41, WM, LOC; statement of Rear Admiral W. F. Fullam to the Aircraft Investigating Committee of Congress, box 38, WM, LOC.

155   *of his life:* Ruth Mitchell, *My Brother Bill*, pp. 223, 266.

156   *to reporters:* Aeronautical Board memo to Secretaries of War and Navy, May 28, 1920, box 46, BD, UNC; Mitchell letter to Menoher, Dec. 23, 1919, box 7, WM, LOC; Mother's telegram to Mitchell, June 9, 1921, box 9, WM, LOC; Report of the Joint Board on Results of Aviation and Ordnance Tests Held During June and July, 1921 and Conclusions Reached, Office of the Chief of Naval Operations, Navy Department, Washington, D.C., Government Printing Office, 1921; "Mitchell Attacks Bomb Test Findings," *New York Times*, Sept. 14, 1921.

156   *troop unit:* Menoher memo to Adjutant General of the Army, July 2, 1920, Menoher memo to Officers on duty with the Air Service, Apr. 21, 1920, Menoher memo to Air Service officers, June 16, 1920, box 8, WM, LOC; "Weeks Tries to End Rift in Air Service," *New York Times*, June 10, 1921; Menoher memo to Adjutant General of the Army, June 8, 1921, box 9, WM, LOC; Rep. Hubert F. Fisher letter to Mitchell, June 11, 1921, box 9, WM, LOC; Mitchell letter to Editor, *New York Tribune*, Nov. 29, 1920, box 8, WM, LOC; Patrick, *United States in the Air*, pp. 83–84; Arnold, *Global Mission*, p. 106; Cooke, *Billy Mitchell*, p. 119; Hurley, *Billy Mitchell*, pp. 68–69.

156   *Mason Patrick:* Drafts of "Exclusives" for *New York Times, New York World, New York Herald* and *New York Tribune,* Box 54, WM, LOC; Arnold letter to Mitchell, Sept. 19, 1921, box 9, WM, LOC.

156   *Billy Mitchell:* White, *Mason Patrick*, pp. 3, 15–19.

157   *Patrick again:* Mitchell memo to Patrick, Oct. 8, 1921, Mitchell memo to Patrick, Oct. 18, 1921, Patrick memo to Mitchell, Nov. 17, 1921; Patrick, *United States in the Air*, pp. 86–89.

157   *at receptions:* Mitchell-Patrick correspondence, Jan. 9, Feb. 6 and June 28, 1923, Aug. 1 and 13, 1924, box 11, WM, LOC; Patrick, *United States in the Air*, p. 89; White, *Mason Patrick*, p. 135; Mitchell letter to Elizabeth, Sept. 12, 1925, GF; Coffey, *Hap*, pp. 121–22; Arnold, *Global Mission*, pp. 116–17; Cooke, *Billy Mitchell*, p. 130; Davis, *Billy Mitchell Affair*, pp. 142–43; Patrick letter to Major Carl Spaatz, Oct. 20, 1922, box 2, SP, LOC.

157   *air ranks:* H. A. Dargue letter to Carl Spaatz, Oct. 2, 1922, box 2, SP, LOC: *Time* cover, July 9, 1923; Eleanor Arnold reminiscences, p. 55, OHC; White, *Mason Patrick*, pp. 72–73, 91–92, 111; Delos C. Emmons reminiscences, no. 388, p. 6, OHC.

157   *he retired:* Patrick, *United States in the Air*, pp. 111–13; White, p. 85; Davis, p. 142; Patrick letter to Maj. Gen. J. E. Fechet, Dec. 18, 1927, IE, LOC.

158   *the system:* White, *Mason Patrick*, pp. 4–6, 66–74, 108–9, 115, 133; Patrick, *United States in the Air*, 123–29, 137, 147–48, 173–74; Confidential Patrick memo, Nov. 10, 1921, box 49, WM, LOC; Patrick memo to Adjutant General, Dec. 19, 1924, box 11, WM, LOC; Dennis Nolan letter to John L. Hines, Feb. 3, 1925, box 31, JH, LOC.

158   *her angry:* Mitchell letters to mother, June 10, 1919, Feb. 1920, box 19B, WM, LOC; diary entries, Mar. 20, 1920, July 1–2, 1920, CS, TF.

158   *ends meet:* Eli Helmick confidential memo to Deputy Chief of Staff, Dec. 15, 1921, file 333.9, Brig., Gen. William Mitchell, box 910, IG, NA; Sworn Statement of Mrs. Caroline Stoddard Mitchell, Dec. 6, 1921, file 333.9, Brig. Gen.

William Mitchell, box 910, IG, NA; Sworn Statement of Brig. Gen. William Mitchell, Dec. 7, 1921, file 333.9, Brig. Gen. William Mitchell, box 910, IG, NA; memo from A. L. Webb with enclosures to General Helmick, Dec. 8, 1921, file 333.9, Brig. Gen. William Mitchell, box 910, IG, NA; diary entries, Apr. 12 and May 25, 1920, CS, TF; Mitchell letter to mother, Feb. 20, 1920, box 19B, WM, LOC.

159　　*they argued:* Eli Helmick confidential memo to Deputy Chief of Staff, Dec. 15, 1921, file 333.9, Brig. Gen. William Mitchell, box 910, IG, NA; Sworn Statement of Mrs. Caroline Stoddard Mitchell, Dec. 6, 1921, file 333.9 Brig. Gen. William Mitchell, box 910, IG, NA; Psychiatric report on William Mitchell Mitchell by Maj. W. L. Sheep and Lt. Col. L. L. Smith, Medical Corps, Dec. 5, 1921, file 333.9, Brig. Gen. William Mitchell, box 910, IG, NA; "Gen. Mitchell, Divorced, Says Wife Threw Bottles at Him," *Washington Times,* Nov. 4, 1922, p. 1; diary entry, May 22, 1921, CS, TF.

159　　*shot her:* Diary entry, Sept. 2, 1920, CS, TF; Sworn Statement of Mrs. Caroline Stoddard Mitchell, Dec. 6, 1921, file 333.9, Brig. Gen. William Mitchell, box 910, IG, NA; Psychiatric report on William Mitchell by Maj. W. L. Sheep and Lt. Col. L. L. Smith, Medical Corps, Dec. 5, 1921, file 333.9, Brig. Gen. William Mitchell, box 910, IG, NA.

159　　*social events:* Sworn Statement of Mrs. Caroline Stoddard Mitchell, Dec. 6, 1921, file 333.9, Brig. Gen. William Mitchell, box 910, IG, NA; Sworn Statement of Brig. Gen. William Mitchell, Dec. 7, 1921, file 333.9, Brig. Gen. William Mitchell, box 910, IG, NA; Psychiatric report on William Mitchell by Maj. W. L. Sheep and Lt. Col. L. L. Smith, Medical Corps, Dec. 5, 1921, file 333.9, Brig. Gen. William Mitchell, box 910, IG, NA; diary entries, Dec. 2 and 17, 1920, June 8, 1921, CS, TF; author interview with Guerdon Trueblood, June 18, 1902; Rebecca McCoy interview; Harriet Mitchell letters to mother, early December 1921 and Dec. 1, 1921, box 19B, WM, LOC.

160　　*awfully suspicious:* Sworn Statement of Mrs. Caroline Stoddard Mitchell, Dec. 6, 1921, file 333.9 Brig. Gen. William Mitchell, box 910, IG, NA; Psychiatric report on William Mitchell by Maj. W. L. Sheep and Lt. Col. L. L. Smith, Medical Corps, Dec. 5, 1921, file 333.9 Brig. Gen. William Mitchell, box 910, IG, NA; "'A Pretty Damn Able Commander'—Lewis Hyde Brereton: Part I," Roger G. Miller, *Air Power History* 47, Winter 2000, p. 17; diary entry, June 14, 1921, CS, TF.

160　　*made public:* Diary entry, July 27, 1921, CS, TF; Daily Journal of Brig. Gen. William Mitchell, May 16 and 21, 1921, box 5, WM, LOC; reminiscences of Adm. Emory S. Land, no. 388, p. 9, OHC.

160　　*"domestic situation":* Diary entries, Nov. 28, 1920, Dec. 4, 1916, CS, TF; Mitchell letter to mother, Nov. 25, 1921, box 19B, WM, LOC; reminiscences of Sen. James W. Wadsworth, no. 109, pp. 323–26, OHC; Martin L. Fausold, *James W. Wadsworth, Jr.: The Gentleman from New York* (Syracuse, N.Y.: Syracuse University Press, 1975), pp. xiii–xvi, 149–50.

160　　*her imprisoned:* William Kelly Jr. letter to Mitchell, Nov. 25, 1921, box 45B, WM, LOC; William Kelly Jr. confidential letter to Mitchell, Nov. 23, 1921, box 9, WM, LOC; Harriet Mitchell letter to mother early December 1921, box 19B, WM, LOC.

161　　*Harriet bragged:* Harriet Mitchell letters to mother early December 1921, Dec. 1, 1921, box 19B, WM, LOC; Ruth Mitchell, p. 251; Daily Journal of Brig. Gen. William Mitchell, Nov. 24 and 28, 1921, box 5, WM, LOC; Harriet Mitchell letters to Katharine Jackson, June 29 and July 27, 1922, BA.

161   *the exam:* Daily Journal of Brig. Gen. William Mitchell, Nov. 23 and 29, 1921,
        box 5, WM, LOC; Psychiatric report on William Mitchell by Maj. W. L. Sheep
        and Lt. Col. L. L. Smith, Medical Corps, Dec. 5, 1921, file 333.9 Brig. Gen.
        William Mitchell, box 910, IG, NA.

162   *psychiatric training:* Edward Shorter, *A History of Psychiatry: From the Era of
        the Asylum to the Age of Prozac* (New York: John Wiley & Sons: 1997), pp.
        145–46, 190–91; Rebecca McCoy interview; Felicity Trueblood interview.

162   *"military duty":* Psychiatric report on William Mitchell by Maj. W. L. Sheep and
        Lt. Col. L. L. Smith, Medical Corps, Dec. 5, 1921, file 333.9, Brig. Gen. William
        Mitchell, box 910, IG, NA.

163   *"national defense":* Daily Journal of Brig. Gen. William Mitchell, Dec. 10, 1921,
        box 5, WM, LOC; White, p. 62; Harriet Mitchell letter to mother, Dec. 5, 1921,
        box 19B, WM, LOC; Bissell letter to Mitchell's sister, Harriet, Jan. 7, 1922, box
        1, WMP, MHS; William Kelly Jr. letter to Mitchell, Dec. 8, 1921, box 45B, WM,
        LOC; reminiscences of Alfred V. Verville, no. 388, pp. 27–42, OHC; Report of
        Inspection Trip to France, Italy, Germany, Holland, and England, Made During
        the Winter of 1921–22, by Brigadier William Mitchell, et al., 1922, p. 124, box
        41, WM, LOC.

163   *each night:* Patrick letter to Mitchell, Dec. 7, 1921, box 11, WM, LOC; corre-
        spondence between Maj. M. Churchill and military attachés in Brussels, Berlin,
        London, Paris, Rome, The Hague, Dec. 2–Mar. 2, 1922, letter from T. Bentley
        Mott to Churchill, Jan. 14, 1922, box 44, MID, NA.

163   *of desertion:* "Gen. Mitchell Divorced," *Milwaukee Journal,* Nov. 3, 1922, p. 1;
        diary entry, Mar. 29, 1922, CS, TF; Perrett, *America in the Twenties,* pp. 152, 156,
        159, 164; "Flapper Jane," *New Republic* 44, Sept. 9, 1925, p. 65–67; Rebecca
        McCoy interview; Felicity Trueblood interview; letter from Aunt Sadie to Caro-
        line Stoddard, early 1920s, TF; Sworn Statement of Mrs. Caroline Stoddard
        Mitchell, Dec. 6, 1921, file 333.9 Brig. Gen. William Mitchell, box 910, IG, NA.

163   *to celebrate:* Diary entry, Sept. 27, 1922, CS, TF; "Gen. Mitchell Divorced," *Mil-
        waukee Journal,* Nov. 3, 1922, p. 1; "Gen. Mitchell Is Divorced by Wife," *Mil-
        waukee Sentinel,* Nov. 4, 1922, p. 7.

164   *of the story:* "Gen. Mitchell, Divorced, Says Wife Threw Bottles at Him," *Wash-
        ington Times,* Nov. 4, 1922, p. 1; Caroline Stoddard letter to Mason Patrick, Nov.
        25, 1922, box 46, BD, UNC.

164   *her place:* Mitchell letters to Elizabeth Mitchell, Dec. 13, 24, and 28, 1922, GF.

165   *society writer:* unidentified newspaper and magazine articles of the Miller-
        Mitchell wedding, box 54, WM, LOC.

165   *show off:* author interview with Tom Gilpin, Aug. 24, 2002; Rebecca McCoy
        interview; unidentified newspaper and magazine articles of the Miller-Mitchell
        wedding, box 54, WM, LOC.

165   *to Caroline:* Tom Gilpin interview; Rebecca McCoy interview; unidentified
        newspaper and magazine articles of the Miller-Mitchell wedding, box 54, WM,
        LOC.

165   *well off:* Tom Gilpin interview; Rebecca McCoy interview; diary entry, Oct. 12,
        1923, CS, TF; Guerdon Trueblood interview.

166   *drive a car:* Rebecca McCoy interview; unidentified newspaper and magazine
        articles of the Miller-Mitchell wedding, box 54, WM, LOC.

166   *bargain clothes:* Tom Gilpin interview; Rebecca McCoy interview.

166   *"all boring":* Undated letter from Mrs. Robert G. Mead, head of Women's
       Bureau to Lucy Miller, two poems written to Elizabeth Miller from her scrap-
       book, undated letter from unidentified corporal to Elizabeth Miller, GF; Ken-
       neth Gilpin interview.

167   *"and the days":* Mitchell letter to Elizabeth Mitchell, Nov. 6, 1922, GF.

167   *"reprehensible thing":* Kenneth Gilpin interview; Rebecca McCoy interview;
       Mitchell letter to Elizabeth Mitchell, Oct. 30, 1922, GF.

167   *first marriage:* unidentified newspaper and magazine articles of the Miller-
       Mitchell wedding, box 54, WM, LOC.

167   *"so absolutely":* Mitchell letters to Elizabeth Mitchell, Oct. 28 and 30, 1922, and
       one written winter 1922–23, GF; Tom Gilpin interview.

CHAPTER 14   TABLES TURNED

Page

168   *or disapproved:* Trial transcript, pp. 295–349, MT, NA; press releases on Reid's
       opening statement, box 1, WMC, NASM; Defense memo on recommendations
       the Chief of the Air Service made to War Department, box 54, WM, LOC.

169   *"court-martial":* "Army Air Force Facing Collapse, Court Informed," Nov. 9,
       1925, Washington newspaper article, Mitchell scrapbooks, WMC, NASM;
       "Mitchell Adds to Air Service Charges; Sees Perjury Plot in Shenandoah Case;
       Three Officers Back Him Before Court," *New York Times,* Nov. 10, 1925, p. 1.

169   *chemical warfare service:* Draft of Fries speech before United States Chemical
       Warfare Association, box 36, WM, LOC.

169–70 from*"From your"* to *sitting down:* Dixie Tighe, "Street Rumbles Drown Trend of
       Mitchell Trial," *Washington Herald,* Nov. 10, 1925.

170   *next war:* Richard Dean Burns, ed., *Encyclopedia of Arms Control and Disarma-
       ment, vol.2,* (New York: Scribner's, 1993), pp. 659–62.

171   *and writings:* trial transcript, pp. 382–429, MJ, NA; David R. Mets, *A Master of
       Airpower: General Carl A. Spaatz,* (Novato, Calif.: Presidio, 1988), p. 37;
       Mitchell, *Memoirs of World War I,* pp. 3–4, 130; Mitchell, *Our Air Force,* pp.
       xxi–xxiii; Mitchell, *Winged Defense,* pp. xv, 14, 16; Hurley, *Billy Mitchell,* pp.
       43–44, 92–93, 111–12, 138.

171   *of Washington:* trial transcript, pp. 372–73, MT, NA; Air Service memo to
       Mitchell, "Handling of Aviation by the War and Navy Departments," box 34,
       WM, LOC.

171   *had made:* Vandiver, *Black Jack,* p. 1060; Air Service memo to Mitchell, "Han-
       dling of Aviation by the War and Navy Departments," box 34, WM, LOC.

172   *San Francisco Bay:* Copp, *A Few Great Captains,* pp. 26–30, 439; War Department
       General Orders No. 123, Dec. 11, 1918, box 20, MT, NA; (Spatz's last name was
       pronounced "Spahtz," but everyone always said "Spats," so he would eventually
       have its spelling legally changed to Spaatz, hoping people would get it right).

172–75 from *Now a major* to *up the dollar:* trial transcript, pp. 351–65, MT, NA; Mets,
       pp. 62–64; Arnold, *Global Mission,* p. 121; "Air Defense 'Wreck,' Spatz Says,"
       Washington Post, Nov. 10, 1925, p. 1; author interview with Eugene Fidell,
       May 8, 2002; Henry Rexach letters to Assistant Chief of Staff, G-2, Feb. 19
       and 24, 1926, with Feb. 18, 1926, news clipping quoting Howze, box 216,
       MID, NA.

175–80   from *The witness* to *on his side:* trial transcript, pp. 374–81, 431–63, MT, NA; Shiner, *Foulois and the U.S. Army Air Corps,* pp. 23–24; James R. Nourse, "Truth Warped to Hide Evils, They Testify for Mitchell," *Washington Herald,* Nov. 11, 1925, p. 1–2; "505 Airmen Killed in Obsolete Craft, Says Aviation Major," *New York Times,* Nov. 11, 1925, p. 1; "Sensational Data Given by Witness to Back Mitchell," *Washington Post,* Nov. 11, 1925, p. 1; *Washington Star* photo of Oldys smoking, Nov. 11, 1925, Mitchell scrapbook, WMC, NASM.

180   *their branches:* Hiram Bingham letter to Dwight Morrow, Oct. 22, 1925, series 9, box 1, DM, ACL; Dwight D. Eisenhower, *At Ease: Stories I Tell to Friends* (New York: Doubleday, 1967), pp. 141, 196; Mitchell, *Winged Defense,* p. 20; George V. H. Moseley letters to Malin Craig, Apr. 18, 1924, Dec. 4, 1926, box 8, GM, LOC; Maj. Francis H. Poole memo, box 37, WM, LOC; War Department press release on Army Housing, Nov. 8, 1925, box 16, WM, LOC; Letter to Maj. George E. Stratemeyer, Aug. 22, 1922, box 2, *SP,* LOC.

180   *in a rut:* Eisenhower, pp. 172–174, 179, 195, 198, 204; Leonard Wood letter to Frank McCoy, Nov. 12, 1925, box 20, *FM,* LOC; reminiscences of John A. Macready, no. 388, pp. 20–34, OHC; War Department press release on International Polo, Mar. 15, 1925, box 16, MT, NA; conversations between Gen. Ira C. Eaker and Capt. Joe Green, 1973, Senior Officers Debriefing Program, box 2, *IE,* AWC.

180–82   from *The next* to *"Yes,sir":* Arnold correspondence May 2–11, 1921, on Violation of War Department Instructions, box 9, WM, LOC; trial transcript, pp. 464–95, MT, NA.

182   *previous week:* Diary entry, Nov. 10, 1925, MB, MHS; "Street Rumbles Drown Trend of Mitchell Trial," Dixie Tighe, *Washington Herald,* Nov. 10, 1925.

182   *"MITCHELL DATA":* John Edwin Nevin, "Army High Command on Trial in Mass of Mitchell Data," *Washington Post,* Nov. 11, 1925, p. 1.

CHAPTER 15   PEARL HARBOR

Page

183   *was wrong:* Dixie Tighe, "Mitchell Trial Halts to Mark Armistice Day," *Washington Herald,* Nov. 12, 1925.

183   *cold feet:* Diary entry, Nov. 11, 1925, MB, MHS.

183–84   from *The generals* to *of the trial:* trial transcript, pp. 554–68, MT, NA; "Mitchell Relying on Testimony for Absolute Defense," *Washington Star,* Nov. 11, 1925, p. 1; Eugene Fidell interview.

185   *chief of staff:* List of senators and congressmen invited to the Hawaiian maneuvers, box 13, MT, NA; Press list for Hawaiian maneuvers, and sample letter to editors by the Secretary of the Navy, Oct. 14, 1924, box 6, MT, NA; John L. Hines, "The Value of the Hawaiian Maneuvers," *Outlook* 139, Apr. 15, 1925, pp. 577–580; "General Hines on Hawaiian Maneuvers," War Department press release, June 7, 1925, box 16, MT, NA; "Honolulu Falls into Hands of Mighty Fleet," *Honolulu Star Bulletin,* Apr. 28, 1925, p. 1.

185   *dirty linen:* "Notes for General Hines—Subject: Grand Joint Army and Navy Exercise No. 3–1925," "Grand Joint Army and Navy Exercise No. 3," by Maj. Gen. J. L. Hines, confidential report, Chief Umpire's memo to Adjutant General, U.S. Army, May 6, 1925, and A. G. Lott memo to Hines, Apr. 2, 1925, box 39, JH, LOC; interview with Gen. Charles L. Bolte, Dec. 9, 1971, vol.1, pp. 3–8,

box 16, CB, AWC; "Army Navy Cooperation: Extracts from the Report of the Commanding General, Hawaiian Department, on Joint Army And Navy Exercise No. 3, July 21, 1925," box 42, WM, LOC; Dennis Nolan letters to Hines, May 9, 1925, box 31, JH, LOC.

186   *"their presence":* trial transcript, pp. 569–576, MT, NA.

186   *Fort Myer:* Dixie Tighe, "Mitchell Trial Halts to Mark Armistice Day," *Washington Herald,* Nov. 12, 1925.

186–91 from *At 11:00 A.M.* to *another bullet:* trial transcript, pp. 576–608, MT, NA; Dixie Tighe, "Mitchell Trial Halts to Mark Armistice Day," *Washington Herald,* Nov. 12, 1925; Eugene Fidell interview; "Letters Sustain Mitchell Charge of Race Air Fixing," *Washington Star,* Nov. 11, 1925; "Notes for General Hines—Subject: Grand Joint Army and Navy Exercise No. 3–1925," "Grand Joint Army and Navy Exercise No. 3," by Maj. Gen. J. L. Hines, confidential report, box 39, JH, LOC.

191–92 from *When the* to *the court:* trial transcript, pp. 612–26, MT, NA; letters from the Secretary of the Navy to Capt. Alfred W. Johnson, Nov. 11, 1925, to Cdr. L. E. Bratton, Nov. 11, 1925, to Col. Sherman Moreland, Nov. 12, 1925, and to Cdr. Garland Fulton, Nov. 11, 1925, letters from Sherman Moreland to the Secretary of the Navy, Nov. 14, 1925, file 6000–1424, NAV, NA.

192–93 from *Reid then* to *not corruption:* trial transcript, pp. 645–53, MT, NA; "Air Race Charges Investigated," John Edwin Nevin, *Washington Post,* Nov. 12, 1925, p. 1; "Letters Sustain Mitchell Charge of Race Air Fixing," *Washington Star,* Nov. 11, 1925; "'R' in Roosevelt Note Likely to Play Part in Mitchell Case," *Washington Star,* Nov. 12, 1925, p. 2; Patrick-Roosevelt correspondence on Pulitzer races, Nov. 10, 1923–July 10, 1924, box 20, MT, NA; "The Dangers of Public Speed Races," *Aviation* 19, Sept. 21, 1924, p. 345.

193   *as a lawyer:* Grumelli, *Trail of Faith,* p. 155.

194   *officer's orderly:* Telegram to Coolidge from American Legion Post 743, Nov. 10, 1925, Dennis Nolan memo to Everett Sanders, Nov. 10, 1925, reel 109, CC, LOC; "Air Veterans Jeer When Mitchell Is Refused N.Y. Trip," Associated Press dispatch, Nov. 12, 1925, in unidentified newspaper, box 56, WM, LOC.

CHAPTER 16 BOMBSHELL

Page

195   *became rowdy:* "Courtroom Comes to Order Unwillingly as Laxity Ends," *Washington Star,* Nov. 13, 1925, p. 5.

195   *the new wards:* Diary entry, Nov. 11, 1925, MB, MHS.

196   *she said:* Arnold, *Global Mission,* pp. 120–121; Coffey, p. 125; Copp, pp. 43–44; Charlotte T. Reid interview; Eleanor P. Arnold reminiscences, pp. 56–57, OHC.

196   *the generals:* Diary entry, Nov. 12, 1925, MB, MHS; Dixie Tighe, "Unawed Widow Of Lansdowne Defends Hero," along with photo of Betty and Mrs. Lansdowne, *Washington Herald,* Nov. 13, 1925, p. 2.

197   *"gone through": New York Times* photo of Mrs. Lansdowne on the witness stand, undated article, Mitchell scrapbooks, WMC, NASM; Bettie Larimore, "Widow of Shenandoah Chief 'Spunky' Figure," *Boston Post,* Nov. 22, 1925; unidentified newspaper photo of Mrs. Lansdowne with her daughter under the headline, "Even Baby Smiles," Mitchell scrapbooks, WMC, NASM.

197–202 from *Reporters had* to *the courtroom:* trial transcript, pp. 659–81, MT, NA; copy

of Mrs. Lansdowne's Oct. 9, 1925, testimony before the Navy's Shenandoah
Court of Inquiry and prosecution memo, "In re testimony of Mrs. Lansdowne,"
box 17, MT, NA; "Mrs. Lansdowne Says Navy Official Asked Her to Give
'Canned' Evidence," *Washington Star*, Nov. 12, 1925, p. 1; "Foley Urged a Lie,
Judges Are Told by Mrs. Lansdowne," *New York Times*, Nov. 13, 1925, p. 1;
"Foley Begged Her to Twist Truth, Widow Tells Judges," *Washington Herald*,
Nov. 13, 1925, p. 1; photo of Moreland standing over Mrs. Lansdowne with
memo, *Chicago News*, Nov. 13, 1925.

CHAPTER 17   REINFORCEMENTS

Page
203   *that duty:* trial transcript, pp. 781–92, 833–34, MT, NA; "Army Fails to Bar
          Charges Made by Mrs. Lansdowne" and "Foley Is Refused Right to Answer Mrs.
          Lansdowne" in later edition, *Washington Star*, Nov. 13, 1925, p. 1; "Foley Asks
          to Quit as Judge Advocate of Shenandoah Quiz," *Washington Post*, Nov. 14,
          1925, p. 4; *Washington Post* cartoon, Nov. 19, 1925; "Up to You, Mr. President,"
          Washington Post, Nov. 15, 1925.

204   *"in disaster":* "Mrs. Lansdowne to Meet Foley in Court 'Showdown,'" *Washing-
          ton Star*, Nov. 14, 1925, p. 1; "Foley to Quit as Shenandoah Judge," *Washington
          Herald*, Nov. 14, 1925, p. 1; "Story of Plot Told in Grill After Judges Eject
          Lawyer," *Washington Herald*, Nov. 19, 1925; "Mrs. Lansdowne Knew Foley's
          Aim Fair, Says Bearer," *Washington Star*, Nov. 18, 1925; Dixie Tighe, "Enemy
          Wives Defend Mates In Foley Quiz," *Washington Herald*, Nov. 19, 1925; diary
          entry, Nov. 16, 1925, MB, MHS; "Attempt to Coerce Mrs. Lansdowne Charged
          to Wilbur," *Washington Herald*, Nov. 19, 1925, p. 1; "Mrs. Lansdowne's Counsel
          Ejected by Marine Guard," *Washington Star*, Nov. 17, 1925; "Shenandoah Case
          Now in Limelight," *Washington Star*, Nov. 15, 1925; *Shenandoah* court of
          inquiry statement, Nov. 20, 1925, box 11, MT, NA; Arthur Brisbane, "Today,"
          Washington Herald, Nov. 19, 1925.

204   *"aching void":* Robert T. Small, "Capital's Longing for a Hero Filled Perfectly by
          Mitchell," *Washington Star*, Nov. 14, 1925, p. 4.

204   *general staff:* "Public Backing Likely to Save Col. Mitchell," *Baltimore Sun*, Nov.
          18, 1925; "Up To You, Mr. President," *Washington Post*, Nov. 15, 1925.

204   *the prosecution:* "General Staff Begins Drive to Convict Col. Mitchell," *Wash-
          ington Post*, Nov. 18, 1925, p. 1.

205   *Reid's evidence:* Francis Bowditch Wilby, War Department profile, biography
          file, AWC; "Gen. Francis B. Wilby, 82, Dies; Headed West Point During War,"
          New York Times, Nov. 21, 1965.

205   *"taking a fee":* "Reid's Wine-Colored Bow Tie Unchanged Since Trial Began,"
          Washington Star, Nov. 15, 1925.

205   *"from his end":* trial transcript, pp. 821–23, MT, NA.

205   *many decades:* Patrick memo to Adjutant General, Mar. 27, 1925, box 38, WM,
          LOC.

206   *ousted president:* Summarized Statement Showing Costs of Anti-Aircraft Tests
          for Summer and Fall of 1925, box 8, MT, NA; Anti-aircraft Experiments at
          Mitchel Field during the months of May, June and July, 1925, box 38, WM, LOC.

206   *his neck:* Information for Official Visitors to Combined Coast Artillery-Air Ser-

vice Tests at Ft. Tilden, N.Y., and Camp Dix, N.J., Aug. 7, 1925, box 38, WM, LOC; trial transcript, p. 980, MT, NA; War Department press release, "Preliminary Report on Anti-Aircraft Firing," July 20, 1925, box 16, MT, NA.

206   *make them:* War Department press release: "Preliminary Report on Anti-Aircraft Firing," July 20, 1925, box 16, MT, NA; trial transcript, p. 393, MT, NA; "Certain Facts and Opinions of Pilots Who Actually Participated in the Operations Concerning the Maneuvers at Fort Tilden and Camp Dix this Summer," statements by 1st Lt. James J. Walker and 1st Lt. William T. Atkinson, box 38, WM, LOC.

207   *two-plane regulation:* Umpire's Report: Joint Exercises Coast Artillery–Air Service, Test No. 2, Exercise 6, July 27, 1925, box 6, MT, NA; trial transcript, pp. 764–69, 774–75, 983–87, MT, NA; "Certain Facts and Opinions of Pilots Who Actually Participated in the Operations Concerning the Maneuvers at Fort Tilden and Camp Dix This Summer," statements by 1st Lt. James J. Walker and 1st Lt. William T. Atkinson, box 38, WM, LOC.

207   *on them:* Trial transcript, pp. 827–29, MT, NA.

207   *towing targets:* Trial transcript, pp. 992–95, MT, NA.

208   *Dargue answered:* Trial transcript, pp. 480–81, 824–27, MT, NA; Col. S. Heintzelman memo to Chief of Staff, newspaper interview by Brigadier General Billy Mitchell, Nov. 18, 1922, box 212, file 183-2-15/18, MID, NA.

208–10 *from Reid now* to *the court:* trial transcript, pp. 829–32, 834–69, 874–87, MT, NA; James R. Nourse, "War Heads Give Up Records to Save Mitchell's Trial," and Dixie Tighe, "Frayed Nerves React to Slap Trial Audience," *Washington Herald,* Nov. 14, 1925, p. 2.

211   *"festive Bill":* Trial transcript, pp. 886–87, MT, NA; "Reid's Wine-Colored Bow Tie Unchanged Since Trial Began," *Washington Star,* Nov. 15, 1925; *Washington Herald* photo headlined "Off for Luncheon," Nov. 14, 1925, p. 2; McCoy letter to Mrs. Louie A. Wood, Nov. 14, 1925, box 177, LW, LOC.

211   *was waging:* Diary entries, Nov. 13–16, 1925, MB, MHS; "'Pagliacci' on Bill of WCAP Tonight," *Washington Star,* Nov. 16, 1925, p. 38.

212   *us all:* "Mitchell, on Radio, Details Advantage of Aircraft in War," *Washington Post,* Nov. 17, 1925.

212   *American Legion:* Diary entry, Nov. 16, 1925, MD, MHS; "'La Tosca' Pleases Large Audience," *Washington Star,* Nov. 17, 1925, p. 5.

CHAPTER 18   PRELUDE

Page

213   *each month:* State of Wisconsin Circuit Court—Milwaukee County: William Mitchell, Plaintiff, vs. Caroline Mitchell, Defendant, court documents filed Aug. 13, 1924, Feb. 9, and Mar. 25, 1925, box 2, WMP, MHS; Wisconsin Supreme Court Journal, series 2030, vol. 46, 1924–26, pp. 213, 226, 319, 351; "Mitchell Loses in Marital Suit," *Milwaukee Journal,* Nov. 17, 1925, p. 1.

214   *with him:* Cicely Banfield interview; Felicity Trueblood interview; diary entries for Dec. 12, 1923, and 1924 and 1925, CS, TF.

214   *"favor any":* Diary entries, July 25, 1923 and Feb. 29, 1924, CS, TF; unidentified news item on Caroline Mitchell, box 57, WM, LOC.

214   *her diary:* Diary entries, June 2, 1924, May 19, Oct. 30, Nov. 11, Dec. 4 and 15, 1925, CS, TF.

214   *judge advocate:* War Department appointment letters for Lt. Clayton Bissell,
        Maj. Francis Wilby, and Maj. Allen Gullion, Nov. 16, 1925, and Navy Depart-
        ment appointment letters for Cdr. Garland Fulton and Lt. Cdr. Holloway H.
        Frost, Nov. 16 and 17, 1925, box 16, MT, NA.

215   *the defense:* Moreland memo to general staff officers, Nov. 18, 1925, box 15, MT,
        NA; Moreland memo to Secretary of War, Nov. 18, 1925, box 17, action reported
        by chief of air service on 127 recommendations of Col. Mitchell, box 15 and 17,
        MT, NA; Weekly Press Review, Military Intelligence Division, G-2, Nov. 18,
        1925, box 58, WM, LOC; Moreland memo to Adjutant General, Nov. 18, 1925,
        box 16, MT, NA; memorandum for Col. Rucker, Nov. 19, 1925, box 15, MT, NA.

215   *Moreland had:* trial transcript, pp. 894–96, MT, NA.

215–19 from *"What do"* to *witness nicely:* trial transcript, pp. 896–944, MT, NA; "All Wit-
        nesses Questioned by Maj. F. B. Wilby," Nov. 18, 1925, *Washington Herald*.

219   *model Zeppelin:* trial transcript, pp. 1022–24, MT, NA; Toland, *The Great Dirigi-
        bles,* p. 81.

220   *flying dirigibles:* Orville Anderson memo to Mitchell, Nov. 19, 1925, box 34, WM,
        LOC; Toland, pp. 86–89.

220   *of storms:* trial transcript, pp. 1024–25, MT, NA; Cooper technical paper; Orville
        Anderson memo to Mitchell, Nov. 19, 1925, box 34, WM, LOC.

220–21 from *Aircraft procurement* to *said gruffly:* trial transcript, pp. 1025–29, MT, NA;
        Orville Anderson memo to Mitchell, Nov. 19, 1925, box 34, WM, LOC; Cooper
        technical paper.

221–22 from *Satisfied, Reid* to *with Mitchell*: author interview with Fred Simpich, Jan.
        1, 2003; author interview with Thomas S. Moorman, Dec. 4, 2002; Allen Wyant
        Gullion biography, biography file, AWC.

222–23 from *"Captain, you"* to *vent gas:* trial transcript, pp. 1029–31, MT, NA; Lans-
        downe memo to Chief of Navy Bureau of Aeronautics, May 12, 1925, and
        response of Chief of Bureau of Aeronautics to Lansdowne, May 28, 1925, box
        10, MT, NA.

224   *dead husband:* Orville Anderson memo to Mitchell, Nov. 19, 1925, box 34, WM,
        LOC; Cooper technical paper.

224   *in dirigibles:* Heinen letter to Mitchell, Nov. 23, 1925, box 11, WM, LOC; Anton
        Heinen, "You are as safe in the air as at sea," *Collier's* 76, Oct. 31, 1925, pp. 9–10;
        Grumelli, *Trial of Faith,* pp. 170–71.

225   *question unanswered:* trial transcript, pp. 1031–33, MT, NA.

225   *not heard:* Notes on Airship Training, unsigned memos No. 1, 5, 19 to Mitchell,
        box 34, WM, LOC; Cooper technical paper; memo to Mitchell on "General con-
        ditions of operating and maintenance of rigid airships of the Naval Air Station,
        Lakehurst, New Jersey," box 38, WM, LOC; William Moffett memo to Aeronau-
        tical Board, Oct. 20, 1923, box 11, WM, LOC; Arnold memo to Mitchell, Oct. 20,
        1925, box 11, WM, LOC.

225–29 from *Reid now* to *weaker ship:* trial transcript, pp. 1034–87, 2432, MT, NA.

229   *aviator's case:* "William Sims: Scholar, Officer, Gentleman," *Time,* Oct. 26, 1925,
        no. 17, p. 9; Coffman, *War to End All Wars,* pp. 90–94, 101–7; Smythe, *Pershing,* p.
        16; Hurley, *Billy Mitchell,* p. 58; Adm. William F. Fullam letter to Sen. Hiram Bing-
        ham, Oct. 5, 1925, and Fullam letter to Patrick, Dec. 22, 1925, box 6, WF, LOC;
        "Should the Army and Navy Be Muzzled?" *Outlook* 124, Feb. 20, 1920, pp. 187–88.

229–32 from *What was* to *"very last":* trial transcript, pp. 1097–1131, MT, LOC: "Sims

Scores 'Uneducated' Admirals," *Washington Herald*, Nov. 19, 1925, p. 1; photo
of Mitchell and Sims, *Washington Herald*, Nov. 19, 1925, p. 2.

232   *"ever saw":* Mitchell, *Memoirs of World War I*, p. 145.

232   *Air Lines:* Mitchell, *Memoirs of World War I*, pp. 156–57; Coffman, pp. 202–03.

232–33   from *"How many"* to *"One":* trial transcript, pp. 1179–82, MT, NA.

233   *different story:* William E. Hunt letter to Wilby, Nov. 17, 1925, box 14, MT, NA.

233–34   from *"Major Rickenbacker"* to *only anecdotes:* trial transcript, pp. 1186–87, MT,
         NA.

235   *use them:* trial transcript, pp. 1192–1207, MT, NA.

235   *audience laughed:* Memorandum for the Press: Report of Adm. R. E. Coontz to
         Chief of Naval Operations, Mar. 3, 1924, box 10, WM, LOC; "Mitchell Defense
         Is Ended Without Colonel on Stand," *Washington Star*, Nov. 11, 1925; "Sheridan
         Charges Bring Hot Retort," *Washington Star*, Nov. 21, 1925; "Navy Flier Here
         Raps Sheridan," *Honolulu Advertiser*, Nov. 23, 1925, p. 1.

235–37   from *Gullion had* to *"old, sir":* trial transcript, pp. 1384–93, 2041–42, MT, NA;
         Aircraft Carrier U.S.S. Langley: Report of Lt. H. W. Sheridan, box 38, WM,
         LOC; letter from Naval Safety Center to author on Class A mishaps on carriers
         compared to total number of landings for Fiscal Years 2000, 2001 and 2002,
         Nov. 5, 2002; photo of Lieutenant Sheridan and other officers playing cards
         before their testimony, unidentified newspaper, Mitchell scrapbooks, WMC,
         NASM; "Mitchell to Take Stand on Monday," *Washington Star*, Nov. 21, 1925.

238   *his face:* "Mitchell Witness Warned of Danger," *Washington Star*, Nov. 23, 1925.

238   *be asked:* Diary entries, Nov. 20–22, 1925, MB, LOC.

CHAPTER 19   CROSS-EXAMINATION

Page

239   *the courtroom:* "Court Bars Move to Show Mitchell Plagiarized Book," *Wash-
         ington Star*, Nov. 24, 1925, p. 1; photo from unidentified newspaper of
         MacArthur and his mother-in-law, Mitchell scrapbooks, WMC, NASM;
         "Mitchell Renews Treason Charge on Witness Stand," *Washington Star*, Nov. 23,
         1925; John Edwin Nevin, "Mitchell Charges Criminal Treason in Defense
         Stand," *Washington Post*, Nov. 24, 1925, p. 1; "Crowd Roped in at Trial," *Wash-
         ington Star*, Nov. 24, 1925, p. 4.

239–46   from *Reid stood* to *"think so":* trial transcript, pp. 1400–1529, MT, NA; Mitchell,
         Memoirs of World War I, pp.159–62; Mitchell, *Our Air Force*, pp. 48–49, 95–98,
         100–102, 186–88.

247   *during Thanksgiving:* Diary entry, Nov. 23, 1925, MB, MHS; memorandum of
         testimony of Col. Mitchell directly relating to Statements #1 and #2, box 37,
         WM, LOC; John Edwin Nevin, "Mitchell Charges Criminal Treason in Defense
         Stand," *Washington Post*, Nov. 24, 1925, p. 1; "Mitchell Renews Treason Charge
         On Witness Stand," *Washington Star*, Nov. 23, 1925; "U.S. Helpless in Air,
         Mitchell Testifies," *Chicago American*, Nov. 23, 1925, p. 1; "Mitchell Hurls New
         Treason Charge," *Washington Herald*, Nov. 24, 1925, p. 1; "Japan Menaces U.S.
         Says Mitchell: Saving Country His Aim," *Washington Times*, Nov. 23, 1925, p. 1;
         collection of headlines from newspapers around the country, Mitchell scrap-
         books, WMC, NASM; Speaking invitations sent to Mitchell during the trial, box
         11, WM, LOC; Mitchell memo to Commanding General, Washington District,

on Thanksgiving request and response, Nov. 24, 1925, box 11, WM, LOC.

247   *and opinion:* Capt. M. G. Cook memo to Director War Plans Division, Jan. 6,
          1926, file 6000–1424, NAV, NA.

247   *Service needs:* Levine, *Mitchell,* pp. 312–13; "Sight Of Companions Dropping Off
          in War Time 'Flaming Coffins' Stirs Mitchell to Action," draft article by Mitchell
          for Bell Syndicate Inc., Feb. 16, 1925, box 28, WM, LOC; "Army Probes Talks on
          Mitchell Case," *Washington Star,* Nov. 20, 1925; "General Staff Held Cause of
          Air Weakness," *Washington Herald,* Feb. 17, 1926, p. 2; "G-2 Will Get You" poem
          by W. G. Schauffler, Feb. 9, 1926, reel 4, HA, LOC.

248   *cross-examination:* "Crowd Roped in at Trial," *Washington Star,* Nov. 24, 1925,
          p. 4.

248   *"in safety":* trial transcript, pp. 1531–34, MT, NA; USAF history of accidents,
          fatalities and flying hours, 1947–2001, Air Force Safety Center website,
          htttp://safety.kirtland.af.mil.

248–52   from *Didn't the* to *"be specified":* trial transcript, pp. 1484–86, 1535–1611, MT,
          NA; Coffman, *War to End All Wars,* p. 205; Kennett, *First Air War,* p. 109; Mauer,
          Aviation in the U.S. Army, pp. 35–36; Mitchell, *Winged Defense,* pp. 102–105;
          "Submarines," Captain T. C. Hart, lecture at General Staff College, Oct. 28,
          1919, General Staff College, 1919–1920, vol.2, Intelligence, part I, Lectures Mis-
          cellaneous, file 241–38, AWC; Capt. Thomas C. Hart memo to Commandant,
          U.S. Army War College, Mar. 20, 1925, and Lt. Col. Kyle Rucker Memo to Gul-
          lion, Nov. 23, 1925, box 14, MT, NA; Maj. M. E. Guerin memo to Gullion, Nov.
          27, 1925, box 16, MT, NA; Hurley, *Billy Mitchell,* p. 139; Meilinger, *Paths of
          Heaven,* pp. xii–xiv, 84, 98; Mets, *The Air Campaign,* pp. 11, 40; Mitchell, *Mem-
          oirs of World War I,* p. 116; "Court Bars Move to Show Mitchell Plagiarized
          Book," *Washington Star,* Nov. 11, 1925, p. 1; "Court Hisses Prosecutor of Air-
          man," Nov. 24, 1925, article from unidentified newspaper, box 56, WM, LOC;
          "Record of Picture of Bomb Failures Barred in Trial," *Washington Star,* Nov. 24,
          1925; "Sensations, Laughter, Hisses, Feature Mitchell Trial," *Washington Her-
          ald,* Nov. 25, 1925, p. 1.

252   *a vengeance:* Diary entry, Nov. 24, 1925, MB, MHS; Maurice Judd, "Part of Col.
          Mitchell's Book And Hart Lecture Identical," *New York Sun,* Dec. 14, 1925.

CHAPTER 20   CRUSHING

Page
253   *told him:* trial transcript, pp. 1612–14, MT, NA.
253   *rivaled Mitchell's:* trial transcript, pp. 1634–38, MT, NA.
253–54   from *A second* to *"very short":* trial transcript, pp. 1639–48, MT, NA; John Edwin
          Nevin, "Mitchell to Test His Defense Today in Court-Martial," *Washington Post,*
          Nov. 25, 1925.
255   *sea commands:* trial transcript, pp. 1660–68, MT, NA.
255   *on Friday:* trial transcript, pp. 1771–73, MT, NA.
256   *following week:* Mitchell letter requesting permission to travel to Middleburg,
          Nov. 25, 1925, box 11, WM, LOC; photo of Mitchell at foxhunt from unidenti-
          fied newspaper, box 58, WM, LOC; Charles Bass interview; Richard Jackson
          interview; Betty Mitchell telegram to Harriet, Nov. 25, 1925, family scrapbook,
          box 11, GH, UWM; "Wife, in Tears, Calls Ruling 'Only Logical,'" Fraser

Edwards, *Washington Herald*, Nov. 26, 1925, p. 2; diary entries, Nov. 26 and Dec. 1, 1925, MB, MHS; Dixie Tighe, "Texas Turkey Gift Of 'Gang' To Mitchells," *Washington Herald*, Nov. 21, 1925; Eugene M. Scheel, *The History of Middleburg and Vicinity* (Warrenton, Va.: Piedmont Press, 1987), p. 121; Elizabeth Mitchell letter to Katharine Jackson, Nov. 8, 1925, BA.

256   *"married Valkyries":* Scheel, pp. 116–19, 126–27, 146; Vicky Moon, *The Middleburg Mystique* (Sterling, Va.: Capital Books, 2001), pp. 1, 18, 30, 33; Middleburg Tennis Club notice to Mitchell, Aug. 24, 1933, box 18, WM, LOC; Tom Gilpin interview.

257   *green pasture:* author's tour of Boxwood, Apr. 30, 2002; advertisement for Boxwood when Elizabeth Byrd sold it in 1943, and National Register of Historic Places Inventory for Boxwood, Dec. 8, 1976, Virginia Historic landmarks Commission Survey Form for Boxwood, file No. 30–91, courtesy of John Kent Cooke; L. G. Collier letter to Betty Mitchell, Feb. 18, 1926, box 12, WM, LOC; Harriet Pillsbury interview; Richard Jackson interview; Elizabeth Mitchell letter to Katharine Jackson, June 27, 1925, BA.

257   *he grew:* Mitchell letters to Michael Cudahy, Jan. 26 and Feb. 10, 1925, box 11, WM, LOC; contract Mitchell signed with Isaac Waddell, June 5, 1925, Waddell's bill for seeds, Waddell letter to Mitchell, July 16, 1926, box 11, WM, LOC; Mitchell letter to Waddell, Dec. 22, 1929, and Waddell's response, Nov. 11, 1930, box 15, WM, LOC.

257   *together there:* Diary entry, Nov. 26, 1925, MB, MHS.

257   *for Moreland:* Moreland memo to McMullen, Wilby, and Gullion, Nov. 25, 1925, box 16, MT, NA.

258   *to reporters:* Memo to Wilby on Aviation, Nov. 16, 1925, Analysis Of Defense Testimony Showing Army Items of Which Evidence Was Introduced, and Memorandum Re: Mitchell Case, box 14, MT, NA: Checklist of Points to Be Rebutted, Evidence for the Defense: Session of Nov. 10, 1925, and Opening Statement—Points Suggested from the Air Service Point of View, box 15, MT, NA; Moreland memo to Adjutant General of the Army, Nov. 21, 1925, box 16, MT, NA.

258   *the accident:* Wilby note to Gullion, box 17, MT, NA; Interrogatory and attachments for Maj. Ralph Royce, box 14, MT, NA; Moreland memos to Adjutant General, Nov. 25 and 27, 1925, box 12, MT, NA.

258   *for them:* Memorandum Re: Mitchell Case, box 14, MT, NA; navy lists of prosecution witnesses, Nov. 27, 1925, box 14, MT, NA; List of [Army] Witnesses For Prosecution In Rebuttal, box 6, MT, NA; "Rebuttal Starts In Mitchell Case as Defense Rests," *Washington Star,* Nov. 25, 1925; Interrogatory for Maj. S. W. Fitzgerald with attachments on Steering Committee and color codes, box 15, MT, NA; Interrogatory for Maj. B. Q. Jones, box 14, MT, NA; Interrogatory for Maj. Gen. Charles Saltzman, box 15, MT, NA.

259   *get-even time:* Lt. Col. Charles Keller memo to Lt. Col. Kyle Rucker, Nov. 21, 1925, box 15, MT, NA; Note to Rucker with suggestions from Drum, box 14, MT, NA; Drum notes to Wilby on prosecution evidence, box 15, MT, NA; Col. Charles S. Lincoln memo to Drum, Nov. 21, 1925, box 12, MT, NA.

259   *witness chair:* Summerall memos to Moreland, Nov. 27, 1925, and Rucker memo to Wilby, Nov. 23, 1925, box 15, MT, NA; Eugene Fidell interview, Sept. 18, 2002; Maj. Gen. Robert C. Davis memo to Summerall, Nov. 20, 1925, box 15, MT, NA.

CHAPTER 21   "DAMNED ROT"

Page

261   *run the trial:* trial transcript, pp. 1794–1802, MT, NA; Eugene Fidell interview,
        Aug. 23, 2002.

261–67 from *Distinguished looking* to *a mistrial:* trial transcript, pp. 1794–1912,
        2769–71, MT, NA; Locher, *Victory on the Potomac,* pp. 17–19; James R. Locher
        III, interview, Nov. 27, 2002; "The Mitchell Court-Martial," Frederic J. Haskin,
        unidentified newspaper, Nov. 28, 1925, Mitchell scrapbooks, WMC, NASM;
        "Mitchell Judge and Lawyer Clash," *New York Times,* Nov. 28, 1925, p. 5;
        "Judge's Irate 'Rot!' Heard by Reid, Halts Mitchell Trial," *Washington Herald,*
        Nov. 28, 1925, p. 2; Eugene Fidell interview, Oct. 31, 2002; "Apology Is Given
        Reid by Gen. King in Dramatic Row," unidentified newspaper, Nov. 27, 1926,
        Mitchell scrapbooks, WMC, NASM.

268   *Reid knew:* John Edwin Nevin, "Mitchell Judge Causes Clash," *Washington
        Post,* Nov. 28, 1925, p. 1.

268   *service's budget:* "Army Lawyers Miss Service Grid Game," William J. McEvoy,
        Washington News, Nov. 28, 1925; Westbrook Pegler, "West Point Cavalry,
        Mounted on Foot, Outrides Navy Team," *Washington Post,* Nov. 29, 1925, p. 21;
        "The Once Over," H. I. Phillips, *Philadelphia Inquirer,* Nov. 28, 1925; John T.
        Lambert, "Plane Route in Commercial Field Desired," *Washington Herald,* Nov.
        30, 1925, p. 2.

268   *his cold:* Diary entries, Nov. 30 and Dec. 1, 1925, MB, MHS; "Mitchell Receives
        Lemon to be Given to Army Counsel," *Washington Star,* Nov. 30, 1925.

268   *Monday afternoon:* trial transcript, pp. 1921–83, MT, NA; Moreland memo to
        McMullen, Wilby, and Gullion, Nov. 25, 1925, box 16, MT, NA.

269   *White House:* "Californians Hail Rodgers and Crew," *New York Times,* Sept. 25,
        1925, p. 1; "Fliers' Own Story of Pacific Flight Told for the Times," *New York
        Times,* Sept. 21, 1925, p. 1; "PN-9 No. 1 Found Off Hawaiian Islands," *Aviation,*
        Sept. 21, 1925, p. 350; "PN-9 Commander Arrives to Testify at Aviation Probe,"
        Washington Post, Oct. 1, 1925, p. 4.

269–72 from *Rodgers settled* to *on land:* trial transcript, pp. 2000–2036, MT, NA; John
        Edwin Nevin, "Flight to Hawaii Chiefly Navigation Test, Rodgers Says," *Wash-
        ington Post,* Dec. 1, 1925, p. 1; Unsigned letters and notes to Mitchell on ques-
        tions to ask of Rodgers's flight, boxes 37 and 38, WM, LOC; telegram to Reid
        Nov. 10, 1925, box 11, WM, LOC.

272   *"the unknown":* "Navy Supports MacMillan," June 22, 1925, release, box 45,
        WM, LOC; Gill Robb Wilson reminiscences, pp. 27–28, OHC; reminiscences of
        Harold McMillan Bixby, no. 388, p. 45, OHC.

273   *snowy day:* trial transcript, pp. 539–41, 957–58, 1166–67, 1496, 2149–81, MT,
        NA; photo of Mitchell with Grover Loening and his amphibian, box 9, MT, NA.

274   *sat down:* trial transcript, pp. 2103–49, MT, NA; "Navy Supports MacMillan,"
        June 22, 1925 Release, box 45, WM, LOC; "Mitchell Attack on Arctic Flight
        Planes Is Backed," *Washington Star,* Dec. 1, 1925.

274   *Washington Star:* trial transcript, pp. 1914–19, MT, NA; "Prosecution Rift
        Causes Sensation in Mitchell Trial," *Washington Star,* Nov. 30, 1925.

275   *"for prejudice":* trial transcript, pp. 2083–88, MT, NA; William J. McEvoy,
        "Mitchell Juror Is Challenged," *Washington News,* Dec. 1, 1925, p. 1; John

Edwin Nevin, "Court Disallows Reid's Challenge of Mitchell Judge," *Washington Post*, Dec. 2, 1925, p. 1.

275   *peace offering:* Diary entry, Dec. 1, 1925, MB, MHS.

CHAPTER 22   SIEGE

Page

277   *Mitchell wanted: Report of President's Aircraft Board: Nov. 30, 1925* (Washington, D.C.: Government Printing Office, 1925).

277   *board's secretary:* Patrick, *United States in the Air,* pp. 182–83; Coolidge Press Conference Dec. 4, 1925, transcript no. 2, vols. 4–7, CCP; White House press release announcing Pershing's appointment as president of the Plebiscite Commission, Mar. 23, 1925, reel 114, CC, LOC; Pershing letter to Martin Egan, Dec. 22, 1925, box 7, *JP,* LOC; Pershing letter to Morrow, Dec. 14, 1926, series 1, box 38, Folder 55, DM, ACL; Pershing letter to William F. Durand, Dec. 22, 1925, series 9, box 1, Folder 2, DM, ACL.

277   *distinguished leaders:* Ruth Mitchell, p. 327; "Mitchell Plan Is Turned Down by Committee," *Chicago Tribune,* Nov. 29, 1925, p. 1.

277   *of the time:* trial transcript, p. 2189, MT, NA; "Warning By Court Brings Tranquility to Mitchell Trial," *Washington Post,* Dec. 3, 1925; "Mitchell Court Rebukes Counsel," *Washington Post,* Dec. 4, 1925; "Even Gen. Howze Has Fallen Victim to Unmilitary Ways of Court-Martial," *Washington Star,* Dec. 4, 1925; "Ban on Insulting Tactics Taken as Rebuke by Reid," *Washington Star,* Dec. 2, 1925, p. 1; "Gullion's Tactics Draw Hot Rebuke in Mitchell Trial," unidentified newspaper, Dec. 2, 1925, Mitchell scrapbooks, WMC, NASM.

278   *against Mitchell:* Kyle Rucker memo to Moreland, Dec. 3, 1925, box 15, MT, NA; Rucker memo to Moreland, McMullen, et al., Dec. 4, 1925, box 14, MT, NA; Rucker memo to McMullen, Dec. 7, 1925, box 16, MT, NA; Unsigned memo to Rucker, Dec. 4, Dec. 4, 1925, box 14, MT, NA; Gen. Hinds telegram to Moreland, Dec. 7, 1925, box 15, MT, NA.

278   *of World War I:* trial transcript, pp. 2541–65, 2688–2708, MT, NA; confidential memo, Office of Naval Intelligence to Naval Operations, May 11, 1925, box 48, WM, LOC.

279   *complex dirigible:* Toland, *The Great Dirigibles,* pp. 91, 227; Mitchell letter to Hugh Allen, Mar. 24, 1934, box 19, WM, LOC; Arnold, *Global Mission,* p. 118; "Survivor of Crashed Airship Refutes 'Slander of the Dead,'" *Milwaukee Journal,* Nov. 19, 1925, p. 1; "Lansdowne Aide Resents Slurs," *Washington Star,* Dec. 12, 1925; Orville Anderson memo to Mitchell, Nov. 19, 1925, box 34, WM, LOC.

279–87 from *Rosendahl began* to *befell it:* trial transcript, pp. 2282–97, 2333–2428, 2436–80, MT, NA; Unsigned memo to Mitchell on general conditions of operating and maintenance of rigid airships at the Naval Air Station, Lakehurst, New Jersey, box 38, WM, LOC; navy repair records for *Shenandoah's* break from the mooring mast, June 30, 1925, box 11, MT, NA; Toland, *The Great Dirigibles,* p. 89; Cooper technical paper; testimony of Cdr. Jerome C. Hunsicker before the Navy's *Shenandoah* inquiry, Oct. 15, 1925, pp. 1182–91, 1220, 1252–54, box 18, MT, NA; C. P. Burgess memo to Chief of Design Section, Bureau of Aeronautics, on Loss of the *Shenandoah,* box 15, MT, NA; Correspondence between Lansdowne and the Department of the Navy on the flight of the *Shenandoah* to the Middle West, June 9–Sept. 1, 1925, box 8, MT, NA; Grumelli, *Trail of Faith*, pp. 205–6.

287–89   from *On Saturday* to *in flight:* trial transcript, pp. 2616–53, MT, NA; Trimble, *Admiral William A. Moffett*, p. 142; List of *Shenandoah* Flights, box 8, MT, NA; Eugene E. Wilson reminiscences, pp. 200–202, OHC; "Lansdowne O.K.'d Airship Orders, Eberle Testifies," *Washington Star*, Dec. 5, 1925; "Eberle Disputes Mitchell's Naval Negligence Claim," *Washington Star*, Dec. 6, 1925.

290   *match it:* Diary entries, Dec. 3 and 7, 1925, MD, MHS; "Strategist Holds Mitchell Erred," *Washington Star*, Dec. 7, 1925; John Edwin Nevin, "Army Will Assail Motives and Facts in Mitchell's Case," *Washington Post*, Dec. 6, 1925; *New Republic*, Dec. 16, 1925, vol. 45, p. 98; Grumelli, *Trail of Faith*, pp. 214–15.

CHAPTER 23   "LAWLESS"

Page

291   *their service:* Prosecution lists of rebuttal witnesses, box 12, MT, NA.

291   *of witnesses:* trial transcript, pp. 3088–91, MT, NA; "Army Will Assail Motives and Facts in Mitchell's Case," John Edwin Nevin, *Washington Post*, Dec. 6, 1925; "Army Begins Attack upon Mitchell Today," *Washington Post*, Dec. 7, 1925; "Mirrors of Washington," *Wall Street Journal*, Dec. 12, 1925, p. 6; "Rickenbacker Hopes Mitchell Is Found Guilty by Court-Martial," International News Service article, Dec. 11, 1925, box 58, WM, LOC.

292   *large expense:* Fox Conner memo to Judge Advocate General on cost of court-martial, Nov. 10, 1925, Oct. 24, Dec. 11, and Dec. 15, 1925, Shipping Tickets from the Quartermaster Corps, First Report of Costs on Court, Nov. 7 and 9, 1925, James A. Willis memo to Moreland, Oct. 28, 1925, box 16, MT, NA; A. W. G. memo to Col. McMullen, Nov. 12, 1925, defense and prosecution witness travel costs, stenographic reports costs, box 12, MT, NA; Stenographic Personal Services bills, box 21, MT, NA.

292–93   from *Moreland had* to *the subject:* Prosecution interrogatory of Ely, box 15, MT, NA; War Department press release on Ely's testimony before Air Board of Inquiry, box 16, MT, NA; Ely letter to Morrow, Dec. 4, 1925, series 9, box 1, folder 2, DM, ACL; James J. Cooke, *Pershing and His Generals* (Westport, Conn.: Praeger, 1997), pp. 86–87; Cooke, *Billy Mitchell*, pp. 211, 222; Coffman, *War to End All Wars*, p. 157.

293–95   from *Ely told* to *said huffily:* trial transcript, pp. 2776–2826, MT, NA; "Says Air Service Failed on Manual," *Washington Star*, Dec. 4, 1925, partial article, Mitchell scrapbooks, WMC, NASM.

295   *air commander:* Gray letter to Mitchell, Oct. 1, 1918, box 6, MT, NA; trial transcript, pp. 3147–3163; Rath telegrams to Moreland, Nov. 20, 21, and 26, 1925, box 15, MT, NA; H. M. Brown telegram to Moreland, Nov. 20, 1925, box 12, MT, NA; Rath telegram to Maj. H. L. Hendrick, Dec. 10, 1925, and Rath telegram to Wilby, Dec. 10, 1925, box 6, MT, NA.

295–300 from *Rath took* to *the jury:* trial transcript, pp. 2955–3007, MT, NA; General Order 123 for Rath's Distinguished Service Cross citation, box 20, MT, NA; "Reid Enraged By Hero Witness; Hissed By Crowd," James O'Donnell Bennett, *Chicago Tribune*, Dec. 12, 1925, p. 7; "Witness Charges Mitchell Sent Men On Death Mission," *Washington Star*, Dec. 9, 1925.

300   *some subjects:* Prosecution interrogatory for Patrick, Dec. 5, 1925, box 17, MT, NA.

300–304 from *The low-key* to *"know that"*: trial transcript, pp. 2943–54, 3022–66, MT, NA; "Patrick Upholds Mitchell in Part," *Washington Star*, Dec. 10, 1925; Nolan letters to Hines, Dec. 10 and 16, 1925, box 31, JH, LOC; Wilby memo to Col. Rucker, Dec. 10, 1925, box 15, MT, NA.

305   *the proceedings:* "Rogers at Mitchell Trial," *New York Times*, Dec. 12, 1925.

305–6   from *The prosecutors* to *look silly:* trial transcript, pp. 3163–3213, 3248–59, 3438–53, MT, NA; "City Defenseless Against Bombers, Gen. Coe Declares," John Edwin Nevin, *Washington Post*, Dec. 12, 1925, p. 1; "Mitchell Scores on Ground Defense," *New York Times*, Dec. 12, 1925; Nolan letter to Hines, Dec. 16, 1925, box 31, JH, LOC.

307   *every year:* "Voice of Santa Is Heard in City Above Cry of Usual Howlers," *Washington Star*, Dec. 12, 1925; Advertisements in *Washington Post*, Dec. 12, 1925; "President Signs Order For Three-Day Holiday," *Washington Post*, Dec. 12, 1925, p. 8.

307   *comedy skits:* Diary entry, Dec. 12, 1925, MB, MHS; "Here After Long Run," *Washington Post*, Dec. 6, 1925, Amusement Section, p. 1.

308   *"eat somewhere":* "Gridiron Pokes Fun at Dawes Campaign," *New York Times*, Dec. 13, 1925, p. 18; "Political Review of 1925 Satirized by Gridiron Club," *Washington Post*, Dec. 13, 1925, p. 1; seating arrangement for Gridiron Club dinner Dec. 12, 1925, box 13, WM, LOC; Perrett, *America in the Twenties*, p. 193; Sobel, *Coolidge*, p. 217.

308–9   from *For the last* to *expressionless:* trial transcript, pp. 3337–94, MT, NA.

310   *"breaking point":* Hugh Aloysius Drum profile, box 1, HD, AWC; George Fielding Eliot, "Hugh Drum" *Scribner's*, Feb. 1939, 105, no. 2, pp. 5–9; Noel F. Busch, "General Drum: Nation's No. 1 Field Soldier Commands Biggest and Handiest Of Four New Armies," *Life*, June 16, 1941, pp. 86–96; Drum profile, Biographies of Army Figures, U.S. Army Center of Military History Library, Ft. McNair; Gen. Hugh A. Drum Dies at Desk at 72," *New York Times*, Oct. 4, 1951, p. 1; Drum letter to Morrow, Dec. 4, 1925, series 9, box 1, file 2, Drum letter to Morrow, Memorandum re possible appointment of Brig. Gen. Hugh A. Drum to a major generalship, and Data Relative to Gen. Drum's Rank in List of Brigadier Generals, series 1, box 18, folder 107, DM, ACL; Drum letter to Hines, June 12, 1920, box 2, JH, LOC; Mary Drum letter to Pershing, 1921, box 8, HD, AWC.

310   *this trial:* Drum letter to Morrow, Sept. 29, 1925, series 9, box 1, folder 2, DM, ACL.

310   *of them:* Col. James H. Reeves memo to Drum with attachments, Dec. 9, 1925, box 14, MT, NA; Drum correspondence with G-2 on his testimony, Feb. 9–24, 1925, file 183–88, MID, NA; Prosecution interrogatory with Drum and accompanying memos, Dec. 12, 1925, box 12, MT, NA; Moreland memo to G-2, Dec. 12, 1925, box 14, MT, NA; trial transcript, pp. 3454–3456, MT, NA.

310–13   from *For more* to *sat down:* trial transcript, pp. 3455–3604, MT, NA; Defense questions for Drum, box 54, WM, LOC; Nolan letter to Hines, Dec. 16, 1925, box 31, JH, LOC; "Gen. Drum and Rep. Reid Have Bitter Clash at Mitchell Court-Martial," *Washington News*, Dec. 12, 1925; "Mitchell Lawless, Weeks Declares," *New York Times*, Dec. 17, 1925, p. 8; John Edwin Nevin, "Gen. Drum Accuses Mitchell Defense of Misquoting Him," *Washington Post*, Dec. 16, 1925; Eugene Fidell interview, Dec. 14, 2002.

313–15   from *The prosecutors* to *final arguments:* trial transcript, pp. 3605–90, MT, NA; General Nolan profile, MIRS Bulletin, Apr. 1936, and Dennis E. Nolan profile,

Assembly, Oct. 1956, box 1, *DN,* AWC; "Gen. Nolan Dies; Aide to Pershing," *New York Times,* Feb. 25, 1956; "Mitchell Lawless, Weeks Declares," *New York Times,* Dec. 17, 1925, p. 8; John Edwin Nevin, "Trial of Mitchell in Final Laps, May Wind Up Tomorrow," *Washington Post,* Dec. 17, 1925, p. 5; Weeks letter to Coolidge, Mar. 3, 1925, box 16, MT, NA; Nolan letter to Hines, Dec. 16, 1925, box 31, JH, LOC.

CHAPTER 24   THE VERDICT

Page

316   *seven weeks:* Statistics on Mitchell Trial, defense document, box 1, WMC, NASM; "Longest Court Martial on Record for Mitchell," *New York World,* Dec. 18, 1925, p. 2.

316   *and unfair:* Diary entry, Dec. 17, 1925, MB, MHS; photo of Betty after the trial, *Washington Herald,* Dec. 19, 1925, p. 4; Rebecca McCoy interview.

316–24 from *"The court"* to *the tables:* trial transcript, pp. 3691–3781, MT, NA; diary entry, Dec. 17, 1925, MB, MHS; Mitchell Case File, box 1, WMC, NASM; Argument by Col. H. A. White, box 1, WMC, NASM; Closing Argument of Judge Frank G. Plain, box 1, WMC, NASM; Press release of Mitchell's final statement, box 1, WMC, NASM; "Col. 'Billy' Mitchell Found Guilty, Pay Stops 5 Years, Stripped of Rank," *Washington Herald,* Dec. 18, 1925, p. 1; "Mitchell Sentence Most Remarkable in 60 Years," *Washington Herald,* Dec. 18, 1925, p. 1; "Mitchell Reduced to Status of Peon for Five Years by Decision of Court," *Washington Star,* Dec. 18, 1925; "Mitchell Found Guilty of Lashing Chiefs; to Be Army Outcast 5 Years," *New York World,* Dec. 18, 1925, p.1; "Buckner for Real or Dead Dry Law," *New York Herald,* Dec. 18, 1925, p. 1; "Valentino Files Suit for Divorce in Paris," *New York World,* Dec. 18, 1925, p. 2; John Edwin Nevin, "Mitchell Found Guilty by Army Court-Martial, Suspended for 5 Years," *Washington Post,* Dec. 18, 1925, p. 1; "Mitchell Is Found Guilty on All Counts; Five-Year Suspension Is Court Verdict; Final Decision Rests with President," *New York Times,* Dec. 18, 1925, p. 1; "Mukden Occupied by Japanese Forces," *New York Times,* Dec. 18, 1925, p. 1; "Swanson, Democrat, Opens Senate Fight for World Court," *New York Times,* Dec. 18, 1925, p. 1; "Mitchell Refuses to Go on with Case and Charges Plot Against Air Force," *Washington Star,* Dec. 17, 1925, p. 1; Howze's notes on verdict and sentence, box 13, MT, NA; photo of judges during the reading of the verdict, unidentified newspaper, Mitchell scrapbooks, WMC, NASM; "Army & Navy," *Time,* Dec. 28, 1925, pp. 6–7; McMullen memo on items taken from the court, Jan. 8, 1925, box 16, MT, NA; Grumelli, *Trial of Faith,* pp. 274, 296.

325   *general voted:* "Mitchell Trial Still a Mystery," *Milwaukee Journal,* May 24, 1951.

325   *not guilty:* Draft of Mitchell article number five on the trial, box 28, WM, LOC; "Mac Backed Billy Mitchell, Says Wiley," *Milwaukee Sentinel,* May 8, 1951, p. 5; James H. Doolittle reminiscences, p. 82–83, OHC; Levine, *Mitchell,* p. 368; MacArthur, *Reminiscences,* pp. 93–94; Tom Gilpin interview; interview with John Gilpin, Dec. 12, 2002; Kenneth Gilpin interview.

326   *"the fight":* Photo of Mitchell and Howze outside the Emery Building, *Washington Herald,* Dec. 18, 1925, p. 1; *Milwaukee Journal* photo Jan. 3, 1926, of Howze and Reid, box 11, GH, UWM; *Washington Post* weather report for Dec. 17, 1925; "Army & Navy," *Time,*, Dec. 28, 1925, pp. 6–7; diary entries, Dec. 1 and 17, 1925, MB, MHS; Elizabeth Mitchell letter to Katharine Jackson, Jan. 12, 1926, BA.

CHAPTER 25   RESIGNATION

Page

327   *of telegrams:* Diary entry, Dec. 18, 1925, MB, MHS; photo of Mitchell with messenger boys, *Washington Star,* Dec. 19, 1925; Elizabeth Mitchell letter to Katharine Jackson, Jan. 13, 1926, BA.

328   *did this:* United Press dispatch Dec. 18, 1925, from St. Petersburg, box 58, WM, LOC; "Halt Mitchell Sentence, Plea of City Council," *Washington Herald,* Dec. 18, 1925; Ray Brooks letter to Mitchell, Dec. 19, 1925, Ray Brooks Collection, Accession No, 1989–0104, NASM; Rep. Horace C. Carlisle letter to Mitchell, Dec. 28, 1925, box 11, WM, LOC; William Jackson letter to Mitchell, Jan. 15, 1926, box 13, WM, LOC; Harriet Young letter to Mitchell, Jan. 8, 1926, box 13, WM, LOC.

328   *War Davis:* V. L. van Newkirk letter to Howze, Dec. 18, 1925, file 6000–1424, NAV, NA; Arthur L. Davis letter to Dwight Davis, Jan. 12, 1925, box 20, MT, NA.

328   *"world's air":* Hector C. Bywater, "The Mitchell Trial; British Views of Case," *Baltimore Sun,* Jan. 13, 1926; Report No. 1914 by Lt. Col. Harry N. Cootes from Austria, Feb. 16, 1926, file 2657–11–68, box 1704, MID, NA; H. R. Knickerbocker, "Soviet Praises Col. Mitchell," International News Service, Dec. 21, 1925, unidentified newspaper, box 58, WM, LOC.

328   *Mitchell bills:* H.R. 5942 introduced Dec. 18, 1925, H.J.Res. 91 introduced Dec. 18, 1925, H.Res. 60 introduced Dec. 19, 1925, and H.Res. 106 introduced Jan. 26, 1926, 69th Congress, 1st Session, box 1, WMC, NASM; Dwight Davis letter to LaGuardia, Jan. 12, 1926, box 21, MT, NA; "LaGuardia Asks Less authority for Army Courts," *Washington Star,* Dec. 18, 1925; "Blanton Opens Bitter Attack Against Peace-Time Courts-Martial," *Washington Star,* Dec. 12, 1925; "Inquiry into Mitchell Court-Martial Asked," *Washington News,* Jan. 26, 1926; "Mitchell Sentence Scored in House as Unusual and Cruel," *Washington Star,* Dec. 19, 1925; Defense press release on "Events Leading Up to Court-Martial of Colonel Mitchell," box 1, WMC, NASM, "Mitchell Verdict Assailed by Reid," *Washington Star,* Dec. 21, 1925; Hurley, *Billy Mitchell,* p. 107–8.

329   *"the court":* Arthur Brisbane, "Today," *Washington Herald,* Dec. 18, 1925; "Colonel Mitchell's Guilt," *Literary Digest,* Jan. 2, 1926, pp. 5–7; "The Mitchell Verdict And Sentence," *New York Times,* Dec. 18, 1925, p. 22; "The Mitchell Verdict," *Milwaukee Journal,* Dec. 18, 1925.

329   *team players:* "Davis Plans Riot Talk in Demanding Army Teamwork," *Washington Post,* Dec. 21, 1925; "Davis Opens War on Friction in Army; Plans Drastic Action," *Washington Star,* Dec. 21, 1925; Davis letter to Morrow, series 9, box 1, folder 2, DM, ACL; "Sweeping Inquiry into Anti-Coolidge Policy Among Air Officers Ordered," unidentified newspaper, box 56, WM, LOC; Arthur Hachten, "High Command Hopes to 'Get' Aviation Chief, Friends Warn," Universal Service, unidentified newspaper, box 58, *WM* LOC.

329   *were over:* Patrick reprimand letter to Arnold, Mar. 2, 1926, reel 4, HA, LOC; Eleanor P. Arnold reminiscences, pp. 52–55, OHC; White, *Mason Patrick,* pp. 126–28; Coffey, pp. 4–6; "Propaganda Probe Brings 2 Airmen Up for Discipline," Associated Press, unidentified newspaper, box 34, WM, LOC.

329   *"military punishment":* Pershing letter to Gen. William M. Wright, Dec. 22, 1925, box 217, *JP,* LOC; Perrett, pp. 52–62

330   *"to society":* Pershing letter to Martin Egan, Dec. 22, 1925, box 7, *JP,* LOC; Maj.

Gem. J. A. Hull memo on Mitchell sentence, Jan. 9, 1926, box 20, MT, NA; Opinion of the Board of the Board of Review, C. M. No. 168771, Office of the Judge Advocate General, Jan. 20, 1926, pp. 103–10 with endorsements from Maj. Gen. J. A. Hull and Dwight Davis, box 1, MT, NA; White House press release on Coolidge amending Mitchell's sentence, Jan. 25, 1926, reel 109, CC, LOC.

330   *the airman:* Press release: Mr. Reid's Statement—Jan. 25, 1926, box 38, WM, LOC; Congressman J. McClintic letter to Everett Sanders, Jan. 25, 1926, Sen. Hiram Bingham letter to Coolidge, Jan. 27, 1926, reel 109, CC, LOC.

331   *said nothing:* Diary entries, Dec. 19, 1925–Jan. 25, 1926, MB, MHS.

331   *Mitchell's resignation:* Diary entries, Jan. 26–27, 1926, MB, MHS; Capt. Kendall J. Fiedler memo on serving Mitchell Court-Martial Order No. 3, Jan. 26, 1926, box 21, MT, NA; "Mitchell Offers Resignation," *Washington News,* Jan. 27, 1926, p. 1; "Mitchell Resigns, Approval of Act Believed Certain," *Washington Star,* Jan. 27, 1926, p. 1; "Mitchell, Disgusted With Verdict, Will Retire," *Washington Herald,* Jan. 27, 1926, p. 1; "Mitchell Escapes Sentence as Davis O.K.'s Resignation," *Washington Star,* Jan. 29, 1926; Draft of Mitchell's article number five after the trial, box 28, WM, LOC; Maydell Blackmon letter to Prescott H. Gatley, Nov. 19, 1933, box 18, WM, LOC; Secretary of War Henry L. Stimson letter to Sen. Robert R. Reynolds, Nov. 13, 1941, in Senate Military Affairs Committee Report No. 933, 77th Congress, 2nd Session, Jan. 6, 1942, p. 2.

332   *processed out:* War Department Pay and Allowance Account Sheet for William Mitchell, June 24, 1926, Maj. W. G. Kilner letter to Finance Officer, Washington, D.C., on property responsibility of William Mitchell, May 5, 1926, and Maj. E. O. Hopkins letter to Finance Officer, Washington, D.C., June 8, 1926, 201, NPRC.

332   *flight pay:* Headquarters, Bolling Field, D.C., certificate of flights Jan. 16, 1926, by Mitchell, and J. R. McCarl letter to Capt. Carl Halla, Mar. 29, 1926, 201, NPRC.

CHAPTER 26   PERIPHERY

Page

333   *household finances:* Diary entries, Feb. 13 and 18, 1926, MB, MHS; Davies telegram to Betty Mitchell, Feb. 13, 1926 and Betty Mitchell letter to Davies, Feb. 21, 1926, box 12, WM, LOC; Mitchell letter to Paul Mixter, Feb. 4, 1926, box 12, WM, LOC; Betty Mitchell letters to Bristol Aeroplane Company, Mar. 15, 1926, and to her brother "Siddy," Feb. 21, 1926, box 12, WM, LOC; Tom Gilpin interview.

334   *an omen:* Diary entry, Feb. 14, 1926, MB, MHS.

334   *the subject:* George Putnam letter to Mitchell with royalty account statement, Jan. 28, 1926, box 12, WM, LOC; Putnam letter to Mitchell, Apr. 1926, box 13, WM, LOC.

334   *an opinion:* Patrick, *United States in the Air,* p. 182.

335   *attorney general:* Mitchell letter to Uncle Wash, Apr. 14, 1926, box 13, WM, LOC; Maydell Blackmon letter to Betty Mitchell, Mar. 5, 1926, box 12, WM, LOC; Mitchell letter to Putnam, Apr. 15, 1926, box 13, WM, LOC; "City Crumbling Under Fire of Giant Bombs from the Air Is Pictured by Col. Mitchell," Cincinnati newspaper clipping, Mar. 4, 1926, box 57, WM, LOC; Davis, p. 334; "Only 250 Buffalonians Hear Mitchell Attack Country's Air Service," *Buffalo Morning*

Express, Feb. 22, 1926; "Duluth Snubs Col. Mitchell," Duluth, Minn., newspaper clipping, box 57, WM, LOC; telegrams from Bingay to Jay G. Hayden, Feb. 1926, White House press release of statement by Everett Sanders, Feb. 17, 1926, Hartwick Lumber Company letter to Sanders, Mar. 8, 1926, with Detroit newspaper clippings, Clarence D. McKean letter to J. Edgar Hoover, Feb. 27, 1926, and Hoover memorandum for the Attorney General, Mar. 1, 1926, reel 109, CC, LOC.

335   *"The Dogs":* Thomas Brady letter to Mitchell, Nov. 5, 1927, box 13, WM, LOC; Mitchell's lecture tour itinerary for 1928, box 58, WM, LOC; Mitchell correspondence with *Field and Stream* editor, Jan. 15 and 22, 1934, box 19, WM, LOC; Raymond J. Brown letter to Mitchell, May 21, 1927, *New York American* invoices for Mitchell, May 22 and 28, 1927, Ronald Millar letter to Mitchell, Feb. 8, 1927, and Mitchell letter to Bradford Merrill, June 1, 1927, box 13, WM, LOC; Elliot Balestier letters to Mitchell, July 25, 1932 and Apr. 20, 1933, and T. V. Ranck letter to Mitchell, Apr. 5, 1933, box 16, WM, LOC; Gordon B. Fulcher letters to Mitchell, Feb. 15 and Mar. 26, 1935, box 19, WM, LOC.

335   *New York Times:* William Mitchell, *Skyways: A Book on Modern Aeronautics,* (Philadelphia: J. B. Lippincott, 1930); William Mitchell, *General Greely: The Story of a Great American* (New York: Putnam, 1936); reprinted *New York Times* review of *Skyways,* box 15, WM, LOC; Walter B. Hayward, "General Greely of Arctic Fame," *New York Times,* Apr. 12, 1936.

336   *in 1935:* Mitchell letter to Joseph D. Holmes, box 15, WM, LOC; Mitchell letter to Bradford Merrill, July 18, 1927, box 13, WM, LOC; Mitchell letter to M. E. Bristow, Mar. 21, 1933, box 17, WM, LOC; Mitchell letter to Frank Miles, Apr. 7, 1933, box 18, WM, LOC; T. V. Ranck letter to Mitchell, Jan. 30, 1935, box 19, WM, LOC; T. V. Ranck letter to Mitchell, Jan. 30, 1935 and undated Mitchell response, Mitchell letter to J. M. Patterson, Mar. 7, 1935, box 19, WM, LOC.

336   *his defense:* Mitchell letter to Sen. Joseph Robinson, Sept. 19, 1929, and Mitchell letter to A. Raymond Brooks, May 3, 1929, box 15, WM, LOC; Mitchell letter to Brisbane, Sept. 4, 1934, and Mitchell letter to Walter Weaver, Dec. 23, 1934, box 19, WM, LOC; Hurley, pp. 130–33; "Gen. William Mitchell Sued," Associated Press news clipping, Mar. 16, 1934, box 53, WM, LOC; Mitchell letter to Frances J. Pratt, Mar. 8, 1934, box 19, WM, LOC.

336   *too radical:* Mitchell letter to Brisbane, Sept. 4, 1934, box 19, WM, LOC; Hurley, *Billy Mitchell,* p. 113; Cooke, *Billy Mitchell,* p. 235.

337   *was feasible:* A. C. MacDonald letter to Charles Kerney, Mar. 4, 1926, Mitchell letter to Kerney, Mar. 15, 1926, Mitchell letter to Sidney Miller, Apr. 15, 1926, and Harriet Mitchell telegram to Mitchell, Apr. 28, 1926, box 13, WM, LOC; Shirley Holladay letters to Mitchell, June 25, 1928, and Feb. 20, 1929, box 14, WM, LOC; "Col. Mitchell Seen as Smith Running Mate," *Morning Telegraph,* Apr. 27, 1927, box 58, WM, LOC; "Democrats Look Upon Mitchell as Logical Candidate," *Wisconsin State Journal* article, undated, and "Urge Col. Mitchell to Run for Senate," unidentified article, box 58, WM, LOC.

337   *he wrote:* Sobel, *Coolidge,* p. 288; Mitchell, *Memoirs of World War I,* pp. 304–5.

337   *"world's millions":* "My Views on Some of the Campaign Issues," Mitchell speech on behalf of Al Smith, box 26, WM, LOC; Mitchell letter to Uncle Wash, Apr. 14, 1926, Mitchell letter to Harriet, Apr. 15, 1926, box 13, WM, LOC; Mitchell letter to M. Robert Guggenheim, Sept. 28, 1928, box 14, WM, LOC;

Mitchell letter to Mr. Cochran, June 21, 1933, box 17, WM, LOC; Mitchell letter to Fay Ingalls, Apr. 21, 1933, and Mitchell letter to E. D. Coblentz with article, July 7, 1932, box 16, WM, LOC; Mitchell memo to Mr. Sherley, box 18, WM, LOC.

338   *trounced him:* "Politics for the Martyr?" *Outlook* 142, Feb. 10, 1926, p. 198; Mitchell letter to James J. Donahue, Oct. 29, 1931, box 16, WM, LOC; Mitchell letter to E. L. Dugger, July 14, 1933, box 17, WM, LOC; Mitchell's Virginia delegate list for state districts, box 54, WM, LOC "Gen. Mitchell Gives Support To Smith," *New York Times*, July 31, 1928; "Mitchell Attacks G.O.P. Record In Address Here," *Chicago Evening Post*, Nov. 1, 1928; Harriet Pillsbury interview; Mitchell letter to John Cudahy, Nov. 30, 1930, box 15, WM, LOC; Sobel, *Coolidge*, pp. 383–85.

338   *defense department:* Mitchell letter to James S. Barron, July 8, 1932, box 16, WM, LOC; Mitchell letter to Henry Breckinridge, July 12, 1932, box 16, WM, LOC; Mitchell letters to Wilmont Hercher and Harold Hartney, Mar. 17, 1933, box 18, WM, LOC; "Roosevelt Said to Favor Unified Air Force; Mitchell, Its Champion, Mentioned as Chief," *New York World-Telegram*, Mar. 18, 1933; Fitzhugh Lee letter to Mitchell, Mar. 2, 1933 and Mitchell reply, Mar. 9, 1933, and Joe Davies letter to Mitchell, Dec. 27, 1932, box 16, WM, LOC; Davies letter to Mitchell, Jan. 26, 1933, Petition to Franklin from the Democratic Party of Michigan on behalf of Mitchell, 1933, Mitchell letter to T. Coleman Andrews, Apr. 25, 1933, and Mitchell letters to John Cudahy, Jan. 9 and Feb. 7, 1933, box 17, WM, LOC.

338   *inaugural committee:* Navy Inter-Office Order on Discontinuance of Aviation, Aug. 31, 1919, and Extract from Testimony Given by Mr. Franklin D. Roosevelt, Acting Secretary of Navy, Before Senate Committee Investigating Reorganization of Army, Sept. 18, 1919, box 31, WM, LOC; Roosevelt-Mitchell correspondence, Aug. 1, 1932–July 4, 1933, box 16, WM, LOC; Ray Baker letter to Mitchell, Jan. 19, 1933, box 18, WM, LOC.

339   *been worried:* Mitchell letter to Sen. Joe Robinson, July 3, 1934, box 19, WM, LOC; Mitchell letter to Roosevelt Jan. 5, 1934, and White House response Jan. 13, 1934, box 19, WM, LOC; Department of Commerce letters to Mitchell July 31 and Sept. 18, 1933, box 17, WM, LOC; Mitchell letter to Brisbane, Mar. 30, 1933, box 17, WM, LOC; Mitchell letter to Richard Crane, Dec. 20, 1933, box 11, WM, LOC; Mitchell letter to Walter Weaver, box 19, WM, LOC.

339   *special time:* Harriet Pillsbury interview; Tom Gilpin interview; Rebecca McCoy interview.

340   *"the reflexes":* Harriet Pillsbury interview; Mitchell letter to William Sturgis, Jan. 26, 1929, box 15, WM, LOC; Mitchell letters to Katharine Jackson, June 15 and July 19, 1930, Sept. 9, 1931, July 10 and 26, 1933, BA; Mitchell letters to Katharine Jackson, June 3, 8, and 12, 1930, June 14, 1933, BA.

340   *George Patton:* Mitchell letter to Harry Jewett, Jan. 29, 1929, Mitchell letter to M. Roy Jackson, Dec. 7, 1929, box 15, WM, LOC; Boxwood Farms inventory of horses for sale, box 14, WM, LOC; Mitchell letter to George Patton, Dec. 9, 1929, box 14, WM, LOC; "William Mitchell, Gentleman Farmer," *Washington Post* Pictorial Section, Nov. 28, 1926.

341   *barroom:* "French City to Honor Mitchell," unidentified newspaper article 1927, box 58, WM, LOC; Capt. Trevor W. Sweet memo to Col. Margetts, Oct. 18, 1927, file 2618–31–7, MID, NA; Maj. George E. A. Reinburg memo on General

Mitchell's Visit to Berlin with 1st Ind. by Col. A. L. Conger, Sept. 13 and 14, 1927, file 51–387–83, box 44, MID, NA; memorabilia from the Mitchell's Oct. 5, 1927, return cruise to New York on the SS *Paris,* box 51, WM, LOC.

341   *vice-commodore:* "Cabin Cruiser Built Here for Gen. Mitchell," unidentified newspaper, Feb. 3, 1929, box 58, WM, LOC; Mitchell letter to Frances P. Garvan, July 1, 1929, box 15, Mitchell letter to Patrick Hurley, Sept. 19, 1929, and Mitchell letter to Hartney, Feb. 8, 1929, box 15, WM, LOC; Harriet Pillsbury interview; Capital Yacht Club letter to Mitchell, Jan. 20, 1931, box 16, WM, LOC.

341   *in Detroit:* Final Account of First Wisconsin Trust Co., executor of the will of Harriet D. Mitchell, Dec. 8, 1923, Milwaukee County Register in Probate, file 53975, envelope 7, Harriet D. Mitchell; First Wisconsin Trust Co. letter to Mitchell, Dec. 29, 1928, box 14, WM, LOC; Milwaukee County Circuit Court Judgment, William Mitchell vs Caroline S. Mitchell, Dec. 4, 1933, box 2, WMP, MHS; Mitchell letter to R. R. DePrez, Dec. 2, 1933, box 18, WM, LOC; Rebecca McCoy interview; H. Huntsman & Sons letter to Mitchell, Mar. 24, 1926, and Mitchell letter to J. G. Vincent, Mar. 18, 1926, box 13, WM, LOC; Wine and liquors list, box 35, WM, LOC; Ritz-Carlton letter to Mitchell, Dec. 23, 1929, box 15, WM, LOC.

341   *$56,000:* Mitchell letters to Brisbane, Nov. 1, 1929 and May 15, 1930, and Mitchell letter to Alan Winslow, Dec. 16, 1929, box 15, WM, LOC; Mitchell letter to Washington Becker, Jan. 20, 1928, box 14, WM, LOC; Mitchell correspondence with Adolfo Pariani and Virginia State Chamber of Commerce, June-July 1933, box 18, WM, LOC; Mitchell correspondence with R.S. Cochran, May-Oct. 1933, box 17, WM, LOC; Mitchell overdraft correspondence with Riggs National Bank, Oct. 3 and Nov. 30, 1928, box 14, WM, LOC; Mitchell loan correspondence with Riggs Bank for 1929 and 1933, box 18, WM, LOC; Central Investment Co. letter to Mitchell, Feb. 27, 1933, box 18, WM, LOC; Maydell Blackmon letter to W. F. Roberts Co., Apr. 18, 1929, box 15, WM, LOC; interview with Rebecca McCoy; interview with Harriet Pillsbury.

342   *they bought:* Interview with Rebecca McCoy; interview with Harriet Pillsbury; Mitchell letter to Standard Oil Co. of New Jersey, Apr. 9, 1929, box 15, WM, LOC; Mitchell letter to W. C. Young, Jan. 30, 1933, box 18, WM, LOC; Mitchell letter to Alexander Klemin, Sept. 16, 1935, box 19, WM, LOC.

342   *Elgin watches:* Veterans Administration pensions certificate for William Mitchell, May 10, 1932, box 16, WM, LOC; John Strickler letter to Mitchell, Nov. 3, 1933, box 18, WM, LOC; Maydell Blackmon letter to Lt. Col. Jacob E. Fickel, Mar. 4, 1934, box 19, WM, LOC; "Mitchell Declines Business Activity," *Washington Post,* Dec. 27, 1925; Mitchell letter to Harlan Wood, Nov. 14, 1929, box 15, WM, LOC; M. V. Little telegram to Mitchell, Oct. 15, 1928, C. E. Standing letter to Mitchell, Nov. 30, 1928, and Maydell Blackmon's response on Dec. 4, 1928, John Callan O'Laughlin letter to Mitchell, Oct. 30, 1928, and Mitchell's response, Nov. 3, 1928, box 14, WM, LOC.

342   *nearby Upperville:* Scheel, pp. 129, 132–134, 144, 150; "Society Turns Out for Whitney Race Meet at Upperville," *Washington Herald,* Nov. 18, 1931; interview with Harriet Pillsbury.

343   *its customers:* Scheel, pp. 127, 134–44.

343–44   from *Mitchell also* to *did Mitchell*: "U.S. Judge Bars South's Claim to Colored Suspect," *New York Daily News,* Apr. 25, 1933; "Demand U.S. Oust Judge Who Freed Colored Slayer" and "Brig. Gen. Mitchell Asked Impeachment," *New York*

Daily News, Apr. 26, 1933; "Judge Upholds Va. Lilly-White [*sic*]" and "All the Elements of a Mystery Novel Surround Case of George Crawford," *African American*, Nov. 11, 1933, p. 1; "Leesburg Folk Believe Crawford Pawn in County Politics," *African American*, Nov. 11, 1933, p. 4; "Made No Effort to Secure Colored Jurors, Says Judge as Crawford Case Opens," *African American*, Nov. 11, 1933, p. 9; "Crawford Girl Friend Spoils Defense Alibi," *African American*, Dec. 16, 1933, p. 2; "Crawford Counsel to Challenge Validity of Jury List," *Loudoun Times-Mirror*, Dec. 17, 1933, p. 1; "End of Crawford Trial In Sight," *Loudoun Times-Mirror*, Dec. 14, 1933, p. 1; "Predict Effort to Lynch Negro," unidentified article, box 18, WM, LOC; Ralph Matthews, "What Happened at Leesburg," *African American*, Dec. 23, 1933, p. 4; Mitchell letter to Howard H. Smith, July 14, 1933, Mitchell letters to Ernest I. White and Sterling Larrabee, Apr. 29, 1933, Mitchell letter to Gov. John Pollard, Apr. 25, 1933, and Statement of George Crawford in Suffolk County Jail, Boston, Jan. 19, 1933, box 18, WM, LOC; Mitchell letter to John Cudahy, May 12, 1935, and T. Coleman Andrews letter to Mitchell, Jan. 20, 1933, box 17, WM, LOC; Scheel, pp. 137–39, 152; Mitchell letters to Katharine Jackson, Apr. 4 and May 17, 1933, BA.

344   *always declined:* Mitchell-Milling correspondence, Nov. 26 and Dec. 21, 1932, box 16, WM, LOC; Thurman Bane letter to Mitchell, Apr. 15, 1928, box 15, WM, LOC; Mitchell letter to Ralph Hills, Nov. 10, 1933, box 18, WM, LOC; Pershing correspondence with William and Elizabeth Mitchell in 1931 and 1932, box 138, *JP*, LOC.

344   *tongue-lashing:* Harriet Pillsbury interview; photo of Mitchell in his office at Boxwood, box 3, WMP, MHS.

344   *"air force":* Mitchell letter to Hugh Straus, Apr. 20, 1929, box 14, WM, LOC; Mitchell letter to Alfred Verville, Mar. 14, 1933, box 17, WM, LOC; International News Service telegram to Mitchell, May 2, 1935, and Mitchell response, box 19, WM, LOC; "Our First Glimpse of the Germany of Today," draft article by Mitchell, Sept. 3, 1927, box 28, WM, LOC.

345   *New York:* "The Center of World Politics," draft article by Mitchell, box 27, WM, LOC; Mitchell letters to Brisbane, Dec. 12, 1934 and Feb. 6, 1935, box 19, WM, LOC; "Suppose Japan Surprised Us," draft article by Mitchell in 1935, box 30, WM, LOC.

345   *looked back:* Mitchell draft articles 3 and 5 for the Bell Syndicate after the trial, box 28, WM, LOC; interview with Harriet Pillsbury, July 13, 2003.

CHAPTER 27   THE END

Page

347   *"three lives":* Reminiscences of Alfred V. Verville, no. 388, pp. 43–45,47, OHC; Mitchell letter to Murphy, Dec. 23, 1934, and Maydell Blackmon letter to B. G. Davis, Feb. 6, 1936, box 19, WM, LOC; Ruth Mitchell, pp. 339–40; Mitchell letters to Katharine Jackson, Dec. 20, 1934, Jan. 9, Nov. 12, and Dec. 14, 1935, BA.

348   *blood pressure:* Statement of medical history in the case of Brig. Gen. William Mitchell, USA, Mar. 13, 1922, and Army Clinical Records for William Mitchell, 1908–1924, 201, NPRC; Mitchell letters to mother, early April, 1915 and Jan. 19, 1916, box 19B, WM, LOC; diary entries, Nov. 29, 1915–Jan. 17, 1916, CS, TF; Harriet Pillsbury interview.

348   *dear friend:* Alfred V. Verville reminiscences, pp. 45–49, OHC; Harriet Pillsbury interview.

348–50 from *On Saturday night* to *4:45 P.M.*: "General 'Billy' Mitchell Dead of Flu Attack," *Chicago Tribune*, Feb. 20, 1935; "Gen. Mitchell Dies; Air Leader in War," *New York Times*, Feb. 2, 1936; "Mitchell Dies; Army Air Chief in World War," *Washington Post*, Feb. 20, 1936, p. 1; Davis p. 341; Harriet M. Fladoes letter to Burke Davis, Aug. 10, 1966, box 56, BD, UNC; Alfred V. Verville reminiscences, p. 48, OHC; Harriet Pillsbury interview; Elizabeth Mitchell letter to Katharine Jackson, Feb. 4 and 13, 1936, BA; Harriet Mitchell letter to Katharine Jackson, Feb. 8, 1936, BA.

350 *of the track:* "Taps Sounded for Gen. Mitchell as Body Is Sent West for Burial," *New York American*, Feb. 21, 1936; Harriet M. Fladoes letter to Burke Davis, Apr. 2, 1966, box 46, BD, UNC; "Gen. Mitchell's Body to Arrive at Home Today," *Milwaukee Sentinel*, Feb. 21, 1936.

351 *in Wisconsin:* "Gen. Mitchell Asked to Be Buried Here," *Milwaukee Sentinel*, Feb. 22, 1936; Boake Carter letter to Sidney T. Miller, Mar. 24, 1936, box 19, WM, LOC.

351 *reached Milwaukee:* "Volleys, Taps Last Honor to Gen. Mitchell," *Milwaukee Sentinel*, Feb. 23, 1936, p. 1; "Mitchell Mourners in Forced Landing," *San Francisco News*, Feb. 23, 1936; Davis, *Billy Mitchell Affair*, pp. 341–42; Harriet Mitchell letter to Katharine Jackson, Feb. 27, 1936, BA.

351 *wintry sky:* "Volleys, Taps Last Honor to Gen. Mitchell," *Milwaukee Sentinel*, Feb. 23, 1936, p. 1; Davis, *Billy Mitchell Affair*, pp. 341–42; Harriet M. Fladoes letter to Burke Davis, Aug. 11, 1966, box 56, BD, UNC.

351 *to complete:* Harriet Pillsbury interview; "Middleburg Mourns Gen. Mitchell," unidentified newspaper, box 59, WM, LOC; Elizabeth Mitchell letter to Katharine Jackson, Mar. 25, 1936, BA.

352 *and basement:* Alfred V. Verville reminiscences, pp. 45–49, OHC; Elizabeth Mitchell letter to Katharine Jackson, Mar. 25, 1936, BA.

352 *$32,998.66 left:* "Mitchell Will Is Filed," *New York Times*, Mar. 26, 1936, p. 3; Davis, *Billy Mitchell Affair*, p. 341; Cooke, *Billy Mitchell*, p. 271; William Mitchell Final Executrix Account, May 20, 1937, Will Book 55, page 422, Fauquier County Circuit Court Clerk's Office, Warrenton, Va.

352 *in the room:* Harriet Pillsbury interview; Elizabeth Mitchell letters to Katharine Jackson, Mar. 25 and May 1, 1936, BA.

EPILOGUE

Page
353–54 from *Neighbors in* to *on July 31:* Felicity Trueblood interview; Cicely Banfield interview; Guerdon Trueblood interview; *The Yale Shingle: 1912 Yearbook* (New Haven, Conn.: Yale University, 1912), p. 99; Helen Ray Hagner, *The Social List of Washington and Social Precedence in Washington: November Edition, 1939* (Richmond, Va.: Lewis Printing Co., 1939), p. 111; Associate Alumnae of Vassar College 1938, Biographical Register Questionnaire for Caroline Stoddard, Mar. 1947, Vassar Alumni Address Register for Mrs. Franklin F. Korell, and Felicity Trueblood letter to Vassar College Alumnae Association, Sept. 12, 1984, in Vassar College Alumni Records for Caroline Stoddard.

354–55 from *After Mitchell* to *seventy-two:* Tom Gilpin interview; Rebecca McCoy interview; Harriet Pillsbury interview; "The Byrds—Their Interests Run From Exploring to Politics to Apple Growing," article from unidentified newspaper, box 19, WM, LOC; Virginia Historic Landmarks Commission Survey Form for

Boxwood Farm, Nov. 14, 1975, file No. 30–91; Elizabeth Mitchell letters to Katharine Jackson, Mar. 25, May 1 and 25, June 12, 1936, and Nov. 14, 1938, BA.

356 *Emery Building:* Davis, *Billy Mitchell Affair,* p. 345; Ruth Mitchell, *My Brother Bill,* p. 326; Correspondence with War Department, 1926–62, requesting access to Mitchell trial transcript, box 21, MT, NA; "Billy Mitchell Back in News: Look at Data Denied," United Press dispatch from unidentified newspaper, box 10, GH, UWM; Maj. Gen. J.C. Lambert letter to Robert D. Loomis, Aug. 7, 1964, box 1, MT, NA.

356 *"senior officers":* "Gen. R. L. Howze, Noted Fighter, Dies," *New York Times,* Sept. 20, 1926, p. 23; Report of Interviews with Gen. Hamilton H. Howze, Apr. 12, 1973, p. 14, box 1, *HH,* AWC.

356 *and died:* "Maj. Gen. Winship Dies at Age of 77," *New York Times,* Oct. 10, 1947, p. 25; War Department profile of Blanton Winship, Aug. 23, 1947, biography file, AWC.

356 *eighty-three:* "S. P. Moreland Dies; Wrote State Act," *New York Times,* Dec. 28, 1951, p. 21.

357 *in the crowd:* Fred Simpich interview; Thomas S. Moorman interview; War Department profile of Allen Gullion, Jan. 15, 1945, biography file, AWC; "Gen. Gullion Drops Dead," *New York Times,* June 20, 1946, p. 25; *The Army Lawyer,* p. 156.

357 *sixty-five:* Charlotte T. Reid interview; "Frank R. Reid Dies; Ex-Congressman," *New York Times,* Jan. 26, 1925, p. 8.

357 *U.S. military:* Harriet Pillsbury interview, July 13, 2003; "Mrs. Fladoes, Sister of Billy Mitchell, Dies," *Milwaukee Journal,* Dec. 26, 1968.

357 *desk drawer:* S. 4286, Aug. 20, 1940, H.Con. Res. 82, June 22, 1940, and S. 4168, June 21, 1941, 76th Congress, 3rd Session; S. 1543, May 20, 1941, H.R. 2756, Jan. 24, 1941, H.J.Res. 240, Oct. 15, 1941, S.J.Res. 109, Oct. 13, 1941, S. 1706, June 30, 1941, and S. 1703, June 30, 1941, 77th Congress, 1st Session; H.R. 2336, Mar. 29, 1943, 78th Congress, 1st Session; S.J.Res. 124, July 17, 1957, H.J.Res. 414, July 16,1957, and H.J.Res. 333, May 14, 1957, 85th Congress, 1st Session; List of Mitchell bills, 1935–1941, 201, NPRC; Henry L. Stimson letters to Sen. Robert R. Reynolds, June 6, 1941, and Aug. 5, 1941, and to Rep. Andrew J. May, May 17, 1943, 201, NPRC; Col. Albert E. Brown memo for Deputy Chief of Staff, July 25, 1941, 201, NPRC; Robert P. Patterson letter to Rep. Andrew J. May, Feb. 25, 1941, 201, NPRC; Wilbur M. Brucker letter to Sen. Richard Russell, Aug. 27, 1957, 201; "Senators Vote Vindication Of Gen. Mitchell, *Chicago Tribune,* Jan. 13, 1942; Sen. Alexander Wiley letter to Elizabeth Byrd with attachment, July 30, 1946, box 19, WM, LOC; Rebecca McCoy interview.

358 *the conviction:* Rebecca McCoy interview; Frank D. Hardin memo for Judge Advocate General of the Army, Apr. 24, 1956, box 21, MT, NA; Wilber M. Brucker letter to Donald A. Quarles, with note from Maj. Gen. Stanley W. Jones to Maj. Gen. W. C. Westmoreland, July 9, 1956, box 21, MT, NA; James Douglas memo for the Chairman, Air Force Board for Correction of Military Records, Mar. 4, 1958, box II:10, *SP,* LOC; "Gen. Mitchell Verdict Won't Be Overturned," *Milwaukee Journal,* March 5, 1958, p. 3.

358 *off Alaska:* "Billy Mitchell Said It!" 1940 *San Francisco Examiner* article, box 1, WMC, NASM; "Prophet—Not Without Honor," *Washington Star,* June 29, 1941,

part 2–Editorial Section; Gordon W. Prange, *At Dawn We Slept: The Untold Story of Pearl Harbor* (New York: McGraw-Hill, 1981), pp. 499–507; Preliminary Report of Inspection, Dec. 10, 1923, p. 39, box 42, WM, LOC; "Mitchell Saw Aleutians as Dagger to Japan—or U.S.," *New York Journal American*, Aug. 2, 1942, p. 2E; Linn, *Guardians of Empire*, pp. 214, 247–51.

358   *in 1923:* Linn, pp. 23, 28, 39, 185, 245–46; Copp, *Few Great Captains*, pp. xv–xvii; R. Earl McClendon, *Autonomy of the Air Arm* (Washington: U.S. Government Printing Office, 1996), pp. 59–60; White, *Mason Patrick*, pp. 128–31; Russell F. Weigley, *The American Way of War* (New York: Macmillan, 1973), p. 402; Locher, *Victory on the Potomac*, pp. 19, 197–99.

359   *Southwest Pacific:* Mets, *The Air Campaign*, pp. 27, 44–45; Meilinger, *Paths of Heaven*, p. 107; Burlingame, *General Billy Mitchell*, p. 189; Weigley, p. 233, 238–40; *Michael S. Sherry, The Rise of American Air Power: The Creation of Armageddon* (New Haven: Yale University Press, 1987), pp. 147, 161–64, 219–21; MacArthur, *Reminiscences*, p. 94.

360   *to resist:* Weigley, *History of the United States Army*, pp. 414, 474–75; Weigley, *The American Way of War*, p. 236; Hurley, *Billy Mitchell*, pp. 136–37; Mets, *The Air Campaign*, pp. 42–53, 76–78; Bilstein, *American Aerospace Industry*, p. 28.

361   *the peace:* Mets, *The Air Campaign*, p. 78; James P. Coyne, *Airpower in the Gulf* (Arlington, Va.: Air Force Association, 1992), p. 173–78; "Conduct of the Persian Gulf Conflict: An Interim Report to Congress, July 1991, U.S. Government Printing Office, Washington, D.C.: pp. 4–1 to 4–6; "Bull's-Eye War: Pinpoint Bombing Shifts Role of GI Joe," Thomas E. Ricks, *Washington Post*, Dec. 2, 2001, p. 1A; Vernon Loeb, "Burst of Brilliance," *Washington Post Magazine*, Dec. 15, 2002, pp. 6–11, 23–27; Vernon Loeb, "Impact of U.S. Bombing Is Felt in Many Ways," *Washington Post*, Dec. 16, 2001, p. 16A; "1's and 0's Replacing Bullets in U.S. Arsenal," Vernon Loeb and Thomas E. Ricks, *Washington Post*, Feb. 2, 2002, p. 1A; "Air War Striking in Ways We Haven't Seen," Stephen Budiansky, *Washington Post*, Apr. 6, 2003, p. 1B.

361   *the troops:* Locher, *Victory on the Potomac*, pp. 16–23, 199–202.

362   *of his name:* Otto Sigfried Samuelsson letter to Frank Reid, Aug. 16, 1941, box 1, WMC, NASM; "Would Name Aleutians the 'Gen. Billy Islands,'" *Milwaukee Journal*, June 12, 1943; "Statue Unveiled in Honor of Airman Billy Mitchell," International News Service article in unidentified newspaper, and "General Billy's Plane" with photo, *New York World Telegram*, 1942 article, box 10, GH, UWM; author interview with Charles Bass, Sept. 17, 2003; author tour of Milwaukee and General Mitchell International Airport.

362   *to emulate:* author interview with Duane J. Reed, Archivist, U.S. Air Force Academy Library, July 20, 2003.

362   *"Star Chamber proceeding":* "The Court-Martial of Billy Mitchell," Republic Pictures Home Video; Warner Bros. advertisement for *The Court-Martial of Billy Mitchell*, box 10, GH, UWM; Col. Ralph K. Johnson memo for the Judge Advocate General, June 10, 1955, box 21, MT, NA.

362   *way he was:* Kenneth Gilpin interview; Harriet Pillsbury interview; Rebecca McCoy interview.

363   *"had it coming":* The Trial of Colonel William Mitchell, analysis by Maj. Abe Goff, in Judge Advocate General's Summary of Court-Martial Proceedings of Colonel William Mitchell, pp. 18–36, box 5, MT, NA; Proceedings of the Air

Force Board for the Correction of Military Records, William Mitchell, 0–63, Docket No. 56–290, box II:10, *SP,* LOC; Arnold, *Global Mission,* pp. 119–20.

363   *"in warfare":* James Doolittle reminiscences, p. 81, OHC; Arnold, pp. 121–22.

364   *needed spark:* Mets, *The Air Campaign,* pp. 65, 68–69; Meilinger, *Paths of Heaven,* pp. xxi–xxix; Thomas E. Ricks, "A Test Case for Bush's Military Reform Pledge?" *Washington Post,* Feb. 20, 2003, p. A13.

Selected Bibliography

MANUSCRIPT COLLECTIONS

Archives and Special Collections, Amherst College Library: Dwight Morrow Papers.

U.S. Army Military History Institute, Army War College: Charles L. Bolte, Dennis Nolan, Hugh Drum, Hamilton Howze, Ira C. Eaker, and Sladen Family papers.

Calvin Coolidge Presidential Library and Museum at Forbes Library: Calvin Coolidge papers.

Library of Congress: Calvin Coolidge, Charles P. Summerall,, Everett Sanders, Frank McCoy, George S. Gibbs, George Van Horn Moseley, George Patton, Henry Arnold, Ira Eaker, Dr. Joel T. Boone, John L. Hines, John J. Pershing, Leonard Wood, Carl Spaatz, William Mitchell, and William F. Fullam Papers.

Milwaukee County Historical Society: William Mitchell Papers.

National Archives: Record Group 18, Hawaiian Department; Record Group 159, Office of Inspector General Correspondence 1917–1934; Record Group 165, Military Intelligence Division Correspondence; Mitchell trial records in Record Group 153, Records of the Judge Advocate General, Entry No. 40; Record Group 80, General Records of the Navy, General Correspondence; Record Group 165, War Plans Division General Correspondence.

National Air Space Museum, Smithsonian Institution: William Mitchell Court-Martial Collection.

National Personnel Records Center: William Mitchell's 201 File.

Southern Historical Collection, Wilson Library, University of North Carolina at Chapel Hill: Burke Davis Papers.

University of Wisconsin–Milwaukee, Golda Meir Library: George Hardie, John L. Mitchell and Mitchell Family Papers.

Wisconsin Historical Society, Writers' Program, Madison, Wisconsin: Alexander, John, and William Mitchell Papers.

FAMILY COLLECTIONS

Cicely Banfield, Tom Gilpin, Harriet Pillsbury, Felicity Trueblood, and Bass Family Papers.

REMINISCENCES

Oral History Collection of Columbia University: Eleanor P. Arnold, Leslie P. Arnold, Carl Spaatz, Ira C. Eaker, James H. Doolittle, Thomas D. Milling, Benjamin D. Foulois, Reed M. Chambers, Alfred V. Verville, Leroy Prinz, Eugene E. Wilson, Emory S. Land, Gill Robb Wilson, James W. Wadsworth, Henry Breckinridge, Frederick Trubee Davison, John A. Macready, Donald Douglas, Harold McMillan Bixby, Joseph J. Clark, and Delos C. Emmons.

AUTHOR INTERVIEWS

Cicely Banfield, Charles Bass, John Cooper, Eugene Fidell, Kenneth Gilpin, John Gilpin, Tom Gilpin, Richard Jackson, Lu Knox, James R. Locher III, John McCain, Rebecca McCoy, Roger G. Miller, Thomas S. Moorman, Harriet Pillsbury, Duane J. Reed, Charlotte T. Reid, Fred Simpich, Felicity Trueblood, Guerdon Trueblood, William H. Webb Jr., and Mitchell Yockelson.

BOOKS, DISSERTATIONS, PERIODICALS, AND GOVERNMENT REPORTS

(A listing of all the works consulted would be prohibitively long, so in most cases only those referred to in the Source Notes are listed here.)

Address of President Coolidge before the Graduating Class U.S. Naval Academy Annapolis, Md., June 3, 1925 . Washington, D.C.: U.S. Government Printing Office, 1925, p. 4.

Allen, Frederick Lewis. *Only Yesterday*. New York: Bantam, 1959.

"America After the War: The President's Omaha Address," *Outlook* 141, Oct. 14, 1925, p. 219.

The Army Lawyer: A History of the Judge Advocate General's Corps, 1775–1975. Washington, D.C.: U.S. Government Printing Office, 1976.

"Army & Navy." *Time*, Dec. 28, 1925, pp. 6–7.

Arnold, H. H. *Global Mission*. New York: Harper & Brothers, 1949.

Bakeless, John. "Contemporary Voices Prophesying War." *Outlook* 142, Mar. 10, 1926, pp. 370–372.

"The Battleship and the Bomb." *Outlook* 128, Aug. 3, 1921, p. 530.

Bilstein, Roger E. *The American Aerospace Industry*. New York: Twayne Publishers, 1996.

Biographies of Army Figures. U.S. Army Center of Military History.

Bliven, Bruce. "The Great Coolidge Mystery."*Harper's*, Dec. 1925, pp. 145–53.

Buford, Charles H. *Alexander Mitchell: Banker, Industrialist, Builder of Railroads, Pioneer of the Great West!* New York: Newcomen Society in North America, 1950.

Burlingame, Roger. *General Billy Mitchell: Champion of Air Defense*. New York: McGraw-Hill, 1952.

Burns, Richard Dean, ed. *Encyclopedia of Arms Control and Disarmament*. Vol. 2. New York: Scribner's, 1993.

Busch, Noel F. "General Drum: Nation's No. 1 Field Soldier Commands Biggest and Handiest of Four New Armies." *Life*, June 16, 1941, pp. 86–96.

Butts, Isaac. *Protection and Free Trade*. New York: Putnam, 1875.

———. *John Butts: His Ancestors and Some of His Descendants*. Poughkeepsie, N.Y.: Press of A. V. Haight.

Cameron, Rebecca H., and Barbara Wittig, eds. *Golden Legacy, Boundless Future: Essays on the United States Air Force and the Rise of Aerospace Power*. Air Force History and Museums Program, 2000.

Cannon, Joseph G. "The National Budget." *Harper's* 139, Oct. 1919, pp. 617–628.

Cesare, Oscar. "Mitchell, The Tireless Flying General," *New York Times Magazine*, Mar. 8, 1925, p.5.

Coffey, Thomas M. *Hap: The Story of the U.S. Air Force and the Man Who Built It, General Henry H. "Hap" Arnold*. New York: Viking Press, 1982

Coffman, Edward M. *The War to End All Wars: The American Experience in World War I*. Lexington: The University Press of Kentucky, 1998.

"Conduct of the Persian Gulf Conflict: An Interim Report to Congress, July 1991." Washington, D.C.: U.S. Government Printing Office.

Connolly, James B. "The Flying Sailor," *Colliers*, Aug. 9, 1919, Vol. 64, pp. 12–13.

Cooke, James J. *Billy Mitchell*. Boulder, Colo.: Lynne Rienner Publishers, 2002.

———. *Pershing and His Generals*. Westport, Conn.: Praeger, 1997.

Copp, DeWitt S. *A Few Great Captains: The Men and Events That Shaped the Development of U.S. Air Power*. McLean, Va.: EPM Publications, Inc: 1980.

"The Court-Martial on Trial." *The Nation* 108, May 3, 1919, p. 679.

Coyne, James P. *Airpower in the Gulf*. Arlington, Va.: Air Force Association, 1992.

"The Dangers of Public Speed Races," *Aviation* 19, Sept. 21, 1924, p. 345.

Davis, Burke. *The Billy Mitchell Affair*. New York: Random House, 1967.

Douhet, Giulio. *The Command of the Air*. Washington, D.C.: U.S. Government Printing Office, 1998 (reprint of 1942 edition by Coward-McCann, Inc.).

Eisenhower, Dwight D. *At Ease: Stories I Tell to Friends*. New York: Doubleday, 1967.

Fausold, Martin L. *James W. Wadsworth, Jr.: The Gentleman from New York*. Syracuse, N.Y.: Syracuse University Press, 1975.

Ferrell, Robert H. *The Presidency of Calvin Coolidge*. Lawrence: University Press of Kansas, 1998.

"Flapper Jane." *New Republic* 44, Sept. 9, 1925, p. 65–67

Foulois, Benjamin D., with C. V. Glines. *From the Wright Brothers to the Astronauts: The Memoirs of Major General Benjamin D. Foulois*. New York: McGraw-Hill, 1968.

Gauvreau, Emile, and Lester Cohen. *Billy Mitchell: Founder of Our Air Force and Prophet without Honor*. New York: E. P. Dutton, 1942.

Gibbs, Sir Philip. "The World in Peril." *Collier's* 75, Feb. 21, 1925, pp. 8–9.

Gilbert, Martin. *The First World War: A Complete History*. New York: Henry Holt, 1994.

Grumelli, Michael. *Trial of Faith: The Dissent and Court-Martial of Billy Mitchell*. Ph.D. Diss., Rutgers University, 1991.

"Guarding the Shenandoah Against Disaster," *Outlook* 136, Sept. 19, 1924, p. 36.

The Habits of Good Society: A Handbook for Ladies and Gentlemen. New York: Rudd & Carlton.

Hagner, Helen Ray, *The Social List of Washington and Social Precedence in Washington: Nov. Edition, 1939*. Richmond, Va.: Lewis Printing Co., 1939.

Hall, Florence Howe. *Social Usages at Washington*. New York: Harper & Brothers, 1906.

Harland, Marion. *The Dinner Year-Book*. New York: Scribner's, 1901.

Hillman, Beth. "Chains of Command," *Legal Affairs*, May/June 2002, pp. 50–52.

John L. Hines. "The Value of the Hawaiian Maneuvers," *Outlook*, Apr. 15, 1925, Vol. 139, pp. 577–580.

Holt, Daniel D., and Leyerzapf, James W. *Eisenhower: The Prewar Diaries and Selected Papers, 1905–1941*. Baltimore: Johns Hopkins University Press, 1998.

Hurley, Alfred F. *Billy Mitchell: Crusader for Air Power*. New York: Franklin Watts, 1964.

In Memoriam: John Lendrum Mitchell, 1842–1904. Milwaukee, Wis., 1925.

Kennett, Lee. *The First Air War*. New York: Free Press, 1991.

Lane, Spencer. *The First World Flight: The Odyssey of Billy Mitchell*. U.S. Press, 2002.

Lee, Clive, and Henschel, Richard. *Douglas MacArthur*. New York: Henry Holt, 1952.

Lemann, Nicholas. "The McCain Code." *New Yorker*, Feb. 4, 2002, p. 53.

Levine, Isaac Don. *Mitchell: Pioneer of Air Power*. New York: Duell, Sloan and Pearce, 1943.

Linn, Brian McAllister. *Guardians of Empire: The U.S. Army and the Pacific, 1902–1940*. Chapel Hill, N.C.: University of North Carolina Press, 1997.

Locher, James R. III.*Victory on the Potomac: The Goldwater-Nichols Act Unifies the Pentagon*. College Station, Tex.: Texas A&M University Press, 2002.

Loeb, Vernon. "Burst of Brilliance."*Washington Post Magazine*, Dec. 15, 2002, pp. 6–11, 23–27.

Lurie, Jonathan. *Military Justice in America: The U.S. Court of Appeals for the Armed Forces, 1775–1980*. Lawrence: University Press of Kansas, 2001.

MacArthur, Douglas. *Reminiscences*. Greenwich, Conn.: Fawcett Publications, 1964.

McClendon, R. Earl. *Autonomy of the Air Arm*. Washington, D.C.: U.S. Government Printing Office, 1996.

A Manual for Courts-Martial: U.S. Army. Washington, D.C.: U.S. Government Printing Office, 1943.

Mason, Herbert Molloy, Jr. *The Great Pursuit*. New York: Random House, 1970.

Mauer, Mauer. *Aviation in the U.S. Army, 1919–1939*. Washington, D.C.: U.S. Government Printing Office, 1986.

Meilinger, Phillip S., ed. *The Paths of Heaven: The Evolution of Airpower Theory*. Maxwell Air Force Base, Ala.: Air University Press, 1997.

Mets, David R. *The Air Campaign: John Warden and the Classical Airpower Theorists*. Maxwell Air Force Base, Ala.: Air University Press, 1999.

———. *A Master of Airpower: General Carl A. Spaatz*. Novato, Calif.: Presidio, 1988.

Miller, Roger G. "'A Pretty Damn Able Commander'—Lewis Hyde Brereton: Part I," *Air Power History* 47, Winter 2000, p. 17.

Millett, Allen R., and Murray, Williamson. *Military Effectiveness, Volume I: The First World War*. Boston: Allen & Unwin, 1988.

Mitchell, Ruth. *My Brother Bill: The Life of General "Billy" Mitchell*. New York: Harcourt, Brace, 1953.

Mitchell, William. "Building The Alaskan Telegraph System," *National Geographic*, Sept. 1904, Vol. 15, pp. 359–361.

———. *General Greely: The Story of a Great American*. New York: Putnam, 1936.

———. *Memoirs of World War I*. New York: Random House, 1960.

———. *Our Air Force: The Keystone of National Defense*. New York: Dutton, 1921.

———. *Skyways: A Book on Modern Aeronautics*. Philadelphia: J. B. Lippincott, 1930.

———. *Winged Defense: The Development and Possibilities of Modern Air Power—Economic and Military*. New York: Putnam, 1925.

Moon, Vicky, *The Middleburg Mystique*. Sterling, Va.: Capital Books, 2001.

Munson, Granville, and Walter H. E.Jaeger. *United States Army Officer's Handbook of Military Law and Court-Martial Procedure*. Washington: National Law Book Co.: 1942.

Murray, Williamson, and Allen R. Millett. *Military Innovation in the Interwar Period*. New York: Cambridge University Press, 1996.

"Our Future Army," *Nation* 109, Nov. 29, 1919, pp. 675–76.

Patrick, Mason. *The United States in the Air*. New York: Doubleday, 1928.

Pound, Edward T. "Unequal Justice," *U.S. News & World Report*, Dec. 16, 2002, pp. 19–30.

Perrett, Geoffrey. *America in the Twenties: A History*. New York: Simon & Schuster, 1982.

Pershing, John J. *My Experiences in the First World War, Volume I*. New York: Da Capo Press, 1995, Frederick A. Stokes, 1931.

———. *My Experiences In The First World War, Volume II*. New York: Frederick A. Stokes, 1931.

"PN-9 No. 1 Found Off Hawaiian Islands," *Aviation*, Sept. 21, 1925, p. 350.

"Politics for the Martyr?" *Outlook* 142, Feb. 10, 1926, p. 198.

Prange, Gordon W. *At Dawn We Slept: The Untold Story of Pearl Harbor*. New York: McGraw-Hill, 1981.

Rainey, James W. "The Questionable Training of the AEF in World War I," *Parameters*. Winter 1992–93. pp. 89–102.

Reardon, George. "Alexander Mitchell: A Wheeler Dealer Par Excellence," *Exclusively Yours*, Mar. 1989, pp. 26–97.

Report of President's Aircraft Board: Nov. 30, 1925. Washington, D.C.: Government Printing Office, 1925.

Scheel, Eugene M. *The History of Middleburg and Vicinity*. Warrenton, Va.: Piedmont Press, 1987.

Sherry, Michael S. *The Rise of American Air Power: The Creation of Armageddon*. New Haven: Yale University Press, 1987.

Shiner, John F. *Foulois And The U.S. Army Air Corps 1931–1935*. Washington, D.C.: U.S. Government Printing Office, 1983.

Shorter, Edward. *A History of Psychiatry: From the Era of the Asylum to the Age of Prozac*. New York: John Wiley & Sons: 1997.

"Should the Army and Navy Be Muzzled?" *Outlook* 124, Feb. 20, 1920, pp. 187–88.

Slater, Kitty. *The Hunt Country of America: Then and Now*. Upperville, Va.: Virginia Reel, Inc., 1997.

Smith, Vme Edom. *Middleburg and Nearby*. Leesburg, Va.: Potomac Press, 1986.

Smythe, Donald. *Pershing: General of the Armies*. Bloomington: Indiana University Press, 1986.

Sobel, Robert. *Coolidge: An American Enigma*. Washington: Regnery, 1998.

Stoddard, Lothrop. "The Japanese Issue in California." *World's Work* 4, Oct. 1920, pp. 585–599.

Toland, John. *The Great Dirigibles: Their Triumphs & Disasters*. New York: Dover Publications, 1972.

Trest, Warren A. *Air Force Roles and Missions: A History*. Washington, D.C.: U.S. Government Printing Office, 1998.

Trimble, William F. *Admiral William A. Moffett: Architect of Naval Aviation*. Washington: Smithsonian Institution Press, 1994.

United States Army Officer's Handbook of Military Law and Court-Martial Procedure. Washington: National Law Book Company, 1942.

Vandiver, Frank E. *Black Jack: The Life and Times of John J. Pershing, Vol. 2*. College Station: Texas A&M University Press.

White, Robert P. *Mason Patrick and the Fight for Air Service Independence*. Washington, D.C.: Smithsonian Institution Press, 2001.

Whitehouse, Arch. *Billy Mitchell: America's Eagle of Air Power.* New York: Putnam, 1962.

Wilson, Al. "Stunt Flying." *Saturday Evening Post,* Sept. 19, 1925, pp. 17–39.

Weigley, Russell F. *History of the United States Army.* New York: Macmillan, 1967.

———. *The American Way of War.* New York: Macmillan, 1973.

Wiener, Frederick B. "The Seamy Side of the World War I Court-Martial Controversy." *Military Law Review* 123, 1989, pp. 109–123.

Winthrop, William. *Military Law and Precedents.* Washington, D.C.: Beard Books, 1896.

Woodward, Helen. *General Billy Mitchell: Pioneer of the Air.* New York: Duell, Sloan and Pierce, 1959.

NEWSPAPERS

African American, Baltimore Sun, Boston American, Boston Post, Buffalo Morning Express, Chicago American, Chicago Evening Post, Chicago Herald Examiner, Chicago Journal, Chicago News, Chicago Tribune, Daily Hampshire Gazette, Daily Journal: Milwaukee, Dearborn Independent, Fellowship Forum, Honolulu Advertiser, Honolulu Star Bulletin, Los Angeles Examiner, Loudoun Times-Mirror, Milwaukee Journal, Milwaukee Sentinel, Morning Telegraph, New York American, New York Daily News, New York Herald, New York Journal, American, New York Sun, New York Times, New York Herald Tribune, Philadelphia Evening Bulletin, Public Ledger and North American, San Antonio Evening News, San Francisco News, Standard Union, Washington News, Washington Herald, Washington Post, Washington Star, Washington Times, Wisconsin News, Wisconsin News and Evening Sentinel, and *Wisconsin State Journal.*

Acknowledgments

The public record on Billy Mitchell's life is voluminous. At least nine biographies had been written on the air general before I began my work. The press of Mitchell's day covered much of his military career in detail. Transcripts of his testimony before Congress number in the thousands of pages. Mitchell himself was a prolific writer, penning four books, hundreds of newspaper and magazine articles, and even more private letters. But parts of his life still remained a mystery for those who had written about him before. Mitchell was a national celebrity, but he was a hard person to get to know. Questions about the man, and his court-martial, remained unanswered. Blank spots needed filling in. My hunt for new material on Billy Mitchell took me all over the country in order to unearth family letters, diaries and government documents never seen before by previous historians or biographers. The discoveries were tucked in archives, packed away in old family chests, even, in one instance, locked in a safe deposit box. It became an exciting treasure hunt.

I had the cooperation of the Mitchell family for this project. I owe a special debt to Tom Gilpin, one of Mitchell's three grandsons from his second marriage, who spent hours recounting for me Mitchell stories passed down from generation to generation, and who eagerly helped me get in touch with other family members. Tom also provided me with copies of more than fifty personal letters written to Betty by Mitchell and others. Those letters, which had never been made public, reveal Mitchell's innermost thoughts on his rivals, contain valuable insights into the women who were important in his life, and shed light on the secret motivation behind his stinging critique of the War and Navy Departments that led to his court-martial. Tom's two brothers, Kenneth Gilpin and John Gilpin, were helpful with recollections of Betty Mitchell. Rebecca McCoy, Mitchell's daughter-in-law, was also generous with her time. I also want to thank John Kent Cooke, the current owner of Mitchell's Middleburg home, who allowed me to tour Boxwood.

I cannot thank enough Harriet Pillsbury, Mitchell's niece, who had a nearly photographic memory of her uncle. Harriet, who was the daughter of Mitchell's sister Harriet, graciously put me up in her northern Wisconsin home for two days of interviews. She then cheerfully endured countless phone calls from me over two years, answering my many follow-up questions about Mitchell and his Wisconsin roots. My only regret is that Harriet did not live to read this book; she died on December 30, 2003, at age eighty-five.

I am also grateful to Representative Charles Bass, one of Mitchell's grandnephews, who allowed me to camp out in the den of his New Hampshire home for a day to pick through an old trunk and box that had been stored in his garage for many years. To my delight they contained some one hundred letters Mitchell and Betty had written to Representative Bass's grandmother, Katharine Jackson, who was one of Mitchell's sisters. Representative Bass also put me in touch with Richard Jackson, one of Katharine's sons, who gave me his recollections of Mitchell.

One of the missing stories has been Mitchell's marriage to his first wife, Caroline. Though she was an important part of his early military career—and was the person who nearly brought him down at his peak—Caroline is largely missing in previous Mitchell biographies. Three of Mitchell's grandchildren by his marriage to Caroline helped me detail her life with him. Cicely Banfield sat down with me for half a day and provided me with early family scrapbooks and material on Caroline's years at Vassar College. Guerdon Trueblood, another grandchild of Caroline's, was helpful. I also spent two days interviewing Felicity Trueblood at her Meadowmere Farm in Florida. She made available to me one of the most important discoveries in my research: twenty years of diaries Caroline had kept (sixteen of which were written during her marriage to Mitchell) that had never been made public.

Relatives of the key lawyers in Mitchell's court-martial were also generous with their time. Charlotte T. Reid aided me greatly with biographical information on her father-in-law, Congressman Frank Reid. William H. Webb Jr. was helpful with information on his father, William Webb, who was a member of the defense team. Fred Simpich and retired general Thomas S. Moorman gave me a rich portrait of their grandfather, Allen Gullion, who was Mitchell's colorful prosecutor.

I learned quickly that the most important person in a historian's life is the archivist. I had some of the best in the business helping me. All the records of Mitchell's court-martial—the trial transcript which numbers 3,781 pages plus thousands and thousands of pages of court documents, prosecution and defense exhibits, correspondence, and lawyers' notes—are located at the National Archives facility in College Park, Maryland. Reference archivist Mitchell Yockelson, an expert in his own right on the World War I U.S. Army, guided me through this vast amount of material and became a valuable adviser during my research. Mitch, I soon discovered, was also a bulldog when it came to fishing important documents out of the billions stored at the archives. He found for me military intelligence files on Mitchell, revealing inspection reports on the army's Hawaiian Department, the psychiatric evaluation Army doctors wrote on Mitchell, confidential army inspector general reports on Mitchell's domestic turmoil with Caroline, and records army investigators had collected on Mitchell's personal finances.

The Library of Congress has the bulk of Mitchell's papers: some twenty thousand letters, army documents, military reports, congressional transcripts, book manuscripts, and scrapbooks that fill more than sixty boxes. Daun van Ee, a historical specialist with the Library's Manuscript Division, was my guide and mentor for this collection. He also pointed me to the papers the Library had stored for sixteen other senior officers and government officials who knew Mitchell.

I found valuable material at eleven other archives, museums and libraries around country. Archivist William Seibert and Preservation Specialist Beverly Mahoney helped me hunt through Mitchell's Army 201 File (his personnel records that fill two large boxes), which is stored at the National Personnel Records Center in St. Louis. Jennifer Macellaro with Columbia University's Oral History Research Office aided me greatly in finding and reviewing the reminiscences of friends, and enemies, of Mitchell. Lu Knox, curator of the Calvin Coolidge Presidential Library and Museum, located at Forbes Library in Northampton, Massachusetts, spent a day guiding me through Coolidge's papers and giving me her insights on him. The staff at the nearby Amherst College

Library's Archive and Special Collections helped me review the Dwight Morrow Papers for material on Mitchell. At the U.S. Army Military History Institute, Carlisle Barracks, Pennsylvania, David Keough and JoAnna McDonald retrieved for me Army War College records on Mitchell as well as the papers of a half dozen senior officers who knew him. The U.S. Army Center of Military History Library at Fort McNair, Washington, D.C., had important background material. Jackie Davis with the Fort Sam Houston Museum sent me detailed information on Mitchell's quarters and office at the army post in Texas. Archivists Marilyn Graskowiak and Mark Kahn helped me sort through the Mitchell defense team's papers deposited with the Smithsonian Institution's National Air and Space Museum; more importantly, they allowed the photographing of some 300 news stories on the court-martial that the defense team had collected in two large scrapbooks. (My thanks to *Time* photo editor Jim Colburn, who photographed the pages for me.)

The Golda Meir Library at the University of Wisconsin-Milwaukee has the George Hardie Papers and the John Lendrum Mitchell Papers, which were important for my research of the Mitchell family in Wisconsin. I also want to thank Dee Grimsrud with the Wisconsin Historical Society in Madison, who helped me review the Alexander and Martha Mitchell Papers in its collection and who tracked down for me Billy Mitchell's divorce records from the Wisconsin State Supreme Court. But my most important find from my week in Wisconsin came at the Milwaukee County Historical Society, where curator Steven Daily hauled out for me eight boxes of the Mitchell Family Collection, as well as Milwaukee court records on Mitchell's divorce. In one of the collection's boxes I found a "1922 Date Book" for Maydell Blackmon, Mitchell's personal secretary. But leafing through the date book, I quickly realized that Maydell had used a spare 1922 book as a diary to record Mitchell's movements, meetings and, in many instances, his thoughts each day from June 1925 to July 1926, the critical period covering his banishment to Texas, the court-martial in Washington, and his speaking tour after the trial.

My book benefited in particular from five previous works on Mitchell: Isaac Levine's *Mitchell: Pioneer of Air Power*, Alfred Hurley's *Billy Mitchell: Crusader for Air Power*, Burke Davis's *The Billy Mitchell Affair*, James Cooke's *Billy Mitchell*, and Michael Grumelli's doctoral dissertation, *Trial of Faith: The Dissent and Court-Martial of Billy Mitchell*. But I want to especially thank Burke Davis, who generously allowed me to review notes on Mitchell's divorce and family correspondence that he had collected for his 1967 book. That material, which Lynn Holdzkom, Beth Getz and Rachel Canada helped me retrieve, is housed in the University of North Carolina at Chapel Hill's Southern Historical Collection.

I consulted with a number of experts throughout the research and writing. Retired Naval Reserve Captain John Cooper, who is also a former Delta Air Lines pilot, reviewed hundreds of pages of accident records on the USS *Shenandoah* and wrote for me a detailed technical analysis of the dirigible disaster and meteorological conditions along its Midwest flight route. Jim Locher, a former assistant secretary of defense and an authority on military bureaucracy, helped me understand the complicated Army organizational issues aired during the Mitchell trial. Attorney Eugene Fidell, founder of the National Institute of Military Justice, answered countless questions from me on court-martial procedures as I read the Mitchell trial transcript. Duane Reed, Chief of the Special Collections Branch Library at the U.S Air Force Academy, gave me advice on air history. Robert Ferrell, who has written an excellent biography of Calvin Coolidge, educated me on the Coolidge Administration and gave me a number of suggestions to improve my manuscript. Roger Miller, a historian with the U.S. Air Force History Office, cheerfully suffered through two years of almost weekly questions from me about early-twentieth-century military air technology and history, then he carefully corrected the errors in my manuscript.

My research became a family affair. My dear wife, Judy, who has been the important first editor for all my books, spent days in libraries collecting hundreds of news articles from the 1920s. My daughter, Colby, spent a week at the National Archives photocopying the Mitchell trial transcript. My son, David, tracked down obscure facts for me. Scott Cooper also hunted for information, while Jane Cooper helped prepare a technical paper.

I want to thank Kristine Dahl, my literary agent and trusted adviser for my books, who brought this project to me. Henry Ferris and Susan Llewellyn at HarperCollins were superb in their editing of the manuscript. I also thank my editors at *Time* for giving me time off to complete the writing.

Finally, this book is dedicated to my brother, Matt, and his wonderful family—with love.

Index

Addams, Jane, 103
Afghanistan, 5
African American, 344
Agriculture Department, U.S., 39
Aguinaldo, Emilio, 61, 78
Aircraft Board, *see* Morrow board
Air Force, U.S., 8
Air Force Academy, 362
Air Force Association, 358
airpower, 2, 5, 6, 7, 56, 126, 130, 155
  in BM's radio address, 211–12
  in future wars, 360–61
  in Morrow board report, 276–77
  unified air force idea and, 37–38,
    140–41
  World War II strategy and, 359–60
  see also Ostfriesland, bombing test
Alexander, Mary, 66
Alfonso XIII, 105–6, 122
Al Qaeda, 5
American Expeditionary Force (AEF),
    119, 138
  bureaucratic wars in, 126–28
American Legion, 25, 31, 32, 37, 40, 53,
    193–4, 212, 233, 335–36, 351, 361
Anderson, Joseph, 12, 15
Anderson, Maxwell, 307
Anderson, Orville, 228–29, 320
Aquitania, 136
Armengaud, Paul, 119, 121
Army Air Corps, U.S., 358
Army of Pacification, 99

Arnold, Eleanor "Bee," 22, 42–43, 58, 196
Arnold, Henry H. "Hap," 22, 32, 34, 43,
    133, 134, 136, 138, 141, 144, 157, 173,
    192, 195–96, 257, 331, 348, 359, 363
  Aircraft Board testimony of, 42
  BM's first meeting with, 34
  court-martial testimony of, 180–82
  Patrick's reprimand of, 329
Aroostook, USS, 270, 271
Articles of War, 85–86
Associated Press, 19, 201

Bain, Jarvis, 263–66
Baltimore News, 39
Baltimore Sun, 84, 204, 328
Bane, Thurman, 146–47, 344
Bass, Charles, 361
Becker, Sherman, 350
Bellamy, Ralph, 362
Berlin, Irving, 307
Billy Mitchell Volunteers, 337
Bingham, Hiram, 24, 41, 92, 330
Bismarck, prince of Germany, 307
Bissell, Clayton, 52, 133, 148, 149,
    151–52, 162, 168, 214, 344, 347
Blackmon, Maydell "Blackie," 3, 9, 10,
    19–20, 22, 33, 44, 45, 132, 135, 238,
    307, 327, 331, 333–34, 341, 342, 344,
    346, 351, 352
Boeing PB-1 biplane, 17
Bonus Army, 336
Booth, Ewing, 49, 60, 179, 211, 323

Bosher, E. W., 342
Bowley, Albert, 48–49, 53, 54, 60, 259
Boxwood (horse), 1, 18
Boxwood estate, 256–57, 333, 340–42, 352, 354–55
Brandt, Gerald, 184–91, 261, 320
Brereton, Helen, 159–60
Brereton, Lewis, 120, 159
Brisbane, Arthur, 10, 25, 31, 48, 204, 328–29, 336, 341, 344
Brother (horse), 101
Bryan, William Jennings, 84
Bureau of Aeronautics, 26
Bureau of Investigation, 335
Byrd, Elizabeth, see Mitchell, Elizabeth "Betty"
Byrd, Harry, 338, 355
Byrd, Richard, 21, 307, 355
  court-martial testimony of, 272–74
Byrd, Tom, 355

Cagney, Jimmy, 362
Camp Dix antiaircraft tests, 207–8, 305, 308
Canvas Back, 341
Capital Yacht Club, 341
Carter, Boake, 350
Cavalry Journal, 98
Chambers, Reed, 140
Chicago Evening American, 39
Chicago Tribune, 23, 24, 62, 103, 110
Chile, 277
China, 55, 56
Churchill, Winston, 136
Clark, Charles, 226–27
Coe, Frank, 304, 305–6
Cold War, 359
Commerce Department, U.S., 337
Congress, U.S., 7, 10, 26, 30, 32, 65, 86, 103, 118, 124, 143, 181, 252, 291, 311, 361
  reaction to verdict in, 328
  Spanish-American War decision of, 70–71
  see also House of Representatives, U.S.; Senate, U.S.
Consolidated PT-1 biplane, 3–4
Constitution, U.S., 85

Cook, M. G., 191, 201, 247
Coolidge, Calvin, 2, 6–7, 12, 21–22, 42, 49, 62, 91, 114, 185, 193, 204, 268, 269, 276, 295, 307, 308, 318, 334, 337
  BM's court-martial and, 30–31, 40–41, 48, 85–86, 92, 117–18
  governing style of, 28–29, 40
  media and, 27–28
  Omaha speech of, 40
  sentence amended by, 330–31
  Weeks' letter to, 313–14, 318
Coolidge, Grace, 12, 27, 91
Coolidge administration, 337
Cooper, Gary, 362
Court-Martial of Billy Mitchell, The (film), 362
Crawford, George, 343
Croix de Guerre, 123
Cuba, 70, 73, 74–76, 96, 105–6
Curtiss-Wright Corporation, 336

Daniels, Josephus, 45, 142, 143–44, 145, 154
Dargue, Herbert, 205–8, 210–11
Darrow, Clarence, 84
Daughters of the Confederacy, 342
Davies, Joseph, 52, 133, 165, 203, 333, 337
Davis, Dwight, 36–37, 42, 48, 85, 91, 116, 328, 329, 331
Defense Department, U.S., 6, 361
De Havilland DH-4 biplane, 9, 20, 58, 141, 177, 248–49, 258, 268
Delaware, USS, 151
DeMille, Cecil B., 9
Democratic Convention of 1892, 65
Dempsey, Jack, 44
Desert Storm, 360
Dewey, George, 73
Distinguished Service Cross, 131, 357
Donovan, William "Wild Bill," 83
Doolittle, Jimmy, 9, 147, 348, 363
Douglas, Donald, 139–40
Douglas, James, 358
Douhet, Giulio, 251
Drum, Hugh, 42, 126, 134, 171, 181, 204, 214, 244, 258–59, 305
  court-martial testimony of, 309–13
Duke, Donald, 215–19

Eberle, Edward, 284–85
  court-martial testimony of, 287–89
Eclipse (horse), 1, 4, 18
Edward, duke of Windsor, 136
Eighth Army Corps, U.S., 2, 32, 110–11
Eisenhower, Dwight D., 180, 359
Eltinge, LeRoy, 260, 261–63, 265
Ely, Hanson, 292–94
Executives Club, 291
Eyes of the Fleet (film), 253

Fairbanks, Douglas, Sr., 9, 129
Farley, James, 339
Fechet, James, 333
Fiedler, Ken, 43–45
Field and Stream, 335
Fighting the Flying Circus (Rickenbacker), 297
First Provisional Air Brigade, U.S., 147
First Pursuit Group, U.S., 120, 175
First Wisconsin Voluntary Infantry, 71
Fladoes, Harriet, *see* Young, Harriet Mitchell
Fladoes, Martin, 357
Flood Tide (horse), 1
Foley, Paul, 198, 199, 202, 203–4
Ford, Henry, 10, 22, 285
Fort Leavenworth, 97
Fort Sam Houston, 1–2, 6, 9–10, 110–11
Fort Tilden antiaircraft tests, 207–8, 305, 308
Fortune, 256
Foulois, Benjamin, 126–27, 128
France, 30, 40, 56, 70, 106, 181
  BM awarded Croix de Guerre by, 123
Frankfurt, 143, 149
Fries, Amos, 169–70, 171, 180
Fullam, William, 155

G-102, 143
Galt, Alexander, 114
George V, king of England, 136
Germany, 70, 137, 223, 242, 344, 358, 359
Gherardi, Walter, 201
Göring, Hermann, 344
Graves, William, 48, 60, 173, 175, 179, 202, 211, 254, 299, 313, 323
  Reid's confrontation with, 274–75

Great Britain, 56, 70, 328, 360
  armed services organization of, 181
Great Depression, 349
Greely, Adolphus, 80, 81–82, 335
Gridiron Club, 307–8
Gullion, Allen, 214–15, 226–29, 238, 257–58, 274–75, 278, 316–17, 324, 328
  BM cross-examined by, 240–46, 248–52
  Eberle cross-examined by, 287–89
  fate of, 356–57
  final argument of, 318–22
  Heinen cross-examined by, 221–25
  La Guardia cross-examined by, 254
  Rodgers cross-examined by, 269–72
  Rosendahl questioned by, 279–82, 286
  Sims cross-examined by, 230–31

Harbord, James, 126, 156–57, 160, 161, 163
Harding, Warren, 29, 144
Harmon, Hubert, 192–93
Hart, Thomas, 250–51
Hartney, Harold, 120
Hawaiian Department, U.S. Navy, 55, 58, 308
Hawaiian Joint Force Exercises, 184–85
Hearst, William Randolph, 25, 31, 70
Heinen, Anton, 19, 219–25
Henderson, USS, 142, 153–54
Hickam, Horace, 25
Hicks, George, 110–11, 114
Highland Chief (horse), 101
Hinds, Ernest, 32, 85
Hines, John, 25–26, 48, 61, 185, 187, 204, 206, 214, 304, 306, 310, 313
Hitler, Adolf, 360
Hoover, Herbert, 30, 338
Hoover, J. Edgar, 335
House of Representatives, U.S., 7, 328
  Aircraft Committee of, 37
  BM promoted posthumously by, 361
  Flood Control Committee of, 357
  Military Affairs Committee of, 254
  Rules Committee of, 103
Houston Press, 19
Howze, Anne, 183, 190
Howze, Hamilton, 356

Howze, Robert, 83, 86, 88, 111–12, 118,
    168, 169, 183–84, 186–87, 193, 195,
    196, 198, 210, 211, 215, 225, 239,
    246, 255, 261, 267, 268, 275, 277,
    297, 299, 303, 305, 313, 316, 319,
    322, 328
  announcement of verdict by, 323–26
  background of, 48, 60–61
  fate of, 356
  witnesses questioned by, 174–75,
    178–79, 182, 190–91, 202, 231–32,
    237, 252, 314–15
Hunsicker, Jerome, 279

Indiana, USS, 145
Iraq, 5, 360
Irwin, George, 48, 60, 214, 323
Isley, Agnes Boeing, 343
Italy, 30, 181

Jackson, Danny, 339
Jackson, Katharine Mitchell, 25, 65–66,
    161, 327, 339, 342, 346, 349, 350,
    352, 355
Jackson, William, 327
Japan, 5, 55, 56–57, 70, 98, 241, 242,
    344–45, 358–60
Jardine, William, 116
Johnson, Alfred, 145, 149, 150, 151–53,
    191
  court-martial testimony of, 253
Joint Aeronautical Board, 262
Joint Army and Navy Board, 262, 265
Joint Chiefs of Staff, 361
Jones, B. Q., 258
Justice Department, U.S., 335
Jutland, Battle of, 143

Kellogg, Frank, 30
Kennedy, Frank, 225–26
Kentucky (horse), 101
King, Edward, 48, 60, 178–79, 239, 269,
    274, 275, 299, 323
  "damned rot" remark of, 266–68
Knox, John, 12
Korean War, 325, 360
Korell, Franklin Frederick, 353–54
Ku Klux Klan, 25

La Guardia, Fiorello H., 194, 253, 320,
    328
  court-martial testimony of, 253–54
Lambert, Florian, 7, 37, 253
Lambert, Samuel, 348, 350
Langley, USS, 185, 187, 234–35, 237
Lansdowne, Margaret, 14, 135, 203, 224,
    282, 284
  court-martial testimony of, 196–202,
    203
Lansdowne, Peggy, 197
Lansdowne, Zachary, 11–16, 27, 44, 135,
    142, 196, 197, 220, 223, 224, 278,
    281, 282, 284–88, 289
Lassiter, William, 176
Lassiter board, 176, 179
Lawson, Walter, 152–53
League of Nations, 137
Lee, Edmund Jennings, 354
Lewis, Sinclair, 29
Lexington, USS, 237
Liberty, 23, 33, 238, 335
Lindbergh, Charles, 336, 354
Lloyd George, David, 136
Loening, Grover, 273, 275
Los Angeles, USS, 12, 202, 280, 284
Luzon, Department of, U.S. Army, 99

MacArthur, Arthur, 49, 77
MacArthur, Douglas, 46, 49–50, 58, 60,
    77, 101, 211, 239, 254, 319, 323, 359
  court-martial vote of, 325
MacArthur, Louise, 46, 50, 211
McCain, John, 8
McCain, John Sidney, 8
McCalla, Kenneth, 19
McCormick, Robert, 62
McCoy, Frank, 49, 60, 211, 319–20, 323,
    351
McDarment, Corley, 133
McKinley, William, 70
McLeary, Harry, 19
McMullen, Joseph, 51, 62, 257, 310–11
Maine, USS, 70, 71
Manchuria, 100
Manual for Courts-Martial, 51
Marshall, Albert, 200–201
Marshall, George C., 180, 351, 359

Martin MB-2 bomber, 142
Mayflower (presidential yacht), 91–92
Meadowmere estate, 65, 66, 69, 95
Mendoza, Captain, 78
Menoher, Charles, 138, 141, 156–57
Metropolitan Club, 346
Mexico, 2, 61, 96–97, 179
Miller, Lucy Trumbull Robinson, 165, 323
Miller, Sidney, 47, 165, 167, 316, 323
Milling, Thomas DeWitt, 104–5, 120, 138, 344
Milwaukee Journal, 329
Milwaukee *Sentinel,* 93
Mitchell, Alexander, 63–64, 68–69
Mitchell, Bianca Cogswell, 64, 161
Mitchell, Caroline Stoddard, 6, 49, 70, 105–6, 125, 136–37, 138, 327, 341, 346
  as army wife, 97–100
  background and personality of, 93–95
  BM's courtship of, 70, 76–77, 82
  BM's papers destroyed by, 353–54
  BM's World War I service and, 129–30
  death of, 354
  failure of first marriage of, 158–64
  last years of, 353–54
  post-divorce lifestyle of, 213–14
  shooting incident and, 159
  Washington social life and, 100–102, 103
  wedding and honeymoon of, 93, 96–97
Mitchell, David, 22, 64, 69
Mitchell, Elizabeth (daughter), 98–99, 160, 213–14
Mitchell, Elizabeth "Betty," 1, 3, 6, 7, 9, 10, 17, 18, 22, 23, 32, 33, 34, 35, 37, 42, 44, 45, 46, 47, 54, 84, 107, 135, 212, 213, 252, 255, 275, 289–90, 307, 325, 327, 333, 334, 344, 347, 356
  background of, 165–66
  BM's marriage to, 164–65
  BM's physical decline and, 348–52
  BM's relationship with, 166–67
  Boxwood estate and, 256–57
  at court-martial, 50, 51, 61, 90–91, 108, 132, 182, 211, 296, 322, 323
  last years of, 330–31, 339, 341–42, 354–55
  Margaret Lansdowne and, 196

Mitchell, Harriet (daughter), 99, 160, 213–14
Mitchell, Harriet (sister), *see* Young, Harriet Mitchell
Mitchell, Harriet Danforth Becker (mother), 63–65, 68, 76, 93–94, 97, 103, 125, 131, 161, 164, 341
Mitchell, Janet, 49, 65
Mitchell, John, Jr., 22, 65–66, 97, 213
  death of, 125
Mitchell, John Lendrum, 63–66, 68–69, 71, 73, 76, 80, 97, 161
Mitchell, John Lendrum III (son), 138
Mitchell, Katharine, *see* Jackson, Katharine Mitchell
Mitchell, Lucy (daughter), 3, 35, 47, 132, 135, 182, 247, 255, 289–90, 327, 330, 333, 339–40, 351, 354
Mitchell, Martha (sister), 65–66, 161
Mitchell, Martha Reed (grandmother), 64, 69
Mitchell, Ruth, 22, 65–66, 71, 161
Mitchell, William, Jr., 339–40, 351, 356, 357–58, 362
Mitchell, William "Billy":
  admirers and enemies of, 3, 7–8, 9
  attempts at exoneration of, 357–58
  background of, 4–5
  birth of, 4, 64–65
  celebrity of, 136, 155, 204
  childhood of, 66–68
  colonialist viewpoint of, 75
  death of, 350
  demotion of, 1–2
  description of, 8–9, 31, 100
  education of, 67, 68, 69–70, 72, 79
  epithets of, 7–8
  estate of, 352
  failed marriage of, 158–64
  as father, 213–14, 339–40
  finances of, 102–3, 213, 257, 332, 340, 341–42, 352
  first airplane experience of, 104–5
  first book on aeronautics of, 139
  first combat experience of, 77
  first marriage of, 93, 96
  first published article of, 98
  funeral of, 350–51

Mitchell, William "Billy" (*cont.*)
  heavy drinking of, 159, 161
  historical interests of, 70–71
  Isley murder case and, 343–44
  joins army, 70–72
  malaria of, 77, 79, 81, 99
  mental examinations of, 161–62
  personality of, 8–9, 67, 68
  physical decline of, 346–50
  political ambition of, 10, 39, 336–39
  postage stamp in honor of, 361
  posthumous honors and stature of,
    361–62
  posthumous promotion of, 361
  predictions of, 5–6, 56–57, 278, 344–45,
    350, 359–61
  racism of, 57–58, 78–79, 343–44
  siblings of, 65–66
  speaking tours of, 333–35, 337
  special medal of honor of, 357
  writing career of, 98, 103–4, 333,
    335–36
Mitchell, William "Billy," court-martial of:
  aftermath of, 327–29
  aircraft safety issue in, 248–49, 251–52,
    268–69, 300–301, 302, 305
  air races issue in, 192–93, 302–3
  air service defects issue in, 173–76
  Anderson testimony in, 228–29
  antiaircraft guns debate in, 205–7,
    233–34, 253–54, 257, 297–99, 310–11
  armed services organization in, 180–81
  Arnold testimony in, 180–82
  Bain testimony in, 263–66
  bill of particulars ruling in, 86–87
  BM relieved of duties in, 32–33
  BM's articles on, 345
  BM's closing statement in, 316–18
  BM's mood in, 195–96
  BM's radio address and, 211–12
  BM's testimony in, 239–46, 248–52
  Brandt testimony in, 184–91
  Byrd testimony in, 272–74
  charges in, 37, 62, 87
  chemical warfare issue in, 169–71
  Clark testimony in, 226–27
  Coe testimony in, 305–6
  congressional reaction to, 328

  cost of, 291–92
  courtroom of, 36–37, 43, 47
  "damned rot" remark in, 266–68
  Dargue testimony in, 205–8, 210–11
  decision for, 32–33
  defense challenges in, 52–56, 59–60,
    62
  defense team in, 51–52
  defense witness list in, 116–17, 133–35
  defense witness phase of, 169–229
  Drum testimony in, 309–13
  Duke testimony in, 215–19
  Eberle testimony in, 287–89
  effect on military of, 329
  Eltinge testimony in, 260–63
  Ely testimony in, 292–95
  film on, 362
  flight pay issue in, 208–10
  foreign reaction to, 328
  formal arraignment in, 45, 61–62,
    89–91
  general staff in, 204–5
  Harmon testimony in, 192–93
  Hawaiian maneuvers in, 184–91,
    234–37, 240–44, 261–66
  Heinen testimony in, 219–25
  jurors acting as prosecutors in, 174–75,
    178–79, 182, 190–91, 202, 231–32,
    237–38, 252, 254, 314–15
  jurors assigned to, 48–50
  Kennedy testimony in, 225–26
  La Guardia testimony in, 253–54
  Lansdowne testimony in, 196–202,
    203
  leadership issue in, 295–97
  legal challenges in, 85–86
  length of, 316
  media and, 46–47, 84, 203–4, 239,
    246–47, 252, 257–58, 268, 274, 275,
    290, 291, 304, 306, 329
  mitigation defense questions in,
    153–54, 215, 260–61, 315, 318
  model airways program in, 215–19
  Morrow board report and, 276–78
  motion to dismiss in, 111–12
  navy advisers in, 191–92, 200–201, 214,
    247
  Nolan testimony in, 313–15

not guilty plea in, 89–91
Oldys testimony in, 175–80
Paegelow testimony in, 227–28
paramount interest principle in, 264–66
Patrick testimony in, 300–304
Perkins testimony in, 253
Pierce testimony in, 191–92
pilot losses in, 191–92
plagiarism accusation in, 250–51, 252
plea for acquittal in, 113–16
prosecution's final argument in, 318–22
prosecution witnesses in, 108–10,
    257–58, 277–78
Rath testimony in, 295–300
Reid-Moreland confrontations in,
    87–88, 110–11, 112, 189, 198–99,
    208–9
Reid's opening presentation in, 168–69
Rickenbacker testimony in, 232–34
Rodgers testimony in, 269–72
Rogers' appearance at, 304–5
Rosendahl testimony in, 278–87
routine of, 108
seating arrangements in, 47
sentence imposed in, 324–25, 330–31
separate air force issue in, 252, 292–95,
    300–302, 310, 312
Shenandoah crash in, 198–200, 203–4,
    219–27, 229–30, 246, 278–79
Sheridan testimony in, 233–37
Sims testimony in, 229–32
Spaatz testimony in, 171–75, 206
Summerall testimony in, 308–9
summons served in, 43–45
Thanksgiving interlude in, 255–57
unified command issue in, 184–91,
    263–66
verdict in, 323–25, 330
War Department's public relations cam-
    paigns and, 33, 39–40, 44–45, 214–15,
    247
Weeks-Coolidge letter and, 314–15, 318
Mitchell, William "Billy," military career
    of:
Alaska assignment of, 80–82
Aviation Section assignment of, 105
Cuba assignments in, 74–76, 99
decorations of, 123, 131

efficiency reports of, 80, 104
enlistment of, 70–72
in European inspection trip, 162–63
first combat experience in, 77
Fort Leavenworth assignment of, 97–99
general staff assignment of, 100–104
insurrecto raid led by, 77–78
Ostfriesland bombing test and, 142–55
Philippines assignments of, 76–79,
    99–100
in postwar era, 137–41
private insignia of, 119
promoted to Brigadier General, 129
promoted to captain, 82
regular army commission in, 79–80
resignation of, 331–32
in World War I, 119–31
Mitchellites, 359, 360
Moffett, William, 14, 18, 22, 40, 142
    BM's rivalry with, 14, 26–27
    Shenandoah flight and, 26–27, 285
Moorman, Thomas S., Jr., 356–57
Moreland, Sherman, 52, 85, 92, 108, 113,
    114, 115–16, 117, 133, 134, 170, 171,
    173, 174, 176, 178, 179, 181, 193,
    204, 205, 210, 214, 215, 221, 247,
    257–58, 260, 262, 274, 278, 291,
    292–93, 310, 313, 315, 319, 322
background of, 51
Brandt testimony and, 188–90
fate of, 356
Lansdowne testimony and, 198–202,
    203
Patrick questioned by, 301–2
Reid's confrontation with, 87–88, 109,
    110–11, 112, 189, 198–99, 208–9
Morrow, Dwight W., 41–43, 92, 116, 276,
    310, 329
Morrow board, 41–43, 92, 116, 134, 310
    report of, 276–77, 290
Mosby, John, 342
Mussolini, Benito, 182

National Aeronautical Association, 336
National Association for the Advance-
    ment of Colored People (NAACP),
    343
National Geographic Society, 21, 272, 273

Navy Department, U.S., 6, 10, 38, 51, 104, 113, 229–30, 231, 257
   Arctic publicity flight of, 21, 272–74
   BM's court-martial and, 133, 191–92, 200–201, 214, 247
   Hawaiian exercises and, 184–91, 234–37, 240–44, 261–66
   Hawaiian publicity flight of, 14, 17–18, 20, 24, 26, 33, 116, 268–72
   in Morrow board report, 276–77
   Ostfriesland bombing tests and, 142–55
   Shenandoah flight and, *see Shenandoah*, USS
Netherlands, 70
Nevin, John, 33, 331
New Deal, 339
New Orleans Times-Picayune, 110
New Republic, 290
New York American, 335
New York Evening Journal, 39
New York Sun, 84, 252
New York Times, 17, 24, 62, 110, 169, 269, 306, 329, 335
New York World, 43
Nolan, Dennis, 26, 62, 126, 304, 306
   court-martial testimony of, 313–15

Office of Strategic Services (OSS), 83
Oldys, Robert, 133, 182, 195
   court-martial testimony of, 175–80
Oldys, Robert, Jr., 176
O'Neill, Eugene, 29
Osprey, 141, 149, 154
Ostfriesland bombing test, 5, 142–55, 161, 240, 253, 317, 345
   aftermath of, 155–56
   BM-navy conflicts in, 148–49, 151–52, 153
   BM's bombing strategy for, 147–48
   BM's preparations for, 146–47
   Navy's rules for, 145–46
   sinking in, 153–54
Our Air Force (Mitchell), 139
"Our Faulty Military Policy" (Mitchell), 104

Paegelow, John, 227–28
Panic of 1893, 69

paramount interest, principle of, 264
Parker, James, 41
Parmer, Charles, 35
Parsons, Henry, 109–10
Patrick, Mason, 1, 7, 22, 26, 55, 59, 162–63, 176, 177, 178, 196, 205, 208, 210, 214, 216, 217, 276, 359, 364
   airpower views of, 157–58
   air races controversy and, 192–3, 302–3
   Arnold reprimanded by, 329
   BM assessed by, 127–28
   BM's bureaucratic challenge to, 156–57
   on condition of air services, 254–55
   court-martial testimony of, 300–304
Patton, George S., 101, 119, 180, 340, 359
Pearl Harbor attack, 5, 56–57, 358, 360
Pearson, Alexander, 192–93
Pennsylvania, USS, 143
Perkins, Randolph, 253
Perry, Matthew, 269
Pershing, John "Black Jack," 41, 50, 52, 54, 58, 61, 119, 124, 126, 128, 130, 131, 136, 141, 142, 155, 160, 161, 180, 233, 240, 258, 276, 299, 310, 311, 337, 344
   BM and, 121–22, 129, 156
   on results of court-martial, 329–30
Peru, 277
Philadelphia Inquirer, 268
Philippines, 70, 71, 76–77, 358
Pierce, O. C., 191–92
Plain, Frank, 52, 133, 317
PN-9 seaplane, 17–18, 20, 33, 268–69
Pointer (dog), 82
Pond, James, 334
Pond Bureau, 333
Poore, Benjamin, 48, 60, 323
Popular Science, 335
Postal Service, U.S., 301
Pravda, 328
Preminger, Otto, 362
President's Aircraft Board, *see* Morrow board
Prohibition, 31, 323, 337, 342
Project B, 146
Pulitzer, Joseph, 70
Pulitzer Trophy, 192, 302–3
Putnam, George, 334

Rath, Howard, 295–300
Reagan, Ronald, 28
Reid, Frank R., 37–40, 43, 44, 45, 46, 51,
    91, 108, 117, 133, 134, 184, 190, 191,
    195, 203, 204, 215, 223, 224, 229,
    236, 238, 239, 249, 250, 251, 255,
    257–58, 259, 262, 263, 269, 272, 281,
    319, 322–23, 326, 328, 330, 331
  Arnold questioned by, 180–81
  background and personality of, 38
  Bain questioned by, 264–66
  bill of particulars request of, 86–88
  BM testimony and, 240, 242–44, 246,
    248
  Brandt questioned by, 186–88
  Byrd questioned by, 273–74
  clothing of, 205
  Coe cross-examined by, 305–6
  courtroom style of, 84–85
  Drum's confrontation with, 311–13
  Eberle questioned by, 288–89
  Eltinge testimony and, 262–63
  Ely cross-examined by, 294–95
  fate of, 357
  Fries questioned by, 169–70
  Graves's confrontation with, 274–75
  Harmon questioned by, 192–93
  Heinen questioned by, 219–21
  juror challenges and, 52–56, 59–60
  Kennedy questioned by, 225–26
  King's "damned rot" remark and, 266–68
  Lansdowne questioned by, 196–200
  Moreland's confrontations with, 87–88,
    109, 110–11, 112, 189, 198–99, 208–9
  motion to dismiss by, 111–12
  Oldys questioned by, 176–78
  Paegelow questioned by, 227–28
  Patrick questioned by, 301–2
  in plea for acquittal, 113–16
  Rath cross-examined by, 297–300
  Rickenbacker questioned by, 232–33
  Rosendahl questioned by, 281, 282–86
  Summerall questioned by, 308–9
Republican Party, U.S., 337
Rich, Corinne, 47
Richthofen, Manfred von, 234
Rickenbacker, Eddie, 10, 39, 157, 247,
    253, 257, 291, 297, 350, 354
  court-martial testimony of, 232–34
Riggs Bank, 341, 352
Rob Roy (dog), 27
Rodgers, John, 18, 26, 33, 307
  court-martial testimony of, 268–72
Rogers, Will, 1–2
  court-martial appearance of, 304–5
Roosevelt, Elliott, 336
Roosevelt, Franklin D., 28, 336, 338–39,
    351, 356
Roosevelt, Theodore, 73, 192
Roosevelt, Theodore, Jr., 192, 193, 303
Root, Elihu, 80
Rosendahl, Charles, 15, 16, 44, 45
  court-martial testimony of, 278–87
Rotterdam, 162
Royal Air Force, 181
Rucker, Kyle, 258

Sacco, Nicola, 84
St. Louis Globe-Democrat, 110
Saint-Mihiel offensive, 119, 121, 128–29,
    296
St. Petersburg Daily News, 327
Saltzman, Charles, 258
San Antonio Evening News, 19
San Antonio Express, 17
San Antonio Light, 108–9
Sanders, Everett, 30, 116, 307, 335
Saratoga, USS, 237
Saturday Evening Post, 7, 251
School of the Line, 99
Scopes, John, 84
Scott, E. D., 33
Sea Gull 3rd, 1
Second Division, U.S., 77
Secretaries Association, 212
Senate, U.S., 65, 69, 71, 78, 118, 137, 323,
    328, 337
  Military Affairs Committee of, 24, 72,
    160
Shawmut, USS, 149, 151–53
Shenandoah, USS, 23, 31, 40, 44, 109,
    116, 133, 268, 320, 323, 330
  BM's critique and, 19–22
  in Coolidge's press statement, 27–28
  in court-martial testimony, 198–200,
    203–4, 219–27, 229–30, 246, 278–79

Shenandoah, USS (*cont.*)
　crash of, 16
　description of, 11–12
　flight of, 11–14
　itinerary of, 14
　media accounts of, 17–18
　Moffett and, 26–27
　structure of, 13
Sheridan, Hiram W., 233–38
Short, Harry, 4, 9, 19, 24
Signal Corps, U.S., 71, 72, 80, 103, 106,
　252
Sims, William Sowden, 229–32, 242, 253,
　320
Skeel, Burt, 192–93
Skyways (Mitchell), 335
Sladen, Fred, 49, 60, 259
Smith, Al, 338
Smithsonian Institution, 361
Spaatz, Carl "Tooey," 195, 359
　court-martial testimony of, 171–75, 206
Spain, 70, 71, 73, 106
Spanish-American War, 4–5, 70–73, 80,
　342
Stearns, Frank, 41
Steele, George, Jr., 202, 284
Steele, Mrs. George W., 202–3
Steiger, Rod, 362
Stimson, Henry L., 357
Stoddard, Caroline (daughter), *see*
　Mitchell, Caroline Stoddard
Stoddard, Caroline (mother), 70, 93–94
Stoddard, Enoch Vine, 70, 94–96
Stoddard, Vine (son), 100, 160
Street, St. Clair, 141–42, 149, 150–51,
　153–54
Summerall, Charles, 48, 51, 53, 62, 206,
　207, 208, 259
　BM's conflict with, 54–56, 58–59
　court-martial testimony of, 308–9
　ousted from jury, 59–60
Supreme Court, Wisconsin, 213

Teapot Dome scandal, 29, 83
Third Attack Group, U.S., 178, 179–80
Thomas Morse MB-3 pursuit plane, 58
"Throwing Our Aeronautics to the Dogs"
　(Mitchell), 335

Time,, 157, 229
Trenchard, Hugh, 123–24, 251
Truman, Harry, 28, 325, 361
20th Century Club, 98
23rd Anti-Aircraft Battery, U.S., 234

U-117, 143
Uniform Code of Military Justice, 86
Union League Club, 335
Universal Services, 35, 39, 47

Vanzetti, Bartolomeo, 84
Versailles, Treaty of, 223
Verville, Alfred, 344, 346–47, 348
Veterans Administration, 342
Veterans Bureau, 208, 210
Vietnam War, 360
Villa, Pancho, 61
Vinson, Carl, 41
Virginia Chamber of Commerce, 341

Waddell, Isaac, 257
Wadsworth, James, 160–61
Wall Street Journal, 291
Walsh, Thomas, 83
War Department, U.S., 2, 5, 6, 7, 10, 19,
　20, 38, 42, 55, 58, 62, 63, 76, 104,
　113, 117, 123, 124, 163, 171, 175,
　205, 247, 252, 255, 257, 262, 328,
　334, 336, 340, 350–51, 355–56, 357,
　358
　air races issue and, 192–93, 302–3
　antiaircraft tests of, 207–8, 305, 308
　BM's resignation accepted by, 331–32
　court-martial decision of, 32–33
　flight pay issue and, 208–10
　Hawaiian exercises and, 186–91,
　　234–37, 240–44, 261–6
　Military Intelligence Division of, 39
　model airways program of, 215–19
　in Morrow board report, 276–77
　Press Relations Section of, 118
　public relations campaign of, 33,
　　39–40, 44–45, 214–15, 247
Warner Brothers, 362
Warren, Francis E., 72
Washington Naval Conference (1921),
　144

Washington Post, 33, 39, 41, 182, 203, 204, 275, 306, 331
Washington Post Radio Hour, 211–12
Washington Star, 24, 89, 204, 274, 304
Washington Times, 61, 164
WCAP, 211
WCAU, 350
Webb, William, 52, 133
Weekly Press Review, 39
Weeks, John, 2, 7, 36–37, 142, 151, 156, 160, 161, 176
  Coolidge letter of, 313–14, 318
West Flying Circus, 172
What Price Glory? (Anderson), 307
Wheeler, Sheldon H., 176–77
White, Herbert, 52, 133, 189–90, 254, 317
Whitney, John Hay, 342
Wilbur, Curtis, 19, 26, 28, 107, 116, 198, 203, 204, 307–8
Wilby, Francis, 204–5, 208, 210, 214, 215, 216–19, 226, 233–34, 235, 252, 257–58, 261–63, 291, 293, 295, 297, 298, 300, 304, 305, 306
Wilson, Eugene, 140, 144
Wilson, Woodrow, 137
Winans, Edwin, 49, 60, 214, 323
Winged Defense (Mitchell), 7, 10, 17, 42, 249, 334
Winship, Blanton, 49, 60, 84–86, 89, 101, 109, 111, 117, 170, 174, 177, 184,

198–99, 203, 209, 211, 215, 217, 223, 226, 237, 239, 244, 246, 251, 261, 266, 274, 281, 288, 299, 303, 311, 313, 317, 323, 356
WOAI, 17, 18
World Almanac, 240
World Court, 323
World's Work, 103
World War I, 5, 106, 119–31, 278, 345, 359
  U.S. air offensive in, 130–31
World War II, 8, 356, 359
Wright, Orville, 307
Wright brothers, 34, 98, 104
WRNY, 194

Yeager, A. H., 108–9
Young, Arthur, 132, 357
Young, Harriet (daughter), 8, 340, 350, 351, 352
Young, Harriet Mitchell, 45, 49, 50, 51, 60, 65–66, 89, 132, 136, 148, 161, 255, 327–28, 337, 338, 341, 342, 351
  background of, 132–33
  BM's death and, 349–50
  fate of, 357

Zenith Corporation, 273
Zeppelin Airship Company, 220
Ziegler, William, Jr., 342